INGRID E. LILLY, Ph.D. (2010) in Hebrew Bible, Emory University, is Assistant Professor of Religious Studies at Western Kentucky University. She is an Assistant Editor for the journal *TC: A Journal for Biblical Textual Criticism* and co-chairs the Textual Criticism of the Hebrew Bible unit at the Society of Biblical Literature's annual conference.

Two Books of Ezekiel

Supplements

to

Vetus Testamentum

Editor in Chief

Hans Barstad

VOLUME 150

The titles published in this series are listed at brill.nl/vts

Two Books of Ezekiel

Papyrus 967 and the Masoretic Text as Variant Literary Editions

By

Ingrid E. Lilly

BRILL

LEIDEN · BOSTON
2012

Library of Congress Cataloging-in-Publication Data

Lilly, Ingrid E.
  Two books of Ezekiel : Papyrus 967 and the Masoretic text as variant literary editions / by Ingrid E. Lilly.
    p. cm. — (Supplements to Vetus Testamentum ; v. 150)
  Includes bibliographical references and index.
  ISBN 978-90-04-20674-8 (hardback : alk. paper)
  1. Bible. O.T. Ezekiel—Criticism, interpretation, etc. 2. Bible. O.T. Ezekiel. Greek—Versions—Papyrus 967. I. Title.

BS1545.52.L55 2012
224'.40486—dc23

2012007362

This publication has been typeset in the multilingual "Brill" typeface. With over 5,100 characters covering Latin, IPA, Greek, and Cyrillic, this typeface is especially suitable for use in the humanities. For more information, please see www.brill.nl/brill-typeface.

ISSN 0083-5889
ISBN 978 90 04 20674 8 (hardback)
ISBN 978 90 04 22245 8 (e-book)

MIX
Paper from
responsible sources
FSC
www.fsc.org   FSC® C004472

PRINTED BY DRUKKERIJ WILCO B.V. - AMERSFOORT, THE NETHERLANDS

This book is dedicated to my family and close friends
who have given me joy, distraction, and support
during the work for this project.

CONTENTS

LIST OF ILLUSTRATIONS

Images are taken with permissions from the following sources:

Johnson, A.C., H.S. Gehman, and J.E.H. Kase. *The John H. Scheide Biblical Papyri: Ezekiel*. Princeton University Studies in Papyrology 3. Princeton: University Press, 1938.

Kenyon, F.J. *Fasciculus VII: Ezekiel, Daniel, Esther*. Volume 2. PLATES. London: Emery Walker Limited, 1937.

Projektes "Digitalisierung der Kölner Papyrusbestände" at http://www .uni-koeln.de/phil-fak/ifa/NRWakademie/papyrologie/Ezechiel/bildereze .html.

Payne, J. Barton. "The Relationship of the Chester Beatty Papyri of Ezekiel to Codex Vaticanus." *JBL* 68 (1949): 265.

Gehman, Henry Snyder. "The Relations Between the Text of the John H. Schiede Papyri and that of the Other Greek MSS. of Ezekiel," *JBL* 57 (1938), 286.

PREFACE

The present study grew out of an idea originally pursued in an independent study on Ezekiel with David Petersen during my doctoral program at Emory University. Upon encountering the scholarship of Johan Lust, I was immediately impressed with the magnitude for potential study of p967. My initial questions took seriously papyrus 967 as a functioning manuscript and edition of Ezekiel with its own distinctive literary features. This initial approach shaped my sense that materialist philology and literary criticism needed to be brought to bear upon textual study, especially in as complex a textual scenario as p967 presented for Ezekiel. In consultation with David Petersen and Carol Newsom, the present study took an early form as a dissertation proposal. Subsequent conversations with Brent Strawn, who was to become my doctoral adviser, gave the project its present shape as a doctoral thesis.

I would like to thank my dissertation committee at Emory University for maintaining a critical and encouraging context for my project. I am grateful for the early guidance of Carol Newsom and David Petersen, who pushed for interesting questions within methodologically clear boundaries. I am fortunate that Eugene Ulrich agreed to be an outside reader on my committee, providing careful and critical feedback, especially in late stages of the manuscript. Finally, I owe many thanks to my dissertation director, Brent Strawn. His energetic conversation, learned instincts, and especially his critical, tireless, and meticulous eye provided necessary guidance and are deeply appreciated. I was fortunate to have a committee of personal mentors. I am a better scholar for my committee's tutelage, and the manuscript is far better for their investment.

A special thanks to Steve Delamarter for reading and commenting on chapter 6, to Juan Hernández for his input on working with Greek manuscripts, to Johan Lust and John Olley for responding to my queries, to Naomi Beeman and Michael Seidler for reviewing my German translations, to Ivy Helman for reviewing the Spanish translations, and to Melissa Warp for assistance with the digital images. A special thanks to Laura DeLancey, Scott Laughlin, and Keaton Brownstead, for helping to compile the indexes. I would also like to thank my colleagues at Western Kentucky University for their support and encouragement in the months leading up to my dissertation defense and to the present publication. Finally, I would like to thank two mentors who are not mentioned above, but without whom I cannot imagine myself as a scholar: John J. Collins and Carolyn Sharp.

I want to thank several institutions that supported my research: The Scheide Library at Princeton University for its generosity and for making their plates of p967 available to me; The Orion Center for the Dead Sea Scrolls who in the Summer of 2007 sponsored me as a research intern in Jerusalem, Israel; and the following program units of the annual conference of the Society of Biblical Literature, whose venues provided important touch stones for the development of the work: "Theological Perspectives on the Book of Ezekiel," "Textual Criticism of the Hebrew Bible," "Greek Bible," and "Papyrology and Early Christian Backgrounds Group." I would also like to thank those involved in the "Graduate Enoch Conference" at Princeton University in June 2008.

Permissions to publish images of p967, as well as the diagrams of Payne and Gehman in the Appendix, are greatly appreciated. I wish to thank Sinéad Ward and the Trustees of the Chester Beatty Library, Robert Daniel of Leipzig with the Köln on-line library of images, Princeton University Press, and Leigh Andersen with the Society of Biblical Literature. I would like to thank the editors of the Madrid portion of p967 for providing information on the plates, though unfortunately I was not able to examine them myself. Hence, there are some minor aspects relating to the codicology chapter that have not been included. Unfortunately, the Schwagmeier dissertation (2004) was unavailable to me, but interested readers will want to take note of it.

Endeavoring to write a study of this length and density was made considerably more enjoyable for the companionship of my Emory doctoral cohort: Katie Heffelfinger and Cameron Howard. I count myself very lucky to have shared our personal lives as well as professional and intellectual formation. In that vein, I would like to thank the additional members of my graduate reading group: Eric Baretto, Mark Delcogliano, and Elizabeth Shively. I want to thank Sarah Scherschligt for her hospitality, especially during the writing intensive summer which brought this project to completion. Several people deserve additional mention for their friendship, informal conversation, and intellectual stimulation, including Kelly Murphy, Meghan Henning, Peter Lanfer, Rachel Mumford, Christopher Hays, Robert Williamson, Amy Robertson, Davis Hankins, Jackie Wyse, Andrea Olsen, Scott Girdner, Jeanne Sokolowski, Amos Marshall, Damien Joseph, Luna Rose, John and Margit Lilly, and Scott Laughlin.

LIST OF ABBREVIATIONS

=	equals, in relation between versions
≈	equals almost/approximately, in relation between versions
86′	86–710
106′	106–410
239′	239–306
403′	403–613
A	Codex Alexandrinus
A″	A-26-544
AB	Anchor Bible
AbrN	*Abr-Nahrain*
AEL	American Essays in Liturgy
Aeth	Aethiopische Übers.
AJBI	*Annual of the Japanese Biblical Institute*
Ambr.	Ambrosius
Arab	Arabische Übers.
Arm	Armenische Übers.
ASP	*American Studies in Papyrology*
ast.	asterisk
ASTI	*Annual of the Swedish Theological Institute*
ATA	Alttestamentliche Abhandlungen
AUDDS	Andrews University Doctoral Dissertation Series
Aug.	Augustinus
α′	Aquila
B	Codex Vaticanus
BEO	Biblica et Orientalia
BETL	Bibliotheca ephemeridum theologicarum lovaniensium
Bib	*Biblica*
BHS	Biblia Hebraica Stuttgartensia
BRS	Biblical Resource Series
BUL	Biblioteca universal Laterza
BIOSCS	*Bulletin of the International Organization for Septuagint and Cognate Studies*
Bo	Bohairische Übers.
BWANT	Beiträge zur Wissenschaft vom Alten und Neuen Testament
BZ	*Biblische Zeitschrift*
BZAW	Beihefte zur Zeitschrift für die alttestamentliche Wissenschaft

C	87-91-490
C'	*C + cI + cII*
cI	49-90-764
cII	130-233-534
CahRB	Cahiers de la Revue biblique
CBQ	*Catholic Biblical Quarterly*
Chr.	Chrysostomus
Co	Coptische Übers.
ConBOT	Conietanea biblica: Old Testament Series
Consult.	I Firmici Materni Consultationes Zacchaei et Apollonii
CRINT	Compendia rerum iudaicarum ad Novum Testamentum
CJ	*Classical Journal*
Cypr.	Cyprianus
Cyr.	Cyrillus Alexandrinus
DBSup	*Dictionnaire de la Bible: Supplément*
DJD	Discoveries in the Judaean Desert
DSD	*Dead Sea Discoveries*
ET	*Expository Times*
ETL	*Ephemerides theologicae Lovanienses*
Eus.ecl.	Eus. Eclogue propheticae
FAT	Forschungen zum Alten Testament
FB	Forschung zur Bibel
FCBS	Fortress Classics in Biblical Studies
fin.	*finis*
GBSOTS	Guides to Biblical Scholarship Old Testament Series
GRBS	*Greek Roman and Byzantine Studies*
GregEl	Gregorius Eliberritanus
HABS	Harper's Annotated Bible Series
HAT	Handbuch zum Alten Testament
Hi.	Hieronymus
Hippol.	Hippolytus Romanus
HS	*Hebrew Studies*
HSM	Harvard Semitic Monographs
HTR	*Harvard Theological Review*
HUBP	Hebrew University Bible Project
IBC	Interpretation, a Bible commentary for teaching and preaching
Ir.	Irenaeus Lugdunensis
θ'	Theodotian
ICA	Initiations au Christianisme Ancien
ICC	International Critical Commentary

IEJ	*Israel Exploration Journal*
ITL	International Theological Library
Iust.	Iustinus Martyr
JAOS	*The Journal of the American Oriental Society*
JBL	*Journal of Biblical Literature*
JBLMS	*Journal of Biblical Literature Monograph Series*
JBS	Jerusalem Biblical Studies
JGK	Johnson, Gehman, and Kase
JNES	*Journal of Near Eastern Studies*
JNSL	*Journal of Northwest Semitic Languages*
JQR	*Jewish Quarterly Review*
JSJSup	Supplements to the Journal for the Study of Judaism
JSNT	*Journal for the Study of the New Testament*
JSOT	*Journal for the Study of the Old Testament*
JSOTSup	*Journal for the Study of the Old Testament Supplement Series*
JSP	*Journal for the Study of the Pseudepigrapha*
JSPSup	Journal for the Study of the Pseudipigrapha: Supplement Series
JTS	*Journal of Theological Studies*
KAT	*Kommentar zum Alten Textament*
L	22-36-48-51-96-231-763
L''	*L + ʄ + ʄl*
ʄ	311–538
ʄl	V-46-449
La	Latein. Übers.
La^C	cod. Constantiensis
La^S	fragmenta Sangallensia
La^W	cod. Wirceburgensis
La^Ver	cod. Veronensis
LBS	Library of Biblical Studies
LD	Lectio divina
LRB	*London Review of Books*
LXX	Septuagint
mg	marginal notation
MPER NS	Mitteilungen aus der Papyrussammlung der Österreichische Nationalbibliothek, Neue Serie
MPI	Monographs of the Peshitta Institute
MSU	Mitteilungen des Septuaginta-Unternehmens
MT	Masoretic Text
NCB	New Century Bible

NIBCOT	New International Biblical Commentary on the Old Testament
NTG	*Neue theologische Grundrisse*
O	Q-88-Syh
o	62-147-407
O′	O + o
obel.	obelus
OBO	Orbis biblicus et orientalis
OG	Old Greek
OLA	Orientalia lovaniensia analecta
OLP	Orientalia lovaniensia periodica
om.	omits
Or.	Origenes
OTL	Old Testament Library
OTS	Old Testament Studies
p967	papyrus 967
p967^{CB}	The Chester Beatty portion of p967
p967^{Köln}	The Köln portion of p967
p967^{Mad}	The Madrid portion of p967
p967^{Sch}	The John H. Scheide portion of p967
PBA	*Proceedings of the British Academy*
Peshitta	Peshitta
PsCypr.	Pseudo Cyprianus
PsVig	Pseudo Vigilius Thapsensis
PTA	Papyrologische Texte und Abhandlungen
Q	Codex Marchalianus
RB	*Revue Biblique*
rel.	*reliqui*
RevQ	*Review de Qumran*
Sa	Sahidische Übers.
SAOC	Studies in Ancient Oriental Civilization
SB	Subsidia Biblica
SBL	Society of Biblical Literature
SBLSCS	Society of Biblical Literature Septuagint and Cognate Studies
SBLSymS	Society of Biblical Literature Symposium Series
SECT	Sources of Early Christian Thought
Spec	*Speculum*
SP	*Studia Papyrologica*
Spec.	Liber De divinis scripturis sive Speculum
STBL	Studies in Biblical Literature

STDJ	Studies on the Texts of the Desert of Judah
Syh	Syrohexapl. Übers.
Syp	Syropaläst. Übers.
σ′	Symmachus
Targ	Targum
TCHB	*Textual Criticism of the Hebrew Bible*
TCS	Text-Critical Studies
TDSA	Testi e documenti per lo studio dell'antichità
TENT	Texts and Editions for New Testament Study
Tert.	Tertullianus
TGI	*Theologie und Glaube*
ThLT	*Theologische Literaturseitung*
Tht.	Theodoretus Cyrensis
TL	*Theologische Literaturzeitung*
TLOT	*Theological Lexicon of the Old Testament*
TS	Texts and Studies
TSAJ	Texts and Studies in Ancient Judaism
TvT	*Tijdschrift voor Theologie*
txt	textual reading
Tyc.	Tyconius Afer
UBS	United Bible Societies
V	Codex Venetus
Vulg.	Vulgata
VT	*Vetus Testamentum*
VTSup	Supplements to Vetus Testamentum
WBC	Word Biblical Commentary
WUNT	Wissenschaftliche Untersuchungen zum Neuen Testament
Z	Ziegler's LXX Göttingen text
ZAW	*Zeitschrift für die alttestamentliche Wissenschaft*
ZNW	*Zeitschrift für die neutestamentliche Wissenschaft und die Kunde der älteren Kirche*

CHAPTER ONE

INTRODUCTION: A MANUSCRIPT APPROACH TO P967

Who took that text out of context?[1]
—Jacques Derrida

1.1. INTRODUCTION

In the late 1930s, a new Greek manuscript of Ezekiel was published in two different locations: among the Chester Beatty Biblical Papyri and at Princeton among the John H. Schiede Biblical Papyri.[2] This manuscript is now known by Rahlf's enumeration p967.[3] p967 is dated to the late second or early third century CE, making it the earliest copy of any Septuagintal codex known at the time.[4] The 1970s turned up two more portions of the Ezekiel manuscript, one at the University of Cologne, and the other in Madrid, Spain.[5]

The significance of p967 for textual studies of Ezekiel was immediately apparent. p967, a Greek uncial, pre-dates Origen's Hexapla and Codex Vaticanus (B) by nearly a century, revealing its importance for study of the Old Greek. In fact, aside from a still missing portion of the beginning of the manuscript (chs. 1–11:24), p967 is the earliest substantial witness to Ezekiel in any language, including Hebrew. The finds among the Judean

---

[1] Cited from a personal conversation with Jacques Derrida by Geoffrey Bennington, "Derrida," (class lecture; CPLT 751 Derrida; Emory University, Spring, 2006).

[2] F.J. Kenyon, *The Chester Beatty Biblical Papyri: Ezekiel* (Fasc. 7. London: Emery Walker, 1937); and A.C. Johnson, H.S. Gehman, E.H. Kase, Jr., *The John H. Schiede Biblical Papyri: Ezekiel* (PUSP 3; Princeton: Princeton University Press, 1938).

[3] The papyrus is now known to be a codex containing Ezekiel, Daniel with its additions of Susanna, Bel and the Dragon, and Esther.

[4] Johnson, Gehman, and Kase, *The John H. Schiede Biblical Papyri*, 5. Earlier Septuagint witnesses exist, most certainly pre-Christian, like Pap. Fouad 266 (Rahlfs 847 and 848) and Pap. Rylands 458 (Rahlfs 957). These are dated between the 2nd century BCE and the 1st century CE

[5] L.G. Jahn, *Der Griechische Text des Buche Ezechiel nach dem Kölner Teil des Papyrus 967* (PTA 15; Bonn: Habelt, 1972); and M. Fernández-Galiano, "Nuevas Paginas del codice 967 del AT griego," *SP* 10 (1971): 7–76.

desert for Ezekiel were scanty and the Ezekiel scroll from Qumran cave 11 was petrified and could not be unrolled.[6]

Perhaps because of this notable lacuna of manuscript data, p967 presents several glaring textual difficulties, particularly with respect to the Masoretic Text (MT). The most notable features of p967 are its omission of ch. 36:23c–38 and its transposition of MT chs. 37 and 38–39, placing the vision of the valley of dried bones after the Gog-Magog battle.[7] Several other unique minuses of significant length (i.e., over 10 letters) are also attested (e.g., Ezek 12:26–28 and 32:24–26).

Despite the significant divergences presented by the new witness, no comprehensive full-length study of p967 has yet appeared. Certainly the protracted publication of the manuscript in four separate critical editions posed challenges for any study of p967.[8] Moreover, the discovery of the Dead Sea Scrolls diverted attention from Septuagintal books whose literary editions were not corroborated by the new Hebrew manuscripts. Septuagintal studies focused on books like Jeremiah, whose shorter LXX edition was corroborated by 4QJer[b]. While studies of Jeremiah, Samuel, and Judges, for example, proliferated and spawned new theories about Hebrew textual traditions and multiple literary editions, the Greek text of Ezekiel went understudied.[9] These conditions are *prima facie* grounds for deeper study of p967.

Initial examination of p967's minuses focused on separate pericopes and usually evaluated these for scribal error. For instance, some scholars argued that p967's omission of ch. 36:23c–38 was due to *homoioteleuton*, or to the loss of a leaf in either a Greek parent codex or the Hebrew

---

[6] See chart 1 below in §1.4.

[7] Chapter and verse references cite the LXX (Z) unless otherwise noted.

[8] For example, despite Walther Zimmerli's access to the Princeton and Chester Beatty manuscripts, he was unable to incorporate information regarding p967's minus of 36:23c–38 because it could not be confirmed that the manuscript lacked it until the Madrid and Cologne publications in the 1970s after most of his work was completed. Walther Zimmerli, *Ezekiel* (trans. Ronald E. Clements; 2 vols.; Hermeneia; Philadelphia: Fortress, 1979), 1:76–77 especially.

[9] For example, Eugene Ulrich first proposed his thinking about "new editions" of the Bible in Eugene Ulrich, "Double Literary Editions of Biblical Narratives and Reflections on Determining the Form to be Translated," in *Perspectives on the Hebrew Bible: Essays in Honor of Walter J. Harrelson* (ed., James J. Crenshaw; Macon, Ga.: Mercer University Press, 1988), 101–116. He further developed the ideas in E. Ulrich, "Pluriformity in the Biblical Text, Text Groups, and Questions of Canon," in *Proceedings of the International Congress on the Dead Sea Scrolls, Madrid, 18–21, March 1991* (ed. J. Trebolle Barrera and L. Vegas Montaner; STDJ 11; Leiden: Brill, 1992), 37–40. It was reprinted as chapter 5 in idem, *The Dead Sea Scrolls and the Origins of the Bible* (Grand Rapids: Eerdmans, 1999), 79–98.

Vorlage.[10] However, none of these proposals involved an argument that could explain *all* of p967's unique features. Thus, p967 continued to present important, unresolved textual issues. In this early phase of scholarship on p967, some scholars like E.H. Kase did suggest that p967 preserved an early (Hebrew?) edition of Ezekiel;[11] however, no work was done to support Kase's impression.

While scholars had long noted p967's minuses, a lack of sufficient study obscured the manuscript's literary significance. Not until Johan Lust's pioneering work in the early 1980s did p967 emerge as an important work of literature with its own distinctive features, as Kase had surmised. In 1981, with the publication of Lust's article, "Ezekiel 36–40 in the Oldest Greek Manuscript," p967 first received attention as a literary work in its own right.[12] In that article, Lust demonstrated that two notable MT variants were exegetically connected: the addition of ch. 36:23c–38 and the transposition of chs. 37 and 38–39. Lust showed that p967's sequence of the Gog-Magog battle before the vision of the valley of bones and the minus of the promise oracle in 36:23c–38 displayed theological and literary coherence.[13] Specifically, Lust demonstrated the significance of p967 as a variant edition of Ezekiel's eschatology. A subsequent literary study by Ashley Crane examined Ezekiel 36–39, concluding that p967 and MT presented variant editions of Ezekiel's views of restoration.[14] Earlier text-critical analysis had not perceived these literary connections.

Lust's approach to p967's text laid the ground work, such that p967 now qualifies for the designation 'variant literary edition.' A variant literary edition, a term coined by Eugene Ulrich, is a textual witness that contains variant passages, chapters, or book-level features that affect both meaning and literary character.[15] In the case of p967, we still do not know:

---

[10] See chapters two and three for a more detailed discussion of this issue.

[11] Kase in Johnson, Gehmen, and Kase, *The John H. Schiede Biblical Papyri*, 10, 67–8.

[12] Johan Lust. "Ezekiel 36–40 in the Oldest Greek Manuscript," *CBQ* 43 (1981): 517–33.

[13] For a good review of the history of discussion on p967's text in chs. 36–39, see D.I. Block, *The Book of Ezekiel: Chapters 25–48*, (NIBCOT; Grand Rapids: Eerdmans, 1998), 339.

[14] Ashley Crane, *Israel's Restoration: A Textual-Comparative Exploration of Ezekiel 36–39* (VTSup 122; Boston: Brill, 2008).

[15] According to Ulrich, a new imaginative model was required that "permits the diachronic complexity of the [biblical] text[s]." Ulrich, *The Dead Sea Scrolls and the Origins of the Bible*, 14. For instance, textual criticism had always assumed the category of *the* canonical text, which Ulrich argues needs to be a decision, not an assumption. Ibid., 51–98. For Ulrich, textual critics needed a sober reminder that all biblical books "passed through successive literary editions." Ibid., x. While redaction criticism had always operated within this imaginative model, textual criticism had not. The explosion of new variant literary

1) how extensive the variant edition is, and 2) whether the status applies to the whole book, or just parts of it. This study addresses the precision still required in the designation 'variant literary edition,' with reference to p967.

Variant literary editions introduce new methodological issues into text-critical scholarship. Simultaneously, p967 is a unique textual witness to as well as a variant literary edition of Ezekiel. Lower critical inquiry cannot proceed without some account of p967's literary character. In other words, both p967's *text* and its *literary edition* are by necessity, interrelated issues. In the case of p967, many text-critical approaches ignored the highly relevant fact that p967 contains a variant literary edition of Ezekiel. Hence, this project must advance a means for integrating text-critical and literary methods.

The story of scholarship on p967 provides an important lesson. An isolated field of inquiry can obscure important, even relevant information about a text. Variant literary editions necessitate a more complex and coordinated methodological approach. Eugene Ulrich points towards the type of methodological creativity required at the outset in the study of variant literary editions. He states

> We should first pay serious attention to our new data, try creatively to allow various possible interpretations to emerge and be sufficiently explored, and only then come to a judgment between competing interpretations.[16]

Maureen Bell makes a similar observation in her introduction to the book, *Re-constructing the Book: Literary Texts in Transmission*.[17] Speaking about texts of great English works such as Shakespeare, Bell's comments nevertheless speak clearly to the issue in biblical studies as well. She notes the way in which "literary critics, textual editors and bibliographers, and historians of publishing have hitherto tended to publish their research as if in separate fields of enquiry."[18] Her collection of essays focuses instead, on the coordinated use of multiple methods for understanding textual criticism in the context of literary history. This literary history involves not

---

editions over which Ulrich poured in his magisterial work as editor of the DJD series are, according to him, the "key to the history of the biblical text." Ibid., 106.

[16] Ulrich, *The Dead Sea Scrolls and the Origins of the Bible*, 102.

[17] *Re-constructing the Book: Literary Texts in Transmission* (eds. Maureen Bell, Shirley Chew, Simon Eliot, et al.; Burlington: Ashgate, 2001).

[18] Maureen Bell, "Introduction: The Material Text," in ibid., 1.

only text-critical issues but also literary, material, and sociological lenses of analysis.[19]

> The long-held expectation of the discovery or re-creation of an *originary* text, "superior" to all others, has been replaced by a (more democratic?) respect for each manuscript or printed witness in its own right. In the case of Shakespeare, for example, the "bad" quartos are being reinspected, reassessed and revalued in terms of printing history and performance practice.[20]

Bell's comments fall into a much broader shift taking place in the textual study of classical works.[21] This shift is especially relevant to how we understand manuscripts: as data used to establish an authoritative modern edition of a text *and* unique artifacts of an historically functioning work of literature. Within biblical studies, such methodological awareness is often made explicit, but rarely made central to a specific study. For example, Gene Tucker summarizes the complexity of the methodological issue well, saying

---

[19] Ibid., 2.

[20] Ibid., 3.

[21] See, for example, J. McGann who states that "textual criticism of modern literatures is reconceiving its discipline." Jerome J. McGann, *A Critique of Modern Textual Criticism* (2d ed.; Charlottesville, Va: University Press of Virginia, 1992), 1. For a similar development in Medieval Studies, see the descriptive yet critical discussion of Howard R. Bloch, "New Philology and Old French," in *Spec* 65 (1990): 38–58. Such a shift is only in nascent stages in biblical studies. For instance, Ulrich, writing explicitly about variant literary editions, emphasizes the fluidity of textual traditions and applies Sanders' process of repetition and resignification to textual witnesses (Ulrich, *The Dead Sea Scrolls and the Origins of the Bible*, 8). The insights of Devorah Dimant offer fresh perspectives on the study of variant literary editions. Focusing on the abundant, yet unexplored evidence for scribal interpretive functions, Dimant notes that "a gradual shift of focus is taking place: side by side with the steady output of traditional philological-historical studies, a growing number of works are being devoted to literary and structural analysis. This new trend in research is producing a more sensitive approach to the interpretive function of Jewish literature of the Hellenistic-Roman period, and additional works are studying the various modes of biblical interpretation current in that literature." See Devorah Dimant, "Literary Typologies and Biblical Interpretation in the Hellenistic-Roman Period," in *Jewish Civilization in the Hellenistic-Roman Period* (ed. Shemaryahu Talmon; JSPSup 10; Sheffield: Sheffield Academic Press, 1991), 73. Similarly, Kristen De Troyer calls into question the scholarly distinction between rewritten Scripture and Scripture. Working with George Nickelsburg's discussion of the terms "rewritten," "expanded," and "supplements" in apocryphal literature, De Troyer notes that supplements resemble what textual critics call interpolations. She asks, "could some of these supplements not be seen simply as the further literary development of the biblical text itself?" While De Troyer does not apply this insight directly to the case of variant literary editions, her discussion pushes some of the boundaries that variant literary editions, by nature, defy. Kristen De Troyer, *Rewriting the Sacred Text: What the Old Greek Texts Tell us about the Literary Growth of the Bible* (TCS 4; Atlanta: SBL, 2003), 4. See also George W.E. Nickelsburg, "The Bible Rewritten and Expanded," in *Jewish Writings of the Second Temple Period* (ed., Michael Stone;CRINT, 2; Philadelphia: Fortress, 1984).

Because all texts and versions of the Bible are historically conditioned docu-
ments, textual criticism must not only try to recover the best text but also
attempt to reconstruct the history of the transmission of texts and versions. In this sense, textual criticism addresses another aspect of the question
explored by literary, form and tradition criticism: what course did the history
of the Bible take? It is not possible to distinguish sharply between the stages
of that history which are treated respectively by the various methods.[22]

Similarly, Ulrich urges that the object of study can no longer be the *Urtext*,
in light of the fluidity of textual production in antiquity. Rather, Ulrich
asks

Should not the object of… text-critical study be, not the single collection of
MT texts [and versions] of the individual books, but the organic, developing,
pluriform Hebrew text—different for each book—such as the evidence
indicates.[23]

Writing about classical texts, J. McGann offers a general ideal taken as
central to this study, stating that

The entire socio-history of [a] work—from its originary moments of production through all its subsequent reproductive adventures—is postulated
as the ultimate goal of critical self-consciousness.[24]

The present study originates in the claim that increased critical awareness
is a pre-requisite to deeper study of variant literary editions. In examining a variant literary edition, the "entire socio-history" of any particular manuscript becomes necessary information that affects the utility of
that manuscript's data to any specific field of inquiry. For example, as
the history of scholarship on p967 demonstrated and as more detailed
analysis below will show, textual analysis, operating in isolation from literary study, obscures the full significance of p967's data. What this proves
is that when working with variant literary editions, a field of inquiry
cannot operate in isolation, without first recognizing that the data it
seeks to interpret is, as Maureen Bell urges, lodged within the "unstable
form" of a book.[25] Hence, the present study takes seriously that a text is
always also a manuscript, a unique historical manuscript of a functioning
literary work.

---

[22] Gene M. Tucker, "Editor's Foreward," in Ralph W. Klein, *Textual Criticism of the Old
Testament: From the Septuagint to Qumran* (GBSOTS; Philadelphia: Fortress, 1974), iii–iv.
[23] Ulrich, *The Dead Sea Scrolls and the Origins of the Bible*, 15.
[24] J. McGann, "Theory of Texts," *LRB* 18 (1988): 20–21.
[25] Bell, "Introduction," 3.

My manuscript approach to p967 takes as central the awareness that p967 is a text in *at least* three different ways. First, p967's text is a mechanically transmitted witness to an earlier 'originary' text, (i.e., the *Urtext* or the Old Greek of Ezekiel.) Second, p967's text is a variant literary edition from the MT with unique literary features. This 'text' can shed important new light on Ezekiel's editorial history. Third, the p967 codex presents a text of Ezekiel that was produced under specific conditions and that functioned in specific ways for historical readers. This manuscript approach encompasses all three definitions of text and implicates several various, potentially related areas of research, which include textual criticism, literary criticism, and codicological criticism.[26]

For reading ease, I shall retain the term 'text' in its traditional text-critical associations. However, from the outset, it is crucial to establish that a text's nature is complex and multiple. While all of the three 'texts' mentioned above are self-consciously treated in the current study, the first two, that of textual and literary criticism, receive greater attention. There is one main reason for this: the weight of scholarly analysis on p967 brings us to the brink of the text-critical question: what is the relationship between p967's text and its literary edition?

Having framed the project in terms of a manuscript approach, and in light of this decision to give more focus to p967's text and its literary edition, further introductory remarks are now relevant. In what follows, I provide a general discussion of methods and variant literary editions and then present more specific work on p967. The discussion reveals the need for a complex and coordinated methodological approach to p967. Hence the present study clarifies and executes an innovative approach to variant literary editions.

1.2. Variant Literary Editions and the Problem of Method

1.2.1. *Integrating Literary and Text-Critical Methods*

Because the phenomenon of variant literary editions is not new to biblical studies, especially since the discovery of the Dead Sea Scrolls, several discussions of procedure and method precede this study.[27] The need to

---

[26] For bibliography on the last, see chapter 6 below.

[27] Ulrich addresses the issue in his chapter on double literary editions, (*The Dead Sea Scrolls and the Origins of the Bible*, esp. 99–120). Emanuel Tov also contributes a chapter on the topic in Emanuel Tov, *Textual Criticism of the Hebrew Bible* (2d ed.; Minneapolis:

integrate literary and text-critical modes of analysis has been widely recognized.[28] As Emanuel Tov states in his chapter, "Contribution of the LXX to the Literary Criticism of the Bible:"

> From the outset it would appear that these issues [i.e. literary ones,] are so far removed from the topics usually treated by textual critics that the relevance of textual data to literary criticism would seem to be remote. This chapter, however, demonstrates that this is not the case. As a rule, too little attention is paid to these aspects in the analysis of textual data.[29]

As Tov indicates, literary methods, while necessary in the analysis of variant literary editions, are held in suspicion by textual critics. At issue is the analytical usefulness of literary categories in the text-critical enterprise. This issue was the subject of debate in the well-known joint project on the David and Goliath variant edition.[30] In that study, four scholars were invited to address the issue of the variant Hebrew and Greek texts by combining literary and text-critical analysis. One question that emerged as central is how to determine an intentional literary variant. Tov and Lust critique the literary procedures and methods of Gooding and Barthélemy for being too subjective.[31] Lust argues that "artful" literary criteria are unhelpful in determining intentional literary variants.[32] For example, David Gooding's literary analysis focused on rhetorical artistry and often argued for text-critical intentionality and priority based on notions of literary taste, completeness, and beauty.[33]

Augsburg Fortress, 2001), 313–50. See also idem, "The Contribution of the LXX to the Literary Criticism of the Bible," in *The Text-Crtical Use of the Septuagint in Biblical Research* (2d ed.; Jerusalem: SIMOR, 1997), 237–63. Kristen De Troyer considers four different case studies of the LXX's relationship to the MT in her *Rewriting the Sacred Text*. Additionally, D. Barthelemy, D. Gooding, J. Lust, and E. Tov provide literary and text-critical case studies on the double edition of 1 Samuel 17–18 in the MT and LXX. See D. Barthélemy, D.W. Gooding, J. Lust, and E. Tov, eds., *The Story of David and Goliath: Textual and Literary Criticism: Papers of a Joint Research Venture* (OBO 73; Göttingen: Vandenhoeck & Ruprecht, 1986). This final study gave students and scholars alike a test case for dealing with the interaction of literary and textual methods in the analysis of variant literary editions.

[28] Lust has argued that "text-critical and literary methods should complement each other." Johan Lust, "Methodological Remarks," in *The Story of David and Goliath*, 126.

[29] Tov, *The Text-Critical Use of the Septuagint*, 237.

[30] Barthélemy et al., *The Story of David and Goliath*.

[31] Tov and Lust also critique Gooding and Barthélemy for their procedural sequence.

[32] Lust, "Methodological Remarks," in *David and Goliath*, 125.

[33] A short list of some of Gooding's literary comments that were used to produce his text-critical evaluation include: "precision of this beautifully structured sequence" (66), "the idea" explained (66), "ways of classical heroes" (67), sections that are "irredeemably inept" (69), "thought-flow of the narrative" (69), "main message of the story" (70), "pedantic and ruinous attempt to get rid of an apparent difficulty" (70), "common theme" (71),

Instead, both Tov and Lust defend a sequential procedure in which textual criticism precedes literary criticism. Tov's "point of departure is the textual level and only the textual level," leaving aside literary questions until late in the analysis.[34] Because the evidence has "been transmitted to us in textual sources," Tov argues that textual, and not literary analysis suits the data.[35] Similarly Lust, who devotes more attention than Tov to the issue of sequencing, argues that textual criticism provides the best starting point for study of textual phenomena.[36] In his own words:

> Discussions may arise concerning sequence in which the respective critical methods should be applied. It is probably preferable to start with textual criticism. Indeed, when one tries to define the relation between different forms of a text...one deals with the history of the text. Such a historical study is not the first aim of rhetorical criticism or of structuralism. These methods may find rhetorical and structural qualities in the text at any stage of its development or of its transmission.[37]

Both scholars emphasize the importance of securing a critical text before conducting literary analysis. However, two major problems immediately present themselves concerning the idea of a critical text. First, textual analysis is not perfectly objective and scientific. Tov himself questions the rule-based nature of textual criteria and admits that common sense ultimately determines one's evaluation.[38] Second, as chapter 2 will demonstrate, complex textual debates such as the theories about the Greek translators, inner-Greek revision, and Hebrew correction militate against the facile establishment of a critical text.

A crucial theoretical issue lies behind these questions about method and the sequence of text-critical and literary methods. It seems overstated if not altogether incorrect to hold that because the variant literary data is transmitted in textual sources, textual criticism must have sequential precedence.[39] Indeed, the literary qualities of textual sources stand alongside their textual nature as equally characteristic of the sources. As discussed above, a manuscript is a text in several ways. This complexity and multiplicity does not provide a facile starting point for methodological

---

"completeness" (74), "logical progression" (74), "consistency" (75), "classical restraint" (75), "good taste" (75), "discrepancy" (79), "time-table difficulty" (81), and "narrative technique" (81).

[34] Tov, "Response," in *David and Goliath*, 94.
[35] Tov, "Conclusion," in *David and Goliath*, 131–132.
[36] Lust, "Methodological Remarks," in *David and Goliath*, 121.
[37] Ibid.
[38] Tov, *Text Criticism of the Hebrew Bible*, 295.
[39] So Tov, "Conclusion," in *David and Goliath*, 131–2.

sequence. Nevertheless, methodological sequencing is possible, although it depends on two important factors: 1) the scholar's orienting questions;[40] and 2) attention to what we mean by 'literary criticism.' The latter warrants some attention, however briefly.

1.2.2. Defining Literary Criticism

Biblical studies offer two ways of understanding literary criticism. Ascendant with the historical critical approach to biblical literature, literary criticism came to mean an interest in the various stages in the development of biblical books.[41] The second meaning of literary criticism comes from literary criticisms that flourish in modern humanities more broadly and has to do with the structure and style of literature, as well as with cultural notions about writing and strategies of reading. Many strands of this type of literary criticism have made deep and successful inroads into biblical studies, such as genre and narrative criticism, to name a few.[42] As indicated above, Lust and Tov critiqued Gooding's literary criticism as being exclusively interested in higher critical features of the variant literary edition, without paying sufficient attention to lower critical issues.[43] What is required is a literary analysis that is rooted in text-critical questions and textual approaches.

The evidence furnished by variant literary editions resembles strata not unlike what redaction critics identify in *Literaturkritik*.[44] In *Literaturkritik*,

---

[40] For example, in the David and Goliath study, Tov's question determines his positions on methodological sequencing. He proposes that "at the initial stage of our discussion there is, in my view, only one question: does the deviating Greek text reflect a deviating Hebrew text or not?" Tov, "Response," in *David and Goliath*, 93. Tov's question reveals his singular interest in the Hebrew *Vorlage* of the LXX without concern for the possibility of subsequent editorial development. Such development could take two forms: inner-Greek editorial development, or inner-Greek correction towards a developed Hebrew text.

[41] See J. Coert Rylaarsdam's comments on the distinct types of literary criticisms within biblical studies which he lays out in the foreward of N. Habel's volume on Literary Criticism. J. Coert Rylaarsdam, "Editor's Foreward" in Norman Habel, *Literary Criticism of the Old Testament*, (GBSOTS; Philadelphia: Fortress, 1971), iii–ix.

[42] See John Barton whose helpful introductory book on the methods of higher criticism operates with the same distinction, calling modern literary criticism, "secular", which I find slightly misleading and unnecessarily loaded. John Barton, *Reading the Old Testament: Method in Biblical Study*, (2d ed.; Louisville: Westminster, 1996), 1–7.

[43] See footnote above.

[44] This study's approach to literary analysis shows affiliation with the types of questions asked in redaction criticism. For the theoretical basis of this view, see S. Talmon who points out that the process of composition blended with the process of transmission. Shemaryahu Talmon, "The Textual Study of the Bible—A New Outlook" in *Qumran and the History of the Biblical Text* (eds. F.M. Cross and S. Talmon; Cambridge: Harvard University

the scholar isolates strata of material that exhibit shared formal features, ideas, or themes that seem secondary to the text. The underlying assumption is that author-scribes introduced such strata. In other words, redaction critics use principles of 'literary coherence' to identify layers of editorial activity. Given that variant literary editions provide a hard set of data for such editorial activity, the types of literary strategies employed by redaction critics can be used to signal intentionality. This approach to textual and literary criticism is adopted in this study and will be referred to as the 'coherence' approach. It now remains to situate this approach within previous scholarship on p967's literary edition.

1.3. Previous Scholarship on p967 as a Variant Literary Edition

1.3.1. *Johan Lust and Ashley Crane*

To date, scholarship on p967 has revealed much about its distinctive literary edition of Ezekiel. However, the types of literary analysis have shifted throughout the history of analysis. The earliest literary study of p967 adopted a tradition-historical approach to the literary analysis of p967's unique text.

Lust recognized the eschatological significance of p967, especially the material in chs. 37–39. In his earliest study, cited above, Lust hypothesized that Pharisaic, anti-apocalyptic theology motivated the transposition in Ezekiel's eschatological chapters. According to Lust, p967's order of chs. 38→39→37 was the more original. The MT displays a later arrangement of these chapters, rejecting the idea that a resurrection followed the eschatological battle. The Pharisaic editor transposed the vision of the valley of dried bones so that it would come before the Gog-Magog battle. Thereby the MT edition disallowed a notion of resurrection at the end times.

Lust was challenged on his Pharisaic proposal, most notably by Daniel Block.[45] Subsequently, Lust abandoned a full-blown argument for sectarian authorship. Instead, he returned to the textual data and in two subsequent

---

Press, 1975, 333. Similar comments can be found in Gene Tucker, "Editor's Forward," iii–iv; See also James Watts, "Text and Redaction in Jeremiah's Oracles against the Nations," *CBQ* 54 (1991): 437, and Kristen De Troyer, *Rewriting the Sacred Text*, 1.

[45] Block, *The Book of Ezekiel: Chapters 25–48*, 337–43. Lust responds in Lust, "Textual Criticism of the Old and New Testaments: Stepbrothers?" in *New Testament Textual Criticism and Exegesis* (Leuven: Leuven University Press, 2002), 28–30. See also Crane's summary of the Block-Lust debate in Crane, *Israel's Restoration*, 236–45.

essays, demonstrated literary coherence among a larger number of p967's variants.[46] Examining the MT pluses in 12:26–28, 32:24–26, and the textual issue in chapter 7, Lust concluded that p967 presents the more apocalyptic edition of Ezekiel than MT. Further, he argued that an MT scribe added material in order to *historicize* p967's more mythologizing tendencies. An MT innovation in 32:24–26 puts Meshech and Tubal in the pit alongside Israel's other historical enemies. The MT also presents its theology of the historical fulfillment of prophecy in 12:26–28. According to this MT plus, Ezekiel's oracles do not linger, but are *immediately* fulfilled. Lust goes on to suggest that these two variants correlate with the MT's plot-sequence in chs. 37–39.

According to Lust's proposals, MT chs. 37–39 represent a later scribal interest to historicize and fix the military events depicted therein. The MT treats Meshech and Tubal as historical leaders. Further, the MT edition interprets Ezekiel's restoration oracles as immediately fulfilled in Israel's post-exilic restoration and subsequent military invasion from the North. These historicizing interpretations work against the earlier edition (p967), which projected Ezekiel's oracles forward to refer not to past or contemporary history but to the end times.

Ashley Crane's dissertation, completed in 2006, adopted and developed Lust's results. He focused on Ezekiel 36–39 in the MT and the Greek uncials using what he called a "text-comparative method."[47] This method explores the interpretive significance of all meaningful textual variants as trajectories of interpretation. Crane was especially interested in Ezekiel's theology of restoration in these chapters, picking up on Lust's eschatological/sectarian conclusions.[48]

Later published in book form, Crane's results advanced scholarly understandings of p967 and the MT as two different literary editions. Crane's characterization of p967 especially highlighted the second half of ch. 37 and its immediate transition to chs. 40–48. In this section, according to Crane, p967 portrays the national unification under a Davidic messiah whose job is

---

[46] Lust, "Textual Criticism of the Old and New Testaments," 15–31; idem, "Major Divergences between LXX and MT in Ezekiel," in *The Earliest Text of the Hebrew Bible: The Relationship between the Masoretic Text and the Hebrew Base of the Septuagint Reconsidered* (ed. Adrian Schenker; SBLSCS 52; Atlanta: SBL, 2003), 83–92.

[47] Crane, *Israel's Restoration*, 1–4. For his evaluation of his comparative Hebrew and Greek witnesses, see ibid., 7–10.

[48] Crane, *Israel's Restoration*, 24.

to shepherd the people peacefully, making sure they are torah-observant (v 24b), as they live under their covenant of peace (v 26). In p967's order, his [the Davidic leader's] greatest purpose is shepherding the people for the building of the sanctuary (v 26b), so God can dwell with his people (v 27).[49]

Since p967's order does not interrupt the covenant of peace in 37:26 with the military scene in chs. 38–39, the transition to the temple vision is seamlessly pacifist.

According to Crane, the later MT edition is the result of shifting Second Temple political realities. The MT edition re-crafted the peaceful vision of Ezekiel to "rally the troops" in a "call to arms."[50] In MT, ch. 37's placement underscores the vision's symbolic significance as Israel's *past* restoration, according to Crane. Chapters 38–39 follow as a text for military hope and confidence in the contemporary *present*; the call to arms is implied.

Aside from the changed chapter order, the best textual support for Crane's reading comes in 37:10. The MT, to describe the revivified bones, uses a military image: an 'exceedingly great army' (חיל גדול מאד מאד). In MT's order of chapters, Israel's restored army faces the military invasion of the following chapters. In contrast, p967 reads instead: 'a very numerous congregation' (συναγωγη πολλη σφοδρα). When read in the context of the changed chapter order, the Greek reading complements the peaceful temple-oriented function for ch. 37 in p967, proposed by Crane. While the variant in 37:10 can certainly take on the significances Crane proposes in light of the changed chapter order, the variant itself is not strong evidence for different views of restoration. p967's reading συναγωγη occurs in all Greek witnesses and therefore cannot necessarily relate to p967's alternate order of chapters. Additionally, Crane's translation 'army' is not restrictive, חיל need not refer exclusively to a military group.[51] Upon closer inspection, Crane's reading of the variant visions of restoration in p967 and MT is not well-supported by a wider set of variants. Nevertheless, Crane's attention to Ezekiel's vision of restoration does offer intriguing literary readings of the two editions.

The work of Lust and Crane provided an important foundation for further understandings of p967 as a literary edition different from the MT. Especially important are Lust's conclusions about the different

---

[49] Crane, *Israel's Restoration*, 251.

[50] Crane, *Israel's Restoration*, 253–54.

[51] For instance, חיל usually refers to a military army, however, it can also refer to a large group of people (1 Kgs 10:2; 2 Chr 9:1) or to leaders (Exod 18:21, 25), worthy men (1 Kgs 1:42) or worthy women (Ruth 3:11).

eschatological horizons and the use of apocalyptic versus historicizing elements. Crane's literary analysis, in the main, highlights important differences regarding Israel's restoration along with a stimulating discussion of Davidic messianism. Most relevant to the present study, however, is Lust and Crane's use of literary and text-critical forms of analysis.

Four types of analysis are clear in Lust and Crane's work: 1) tradition-historical analysis, 2) historical criticism, 3) a 'text-comparative' approach,[52] and 4) a coherence approach. Both Lust and Crane attend to literary issues in conjunction with text-critical questions to varying degrees of success. Their appraoches require evaluation to determine how well they make sense of p967's unique textual features.

1.3.2. *Lust's Tradition History Approach*

Lust insightfully recognized the significance of p967's edition of Ezekiel 36–40 to beliefs about resurrection and eschatology. This observation remains relevant to a history of theology. However, the utility of this approach to text-critical questions was swiftly refuted by Block. Specifically, Block challenged Lust's claim that a sectarian theological view on eschatology was the editorial motivation which produced the MT.[53] Block pointed out how difficult such sectarian and theological arguments are to substantiate,

> Indeed, one could argue with equal if not greater force that the growth of apocalypticism in the late intertestamental period stimulated the rearrangement of oracles in the text-form, so that the resurrection of the dead is seen as the final eschatological event prior to the reestablishment of a spiritual Israel, rather than simply a metaphor for the restoration of the nation from exile.[54]

In short, as Block suggests, the history of ideas about resurrection and eschatology provides an unstable basis upon which to make claims about textual priority. Lust fully accepted the critique, modifying his position

---

[52] "Text-comparative" is Crane's term.

[53] Lust's original proposal understood the MT transposition as a Pharisaic attempt to disallow resurrection at the end times, thus placing ch. 37 (the vision of dried bones) before chs. 38–39 (the Gog-Magog battle). Lust, "Ezekiel 36–40," 531. Block's retort is the sixth argument he levies against Lust, and in my estimation, his only successful one. Block, *The Book of Ezekiel.*

[54] Block, *The Book of Ezekiel,* 341.

and stating that MT's "'plusses' are *somehow* connected with the editor's opinions concerning eschatology and apocalypticism."[55]

1.3.3. *Crane's Historical-Critical Approach*

Crane's study is framed by Lust's tradition-historical approach. Focusing on 'restoration' instead of eschatology, Crane focuses on the same block of text: Ezekiel 36–39. However, Crane's analysis, presented above, is inadequate in two respects. First, Ezekiel's material about restoration extends beyond the scope of Crane's study. Several promise oracles throughout Ezekiel bear heavily on Ezekiel's theology of restoration which is in fact the stated goal of Crane's literary analysis. Chapter 34 is a promise oracle to Israel using the metaphor of a shepherd gathering his mishandled sheep. Ezek 30:39–44 deals with God gathering Israel to his holy mountain. Ezek 17:22–24 advances the vine metaphor and depicts its replanting on the mountain height of Israel. Finally, Ezek 11:14–25 uses much of the same purity language as 36:23c–38 to describe how God will restore Israel. These four passages bear on Ezekiel's theology of restoration, and yet Crane does not consider them in his study. Hence, Crane's study does not encompass the relevant scope of this theme in Ezekiel.[56]

Second, Crane's conclusions about p967 and MT's different views of restoration draw heavily on the world outside the text. He relies on Second Temple and Maccabean political realities to develop his characterization of the MT as the later edition. While this produces a stimulating reading, Crane's real error is in formulating his decisions about textual priority on the basis of historical-critical arguments that are underdeveloped and therefore over-generalized. This is especially the case in his treatment of 36:23c–38.

Crane does not deal with the theological content nor literary impact of the MT plus 36:23c–38.[57] In lieu of an exegetical analysis of the MT plus,

---

[55] Lust, "Major Divergences," 92. Italics mine. See also idem, "Textual Criticism of the Old and New Testaments," 54.

[56] For example, p967 presents an extensive minus in a passage about restoration in 33:25 where the MT, as the longer text, reads עַל הַדָּם תֹּאכֵלוּ וְעֵינְכֶם תִּשְׂאוּ אֶל גִּלּוּלֵיכֶם וְדָם תִּשְׁפֹּכוּ וְהָאָרֶץ תִּירָשׁוּ, (you eat with blood, your eyes gaze upon your idols, and you pour out blood. Will you then possess the land?) Crane does not deal with this variant.

[57] When Crane applies his text-comparative approach (discussed below) to the variants in 36:22–38, he understandably excludes p967 since it lacks vv. 23c–38. However, as a result, his analysis of 36:22–38 focuses only on the rare textual differences among the MT, Vaticanus, and Alexandrinus. In his own words,

Crane assumes these verses participate in the MT's 'call to purity' (along with ch. 37). His discussion of the reason for 36:23c–38's presence in MT is brief, saying only

> as the chapter reorder [in the MT] appears to be a call to arms, this inserted pericope *appears to be* a call to purity. It introduces and supports the "new" moral and/or spiritual resurrection metaphor for the dry bones, and the unity of the united nation under a military Davidic leader.[58]

Aside from this remark, Crane is uncharacteristically inattentive to this unit. He turns to Lust in order to support his conclusions.[59] In Crane's words,

> the main significance for us is that Lust's changing eschatological proposal provides a plausible theological reason for the chapter re-order, resulting in the creation and insertion of 36:23c–38 in later MSS.[60]

Crane thus abandons his text-comparative method, discussed below, when he encounters the largest, most obvious variant in his chosen unit. Instead Crane's arguments about the MT plus in ch. 36 rely on highly speculative historical-critical analyses. In fact, Crane resurrects Lust's Pharisaic proposal, attributing the MT edition to "a sector of the Jewish community that may have felt so strongly about their theology to have interacted with the text, changing the text to reflect their sifting [*sic*] theology."[61] Ultimately, Crane places MT's editorial activity in Hasmonean times as a call to arms. Crane's case for the priority of p967's text is far from proven; indeed his conclusion may well prove to be incorrect. Indeed, Block's refutation of Lust's work applies equally well to Crane's. In short, Crane's historical-critical approach cannot support his text-critical conclusions about priority.[62]

---

as our goal is to observe variants as possible theological interpretations, we will not discuss verses where agreement is found... Our discussion of vv. 22–38 may therefore appear disjoined owing to the omission of the majority of the verses. Crane, *Israel's Restoration*, 74–75.

[58] Crane, *Israel's Restoration*, 255. Italics mine.

[59] Here Crane uncritically adopts Lust's 2003 work which used the tradition-historical approach to Ezek 36:23c–38. However, Lust's goal in that study was to show why 36:23c–38 was an appropriate introduction to ch. 37. He never claimed to be attending to the entire plus as a unit of composition. Crane fails to recognize the limited and circumstantial nature of Lust's comments.

[60] Crane, *Israel's Restoration*, 235.

[61] Ibid.

[62] Indeed, Crane eschews text-critical methods at the outset of his study. Crane, *Israel's Restoration*, 4.

1.3.4. *Crane's Text-Comparative Approach*

The body of Crane's analysis consists of what he calls a text-comparative approach. This approach affirms the integrity of each source/manuscript witness as a final text of Ezekiel. Consistent with this affirmation, Crane examines meaningful textual variants as "trajectories of interpretation." By this, Crane presupposes that textual variants are the result of intentional scribal interpretation, and that a comparison within a textual tradition will show various 'trajectories' of interpretation.

Further, in keeping with the affirmation of a manuscript as a final text, Crane even includes paratextual information for each witness, such as paragraphing. Overall, his text-comparative approach represents a legitimate challenge to textual criticism's romance with the *Urtext* and obsession with textual differences as solely derived from scribal error or contamination. Instead of going behind the witnesses to find an ideal text, Crane's approach affirms the form of the text in which each particular manuscript presents it.

Crane's text-comparative approach shares a major objective with the present study, namely to reframe textual criticism in the service of study of variant literary editions. As I will discuss below, my codicological analysis in chapter 6 will deepen Crane's approach to the particularity of each manuscript, more fully affirming the idea that each manuscript is its own edition of Ezekiel.[63]

1.3.5. *Lust's Coherence Approach*

Lust's second phase of literary analysis adopted a 'coherence' approach to the literary analysis of p967's variants. He examined a wider scope of variants between p967 and MT than previously or subsequently considered. Showing coherence across a larger data set more strongly supports theories of intentional editorial activity. For example, Lust was able to show that all of MT's pluses he examined historicized Ezekiel's oracles. In every case, p967's edition presented the more mythologizing edition.

Lust's coherence approach suggests that at some unknown stage, redactors altered Ezekiel's textual tradition according to particular interests. As indicated above, this approach comes into close alignment with *Literaturkritik* and discerns literary layers from a circumscribed data set of variants. In this sense, Lust's coherence approach adeptly combines

---

[63] See more on the codicological analysis of p967 in chapter 6.

literary analysis and text-critical approaches in the study of p967's variant literary edition.

Having examined the four types of literary analysis already deployed on p967's text, it remains to return to the text-critical discussion.

1.4. RETURNING TO TEXTUAL CRITICISM OF P967

Both Lust and Crane deal with textual issues in their literary analyses, although in often incomplete or even incorrect ways. Specifically, they addressed two important text-critical questions: 1) Are the meaningful variants that distinguish p967 and MT as variant literary editions intentional? and 2) assuming editorial activity, which edition of Ezekiel, p967 or MT, represents the earlier edition?

First, both scholars recognized the need to show that p967's variants are not a result of transmission error. Lust's work has gone a long way to defend the text of p967. He adduced factors such as the literary coherence among MT's pluses, late linguistic features, the weakness of text-critical arguments for mechanical error, and the independent witness of Latin manuscript Wirceburgensis (La[W]), which supports p967's edition of Ezekiel 36–39 (the omission and re-order of chapters).[64] Additionally, Crane adduced indirect evidence for p967's edition of chs. 36–39 in Daniel, Revelation, Targum Neofiti, and Pseudo-Jonathan to Numbers 11:26.[65] Crane shows that these 'witnesses,' perhaps his most important contribution to study of p967, knew p967's order of chapters 36–39. Hence, he argues that a robust reception history would challenge claims that p967's order of chapters is merely a scribal mistake, if erroneous at all. Crane's work finally concludes about p967's edition,

---

[64] Codex Wirceburgensis, a 6th century manuscript, represents one of the two earliest and best preserved Latin witnesses to Ezekiel. It was published by E. Ranke, *Par palimpsestorum Wirceburgensium antiquissimae Veteris Testamenti latinae fragmenta e codd. Rescriptus* (Vienna: G. Braumüller, 1871). For Lust's demonstration that La[W] represents an independent textual witness to p967 chs. 36–39, see Lust, "Ezekiel 36–40," 518. A more detailed analysis of the manuscript and its significance for p967 can be found in P.M. Bogaert, "Le témoignage de la Vetus Latina dans l'étude de la tradition des Septante Ézéchiel et Daniel dans le Papyrus 967," *Bib* 59 (1978): 390–391. See also Kase, "Relation to the Old Latin Version," in *The John H. Schiede Biblical Papyri*, 42–48.

[65] Crane, *Israel's Restoration*, 245–9. Lust had already substantially argued for Revelation's connection to p967 in Lust, "The Order of Final Events in Revelation and in Ezekiel," in *L'Apocalypse johannique et l'Apocalyptique dans le Nouveau Testament* (ed. J. Lambrecht; BETL 53; Louvain: Leuven University Press, 1980), 179–83.

p967 is not an innovative or maverick text, but representative of an existing textual tradition.[66]

Thus, he affirms what Lust had also argued, that several of MT's pluses represent a coherent and distinct literary edition from p967. Nevertheless, debates persist, despite the strong evidence mounted by Lust and Crane.

Second, a textual argument mounted by both Lust and Crane is that the MT is the later edition, expanded from a Hebrew text best represented by p967's *Vorlage*. For instance, Lust showed that the pluses in MT and in several other LXX manuscripts included late linguistic features.[67] This constitutes important evidence in any evaluation about priority. However, it is premature to declare that the *entire* text of p967 traces back to a variant Hebrew *Vorlage*.

Indeed, several critical editions of the Ezekiel LXX remain ambivalent about p967's text. Four examples will demonstrate this ambivalence. First, the Hebrew University Bible Project (HUBP), a self-declaring 'conservative' approach to the witnesses, does not assign much value to p967 readings.[68] The editors of HUBP construct a diplomatic text, using the Aleppo Codex as the base text, but they developed a strict set of criteria for the variants they record in the apparatus, the most important of which is rejection of retroverted readings. Since most of p967's unique variant

---

[66] Crane, *Israel's Restoration*, 208.

[67] Lust, "Ezekiel 36–40," 521–5.

[68] Apparatus I in HUBP, devoted to the versions, often does not record p967's variants, as in 12:26–28 and 32:24–26. By way of explanation, the editors do not view the *Urtext* as their supreme goal (xi §3,) but are rather interested in the proto-MT text tradition (xiii §11). The system of apparatuses which organize the editors' opinions about the integrity of a reading center on the Hebrew text. For them, "study of the versions has shown that retroverted readings cannot have a claim to certainty, unless attested in a Hebrew source" (xii §6). Of course, the editors acknowledge that the literal translation technique observed for Greek Ezekiel implies that several unique readings may reflect a Hebrew *Vorlage*. As one would expect, they state that the "retroverted readings from the ancient version in Apparatus I present the most difficult problems of method" (xvii §29). Apparatus I supplies the readings which in the editors' view, reflects the period of textual pluriformity characteristic of the second and third century BCE, while the readings that appear in Apparatuses II–IV are characterized as reflecting a later stage (xiii §9). For LXX readings, the editors follow Ziegler's 1977 edition for quotations, and refer to his text as the Old Greek (LXX). Because p967 was new to Ziegler's 1977 edition and discussion appeared only in the Supplement (*Nachtrag*), the HUBP editors simply note when a reading derives specifically from p967, avoiding any judgment about whether it reflects the OG. (Chapter 36:23–38 appears as such a note in Apparatus I.) In the end, the editors demur, "the question of the importance of 967 as a witness to the Old Greek and its possible reflection of a variant Hebrew tradition cannot be treated here" (xxii §49 note 43).

readings are unsupported by Hebrew texts, the readings do not appear in the apparatus.

Second, Ziegler had access to the John H. Scheide (Princeton) and Chester Beatty (Dublin) portions of the p967 manuscript when he published his Göttingen edition of LXX Ezekiel (1952). Later, in part stimulated by the publication of the Madrid and Köln portions of p967, Detlef Fraenkel supplied a 22-page Supplement (*Nachtrag*) in the second edition (1977).[69] Fraenkel outlines how the complete evidence from p967 was evaluated for the second edition, and echoes Ziegler's overall positive assessment of p967's usefulness for determining the OG. However, Codex Vaticanus (B) was still given pride of place as the base text for the 1977 edition. Fraenkel notes the considerable amount of work required by the new evidence as something of an apologia for its incomplete incorporation into the eclectic, critical text.[70]

Third, in his *Textual Criticism of the Hebrew Bible*, Tov characterized the LXX of Ezekiel as a variant literary stratum, earlier than the MT. Although he cites Lust's work on p967, and presumably considered the evidence of p967 for himself, Tov's presentation lacks analysis of any p967 variants.[71] According to Tov, the stratum of recensional rewriting "is not extensive; it is extant in chapter 7 only."[72] One is left to conclude that Tov does not currently attribute much value to p967 in determining this "shorter and earlier edition."

Fourth, Walther Zimmerli had full recourse to the Chester Beatty and John H. Scheide portions of p967 for his Hermeneia commentary on Ezekiel, but that work appeared before the critical editions of Jahn and Fernández-Galiano were prepared. Although Zimmerli acquired transcriptions of the latter portions, and therefore knew with certainty that p967 presented an alternative order of chs. 36–39, he does not mention this

---

[69] Detlef Fraenkel, "Nachtrag zur 1. Auflage von 1952," in *Ezechiel* (ed. Joseph Ziegler; Septuaginta: Vetus Testamentum Graecum auctoritate Academiae Scientiarum Gottingensis 16:1; 2d ed.; Göttingen: Vandenhoeck & Ruprecht, 1977), 331–352. Hereafter Ziegler, LXX.

[70] Fraenkel, "Nachtrag" in Ziegler, LXX, 333.

[71] The space and the genre of the book precluded any lengthy analysis of specific variants.

[72] Emanuel Tov, *Textual Criticism of the Hebrew Bible*, 333–4. See also idem, "Recensional Differences Between the MT and the LXX of Ezekiel," *ETL* 62 (1986): 89. Tov concludes that the literary layer reflected in the MT was added to "a shorter and earlier edition as represented by LXX." He argues on the basis of parallel elements and synonymous words contained in the MT pluses. Tov, *Textual Criticism of the Hebrew Bible*, 334.

in his discussion of Ezekiel's textual history. In fact, Zimmerli places the discussion of p967 in his section on "The Later History of the Book and Its Text" thereby apparently denying any merit to p967 as an early witness.[73]

The four cases mentioned above share a minimalistic approach to p967's text. None attribute much value to p967 as a witness to a Hebrew parent text, in contrast to Lust and Crane's assertions. Even Ziegler's eclectic Greek text defers to B as the best witness to the Old Greek. Moreover, textual debates continue over individual p967 variants. From a text-critical perspective, more work is certainly required on p967, especially if it is to be taken seriously as reflecting an early edition of Ezekiel.

One of the primary issues involved in determining textual priority is genetic relations; indeed, p967's text-type remains a somewhat open question. Additionally, inner-Greek revision must be considered. The relationship among p967, B, and the Old Greek is far from resolved. Lust's argument for the priority of p967 over MT is at least based on translation and linguistic analysis. But, as I will discuss below, Lust overstates his case by implying that the status of textual priority extends to all of p967's textual features.

Crane uncritically accepts that p967 is closest to the Old Greek. In so doing, he conflates p967 with the OG and assumes p967 reflects the Hebrew *Vorlage* of the OG. The result is that when Crane speaks about the priority of p967 over the MT, he has abandoned textual criticism's well-established text groups and stemmata of textual relations.[74] In point of fact, these and other issues, such as translation technique, render comprehensive positions on priority premature.[75]

---

[73] Walther Zimmerli, *Ezekiel* (2 Vols.; trans. Ronald E. Clements; Hermeneia; Philadelphia: Fortress, 1979), 1:76–77.

[74] To be sure, Crane's is not a traditional text-critical project. Nevertheless, his study does not adequately interact with textual criticism. For instance, he defines scribal errors as "variants without discernible interpretive intent." Crane, *Israel's Restoration*, 2. This definition radically diverges from textual criticism's well established principles for transmission error. See Tov, *Textual Criticism of the Hebrew Bible*, 232–75. This sort of inadequate appropriation of text-critical principles is characteristic of a project whose method over-privileges final forms. Crane's text-comparative method insists that texts were read in their final form as manuscripts and therefore must be respected for their differences. While I embrace this presupposition whole-heartedly, it does not eliminate the need for textual criticism. He attempts to assign priority throughout, often on the basis of literary considerations alone. Crane eschews text-critical analysis and yet seeks to draw textual conclusions.

[75] This will be discussed more fully in chapter 3.

Indeed, scholars have taken issue with the conclusion that p967 is earlier than the MT. Daniel I. Block directed a seven-point challenge against the priority of p967.[76] Block's seven critiques defended the integrity of the MT as the ancient standardized form and thus the preferred basis for his exegetical work.[77] According to Block, p967's witness provides not a *real* but at best a *hypothetical* reconstruction of an early Hebrew text which can therefore *not* be used to supplant the actually extant Hebrew of MT. In the end, Block affirms that p967 "may still represent an old text form,"[78] but he avoids taking a conclusive stance on priority.[79]

Block's implicit position on priority is made explicit in the recent article of Hector M. Patmore. Patmore argues that priority cannot be defended for either p967 or MT; all that can be said for certain is that we have in these two witnesses, parallel ancient editions of Ezekiel. Referring to the Hebrew evidence for the wide circulation of 'proto-MT' texts at Qumran and Masada, Patmore concludes

> The available data are better explained by the conclusion that two different texts of Ezekiel [MT and p967] must have been in circulation concurrently for a prolonged period of time and that the historical precedence of either text cannot be established legitimately.[80]

Patmore's work is based on the arguable strength of the 'proto-MT' textual tradition. Indeed, he reminds us that we have a total of 340 words of Ezekiel in Hebrew preserved in the various fragments from the Judean desert but only from chapters 1, 10, 11, 23, 24, 35–38, and 41 many of which support MT readings over LXX or p967 ones (see chart 1).

---

[76] Block, *The Book of Ezekiel*, 337–42. For a good discussion of Block's seven points, see Crane who often favors Lust. Crane, *Israel's Restoration*, 290–300.

[77] Block, *The Book of Ezekiel*, 342.

[78] Ibid.

[79] Block's ambivalence on the issue of priority can be seen in his comments about the originality of the MT plus at 36:23c–38. Block concedes that the passage in the LXX was brought into conformity with the received Hebrew text, and shows distinct literary style from its literary environment. Thus, Block allows that the passage could be a secondary addition, saying it "may point to the hand of a redactor," albeit a thoroughly Ezekielian one. Block, *The Book of Ezekiel*, 343.

[80] Hector M. Patmore, "The Shorter and Longer Texts of Ezekiel: The Implications of the Manuscript Finds from Masada and Qumran," *JSOT* 32 (2007): 231–42.

Chart 1. *Hebrew Manuscripts of Ezekiel from the Judean Desert*

	Preserved	Script	Date
1Q9[81]	Two fragments within 4:16–5:1	"assez classique"[82]	(not dated)
3Q1[83]	One complete word, a hapax in 16:31	Herodian	End of the first century BCE or the beginning of the first century CE
4Q73 (4QEzek[a])[84]	10:6–11:11; 23:14–15, 17–18, 44–47; 41:3–6	Late Hasmonean/ early Herodian[85]	Middle of the first century BCE
4Q74 (4QEzek[b])	Multiple fragments from 1:10–24	Herodian	Early first century CE
4Q75 (4QEzek[c])	24:2b–3	Hasmonean	First or middle of the first century BCE
11Q4[86]	Words from 4:3–6; 5:11–17; 7:9–12; 10:11; and 13:17[87]	Mid-Herodian/ possibly late-Herodian	c. 10 BCE–30 CE[88]
MasEzek[89]	35:11–38:14	Early Herodian hand	Second half of the first century BCE

---

[81] 1Q9 consists of two small fragments of Ezek 4:16–5:1 and is published in Dominique Barthélemy, "Ézéchiel (Pl. XII)," in Dominique Barthélemy and Józef Tadeusz Milik, *Qumran Cave I* (DJD 1; Oxford: Clarendon , 1955), 68–9.

[82] Ibid.

[83] 3Q1 is extremely fragmentary and difficult to read. Only one full word, לקלס can be discerned, which only appears in Ezek 16:31. The manuscript is published in Maurice Baillet, "Ézéchiel (Pl. XVIII)," in Maurice Baillet, Józef Tadeusz Milik, and Roland de Vaux, *Les 'petites grottes' de Qumrân: exploration de la falaise, les grottes 2Q, 3Q, 5Q, 6Q, 7Q, à 10Q, le rouleau de cuivre* (DJD 3; Oxford: Clarendon, 1962), 94.

[84] 4Q73–75 together form eight fragments from three scrolls. 4QEzek[a, b, c] are published in Judith E. Sanderson, "Ezekiel," in *Qumran Cave 4. X. The Prophets* (eds. Eugene Ulrich et al.; DJD 15; Oxford: Clarendon, 1997), 209–20. See also Lust's preliminary assessment in Lust, "Ezekiel Manuscripts in Qumran: Preliminary Edition of 4Q Ez a and b," in idem, *Ezekiel and His Book*, 90–100.

[85] Sanderson, "Ezekiel," 209. This date is supported by Lawrence A. Sinclair, "A Qumran Biblical Fragment 4QEzek[a] (Ezek 10, 17–11, 11)," *RevQ* 14 (1989): 100.

[86] 11Q4 is published in Edward D. Herbert, "11QEzekiel (pls. II, LIV)," in Florentino García Martínez, Eibert J.C. Tigchelaar, and Adam S. van der Woude, *Qumran Cave 11 2: 11Q2–18, 11Q20–31* (DJD 23; Oxford: Clarendon, 1998), 15–28. It is likely a full scroll, albeit a "dense, unopenable mass" of Ezekiel. Only a few fragments were recovered. See also William H. Brownlee, "The Scroll of Ezekiel from the Eleventh Qumran Cave," *RevQ* 4 (1963): 12.

[87] Brownlee, "The Scroll of Ezekiel," 16–17.

[88] Herbert assumes the dating scheme of F.M. Cross, and refutes Brownlee's dating to c. 55–25 BCE as too early. Herbert, "11QEzekiel," 21.

[89] MasEzek contains Ezek 35:11–38:14 and is analyzed by Talmon in Shemaryahu Talmon, "1043–2220 (MasEzek) Ezekiel 35.11–38.14," in *Masada 6: The Yigael Yadin Excavations*

Patmore's study is a very useful reminder that the LXX textual tradition has no extant Hebrew support. "What we can say *positively* is that what [Hebrew] data we do have *do not* reflect a prototype of the Greek recensions."[90]

However, Patmore's study contains some errors and further illustrates the types of methodological pitfalls that await students of Greek texts and p967, specifically.[91] For instance, the Hebrew texts of Ezekiel may not represent as strong a textual tradition for the MT as Patmore supposes. Many of the manuscript fragments that Patmore cites (4Q73–75) have been cautiously identified as excerpted or abbreviated biblical manuscripts.[92] These types of manuscripts do not represent full copies of Ezekiel, and thus provide a rather complicated 'witness' to the biblical text.[93] Julie A. Duncan has noted the "expansionist tendencies" of many of the excerpted and

---

1963–1965 (eds. S. Talmon and Y. Yadin; Jerusalem: Israel Exploration Society and the Hebrew University of Jerusalem, 1999), 59–75. For a description of the excavation in which MasEzek was found, (beneath the floor of the synagogue), see Yigael Yadin, *Masada: Herod's Fortress and the Zealots' Last Stand* (London: Weidenfeld & Nicolson, 1966), 168–89.

[90] Patmore, "The Shorter and Longer Texts," 237.

[91] For instance, Patmore incorrectly represents Tov's position on p967. See Tov, "Recensional Differences," 99–101. Additionally, he pays little attention to Lust's work on p967, even citing him incorrectly as calling 7:6–9 a *variation* in p967. In fact, Ezekiel 1–11 is not extant in p967. See Patmore, "The Shorter and Longer Texts," 239.

[92] The excerpted status of 4Q73 (4QEzek[a]) is the most probable, with its possible thematic selection of texts. Strawn lists it in Table 1 "List of Excerpted and Abbreviated Manuscripts at Qumran" in Brent A. Strawn, "Excerpted 'Non-Biblical'" Scrolls at Qumran? Background, Analogies, Function," in *Qumran Studies: New Approaches, New Questions* (eds., Michael T, Davis and Brent A. Strawn; Grand Rapids: Eerdmans, 2007), 119. 4Q73 is discussed in Tov, "Excerpted and Abbreviated Biblical Texts from Qumran," in *Hebrew Bible, Greek Bible and Qumran: Collected Essays* (TSAJ 121; Tübingen: Mohr Siebeck, 2008), 37; and idem, *The Texts from the Judean Desert: Indices and an Introduction to the Discoveries in the Judaean Desert Series* (eds. Emanuel Tov et al.; DJD 39; Oxford: Clarendon, 2002), 46. For the most thorough discussion of 4Q73, see George J. Brooke, "Ezekiel in Some Qumran and New Testament Texts," in *The Madrid Qumran Congress: Proceedings of the International Congress on the Dead Sea Scrolls Madrid 18–21 March 1991* (2 vols.; eds., Julio Trebolle Barrera and Luis Vegas Montaner; STDJ 11; Leiden: Brill, 1992), 1:317–37. Brooke also raises the possibility that 3Q1 (3QEzek) may be excerpted as well. For an opposing position, see Mladen Popović, "Prophet, Books and Texts: Ezekiel, Pseudo-Ezekiel and the Authoratativeness of Ezekiel Traditions in Early Judaism," in M. Popović (ed.), *Authoritative Scriptures in Ancient Judaism* (JSJSup 141; Leiden: Brill, 2010), 227–251.

[93] For a good discussion of these texts, see Tov, "Excerpted and Abbreviated," 28; and Brent A. Strawn, "Excerpted Manuscripts at Qumran: Their Significance for the Textual History of the Hebrew Bible and the Socio-Religious History of the Qumran Community and its Literature," in *The Bible and the Dead Sea Scrolls*, Vol. 2: *The Dead Sea Scrolls and the Qumran Community* (ed. J.H. Charlesworth; Waco: Baylor University Press, 2006), 112–113. His essay also includes impressive bibliographic references to the pioneering work of Patrick Skehan, Sidnie White Crawford, Julie Duncan, and Emanuel Tov with excerpted texts, as well as numerous other scholarly mentions of the phenomenon.

abbreviated manuscripts.[94] Judith Sanderson argues that 4QEzek[b] cannot be a full text of Ezekiel, but rather a manuscript with what seem to be "edited highlights" of the prophet's visions.[95] Additionally, Brent A. Strawn observes that excerpted manuscripts were probably more than *just* a copy of a biblical text—indeed, function may dictate the text's form, if not type, in the case of these manuscripts (i.e., liturgical texts). Materialist philology "warrants caution when comparing the excerpted manuscripts' textual data with other witnesses to the biblical text."[96] Finally, it may be significant that MasEzek, the strongest textual support for MT's 'eschatological edition,' was uncovered in a synagogue at Masada. The ancient function of the manuscript no doubt plays an important role in how we understand its textual information.

In sum, while Patmore's study should be viewed with caution, he is correct that it is still too early to establish textual priority definitively between p967 and MT's texts. Lust and Crane have not yet conclusively proven their positions on textual priority, although Lust's work has clearly made the stronger case. While textual priority is still undecided, Lust did lay important groundwork for further study of p967 as a variant literary edition of Ezekiel.

1.5. THE CONTENTS OF THE PRESENT STUDY

The present study represents a manuscript approach to p967. Primarily, the study seeks to provide a deeper understanding of the literary history of Ezekiel through the lens of p967's text. In addition, the preceding discussion has revealed a number of issues which this project will address. A central issue is the way in which textual criticism interacts with and complements various other critical approaches. For the time being, I accept Tov and Lust's insistence that textual criticism takes sequential precedence, methodologically. Hence, this project begins and is everywhere rooted in text-critical questions. To that end, chapter 2 contains a

---

[94] Julie A. Duncan, "Excerpted Texts of Deuteronomy at Qumran," *RevQ* 18 (1997): 43–62.

[95] Sanderson, "Ezekiel," 216. 4QEzek[b] is listed as a "biblical scroll of small dimensions" in Tov, "The Dimensions of the Qumran Scrolls," *DSD* 5 (1998): 77–79. Such small scrolls were almost certainly portable, and probably only contained a small amount of text. See further S.J. Pfann, "4Q298: The Maskil's Address to All Sons of Dawn," *JQR* 85 (1994): 213 n.14.

[96] Strawn, "Excerpted Manuscripts," 132. For the term, "materialist philology," see Siegfried Wenzel and S.G. Nichols, eds., *The Whole Book: Cultural Perspectives on the Medieval Miscellany* (Ann Arbor: University of Michigan Press, 1996), 1.

comprehensive discussion of prior study of p967's text. Textual criticism assumes priority in order to orient the study within the state of discussion on p967's text. However, my thoughts on methodological sequence do diverge from the positions of Tov and Lust. Indeed, several unresolved and outstanding textual issues demonstrate the need for this literary study of p967. Thus, while Chapter 2 provides a text-critical orientation to the unique features of p967's text, the 'coherence approach' overturns the methodological sequence and gives momentary priority to literary analysis. As per the coherence approach, only those literary features which can be shown to participate in *Tendenzen* sufficiently complement strictly text-critical evaluations.

Hence, in chapters 3, 4, and 5, I combine textual criticism with the 'coherence' approach to literary criticism. These chapters drive towards the question: what is the scope and nature of p967's variant literary edition? A comprehensive study of p967's variants is needed. In what way(s) does p967 represent a variant literary edition from other known witnesses, especially the MT? Only a comprehensive study of p967's 'literary' variants can shed new light on the meaningful divergence in Ezekiel's text history. Hence, chapters 3, 4, and 5 examine only those variants that my 'coherence approach' deemed meaningful to the divergent editions of p967 and MT.

Chapter 3 describes and develops the coherence approach and introduces the data set for chapters 4 and 5: those variants which participate in the larger scope of p967's variant literary edition. Chapter 4 is strictly text-critical. In it, I submit my data-set to text-critical analysis, and consider such issues as p967's relation to the Old Greek and its Hebrew *Vorlage*. Then, chapter 5 turns to a literary analysis of the same set of variants. This chapter is largely exegetical, presenting the meaningful differences between p967 and MT as variant literary editions according to literary tendencies.

Chapter 6 provides a comprehensive codicological analysis of p967. The chapter begins with a descriptive analysis of p967's paratextual features, such as format, text-arrangement, and marginal marks, including several Greek notations. The second half of the chapter interprets the significance of p967's paratextual marks for its literary edition.

Finally, chapter 7 presents conclusions about p967 as a text, a variant literary edition, and an artifact of the book of Ezekiel. The evidence furnished by p967 for Ezekiel's textual history places Ezekiel with Daniel, Jeremiah, and Esther, along with sections of Judges, Exodus, and 1 Samuel all of which preserve evidence for at least two editions.[97] This study will thus help to rectify our heretofore limited understanding of the different books of Ezekiel. The study will also impact our understanding of Ezekiel's composition history, as some conclusions about Ezekiel's transmission will be possible.

---

[97] Ziegler's LXX Ezekiel is 6% shorter than the MT. Even without considering p967, this was enough for Emanuel Tov to call the LXX a variant literary edition of Ezekiel. Tov, *Textual Criticism of the Hebrew Bible*, 333.

CHAPTER TWO

UNDERSTANDING P967'S TEXT:
HISTORY OF TEXT-CRITICAL SCHOLARSHIP

2.1. INTRODUCTION

The publication history of p967, as indicated in chapter 1, is complex and variegated. p967 Ezekiel was published over the course of four decades in four critical editions in three different languages and is housed in four international locations.[1] Access to information on p967 is not straightforward. Additionally, the information, once accessed, is almost as variegated as its publication history. About the conditions of p967's availability to his work, Joseph Ziegler lamented,

> Der Papyrus 967 hatte nicht nur das Mißgeschick, daß viele seiner Blätter verloren ginge, sondern daß er auch in verschiedene Hände geriet, die ihn gesondert veröffentlichten.[2]

This comment referred to Ziegler's preparatory work with p967 for his 1952 Göttingen *Septuaginta Ezechiel*. His critical edition is the most important contribution to Ezekiel Septuagint studies and serves as the base text for several modern Septuagint translation projects.[3] For the edition, Ziegler only had p967[Sch+CB] available to him. The 1977 updated edition was largely catalyzed by availability of the Köln and Madrid portions of p967. Despite

---

[1] For clarity, the portions of p967's manuscript will be referenced as: Chester Beatty = p967[CB], Schiede/Princeton = p967[Sch], Universität Köln = p967[Köln], Madrid = p967[Mad].

[2] "Papyrus 967 not only has the misfortune that many of its sheets are incomplete, but also that it ended up in the hands of various people who published it in different forms." Joseph Ziegler, "Die Bedeutung des Chester Beatty-Schiede Papyrus 967 für die Textüberlieferung der Ezechiel-Septuaginta," *ZAW* 61 (1945/1948): 76.

[3] Three modern translation projects rely on the 1977 Göttingen second edition. Joseph Ziegler, ed., *Ezechiel, Septuaginta* (2d ed.; Göttingen: Vandenhoeck & Ruprecht, 1977); The NETS project refers to Ziegler's LXX, but uses the NRSV as its base text. *La Bible d'Alexandrie* and *Septuaginta Deutsch* offer new translations from Ziegler's LXX. Albert Pietersma and Benjamin G. Wright, eds., *A New English Translation of the Septuagint* (Oxford: Oxford University Press, 2007); Marguerite Harl with the assistance of Gilles Dorival and Oliver Munnich are working on *La Bible d'Alexandrie*; Wolfgang Kraus and Martin Karrer are the editors for *Septuaginta Deutsch*. The translation work is divided into three sections: chs. 1–19 Hermut Löhr; chs. 20–39 Almut Hammerstaedt-Löhr and Knut Usener; chs. 40–48 Michael Konkel and Johan Lust (Fachberater).

full access to p967$^{\text{Köln+Mad}}$, the 1977 editor, Detlef Fraenkel, notes the considerable work still required on the manuscript, making its usefulness to even the second edition less than complete.[4]

The protracted availability of information on p967 affects more general issues in Ezekiel studies as well. Walther Zimmerli's Hermeneia Commentary on Ezekiel, originally published in 1969 suffered the lack of p967's important evidence for the final stages of Ezekiel's redaction history. Zimmerli had full recourse to p967$^{\text{CB+Sch}}$, but his commentary was published before the critical editions of p967$^{\text{Köln+Mad}}$ were prepared. Although Zimmerli had transcriptions of those portions, and therefore knew with certainty, for instance, that p967 lacked 36:23c–38, he does not address this or other relevant textual issues in his introduction.[5] In fact, Zimmerli places the discussion of p967 in the introduction under "The Later History of the Book and Its Text," thus qualifying the witness as important only to the Greek tradition and denying any merit to p967 as a witness to the Hebrew.[6] Certainly, if Zimmerli had benefitted from a complete critical commentary on p967 and subsequent textual debates, he would have been more attentive to the value of p967's witness.

Although the publication history of p967 negatively impacted important Ezekiel studies, the multiple editions and editorial work have afforded considerable scholarly discussion, as M. Fernández-Galiano points out,

---

[4] Detlef Fraenkel, "Nachtrag," 333. For a similar problem in Ziegler's edition of Daniel, see Alexander A. Di Lella, "The Textual History of Septuagint-Daniel and Theodotian-Daniel," in *The Book of Daniel: Composition and Reception* (vol. 2 of *The Book of Daniel*; eds. John J. Collins and Peter W. Flint; Boston: Brill, 2002), 590–591. Di Lella points out that Ziegler provides a conjectured reading in Dan. 7:13 regarding the important actions of the one like a son of man. Ziegler, however, seems not to have consulted the 1968 publication of p967 where, according to Di Lella, the OG reading appears and finds the support of other OG mss.

[5] On the notable minus of 36:23b–38, Walther Zimmerli only knew p967$^{\text{CB+Sch}}$ and was not yet aware of the Madrid or Köln portions, thus he cast doubt on the reliability of the new witness' omission. Zimmerli states, "in 37:4 the surviving text breaks off....it is not absolutely necessary to conclude that 36:23ff, a section which is so significant from the content point of view, could still not have followed after chapter 37. It is not probable, but not absolutely impossible. Perhaps the discovery of the missing sheets of p967 will one day give us more certain information." Zimmerli, *Ezekiel*, 2:242. *Pace* Lust, who claimed that Zimmerli "did not offer any further suggestions concerning this phenomenon." Lust, "Ezekiel 36–40," 519. Zimmerli elsewhere, takes a more bold position that the minus is an inner-Greek error. "The possible absence of the passage from p967 and the peculiar character of the translation of it would then be a problem for the history only of LXX, but not of MT." Zimmerli, *Ezekiel*, 2:245.

[6] Zimmerli, *Ezekiel*, 1:76–77.

> Pero tampoco, creemos, ha sido enteramente prejudicial para el estudio del
> códice el hecho de que se hayan producido forzosos intervalos en la pub-
> licación de sus diferentes partes: al contrario, el manuscrito 967 ha tenido
> así varias oportunidades de estudio y confrontación por parte de diversas
> personas a lo largo de más de seis lustros.[7]

Each of the four p967 publications offered independent analysis of the
witness. These and other published analyses comprise a rich international
conversation about textual issues and Ezekiel/Septuagint studies. However, these conversations do not achieve consensus on most issues.

A unified critical edition of the text is urgently needed. Lacking such an
edition, p967 suffers from incomplete and at times incommensurate analysis. The present chapter attempts to synthesize the history of research
on p967, to highlight important debates, and to appreciate the light that
has been shed on this important Greek witness. I will discuss text groups,
patterns of alignment, and the way p967 has figured in debates concerning the Old Greek. I will discuss issues in translation including translation
technique and the multiple translator theory. Finally, I will consider the
quality of p967 as a textual witness, focusing on specific debates about
textual errors. At the end of these discussions, it will be possible to defend
the enormous importance of p967 for Ezekiel's textual history, and to situate the present literary study of its variant status among the relevant textual debates. I turn first to a description of the critical publications.

2.2. The Critical Publications of p967

The four volumes in which p967 is published address a wide range of concerns and achieve varying depths of discussion. For instance, the Princeton publication is unique in providing qualitative analysis of p967 with
respect to contemporary Septuagint debates. By way of contrast, the Universität Köln publication provides numerous quantitative lists. Despite
their differing emphasis on quantitative vs. qualitative information, these
thorough and helpful volumes are themselves to be contrasted with the
minimal information provided in the Chester Beatty publication, a deficit

---

[7] Fernández-Galiano, "Nuevas Paginas," 7. "But, neither, do we believe, it has been
entirely prejudicial toward the study of the codex the fact that there have been inevitable
intervals between the publication of its different parts; on the contrary, the manuscript
967 has had so many various opportunities for study and interaction on the part of various
different people. In fact more than six five-year studies have been completed on it."

remedied by subsequent publications.[8] A short description of the contents and approaches of the four volumes follows.[9]

2.2.1. *p967^{CB}: Chester Beatty*

Frederic C. Kenyon, the director and principal librarian of the British Museum, edited all of the volumes in the Chester Beatty library. A voluminous task, Kenyon understandably provided very little analysis of the Ezekiel portion of the p967 manuscript.[10] However, as the first publication of the codex, it fell to Kenyon to describe the origins, contents, and features of the then incomplete codex, much of which was therefore speculative.[11] In his publication, Kenyon lamented, "the Beatty leaves are all imperfect, nearly half having been lost from the bottom of each leaf."[12]

Two subsequent publications rectified the short-comings in the Beatty publication. First, the damaged pages of p967^{CB} were made complete in 1972 by p967^{Köln}, thus Jahn incorporates all of p967^{CB} into his transcription and analysis.[13] Jahn's transcription supplies enough text to successfully compare the full text with the other Greek versions. Second, Kenyon's half page of analysis was rectified by Payne who wrote an article in 1949

---

[8] John Barton Payne conducted the lacking analysis of p967^{CB} in J. Barton Payne, "The Relationship of the Chester Beatty Papyri of Ezekiel to Codex Vaticanus," *JBL* 68 (1949): 251–265. Jahn republished a transcription of p967^{CB}, producing more of the text than Kenyon's volume in Jahn, *Der Griechische Text.*

[9] See also Table I for a detailed list of contents, including the passages transliterated in each portion.

[10] p967^{CB} consists of 8 leaves of Ezekiel running from 11:25—17:21; however, Kenyon's 3–page textual analysis covers a total of 29 leaves of the codex: Ezekiel (8 leaves), Daniel (13 leaves) and Esther (8 leaves). Thus very little analysis of Ezekiel is present in the Chester Beatty publication. Only one half of one page is devoted to p967^{CB}.

[11] In his *General Introduction*, published in 1933, Kenyon had not perceived the connection between the Ezekiel/Esther and the Daniel portions of the codex. By 1937, when he published *Ezekiel, Daniel, Esther*, Kenyon benefitted from both the presumably spoken observations on handwriting of A.S. Hunt and the photographs of p967^{Sch} in working out his description of the codex. F.J. Kenyon, *General Introduction: The Chester Beatty Biblical Papyri Descriptions and Texts of Twelve Manuscripts on Papyrus of the Greek Bible* (Fasc. 1; London: Emery Walker, 1933), 1–18.; Kenyon, *The Chester Beatty Biblical Papyri: Ezekiel, Daniel, Esther* (Fasc. 7; 2 vols.; London: Emery Walker, 1937). For additional discussion on the early speculated contents of the codex, see Johnson et al., *The John Schiede Biblical Papyri*, 1–3. In 1971, M. Fernández-Galino was able to refine Kenyon and Johnson's work with the codex, with the new portions, p967^{Madrid} and p967^{Köln}. M. Fernández-Galiano, "Nuevas Paginas," 11–16. See chapter 6 "Codicology" of the present work for more detailed information on the contents, description, and nature of the codex.

[12] Kenyon, *Ezekiel*, v.

[13] The German leaves included the missing bottom halves of the p967^{CB} columns.

addressing the critical comparison of p967^{CB} with the other uncials, specifically with B.[14]

2.2.2. p967^{Sch}: Schiede/Princeton

Allan Chester Johnson, Henry Snyder Gehman, and Edmund Harris Kase, Jr. (hereafter JGK) divided the editorial work of p967^{Sch} to produce the impressive 1938 Princeton publication.[15] JGK supply thorough analysis of collations and issues of alignment among the Greek uncials and minuscules and the Latin versions, and include extensive discussion of the Syro-Hexaplar and Origin's textual marks. Distinctive among the publications, the Princeton volume provides qualitative discussion about the role of p967^{Sch} in Septuagint debates in 79 pages of analysis. In particular, Kase's essays bring p967^{Sch} to bear on the development of the *nomina sacra* and Ezekiel translation studies.

2.2.3. p967^{Mad}: Madrid

In 1971, when new pages of the p967 codex appeared in Madrid, M. Fernández-Galiano undertook the task of their publication in "Nuevas Paginas del codice 967 del A.T. griego." The volume includes a short history of scholarship, including the intervening discussions of the Göttingen school. The Madrid volume also tells the history of how these leaves, originally in separate hands, came together in one publication. The remaining discussions are particularly strong on the description of the graphic elements of the codex. However, the Madrid volume does not include significant textual analysis or discussion.

2.2.4. p967^{Köln}: Universität Köln

The following year, P. Leopold Günther Jahn and his team published the fourth and final volume on p967 entitled, *Der griechische Text des Buches Ezechiel, nach dem Kölner Teil des Papyrus 967*. Jahn not only supplied a new transcription of the entirety of p967^{CB} as noted above, but also reread 19:12–20:4a; 21:8(3)c–14(9)a; and 25:5–26:9, initially included among

---

[14] Payne, "The Relationship," 251–265.

[15] Gehman wrote "Relation to Hebrew, Syro-Hexaplar, and Greek Texts" (73–80) as well as the enormous "Observations Criticae" (80–140); Kase assisted with the transcription and wrote "Relation to the Old Latin Version" (42–48), "The *nomen sacrum* in Ezekiel," (48–52) and "The Translator(s) of Ezekiel" (52–73). Johnson is responsible for the remainder of the volume.

the p967[Sch] leaves. These last sections appeared on leaves that were torn rather bizarrely by the dealers, with a narrow strip of the column appearing in the Princeton volume, now supplemented by the remainder of the column among the *Köln* leaves.

> Zu den Stücken, welche die von Kenyon und Johnson veröffentlichen Teile ergänzen, wurden die entsprechenden schon edierten Text emit wiedergegeben, zusammen mit dem jeweiligen wurde bis auf kleinere Vereinfachungen bzw. Korrekturen, wo diese angebracht erschienen.[16]

The Köln publication supplies useful textual data and analysis. Most distinctive is the quantitative data from p967[Köln] organized according to Hexaplaric analysis. This arrangement of the data betrays an interest in the larger Origenian project within German Septuagintal studies especially, as well as the Lagardian approach to text criticism of the Old Greek.[17] One weakness of Jahn's critical apparatus owes to this interest; he is not as thorough as JGK with the uncial and minuscule readings when they do not contribute much beyond errors of text-type. However, these variants are significant to dominant text-critical approaches adopted by this dissertation.

2.2.5. *Summary of Publications*

The Princeton and Köln publications offer the strongest basis for study of p967. However, as I indicated above, they organize data differently and emphasize different Septuagintal discussions. JGK seize upon the value of p967 as a pre-hexaplaric witness for the Old Greek and the Hebrew *Vorlage*. Their analysis, therefore, takes account of p967's relationship to all the versions. Subsequent scholarship written predominantly in English adopts their general approach to p967. German scholarship tended to adopt a different trajectory of analysis based on Ziegler's work with p967 for the preparation of his 1952 *Ezechiel* critical Septuagint edition. This trajectory attempts to purify the LXX from Origen's effects, a trajectory that influenced the publication of p967[Köln]. This difference proved to be consequential in the evaluation of p967, particularly for its testimony to the Hebrew and its relationship to the OG, as this chapter will reveal.

---

[16] Jahn, *Der Griechische Text*, 15. "The sections which complete those that Kenyon and Johnson published were reproduced with the corresponding edited text, together with the respective critical apparatus. The attached sections were essentially unchanged, except for small simplifications and/or corrections where required."

[17] See discussion of De Lagarde below.

These discussions break not only into different trajectories but into different chronological phases of research, beginning with the Princeton editors and subsequent scholarship's high esteem of p967.

2.3. Text Groups, Alignment, and the Old Greek:
Three Phases of p967 Research

2.3.1. *Phase 1—High Esteem for p967:*
Kenyon, Johnson, Gehman, Kase, and Payne

Early scholars counted p967's unique variants, and collated its readings with the other uncials in order to place the new version into a text group. Kenyon provided a table enumerating the instances where p967[CB] agrees and disagrees with the other available uncials: A, B, Q and Γ.[18] (See Table II.) From this comparison, he states,

> It will be seen that there is a very marked preponderance of agreement with B, though the number of singular readings is enough to prove the independent character of the papyrus.[19]

Johnson's collations of the uncials confirmed Kenyon's conclusions. p967 has the closest textual affinity with Codex Vaticanus (B).

> Since B and Sch. are evidently pre-Origenian, their closer affiliation is not surprising, although the fact that there are some 660 variants in these 42 pages of text shows that one or other has diverged far from their common ancestor.[20]

The amount of variance between p967 and B that Johnson described underscores Kenyon's claim for the independent character of p967. Adding further evidence, Johnson enumerates 550 p967[Sch] variants "not found in any other uncial MS."[21] As Johnson notes, many of these variants are unimportant. Several of the unique readings among the uncials, however, are supported by various minuscules; in particular, manuscripts 22, 23, 36, 48, 51, and 231 emerge as a "fairly consistent group."[22] The support of

---

[18] Γ = The Grotta Ferrata palimpsest (Kenyon, *Ezekiel*, x).
[19] Kenyon, *Ezekiel*, x.
[20] Johnson, in Johnson, et al., *The John H. Schiede Papyri*, 35.
[21] Johnson, in Johnson, et al., *The John H. Schiede Papyri*, 18.
[22] Johnson, in Johnson, et al., *The John H. Schiede Papyri*, 21. Johnson considers the minuscule groupings proposed by Field, Cornill, and Swete and supplies a brief discussion of their disagreements on page 78–79. Frederick Field, *Origenis hexaplorum quae supersunt, sive veterum interpretum Graecorum in totum Vetus Testamentum fragmenta* (2 vols.;

a group of minuscules for some of p967's unique readings suggests that p967 represents a viable text tradition which JGK determine to be closest to the Old Greek against B.

Bringing in other versions, the picture according to JGK begins to acquire focus. They determine that p967[Sch] represents the text most closely resembling the base text for the Old Latin.[23] The Syro-Hexaplar, on the other hand, generally agrees with B against p967[Sch].[24] This divided alignment, along with their results about the Greek versions, lead JGK to conclude,

---

Oxford: Oxford University Press, 1875), lxxxvi–lxxxviii; Carl Heinrich Cornill, *Das Buch des Propheten Ezechiel.* (Leipzig: J.C. Hinrichs, 1886); and Henry Barclay Swete. *Introduction to Old Testament in Greek* (Cambridge: Harvard University Press, 1900), 165–168. The minuscule numbers follow the Holmes Parson edition. R. Holmes and J. Parsons, *Vetus Testamentum Graecum cum Variis Lectionibus* (Vol. IV; Oxford: Clarendon, 1827). It is interesting to note the close affinity between the minuscules listed by Johnson and the Lucianic text group. E. Tisserant, in 1911, worked on Ezekiel's Lucianic group of mss, which included 22, 36, 48, 51, and 231. E. Tisserant, "Notes sur la recension lucianique d'Ézéchiel," in *RB* 8 (1911): 384–390. J. Ziegler added 46 and 449 (H-P numbering) to the siglum L group, which according to his enumeration, included: 22, 36, 48, 51, 96, 231, and 763. Ziegler, *Ezechiel* (1952), 44–57. Except for 23, all of Johnson's p967 minuscules are Lucianic.

[23] Johnson, et al., *The John H. Schiede Papyri,* 46. It should be noted that JGK did not conduct a full study of p967[Sch] against the Latin witnesses; they urge that "an examination of the entire text of each Old Latin authority is required....The original translation of the Old Latin version was made from a text closely resembling that of the Schiede papyri and probably of Egyptian origin, and the text of the Codex Wircenburgensis, although it gives evidence of some revision and has suffered much at the hands of an ignorant copyist, stands close to the fountainhead of the Old Latin tradition." Johnson, et al., *The John H. Schiede Papyri,* 46–48. One study reviews the significance of Codex *Wirceburgensis* for the transposition of chs. 38–39 in p967: P.M. Bogaert, "Le témoignage de la Vetus Latina," 384–395. Eugene Ulrich defends the usefulness of the Old Latin for determining the OG. Ulrich, "The Old Latin Translation of the LXX and the Hebrew Scrolls from Qumran," in *The Dead Sea Scrolls and the Origins of the Bible* (Grand Rapids: Eerdmans, 1999), 270.

[24] The Syriac witness poses a more complicated problem which JGK address in their argumentation. If S-H and B agree against p967, the former would seem to best represent the original LXX. According to this view,

> we should have to assume that someone revised this early version of Ezekiel on the basis of the Hebrew to produce the Schiede text, and that this revision was sporadic and individual and did not become the accepted version...[and] was intended for private use rather than for the Church in general. Johnson, et al., *The John H. Schiede Papyri,* 75.

However, JGK are careful to point out the problems with this hasty conclusion, noting especially that the Syro-Hexaplar only continues one tradition of LXX in Alexandria, faithfully relying on Origen's 5th column as it was understood in the early 7th century CE Johnson, et al., *The John H. Schiede Papyri,* 75. Further, the idea that p967 represents a revised text is difficult to square with its sporadic and at times erroneous unique readings of the Hebrew. "We should naturally expect him [i.e. the scribe] to work in the direction of improvement rather than of error." Johnson, et al., *The John H. Schiede Papyri,* 77.

there were at least two pre-Origenian traditions of the LXX; one of these is represented by Sch.; the other by B and the Syro-Hexaplar.[25]

Several English studies followed to substantiate JGK's high evaluation of p967. Two *JBL* articles, by Gehman in 1938 and J.B. Payne in 1949, affirm the conclusion that p967 and B represent two pre-hexaplaric traditions of Greek Ezekiel, with p967 standing closer to the Old Greek. Gehman's article showcased the previously under-known work of Otto Procksch, who concluded that there were two pre-hexaplaric texts on the basis of p967[Sch], with p967 standing closer to the OG and B representing a recension.[26] Gehman adduces the independence of this study as impressive support for his similar conclusion.

Payne's study of p967[CB] found that its 122 variants were supported by the minuscules: "all groups variously support Be [p967[CB]] as opposed to B."[27] (See Table II.) Payne makes explicit what was implied by JGK's study, that since p967 readings have "been perpetuated against B in all manuscript families," p967 must lie closer to the original Greek, before transmission splintered into the groups identified today.[28]

For both Gehman and Payne, the importance of p967 among the uncials not only decreased the value of B, but increased the value of A's readings. In fact, Payne goes so far as to say that A's witness competes with B if its hexaplaric revisions are removed.[29] Gehman and Payne included diagrams with their early studies, which help to communicate their evaluation of p967 among the principle textual witnesses to Greek Ezekiel. (See Table III.)

Gehman wrote a second article in 1938 on p967's relation to the Hebrew text.[30] There he advanced the argument, originally presented in the Princeton volume, that many of p967's unique readings demonstrate reliance on the Hebrew. 43 passages are an "exact translation" of the Hebrew, 11 are "close translations," and 20 show "possible Hebrew influence."[31]

---

[25] Johnson, et al., *The John H. Schiede Papyri*, 76.

[26] Gehman, "The Relations between the Text of the John H. Schiede Papyri and that of the other Greek Mss. of Ezekiel," *JBL* 72 (1938): 281–287. Otto Procksch, *Studien zur Geschichte der Septuaginta-Die Propheten* (Leipzig: J.C. Hinrichs, 1910).

[27] Payne, "The Relationship," 257.

[28] Payne, "The Relationship," 260.

[29] Payne, "The Relationship," 362.

[30] Gehman, "The Relations between the Hebrew Text of Ezekiel and that of the John H. Schiede Papyri," *JAOS* 58 (1938): 92–102.

[31] Johnson, et al., *The John H. Schiede Papyri*, 74. They note 43 exact translation passages: 20:13, 41; 21:6(11), 7(12), 22(27), 23(28), 28(33), 30(35); 22:4, 8; 23:17, 32, 33; 24:17; 26:13, 18; 27:4, 8, 27, 33; 28:7, 13; 30:5, 7, 13, 17, 21; 32:3, 4, 20, 21, 24; 34:13, 15, 28, 31; 36:8; 37:1; 38:8, 11,

Additionally JGK discussed 20 cases where p967[Sch] reflects a misreading of the Hebrew, or else a faulty Hebrew parent text.[32] Gehman's article offered textual analysis and evaluation of each of those passages. Gehman's work suggests that the Old Greek was more faithful to its Hebrew parent text than previously thought.

John W. Wevers, in a 1951 article on the *status constructus* in p967[Sch], draws the same conclusion.[33] Wevers compared the Greek uncials with the MT, reasoning that the more original readings would preserve Hebraized syntax. Indeed, p967[Sch] frequently renders the MT's את with a Greek article. "New evidence for the fact that Sch. [p967[Sch]] represents such an earlier witness to the original LXX has [now] been found."[34] By implication, Wevers' study affirms that the OG according to p967 is closer to the Hebrew than was previously thought.

This first phase of primarily English scholarship largely served to substantiate and refine the conclusions already made in the Princeton volume. According to this trajectory, p967 stands as the most important Greek version of Ezekiel, shedding new light on the complications of pre-hexaplaric transmission. Five consensus conclusions emerged:

1. p967 is most closely aligned with B, though they are distinct.
2. p967, as an independent text type, and B represent two pre-hexaplaric traditions of Greek Ezekiel.
3. Of the two, p967 is closest to the Old Greek.
4. p967 shows that the Old Greek was closer to the Hebrew than previously thought.
5. Work on p967 reveals the increased value of A's witness.[35]

16–17; 39:4, 8. They note 11 close translation passages: 22:7; 23:25; 24:4, 20; 25:3; 26:16; 27:14; 32:21; 38:11, 17; 39:4. They note 20 possible Hebrew influence passages: 20:41, 44; 21:21(26); 22:25; 24:14; 26:14; 27:19, 30, 33; 28:13; 29:14; 30:4, 8; 31:8, 16, 18; 34:14, 19; 35:11; 36:3.

[32] Johnson, et al., *The John H. Schiede Papyri*, 75. 24:2; 36:2; 32:18; 27:16; 28:16; Dittography of a Hebrew letter: 29:20; 30:9; 31:4, 7; 32:22; 34:27; 36:3; 38:15, 18; 39:14, 23; Haplography in the Hebrew text: 38:14; 39:18, 23, 27.

[33] Wevers' four conclusions are listed on the final page of his article. John W. Wevers, "Evidence of the Text of the John H. Schiede Papyri for the Translation of the *Status Constructus* in Ezekiel," *JBL* 70 (1951): 216.

[34] Wevers, "Evidence," 211.

[35] Not only Gehman and Payne, but Wevers makes this observation as well, saying, "the conclusion that A (minus the Hexaplaric additions) is to be considered more valuable as a witness to the original LXX, sometimes at the expense of B, is now strengthened." Wevers, "Evidence," 216.

2.3.2. Phase 2—Distancing p967 from the Old Greek:
Joseph Ziegler and the Göttingen Septuaginta Ezechiel

The question of p967's status was put to the test for the first time with the Göttingen Septuaginta Project. This project aimed to reconstruct an eclectic critical text of the Old Greek, thus the question of original readings achieved great significance. From 1939 to 1957, Joseph Ziegler was busy at work preparing all sixteen prophetic books for publication. He published *Ezechiel* in 1952 with the full benefit of p967[CB+Sch] and grouped the new manuscript among the chief B-text witnesses (see Table IV).[36] With respect to the conclusions of Gehman and his fellow editors, Ziegler acknowledged the special value of p967, but he conservatively simplified the situation in two ways.

First, Ziegler placed p967 squarely in the B-text group. While the first phase scholars recognized the relatively close affinity with B, Kenyon and JGK emphasized the independent character of the papyrus. Gehman, Procksch, and Payne even proposed that B and p967 preserved two different, pre-hexaplaric transmission traditions. The implications of these conclusions were flattened in Ziegler's decision to place p967 in the B-text group, and to ignore the new confidence in A echoed by Gehman, Payne, and Wevers. Second, Ziegler treated B as the principal witness and base text for the critical edition rather than p967.[37] This decision contradicts the most widely sounded conclusion from phase one, that

> The authority of B as our best source for the original LXX must yield to this new evidence [from p967].[38]

Herein lies Ziegler's most clear departure from phase one scholarship.

In his 1952 discussion, Ziegler affirms that we are on strongest ground for the OG when p967, the Latin, and Coptic agree with B. He esteems such readings as almost certainly the original Greek, especially when they confirm a hexaplaric omission.[39] However, in choosing B as his base text, he is willing to read with B, even when it stands alone.

---

[36] Ziegler, *Ezechiel* (1952).

[37] Ziegler, *Ezechiel* (1952), 23–28.

[38] Johnson, et al., *The John H. Schiede Papyri*, 79. The quote appears in five other publications: Gehman, "The Relations," *JAOS*, 102; Gehman, "The Relations," *JBL*, 287; Payne, "The Relationship," 265; Ashley Crane, "The Restoration of Israel: Ezekiel 36–39 in Early Jewish Interpretation: A textual-comparative study of the oldest extant Hebrew and Greek," (PhD. Diss., Murdoch University, 2006), 256; Leslie John McGreggor, *The Greek Text of Ezekiel: An Examination of its Homogeneity* (Atlanta, GA: Scholars Press, 1985), 10.

[39] "967 ist als ältester Zeuge eine wertvolle Stütze von B (und einigen anderen alten Zeugen, namenlich der altlateinischen und koptischen Überlieferung) in der Auslassung

Eine Reihe von Lesarten wird nur von B, dem häufig der Papyus 967, die Vetus Latina und die koptischen Übersetzungen sowie gelegentlich einige Minuskeln zur Seite treten, bezeugt.[40]

Ziegler relies heavily on B because he deems it the only witness which is free from hexaplaric effects. Especially important are the 150 cases where B omits an asterisked passage, revealing itself both closer to the Old Greek and immune from correction towards the Hebrew in the pre-hexaplaric period. Using the same criterion, Ziegler concludes that p967 has been corrected towards the Hebrew. Seemingly on this basis alone, Ziegler adopts B and not p967 as the most reliable base-text for the OG.[41] However, as Peter Katz would later comment, Ziegler's conservative decision to rely so heavily on B subtly makes it, and not the OG, the object of/basis for the critical edition.[42]

Ziegler summarizes his use of p967 as follows:[43]

1. Where B was previously the only witness, p967 lends support for the oldest, pre-hexaplaric, original reading.

hexaplarischer, asterisierter Stellen." "As the oldest witness, 967 is a valuable support for B (and some other older sources, particularly the Old Latin, and Coptic traditions) in the omission of hexaplaric asterisked passages." Ziegler, "Die Bedeutung des Chester Beatty-Schiede Papyrus 967 für die Textüberlieferung der Ezechiel-Septuaginta," *ZAW* 61 (1945/1948): 77.

[40] "One set of readings is attested only by B, leaving aside the numerous readings of [papyrus] 967, the Old Latin, and the Coptic traditions as well as occasionally, some of the miniscules." Ziegler, *Ezechiel* (1952), 23.

[41] Ziegler describes the official principles he used for the B-texts in the section entitled, "Kurze Charakteristik der Hauptzeugen B 967," where he describes the characteristics of the principal witnesses. He focuses the bulk of his conversation on B. He discusses B's pluses, minuses, rearrangements, and alternative wordings against the MT. In offering his principles of assessment, he concentrates on the cumulative evidence of other versions and the assistance of Origenian marks, and refers to the pre-967 work of Rahlfs and Cornill throughout. P967's role as a "Hauptzeuge" receives only brief mention at the end of the section. Judging merely from the space devoted for discussion, Ziegler clearly values B far above p967. Ziegler presents his work on p967, not in the 1952 publication, but in an article he wrote for *ZAW* in the previous year. Ziegler, "Die Bedeutung," 76–94.

[42] Peter Katz, "Zur Textgestaltung der Ezechiel-Septuaginta," *Bib* 35 (1954): 29–39.

[43] Ziegler, *Ezechiel* (1952), 28. This list refers to Ziegler's conclusions in his *ZAW* article from 1945/48.

1. Pap. 967 stützt die bisher von B als einziger Handschrift vertretenen ältesten, vorhexaplarischen, ursprünglichen Lesarten.

2. An einigen Stellen hat 967 allein die ursprüngliche Lesart bewahrt, z.B. 26:16 στυγνασουσιν und 36:8 εγγιζουσιν.

3. Die größte Bedeutung hat 967 deshalb, weil er zeigt, daß bereits in vorhexaplarischer Zeit die Ez.-LXX nach dem hebr. Text korrigiert wurde.

2. In a few passages p967 alone preserves the original reading, e.g., 26:16 and 36:8.

3. p967 is most valuable for showing that already in the pre-hexaplaric stages, LXX Ezekiel was corrected toward the Hebrew.

4. What emerges from the vocabulary of p967 is that some renderings were more consistent than previously could be supposed. So, for example, p967 shows in every instance, שׁמם was translated with στυγναζειν and בור was translated with βοθρος.

5. The occasional alignment of p967 with readings of the Alexandrian texts, the Lucianic recension, and the Catena-group, shows that these witnesses sometimes have drawn on older pre-hexaplaric sources.

Ziegler embraces the witness of p967 as primarily providing important support to B and in only a few cases, standing alone as the original Greek. p967's lexical consistency offers new confidence for previously conjectured readings. As a final modest appraisal, Ziegler posits pre-hexaplaric status for p967 readings which have widespread alignment across the Greek text groups. Nevertheless, Ziegler does not value p967 overall nearly as highly as he does the B text.

One year after the publication of *Ezechiel*, Ziegler still needed to defend his conservative B-centered approach with a 1953 *Biblica* article devoted to continued textual evaluation of p967. The earlier studies of Peter Katz and J.A. Bewer, that would challenge his editorial decisions with p967, remained to be addressed.[44] Throughout Ziegler's study of and response to specific textual evaluations, he remains steadfast in his high evaluation of B, and reiterates his opinion that p967, when it reads with B, provides excellent proof for the original OG.[45] However, he expresses caution when

---

4. Aus dem Wortschatz von 967 geht hervor, daß manche Wiedergaben konstanter waren als man bisher annehmen konnte; so ist, wie 967 zeigt, an allen Stellen שׁמם mit στυγναζειν und בור mit βοθρος wiedergegeben worden.

5. Das gelegentliche Zusammengehen von 967 mit Lesarten des alexandrinischen Textes, der lukianischen Rezension und der Catenen-Gruppe zeigt, daß diese Zeugen manchmal aus alten vorhexaplarischen Quellen geschöpft haben.

[44] P. Katz, "Rez. A. Rahlfs, Septuaginta," *ThZ* 61 (1936): 265–87; Julius A. Bewer, "Review of Johnson, Gehman, and Kase (eds.), *The John H. Schiede Biblical Papyri: Ezekiel*," *JBL* 57 (1938): 421–425.

[45] In this article, Ziegler notes that frequently the two oldest witnesses (967 and Tyc.) support the B-Text. Because of the value Ziegler assigns p967 and Tyc. as old witnesses to the LXX, he declares that when p967 and Tyc. support B, we have first-rate proof that we are close to the Old Greek. ("Häufig stützen diese beiden alten Zeugen (967 und Tyc.) den B-Text und beweisen so seine Vorzüglichkeit.") See Ziegler, "Zur Textgestaltung," 436.

p967 stands alone or is weakly attested.[46] Ziegler's evaluative comments about p967 when it reads against B may be summarized as follows:

1. Because p967 is corrected toward the Hebrew, it is only the original when it has considerable support.[47]
2. When p967 and a version read against the MT, they constitute good evidence for the OG.[48]
3. When p967 reads with the MT, either alone or with weak support (for instance, when it is accompanied by L and O or by representatives of these Resensions respectively,) then the reading is secondary.[49]

Ziegler's post-1952 *Ezechiel* work on p967 reveals the disputes that still lie beneath the surface of the Göttingen edition. It solicited a direct response by Katz in the 1954 issue of *Biblica*. Katz, writing an article with the same title as Ziegler's 1953 *Biblica* study, "Zur Textgestaltung der Ezechiel-Septuaginta," re-activated his earlier positions. Specifically, Katz shows that p967 is not corrected in every instance where it reads with the MT.[50] Despite obvious unresolved debate, both between Ziegler and phase one scholarship and in the Katz-Ziegler exchange that appeared in *Biblica*, Ziegler's decision to take p967 as a *Rezension* served as the basis for its minimal role in the 1952 Göttingen Septuaginta *Ezechiel*.

---

[46] "Fur jeden Herausgeber eines Textes ist es immer eine schwere Entscheidung, eine nur dünn bezeugte Lesart oder gar ohne jegliche Grundlage eine Konjektur in den Text aufzunehmen." "For the editor of a text, it is always a difficult decision whether to take up one flimsily attested version, or whether to introduce conjectures into the text." Ziegler, "Zur Textgestaltung," 436.

[47] "Mit Vorsicht ist das Zeugnis von 967 aufsurefen, wenn er mit M geht, da deutlich erwiesen ist, dass er nach dem Hebr. Korrigiert ist. Wenn 967 mit vielen anderen Zeugen eine mit M übereinstimmende Lesart überliefert, kann diese Lesart als ursprünglich in den Text aufgenommen warden, so 27,28." "The evidence of p967 should be called upon cautiously when it agrees with MT, as this proves clearly that it is corrected according to the Hebrew. If p967, along with many other witnesses, passes on a reading which agrees with MT, this reading can be held as original to the text, so 27:28," (Ziegler, "Zur Textgestaltung," 436). To explain the inconsistent nature of p967's alignment with MT, Ziegler compares it to the situation of Theodotian, Symmachus, and Aquila. The Three did not consistently revise toward the Hebrew, but rather only occasionally made corrections. Ziegler, "Die Bedeutung," 94.

[48] "Wenn 967 eine Lesart gegen M vertritt, so verdient sie Vertauen, besonders wenn sie von alten Zeugen wie B und Tyc. gestützt wird." Ziegler, "Zur Textgestaltung," 437.

[49] "Wenn 967 allein oder von nur wenigen Zeugen, so von L und O, bzw. Einigen Vertretern dieser Rezensionen begleitet, eine mit M übereinstimmende Lesart bezeugt, dann ist hier eine spätere sekundäre Variante anzunehmen. (Dies gilt für Stellen wie 20,4; 26,13; 28,15; 28,16; 32,32)." Ziegler, "Zur Textgestaltung," 438.

[50] Katz, "Zur Textgestaltung," 38.

2.3.3. *Phase 3—No New Ground: The 1977 Göttingen Septuagint*

In his 1952 Göttingen edition, Ziegler did not have the benefit of the entire p967 manuscript. The 1977 edition of Göttingen *Ezechiel* reprints the exact 1952 text and introduction, only adding a twenty-two page supplement written by Detlef Fraenkel.[51] The new portions of p967$^{Mad+Köln}$, in part, prompted the supplement to Ziegler's edition.[52] Of note, Fraenkel reassesses a whole category of Ziegler's omitted readings where a version of a patristic citation stood against the entire tradition. In these cases, where the readings are established by p967, they are included in the supplement, (e.g., 34:3).[53]

Overall, Fraenkel's supplement calls p967 a chief witness (*Hauptzeuge*), but does not incorporate any new readings from p967 into the critical text. p967 readings appear in Fraenkel's critical apparatus, making them available for consultation, but the edition does not represent an evaluative update in the scholarly discussion.

2.3.4. *Summary and Discussion of p967 and its Hebrew* Vorlage

Debates about the relationship between p967 and the Hebrew were at work at several points in the preceding discussion. Indeed, whether a pre-hexaplaric witness is corrected toward the Hebrew remains a highly contested issue. It is, as most agree, difficult to evaluate the evidence with respect to the Hebrew. Ziegler admits as much:

> Hier ist es nicht ganz klar, ob 967 nach MT korrigiert ist oder ob er die ursprüngliche LXX-Lesart bewahrt hat, die in den anderen Hss. durch innergriechischen Einfluß verlorengegangen ist.[54]

---

[51] About this edition and Fraenkel's "Nachtrag"—Lust says, "It should also be noted that, in Ziegler's edition, some of the variants of the papyrus are not accepted in the critical text, but are relegated to the critical apparatus. The appendix published in the anastatic re-edition of 1982 . . . carefully notes all the variants in the newly published fragments, but does not incorporate them in the critical text." Johan Lust, "The Septuagint of Ezekiel According to papyrus 967 and the Pentateuch," *ETL* 72 (1996): 131 n. 4.

[52] More fragments of p988, the Antinoopolis papyri, surfaced as well. See Fraenkel, "Nachtrag," 331.

[53] Fraenkel, "Nachtrag," 334.

[54] Ziegler, "Die Bedeutung" 84. "Here it is not completely clear whether p967 is corrected toward the MT, or whether it has preserved the original reading of the LXX, that in the other manuscripts has been lost through inner-Greek influence." P. Leopold Günther Jahn seconds the sentiment, "Ob eine Lesart in 967 ursprunglich oder korrigiert ist, kann an den meisten Einzelstellen nicht mit Sicherheit entschieden werden." "In most individual cases, it cannot be decided with certainty whether a reading in p967 is original or corrected." Jahn, *Kölner Teil Papyrus*, 155.

In general, German scholars like Ziegler, followed by Jahn in the 1970s, rely on two criteria. (1) Ziegler is suspicious of p967 when it reads with the MT. (2) More importantly, Ziegler consults Origen's marks to assess whether p967 has been corrected towards the hexaplaric tradition.[55] Of primary concern is Origen's asterisk which was affixed to readings that were present in the Hebrew text and needed to be added in the Greek.[56] So Ziegler assigns priority to the Greek witness which omits the asterisked passages. When p967 includes the asterisked reading, Ziegler concludes that it was likely corrected toward a pre-hexaplaric Hebrew text. Ziegler identified six passages in p967[CB+Sch] where one should make such an evaluation.[57] Jahn argues along the same lines about five asterisked additions in p967[Köln].[58]

This discussion clearly cautions against facile conclusions about the Hebrew base text of p967. However, some important points should be made in light of the above discussion. While Origen's marks do provide useful data, they alone cannot determine the integrity of the pre-hexaplaric Greek in relation to the Hebrew. For instance, JGK do not place much trust in Origen's marks because of the ambiguity involved in using them for evaluation. p967[Sch] omits 10 out of 49 possible obelized readings,

---

[55] Indeed, the goal of a critical Old Greek text, since de Lagarde, has been to purify the LXX of hexaplaric effects. Thus de Lagarde emphasized the importance of the Three for working back to the *Ur-Translation*.

[56] For general information about using Origen's hexaplaric marks for text criticism, see Tov, *Text Criticism of the Hebrew Bible*, 147–148; and Ernst Würthwein, *The Text of the Old Testament: an Introduction to the Biblia Hebraica* (trans. Erroll F. Rhodes; Grand Rapids: Eerdmans, 1979), 57–58.

[57] 24:25; 27:2; 31:14; 32:4; 32:13; and 38:16. Ziegler, "Die Bedeutung," 86. Here Ziegler dismisses the p967 asterisked passages, 21:27(32) and 23:33, as probably preserving the original reading. He also misreads Johnson's Origenian evalution. Ziegler reduces Johnson's list of 20 asterisked passages to 8, critiquing Johnson's analysis. However, Johnson himself refines the list of 20 down to 5 that appear uniquely in p967[Sch]. For Johnson's original list of 20, see Johnson, et al., *The John H. Schiede Papyri*, 40.

[58] Jahn lists 13 passages where "Asterisierte Stellen...in 967 vorkommen." Of these 13, 5 passages, "an denen der betr. Zusatz in 967 unvollständig oder in veränderter Form erscheint, zeigen deutlich, daß diese Einfügungen vorhexaplarische Korrekturen nach dem. Hebr. sind (18:24; 20:23; 46:16; 47:17; 48:10.)"—"where 967's addition appears incomplete or in a different form, [these] clearly show that these prehexaplaric insertions are corrections toward the Hebrew." Jahn, *Kölner Teil Papyrus*, 145. It should be pointed out that a mere και is asterisked in 20:23 which could equally likely be an error in the Hebrew transmission tradition, and the p967 plus of του affixed to the aorist infinitive is a common Greek syntactic construction in p967. Jahn finds particularly strong evidence in a very interesting case passage, 20:40. In p967, the hexaplaric asterisked Ισραηλ is inserted above the line as a correction, which Jahn argues is the work of a copyist and not a later scribe. By this, it would seem that the copyist knew the hexaplaric tradition and corrected his text accordingly.

and includes 5 passages marked with the asterisk that are missing in B.[59] Johnson states,

> if we are to judge by the sole criterion of the omission of obelized passages and the inclusion of those marked with the asterisk, the new text is better than B.[60]

Johnson's logic poses a challenge since Ziegler considered the presence of any asterisked readings in p967 to be a sign that it was *corrected* toward a pre-hexaplaric Hebrew text, and thus *not* the better text, contra Johnson. In truth, deciding between Johnson and Ziegler is very difficult—the evidence could be read either way, and without a thick evaluation which takes other versions and readings into account, Origen's marks alone cannot determine much about the Old Greek or its Hebrew *Vorlage*.

In addition to the difficulty of how to interpret Origen's marks, JGK rightly question the accuracy of the hexaplaric transmission tradition. Johnson notes the variety in the testimony. For instance,

> Q and 86 preserve a tradition of the asterisk which is not found elsewhere... Similarly the texts do not always agree in their testimony about the same passage.[61]

These two factors, interpretive ambiguity and inconsistent testimony, remind us that Origen's marks are just one factor, and an insecure and ambiguous one at that, in the evaluation of p967's relation to the Hebrew.

JGK and Payne weigh a wider variety of data to make their evaluation that p967, as a witness to the OG, is closer to the Hebrew than was previously thought.[62] The strongest case is mounted by Gehman in his

---

[59] Johnson, et al., *The John H. Schiede Papyri*, 37, 40.

[60] Johnson, et al., *The John H. Schiede Papyri*, 40–41.

[61] Johnson in Johnson, Gehman, and Kase, *The John H. Schiede Papyri*, 40. Eugene Ulrich points out one complicating factor of Origen research, "the oldest extensive manuscripts of the Septuagint that are extant are dated in the fourth century, at least a century after Origen, so we cannot always be certain that our Septuagint text corresponds to that of his day." Ulrich., *The Dead Sea Scrolls*, 203.

[62] For instance, JGK consider information from the isolated Septuagint debate about the *nomina sacra*. JGK state, "Perhaps the most striking characteristic of the Schiede text is the use of the singular (κς) in designating the *nomen sacrum*." Johnson, et al., *The John H. Schiede Biblical Papyri*, 19. Kase argues, "the frequent substitution in B of κυριος κυριος for an original κυριος, and the occasional occurrence of κυριος ο θεος in the Schiede codex, can be attributed to sporadic revision of the Septuagint based on a Hebrew text in which the original reading יהוה had been systematically expanded to אדני יהוה, the reading of the present Massoretic text." Kase in Johnson, et al., *The John H. Schiede Papyri*, 51. Here Kase relies on the original proposal of von Baudissan that a singular κυριος was the original

evaluation of Greek readings that clearly evince reliance on the Hebrew. Gehman adduces evidence for alignment between p967 and a variant Hebrew base text, not with the MT, as in Ziegler's analysis.[63] Gehman analyzed a total of 74 passages along with the 20 cases where he found a faulty reading of the Hebrew. This data constitute excellent evidence for an early Hebrew *Vorlage*.

> The influence of the Hebrew is somewhat surprisingly established by errors due to misreading the original or by clear evidence of the use of a Hebrew text which was not always flawless.[64]

Especially in these 20 cases where an error stands between the Greek and the Hebrew, the criteria of *lectio dificilior* obtains, since it is difficult to imagine that a corrector would propogate an erroneous Hebrew text, or so

---

reading in Ezekiel 1–39. W.W. Graf von Baudissin, *Kyrios als Gottesname im Judentum und seine Stelle in der Religionsgeschichte*, 1:525–602. Kase, however, is probably wrong that the original Hebrew had יהוה alone. See Lust, "אדני יהוה in Ezekiel and its Counterpart in the Old Greek, *ETL* 72 (1996): 138–145. Lust considers the Masada evidence sufficinetly early to erase the possibility of an original singular reading in the Hebrew. Lust, אדני יהוה, 145. Thus, the evidence of p967's *nomina sacra* cannot be adduced to argue p967's affinity with the Hebrew. For more on divine name debates, see below.

[63] In one case, Ziegler and JGK independently offer opposite evaluations of a specific passage, 28:16. Because p967 reads with the MT, Ziegler concludes that it is a secondary correction toward the Hebrew. Ziegler, "Die Bedeutung," 85–86. JGK determined the opposite, that p967 misread the Hebrew and thus could not be characterized as a correction. Johnson, et al., *The John H. Schiede Papyrus*, 75. Gehman took up a more detailed analysis of the claim in Gehman, "The Relations," *JOAS*, 99.

MT	הסכך	(Qal ptc.)	
p967	το χερουβ τοσεχ		εκ μεσων
C (OL)	*cherubin sech*		*de medio*
Q	το χερουβ το συσκιαζον		εκ μεσων
BA	το χερουβ _____		εκ μεσων

Gehman argues that p967 mistook the Qal ptc. as a proper name, and incorrectly transliterated τοσεχ, or else correctly transliterated הסך, a mistake in the Hebrew *Vorlage*. Whichever, the Latin witness, C, took p967's reading up and assumed that το was the article and could be dropped. Q corrected the mistake and offered the proper translation of the Hebrew/MT. BA omitted the word altogether.

Julius Bewer found no grounds for a faulty Hebrew parent text, but accepted Gehman's evaluation of the witnesses. Bewer, "Review of Johnson, Gehman, and Kase," 423.

The same disagreement ensued for 24:2, where Ziegler called p967 secondary due to agreement with the MT, and JGK and Bewer thought internal evalution led to the opposite conclusion.

Peter Katz similarly critiqued Ziegler's argument in a 1954 *Biblica* article. Katz says, "Nicht überall, wo 967 mit *M* übereinstimmt, ist er notwendig sekundär. Innere Gründe entscheiden hier in der andern Richtung." "Where 967 corresponds with MT, it is not necessarily secondary in every case. Internal grounds here decide in the other direction." Peter Katz, "Zur Textgestaltung der Ezechiel-Septuaginta," *Bib* 35 (1954): 38.

[64] Gehman, "The Relations," *JOAS*, 93.

egregiously misread the Hebrew. Wevers' study of p967's Hebraized syntax provides additional support. While evaluations of each passage require attention to the possibility of correction toward the Hebrew, in general, p967 does offer reliable evidence for its Hebrew *Vorlage*. In brief, Gehman and Wevers' studies are more convincing than Ziegler's method.[65]

2.3.5. *Summary and Discussion of p967, the Hebrew and the Old Greek*

It remains to clarify the relationship among p967, its Hebrew *Vorlage*, and the OG. Gehman used p967 to show that the OG was closer to the Hebrew than previously thought. For Gehman, this conclusion assumed the OG was an *Ur-Translation* from which all manuscript evidence descends. His adoption of this model is most obvious in his diagram of LXX transmission history (see Table III). Payne's diagram likewise adopts the model. According to this model, p967 and B are trajectories of inner-Greek development, with p967 lying closer to the *Ur-Translation*.

Belief in an *Ur-Translation* reflects the Lagardian model of LXX textual studies. De Lagarde's proposal of an *Ur-Text* or *Ur-Translation* posited an original translation that split into the variety of manuscripts that we know today.[66] The perennial appeal of the Lagardian model is its continued ability to explain the manuscript data.[67]

However, as Emanuel Tov has pointed out, the Lagardian approach is often guilty of blurring the distinction between the archetype and the autograph, where 'archetype' is the goal of text criticism, and 'autograph' is the actual translated text that lies behind our scholarly construct.[68] Further,

---

[65] Emanuel Tov also questions Ziegler's eclectic OG text, saying,
The text-critical analysis of the LXX must take all extant Greek readings into consideration, because at the outset one does not know which reading is original, and it may have a bearing on the text of the Hebrew Bible. In principle, any reading found either in the reconstructed text or in the apparatus of one of the Göttingen editions or of Rahlfs, *Septuaginta*, may have been part of the Old Greek translation. Tov, *Text-Critical Use*, 51.

[66] Paul A. De Lagarde, "Introduction," in *Anmerkungen zur griechischen Übersetzung der Proverbien* (Leipzig: Brockhaus, 1863); see also idem, *Mittheilungen I* (Göttingen: Dietrich, 1884), 19–26.

[67] Supporters for the Lagardian hypothesis have far outnumbered detractors. The entire Göttingen school is Lagardian; Alfred Rahlf himself was pupil and successor to De Lagarde. Even the diplomatic Cambridge edition of the Septuagint affirmed the existence of the Old Greek translation, disagreeing only that it was not yet time to establish a critical text.

[68] Emanuel Tov, "The Septuagint," in M. Mulder (ed.), *Mikra: Text, Translation, Reading, and Interpretions of the Hebrew Bible in Ancient Judaism and Early Chrsitianity* (Assen: Van Gorcum; Philadelphia: Fortress, 1988), 165. See also Jennifer M. Dines who highlights

variations on the theory of the original and famous detractor Paul E. Kahle routinely challenge the Lagardian model. Kahle's main contribution lies in his comparing the collection of LXX translations to the Aramaic Targums.[69] Similar to what we see in the Targums, translations of the Greek Bible were at first oral and piecemeal, and served multiple functions. Over time, numerous 'unofficial' Greek versions came into existence. Thus according to Kahle, one cannot think in terms of an *Ur-Translation* but rather of multiple versions.

The *Ur-Translation* model seemed unthreatened by p967 at first. Harry Orlinsky used the manuscript data from p967[CB+Sch] to extend the textual construct of the *Ur-Translation* even earlier than had previously been suggested. Defending the Lagardian position, he says,

> The new pertinent manuscript data, such as the Chester Beatty [p967[CB],] Rylands, and Schiede papyri [p967[Sch],] serve to push back the problem of recension and of the Proto-Septuagint chronologically nearer to its date of composition; they do not alter the problem.[70]

However, as was the case with Zimmerli's redaction-critical work, (see above,) Orlinksy was not able to appreciate the full impact of p967's evidence. Orlinsky's article was originally published in 1941, long before p967[Mad+Köln] surfaced.[71] Like Zimmerli, Orlinsky lacked the full manuscript evidence and the benefit of sufficient scholarly assessment.

p967, as a variant literary edition *may*, in fact, challenge the *Ur-Translation* theory. The importance of Lust's demonstration that there are two literary editions of Ezekiel in our manuscript evidence must not be underestimated. In brief, with p967 we face the problem of the relationship between the Hebrew, LXX transmission and the OG, which is further complicated by the apparent existence of double literary editions. Needless to say, these issues cannot be resolved here.

Even so, three viable models can describe the possible relationship of p967 to the Hebrew text of Ezekiel. Simplifying matters considerably,

---

the importance of what she calls, the "Göttingen gap" to maintain the distinction that Tov names. J.M. Dines, *The Septuagint* (New York: T&T Clark, 2004), 59.

[69] P. Kahle, *The Cairo Genizah* (London: Oxford University Press for the British Academy, 1947), 214; *The Cairo Genizah* went through eight editions, the most recent being, (8th ed.; Oxford: Blackwell, 1980).

[70] Harry M. Orlinksy, "On the Present State of Proto-Septuagint Studies," in S. Jellicoe and H.M. Orlinsky (eds.), *Studies in the Septuagint: Origins, Recensions, and Interpretations* (New York: Ktav, 1974), 96.

[71] Reprinted from *JAOS* 61 (1941): 81–91.

I will conceptualize these in terms of the divergence in text type, observed by Gehman and Payne, between p967 and B.

(1) According to Gehman and Payne's *Ur-Translation* model (Table III), p967 and B share a common OG ancestor. Their divergence and status as variant literary editions should be attributed to inner-Greek development.

The second and third models accept the probable conclusion that significant literary development occurred in the Hebrew stages of transmission to produce the variant literary editions of B and p967 (where B's literary edition is closer to the MT). Lust's work with p967 finds solid basis to view p967 as reflecting an early Hebrew edition.[72] Eugene Ulrich's work with double literary editions more generally shows that the Hebrew text was pluriform and that multiple editions circulated in antiquity.[73] About the OG translation, Ulrich has little to say, but he *has* commented,

> There was a wide variety of Hebrew texts available and in use when the OG translation of the various books was made and for several centuries during the early transmission of the OG. One must treat the elasticity of the Hebrew text with caution, to be sure, but one also must not underrate the variation in the Hebrew text abundantly demonstrated by the Qumran manuscripts and the versions. To underrate it will cause distortion in the understanding of the LXX and the forces behind its translation and transmission.[74]

(2) In this light, the second model may be called the Kahle approach to the OG. Kahle's arguments about the OG translation are not incompatible with Ulrich's multiple and fluid Hebrew text theory (although Ulrich does not assent to Kahle's theory of translation). According to this model, the Hebrew text of Ezekiel was multiple and fluid, allowing (but not requiring) a view of 'the Old Greek' translation as multiple or even a composite collection of section-translations of Greek Ezekiel. B and p967, then, represent or contain two or more separate translations of the multiple Hebrew texts.

(3) The third model, which carries the most weight in my mind, draws on the LXX transmission theory articulated by Frank Moore Cross. Using the Qumran evidence, and particularly Barthélemy's *kaige* recension, Cross outlines four stages of interdependence between Hebrew and Greek text

---

[72] Lust, "Ezekiel 36–40," 517–533; idem, "Major Divergences," 83–92.

[73] Ulrich insists that Qumran texts show a continuity with earlier processes of the "composition of scriptures." Eugene Ulrich, "The Community of Israel and the Composition of Scriptures," in *Dead Sea Scrolls*, 9–15 especially.

[74] Eugene Ulrich, "The Septuagint Manuscripts from Qumran: A Reappraisal of Their Value," in Ulrich, *Dead Sea Scrolls*, 179.

transmission.[75] The first stage is that of the Old Greek translation dated to the 3rd–2nd centuries BCE (depending on the book). The second stage is the proto-Lucian, generalized revision of the OG towards the contemporary Hebrew text in the 2nd to 1st century BCE.[76] Then in the mid-1st century CE, the *kaige* revision brought the LXX again towards the Hebrew of the proto-MT. The final stage is Aquila's version, arguably a revision or a translation, adopting a more extreme literalness of translation than even the *kaige*.

What is clear in Cross' model is that the Greek text was consistently brought into alignment with what is considered to be a developing Hebrew text. Support for this view can point to Ulrich's observation that the Hebrew text tradition was fluid. As Jellicoe states,

> It is now clear that up to the time of its fixation under Aqiba there was development within the Hebrew text. Mgr. Skehan has consistently drawn attention to what he calls, 'an exegetical process at work within the transmission of the text itself, in Hebrew.' Ziegler, more than a generation ago, illustrated this from Isaiah, demonstrating that the Greek translators had faithfully reflected the expansionist, harmonizing, and exegetical technique of the Hebrew *Vorlage*. Ezekiel is another case in point, and the same process would appear to account for the longer text of Jeremiah and possibly the Book of Job.[77]

According to this model, p967 and B represent subsequent corrections towards a developing Hebrew text. This model absorbs Ziegler's emphasis on the phenomenon of correction towards the Hebrew, but it also allows development in the Hebrew text-tradition, and consequently also inner-Greek development.

No easy decision about these models can be advanced with absolute certainty, especially at this stage of research and with the paucity of evidence for Ezekiel's transmission. However, I think it highly unlikely that p967 and B represent two separate translations; they have too much in common. Hence, a radical version of the second model above finds no

---

[75] Frank M. Cross, *The Ancient Library of Qumrân and Modern Biblical Studies* (Rev. ed.; Garden City, NY: Doubleday, 1961); idem, "The History of the Biblical Text in Light of the Discoveries in the Judaean Desert," *HTR* 57 (1964): 281–99; and idem, "The Contribution of the Qumrân Discoveries to the Study of the Biblical Text," *IEJ* 16 (1966): 81–95. These three publications combine to provide his approach to the history. See Jellicoe's helpful digest of Cross' points, in S. Jellicoe, "Prolegomenon," in *Studies in the Septuagint: Origins, Recensions, and Interpretations: Selected Essays* (eds., S. Jellicoe and H.M. Orlinsky; New York: Ktav, 1974), XLVI–LI.

[76] This was the text used by Josephus.

[77] Jellicoe, "Prolegomenon," XLIX.

p967 according to Frank M. Cross' Model of LXX Transmission

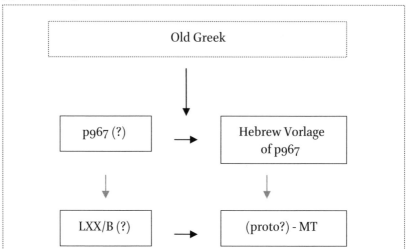

support in p967's evidence. The third model remains most compelling for absorbing the textual complexities already examined above. However, issues in translation technique, to which we will now turn, suggest that some piece-meal translation may have been at work in the production of the OG. Some of this piece-meal translation could be the result of developing and hence variant Hebrew texts, as reflected in MT and p967. In the end, Cross' model is the most compelling for the evidence available.

2.4. p967, Literal Translation Technique, and Linguistic Non-Homogeneity

Text-critical scholars who use Septuagintal texts for comparison with the Hebrew emphasize the importance of translation technique. A critic can trust Greek evidence if the text displays a literal rather than free translation technique.[78] Emanuel Tov calls the LXX translation of Ezekiel

---

[78] For a general discussion of translation technique and the terms, "literal" and "free," see Tov, *Text Critical Use*, 17–29. James Barr's early study often serves as the model for such evaluation. James Barr, *The Typologies of Literalism in Ancient Biblical Translations* (MSU 15; Göttingen: Vandenhoeck & Ruprecht, 1979).

"relatively literal."[79] Johan Lust strengthens the claim, stating that Ezekiel is, "rendered word for word, preserving word-order and syntax of the Hebrew."[80] Gehman's work on p967 argued for its fidelity to the Hebrew parent text, leading him to conclude that the OG translation was more faithful than previously thought.[81]

We have already seen that this straight-forward evaluation of p967's faithful preservation of the Hebrew was challenged by Ziegler's correction theory. Indeed, Ziegler also examined whether the translator gave an exact or a loose translation, noting

> dass er keine starre Konsequenz in der Wirdergabe der gleichen Wörter und Wendungen zeigt; diese ist ein Kennzeichen des Aquila.[82]

Ziegler advocated calling p967 a "Rezension," making it less reliable as a witness to the OG and thus the Hebrew *Vorlage*. While I found Ziegler's argument that p967 was a corrected *Rezension* flawed, possible correction and recensional issues cannot be dismissed prematurely.

Translation studies of Ezekiel do challenge any simple evaluation for a homogeneous literal translation technique. Already in 1903, H. St. J. Thackeray observed the linguistic non-homogeneity of LXX Ezekiel. By linguistic non-homogeneity, I am primarily referring to Greek lexical inconsistencies, but divergent syntax or linguistic conventions also occur across the Greek book. Over several lectures and four publications, Thackeray developed his two-translator hypothesis to account for the linguistic variety he found, not only in Ezekiel, but in Jeremiah, the Minor prophets, and other books.[83] Proposing a wide-spread scribal practice of bi-sectioning books

---

[79] Emanuel Tov, *The Text Critical Use of the Septuagint in Biblical Research*, (2d. ed.; JBS 8; Jerusalem: SIMOR, 1997), 250.

[80] Johan Lust, "Major Divergences between LXX and MT in Ezekiel," in *The Earliest Text of the Hebrew Bible: The Relationship between the Masoretic Text and the Hebrew Base of the Septuagint Reconsidered* (ed. A. Schenker; SBLSCS 52; Atlanta: SBL, 2003), 83.

[81] Gehman, "The Relations," 92–102.

[82] "That he does not exhibit any rigid consistency in the rendering of identical words and expressions; this is a distinguishing characteristic of Aquila." Ziegler, "Zur Textgestaltung," 440.

[83] Thackeray first proposed the idea of bi-sectioning books in H. St. J. Thackeray, "The Greek Translators of Ezekiel," *JTS* 4 (1903): 398–411. He adds Exodus, Leviticus, and the Psalter in Thackeray, "The Bisection of Books in Primitive Septuagint Mss.," *JTS* 9 (1907): 88–98. Ziegler questions Isaiah and the Minor Prophets in Ziegler, *Untersuchungen zur Septuaginta des Buches Isaias* (ATA 12/3; Muinster: Aschendorffsche Verlagsbuchhandlung, 1934), 31–46. See the discussion and footnotes of Shemaryahu Talmon, "The Textual Study of the Bible—A New Outlook," in *Qumran and the History of the Biblical Text* (eds., F.M. Cross and S. Talmon; Cambridge: Harvard University Press, 1975), 324.

for translation,[84] Thackeray modified the theory somewhat to fit Ezekiel's unique evidence. Ezekiel's anomaly was the presence not of two, but three linguistic sections. Thackeray broke the units as follows: α = chs. 1–27; β = chs. 28–39; γ = chs. 40–48.[85]

Roughly contemporary with Thackeray, Johannes Herrmann and Josef Schäfers conducted independent studies on Ezekiel leading to similar conclusions.[86] The three scholars differed about the division of the sections and the number of translators, but the results of the three studies affirmed the problem of the non-homogeneous translation of Ezekiel.

The discovery of p967 had a large impact on these debates. The *nomina sacra* evidence in p967 threatened one of the main arguments adduced by proponents of the multiple translator theory. Indeed, Schäfers relied on variation in the divine name alone for his section divisions, and Thackeray also used them as evidence. Interestingly, p967 has a singular ϗϛ[87] where MT has the double form, יהוה אדני. In the remaining 15 cases, p967 has ϗϛ ο θϛ. At first, this new data showed the Greek double form to be a later correction toward the MT tradition, thus eliminating the *nomina sacra*

---

[84] One particularly strong piece of support to Thackeray's theory of bi-sectioning is the ancient attestation to the practice by Epiphanius who says, "translators worked in pairs." Epiphanius, *De Mensuris et Ponderibus*, 3ff. see F. Hultsch, *Metrologicorum scriptorium reliquiae* (Vol. 1; Leipzig: Teubius, 1864), 259–279.

[85] The break between α and β occurs at the end of ch. 27, which according to the chapter divisions in codex Marchalianus (Q) falls at the halfway point of the 48 chapter book. Additionally, Q displays two slanted lines at the end of ch. 27, indicating a pause. This evidence correlates with the situation presented in B. Thackeray discovered a similar phenomenon in the book of Jeremiah. Thackeray, "The Greek Translators," 409. He thus concludes that Greek translators commonly divided a book in half without regard to subject matter. He states, "it appears...that there is some truth to the statement of Epiphanius that *the translators worked in pairs*" (original emphasis.) To explain the strange situation of the three sections in Ezekiel, Thackeray reasons that the two scribes must have been contemporaries, and that the second who was responsible for β had to defer to the expertise of the first for the difficult terminology of chaps. 40–48. In this way, the first translator was responsible for the more difficult sections of α and γ. Thackeray, "The Greek Translators," 410–411.

[86] In 1923, Johannes Herrmann proposed divisions, chaps. 1–27; 28–29; 40–48, (the same as Thackeray's,) and argued for three separate translators. Josef Schäfers also found three translators, but used the divine name alone as his criteria, breaking the book into chaps. 1–11; 13–39; 40–48. Johannes Herrmann, "Die Septuaginta zu Ezechiel das Werk dreier Übersetzer," in J. Herrmann and F. Baumgärtel (eds.,) *Beiträge zur Entstehungsgeschichte der Septuaginta* (Berlin: Verlag von W. Kohlhammer, 1923), 1–19. See also Herrmann, *Die Gottesnamen im Ezechieltexte* in R. Kittel (ed.), *Alttestamentliche Studien: Rudolf Kittel zum 60. Geburtstag* (BWANT 13; Leipzig: J.C. Hinrichs, 1913), 70–87; and Herrmann, *Ezechielstudien* (BWANT 2; Leipzig: J.C. Hinrichs, 1908). Josef Schäfers, "Ist das Buch Ezechiel in der Septuaginta von einem oder mehreren Dolmetschern übersetzt?" *TGI* 1 (1909): 289–291.

[87] p967 has abbreviations for the divine name, so ϗϛ for κυριος and θϛ for θεος.

evidence from any translation debates.[88] However, the matter seems far from resolved.[89]

The most impressive work on the Greek translator(s) of Ezekiel, subsequent to the emergence of p967 was done by Leslie John McGregor. In his dissertation, published in 1985, McGregor points out that the convention and transmission of the divine name is entirely discontinuous with the translation and transmission of the text:

> The distribution of variants [in divine name] cannot be taken on its own as support for an early (fully recensional) revision of some part of the text. The early stage of transmission of the word <<yhwh>> was a unique, scribal phenomenon.[90]

---

[88] See §2.3.4 above for an earlier discussion of the *nomina sacra* debate.

[89] McGregor supplies an impressive digest to the history of debate on the *nomina sacra* in Ezekiel, including how p967 affected matters. McGregor identified what he calls the consensus position, that the singular κυριος that appears throughout p967 was considered earlier than the double forms, and moreover, the singular form reproduced an originally singular Hebrew form where אדני is a later addition. However, McGregor argues against this position and maintains that the double form was in the earliest Hebrew text. To explain p967 and the Greek, McGregor argues that the double *nomen sacrum* is original to both the Hebrew and the Greek which read, κυριος יהוה, while the singular rendering κυριος reflected a later scribal choice to omit the Hebrew tetragrammaton. McGregor, *The Greek Text*, 57–93.

The *nomina sacra* debate is an entirely complex one and cannot be resolved here. Ludwig Traube offered the pioneer study, coining the term, *nomina sacra*, in Traube, *Nomina Sacra: Versuch einer Geschichte der christlichen Kürzung* (Munich: Beck, 1907; repr. Darmstadt: Wissenschaftliche Buchgesssellschaft, 1967). His work is taken up in codicological debates that largely focus on the Christian phenomenon of contraction in the divine name. For a review of this scholarship and his argument see Larry W. Hurtado, *The Earliest Christian Artifacts: Manuscripts and Christian Origins* (Grand Rapids: Eerdmans, 2006), 95–134. Indeed, bringing in Qumran studies, where the divine name could be rendered as four dots, four diagonal strokes, in paleohebrew, etc. shows the complexity and vastness of the evidence. For the Qumran evidence, see E. Tov, *Scribal Practices and Approaches Reflected in the Texts Found in the Judean Desert* (STDJ 54; Leiden: Brill, 2004), esp. 218–221, 238–246; and Patrick Skehan, "The Divine Name at Qumran, in the Masada Scroll, and in the Septuagint," *BIOSCS* 13 (1980): 14–44. Lust provides a discussion specific to Ezekiel where he also identified the importance of the separate but related Christian phenomenon of the developing divine name in Lust, "אדני יהוה," 140. However, Lust does not attempt to solve the matter.

In weighing the state of the discussion, I will have to agree with McGregor, that the development of the *nomina sacra* cannot be attributed to 'literary' recensional activity but rather to early scribal practice and convention. I take the transmission patterns of the divine name to be largely separate from the literary recension(s) in the text transmission. For example, I could find no literary coherence among the 15 verses in which p967 has κς ο θς; If these are examples of scribal recensions they appear sporadic and without larger literary significance. Even so, Zimmerli's discussion of the different Hebrew renderings of the divine name in Ezekiel's prophetic literary forms deserves further consideration. Zimmerli, *Ezekiel*, 2:556–562.

[90] McGregor, *The Greek Text*, 92.

So, eschewing data on the divine name alone, McGregor weighs the total linguistic evidence for Greek translation. With meticulous attention to method, perfecting the linguistic evaluations of the studies that preceded him, McGregor finally agreed with Thackeray that the linguistic non-homogeneity of Ezekiel resulted from the different styles of more than one translator. He modified Thackeray's unit divisions to chs. 1–25 (S1); 26–39 (S2); 40–48 (S3) (where S stands for section). McGregor's careful, comprehensive work makes his study the best synthesis of evidence for the multiple translator theory (See Table V).[91]

While McGregor's work presents a formidable conclusion about the translation of Ezekiel, several alternative arguments interpret the evidence differently, all appealing to explanations based on recensional not translation activity. The recension-arguments often use the same evidence as the multiple translator arguments, thus deciding between them can be difficult. Further, many of them have not been worked out in as much detail as the multiple-translator theories. However, a brief presentation of them will highlight their pervasive appeal.

Already in 1938, Kase used p967[Sch] to challenge Thackeray's multiple translator hypothesis. Kase concluded that Greek Ezekiel had one translator, and attributed linguistic divisions in the book to a revision.[92] Chapters 1–27, according to Kase, underwent a revision to render the Hebrew more literally.[93] Kase's argumentation relied heavily on what might be

---

[91] Table V shows McGregor's summary of the linguistic evidence that distinguishes S1 from S2.

[92] Kase "The Translator(s) of Ezekiel" in Johnson, et al., *The John H. Schiede Papyri*, 52–73. Ziegler largely follows Kase, only he detects sporadic correction in section β. Ziegler "Die Bedeutung," 88. In a separate discussion of the *nomina sacra*, Johnson ascribes the doublet forms in chaps. 20–39 (roughly section β) to a later redactor of the original edition. However, Ziegler does not mention the Princeton editor's proposal. Johnson, et al., *The John H. Schiede Papyri*, 41. For a full discussion of Kase and Ziegler, see McGregor, *The Greek Text*, 11–13.

[93] Whereas previous theories attributed the linguistic divisions to a bi-section by translators of Ezekiel, Kase attributes them to a series of bi-sections in the history of transmission of the book such that p967 represents a text comprised of unmatched sections. Springing from the linguistic evidence and the dispersion of the *nomina sacra*, he offers the following transmission history:

(1) Chaps. 40–48 circulated separately at first. When they were joined to Ezekiel, the late oracles of chaps. 38–39 were inserted as a connection between the two sections of the Hebrew book. This explains the division of *nomina sacra* forms found at ch. 40. Thus, chaps. 1–48 were translated by one hand.

(2) A later, conservative reviser who sought to bring the LXX closer to the Hebrew made some changes, but we only see his version in chaps. 1–27 because of the practice of bi-secting books. This explains the linguistic division between chaps. 27/28. Thus, accord-

called the consensus position on the *nomina sacra* evidence, but as we saw above, that evidence remains ambiguous.

Emanuel Tov offered his own theory of revision. Although his 1976 study focused on Jeremiah, Tov spelled out the implications of his conclusions for Ezekiel, arguing that one type, Ezekiel α, preserves the Old Greek.[94] Tov detected a different text type in β, possibly owing to a revision. He argues,

> The assumption that Ez β represents a later revision may further be corroborated by the following:
>
> 1. Thackeray, "Ezekiel," and Herrmann listed differences between the two (three) different "translators" Ez α, γ, and β. Yet, at the same time, Thackeray acknowledged the existence of important similarities between Ez α and β.
> 2. Approaching the question from a different angle, Barthélemy, *Devanciers*, 47, assigned Ez β to a kaige-like revision.
>
> The correctness of this hypothesis has yet to be verified by a minute inner-Greek analysis of Ez-LXX.[95]

Dominique Barthélemy's study, cited by Tov, makes extremely brief mention of Ezekiel. Discussing the translation, καὶ γαρ for גם, Barthélemy notes that the two Ezekiel cases, in 31:17 and 39:16, fall into Thackeray's section β. "Je n'entends pas prendre position sur ce point, mais seulement situer mon etude par rapport à cette hypothése."[96]

One further study worth bringing into the present conversation is E. Tisserant's 1911 study on the Lucianic manuscripts of Ezekiel. Tisserant argued that in minuscules 22, 36, 48, 51, 231 (according to Holmes Parsons edition), Ezek 22:19–32:32 was not Lucianic.[97] Picking up with Tisserant's observation, N. Fernández-Marcos says,

---

ing to Kase, we have chs. 1–27 in a revised form, and chaps. 28–48 in an unrevised form. Kase, "The Translator(s) of Ezekiel," in Johnson, et al., *The John H. Schiede Papyri*, 72–73.

[94] Tov, "The Relationship Between the LXX of Jer, Ez, and the MT," in *The Septuagint Translation of Jeremiah and Baruch: A Discussion of an Early Revision of the LXX of Jeremiah 29–52 and Baruch 1:1–3:8* (HSM 8; Missoula: Scholars Press, 1976), 135–155.

[95] Tov, *The Septuagint Translation*, 151.

[96] "I do not intend to take a position on this point, but only to situate my study in relation to this hypothesis." D. Barthélemy, *Les Devanciers D'Aquila* (Leiden: Brill, 1963), 42–4, n. 4.

[97] Tisserant adduces the Attic forms and typical Lucianic family formula of ταδε λεγει αδωναι κυριος that are replaced by general LXX koiné forms and the expression, ταδε λεγει κυριος in this section of Ezekiel.

It is possible that the archetype of the seven manuscripts (L) suffered a lacuna that was filled with another manuscript of a different character. Manuscripts may change their textual affiliation from book to book, but the change may occur within a book as in this section of Ezekiel.[98]

The presence of a different text-type in the L minuscules is particularly relevant to p967, since, as JGK noted, p967[Sch] was often supported in its unique readings by these minuscules, along with 23.[99] Tisserant and Fernández-Marcos' Lucian studies provide further data about the non-homogeneous texture of Greek Ezekiel's linguistic features.

The linguistic non-homogeneity of Ezekiel invites several explanations. McGregor's careful work supports an updated version of Thackeray's multiple-translator theory. Certainly, his summary of the evidence provides scholarship an invaluable service for all future lines of inquiry. (See Table V.) Above, I presented several iterations of one such line of inquiry, namely whether the linguistic patterns and sections in Ezekiel can be attributed not to the translator, but to inner-Greek revision.[100] Ziegler, Kase, Tov, and Barthélemy each suggested theories of revision to explain their findings. I critiqued the method Ziegler used to argue that p967 is a corrected *Rezension* in §2.4. above. However, Ziegler's attention to the well-founded fact of Greek correction toward a developing Hebrew text deserves attention.[101] Indeed, Kase argued for an inner-Greek correction toward the Hebrew in section α, chs. 1–27.[102] However, Tov took the same section to be the Old Greek and section β, chs. 28–39 as the revision, in part relying on Barthélemy's suggestion that section β exhibits kaige-like features. I noted the studies of Tisserant and Fernández-Marcos, simply to connect a linguistic-section break in the Lucianic manuscripts with the

---

[98] His study suggests a variant section division from Tisserant's: chaps. 22:4b–27:27. N. Fernández Marcos, "On Symmachus and Lucian in Ezekiel," in *Interpreting Translation: Studies on the LXX and Ezekiel in Honour of Johan Lust* (eds., F. García Martínez and M. Vervenne; Leuven: Leuven University Press, 2005), 153.

[99] Johnson, et al., *The John H. Schiede Papyri*, 21. See discussion above.

[100] For a review of revision theories which challenge translation debates in other books, see S. Talmon, "A New Outlook," 324; Lester Grabbe, "The Translation Technique of the Greek Minor Versions: Translations or Revisions?," in *Septuagint, Scrolls, and Cognate Writings* (eds., George J. Brooke and Barnabas Lindars; SBLSCS 33; Atlanta: SBL, 1992), 505–517 especially.

[101] Emanuel Tov likewise emphasized the phenomenon of correction, stating that the LXX was, "always corrected towards the Hebrew in the later mss. of LXX." Tov, *Text Criticism of the Hebrew Bible*, 313.

[102] Engaging JGK's query about whether there may not have been a pre-Theodotianic revision evinced by p967[Sch], Wevers shows that if there was one—it was thoroughgoing and made its way into all of the versions. Wevers, "Evidence," 216.

present discussion. Since p967's unique readings were often supported by the Lucianic minuscules, a more detailed study may use this line of inquiry to shed light on the larger issue of Ezekiel's linguistic non-homogeneity.

Despite the above debates, three conclusions have emerged: (1) We learn from the above discussions that Thackeray's divisions of Greek Ezekiel into linguistic sections held wide support by both multiple-translation proponents like Herrmann and McGreggor and revision proponents like Kase and Tov; (2) the case for revision is very much open and understudied; and (3), despite the linguistic complexity pointed out in the different theories, the overall translation technique of Greek Ezekiel, especially p967, may still be considered fairly literal. Indeed, Ziegler's arguments for correction, while not misplaced, were shown to be less than satisfactory.

2.5. Quality of p967 as a Textual Witness—Assessing Arguments for Errors

Despite its literalness, p967 is not a pristine text. Eugene Ulrich notes its "numerous errors" and "expansions" which he claims are "clearly attributable to the vulnerabilities inherent in the process of transmission history."[103] Johan Lust, who along with Ashley Crane, is the strongest proponent for p967's integrity as an early variant edition of Ezekiel, concedes that the manuscript contains errors.[104] These impressions should be tempered somewhat with the opinion of the first critical editors of p967[Sch] that "actual mistakes in copying seem to be comparatively few."[105] Nevertheless, most of p967's unique readings are listed in the critical publications, especially in Jahn's edition, as owing to *homoioteleuton*.[106]

Several challenges to p967's textual integrity focus on its omission of 36:23c–38.[107] The Princeton editors themselves offered multiple explanations.[108] In 1943, Floyd Filson focused the discussion and concluded that

---

[103] Ulrich, *The Dead Sea Scrolls*, 241.
[104] Lust, "Ezekiel 36–40," 519.
[105] Johnson, et al., *The John H. Schiede Papyri*, 7.
[106] Jahn, *Der griechische Text*, 126–128. Johnson, et al., *The John H. Schiede Papyri*, 7–8. See also Lust, "Ezekiel 36–40," 519, n. 14.
[107] For my textual evaluation of this passage, see chapter 4.
[108] For a good discussion on Johnson and Kase' early proposals, see Floyd V. Filson, "The Omission of Ezek 12:26–28 and 36:23b–38 in Codex 967," *JBL* 62 (1943): 29–30. See Johnson, et al., *The John H. Schiede Papyri*, 8–9. On the omission, Kenyon says, "the exact explanation is not clear. It looks, however, as though either it were not in the original LXX, or a version of it, current earlier in liturgical use, had been incorporated by the translators

the major p967 minus of 36:23c–38 was a mechanical error. He favored an explanation due to *homoioteleuton*, but listed several possibilities, including a lost sheet in a parent codex, or a skipped column in a parent roll.[109] These arguments about 36:23c–38 would be remounted by Wevers in 1969 and Spottorno in 1981.[110]

William A. Irwin, writing a year after Filson, disagreed and moreover, considered the issue conclusive. In his commentary, he reviewed the textual data and Thackeray's liturgical argument described below; he decided that the "convergence of two cogent lines of evidence establishes conclusively that the passage was not in the Hebrew text at the time of its translation into Greek."[111] He found this conclusion so convincing, and Filson's argument so unsatisfactory, that he conducted a point-by-point refutation of Filson in a footnote.[112]

Indeed, the argument for *homoioteleuton* for this omission is quite unreasonable.[113] Ziegler, finding Thackeray's linguistic liturgical explanation tenuous, nevertheless, dismissed Filson's *homoioteleuton* argument altogether.

> Eine befriedigende Erklärung der Auslassung läßt sich nicht geben, wie Kenyon, JThSt 39 (1938) 276 sagt, "the exact explanation is not clear."[114]

P.M. Bogaert, writing in 1978, finds p967 to preserve an intact text according to comparative analysis with the Latin versions.[115]

D.I. Block offered seven critiques against Lust;[116] Block's work is often hailed as *the* counter argument, proving that 36:23c–38 was erroneously

---

of the LXX. The latter explanation seems *a priori* more probable." F.J. Kenyon, "Reviews," *JTS* 39 (1938).

[109] F.V. Filson, "The Omission," 28. See chapter 4 for more detailed engagement with the textual arguments about this passage.

[110] J.W. Wevers, *Ezekiel* (NCB; London: Nelson, 1969), 273. M.V. Spottorno, "La omisión de Ez. 36, 23b–38 y la transposición de capítulos en el papiro 967," *Emerita* 50 (1981): 93–99.

[111] W.A. Irwin, *The Problem of Ezekiel: An Inductive Study* (Chicago: University of Chicago Press, 1943), 62. Irwin includes a more general discussion of the value of LXX on pp. 294–301. Irwin offered an initial and similar evaluation in W.A. Irwin, *The Prophets and Their Times* (ed., J.M. Powis Smith; Rev. ed.; Chicago: University of Chicago Press, 1941), 203.

[112] Irwin, *The Problem*, 62–63, n. 3.

[113] See the thorough discussion of Ashley Crane who rules in favor of the integrity of p967. Ashley Crane, *Israel's Restoration*.

[114] "A satisfying explanation of the omission cannot be given, as Kenyon says, 'the exact explanation is not clear.'" Ziegler, *Ezechiel*, (1952), 10, n. 1.

[115] P.M. Bogaert, "Le témoigne de la Vetus Latina," 390–391.

[116] D.I. Block, *The Book of Ezekiel: Chapters 25–48* (NIBCOT; Grand Rapids: Eerdmans, 1998), 337–342. For a discussion of Block's seven points see Crane who often favors Lust. Crane, *Israel's Restoration*.

omitted in p967. However, he mounts his arguments in his running commentary/discussion of the MT. Thus his discussion of p967 is framed by his larger goal to defend the integrity of the MT as an ancient standardized form and thus the preferred basis for his exegetical work.[117] According to Block, p967's witness provides not a *real* but at best a *hypothetical* reconstruction of an early text which can therefore not be used to supplant the viable Hebrew of the Masoretic text. Block, in the end, affirmed that p967 "may still represent an old text form,"[118] but evaded the opportunity to take a conclusive stance on priority.[119] Thus even Block, while mounting some important considerations, does not levy a fatal blow against understanding p967 as an early text. Indeed, Lust responded to each of Block's seven critiques to prove the integrity of p967 as often reflecting an early Hebrew witness.[120]

Johan Lust, using an innovative approach, argued for the integrity of p967's witness. On the basis of literary/theological analysis, Lust argued that the MT addition 36:23c–38 cohered with several other pluses, making a strong case for, if not the originality of, the integrity of p967's version.[121] Even before the discovery of p967, Thackeray had already singled out 36:23c–38 for its linguistic distinctiveness in the Greek tradition. Supposing it to be an early Jewish liturgical addition to the book, Thackeray offered a near prophetic prediction of what p967 demonstrated, that:

> early in our era, a later version of this lectionary passage [36:22–38] supplanted that of the original Alexandrian company in the parent MS, from which all of our MSS are descended.[122]

---

[117] Block, *The Book of Ezekiel*, 342.

[118] Block, *The Book of Ezekiel*, 342.

[119] Block's ambivalence on the issue of priority can be seen in his comments about the originality of MT plus, 36:23c–38. Block concedes that the passage in the LXX was brought into conformity with the received Hebrew text, and shows distinct literary style from its literary environment. Thus, Block allows that the passage could be a secondary addition, saying it "may point to the hand of a redactor," albeit a thoroughly Ezekielian one. Block, *The Book of Ezekiel*, 343.

[120] Johan Lust, "Textual Criticism of the Old and New Testaments: Stepbrothers?," in *New Testament Textual Criticism and Exegesis* (ed. A. Denaux; Leuven: Leuven University Press, 2002), 15–31. See especially pp. 20–31.

[121] Johan Lust, "Ezekiel 36–40," 517–533; idem, "Major Divergences," 83–92; idem, "De samenhang van Ez. 36–40," *TvT* 20 (1980): 26–39. In addition to the literary coherence, Lust found late biblical Hebrew syntax and morphology as well as phrases identified as later strata in the book of Jeremiah.

[122] H. St. J. Thackeray, *The Septuagint and Jewish Worship: A Study in Origins* (2nd ed.; The 1920 Schweich Lectures; London: Oxford University Press, 1923), 129. Thackeray first proposed his lectionary theory in 1903 where he noted the linguistic similarity of the passage to Theodotian. At that time, he preferred the Jewish synagogue as the liturgical

Together, then, Lust and Thackeray provided compelling reasons to trust many of p967's readings as a viable witness to the Greek text of Ezekiel in antiquity.[123]

The arguments presented about p967's minus in ch. 36 do not change the general assessment that p967 contains some errors. Ulrich, Lust, and the editors of the critical editions all point to cases of *homoioteleuton* as well as other errors of textual transmission. However, the case of Ezek 36:23c–38 is instructive. Several scholars hastily took the p967 minus for an error. Such a negative assessment of the reading is no longer tenable.[124] The example of 36:23c–38 invites a similar reappraisal of p967, as the present 'manuscript approach' to p967 endeavors to accomplish.

2.6. CONCLUSION

The preceding discussion of scholarship on p967 has yielded important results. All scholars recognize the significance of p967 to a greater or lesser extent, as the earliest Greek witness. Joseph Ziegler exhibited the most skeptical approach to p967, questioning its originality with an argument for correction to a pre-hexaplaric Hebrew text. On this basis, Ziegler deferred to B's witness, which he found relatively free from hexaplaric effects and thus the best representative of the OG. Ziegler's work introduced a cautionary note into the evaluation of p967. However, his conservative approach to p967 seems generally unfounded and has not won wide support. Gehman's analysis of the relationship to the Hebrew is more satisfactory. Gehman pointed to 74 readings where p967[Sch] relied on a non-MT base text. Further, he demonstrated 20 cases where p967[Sch] preserved errors in the Hebrew tradition; both types of readings work against the Hebrew correction theory as articulated by Ziegler.

---

context, but adopted a Christian lectionary theory in 1909. By 1923 in his book, Thackeray is ambiguous about the nature of the liturgical context in which the passage was produced. H. St. J. Thackeray, "Notes and Studies: The Greek Translators of Ezekiel," *JTS* IV. (1902–1903): 407–408. See also, idem, *Grammar of the Old Testament in Greek*, (Vol. 1; Cambridge: Cambridge University Press, 1909), 12.

[123] See Emanuel Tov's favorable discussion of Lust's arguments in Tov, "Recensional Differences between the Masoretic Text and the Septuagint of Ezekiel," in *The Greek and Hebrew Bible: Collected Essays on the Septuagint* (ed., Emanuel Tov; Boston: Brill, 1999), 408–410.

[124] See chapter 4 for my complete analysis of the variant.

In general, p967's text shows closer fidelity to the Hebrew parent/tradi-
tion than the rest of the LXX versions previously exhibited. This conclusion immediately raises the question of the inter-relationship among p967,
the other LXX-text traditions, the Hebrew, and the OG. I proposed three
models within which to understand p967 as a variant literary edition.

1. Gehman and Payne's Lagardian model: p967 and B are inner-Greek
   developments subsequent to the OG translation.
2. Kahle's multiple translations (supported by Ulrich's fluid Hebrew):
   p967 and B are two separate translations of a fluid Hebrew text; thus
   there are two Old Greek texts preserved in p967 and B.
3. Cross' correction to changing Hebrew text: p967 and B represent corrected texts towards a developing Hebrew text (with the possibility of
   inner-Greek development left open.)

All three models affirm the conclusions of Gehman and Payne, that there
were two, pre-hexaplaric, Greek traditions of Ezekiel, with p967 standing
closer to the Old Greek and its Hebrew *Vorlage*.

Any adjudication among the models will need to address p967's reliability as a viable textual witness. This is particularly true for any arguments about the Hebrew parent text of p967. As we saw, the case of
36:23c–38 confirmed the importance of robust evaluations which consider
arguments for error alongside literary assessments. Lust's demonstration
that 36:23c–38 coheres with several other variant readings makes a reex-
amination with literary sensitivities a necessity. Such a literary analysis
will provide a new angle on textual analyses, revealing many weaknesses
or cases for debate.

The same literary approach will offer new insight into the debates about
the Greek translation of Ezekiel. The possibility that a section of p967 is
a revision or a recension arose in the debates about the linguistic non-
homogeneity in Ezekiel. What McGregor attributes to a multiple translator theory was alternately interpreted by Tov as evidence for a recension.
I presented several studies that found basis for a revision in some part of
Greek Ezekiel. Tov's recension, Barthélemy's revision, Ziegler's correction,
JGK's revision, and Tisserant/Fernandex-Marcos' Lucianic gap all require
further inquiry. The literary study of p967's variant readings found below
will add further data necessary for evaluating these various proposals.

The textual issues that have emerged in the course of study on p967
cannot be easily resolved. The present chapter described stalemates

within text-critical studies on several fronts. These stalemates confirm what was proposed in the introduction to this project, that text-critical analysis alone is not equipped to decide these matters. Text-critical analysis, rather, situates the critic within the matrix of textual issues, and prepares us to explore different types of literary analysis and the light that they will shed on p967's text.

CHAPTER THREE

A COHERENCE APPROACH TO LITERARY ANALYSIS: DISCERNING *TENDENZEN*

3.1. INTRODUCTION

No doubt, editorial activity occurred at some phase of Ezekiel's transmission, resulting in the variant literary editions under discussion. As we saw in chapter 2, several textual approaches assumed some type of editorial activity, whether attributed to the Old Greek translation, to an inner-Greek revision, or to a fluid Hebrew textual tradition behind MT and p967. However, we also saw that these proposals were not easily defended using text-critical analysis alone. Chapter 2 revealed the pressing necessity for literary analysis.

It also became clear in chapter 1 that the scholar of variant literary editions must specify: what type of literary analysis can assist in answering text-critical questions? *Both* the text-critical question *and* the type of literary analysis must be made explicit. The specific question addressed in the present chapter, as well as in chapters 4 and 5, is: what is the scope of variants that distinguish p967 from MT as variant editions of Ezekiel? The theories presented in chapter 2 about the role of translators, revisers, or composers require a more specific data set. Indeed, only until we understand the extent of p967's variant literary edition can any further advances be made on these types of textual questions. Hence, the scope and character of the variants is the primary object of study in chapters 3, 4, and 5.

Lust mounted a strong case for p967's status as a variant literary edition in chs. 36–39, 12:26–28, and 32:24–26. As Tov notes in the case of 1 Samuel, "if recensional difference is recognized within a certain book..., the complete book is likely to reflect such features elsewhere including in small details."[1] Chapters 3, 4, and 5 of this project are oriented by Tov's proposal, that a wider scope of details further distinguishes MT and p967, beyond those variants already identified by Lust. Beginning with Lust's data set,

---

[1] Tov, *The Text Critical Use of the Septuagint*, 242.

the present study identifies the tendencies of coherence that characterize a wider scope of variants. The result is a more specific typology of literary tendencies that distinguish MT and p967's editions. I designate these using the term 'literary *Tendenzen*' or *Tendenzen* for short.

3.2. Procedure: Organizing Variants according to *Tendenzen*

It remains to explain the procedure of identifying variants according to *Tendenzen*. The first step involved working through p967's text comprehensively, identifying all meaningful variants in comparison with MT. The second step adopted the coherence approach (described in chapter 1) to characterize trends across the large number of meaningful variants. The second step was more involved, and deserves fuller attention.

As indicated in chapter 1, Lust's coherence approach established the significance of Ezek 12:26–28; 32:25–26; 36:23c–38; and the variant sequence of chaps. 37 and 38–39 for the different editions of Ezekiel. In light of Lust's work, and upon further consideration of the meaningful variants, it became clear that each of Lust's major variants occurred within what can be called 'intertextual centers.' The emergence of intertextual centers confirmed, to some extent, Tov's proposal, that minor details participate in the differences already identified in more major variant features.[2] The four intertextual centers are thus:

1) 'Disputation on Prophecy' in Ezekiel 12–13;
2) 'Israel's Enemies in the Underworld' in Ezekiel 32:17–32;
3) 'The Vision of Dried Bones' in Ezekiel 37; and
4) 'Gog and Magog' in Ezekiel 38–39.

The intertextual centers house, in addition to the four variants significant to Lust's work, the themes, terms, and forms which proved to characterize variants in detail outside of the centers. In other words, the four intertextual centers formed the *qualitative* framework for my quantitative analysis. In my quantitative analysis, I identified all the variants, what Tov called the "smaller details," that could be grouped into *Tendenzen* related to each intertextual center.

---

[2] See chapter 5 for more attention to Tov's proposal.

A '*Tendenz*' is a theme, *stichtwort*, or form present in the intertextual center that characterizes variants elsewhere across Ezekiel. So for example, the 'Fate of the Slain' *Tendenz* includes variants related to the major theme of death and the location of the dead. This *Tendenz* was highly concentrated in Ezek 32:17–32, the intertextual center. In chapter 5, *Tendenzen* such as this one are brought to bear on the literary differentiation between p967 and the MT editions of Ezekiel.

Only textual readings that could be proved to relate to the *Tendenzen* are included in the present data set. That is to say, many other meaningful variants are omitted from the present discussion.[3] The coherence approach is not interested in isolated literary features, but rather trends that more likely signal layers of authorial activity.

3.3. Introduction to the *Tendenzen*

Chapter 5 will focus on literary readings of the *Tendenzen*. However, an outline of the *Tendenzen* here provides a brief overview of their nature and the number of variants encompassed by each one:[4]

Prophecy *Tendenzen*	87 variants
Fate of the Slain *Tendenz*	99 variants
Tendenzen Related to Ezekiel 36:23c–38	21 variants
'Gog-Magog' *Tendenzen*: Variants Related to Ezekiel 38–39	49 variants

3.4. Textual Lemmata according to *Tendenzen*

The variants are grouped according to *Tendenzen* in the Textual *Lemmata* below. For cross-referencing purposes, the numerical outline follows the paragraph sections in chapter 5, in which the variants are submitted to exegetical analysis.

---

[3] For example, one of the longest of p967's minuses omitted from the present discussion occurs in 33:25 where the MT reads עַל הַדָּם תֹּאכֵלוּ וְעֵינֵכֶם תִּשְׂאוּ אֶל גִּלּוּלֵיכֶם וְדָם תִּשְׁפֹּכוּ וְהָאָרֶץ תִּירָשׁוּ, ("you eat with blood, your eyes gaze upon your idols, and you pour out blood. Will you then possess the land?")

[4] Some variants are counted twice if, in chapter 5, they could be exegetically connected to more than one *Tendenz*. The actual total number of variants equals 230, as indicated in chapter 4.

'Prophecy' *Tendenzen* (§5.2)

Intertextual Center: Disputation on Prophecy in Ezekiel 12–13 (§5.2.1)

12:26 (minus) 967] και εγενετο λογος κυριου προς με λεγων Z rel. = וַיְהִי דְבַר יְהוָה
אֵלַי לֵאמֹר MT

12:27 (minus) 967] υιε ανθρωπου ιδου οικος ισραηλ ο παραπικραινων λεγοντες
λεγουσιν η ορασις ην ουτος ορα εις ημερας πολλας και εις καιρους
μακρους ουτος προφητευει Z ≈ rel. ≈ בֶּן אָדָם הִנֵּה בֵית יִשְׂרָאֵל
אֹמְרִים הֶחָזוֹן אֲשֶׁר הוּא חֹזֶה לְיָמִים רַבִּים וּלְעִתִּים רְחֹקוֹת
הוּא נִבָּא MT

12:28 (minus) 967] δια τουτο ειπον προς αυτους ταδε λεγει κυριος ου μη μηκυνωσιν
ουκετι παντες οι λογοι μου ους αν λαλησω λαλησω και ποιησω
λεγει κυριος Z ≈ rel. ≈ לָכֵן אֱמֹר אֲלֵיהֶם כֹּה אָמַר אֲדֹנָי יְהוָה
לֹא תִמָּשֵׁךְ עוֹד כָּל דְּבָרָי אֲשֶׁר אֲדַבֵּר דָּבָר וְיֵעָשֶׂה נְאֻם אֲדֹנָי
יְהוָה MT | δια τουτο ειπον προς αυτους ταδε λεγει κυριος (om.
ου μη μηκυνωσιν—*fin.*) 410

13:2 προφητευσεις 967 (obel. *O*) Z B Sa Hi.] (ast. *O*) τους προφητευοντας rel. =
הַנְּבִאִים MT
προς αυτους 967 (obel. *O*) ZB Sa Hi.] (ast. *O*) τοις προφηταις τοις προφητευουσιν
απο καρδιας αυτων rel. θ'α' ≈ לִנְבִיאֵי מִלִּבָּם MT | לִנְבִיאֵי אֲלֵיהֶם
מִלִּבָּם HUBP[III-96]

13:3 προφητευουσιν 967 Z rel. (recon. הַנְּבִיאִים] הַנְּבָאִים MT
απο καρδιας αυτων 967 Z rel.] (ast. *O*) τοις πορευομενοις οπισω του πνευματος
αυτων *O' L"* 403 410 Arm Or. Tht. ≈ הַנְּבָלִים אֲשֶׁר הֹלְכִים אַחַר
רוּחָם MT

13:7 (minus) ZB Sa Hi.[(967 not preserved)]] (ast. *O*) και ελεγετε φησι(ν) κυριος και εγω
ουκ ελαλησα Q θ' ≈ A Arab rel. = וַאֲמַרְתֶּם נְאֻם יְהוָה וַאֲנִי לֹא
דִבַּרְתִּי MT

'Prophetic Temporality' *Tendenz*: Time and Fulfillment in Ezekiel (§5.2.2)

Programmatic Statements about Prophecy and Fulfillment (§5.2.2.1)

7:13 (minus) ZB 233 La^S Co Hi.[(967 not preserved)]] (ast. *O* 86') και ετι εν ζωη το ζην
αυτων οτι ορασις εις παν το πληθος αυτης ουκ ανακαμψει rel. ≈
α'σ'θ' = וְעוֹד בַּחַיִּים חַיָּתָם כִּי חָזוֹן אֶל כָּל הֲמוֹנָהּ לֹא יָשׁוּב MT

8:18 (minus) ZB La^S Hi.[(967 not preserved)]] και κεκραξονται εις τα ωτα καλεσουσιν εν
τοις ωσιν μου φωνη μεγαλη και ου μη εισακουσω αυτων *L*-311-
V-46-*Z^V* Tht. | (ast. *O*) και καλεσουσιν εν τοις ωσιν μου φωνη
μεγαλη και ου μη εισακουσω αυτων ≈ rel. = וְקָרְאוּ בְאָזְנַי קוֹל
גָּדוֹל וְלֹא אֶשְׁמַע אוֹתָם MT

22:28 αλειφοντες αυτους 967 Z rel.] ηλειφον αυτους Q ≈ טָחוּ לָהֶם MT | חֹזֶה לָהֶם
HUBP[III-96]
πεσουνται 967 Z rel. (recon. יִפֹּלוּ)] αναρτυτω πεσουνται Q^mg *III* (recon. תִּפֹּל
יִפֹּלוּ) | (ast.^sub Q) πηλω Q = תָּפֵל MT

24:14 ουδε μη ελεησω 967 Z rel.] ου φεισομαι ουδε μη ελεησω *L* 86 | ουδε μη ελεησω
(ast. *O*) ουδ ου μη παρακληθω *O'*-62 Arm Hi. ≈ ουδε φεισομαι και
ου μη παρακληθω 62 *III* Tht. ≈ וְלֹא אָחוּס וְלֹא אֶנָּחֵם MT | וְלֹא
אָחוּס וְלֹא אֲרַחֵם HUBP[I-Targ] (cf. וְלֹא אֲרַחֵם HUBP[I-Peshitta])

38:8   επ εσχατων ετων 967 ≈ Z rel.] (minus) 106| באחרית השנים MT | באחרית
        השנה HUBP[III-96]

38:17   των προφητων ισραηλ 967 ≈ Z rel.] των προφητων ισραηλ (ast. O) των
        προφητευσαντων O-62 L" Bo Tht. σ'θ' = הַנְּבָאִים נביאי ישראל
        נשיאי ישראל HUBP[III-30] (om. נביאי ישראל) | הַנְּבָאִים MT |
        הַנְּבָאִים HUBP[III-96]

Date Reckoning (§5.2.2.2)

26:1   δεκατω 967 538 cII-86 26 544 Bo] ενδεκατω Z rel. = עשתי עשרה MT |
        δωδεκατω A

29:1   δεκατω 967 Z rel. = הָעֶשְׂרִית MT] δωδεκατω B Syh[mg]-62' L[-36]-311 233–613
        927 Co Arab Hi.

30:20   δεκατω 967 62' 763*-lI] ενδεκατω BAQΓ Syh rel. = אחת עשרה MT

31:1   δεκατω 967 Q-62' 490–534 106 Tht.] ενδεκατω BA Γ Syh rel. = אחת עשרה
        MT

32:1   δωδεκατω 967 B Syh duodecimo La[H] rel. = שתי עשרה MT] ενδεκατω Z A"-
        106 534–239' | δεκατω 88 L'-449* 130* 410 Tht. decimo Hi.

32:17   δεκατω 967 88 763–449 Tht. 86 α'θ'] δωδεκατω ZBAQ Syh duodecimo La[H] =
        שתי עשרה MT

33:21   δεκατω 967 88-Syh[txt] 449* 86] δωδεκατω Z BA rel. = שתי עשרה MT |
        ενδεκατω L

Ezekiel's Temporal Structure (§5.2.2.3)
The Number of Years for Israel's Guilt

4:4   πεντηκοντα και εκατον Z rel. (obel. O) [(967 not preserved)]] ενενηκοντα και εκατον
        O Q[mg]-147 538 534–239'-710 | ενενηκοντα και τριακοσιας 410 |
        (minus) C' = MT

4:5   ενενηκοντα και εκατον Z rel. [(967 not preserved)]] ενενηκοντα και τριακοσιας C'-403'
        410 Hi. = שלש מאות ותשעים MT

4:6   το δεξιον Z rel. [(967 not preserved)]] το δεξιον (obel. O) δευτερον O-62 Arm = הימיני
        שנית MT ≈ L"-311 Tht. 147'

'On that Day'

20:5–6 τη χειρι μου αυτων του εξαγαγειν 967 534 106] [(v 5)] τη χειρι μου αυτων λεγων
        εγω κυριος ο θεος υμων [(v 6)] εν εκεινη τη ημερα αντελαβομην τη
        χειρι μου αυτων του εξαγαγειν Z rel. = MT

23:38   (minus) 967 Z ≈ cII-239' lI 26' 544 Cyr.] (ast. O) εν τη ημερα εκεινη O' lII
        Arm Tht. Q[txt] 86 = ביום ההוא MT

23:39   (minus) 967 Z rel.] (ast. O) εν τη ημερα εκεινη O' V-449 Aeth Tht. α'σ'θ'
        Q[txt] 86 = ביום ההוא MT | αφυλακτως 26' 239' 403' 410 544 |
        αφυλακτως εν τη ημερα εκεινη A

24:2   γραψον εχει σεαυτω εις ημεραν 967] γραψον σεαυτω εις ημεραν Z rel. |
        γραψον σεαυτω το ονομα της ημερας lII Tht. = כתוב לך את
        שם היום MT cf. omnia (nomen?) in diem La[S]
        απο της ημερας ταυτης 967 Z rel.] ταυτης 449 Tht. |הזה את עצם היום MT
        απο της ημερας της σημερον 967 Z rel.] απο της ημερας ταυτης σημερον L[·36]
        ≈ הזה בעצם היום MT | (minus) 46

24:27 (minus) 967] εν εκεινη τη ημερα ZB *L''* La^{CS} Tht. | εν τη ημερα εκεινη rel. = ביום ההוא

38:14 και εν τη ημερα εκεινη 967] ουκ εν τη ημερα εκεινη Z B O' 106 198 239' = *in die non* La^W] | ουχι εν τη ημερα εκεινη = הלוא ביום ההוא MT rel. = *nonne in die illa* La^{Amb}

38:18 η ημερα εκεινη εν 967] εν τη ημερα 534 La^W | εν τη ημερα εκεινη εν ημερα Z rel. = ההוא ביום ביום MT

40:1 εν τη ημερα εκεινη 967 Z rel.] εν οστεω τη ημερα εκεινη 62' = בעצם היום הזה MT | בעצם הזה היום הזה HUBP^{III-93}

'Divine Speech' *Tendenz*: Prophetic and Oracle Formulae (§5.2.3)
Formulae of Prophetic Speech (§5.2.3.1)
Divine Messenger Formula: "Thus says the Lord" (ταδε λεγει αδωναι κυριος / כה אמר אדני יהוה)

16:59 (minus) 967 Z rel.] (ast. O^{-Q}) οτι O^{-Q}-62 Arm = כי MT | *propter quod* Or.^{lat}

17:9 (minus) 967 La^C] ταδε λεγει κυριος Z rel. = כה אמר אדני יהוה MT

21:3(8) δια τουτο 967 Z rel.] (minus) MT

21:3(8) ταδε λεγει κς 967 B^{mg} rel. (ast. Q) = כה אמר אדני יהוה MT) [minus (Z B^{txt} 106 | כה אדני יהוה HUBP^{III-150} | כה אמר אדני יהוה HUBP^{III-30, 93, 96}, G-BEb 22

25:15 οτι 967] δια τουτο Z rel. | (minus) 106 147 239 *III* Bo Aeth Tht. = MT

33:25 (minus) 967 Z rel.] כה אמר אדני יהוה MT

33:25 (minus) 967 Z B La^{CS} Co Hi.] (ast. O 449 534) επι τω αιματι φαγεσθε και οφθαλους υμων λημψεσθε προς ειδωλα υμων και αιμα εκχειτε και την γην κληρονομησετε ⁽²⁶⁾ εστητε επι τη ρομφαια υμων εποιησατε βδελυγμα και εκαστος τον πλησιον αυτου εμιανατε και την γην κληρονομησετε ≈ rel. = על הדם תאכלו ועינכם תשאו אל גלוליכם ודם תשפכו והארץ תירשו ⁽²⁶⁾ עמדתם על חרבכם עשיתן תועבה ואיש את אשת רעהו טמאתם והארץ תירשו MT cf.^{39:17–19}

36:7 (minus) 967 Z rel.] (ast. O) ταδε λεγει αδωναι κυριος O-62' *L''* Arm Tht. Hi. = כה אמר אדני יהוה MT

44:9 δια τουτο 967 Z rel.] (minus) MT

Formula for a Divine Saying: "Oracle of the Lord" (λεγει αδωναι κυριος / נאם אדני יהוה)

18:32 (minus) 967] λεγει κυριος ZB La^S Co rel. = נאם אדני יהוה MT

18:32 (minus) 967 ZB La^S Co Arab Hi.] (ast. O) και επιστρεψατε και ζησατε ≈ rel. = והשיבו וחיו MT | επιστρεψατε και ζησατε 534 = השיבו וחיו HUBP^{III-96-150} | ως το επιστρεψαι αυτον απο της οδου αυτου της πονηρας και ζην αυτον λεγει αδωναι κυριος και επιστρεψασται και ζησεται επιστρεψατε ουν και ζησατε ≈ *L''* Arm Tht. 62

20:6 τη χειρι μου αυτων του εξαγαγειν 967 534 106] ^(v 5) τη χειρι μου αυτων λεγων εγω κυριος ο θεος υμων ^(v 6) εν εκεινη τη ημερα αντελαβομην τη χειρι μου αυτων του εξαγαγειν Z rel. = MT

20:33 δια τουτο 967 Z rel. (obel. *O*)] (minus) 62 Tyc. = MT
24:14 δια τουτο 967 Z (obel. *O* Hi.)] (minus) MT
εγω κρινω σε κατα τα αιματα σου και κατα τα ενθυμηματα σου κριθησει λεγει
κς η ακαθαρτος η ονομαστη και πολλη του παραπικραινειν 967
≈ Z rel. (obel. *O* Hi.)] η ακαθαρτος η ονομαστη και πολλη του
παραπικραινειν *ll* 764 La[S] | (minus) MT
κριθησει λεγει κς 967] κρινω σε Z rel. | (minus) La[W] | (minus in context) *ll*
764 La[S] = MT
33:27 (minus) 967 Z rel. = MT] נאם אדני יהוה HUBP[III-30]
36:23 (minus) 967 Z B 46 Bo La[Ver] Tyc. PsCypr.) (ast. *O*) λεγει αδωναι κυριος rel.
= MT נאם אדני יהוה
(minus) 967] Ezek 36:24–38 Z ≈ rel. ≈ MT
37:28 (minus) 967 Z rel. = MT] λεγει κυριος A'-410 Arab Tyc.

"Behold" (ιδου / הנה)

16:44 ταυτα εστιν 967 Z rel.] הנה MT
17:12 οταν 967 Z Syh[mg] rel.] ιδου Q[mg]-Syh *L''* Chr.II 193 Tht. 86 α'σ'θ' = הנה MT
21:3(8) ιδου εγω 967 Z rel. = הנני MT] (minus) B[txt]
22:13 εαν δε 967 Z rel.] ιδου ουν *L'-36* Tht. ≈ הנה HUBP[III-150] | και ιδου θ' 86 = והנה
MT | *ecce* Arm | *et ego* Arab
24:14 (minus) 967 Z rel.] ιδου Q 26 Tht. | (minus in context) MT
25:7 (minus) 967 ZB 87 *L'-36* La[C] Bo] (ast. *O*) ιδου εγω rel. = הנני MT
37:2 (minus) 967 ZB Bo GregEl.Ambr.Ir.[lat] Aeth Arm Hi.] και ιδου AQ = והנה
MT
39:8 ιδου ηκει και εσται 967] הנה באה וְנִהְיָתָה MT | ιδου ηκει και γνωση οτι
εσται Z rel. (cf. *scies quia erit* La[Sg] *scies quoniam erit* La[H]
43:12 (minus) 967 ZB 106] (ast. *O*) εισιν rel. ≈ הנה MT
(minus) 967 ZB] (ast. *O*) ουτος ο νομος του οικου rel. = זאת תורת הבית MT

Other Types of Prophetic Speech

12:26 (minus) 967] και εγενετο λογος κυριου προς με λεγων Z rel. = ויהי דבד
יהוה אלי לאמר MT
21:2(7) δια τουτο προφητευσον υιε ανθρωπου 967 Z rel.] υιε ανθρωπου δια τουτο
προφητευσον A''0239'-403' Bo Arab | δια τουτο υιε ανθρωπου
προφητευσον La[S] Tyc. | υιε ανθρωπου *O*-Q-147 *C''*- 86' 106 = בן
אדם MT
και προφητευσον επι 967 26' 147' Hi. = והנבא אל MT] και προφητευσον
περι *L''-449* Tht. | και προφητευσεις επι Z rel.
21:3(8) (minus) 967 48 *C'-233* 544 Sa Tyc.] και ερεις προς την γην του ισραηλ Z rel.
= ואמרת לאדמת ישראל MT
33:27 (minus) 967 ZB La[CS] Co Hi.[test]] ερεις προς αυτους Syh + δια τουτο ειπον
αυτοις *O*-Syh *L''* 62 | δια τουτο ειπον αυτοις rel.-Syh | ταδε ειπον
αυτοις 106 (recon. ειπον אָמַר) ≈ כה תאמר אלהם MT
34:9 (minus) 967 ZB Bo] (ast. *O*) ακουσατε λογον κυριου rel. = שמעו דבר יהוה
MT
37:4 προφητευσον 967 ZB A V-449 Bo Aeth Or.IV 210 Tht.Tert.GregEl.Ambr.
Ir.[lat]Consult = הנבא MT] προφητευσον υιε ανθρωπου *L'-403*

Or.XI 387 Lo. | προφητευσον υιε ανθρωπου προφητευσον 26 544
613 | (obel. Q) υιε ανθρωπου προφητευσον rel.

επι τα οστα ταυτα 967 Z rel. = עַל הָעֲצָמוֹת הָאֵלֶּה MT] επι τα οστα ταυτα
προφητευσον υιε ανθρωπου V-449 Tht. | (minus) L'-46 Or.XI
387 Lo.

37:7   εν τω με προφητευσαι 967 ZB Ambr.Ir.[lat]] εν τω με προφητευσαι φωνη 233 |
(ast. O) φωνη εν τω με προφητευσαι rel. = קוֹל כְּהִנָּבְאִי MT

37:9   προφητευσον επι το πνα προφητευσον υιε ανθρωπου 967 Z rel. = MT] υιε
ανθρωπου προφητευσον επι το πνευμα προφητευσον A''-106 υιε
ανθρωπου προφητευσον επι το πνευμα C''- 239'-403' Arab Arm
Hi. | προφητευσον υιε ανθρωπου 407 Ambr.

37:12   προφητευσον και ειπον 967 Z rel. = MT] προφητευσονται υιε ανθρωπου και
ειπε L'' Tht.

(minus) 967 ZB Cypr.Ambr.Tyc.Spec.] (ast. O) προς αυτους rel. = אֲלֵיהֶם MT

Recognition Formula: "They/you will know that I am the Lord" (και γνωσονται οτι εγω ειμι κς ο θς / וִידְעוּ כִּי אֲנִי יְהוָה) (§5.2.3.2) and Nation-Recognition Formula (§5.2.3.3)

20:5   (minus) 967 534 106] λεγων εγω κυριος ο θεος υμων Z rel. = לֵאמֹר אֲנִי יְהוָה
אֱלֹהֵיכֶם MT

20:6   τη χειρι μου αυτων του εξαγαγειν 967 534 106] [(v 5)] τη χειρι μου αυτων λεγων
εγω κυριος ο θεος υμων [(v 6)] εν εκεινη τη ημερα αντελαβομην τη
χειρι μου αυτων του εξαγαγειν Z rel. = MT

20:26   (minus) 967 ZB La[CS] Sa Iust.Hi.[test]] (ast. O) ινα γνωσιν οτι εγω κυριος rel. =
לְמַעַן אֲשֶׁר יֵדְעוּ אֲשֶׁר אֲנִי יְהוָה MT

28:26   (minus) 967 62 = MT] (obel. O[-Syh]) και ο θεος των πατερων αυτων Z rel.

34:15   (minus) 967 Aug. = MT] (obel. O 86) και γνωσονται οτι εγω ειμι κυριος Z ≈
rel. = et scient quod ego sum dues La[Sg]

34:30   (minus) 967 Z rel.] (ast. O) μετ αυτων O (Q[mg])-62' L'' Arm Tht. = אִתָּם MT

36:38   (minus in context) 967] και γνωσονται οτι εγω ειμι κυριος A''-410 L'-46 233'-403'
| και γνωσονται οτι εγω ειμι κυριος Z rel. = וְיָדְעוּ כִּי אֲנִי יְהוָה MT

36:23   (minus) 967] εν τω αγιασθηναι με εν υμιν κατ οφθαλμους αυτων Z rel. =
בְּהִקָּדְשִׁי בָכֶם לְעֵינֵיהֶם MT

36:36   (minus in context) 967] και γνωσονται τα εθνη οσα αν καταλειφθωσι
κυκλω υμων οτι εγω κυριος ωκοδομησα τας καθηρημενας και
κατεφυτευσα τας ηφανισμενας Z ≈ rel. ≈ וְיָדְעוּ הַגּוֹיִם אֲשֶׁר
יִשָּׁאֲרוּ סְבִיבוֹתֵיכֶם כִּי אֲנִי יְהוָה בָּנִיתִי הַנֶּהֱרָסוֹת נָטַעְתִּי
הַנְּשַׁמָּה MT

37:28   και γ[ν]ωσονται τα εθνη οτι εγω ειμι κς 967 Z rel. = וְיָדְעוּ הַגּוֹיִם כִּי אֲנִי
יְהוָה MT] et scient omnes gentes quia ego Dominus La[W] | και
γνωσονται οτι εγω ειμι κυριος A Aeth Arab

38:14   εγερθηση 967 Z rel. (recon: תֵּעֹר)] εξεγερθηση A''; απαντηση 46; γνωση και
εγερθηση L'' Tht. | תֵדַע MT

38:16   γνωσιν παντα τα εθνη 967 L''-449 La[W] Tht.] γνωσι παντα τα εθνη εμε Z rel. =
דַּעַת כָּל הַגּוֹיִם אֹתִי HUBP[III-30] | sciant me omnes gentes quod
ego sum dominus dues La[S] | דַּעַת הַגּוֹיִם אֹתִי MT | הַגּוֹיִם אֹתִי
HUBP[III-93]

38:20 ινα γνωσιν παντα τα εθνη εμε εν σοι ενωπιον αυτων 967] (minus) Z rel. = MT

39:8 ιδου ηκει και εσται 967] הנה באה וְנִהְיָתָה MT | ιδου ηκει και γνωση οτι εσται
Z rel. (cf. *scies quia erit* La^Sg *scies quoniam erit* La^H

'Fate of the Slain' *Tendenzen* (§5.3)
Intertextual Center: The Pit in Ezekiel 32:17–32 (§5.3.1)
Population of the Pit

32:18 τα εθνη 967 ≈ tr. Z rel.] גוים אדרם MT | גוים אֹרִידִים HUBP^III-96
τας θυγατερας νεκρας 967 ≈ tr. Z rel.] בנות MT

32:26 (minus in context) 967] μοσοχ και θοβελ και πασα (recon. θοβελ (ותבל
Z rel. ≈ משך תבל וכל MT | μοσοχ και θοβελλι και πασα (recon.
θοβελλι (תבלי 233 | μοσοχ και βοβελ και πασα (recon. βοβελ
בבל) 538 | cf.^v 25 *cubile eorum* Hi. σ'θ' (HUBP^V-recon. /משכבם
משכב להם cf.^v 25)

32:29 εδοθησαν 967 ZB Q^mg-Syh^mg Co] εδωμ rel. = אדום MT
(minus) 967 ZB La^C Co] (ast.O) και οι βασιλεις αυτης και παντες ≈ rel. ≈ מלכיה
וכל MT | και μοσοχ οι βασιλεις αυτης και παντες minisc.
οι αρχοντες ασσουρ 967 Z ≈ A] οι αρχοντες 130' | οι αρχοντες αυτης O (Q^txt)
L" C'-233– 86 106' La^C Arab Arm (= נשיאיה MT) | נשיאיה
אשר MT

32:30 στρατηγοι ασσουρ 967 Z rel.] צדני אַשֶׁר MT | צדְנִי אַשֶׁר HUBP^III-G-BEb 10 |
σιδωνιοι α'σ' | σεδεκ θ' | *venatores qui* Vul

Circumcision in the Pit

32:19 (minus) 967 ZB Co Arab Hi.^test] (ast. O 449 Hi.) εξ υδατων ευπρεπους
καταβηθι και κοιμηθητι μετα απεριτμητων rel. ≈ ממי נעמת
רדה והשכבה את ערלים MT

32:21 μετα απεριτμητων 967 Z rel. (recon. ערלים])בערלים) MT | ערלים
HUBP^III-30 | כערלים HUBP^III-93

32:26 (minus in context) 967] παντες απεριτμητοι C 26 = ערלים כלם MT | כלם
חללים HUBP^III-30 | παντες (obel. Q) τραυματιαι αυτου παντες
απεριτμητοι ≈ Z rel.

32:27 απ αιςνος 967 Z rel.] מערלים MT

32:29 τραυματιων 967 Z rel.] ערלים MT | הערלים HUBP^III-30

Shame of the Pit

32:24 (minus) 967] ελαβοσαν βασανον αυτων Z ≈ rel. | וישאו כלמתם MT
(= ατιμιαν θ' 86 cf.^16:52; 36:7; 39:26 ≈ αισχυνην α'σ') | וישאו את
כלמתם HUBP^III-96

32:25 (minus) 967 Z rel.] (ast. 86) και αρουσιν εντροπην αυτων 86 | וישאו כלמתם
MT

32:30 και απηνεγκαν την βασανον αυτων 967 Z rel.] και ελαβον την βασανον αυτων
A"-106' L"-456 Tht. | וישאו את כלמתם MT וישאו כלמתם
HUBP^III-96
(minus) 967 Z rel.] (ast. Q^txt 86) αισχυνομενοι O Arm Hi. ≈ L"-456 Tht. =
בושים MT

Giants in the Pit

32:21   και ερουσιν 967 87 Bo ≈ יֹדברו (om. copula) HUBP[III-96]] και ερουσιν σοι Z
        rel. ≈ 407 | ידברו לו MT

        οι γιγαντες 967 Z rel.] אֵלֵי גבורים MT | גבורים HUBP[III-93 150] | אילי גבורים
        καταβηθι 967 Z rel. (recon. רד)] יְרְדוּ MT
        κοιμηθητι 967 Z rel. (recon. שֹכב)] שָׁכְבוּ MT
        μετα απεριτμητων 967 Z rel. (recon. בערלים)] הערלים MT | ערלים
        HUBP[III-30] | כערלים HUBP[III-93]

32:27   και 967 Z rel.] και (ast.) ουκ O(Q*) Arm[p] Hi. = ולא MT
        γιγαντων 967 Z rel. = גבורים MT] גבורים בארץ HUBP[III-96]
        απ αιϛνος 967 Z rel.] מערלים MT

'Fate of the Slain' *Tendenzen:* Variants across the Rest of Ezekiel (§5.3.1)

Tyre's Fate in the Midst of the Sea (§5.3.2.1)

26:20   μη δε αναστᾳθης 967 Z ≈ μη δε αναστῃς B *lll* Tht.] ונתתי צבי MT | תשב
        צבי HUBP[III-30(pm) 89(pm)]

        επι [της] ζωης 967 *ll* 91–764] επι γης ζωης Z ≈ rel. = בארץ חיים MT
26:21   ετι 967 ZBL La[CW] Co Arab] ετι (ast.) και ζητηθηση και ουχ ευρηθηση (+ ετι
        62) rel. = ותבקשי ולא תמצאי עוד MT
27:32   (minus) 967 ZB Co Arab Tyc.Hi.[test]] (ast. O) τις ωσπερ τυρος κατασιγηθεισα
        εμμεσω θαλασσης ≈ rel. = מי כצור כדמה בתוך הים MT
28:8   (minus) 967 rel. Z] לשחת MT
28:10(9)   εν πληθει 967 Z rel.] εν χειρι L" Tht. = ביד MT
        απεριτμητων 967 ZB La[C] Co Arab Hippol. Tyc.] (ast. O[-Syh]) τραυματιζοντων
        σε θανατοις απεριτμητων ≈ rel. = מחללי מותי ערלים MT
32:19   (minus) 967 ZB Co Arab Hi.[test]] (ast. O 449 Hi.) εξ υδατων ευπρεπους
        καταβηθι και κοιμηθητι μετα απεριτμητων rel. ≈ ממי נעמת
        רדה והשכבה את ערלים MT

"Hordes" *Tendenz:* The End for Enemy Hordes (§5.3.2.2)

Hamon-gog's Hordes

39:11   το γαι το πολυανδριον του γωγ 967 Z rel.] גיא המון גוג MT | המון גוג
        HUBP[III-96] | גיא המון גיא HUBP[III-150]

        εκει τον γωγ και παν το πληθος αυτου 967 rel. = שם את גוג ואת כל
        המונה MT

39:15   πολυανδριον 967 Z rel.] πληθος σ' | εβρ' αμωνα θ' Syh = המונה MT

Egypt's Hordes

32:18   ισχυν 967 Z rel.] πληθος 86 σ'* θ' Syh.* = *multitudinem* Hi. = המון MT |
        γην A
32:20   πασα η ισχϑς αυτης 967 Z rel.] (ast. α'σ'θ') το παν πληθος αυτης 86 α'σ'θ' ≈
        וכל המוניה MT
32:24   δυναμις αυτου 967 Z rel.] המונה MT | δυναμις αυτου και παν το πληθος
        αυτου L Tht. (Heb = fs. suffix vs. 967 ms. indep. pron.)
32:25   (minus in context) 967 Z rel.] (obel. pro ast. L) συν παντι τω πληθει
        εκαστου L 62 ≈ בכל המונה MT

32:26 (minus in context) 967] η ισχυς αυτων Z rel. | η ισχυς εκαστου L | המונה
MT

32:31 ισχυν αυτων 967 ZB La^C Co Arab] ισχυν αυτων (ast. *O*) τραυματιαι μαχαιρας
φαραω και πασα δυναμις αυτου rel. = המונה חללי חרב פרעה
וכל חילו MT

32:32 πληθος αυτου 967 Z rel. = המונו HUBP^III-G-BEb 10 (sm) | המונה MT (q המונו /k
המונה HUBP^III-G-BEb 10 (pm))

29:19 (minus) 967 BZ La^S (vid.) Co] (ast. Q) και λη(μ)ψεται το πληθος αυτης rel. =
ונשא המנה MT

30:4 (minus) 967 Z B La^S Co Tyc.] (ast. *O*) και λη(μ)ψονται το πληθος αυτης rel.
= ולקחו המונה MT

32:6 απο του πληθους 967] απο του πληθους σου Z rel. | מדמך MT

Tyre's Hordes
Textual Variants:

27:25 εν τω πληθει 967 Z rel.] εν αυτοις καρχηδονιοι Q^mg | εν τω πληθει εμποροι σου
O' 106 Aeth Arab Arm | (minus) MT

28:9 εν πληθει 967 ZB La^C Co Arab Hippol. Tyc.] εν χειρι (ast. *O*^-Syh) τραυματιζοντων
σε ≈ rel. = ביד מחלליך MT

29:17 δια πληθος αμαρτιων σου 967 Z (obel. *O*)] (minus) MT

Translation Variants:

26:10 απο πληθους 967 ≈ Z rel.] משפעת MT | מרפסת Tar ≈ HUBP^I-Peshitta
(HUBP^V-שפע-II, 'stamp (hoofs)')

27:12 απο πληθους πασης ισχυος σου 967 Z rel.] απο πληθους πασης δυναμεως σου
III Tht. | מרב כל הון MT

27:16 απο πληθους του συμμεικτου σου 967 Z rel.] מרב כל הון MT | מרב מעשיך
HUBP^III-30

27:18 εκ πληθους δυναμεως σου 967 Q 233 Arab] εκ πληθους πασης δυναμεως
σου Z rel.| (ast. *O*^-Syh) εν πληθει εργων σου εκ πληθους πασης
δυναμεως σου *O'* L' Tht. Hi. = ברב מעשיך מרב כל הון MT
| מרב ≈ ברב HUBP^III-30 ≈ 93

27:33 απω του πληθους σου 967 Z rel.] απω του πληθους σου του πλουτου 62' ≈ ברב
הוניך MT

28:16 απο πληθους 967 Z rel.] ברב MT

28:18 δια το πληθος των αμαρτιων σου 967 Z rel.] δια το πληθος των ανομιων σου
Syh^mg L' Tht. = מרב עוניך MT

Hordes on the Day of the Lord

7:12 (minus) ZB La^S Co Aeth ^(967 not preserved)] (ast. *O*) οτι οργη εις παν το πληθος
αυτης rel. = כי חרון אל כל המונה MT

7:13 (minus) ZB 233 La^S Co Hi.^(967 not preserved)] (ast. *O* 86') και ετι εν ζωη το ζην
αυτων οτι ορασις εις παν το πληθος αυτης ουκ ανακαμψει rel. ≈
α'σ'θ' = ועוד בחיים חיתם כי חזון אל כל המונה לא ישוב כי
MT

7:14 (minus) ZB La^S Co Hi. $^{(967\ not\ preserved)}$] (ast. O 86 449) και ουκ εστι(ν) πορευομενος εις τον πολεμον οτι η οργη μου εις παν το πληθος αυτης rel. = MT ואין הלך למלחמה כי חרוני אל כל המונה

Israel's Hordes

37:26 (minus) 967 Z rel.] (ast. O) και δωσω αυτους και πληθυνω αυτους ≈ O-62' L'' 87^{mg}–91^{mg} Bo Arm Tht.Hi. = MT ונתתים והרביתי אותם

'Death on the Field' *Tendenz* (§5.3.2.3)

Textual Variants

26:10 εκ πεδιου 967 Z rel. (recon. [מִבְקָעָה] מְבִקְעָה MT
29:5 περισταλης 967 Z rel.] συσταλης 26 | תקבץ MT
35:8 (minus) 967 Z rel.] τα ορη σου L'' | (ast. O) τα ορη αυτου O-62 = הריו MT | montes Arm

πεδιοις σου 967 Z rel.] אפיקיך MT

εσονται 967] (minus) Z rel. = MT

πεσουνται εν σοι 967 Z rel.] יפלו בהם MT) | minus (HUBP$^{III-150}$
37:10 συναγωγη 967 Z rel.] δυναμις 87–91 Syh = *valentia* Tert. = חיל MT

πολλη 967 Z rel.] μεγαλη A''-106'-403' Bo Tert. = גדול MT

σφοδρα 967 Z rel.] σφοδρα (ast. O) σφοδρα O-62' 534 Arab Arm^p Hi. = מאד מאד MT
37:12 (minus) 967 Z rel.] (ast. O) λαος μου O' Bo Arab Arm Tert.Hi. = עמי MT
37:19 εν τη χειρι ιουδα 967 Z rel.] בידי MT
37:25 (minus) 967 ZB La^W Eus.ecl.Tyc.] (ast. O^{-Syh}) και οι υιοι αυτων και οι υιοι των υιων αυτων εως αιωνος ≈ rel. = MT ובניהם ובני בניהם עד עולם

πεδιον *as Greek Translation*

3:22 πεδιον 967 Z rel. = בקעה MT
3:25 πεδιον 967 Z rel. = בקעה MT
16:5 πε[διου] 967 Z rel. = שדה MT
17:5 πεδιον Z$^{(967\ not\ preserved)}$ = שדה MT
17:8 πεδιον 967 Z rel. = שדה MT
17:24 πεδιου Z$^{(967\ not\ preserved)}$ = αγρου A'-403'–410 62 449 = שדה MT
26:10 εκ πεδιου 967 Z] מבקעה MT
29:5 πεδιου σου 967] πεδιου Z = שדה MT
31:4 πεδιου 967 Z = שדה MT
31:5 πεδιου 967 Z = שדה MT
31:6 πεδιου 967 Z = שדה MT
31:15 πεδιου 967 Z = שדה MT
33:27 πεδιου 967 Z = שדה MT
34:8 πεδιου 967 Z = αγρου A''-106' L''-449 Arab Arm = שדה MT
35:8 πεδιοις σου 967 Z = אפיקיך MT
37:1 πεδιου 967 Z = בקעה MT
37:2 πεδιου 967 Z = בקעה MT
38:20 πεδιου 967 Z = שדה MT
39:4 αγρου 967 410] πεδιου Z rel. = שדה MT

39:5   πεδιου 967 Z = שדה MT
39:10 πεδιου 967 Z = שדה MT
39:17 πεδιου 967 Z = αγρου A''-410 L'' Arab = שדה MT] γης 36

"Bones" Tendenz (§5.3.2.4)

24:2   γραψον εκει σεαυτω εις ημεραν 967] γραψον σεαυτω εις ημεραν Z rel. | γραψον
       σεαυτω το ονομα της ημερας *lII* Tht. = כתוב לך את שם היום
       MT cf. *omnia (nomen?) in diem* La[S]
       απο της ημερας ταυτης 967 Z rel.] ταυτης 449 Tht. | את עצם היום הזה MT
       απο της ημερας της σημερον 967 Z rel.] απο ταυτης σημερον L'-36
       ≈ הזה בעצם היום MT | (minus) 46
24:4   και εμβαλε 967 Z rel.] אסף MT
       εξεσαρκισμενα απο των οστεων 967 ≈ Z rel.] מבחר עצמים MT
       (minus) 967 Z rel.] πληρη 62 θ' (recon. הַמָּלֵא) | (ast) πληρης α' | πληρωσον
       σ' = מָלֵא MT | מלאו HUBP[III-89]
24:5   υποκαιε 967 Z rel.] דור MT
       τα οστα 967 Z rel. = העצמים MT] העצומים HUBP[III-96]
24:9   (minus) 967 ZB *ll* La[SW] Sa] (ast. *O*) ουαι πολις των αιματων rel. = אוי עיר
       הדמים MT
       δαλον 967 Z rel.] λαον B 130 La[S] | מדורה MT | תברה HUBP[I-Tar] מעמרא
       HUBP[I-Peshitta]
24:10 τα ξυλα 967 Z rel. = העצים MT] העצם HUBP[III-93] ≈ *ossa* Vul.
       (minus) 967 ZB *ll* 106 La[SW] Co Ambr.] (ast. *O*) και τα οστα συνφρυγησονται
       rel. = והעצמות יחרו MT
24:11 ανθρακας 967 ZB *ll* La[SW] Co] ανθρακας (ast. *O*) αυτης rel. = גחליה MT
       (minus) 967 ZB *ll* La[SW] Co] (ast. *O*) αυτης εξηψηθη Q V-46 C'-86'-239'-403'
       106' 544 Aeth ≈ A' O'-Q 48–449 130–233 Arm. Tht.Hi.| κενη
       εξηφθη L[-36] 48 cf.[MT] רקה MT (= κενη)
37:1   οστω(ν) 967 Tert.Ir.[lat]Consult = עצמות MT] οστων ανθρωπινων Z rel.| οστων
       ανθρωπων L'' 130*-534–403' Bo Arm Or.Tht.Hi.
37:4   επι τα οστα ταυτα 967 Z rel. = על העצמות האלה MT] επι τα οστα ταυτα
       προφητευσον υιε ανθρωπου V-449 Tht. | (minus) L'-46 Or.XI
       387 Lo.
37:7   τα οστα 967 Z rel. = העצמות HUBP[II-PirkeRE32(201) ≈ MasEzek]] (minus) HUBP[III-96] |
       עצמות MT
       εκαστον προς τη αρμονιαν αυτου 967 Z rel.] οστεον προς τη αρμονιαν αυτου
       O (Q[mg)] C'- 130'-239'-403' 410 Arab Arm | οστεον προς οστεον
       εκαστον L''-48-46 Tht. = עצם אל עצמו MT
40:1   εν τη ημερα εκεινη 967 Z rel.] εν οστεω τη ημερα εκεινη 62' = בעצם היום הזה
       MT | בעצם הזה היום הזה HUBP[III-93]

'New Life' Tendenz (§5.3.2.5)

17:23 και τα κληματα αυ]του αποκ[αταστασθησεται] 967 ≈ (obel. O Hi.) Z rel.]
       (minus) 764 = MT
18:32 (minus) 967 ZB La[S] Co Arab Hi.] (ast.O) και επιστρεψατε και ζησατε ≈ rel.
       = השיבו וחיו MT | επιστρεψατε και ζησατε 534 = והשיבו וחיו

HUBP[III-96-150] | ως το επιστρεψαι αυτον απο της οδου αυτου της πονηρας και ζην αυτον λεγει αδωναι κυριος και επιστρεψασται και ζησεται επιστρεψατε ουν και ζησατε ≈ L" Arm Tht. 62

26:20 μη δε αναστᾳθης 967 Z ≈ μη δε αναστης B *III* Tht.] וְנָתַתִּי צְבִי MT | תָּשֵׁב צְבִי HUBP[III-30(pm) 89(pm)]

26:21 ετι 967 ZBL La[CW] Co Arab] ετι (ast) και ζητηθηση και ουχ ευρηθηση (+ ετι 62) rel. = וּתְבֻקְשִׁי וְלֹא תִמָּצְאִי עוֹד MT

31:17 ζωης αυτου απωλοντο 967 ≈ Z rel.] גוֹיִם MT

37:1 *init.* (minus) 967 Z rel. = MT] νεκρων αναβιωσις Q[mg] | περι αναστασεως των νεκρων Syh[mg]

37:5 πνα (πνευμα) ζωης 967 Z rel.] *spiritum et vivetis* Bo Tert. = רוּחַ וִחְיִיתֶם MT

38:14 εγερθηση 967 Z rel. (recon: תֵּעוֹר)] εξεγερθηση A"; απαντηση 46; γνωση και εγερθηση L" Tht. | תֵּדַע MT

Tendenzen Related to Ezekiel 36:23c–38 (§5.4)
Intertextual Center: The Promises in Ezekiel 36:23c–38 (§5.4.1)

36:23 οτι εγω κς 967 62' 534 PsCypr. = כִּי אֲנִי יְהוָה MT] οτι εγω ειμι κς Z rel.

(minus) 967 Z B 46 Bo La[Ver] Tyc. PsCypr.] (ast. *O*) λεγει αδωναι κυριος rel. = נְאֻם אֲדֹנָי יְהוִה MT

(minus) 967] εν τω αγιασθηναι με εν υμιν κατ οφθαλμους αυτων Z rel. = לְעֵינֵיהֶם בָּכֶם MT

(minus) 967] Ezek 36:24–38 Z ≈ rel. ≈ MT

"Heart/Spirit" *Tendenz* (§5.4.2)

13:2 προς αυτους 967 (obel. *O*) ZB Sa Hi.] (ast. *O*) τοις προφηταις τοις προφητευουσιν απο καρδιας αυτων rel. θ'α' ≈ לִנְבִיאֵי מִלִּבָּם MT | לִנְבִיאֵי מִלִּבָּם אֲלֵיהֶם HUBP[III-96]

13:3 απο καρδιας αυτων 967 Z rel.] (ast. *O*) τοις πορευομενοις οπισω του πνευματος αυτων *O'L"* 403 410 Arm Or. Tht. ≈ הַנְּבָלִים אֲשֶׁר הֹלְכִים אַחַר רוּחָם MT

16:30 την θυγατερα 967 Z ≈ rel. (recon. לְבָתֵּךְ)] την καρδιαν *O* (Syh[txt])-62' *L"* Tht. Or.[lat]VIII400.401 Hi. = לִבָּתֵךְ MT | *testamento* Bo (διαθηκη) Arab

17:22 κορυφης 967 B La[c] Bo Arab Cyr.II372 Or.[lat]VIII438 Spec.Hi.[test]] κορυφης + (ast. *O* 86 Hi.) και δωσω απο κεφαλης παραφυαδων αυτης ≈ rel. = וְנָתַתִּי מֵרֹאשׁ יְנִקוֹתָיו MT

καρδιας αυτων 967 Z rel.] εκ καρδιας κορυφης αυτης *L"* Tht. | יְנִקוֹתָיו רַךְ MT

20:24 καρδιων αυτω(ν) 967 147' 407 106 (*cordis* Ir.[lat])] πατερων αυτων Z rel. = אֲבוֹתָם MT

21:12 παν πνα (πνευμα) 967 = כָּל רוּחַ MT] (obel. *O*) πασα σαρξ και παν πνευμα Z rel. | παν πνευμα πασα σαρξ 62

22:15 η καρδια σου 967] η ακαθαρσια σου Z rel. = טֻמְאָתֵךְ MT | (minus) Peshitta

22:27 (minus) 967 rel.] (ast. *O*) του απολεσαι ψυχας *O' III* Arm. Tht. = לֶאֱבָד נְפָשׁוֹת MT (pr. copula HUBP[III-150]) | נְקִי לֶאֱבָד נְפָשׁוֹת HUBP[III-96]

29:16 αυτων 967 Z rel. = MT] των καρδιων A''-410 Syh 36 C'-86–239'-403' Arm

31:10 και ειδον 967 Z rel.] και επηρθη η καρδια αυτου Syh^{mg} L'' Tht. = ורם לבבו MT
    | και επηρθη το πνευμα η καρδια αυτου 46

36:5 (minus) 967 Z rel.] εξ ολης καρδιας 62 L''-46 Tht. = כל לבב MT
    εν προνομη 967 Z rel.] εις προνομην 147' 46 cII = בז MT | לבב HUBP^{III-93}

37:1 πνι κυ (πνευματι κυριου) 967 rel.] πνευματι κυριος ZB A' 62' Tert.Ambr.Ir.^{lat} |
    πνευματι τω αγιω κυριου Q^{mg} | πνευματι Or. Lo.] רוח יהוה MT

37:9 σου πνευματω(ν) 967] πνευματων Z rel. = רוחות MT] ανεμων 407 36^{txt}-V |
    ανεμων του ουρανου A'' Arab Ambr.Spec.Aug.
    (minus) 967 Z rel.] (ast. O) το πνευμα A''-403' O' L' Bo Arab Arm Tht.Tert.
    Ambr.Ir.^{lat} Spec.Consult.Hi.PsVig. = הרוח MT

39:29 εξεχεα τον θυμον μου 967 Z rel.] שפכתי את רוחי MT

'Gog-Magog' *Tendenzen*: Variants Related to Ezekiel 38–39 (§5.5)

38:3 (minus) 967 B Arm] γωγ Z rel. = גוג MT | μαγωγ 87 | γωγ και μαγωγ Tht.

38:4 (minus) 967 Z rel.] (ast. O) και περιστρεψω σε κυκλοθεν και δωσω χαλινον
    εις τας σιαγονας σου O' L'' 87^{mg}-91^{mg}-239' 26 Bo Aeth Arm Tht.
    ≈ ושובבתיך ונתתי חחים בלחייך MT
    συναξω σε 967 Z rel.] πλανησω σε 147 26 239' Aeth | והוצאתי אותך MT
    ενδεδυμενους θωρακας παντας 967 Z rel.] לבשי מכלול MT
    και μαχαιραι 967 Z rel.] επιλαμβανομενους και μαχαιραι 62 cf. תפשי MT | και
    μαχαιραι (ast. O) παντες αυτοι O 26 239' Arm θ' ≈ חרבות כלם
    (תפשי) MT

38:6 και παντες οι περι αυτον 967 Z rel.] και παντα τα υποστηριγματα αυτου Syh
    θ' | וכל אגפיה MT

38:8 επ εσχατων ετων 967 ≈ Z rel.] (minus) 106| באחרית השנים MT | באחרית
    השנה HUBP^{III-96}
    επι την γην ισραηλ 967 62' V-449 26 403' 410 544 ≈ Z rel.] επι την ιερυσαλημ
    233 | על הרי ישראל MT

38:9 και παντες οι περι σε 967 Z rel.] וכל אגפיך MT

38:11 γην απεριμμενων 967 ≈ γην απεριμμενην Z rel.] ארץ פרזות MT

38:16 γωγ 967 O-62 La^{SW} (ast. O) = גוג MT] (ast. V) ω γωγ L''-46 Tht. o Gog Vul. |
    (minus) Z rel. (Z rel.$^{-Bo}$ tr.$^{v 17}$ (obel.O) γωγ)

38:17 συ ει περι ου 967 Z rel.] האתה הוא זה אשר MT | אשר
    HUBP^{III-30}
    του αγαγειν σε επ αυτους 967 Z ≈ rel. ≈ להביא אתך עליהם MT] להביא
    אתך עולם HUBP^{III-93}

38:21 και καλεσω επ αυτον παν φοβον μαχαιρας 967 ≈ (om. μαχ.) Z rel.] και καλεσω
    επι αυτον και παν φοβον B | + (ast. L) εις παντα τα ορη μου Syh
    ≈ L'' Tht. cf.^{MT} | וקראתי MT | וקראתי עליו לכל הרי חרב
    עליו למפל הרי חרב Tar

38:22 και επι παντας τους μετ [αυ]του 967 Z rel.] ועל אגפיו MT

39:4 και ου βεβηλωθησεται το ονομα το αγιον 967 cf.$^{39:7}$] (minus) Z rel. = MT

39:6 επι γωγ 967 Z rel.] μαγωγ O^{-Q} C'-198–393–403' 106' Arm = במגוג MT

39:11 εκει τον γωγ και παν το πληθος αυτου 967 rel. = שם את גוג ואת כל המנה
    MT

εν ισραηλ 967 Z rel. = בִישְׂרָאֵל MT] εν ιερουσαλημ 26' | (minus) A*
(minus) 967 Z rel.] ανατολης L'' Tht. = קָדְמַת MT
τοπον ονομαστον μνημειον 967 Z rel. = *locum nominatum* ... La^S Vul ≈ מְקוֹם
שָׁם קֶבֶר HUBP^III-96 G-BEb24 | τοπον εχει ονομαστον μνημειον 62
cf.^MT | (לֵבֵית) מָקוֹם שָׁם קֶבֶר MT | אֲתַין לְגוֹג אֲתַר כְּשֵׁר
(קְבוּרָא) Tar (אֲתַר כְּשֵׁר cf. שָׁם MT)

39:28 εν τω επιφανηναι με αυτοις 967 Z rel. (recon. בְּהַגְלוֹתִי)] בְּהַגְלוֹתִי אֹתָם MT
εν τοις εθνεσιν 967 Z rel.] + (ast. *O*) και συναξω αυτους επι την γην αυτων και
ου καταλειψω απ αυτων ουκετι εκει L''-403' 87^mg Bo Arm Tht. ≈
O-62' = מֵהֶם שָׁם וְכִנַּסְתִּים עַל אַדְמָתָם וְלֹא אוֹתִיר עוֹד MT

Related to Meshech and Tubal

27:13 και συμπασα ^και τα παρατεινοντα 967 Z rel. (recon. συμπασα ≈ תֶּבֶל or הַכֹּל)]
και μοσοχ και θοβελ 87–91 86 α'σ' ≈ (tr.) תֶּבֶל וּמֶשֶׁךְ MT (תּוּבַל
HUBP^III-30 96 150)

32:26 (minus in context) 967] μοσοχ και θοβελ και πασα (recon. θοβελ (וְתֻבָל
Z rel. ≈ מֶשֶׁךְ תֻּבַל וְכָל MT | μοσοχ και θοβελλι και πασα (recon.
θοβελλι (תֻּבְלִי) 233 | μοσοχ και βοβελ και πασα (recon. βοβελ
בֹּבֶל) 538 | cf.^v 25 *cubile eorum* Hi. σ'θ' (HUBP^V-recon. /מִשְׁכְּבֹם
מִשְׁכַּב לָהֶם cf.^v 25)

32:29 (minus) 967 ZB La^C Co] (ast.*O*) και οι βασιλεις αυτης και παντες ≈ rel. ≈
מְלָכֶיהָ וְכָל MT | και μοσοχ οι βασιλεις αυτης και παντες
minisc.

38:2 ρως μεσοχ 967 B ≈ Z rel. = *ros mosoch* Hi. (translit. רֹאשׁ)] ρωμεσοχ 410 ≈
106 239' Arm | κεφαλης ρως μεσοχ 62 | κεφαλης μοσοχ α' Tht.
= *capitis* μασεχ Bo = רֹאשׁ מֶשֶׁךְ MT

38:3 ρως μοσοχ 967 Z ≈ rel. (translit. רֹאשׁ)] ρωμεσοχ 410 ≈ 106 239' Arm | *capitis*
μασεχ Bo = רֹאשׁ מֶשֶׁךְ MT

39:1 ρως μοσοχ 967 Z ≈ rel. (translit. רֹאשׁ)] ρωμεσοχ 410 ≈ 106 Arm | *capitis*
μασεχ Bo = רֹאשׁ מֶשֶׁךְ MT | γης ρως μοσοχ L

Geographic *Tendenz*: Gog's Entourage of Nations (§5.5.1)
Related to Gog's burial

39:11 εν ισραηλ 967 Z rel. = בִישְׂרָאֵל MT] εν ιερουσαλημ 26' | (minus) A*
το πολυανδριον του γωγ 967 el.] הֲמוֹן גּוֹג MT
(minus) 967 Z rel.] ανατολης L'' Tht. = קִדְמַת MT
τοπον ονομαστον μνημειον 967 Z rel. = *locum nominatum* ... La^S Vul ≈ מְקוֹם
שָׁם קֶבֶר HUBP^III-96 G-BEb24 | τοπον εχει ονομαστον μνημειον 62
cf.^MT | (מָקוֹם שָׁם קֶבֶר MT | (אֲתַר כְּשֵׁר לְבֵית) אֲתַין לְגוֹג אֲתַר
(קְבוּרָא) Tar (אֲתַר כְּשֵׁר cf. שָׁם MT)
γαι 967 Z rel. = גֵּיא MT ≈ γε O (γη Syh) C^'-233 410 La^S (*ge*) Arm Ambr.Hi.] τε
B 26 Cyr.[5] | (minus) 106 Arab

---

[5] See also τε in v. 11 of B.

Related to 38:5—Gog's military entourage

30:5 περσαι 967 Z rel.] αιθιοπια 86 α'σ'θ' = כוש MT
και κρητες 967 Z rel.] και φουδ 86 α'σ'θ' = ופוט MT
και λυδοι 967 Z = ולוד MT] wlwby' HUBP[I-Peshitta]; tr. L" Tht. (cf.[below])
και λιβυες 967 Z rel.] και λιβυες και αιθιοπες και λυδοι και πασα η αραβια L"
Tht. | (minus) MT
οι επιμεικτοι 967 Z rel. (recon. ~ הָעֶרֶב) ≈ reliquum] αραβια 86 Hi.[lat.] α' ≈ σ'
= הערב MT | + (ast. 86) και χουβα α'σ'θ' = וכוב MT

Related to 38:13—those who speak about Gog

27:15 ροδιων 967 Z rel.] αραδιων A"-106 | drn HUBP[I-Peshitta] | δαδαν 86 α'σ'θ' Hi. =
דדן MT

27:23 (minus) 967 ZB L' Co Arab] (ast. O) και δαιδαν rel. (recon. ודדן) | וְעֶדֶן MT
(= edne Hi.)
ουτοι εμποροι σου 967 ZB L' Co Arab = (obel. Syh)] ουτοι εμποροι σου (ast.
O[-Q]) σαβα O[-Q]-62' α'σ'θ' 86 (sabba Hi.) cf.[MT] | רכלי שבא MT
(שבה HUBP[III-96])

Word Plays with Meshech משך (§5.5.2)

12:28 (minus) 967 410] ου μη μηκθνωσιν Z rel. = לא תמשך

32:20 και κοιμηθησεται 967 Z rel. (recon. והשכב cf.[v 32])] και ηλκυσαν αυτην 62'
= משכו אותה MT (om. copula) | και εξειλκυσαν αυτην 86
α'σ'θ'

32:25 (minus in context) 967 Z rel.] (obel. pro ast. L) κοιτη αυτης συν παντι 62'
L" Tht. = משכב לה בכל MT | וכל משכב לה HUBP[III-96 150]

32:26 (minus in context) 967] μοσοχ και θοβελ και πασα (recon. θοβελ) (ותבל) Z
rel. ≈ משך תבל וכל MT | μοσοχ και θοβελλι και πασα (recon.
θοβελλι) (תבלי) 233 | μοσοχ και βοβελ και πασα (recon. βοβελ
בבל) 538 | cf.[v 25] cubile eorum Hi. σ'θ' (HUBP[V-recon.] /משכבם
משכב להם cf.[v 25])

Plunder and Spoil Tendenz (§5.5.3)

29:19 (minus) 967 BZ La[S] (vid.) Co] (ast.Q) και λη(μ)ψεται το πληθος αυτης
rel. = ונשא המנה MT

30:24 και προνομευσει την προνομην αυτης και σκυλευσει τα σκυλα αυτης 967
Z rel.] ונאק נאקות חלל לפניו MT (לפניו] cf. ενωπιον αυτου
62')

34:8 (minus) 967 26 306* 410 La[CS] Aug.] (ast. 88) εις προνομην και γενεσθαι τα
προβατα (subst. ποιμνια L") μου Z rel. ≈ לבז ותהיינה צאני MT |
צאני) לבז ותהיינה (om. HUBP[III-96]

CHAPTER FOUR

THE *TENDENZEN*: TEXT-CRITICAL ANALYSIS

4.1. INTRODUCTION

Chapter 2 revealed that while previous textual scholarship on p967 has been thoroughgoing, many textual issues require additional clarification. The goal of the present chapter is to refine our understanding of how p967 relates to the Greek witnesses, OG, and the Hebrew *Vorlage* of OG. While the foundation was laid by the studies discussed in chapter 2, several heretofore unresolved textual issues surfaced throughout the history of study that can only be examined through closer inspection of individual variants.

As indicated in chapter 3, the present chapter's data set is the result of literary study, specifically, the coherence approach to variants between p967 and MT. This data set is unique in a few ways. The data set excludes variants that are inconsequential to the meaning of the text, such as orthographic differences, but more importantly, it excludes variants that could not be shown to participate in the *Tendenzen* identified in chapter 3 and discussed in chapter 5. Hence, this data set would already appear to be the result of intentional editorial activity. While textual evaluations for error are considered in the following discussion, the central aim of the present chapter is to provide a textual explanation for the divergence between p967 and the other Greek and Hebrew witnesses (primarily), to note how extensively the witnesses attest specific variants, and to explain isolated features. More specifically, the textual relationship among Codex Vaticanus (B), the Masoretic Text (MT), and p967 are of central concern.[1] Hence, the discussion breaks into sections dealing with the following five questions:

---

[1] The significance of B to study of p967 was demonstrated in chapter 2. While this chapter focuses mainly on the Greek and Hebrew witnesses, one can consult the following critical editions for the Versions: for the critical Latin text, see Robertus Weber, et al., eds., *Biblia Sacra Iusta Vulgata Versionem*, 3d ed. (Stuttgart: Deutsche Bibelgesellschaft, 1983); For the Syriac, see Martin J. Mulder, ed., *The Old Testament in Syriac According to the Peshitta Version*, 3/3, *Ezekiel* (Leiden: Brill, 1985). For the Aramaic Targum Jonathan, see Alexander Sperber, *The Bible in Aramaic. Vol. 3 The Latter Prophets according to Targum Jonathan* (Leiden: Brill, 1962).

1. What do Origen's text-critical marks indicate about p967's readings?
2. How do we evaluate p967's unique readings? Are they the result of scribal error and if so, at what stage?; or can they be explained as intentional variants? This question is also taken up under question 5 below.
3. When p967 and B disagree, as the best witnesses to the Old Greek, how do we explain the divergence?
4. Does p967 reflect a Hebrew *Vorlage* different from the MT? If so, can we explain its divergence from the MT?
5. How convincing are arguments for scribal error where they apply to p967's three major minuses (12:26–28; 32:25–26; and 36:23c–38)?

These questions are the basis for the selection of individual variants to be analyzed below. Before turning to those analyses, a more general discussion of the alignment for this specific data set begins our textual discussion.

4.2. TEXTUAL DISCUSSION

4.2.1. *General Alignment*

Out of the 230 meaningful variants that form the data set of chapters 3–5, the statistics for alignment are as follows:[2]

	Agree	*Diverge*
p967 and B	164	58
p967 and A	126	96
p967 and O-group	88	103
p967 and MT	30	191
MT and O-group	110	93
MT and L-group	98	117
MT and B	50	179
MT and p967	30	191

MT reads alone: 68 times
p967 reads alone: 31 times
B reads alone: 2 times

---

[2] Alignment was tabulated among the major Greek manuscripts and groups (i.e., p967 B A O-L-groups and the MT). I tabulated the O-L-groups only when nearly the entire group presented the same reading. Additionally, p967 is missing in some verses in which I tabulated alignment for MT with B and the O-L-groups. These factors explain why the numbers of variants counted in each case are not equal.

Deciding alignment for textual readings is somewhat subjective. I was overly conservative in marking divergence, deciding that texts were aligned only when the readings were *identical*. Such a rigorous criterion for alignment furnishes a table that highlights mechanical relationships among witnesses. In other words, the table shows instances where a reading was transmitted accurately, according to a copyist function. While this strict criterion ultimately sheds light on the transmission history of Ezekiel's different literary editions, there were also negative implications to this decision. Often overlooked are the potentially important number of times where readings had partial support, for example in 18:32 where L's reading included the MT plus, but in the context of L's considerably longer addition; or conversely in 32:25 when only the first half of MT's plus agreed with L. These two instances of partial agreement were tabulated as disagreement, since the textual readings were not identical. Additionally, the table is blind to factors such as translational vs. transmissional vs. compositional variants. If a variant participated in a *Tendenz* no matter its possible origin, it is included in the tabulation. Subjective factors such as these shed light on the utility of the above table; a table of alignment reveals trends, but not hard facts.[3]

With the above caveats duly noted, we can nevertheless use the table to draw conclusions about the textual relationships among the 'literary editions' of Ezekiel. The notable agreement between B and p967 represents a strong testimony for the early divergence of the Greek literary edition from the MT. However, consistent with Gehman's observation about the divergence between p967 and B's text types,[4] there are still 58 occasions on which p967 and B's literary editions diverge as well.

The number of times p967 and B agree with the MT is especially interesting given the divergence just noted. p967 reads with the MT 30 times; this requires examination, especially in a project explicitly searching for the *divergent* variants between p967 and MT. In most of the cases in which p967 and MT read together, either A or L primarily, but also sometimes B presented the divergent reading. These isolated divergences in the Greek tradition, while small in number, indicate that p967 is not the only version which houses readings that could be characterized as 'variant literary' readings.[5] The other instances in which p967 and the MT agree

---

[3] This is all the more the case when dealing with variant literary editions. For example, the redaction critic may see "support" where the textual critic marks disagreement.

[4] Gehman in Johnson, Gehman, and Kase, *The John H. Schiede Papyri*, 76.

[5] This was notably the case with date references and the recognition formula.

are occasioned by divergent readings in the medieval Hebrew witnesses, for example οστα for עצמים (Hebrew variant: עצום) in 24:5, ξυλα for עצים (Hebrew variant: עצם) in 24:10, and γιγαντων for גבורים (Hebrew variant: גבורים בארץ) in 32:27. B reads with the MT 20 more times than does p967, indicating its closer relationship with MT's literary edition. In most of these 20 cases, p967 is the divergent reading with modest or no support. Two conclusions seem possible: 1) that p967 is a maverick Greek text in these instances; and/or 2) that B is more representative of the known Greek tradition, with p967 being an Old Greek version that was *not* taken up into the dominant stream of Greek transmission. The latter possibility would explain the strikingly few number of times B reads alone: twice. The issue of p967's unique or weakly supported readings will be examined in greater detail below in §§4.3.1 and 4.3.2.

Finally, the MT is most strongly supported by the L- and O-group manuscripts, 98 and 110 times respectively. However, MT reads alone 68 times. These isolated MT readings, unsupported by the versions, show some clustering in ch. 24:1–14 (10 times); ch. 32:17–32 (16 times); and chs. 38–39 (17 times).

4.2.2. *Hexaplaric Notations*

Out of the roughly 233 variants pertinent for the present study, there are 75 readings in which Hexaplaric notations appear. The obelus occurs 17 times and the asterisk occurs 64 times.

Asterisked readings:

MT	63
L/(L)	47
A	35
p967	2 (both agree with MT)
B	1 (agrees with MT)

Obelus readings:

L	14
B	12
A	10
p967	7
MT	0

The asterisk marks a reading that was not original to the Greek text, and that therefore Origen added on the basis of his Hebrw text. It indicates a reading that was likely not original to the Old Greek nor its Hebrew *Vorlage*. We have already noted the challenges involved in using Origen's marks for text-critical questions (§2.3.4). Nevertheless, some notable trends do warrant brief attention.

In the data collated here, the asterisk occurs 64 times, 63 of which mark an MT variant. In contrast, p967 and B are virtually free of asterisked readings. When an MT reading receives the asterisk, p967 and B often present either a minus, or an obelized reading. This trend underscores what was repeatedly discussed in chapter 2, the close relationship of p967 and B to the Old Greek. More importantly, however, the trend in the Hexaplaric data sheds new light on MT. The overwhelming trend for the asterisk in MT readings suggests that MT represents a text much developed beyond the Old Greek translation.

Equally striking is how often MT shares an asterisked reading with L and/or A against B and p967. MT is supported by L 45 times and by A 35 times in its asterisked reading.[6] This substantial evidence suggests that the Lucianic texts especially were corrected back to a Hebrew *Vorlage* quite similar to the MT.[7] If Cross' model of Greek transmission, described in chapter 2, is correct, MT can be characterized as a Hebrew text developed beyond the OG, but that preceded the Lucianic stage of the LXX corrections/revisions.

4.3. TEXT-CRITICAL ANALYSIS OF VARIANTS

What follows is a text-critical examination of p967's relationship with the Old Greek translation and its Hebrew *Vorlage*. For such an examination,

---

[6] MT and L: 7:12, 13, 14; 8:18; 13:2(2x), 3, 7; 17:22; 20:26; 21:3, 12; 22:27, 28; 23:38; 24:9, 10, 11(2x), 14; 27:18, 32; 28:9, 10; 29:19; 30:4; 32:19, 25(3x), 29, 30, 31; 33:25; 34:8, 9, 30; 35:8; 36:7, 23; 37:4, 9, 12, 25, 26; 38:4, 17, 21; 39:28; 43:12(2x) | and MT and A: 7:12, 13, 14; 8:18; 13:2(2x), 7; 17:22; 18:32; 20:26; 24:9, 10, 11(2x); 25:7; 26:21; 27:32; 28:9, 10; 29:19; 30:4; 32:19, 29, 31; 33:25; 34:8, 9; 36:23; 37:4, 9, 12, 25; 43:12(2x).

[7] The idea that the Lucianic texts represent a correction is sometimes disputed. However, Cross' model of Greek transmission describes the second stage as the proto-Lucianic revision of the OG towards the contemporary Hebrew text in the 2nd to 1st century BCE. Frank M. Cross, *The Ancient Library of Qumrân and Modern Biblical Studies*, (rev. ed.; Garden City, NY: Doubleday, 1961); and idem, "The History of the Biblical Text in Light of the Discoveries in the Judaean Desert." *HTR* 57 (1964): 281–99, and idem, "The Contribution of the Qumrân Discoveries to the Study of the Biblical Text." *IEJ* 16 (1966): 81–95. These three publications combine to provide his approach to the history. See discussion on pp. 48–50 of chapter 2.

three categories of variants require specific attention. First, p967's unique variants remain unexplained. Above, I offered that they could represent maverick, inner-Greek developments, or they reflect OG readings that were not taken up in the dominant stream of Greek transmission. These questions will be addressed in the analysis of unique p967 readings.

Second, the variants between p967 and B reflect divergence in the Greek tradition. Examination of these variants can further clarify the relationship of p967 and B to the OG. A third line of inquiry includes those instances where issues in the Hebrew can best explain p967 variants. This set of variants illuminates the relationship between p967 and its possible Hebrew parent texts, either the *Vorlage* of the OG, or the text to which the Greek tradition was corrected. In all three sections, the set of variants is listed, followed by text-critical analysis of only those variants that have clear text-critical information to yield. Variants that yielded only shallow and ambiguous evaluations are not interpreted text-critically in the following discussion.

An additional text-critical issue requires clarification about the following analysis. The medieval manuscripts found in HUBP apparatus III often support p967 readings or help clarify textual issues in the Hebrew. These manuscripts are collated in the third apparatus of HUBP, which serves primarily to clarify the text of Allepo (that which is reproduced in the running text). While the editors suggest that the medieval manuscripts primarily provide information about transmission of the Hebrew in the medieval period, they allow that a critic must choose to use the apparatus as they see fit. The striking number of times that these medieval manuscripts contained text-critically important information vis-à-vis p967 shows their importance to the present analysis. Additionally, the entire MT textual tradition is late, so to *include* MT and *exclude* its contemporary witnesses would be misguided. Hence, consideration of the medieval Hebrew manuscripts occasionally yields important text-critical information for p967's text and its parent textual tradition.

4.3.1. *Isolated p967 Variants*

p967 relative to B's readings (alignment of MT noted)

12:26–28*	(minus)] full three verses = MT	
18:32	(minus)] λεγει κυριος = MT	
22:15	η καρδια σου] η ακαθαρσια σου = MT	
24:2	εκει] (minus) | MT	
24:14	κριθησει λεγει κς] κρινω σε | MT	

24:27	(minus)] εν εκεινη τη ημερα ≈ tr. MT
25:15	οτι] δια τουτο | MT
32:6	(minus)] σου = MT
32:24	(minus)] ελαβοσαν βασανον αυτων | MT
32:26*	(minus)] full verse = MT
35:8	εσονται] (minus) = MT
36:23c–38*	(minus)] full 15 ½ verses = MT
37:9	σου] (minus) = MT
38:14	και] ουκ = MT
38:18	η ημερα εκεινη εν] εν τη ημερα εκεινη εν ημερα = MT
38:20	ινα γνωσιν παντα τα εθνη εμε εν σοι ενωπιον αυτων] (minus) = MT
39:4	και ου βεβηλωθησεται το ονομα το αγιον] (minus) = MT
39:8	εσται] γνωση οτι εσται | MT

* dealt with below in §4.4 as major variants

22:15—καρδια

p967   και εκλειψει η καρδια σου εκ σου

MT   והתמתי טמאתך ממך

και—σου 967] והתמתי—ממך MT | (minus) HUBP[I-Peshitta]

η καρδια σου 967] η ακαθαρσια σου Z rel. = טמאתך MT | (minus) HUBP[I-Peshitta]

p967's unsupported variant stands against all other Greek witnesses reading η καρδια σου for טמאתך. The rest of the Greek witnesses read η ακαθαρσια σου, without exception, reproducing the MT in a word for word correspondence (i.e., literally). p967's reading could represent a mistaken (intentional?) inscription of καρδια for ακαθαρσια. Thus, p967 would be an inner-Greek development subsequent to the OG.

Nevertheless, further inquiry reveals that p967's variant may just as likely highlight scribal activity in the Hebrew tradition. טמא was transmitted with some textual variety in ch. 22. In v. 3, mss. 89 and 96 strengthen טמא with the Piel over MT's Qal. Manuscript 96 replaces the adj. with a Pual 2m/fs verb טומאת in vv 5 and 10. Again in vv 26 and 27, ms. 96 presents textual variation in טמא and נקי respectively, the former also supported by ms. 150. Manuscript 96 also brings additional emphasis to טמא in v. 4aα where its omission of אשמת leaves טָמֵאת to govern two phrases. In addition to these grammatical variations in terminology and emphasis, ms. 30 uniquely presents a 10-word plus at the beginning of v. 7b.

It reads טמאת הנדה ענו .טמאת הנדה ענו בך שחד לקחו בך למען שפך דם
בך is probably drawn from the same phrase in 22:10b and שחד לקחו בך
למען שפך דם from 22:12a. Finally, the noun טֻמְאָה with a possessive suffix
occurs seven times in Ezekiel: 24:11, 13(2); 36:25, 29; 39:24, and here. It is
worth noting that these instances occur in sections of particular import
in the data set of this dissertation: two occur in p967's large minus of
36:23c–38 (vv 25 and 29), and one occurs in each ch. 39 and ch. 24, which
will be treated further below.

In addition to the textual fluidity in the Hebrew tradition related to the
term טמא, warrant for p967's reading occurs in the Hebrew elsewhere. In
36:5, MT is likely the developed text with its plus about the heart (כל לבב),
and later in the same verse, ms. 93 changes לבז to לבב.[8]

In short, adjudication between the textual evidence complicates a
determination regarding whether p967 is an inner-Greek development or
reflects a variant Hebrew *Vorlage*. The Peshitta's omission of the entire
phrase could support the latter, and hence testify to a short Hebrew
text that expanded in two directions. One of these could have been the
Hebrew parent text of p967, reading לבך (cf. Ezek 22:14.) However, taken
in isolation, p967's variant in 22:15 is probably an inner-Greek development; certainty eludes.

24:14—κριθησει λεγει κς

p967 εγω κρινω σε κατα τα αιματα σου και κατα τα ενθυμηματα σου κριθησει
   λεγει κς η ακαθαρτος η ονομαστη και πολλη του παραπικραινειν
MT (minus)

  εγω—*fin.* 967 ≈ Z rel.] (minus) *ll* 764 La^S | (minus in context) MT
  κριθησει λεγει κς 967] κρινω σε Z rel. | (minus) La^W | (minus in context)
    ll 764 La^S = MT

Both p967 and Z rel. expand v. 14 beyond the MT. The plus material is
drawn from the first half of the verse, as well as from the vocatives of
22:5b, as most critics point out.[9] Standard principles of textual criticism

---

[8] See both the discussion on 36:5 in §4.3.1. and the variants related to the heart *Tendenz*
in chapter 5.

[9] So G.A. Cooke, *A Critical and Exegetical Commentary on the Book of Ezekiel* (ICC; Edinburgh: Clark, 1936), 275; Leslie C. Allen, *Ezekiel 20–48* (WBC 29; Dallas: Word Books, 1990),
55; Zimmerli, *Ezekiel*, 1: 496. The vocatives in 22:5 include טמאת השם and רבת המהומה.
The former agrees with η ακαθαρτος η ονομαστη, while the πολλη του παραπικραινειν is
close to the latter, likely רבת המרי. In both cases, the Hebrew should be seen as strongly

leave no basis for an MT omission; the plus is undoubtedly secondary. However, p967 strengthens the case already supposed by Zimmerli, Allen, and Cooke, that the plus appeared already in the OG's Hebrew *Vorlage*.[10] p967's reading και κατα τα ενθυμηματα σου κριθησει λεγει κς is closer to the Hebrew of v. 14a: ‏וכעלילותיך שפטוך נאם אדני יהוה.[11] However v. 14a was translated in ZBAQ as και κατα τα ενθυμηματα σου κρινω σε λεγει κυριος, which, minus λεγει κυριος, is also what appears in v. 14b in ZBAQ. κρινω σε would thus be the less literal translation, except that ms. 96 emends ‏שפטוך to ‏שפטתיך in v. 14a, thereby providing a textual rationale for the variation in the Greek. In short, the differences between the Greek readings in v. 14 are best explained on the basis of variant Hebrew expansions.[12]

32:6—minus σου

p967	απο του πληθους επι των ορεων
MT	‏מדמך אל ההרים

απο του πληθους 967] απο του πληθους σου Z rel. | ‏מדמך MT

Neither p967 nor Z rel. translate the ‏מדמך from the MT, although p967 lies further away since it lacks the 2s possessive pronoun. Against Allen who considers MT's form related to ‏ממך at the end of the verse, a baseless position, the strongest Greek text tradition απο του πληθους σου probably translated ‏מרבך.[13] This would require that the scribe of the Hebrew

---

emphatic, even superlative, since the adjective is determined as the *nomen regens* of a construct. See Wilhelm Gesenius, *Hebrew Grammar* (Rev. and enl. by E. Kautzsch; Oxford: Clarendon, 2003), §133g and 132c. The Greek loses this emphasis with a string of three substantive adjectives limited by the genitive articular infinitive, Herbert W. Smyth, *Greek Grammar* (Rev. by Gordon M. Messing; Cambridge: Harvard University Press, 1984), §1322 and 2032a.

[10] Zimmerli regards the plus as an addition. However, in consideration of Ewald, Hitzig, and Smend, who take it to be original to the Hebrew, Zimmerli suggests that the plus may have been found in the Hebrew *Vorlage* of the OG. Cooke and Allen more assertively draw this conclusion. Ibid.

[11] As Gehman notes of p967, κριθησει is possibly based on ‏שפטוך in the shared material from earlier in the verse. Gehman, "The Relations," JAOS 58 (1938): 97. p967's επιτηδευματα ("practices") in v. 14a for ενθυμηματα ("thoughts," "devices") found in Z is supported by the margin of the Syro-Hexaplar as well as the Catena group witnesses. επιτηδευματα is also found in two restoration passages: several times in ch. 20, as well as in 36:31.

[12] Another similar textual phenomenon may be found in 35:6. Here it is the *MT* which preserves a plus in the second half of the verse: ‏אם לא דם שנאת ודם ירדפך. Like 24:14, the plus is repetitive of material from v. 6a. The term "blood" appears in both pluses.

[13] For the suggestion, see Cooke, *A Critical and Exegetical Commentary*, 356. *Pace* Allen, *Ezekiel*, 2:129, who apparently follows the lead of BHS.

Vorlage or the Greek translator confused ד for ר and מ for ב, which, as Cooke points out, are often confused.[14] It cannot be known whether the Greek translator or a Hebrew *Vorlage* with the reading מרבך is responsible for the variant. Nevertheless, p967's minus of σου likely occurred in Greek transmission, perhaps owing to haplography of the -ους ending immediately preceding.

32:24—minus βασανον αυτων

p967 (minus)
MT וישאו כלמתם את יורדי בור

(minus) 967] βασανον αυτων Z ≈ rel. | αισχυνην α'σ' | ατιμιαν θ' 86 =
כלמתם MT (cf.[16:52; 36:7; 39:26] | את כלמתם HUBP[III-96]
(minus) 967 *ll*] μετα των καταβαινοντων Z rel. = את יורדי MT

p967's minus at the end of v. 24 should be considered as part of its major variant, discussed in §4.4.3 below. Nevertheless, Z rel. do not reproduce the contested phrase exactly either. βασανον "torment" does not literally translate כלמה "shame" or "insult," although the same equivalent occurs in v. 30.[15] The Hexaplaric three come closer to the Hebrew, especially ατιμιαν in θ' 86 which translates כלמה elsewhere in Ezekiel.[16]

In addition to these issues of translation, which call the phrase into question, the two Lucianic witnesses that omit μετα των καταβαινοντων suggest possible scribal emendation. Whether p967's minus may be taken as reflecting a Hebrew parent text is largely connected to textual issues involved with the remainder of the minus. However, the above considerations raise some textual suspicion about v. 24bβ, discussed further in §4.4.3 below.

---

[14] Cooke, *A Critical and Exegetical Commentary*, 357.
[15] βασανος occurs 7 times in the LXX of Ezekiel. Four of those cases translate כלמה (16:52, 54; 32:24, 30). However, the *Vorlage* is not consistent: once דאגה (12:18) and twice מכשול (3:20 and 7:19).
[16] In Ezekiel αισχυνη usually translates ערוה.

35:8—εσονται

p967   και εν πασι τοις πεδιοις σου εσονται τετραυματισμενοι μαχαιρα πεσουνται

      εν σοι

MT   וכל אפיקיך חללי חרב יפלו בהם

      πεδιοις σου 967 Z rel.] אפיקיך MT

      εσονται 967] (minus) Z rel. = MT

      πεσουνται εν σοι 967 Z rel.] יפלו בהם MT | (minus) HUBP[III-150]

p967's εσονται plus clarifies the potential confusion at the end of the verse; MT's בהם refers back to the land forms (hills, channels, etc.) while εν σοι in the LXX confuses the syntax. p967's text is probably an inner-Greek addition to clarify the syntax of the verse.

38:20—Recognition Formula

p967   ινα γνωσιν παντα τα εθνη εμε εν σοι ενωπιον αυτων
MT   (minus)

      ινα—αυτων 967] (minus) Z rel. = MT

p967's 'nation recognition' formula in v. 20 is unattested by any other witnesses. JGK suggest that it has been lifted from v. 16.[17] While possible, it is more important to note that within the 'nation-recognition' *Tendenz*, textual alignment among the witnesses is notably inconsistent. There is no textual basis to suppose that this phrase occurred in the Hebrew *Vorlage*; it was probably a Greek addition found only in p967's text. (See discussion of 38:18 below for additional considerations.)

39:4—και ου βεβηλωθησεται το ονομα το αγιον

p967   και ου βεβηλωθησεται το ονομα το αγιον
MT   (minus)

      και—αγιον 967 cf.[39:7]] (minus) Z rel. = MT

p967 is unsupported in its seven word plus. As in 38:20, the phrase is probably a harmonizing addition, anticipating 39:7.

---

[17] Johnson, Gehman, and Kase, *The John H. Scheide Biblical Papyri*, 131.

39:8—εσται

p967 ιδου ηκει και εσται
MT   הִנֵּה בָאָה וְנִהְיָתָה

εσται 967] וְנִהְיָתָה MT | γνωση οτι εσται Z rel. (cf. *scies quia erit* La^Sg
scies quoniam erit La^H)

p967 is alone among the versions in its reading εσται. However, this reading comes closest to the MT וְנִהְיָתָה. The Niphal of היה is rare in the MT;
p967 probably (mis?)-translated its Hebrew *Vorlage*, while Z rel. represent
either a variant *Vorlage* or a developed Greek text.

24:2, 27 and 38:14, 18—Four Variants Related to "On that Day"

24:2 p967 γραψον εκει σεαυτω εις ημεραν
      MT   כתוב לך את שם היום

 εκει 967] (minus) Z rel. | το ονομα *lll* Tht. = שֵׁם MT cf. *omnia*
(*nomen?*) La^S

24:27 p967 (minus)
       MT   ביום ההוא

(minus) 967] εν εκεινη τη ημερα ZB *L"* La^CS Tht. | εν τη ημερα
εκεινη rel. = ביום ההוא MT

38:14 p967 και εν τη ημερα εκεινη εν τω κατοικισθηωαι μου τον λαον ισραηλ επ
             ειρηνης εγερθηση
       MT   הלוא ביום ההוא בשבת עמי ישראל לבטח תדע

και εν τη ημερα εκεινη 967] ουκ εν τη ημερα εκεινη Z B *O'* 106 198
239' | ουχι εν τη ημερα εκεινη rel. | *in die non*
La^W | *nonne in die illa* La^Amb = הלוא ביום
ההוא MT
εγερθηση 967 Z rel. (recon: תֵּעַר)] εξεγερθηση A"; απαντηση 46;
γνωση και εγερθηση *L"* Tht. | תדע MT

38:18 p967 και εσται η ημερα εκεινη εν η αν ελθη γωγ
       MT   והיה ביום ההוא ביום בוא גוג

και εσται 967Z rel. = והיה MT] (minus) Peshitta
η ημερα εκεινη εν 967] εν τη ημερα 534 La^W Peshitta| εν τη ημερα
εκεινη εν ημερα Z rel. = ביום ההוא ביום MT

24:2—εχει

p967 differently interpreted the unvocalized Hebrew text, reading שָׁם
where MT has שָׁם.

24:27—minus: εν τη ημερα εχεινη

p967's minus in 24:27a, as with its minus in 20:6a, stands against Z's εν
εχεινη τη ημερα. However, Z's word order is inverted from MT. The order,
εχεινη + ημερα appears only in 24:26 and 45:22 in p967. Elsewhere, the
order ημερα εχεινη occurs, which is more reflective of the Hebrew phrase,
(see 29:21; 30:9; 38:10, 14, 18, 19; and 39:11). Indeed, Allen determines that
"on that day" in 24:27 is the result of a marginal gloss.[18] It is not possible
to adjudicate Allen's proposal on the basis of this evidence; however, p967
may not be an erroneous omission.

38:14—χαι

In 38:14, χαι stands alone in p967. All other witnesses to Ezekiel 38:14 render "on that day" with the negative particle. JGK explain p967's omission:
"it seems that Sch. [p967[Sch]] was based on a text in which הלוא, on account
of its resemblance to what precedes and follows, was omitted through
haplography."[19] However, neither ουχ nor הלוא resemble the words immediately surrounding them (Heb: יהוה הלוא ביום and Greek: χυριος ουχ εν τη)
necessary to make an evaluation based on haplography. There is no basis,
at least according to textual criteria, for error in p967's text.[20]

Grammar and syntax, as well as the second half of the verse, warrant
viewing p967 as a viable text with a variant Hebrew *Vorlage*. First, the
Hebrew "הלוא is sometimes used with a certain exclamatory nuance."[21]
Likewise the negative particles ουχ and *nonne* expect a positive response.[22]
Thus, the interrogative negative particles in MT and La[Amb] support the

---

[18] He does so based on the chronological problem already set up in v. 26 between the
fall of Jerusalem and Ezekiel's dumbness "as the Aram. inf להשמעות 'to cause to hear'
suggests. Fohrer, 143; cf. Zimmerli, 503 . . .)." Allen, *Ezekiel*, 2:56.

[19] Johnson, Gehman, and Kase, *The John H. Scheide Biblical Papyri*, 130.

[20] In fact, some critics believe the negative particle is a later addition. For redaction-
critical reasons, Zimmerli takes vv. 14–16 as the interrogative reflection of a later redactor,
noting that the "introductory formula has therefore been changed from the normal form,
והיה ביום ההוא ('and it will be on that day') to the question הלוא ביום ההוא ('will it not
be on that day?')." Zimmerli, *Ezekiel*, 2:312.

[21] Paul Joüon and T. Muraoka, *A Grammar of Biblical Hebrew*. (Parts 1 and 2; SB 14/1;
Rome: Editrice Pontificio Istituto Biblico, 2003), 2:§161c, 610. Genesius, *Hebrew Grammar*,
§150e.

[22] Smyth, *Greek Grammar*, §2651.

syntax of p967 and may have been variant readings differing only in emphasis. However, the Greek particles ουκ and the more emphatic ουχι would
expect a positive answer only if the context dictates they be understood
interrogatively. Since the context does not demand the interrogative, the
Greek negative particle could also represent a contrary to fact declarative
statement, as La^W seems to take it.[23] These grammatical considerations at
least show that p967 is not as singular a reading as the tables of alignment
would indicate and is certainly not necessarily an erroneous text.

Second, v. 14b is the statement to which the contested phrase is directed.
p967's εγερθηση likely read תדע as תֵּעֹר. The metathesis of ע and ד could
have been the mistake of the translator; however, given that no other versions follow MT, the error likely occurred in the Hebrew. This may be
supported by the mediating role of the later Lucianic witnesses, which
preserve *both* p967 and the MT's readings as viable textual traditions.

In conclusion, the variant in v. 14b probably arose during Hebrew
stages of transmission, which strongly suggests that the v. 14a variant did
as well.

38:18—η ημερα εκεινη εν

In 38:18, the syntax of p967 modifies the expected formal phrase εν τη
ημερα εκεινη / ביום ההוא. However, Z rel. and MT expand the phrase with
an added εν ημερα / ביום, syntax unattested elsewhere in neither Z nor
MT.[24] Because the Greek witnesses provide strong testimony for MT, we
should examine the divergence in the Greek first.

The syntax of both p967 and Z makes sense. p967 starts with a temporal phrase και εσται η ημερα εκεινη followed by a relative-prepositional
construction εν η and a subjunctive verb αν ελθη to complete the temporal clause. The translated phrase runs "it will be that day, whenever Gog
comes up."[25] This Greek temporal clause is more vivid. It is also definite,

---

[23] Smyth, *Greek Grammar*, §2688b.

[24] Allen notes the accentuation in v. 18a, but refers to Zimmerli. Allen, *Ezekiel*, 2:202. Cf.
Zimmerli, *Ezekiel*, 2:288. Cooke decides, "for the softening of expressions regarded by the
versions as unsuitable, see notes on 8:1 11:24; 20; 43:2; 44:7." Cooke, *A Critical and Exegetical
Commentary*, 417. However these citations do not provide much clarity for Cooke's point.
Crane dismissed Eichrodt's posposal to see a gloss here. However, Crane overlooks the
textual evidence of the Peshitta, and offers no study for the varied syntax in the Greek.
Crane, *Israel's Restoration*, 166.

[25] The temporal condition is set by the future indicative verb εσται and refers to a
definite future. However a temporal clause with a future verb is rare in Greek "because it
does not make clear the difference between action continuing and action simply occurring in the future." Smyth, *Greek Grammar* §2398. The principle clause that follows uses

indicating that "that day" *will* occur. Yet it leaves open the possibility that "Gog coming up" recurrs as a "repeated customary action or a general truth."[26] Thus, in its syntax, p967 captures the anxiety of an impending one-time invasion versus a continuous mythic but real threat; in both cases, the (repeated) event(s) will be on "that day," the day predicted across the book of Ezekiel.

Z does not provide an immediate predicate for its definite future verb εσται; *what* will be is unidentified, leaving the future to the same rhetorical forces as summoned by the phrase elsewhere in Ezekiel. Probably, in the last part of the verse, the future indicative phrase αναβησεται ο θυμος μου provides the *what*: "my wrath."

Turning to the Hebrew, the syntax of MT 38:17–19 is uncertain because of אם לא in v. 19. There are two equally valid possibilities: (1) אם לא is to be understood as a conditional construction, with אם לא ביום ההוא as the protasis. The phrase omits the verb, but because of ביום ההוא, refers back to והיה ביום ההוא (v. 18). As in Z above, והיה implies תעללה חמתי (v. 18bβ). Thus, the conditional clause implies the protasis, "if my wrath does not go up on that day." The apodosis commences in v. 19bβ with the imperfect יהיה רעש.[27] The meaning of the entire conditional construction would thus be: "my wrath will flare on the day Gog invades; if it does not flare up, there will be a great shaking."[28] (2) אם לא refers to the self-imprecation of God's speech in v. 18bβ and thus functions as the oath formula "certainly."[29] In this meaning, God *certainly* promises a seismic event on the day Gog invades, but this event is to be understood as the *fulfillment* of God's wrath.

Because the Hebrew grammar invited two interpretations of vv. 17–19, we can now correlate the syntax of (1) with Z's translation. p967 does not follow option (2), and is thus likely an inner-Greek reinterpretation of Z's syntax. The following explanation can also explain p967's unique plus of the recognition formula in v. 20 as well.

In v. 18aα, p967's unique temporal construction is oriented towards a desired interpretation of v. 18, that would appreciate the possible

---

αν plus a subjunctive. As a "future more vivid" clause, it refers to the future indefinitely. For more on the differences between definite and indefinite temporal clauses, see Smyth, *Greek Grammar*, §§2390–2394.

[26] Smyth, *Greek Grammar*, §2409.

[27] Gesenius, *Hebrew Grammar*, §159rb.

[28] The latter event, the great shaking, implies the divine intervention that produces the good end for Israel, that Gog is thwarted and conquered on the land of Israel.

[29] Gesenius, *Hebrew Grammar*, §149a.

repeatability of Gog's invasion (see above). With this modification, p967 severed ει μην εν τη ημερα εκεινη in v. 19bα from και εσται εν ημερα εκεινη in v. 18aα. Thus, the ει μην required an innovative interpretation. p967 probably read ει μην as "except," a modification of the protasis. This syntax would then point to p967's unique recognition formula plus in v. 20. Thus we read "except on that day there will be a great shaking... in order that they will know."

It is possible that a Hebrew *Vorlage* lay beneath p967's syntax. ει μην in v. 19 could have translated כי אם. η ημερα εκεινη εν η could have translated היום ההוא באשר.[30] The Peshitta reading in v. 18aα (Syriac for εν τη ημερα), partially supported by 534 and La^W, could not syntactically correlate with v. 19's ει μην εν τη ημερα εκεινη, just as in p967.[31] However, these speculations cannot compare with the safer conclusion, namely that p967 is an inner-Greek reinterpretation of the Greek syntax.

4.3.1.1. *Summary of Results*

Above, I analzed twelve of the eighteen isolated p967 readings; three more receive more extensive discussion below in §4.4. Of these twelve, four are definitely or arguably based on a Hebrew *Vorlage*: 24:2; 24:14; 32:24; and 38:14. Four more *could* reflect a Hebrew *Vorlage*: 22:15; 24:27; 32:6; and 39:8. Four were probably inner-Greek developments: 35:8; 38:20; 38:18; and 39:4.

4.3.2. *Variants between p967 and B*

In the following variants, p967 has manuscript support but reads against B.

	p967 relative to B's readings (alignment of MT noted)
12:28*	(minus)] ου μη μηκυνωσιν ουκετι παντες οι λογοι μου ους αν λαλησω λαλησω και ποιησω λεγει κυριος = MT
16:59	(minus)] ταδε λεγει κυριος = MT
20:5	(minus)] λεγων εγω κυριος ο θεος υμων = MT
20:5–6	(minus)] ^(v. 5) τη χειρι μου αυτων λεγων εγω κυριος ο θεος υμων ^(v. 6) εν εκεινη τη ημερα αντελαβομην = MT
20:24	καρδιων] πατερων = MT
21:3(8)	(minus)] και ερεις προς την γην του ισραηλ = MT

---

[30] Cf. 2 Chr 18:24 and 1Kgs 22:25.
[31] Zimmerli notes the connection here with the Peshitta's reading in 38:10 as well. Zimmerli, *Ezekiel*, 2:288.

21:3(8)   ταδε λεγει κς = MT] (minus)
21:12   (minus) = MT] πασα σαρξ και
22:13   χειρα μου προς] (minus) = MT
24:9   δαλον] λαον | MT
26:1   δεκατω] ενδεκατω = MT
26:20   της] γης = MT
27:18   (minus)] πασης | MT
28:26   (minus) = MT] και ο θεος των πατερων αυτων
29:1   δεκατω = MT] δωδεκατω
30:20   δεκατω] ενδεκατω = MT
31:1   δεκατω] ενδεκατω = MT
32:17   δεκατω] δωδεκατω = MT
32:18   τα εθνη τας θυγατερας νεκρας] tr. τα εθνη / τας θυγατερας | MT
32:21   (minus)] σοι | MT
32:25*   (minus)] εν μεσω τραυματιων
33:21   δεκατω] δωδεκατω = MT
34:8   (minus)] εις προνομην και γενεσθαι τα προβατα μου ≈ MT
34:15   (minus) = MT] και γνωσονται οτι εγω ειμι κυριος
37:1   κυ = MT] κυριος = MT (יהוה MT)
37:1   (minus) = MT] ανθρωπινων
38:16   γωγ = MT] tr.ᵛ· ¹⁷
38:16   (minus)] εμε = MT
38:21   παν φοβον μαχαιρας] και παν φοβον | MT
39:11   γαι = MT] τε

20:5–6—(minus) 967
See discussion of 24:27 in §4.3.1 above.

21:3 (MT v. 8)—967 vs. Bᵗˣᵗ in three prophetic speech formulae

p967   ² και προφητευσον επι την γην του ισραηλ ³ ταδε λεγει κς ιδου εγω προς σε
MT   ² והנבא אל אדמת ישראל ³ ואמרת לאדמת ישראל כה אמר יהוה
          הנני אליך

          (minus) 967 48 *C*'-233 544 Sa Tyc.] και ερεις προς την γην του ισραηλ Z
                rel. = אל אדמת ואמרת לאדמת ישראל MT (אדמת
                HUBPᴵᴵᴵ⁻ᴳ⁻ᴮᴱᵇ ²²)
          ταδε λεγει κς 967 Bᵐᵍ rel. (ast. Q) = כה אמר יהוה MT] (minus) Z
                Bᵗˣᵗ 106 | כה אדני יהוה HUBPᴵᴵᴵ⁻¹⁵⁰| כה אמר אדני HUBPᴵᴵᴵ⁻³⁰, ⁹³, ᴳ⁻ᴮᴱᵇ ²²
                יהוה HUBPᴵᴵᴵ⁻³⁰, ⁹³, ⁹⁶, ᴳ⁻ᴮᴱᵇ ²²
          ιδου εγω 967 Z rel. = הנני MT] (minus) Bᵗˣᵗ

Of the three prophetic formulae in v. 3, B^{txt} and p967 preserve exact oppo-site elements, but together translated the MT. ואמרת לאדמת ישראל is represented in B^{txt} with και ερεις προς την γην του ισραηλ, and כה אמר יהוה הנני אליך is represented in p967 with ταδε λεγει κς ιδου εγω προς σε.

All three prophetic formulae are likely additions, an accretion of pro-phetic forms onto an originally short text. MT preserves some textual vari-ety that hints at types of Hebrew development. אל אדמת in ms. G-BEb 22 not only brings the morphology closer to v. 2(7)b והנבא אל אדמת, but it suggests a clarification of the object of הנני אליך later in v. 3(8). Likewise, ms. 150 reflects a text in which the messenger formula was not present, since its reading brings emphasis instead to the subject, כה אדני יהוה הנני. MT could have corrected to the standard messenger formula, while four Hebrew manuscripts: 30, 93, 96, and G-BEb 22, probably over-compen-sated for the Hebrew reading.

The only phrase that is well-supported is הנני אליך / ιδου εγω προς σε. Even B provides partial support for the phrase, omitting only ιδου εγω. B^{txt}'s lone προς σε elicited the marginal correction ιδου εγω to make sense of B's text. Also, the Hebrew variants just discussed are all oriented towards clar-ifying הנני אליך, suggesting that this phrase generated the scribal editing. Probably, the asterisked messenger formula was ultimately an attempt to harmonize the form of הנני אליך with the rest of Ezekiel.[32]

Most likely, p967 and B both preserve their respective Hebrew *Vorla-gen*, although B required some inner-Greek correction. Nevertheless, the B^{txt} likely reflects a variant *Vorlage* which omitted כה אמר יהוה הנני אליך on account of perceived Hebrew corruption. This text either added ואמרת לאדמת ישראל for clarity, or incorporated a gloss.[33] Needless to say, these proposed Hebrew stages of scribal activity lie behind our current wit-nesses. However, the simplest explanation for the MT is that it combined *both* Hebrew readings, resulting in the longer Hebrew edition. According to this solution, p967 and B reflect variant Hebrew *Vorlagen*.

21:12—(minus) 967 vs. πασα σαρξ και B

παν πνα (πνευμα) 967 = כל רוח MT] (obel. *O*) πασα σαρξ και παν πνευμα Z rel. | παν πνευμα πασα σαρξ 62

---

[32] As Zimmerli points out, the messenger formula precedes הנני אליך in Ezekiel 13 of the 14 times. Zimmerli, *Ezekiel*, 1:175 comments on 5:8.

[33] The phrase reasserts that the oracle that follows should be understood as directed at the "land" of Israel, perhaps to distinguish from Israel as "the people" who were usually addressed by הנני אליך.

p967 agrees with the MT; however, there is no reason to suppose Z rel. added πασα σαρξ, especially since the phrase receives the obelus. Likely, both Greek readings reflect alternate Hebrew *Vorlagen*, although the evidence cannot provide any certainty either way.

22:13—προς χειρα μου 967 vs. (minus) B

p967 επαξω χειρα μου προς χειρα μου
MT הכיתי כפי

χειρα μου προς χειρα μου 967 Z rel.] χειρα μου B V 490 Co = כפי MT

The reconstructed *Vorlage* of p967 probably agrees with the Hebrew of אכה כפי אל כפי 21:22. There, only in ms. 89 do we find the same reading, (minus אל כפי) as the MT of 22:13. With its considerable support from other witnesses, p967 probably reflects a variant Hebrew *Vorlage*.

24:9—δαλον 967 vs. λαον B

δαλον 967 Z rel.] λαον B 130 La^S | המדורה MT | תברה HUBP^I-Tar | מעמרא HUBP^I-Peshitta

(minus) 967 ZB *ll* La^SW Sa] (ast. O) ουαι πολις των αιματων rel. = אוי עיר הדמים MT

δαλον in p967 is the majority reading and best represents the Old Greek. B's λαον can be explained as inner-Greek error: a metathesis of α and λ and a dropped δ, a reading taken up by a few witnesses.[34]

The more difficult variant lies between p967 and the MT. מדורה is only translated in one other LXX book, Isa 30:33. There the translation of the verse is not word for word, and in any case, the Greek scribe, who used the verb κειμαι, seems to have misread מְדֻרָתָה as a verbal form of ירד (a Polal passive fem. pl. participle, reconstructed מְדוּרָתות). A better solution lies in a variant Hebrew *Vorlage* to the Old Greek δαλον (firebrand), a literal translation of האור (firebrand) in lieu of המדורה in the MT.

Two textual issues in the surrounding context support this evaluation. The MT plus in the first half of the verse, אוי עיר הדמום, which is likely a post-OG addition to the Hebrew, further suggests that the verse was

---

[34] So Cooke, who calls B's reading "τον λαον ? a corruption of τον δαλον." Cooke, *A Critical and Exegetical Commentary*, 274.

edited in Hebrew stages of the textual tradition.[35] Second, the MT's use of דור as a verb, "pile up," in v. 5 is not only a hapax, but all Greek witnesses translate υποκαιε "burn."

26:20—της 967 vs. γης B

επι ᵗⁿˢ ζωης 967 *ll* 91–764] επι γης ζωης Z ≈ rel. = בארץ חיים MT

p967's reading της appears above the line as a secondary correction in the manuscript. The corrector brought p967's reading into agreement with texts like *ll* 91–764 and not the MT or Z rel. The graphically similar substitution in the phrase επι γης/της ζωης recurs four other times in Ezekiel with inconsistent renderings across the versions:

	γης	της
32:23	Z B	967 A
32:24	Z	967 BA
32:26	Z	BA (context of p967 minus)
32:32	Z	967 BA
26:20	Z BA	967

With considerable support in 26:20, Ziegler understandably reads γης with BA. However, the textual evidence in 32:23, 24, 26, 32 should have the OG reading της, against Ziegler. p967's correction to της, as well as the evidence from the verses in ch. 32 suggest that here in 26:20, p967 corrected its text to reflect the reading of the OG.

27:18—(minus) 967 vs. πασης B
See discussion of 27:16 in §4.3.3.1 below.

28:26—(minus) 967 vs. και ο θεος των πατερων αυτων B

p967	και γνωσονται οτι εγω ειμι κς ° ᵠˢ αυτων
B	και γνωσονται οτι εγω ειμι κυριος ο θεος αυτων και ο θεος των πατερων αυτων
MT	וידעו כי אני יהוה אלהיהם

(minus) 967 62 = MT] (obel. *O*⁻ˢʸʰ) και ο θεος των πατερων αυτων Z rel.

---

[35] On the MT plus in v. 9a, Allen takes it to be a later "mechanical assimilation" to v. 6. Allen, *Ezekiel*, 2:55. So also Cooke, *A Critical and Exegetical Commentary*, 268; and following Cornill, Bertholet, and Fohrer, also Zimmerli, *Ezekiel*, 1:494.

p967 lacks the Z rel. plus και ο θεος των πατερων αυτων. In its shorter reading, the corrected p967 probably represents the OG, since there is no good reason for MT or p967 to have eliminated the phrase. B, supported by most of the versions, shows expansion of θεος αυτων with a common formula.[36] θεος αυτων / אלהיהם is not a common form for the recognition formula and may have invited such emendation.[37] Since the B reading has an obelus in the Hexaplaric tradition and is supported by so many witnesses, the addition may have occurred in a now lost Hebrew text, although inner-Greek activity is also possible.

32:18—τα εθνη τας θυγατερας νεκρας—967 vs. B on Word Order

967	και καταβιβασουσιν αυτης τα εθνη τας θυγατερας νεκρας
B	και καταβιβασουσιν αυτης τας θυγατερας τα εθνη νεκρας
MT	והורדהו אותה ובנות גוים אדרם

αυτης 967 Z rel. ≈ tr. L'-46 Arm Tht.Hi.] אותה MT | אַתָּה HUBPIII-30
τα εθνη 967 ≈ tr. Z rel.] tr. גוים אדרם MT | גוים אֹרִידִים HUBPIII-96
τας θυγατερας νεκρας 967 ≈ tr. Z rel.] tr. בנות MT

p967 and B differ only in word order. However, neither translates the MT exactly. The MT is to be questioned here, not only for its disagreement with all of the versions, but also because of the meaningful variants in mss. 30 and 96, discussed below. Since B follows the word order of MT, it more likely represents a correction back to the MT, while p967 is closest to the OG. It is possible to explain all of the variants among the witnesses with the following reconstruction. Largely on the basis of p967, I propose a hypothetical *Vorlage* to illustrate the developments that are textually supported by Hebrew witnesses.

Vorlage:	והורדוה הגוים את הבת המתה
OG:	και καταβιβασουσιν αυτης τα εθνη της θυγατρος νεκρας

At least two developments could have occurred in the Hebrew, as evinced in mss. 30 and 96. If correct, the two hypothetical developments could explain MT's text. First, a scribe could have written אוֹרִידֵם "I will bring

---

[36] The phrase, θεος των πατερων / אלהי אבי... appears frequently in the Exodus chapters distinctly related to the revelation of the divine name, thus the association with the recognition formula.

[37] אלהיהם appears in the recognition formula only in Ezek 34:30; 39:22; and 39:28; θεος αυτων occurs in these three verses and 35:15.

them down" in the margin. This paratextual note indicates that the nations fall by God's agency, not on their own, as p967 and its proposed *Vorlage* would have it. Manuscript 96 likely reflects this reading in its variant אֹרִידֵים.

Then, a scribe could have re-arranged words and slightly emended the consonantal text to give the agency to Ezekiel.

והורדהו אתה את בנות הגוים	you, bring him down with the daughters of the nations

Manuscript 30, which preserves אַתָּה, supports this proposal. The emendations necessary were metathesis of ו and ה on the end of the verb to create a 3ms direct object and to harmonize the verb with the 2ms pronoun. אתה may have been the result of a transposition and emendation of the graphically similar המתה. In keeping with this explanation, MT's reading mediates among these developments. Most creatively, MT took אוריֵדֶם as the adjective אַדְּרֵם for modifying הגוים.

The Greek is easier to explain. p967's θυγατερας is simply the plural of θυγατρος. Whether by mistake or intentionally, the change was in part allowed by the adjective νεκρας, which is the same in the Gen fs and fpl. B rel. is the result of changed word order to bring the Greek closer to the Hebrew of the MT, although νεκρας was not exchanged for an equivalent of אַדְּרֵם.

34:8—(minus) 967 vs. εις προνομην και γενεσθαι τα προβατα B

967	του γενεσθαι μου τα προβατα εις καταβρωμα
MT	היות צאני לבז ותהיינה צאני לאכלה

(minus) 967 26 306* 410 La^{CS} Aug.] (ast. 88) εις προνομην και γενεσθαι τα προβατα (subst. ποιμνια *L''*) μου Z rel. ≈ לבז ותהיינה צאני MT | צאני (om. לבז ותהיינה) HUBP^{III-96}

Ziegler's apparatus attributes p967's minus of the phrase εις προνομην και γενεσθαι τα προβατα μου, found in B and the MT, to *homoioteleuton*. However, p967 does not replicate B's word order for "my sheep." The text places the possessive pronoun before the article: μου τα προβατα. Thus, p967's text cannot have produced scribal paraplepsis to lead to its current minus. The MT does reproduce צאני in both instances. However, additional considerations obviate paraplepsis in the Hebrew as well. First, the verbal elements are quite different, היות and ותהיינה. Second, the second צאני is omitted in ms. 96 and is otherwise textually suspect. Not only do the Lucianic witnesses show variance for this term, but later in the verse, MT's רעי was "wrongly changed" from (ה)רעים according to most critics.[38] The weakness of the argument for *homoioteleuton*, as well as the asterisk in the B reading, suggests that p967's minus represents the OG.

37:1—κυριου 967 vs. κυριος B

πνι κυ (πνευματι κυριου) 967 rel.] πνευματι κυριος ZB A′ 62′ Tert.Ambr.Ir.[lat] | πνευματι τω αγιω κυριου Q[mg] | πνευματι Or. Lo. | רוח יהוה MT

The syntax of MT in 37:1 is ambivalent, leading to the two possible inter-pretations reflected in p967 and B's readings. רוח יהוה as a construct chain reflects p967's translation πνευματι κυριου. The second option is for יהוה to be the subject of the earlier verb ויוצאני. B reflects this interpretation. Though an accurate translation of the Hebrew, p967 probably reflects an inner-Greek development; B is more reflective of the OG.

37:1—(minus) 967 vs. ανθρωπινων B

οστω(ν) 967 Tert.Ir.[lat]Consult = עצמות MT] οστων ανθρωπινων Z rel.| οστων ανθρωπων L″ 130*-534-403′ Bo Arm Or.Tht.Hi.

The adjective ανθρωπινος in B is likely a stylistic modification on L's οστων ανθρωπων. It is possible that a variant Hebrew text lay beneath this stream in the Greek.[39] What is more certain is that p967's shorter reading, reflect-ing the MT, derives from a Hebrew *Vorlage*.

39:11—γαι 967 vs. τε B

γαι 967 Z rel. = גיא MT ≈ γε O (γη Syh) C′-233 410 La[s] (*ge*) Arm Ambr.Hi.] τε B 26 Cyr.[40] | (minus) 106 Arab

B is easily explained as an error, reproducing τε as opposed to γε. p967's γαι reflects a Hebrew *Vorlage* and is probably earliest, although the vari-ant spellings may not require a textual explanation. Both γαι and γε are transliterations for the Hebrew גיא so variety can be expected.

---

[38] Zimmerli, *Ezekiel*, 2:206. Allen, *Ezekiel*, 2:157. The un-suffixed conjecture is supported by all LXX mss., the Latin, and the Peshitta.

[39] The MT plus in 34:31 אדם אתם "you are men" and in 36:37 כצאן אדם "like a flock of men," both promise oracles leading up to chapter 37, make the proposal quite possible that the Hebrew of 37:1 once included the term אדם.

[40] τε occurs in v. 11 of B meaning "and" as an enclitic weak particle.

4.3.2.1. *Summary of Results*

Thirteen of the 30 variants between p967 and B, where p967 has some textual support, were analyzed above; for one more see §4.4.2 below.[41] Of these 13 variants, seven definitely or arguably reflect variant Hebrew *Vorlagen*: two in 21:3(8); 22:13; 24:9; 26:20; and 32:18. Four more likely reflect variant Hebrew *Vorlagen*: 21:12; 27:18; 28:26; 34:8. One more, 37:1, shows that the Greek witnesses propagated two valid interpretations of the Hebrew; thus there was only one Hebrew *Vorlage*. The only other variant that cannot reflect two variant Hebrew *Vorlagen* is in 39:11.

As the above discussion indicates, the B reading could often be attributed to a variant Hebrew text, twice in 21:3(8); 21:12; 22:13; 24:9; 26:20; 27:18; 28:26; 32:18; 34:8; and 37:1. Twice, B can be explained as a correction towards the MT, with p967 representing the OG (32:18 and 34:8). Twice, B's reading was shown to be an inner-Greek error (24:9 and 39:11). I did not find one instance where a p967 reading resulted from an error. However, in three cases, p967 definitely or arguably represents a corrected text, twice to the Hebrew in 37:1 and once to the OG in 26:20.

4.3.3. *MT and the Hebrew* Vorlage *of p967*

4.3.3.1 *p967 Variants Based on a Variant Hebrew* Vorlage

Several variants provide strong evidence for editorial activity in the Hebrew. The following variants shed light on the relationship among p967, the MT, and the Hebrew *Vorlage* to the Old Greek.

4:4–6   p967 not preserved; B] MT (presented below)

13:2   MT לנביאי מלבם [967 προς αυτους

24:10   MT והעצמות יחרו [967 (minus)

---

[41] Six additional variants are date references. Except in 26:1, they are difficult to adjudicate textually, thus were not dealt with here. Even before p967's witness, a textual problem was already recognized for the year in 26:1. Allen points out that the MT עשתי עשרה "the eleventh year" renders the ordinal differently than elsewhere in Ezekiel אחת עשרה (30:20; 31:1). Allen, *Ezekiel*, 2:71. Most take עשתי as a corruption of שתי "twelfth." In this decision, critics follow Carl Steuernagel, *Lehrbuch der Einleitung in da AT mit einem Anhang über die Apokryphen und Pseudepigraphen* (Tübingen: J.C.B. Mohr (P. Siebeck), 1912), 576. See Zimmerli, *Ezekiel*, 1:26; Cooke, *A Critical and Exegetical Commentary*, 288, 294; Allen, *Ezekiel*, 2:71. This same mistake also occurred in 40:49 which increases the likelihood that twelfth was original. Bewer, who also prefers the twelfth year, does so only on the basis of A's witness. Bewer, *English Bible 1949 Authorized* (HABS; New York: Harper & Bros., 1950), 2:15.

24:14 διαστελω 967] אפרע MT
ουδε μη ελεησω 967] ולא אחוס ולא אנחם MT
26:10 εκ πεδιου 967] מִבְקָעָה MT
27:16 ανθρωπους 967] ארם MT
απο πληθους του συμμεικτου σου 967] מרב מעשיך MT
29:5 περισταλης 967] תקבץ MT
32:30 στρατηγοι ασσουρ 967] צדני אשֵׁר MT
32:32 πληθος αυτου 967] המונה MT
36:5 (minus) 967] כל לבב MT
εν προνομη 967 = MT] לבב HUBP[III-93]
37:7 τα οστα 967] עצמות MT
39:11 ονομαστον 967] שֵׁם MT
39:28 εν τω επιφαναι με 967] בהגלותי MT
(minus) 967] וכנסתים על אדמתם ולא אותיר מהם עוד שם MT

13:2—אליהם

p967   και ερεις προς αυτους
MT   ואמרת לנביאי מלבם

προς αυτους 967 (obel. O) ZB Sa Hi.] (ast. O) τοις προφηταις τοις
προφητευουσιν απο καρδιας αυτων rel. θ'α' ≈ לנביאי
אליהם לנביאי מלבם MT | מלבם HUBP[III-96]

אליהם in ms. 96 strongly suggests that p967 and B's προς αυτους was
originally a Hebrew reading; p967 and B probably reflect their *Vorlage*
faithfully. The Hexaplaric obelus makes it difficult to determine the OG;
however, p967 and B are certainly closer to it than rel θ'α'. Thus, the OG
Vorlage and MT represent variant texts. The MT's לנביאי מלבם is likely
the later development, according to the loosely translated asterisked reading of the Hexaplaric texts: τοις προφηταις τοις προφητευουσιν απο καρδιας
αυτων.

24:10—העצם

p967   και πληθυνω τα ξυλα και ανακαυσω το πυρ οπως τακη τα κρεα οπως
       ελαττωθη [ο] ζωμος
MT   הרבה העצים הדלק האש התם הבשר והרקח המרקחה והעצמות יחרו

τα ξυλα 967 Z rel. = העצים MT] העצם HUBP[III-93] ≈ *ossa* Vul.
(minus) 967 ZB *ll* 106 La[SW] Co Ambr.] (ast.O) και τα οστα συνφρυγησονται
rel. = והעצמות יחרו MT

Manuscript 93 is alone in reading העצם, although the Vulgate suggests a similar reading העצמות. The weight of evidence indicates that the MT העצים represents the *Vorlage* to the OG τα ξυλα. Thus, ms. 93 is a later Hebrew variant, easily explained as an error except for the second half of the verse. The same lexeme is contested at the end of the verse in the MT plus והעצמות יחרו. However, here too, p967 and B indicate the phrase was probably missing in the *Vorlage* to the OG. Taken together, והעצמות יחרו in MT (an asterisked reading) and העצם in ms. 93 testify to a *Tendenz* in the Hebrew transmission involving the lexeme עצם.

24:14—ולא ארחים

p967	ου διαστελω ουδε μη ελεησω
MT	לא אגרע ולא אחוס ולא אנחם

διαστελω 967 Z rel.] אפרע MT | אמנע TarJ | אגרע HUBP[III-96]

ουδε μη ελεησω 967 Z rel.] ου φεισομαι ουδε μη ελεησω *L* 86 | ουδε μη ελεησω (ast. *O*) *O*'-62 Arm Hi. ≈ ουδε φεισομαι και ου μη παρακληθω 62 *lII* Tht. ≈ ולא אחוס ולא ארחים MT | ולא אחוס ולא אנחם HUBP[I-TarJ] (cf. ולא ארחם HUBP[I-Peshitta])

p967, B, and several other witnesses that read ουδε μη ελεησω omit the second expression in MT's phrase ולא אחוס ולא אנחם. ולא אנחם cannot have been in the OG, especially as it is variously represented among the versions in which it appears.[42] The Hexaplaric manuscripts translate אנחם with the asterisked παρακληθω, reading a Piel אֲנַחֵם "I will comfort" where MT vocalized a Nifal אֶנָּחֵם "I will be sorry."

Missing from the OG, the נחם-expression was probably a later Hebrew addition.[43] Such an evaluation is made more likely by the alternate term in TarJ ולא ארחים "and I will not have compassion" which is likely the result of an accretion of similar expressions in the Hebrew. Variety in the first Hebrew term, MT's פרע "to let go," TarJ's מנע "to withhold," and ms. 96's

---

[42] Zimmerli, noting its omission in the Greek and Latin witnesses, determines that ולא אנחם "is certainly an addition, since it adds a third statement to the two preceding parallel expressions." Zimmerli, *Ezekiel*, 1:496.

[43] While Allen asserts the originality of the expression in the Hebrew, his reasons may equally apply to a later addition. He makes the case that a word-play exists in ch. 24 on the consonants חם, focusing poetic attention on the divine חמה. Allen prefers אנחם in order to fulfill the חם-word-play. Allen, *Ezekiel*, 58.

גרע "to diminish/restrain," similarly reflects fluidity in the Hebrew.[44] The latter two may lie behind φειδομαι "to spare," which appears in *L* 86 and is transposed in 62 *lll* Tht. as a Greek correction back to the Hebrew.

מבקעה—26:10

εκ πεδιου 967 Z rel. (recon. מְבֻקָּעָה)] מְבֻקָּעָה MT

εκ πεδιου in the LXX witnesses reflects a variant pointing of בקעה. The MT "breached" is a 3fs Pual ptc. of בקע pointed מְבֻקָּעָה. The Greek translated εκ πεδιου "from the plain" and reads a noun with a prefixed preposition: מִבְּקְעָה. It is possible this vocalization represented a Hebrew tradition, although no textual evidence could prove the matter.

מרב and כל הון—27:16

p967	ανθρωπους εμποριαν σου απο πληθους του συμμεικτου σου
MT	ארם סחרתך מרב מעשיך

ανθρωπους 967 Z rel. (recon. אָדָם)] ארם MT | (εδωμ) Peshitta (recon. אדם)
απο πληθους του συμμεικτου σου 967 Z rel.] מרב מעשיך MT | מרב כל הון HUBP[III-30]

Several textual issues are involved in the evaluation of 27:16. MT's מרב מעשיך is translated in all Greek witnesses, with the support of the versions as απο πληθους του συμμεικτου σου. Cooke reconstructs the Hebrew *Vorlage* of συμμεικτου σου as מערבך and cites vv. 17 and 19 for support; we should add vv. 27(2x), 33, and 34 as further evidence.[45] In all these instances, συμμικτος "comingled" translates מערב, probably working from the Hebrew עֶרֶב "mixed company," although the Aramaic מְעָרַב, a Pael pass ms ptc meaning "mixed" is even more similar.[46] The root מערב has several meanings in the Hebrew, as the Greek indicates in v. 9 δυσμη "west"

---

[44] גרע appears in 5:11 in a similar sequence of divine promises about the efficacy of prophecy. מנע has no association with the content or form of 24:14, however it is used in Ezekiel with respect to *Sheol* in 31:15. MT's פרע has invited some critical comments. Zimmerli gratuitously notes in his textual comments that the verb does not appear elsewhere in Ezekiel. Zimmerli, *Ezekiel*, 1:496. Cooke supplies more relevant information about Rabbinic sources that noted and discussed the verb. Cooke, *A Critical and Exegetical Commentary*, 275.

[45] Cooke, *A Critical and Exegetical Commentary*, 310. Allen and Zimmerli do not comment. Zimmerli, *Ezekiel*, 2:47–8. Allen, *Ezekiel*, 2:82.

[46] This term is found twice in Daniel 2:41, 43 to describe the mixed materials of the statue representing the four kingdoms.

and v. 13 εμπορια "business," both literal translations. The context of 27:16 warrants the translation "merchandise," which εμπορια would have best captured. Nevertheless, all LXX witnesses read συμμικτος, and this, with Cooke, probably indicates a variant Hebrew *Vorlage*. Manuscript 30's כל הון for מעשיך affirms that the Hebrew was somewhat fluid (cf. 27:18 where MT reads מרב כל הון). Additionally, two verses later in v. 18, the phrase ברב מעשיך (corrected in ms. 30 to מרב, partially supported by ms. 93) is not attested in the best Greek witnesses. These anamolies suggest that the Hebrew of the MT in 27:16 was fluid, even after the OG translation.

If p967 accurately reflects its *Vorlage* and מערבך lay in the Hebrew, as I am suggesting, the similarity of מערבך to מרב, the MT's *nomen regens*, may have produced the MT reading. Further, based on כל הון in ms. 30 (and v. 18), it is possible that the graphically similar המון, a common Hebrew equivalent for πληθος, was also a part of the expression in the Hebrew *Vorlage*. If the *Vorlage* to the OG read מהמון מערבך, the Hebrew readings can both be explained through (deliberate?) haplography, although this proposal is purely speculative. What is certain is that the Greek witnesses point to a Hebrew text different from that of MT.

תקבץ—29:5

περισταλης 967 Z rel.] συσταλης 26 | תקבץ MT

The different readings probably emerged because of two different Hebrew interpretations: תקבץ "to be gathered" and תקבר "to be buried."[47] The reading תקבר could certainly have appeared in a Hebrew text, where a Hebrew scribe miscopied the final letter of very simital verbs: קבץ and קבר. At the very least, the Greek reading is the result of a misunderstanding of the Hebrew and not a complete innovation in translation. However, the variant could also point to a variant Hebrew *Vorlage* for p967 and the rest of the LXX tradition.

צדני—32:30

στρατηγοι ασσουρ 967 Z rel.] צדני אֲשֶׁר MT | צֹדנִי אֲשֶׁר HUBP[III-G-BEb 10] | σιδωνιοι α'σ' | σεδεκ θ' | *venatores qui* Vul

Zimmerli raises the possibility that LXX misread צדני as a plural construct form of סרני "tyrants/governors" to produce its reading στρατηγοι. Cooke

---

[47] Thanks to Brent A. Strawn for making this suggestion.

determines that Zimmerli's explanation offers the decisive solution. However, across the LXX, στρατηγος as the translation of סרן occurs only once, and never in Ezekiel. Instead we find αρχων (4 times) or σατραπης (8 times) across the LXX. Much more commonly, we find סגן beneath στρατηγος, most importantly three times in Ezekiel (23:6, 12, 23).

Zimmerli's hesitation, signaled by his question mark, is prudent. סגני is not similar enough to צדני graphically to explain on the basis of error. Hence, it is better to conclude with Zimmerli, that "the whole expression [וכל צדני אשר] has surely been added secondarily."[48] How the reading was produced is now lost to us, although certainly we have variant interpretations of the unvocalized אשר: a proper noun in LXX and the relative particle in MT. The reading צדנִי in ms. G-BEb 10 reflects a now lost construct chain, providing additional Hebrew support to LXX's reading. However the witness neither equals the Greek, nor understands אשר as a proper name. Nevertheless, interpretive fluidity in the Hebrew best explains the Greek variant.

32:32—המונו

πληθος αυτου 967 Z rel. = המונו HUBP[III-G-BEb 10 (sm)] | המונה MT (q המונו /k המונה /k HUBP[III-G-BEb 10 (pm)])

The ketib-qere reading in ms. G-BEb 10 (pm) המונו supports the ms possessive pronoun of the Greek witnesses. This constitutes important evidence suggesting that the LXX variant was based on a different Hebrew text from the MT.

36:5—לבב

(minus) 967 Z rel.] εξ ολης καρδιας 62 L '[+46] Tht. = כל לבב MT
εν προνομη 967 Z rel.] εις προνομην 147' 46 cII = לבז MT | לבב HUBP[III-93]

The textual information supplied by ms. 93's reading לבב is relevant to the LXX minus in the beginning of the verse. לבב could be explained as an erroneous reproduction of לבז. However, taking all the textual information together, ms. 93 complies with the Tendenz found in the MT plus כל לבב in the first half of the verse. More likely, לבב was an intentional modification of לבז. In the first half of the verse, p967 Z rel.'s minus accurately reflects its Hebrew Vorlage as a variant Hebrew edition.

---

[48] Zimmerli, Ezekiel, 2:168–169. However, note phonetic similarity.

37:7—העצמות

τα οστα 967 Z rel. = **העצמות** HUBP[II-PirkeRE32(201)] ≈ MasEzek] (minus) HUBP[III-96] |
עצמות MT

LXX is based on a Hebrew text type represented by the supplied article in ms. PirkeRE32(201) (partially supported by MasEzek).[49] The minus in ms. 96 suggests that a shorter Hebrew text circulated, once again, affirming fluidity in the Hebrew.

39:11—מקום שָׁם קבר

τοπον ονομαστον μνημειον 967 Z rel. = *locum nominatum...* La[S] Vul ≈ מקום שָׁם קבר HUBP[III-96 G-BEb24] | τοπον εχει ονομαστον μνημειον 62 cf.[MT] |
(קבורא אתין לגוג אתר כשר (לבית MT | מקום שָׁם קבר
Tar (אתר כשר cf. שָׁם MT)

The Hebrew that likely lay beneath 967 Z rel.'s ονομαστον occurs in ms. 96 G-BEb24 with שָׁם. Manuscript 62 harmonizes between the two vocalizations of שם by supplying both εχει and ονομαστον. MT's שָׁם is only loosely supported by the Targum's phrase אתר כשר "a fitting place" which captures the sense. The two Hebrew manuscripts 96 and G-BEb24 show that the LXX reflects a vocalization alternative to the MT tradition, and based on the testimony across the versions, likely preceding it.

4:4–6—*The Number of Years for Israel's Guilt*

4:4
Z   και συ κοιμηθηση επι το πλευρον σου το απιστερον και θησεις τας αδικιας του
     οικου ισραηλ επ αυτου κατα αριθμον των ημερων
     πεντηκοντα και εκατον ας κοιμηθηση επ αυτου και
     λημψη τας αδικιας αυτων

MT   ואתה שכב על צדך השמאלי ושמת את עון בית ישראל עליו מספר
     הימים אשר תשכב עליו תשא את עונם

πεντηκοντα και εκατον Z rel. (obel. O) [(967 not preserved)]] ενενηκοντα και εκατον
O Q[mg]-147 538 534–239'-710 | ενενηκοντα και
τριακοσιας 410 | (minus) C' = MT

---

[49] Manuscript 96's minus raises some question about the originality of the term, especially since עצם has been identified as the theme word for the Bones-*Tendenz*.

4:5

Z   και εγω δεδωκα σοι τας δυο αδικιας αυτων εις αριθμον ημερων ενενηκοντα και
εκατον ημερας και λημψη τας αδικιας του οικου
ισραηλ

MT   ואני נתתי לך את שני עונם למספר ימים שלש מאות ותשעים יום
ונשאת עון בית ישראל

init. Z rel. MT] ואני נתתי לך את עונם HUBP[III-30]

ενενηκοντα και εκατον Z rel. [(967 not preserved)]] ενενηκοντα και τριακοσιας C'-403'

שלש מאות ותשעים MT = 410 Hi.

δυο Z rel.] שני MT (שְׁנֵי) | שתי HUBP[III-96] | om. V

αδικιας αυτων Z rel.] עונם MT | עולם HUBP[III-G-BEb61]

εις αριθμον Z rel.] למספר MT | מספר HUBP[III-30]

4:6

Z   και συντελεσεις ταυτα παντα και κοιμηθηση επι το πλευρον σου το δεξιον και
λημψη τας αδικιας του οικου ιουδα τεσσαρακοντα
ημερας ημεραν εις ενιαυτον τεθεικα σοι

MT   כלית את אלה ושכבת על צדך הימיני שנית ונשאת את עון בית יהודה
ארבעים יום יום לשנה יום לשנה נתתיו לך

το δεξιον Z rel. [(967 not preserved)]] το δεξιον (obel. *O*) δευτερον *O*-62 Arm = הימיני

שנית MT ≈ *L*''-311 Tht. 147'

ιουδα Z rel. = יהודה MT] יהוהה HUBP[III-93!]| ישראל HUBP[III-96]

Critics have long known that variants exist between the LXX and MT in
4:4–6; p967, missing in these chapters, does not provide any new information. Nevertheless, the textual issues resemble those examined above.

In v. 4, LXX πεντηκοντα και εκατον is a plus over MT. In v. 5, LXX has
ενενηκοντα και εκατον for MT's שלש מאות ותשעים.

Two scholars come to opposite conclusions about the text of vv. 4–6.
Zimmerli takes the MT to be an expanded form of an originally unspecified
sign action, but in a form earlier than Z.[50] Brownlee concludes the opposite, taking the 190 days in Z v. 5 and consequently v. 4, as the original.[51]

As Brownlee points out, the variation between the numbers in MT and
Z are, at least in part, the result of two valid readings of שני עונם in v. 5:
"both sets of their iniquity" and "the years of their iniquity." Z, supported
by all of the versions, reads the former for שני, δυο "two."[52] In accordance
with this reading, v. 5 reports the total of the two date reckonings: "150"

---

[50] Zimmerli, *Ezekiel*, 1:165–168.
[51] Brownlee, *Ezekiel*, 1:60 n6b, 68.
[52] While rare, the numerals between 2–10 can take a singular object, as is the case with
עונם. Gesenius, *Hebrew Grammar*, §134e. The Greek cannot be considered a mistake.

(v. 4) plus "forty" (v. 6) = 190 (v. 5).[53] Thus, Z exhibits arithmetic coherence not explicitly found in MT and would therefore represent the *lectio facilior*. Additionally, the variant readings in v. 4, πεντηκοντα και εκατον (150), ενενηκοντα και εκατον (190), and ενενηκοντα και τριακοσιας (390), all pluses, indicate that the Greek tradition splintered into different interpretative calculations. These two considerations seem to indicate that the Greek scribes were responsible for the textual variance in these verses.

However, there are several indications that scribal activity occurred in the Hebrew stages and produced the present variant editions. Manuscript 96 shows how the Greek reading δυο in v. 5 could be the product of Hebrew activity. The scribe substituted שתי, the *feminine* construct form of שני for the masculine noun, עון, in order to guarantee the contested reading, "two punishments."[54] Later in v. 6, ms. 96 substitutes "Israel" for "Judah," perhaps to eliminate the problems with the "house of Israel" throughout the three verses. These two Hebrew variants show how generative interpretations occurred in Hebrew stages of scribal transmission. Further, an unusual density of Hebrew variance in v. 5, including an entire phrase in ms. 30, show there was fluidity in Hebrew stages. The obelus reading in v. 4 ενενηκοντα και εκατον (190) may also be adduced in support.[55]

Finally, Z is not the *lectio facilior*; MT also presents a similar interpretive scheme for its numbers. As Zimmerli points out, the number forty in v. 6 plays an important role in the Exodus narrative. In MT, "390" of v. 5 and "forty" of v. 6 add up to 430, which, given the context of Egypt, is probably a reference to the same number in Exodus 12:40.[56] While accurate arithmetic explained Z's readings, *meaningful* arithmetic can explain MT's variant numbers.

Zimmerli may be correct that the unspecified number in MT v. 4 מספר הימים "the number of days" was original to an early proto-type of the passage:[57]

---

[53] Brownlee notes that vv. 4–6 would make more sense in a different order—such that v. 5 was displaced from after v. 6, obscuring its role as the total of vv. 4 and 6. The displacement occurred so that Jerusalem (v. 7) could come immediately after Judah (v. 6)—preserving geography, but not arithmetic. Brownlee, *Ezekiel*, 1:64.

[54] Not common in Ezekiel, שתי in Ezek 35:10 refers to the two nations of Israel, similar to the sign act in Ezek 4:4–6. For the opposite position to my evaluation, see Cooke, *A Critical and Exegetical Commentary*, 64. On the issue of gender disagreement between numerals and their nouns, see Gesenius, *Hebrew Grammar*, §97a.

[55] Indeed, Z's 150 is probably the result of Greek activity "obtained by subtracting the 40 years of Judahs' captivity (v. 6) from the total 190." with Cooke, *A Critical and Exegetical Commentary*, 52.

[56] Zimmerli, *Ezekiel*, 1:167.

[57] Zimmerli, *Ezekiel*, 1:165–66.

It appears probable that we are not dealing with one single addition, made at one time, but that several phases of such activity are discernible. In the different numbers given in MT and LXX, which are not simple scribal errors, we can follow still further the interpretive work which molded the text.[58]

In sum, the disagreements among the witnesses show a protracted phase of scribal activity. Some of this variation could have occurred in the Greek process of transmission. However, it is clear that significant activity occurred in the Hebrew stages as well, especially the important development of "two punishments" as represented by the variant in ms. 96. The variants between the MT and LXX largely reflect variant Hebrew editions.[59]

4.3.3.2. Pseudo-Ezekiel: *A Variant Hebrew Literary Edition of Ezek 37:2–10*

In addition to the 12 verses just discussed for their relationship to the Hebrew, four variants in Ezekiel 37 will benefit from text-critical comparison with *Pseudo-Ezekiel*. *Pseudo-Ezekiel* was found in several copies among the Dead Sea Scrolls.[60] 4Q386 preserves the unambiguous evidence from three successive columns of the text whose sequence is based on Ezekiel. Its contents include a paraphrase of the valley of dried bones in column i, a gathering on the wasted land of Israel, and the oppressive threat of Belial

---

[58] Zimmerli, *Ezekiel*, 1:164.

[59] One suggestion is that the phrase at the end of v. 4 תשא את עונם (with copula in ZB rel.) could be the basis for MT's unique ותשעים in v. 5. There may also be a key to development of the different numbers in v. 4 with the obelus reading ενενηκοντα και εκατον "190" and 410's variant ενενηκοντα και τριακοσιας "390," both occurring in v. 5 of Z and MT, respectively.

[60] Devorah Dimant offers a reconstruction of the manuscripts and fragments in six columns to reflect one singular composition of *Pseudo-Ezekiel*. There are five fragments of *Pseudo-Ezekiel*: 4Q385, 4Q386, 4Q387, 4Q388, 4Q391. Dimant relies most heavily on 4Q385since its six fragments preserve a significant amount of *Pseudo-Ezekiel*. 4Q385, along with 4Q386 and 4Q388, includes the paraphrase of the vision of the dried bones, but their contents cover separate portions of Dimant's reconstructed text. See especially Dimant's graphic though partial reconstruction in Devorah Dimant, *Qumran Cave 4 XXI: Parabiblical Texts, Part 4: Pseudo-Prophetic Texts*, (DJD 30; Oxford: Clarendon Press, 2001), 18. Hartmut Steggemann proposed a different order for 4Q385's fragments wherein the valley of dried bones in fragment 2 appears in the last column of the work. Thus 4Q385 would represent a variant edition and sequence from 4Q386. Reference to Steggemann's work appears in D. Dimant and J. Strugnell, "4Q Second Ezekiel," *RevQ* 13 (1988): 45–46 n1a. I have not been able to locate his proposal elsewhere. Given the importance of this question, I will follow Dimant's reconstruction only of columns I–IV. "The reconstruction of cols. I–IV rests solely on material grounds, and therefore may be considered certain. The remaining columns in the restoration, designated cols. V–VI, lack this material certainty, but display other features which permit their placement in the sequence with a high degree of plausibility." Dimant, *Qumran Cave 4 XXI*, 19.

in column ii. 4Q385 also preserves the edition of Ezekiel 37. Because *Pseudo-Ezekiel* has been characterized as 'rewritten Scripture,'[61] it does not represent a 'textual witness' to Ezekiel in the traditional sense. However, rewritten scripture can still provide important text-critical information, especially in study of variant literary editions. Kristen De Troyer critiques the text-critical distinction between rewritten Scripture and Scripture, arguing that the same compositional effects we see in so-called 'rewritten Scripture' may closely resemble those we see *within* our canonical textual traditions.[62] The copies of *Pseudo-Ezekiel* found at Qumran are all written in Hebrew, a fact which underscores the kind of fluidity we have been exploring in the Hebrew text of Ezekiel. Since Ezekiel's text became an active site of scribal expansion, interpretation, and/or composition, a manuscript like *Pseudo-Ezekiel* holds important information for text-critical analysis of variant literary editions.[63] 4Q385 and 4Q386 are below compared with four variants from the *Tendenzen* data set: 37:4, 7, 9, and 10.

37:4 (4Q 385 line 5a and 4Q386 line 4)

MT	ויאמר אלי הנבא על העצמות
4Q385 and 4Q386	ויאמר בן אדם הנבא על העצמות
p967	και ειπεν προς με προφητευσον επι τα οστα

προφητευσον 967 ZB A V-449 Bo Aeth Or.IV 210 Tht.Tert.GregEl.Ambr.
Ir.[lat]Consult = הנבא MT] προφητευσον υιε ανθρωπου
L'-403 Or.XI 387 Lo. | προφητευσον υιε ανθρωπου
προφητευσον 26 544 613 | (obel. Q) υιε ανθρωπου
προφητευσον rel.

επι τα οστα ταυτα 967 Z rel. = העצמות האלה על MT] επι τα οστα ταυτα
προφητευσον υιε ανθρωπου V-449 Tht. | (minus)
L'-46 Or.XI 387 Lo.

---

[61] George Brooke includes both *Pseudo-Ezekiel* and the *Apocryphon of Jeremiah* in his discussion of rewritten Bible. Brooke, "Rewritten Bible," *Encyclopedia of the Dead Sea Scrolls* vol. 2, (eds. Lawrence H. Schiffman and James C. VanderKam; New York: Oxford University Press, 2000), 779.

[62] Working with George Nickelsburg's discussion of the terms, "rewritten," "expanded," and "supplements" in apocryphal literature, De Troyer notes that supplements resemble what textual critics call interpolations. She asks, "could some of these supplements not be seen simply as the further literary development of the biblical text itself?" While De Troyer does not apply this insight directly to the case of variant literary editions, her discussion pushes some of the boundaries that variant literary editions, by nature, defy. De Troyer, *Rewriting the Sacred Text*, 4.

[63] See also Dimant who edited *Pseudo-Ezekiel* for the DJD series and suggests that a host of unexplored manuscripts can help us further understand the types of "scribal interpretive functions" that would have produced variant literary editions. Devorah Dimant, "Literary Typologies," 73.

Both *Pseudo-Ezekiel* manuscripts contain the title בן אדם in place of MT's
אלי. Although transposed, the title is present in the L- and O-groups in a
plus over p967, B, and the MT. The title receives the obelus in manuscript
Q, which indicates that Origen considered it a faulty Greek reading. The
term בן אדם / υιε ανθρωπου is also transposed/plus in Greek witnesses to
37:9 and 12 as well.

The επι τα οστα minus in L remains a divergent reading, since על
העצמות is present in 4Q385 and 4Q386.

37:7 (4Q 385 frag. 2 line 5b and 4Q386 frag. 1 line 5)

MT   ותקרבו עצמות עצם אל עצמו
4Q385 and 4Q386   הקרבו עצם אל עצמו ופרק אל פרקו
p967   και προσηγαγεν τα οστα εκαστον προς τη αρμονιαν αυτου

τα οστα 967 Z rel. = העצמות HUBP[II-PirkeRE32(201) ≈ MasEzek]] (minus) HUBP[III-96] |
עצמות MT

εκαστον προς τη αρμονιαν αυτου 967 Z rel.] οστεον προς τη αρμονιαν αυτου
O (Q[mg]) C'-130'-239'-403' 410 Arab Arm | οστεον προς
οστεον εκαστον L[''-48-46] Tht. = עצם אל עצמו MT

The *Pseudo-Ezekiel* reading is strikingly different from MT and the versions. However, the Greek and Hebrew diverges enough to warrant the
comparison. Indeed, *Pseudo-Ezekiel* provides some important but partial
support for both Hebrew and Greek readings. It lacks העצמות like ms. 96;
it agrees with MT's עצם אל עצמו which is taken up in L's reading οστεον
προς οστεον εκαστον; and פרקו shows that Hebrew scribes produced the
reading present in p967: αρμονιαν αυτου "its joint."[64] These types of inner-
Hebrew variants demonstrate the probability that p967's variants were
present already in its Hebrew *Vorlage*.

37:9 (4Q 385 line 7b and 4Q386 line 8b)

MT   מארבע רוחות
4Q385 and 4Q386   על ארבע רחות השמי
p967   εκ των τεσσαρων σου πνευματω(ν)

σου πνευματω(ν) 967] πνευματων Z rel. = רוחות MT] ανεμων 407 36[txt]-V |
ανεμων του ουρανου A'' Arab Ambr.Spec.Aug.

---

64 Dimant, *Qumran Cave 4 XXI*.

Pseudo-Ezekiel השמים provides warrant for A's reading του ουρανου "of heaven". p967's unique σου remains unsupported.

37:10 (4Q385 lines 8–9 & 4Q386 lines 9b–9c–10)

MT	ויעמדו על רגליהם חיל גדול מאד מאד
4Q385 & 4Q386	ויעמד עם רב אנשים וברכו את יהוה צבאות אשר חים
p967	και εστησαν επι των ποδων αυτων συναγωγη πολλη σφοδρα

συναγωγη 967 Z rel.] δυναμις 87–91 Syh = *valentia* Tert. = חיל MT

πολλη 967 Z rel.] μεγαλη A''-106'-403' Bo Tert. = גדול MT

σφοδρα 967 Z rel.] σφοδρα (ast. O) σφοδρα O-62' 534 Arab Arm^p Hi. = מאד מאד MT

4Q385 and 4Q386 read עם רב אנשים instead of MT's חיל גדול מאד מאד. p967 Z rel.'s reading does not match either, although its term πολλη comes closer to רב then MT's גדול. While genetic textual agreement is not justified here, 4Q385 and 4Q386 prove that the term for *who* was raised in the bones-vision was in flux in the Hebrew literary tradition.

In 4Q385 and 4Q386, a unique plus follows וברכו את יהוה צבאות אשר חים "and they blessed the Lord of Hosts who brought them to life." This plus is not found in our manuscripts of Ezekiel. However, elements of it anticipate the literary *Tendenz* of p967's reading. p967 and Z rel.'s term συναγωγη is more in keeping with an act of blessing the Lord, which is described in 4Q385 and 4Q386's edition.

4.3.3.3. *Summary of Results*

I analyzed eighteen variants which support the argument that behind p967's text lies scribal activity in the Hebrew. In all eighteen instances, p967's reading is closest to the OG.

Fifteen cases definitely or arguably reflect two variant Hebrew texts for the Greek tradition: 4:4–6; 13:2; 24:10; 24:14; 27:16; 32:32; 36:5; 37:4; 37:7; 37:7; 37:9; 37:10; 39:11; and 39:28. The remaining three cases could possibly reflect variant Hebrew texts: 26:10; 32:30; and 37:10. In almost all of these cases, the MT represents the more developed text. Only in 24:10 and 37:9 can MT be considered the earliest reading.

4.4. Textual Discussion of 12:26–28, 32:24–26, and 36:23c–38

4.4.1. *Introduction*

The final text-critical objective of the present chapter is to evaluate the case for error in p967's text. Specific attention must be paid to 12:26–28, 32:24–26, and 36:23c–38. These three variants serve as 'intertextual centers' in chapter 5's literary analysis. Hence, their status as 'intentional' or what I call 'viable' textual readings requires analysis and defense.

4.4.2. *Ezek 12:26–28*

p967

²⁵ διοτι εγω κς λαλησω τους λογους μου λαλησω και ποιησω και ου μη μηκυνω ετι οτι εν ταις ημερας υμων οικος ο παραπικραινων λαλησω λογον και ποιησω λεγει κυριος ²⁶⁻²⁸ (minus)

¹³:¹⁻² και εγενετο λογος κυριου προς με λεγων υιε ανθρωπου

MT

²⁵ כי אני יהוה אדבר את אשר אדבר דבר ויעשה לא תמשך עוד כי בימיכם בית המרי אדבר דבר ועשיתיו נאם אדני יהוה ²⁶ ויהי דבד יהוה אלי לאמר ²⁷ בן אדם הנה בית ישראל אמרים החזון אשר הוא חזה לימים רבים ולעתים רחוקות הוא נבא ²⁸ לכן אמר אליהם כה אמר אדני יהוה לא תמשך עוד כל דברי אשר אדבר דבר ויעשה נאם אדני יהוה

¹³:¹⁻²ויהי דבר יהוה אלי לאמר בן אדם

Floyd Filson's 1943 study made the case for error in p967's text, pointing out the repeated phrases in 12:25bβ–12:27aα' and 12:28–13:2aα' (...ועש נאם אדני יהוה ויהי דבר יהוה אלי לאמר בן אדם) for a total of 11 words.[65] According to Filson, the scribe of p967 omitted the verses through parablepsis.[66] When Jahn re-published p967^Köln, he independently agreed that the omission was "per *homoioteleuton*."[67] Filson suggests that such an error may have been facilitated by the fact that the verses *might* have

---

[65] Filson, "Omission," 28.

[66] Filson follows JGK's general observation that the p967 manuscript contains many errors through omission. However, the present study evaluates several of these "omissions" differently.

[67] Jahn, *Der Griechische Text*, 23. For a thorough presentation of the commentaries on this passage, some with awareness of the issue presented by p967, see Lust, "Major Divergences," 86 n86.

filled nearly an entire column.[68] However, I agree with Lust that that this later consideration is of little to no text-critical value since the conjecture is probably materially incorrect.[69] Nevertheless, the *homoioteleuton* argument is quite strong for this variant and understandably holds many adherents.[70]

Lust mounted counter-arguments with equal merit.[71] He adduced literary and linguistic features to support the integrity of p967's text.[72] For discussion of Lust's literary arguments, see chapter 5 of the present study (§5.2.1). Indeed, the literary arguments against text-critical evaluations for error in p967's text are strong. Thus, an argument for an *erroneous* minus is weakened, although adjudication between literary and textual arguments is not straight-forward.

In addition to a literary argument, Lust found linguistic reasons to see the section as a late addition to the Hebrew text. Four specific phrases occur within the MT plus—"vision" (חזון), "times" (עתים), and "for many years ahead" (לימים רבים)—appear only in later works like Daniel, and Chronicles.[73] Moreover, "for distant times" (לעתים רחוקות) is a *hapax*.[74]

Textual critics have also long noted the difficulty in v. 28 with the phrase לא תמשך עוד כל דברי אשר אדבר דבר ויעשה. Syntactically problematic, לא תמשך is repeated from v. 25 where it is often called "formally neutral."[75] However, this explanation only mollifies the textual difficulty. At issue is the 3fs conjugation of the verb תמשך without a corresponding subject in either context. In v. 25, the 1cs divine speech yields to the 3ms subject דָּבָר once, but the noun requires a 3ms conjugation. Likewise, in v. 28, two options for the subject present themselves. Syntactically,

---

[68] Filson adduces the speculative reconstruction, by JGK, that the dimensions of p967's base-text indicated that the present minus filled a little over a column; however, the speculative nature of his evidence renders the argument untrustworthy. Filson, "The Omission," 28. See Johnson, Gehman, and Kase, *The John H. Sheide Biblical Papyri*, 8.

[69] See Lust, "Textual Criticism of the Old and New Testaments," 24–25.

[70] Several scholars have taken up Filson's evaluation for error in p967, including Brownlee's critical, eclectic translation on the basis of Filson's 1943 study. Brownlee, *Ezekiel*, 1:182. See also Zimmerli, *Ezekiel*, 1:283.

[71] While p967 is alone among the witnesses, La^W, which frequently supports p967 minuses, does not preserve this section.

[72] Lust, "Major Divergences," 85–86; idem, "Textual Criticism of the Old and New Testaments," 24–26.

[73] Lust is careful to point out that "vision" is not a new term, but has the connotations common of later apocalyptic works. Lust, "Textual Criticism of the Old and New," 26.

[74] For Lust's analysis of the Greek of this passage, see ibid., 26.

[75] So Zimmerli, *Ezekiel*, 1:283; see also Ehrlich, *Randglossen*, 43; Cooke, *A Critical and Exegetical Commentary*, 137.

כָּל דְּבָרֵי ought to serve as the subject. However, the *nomen regens* כָּל is an attribute of the genitive, such that "the predicate usually agrees in gender and number with the genitive," which in this case is a masculine plural noun.[76] The other option is syntactically problematic: דָּבָר stands in the following clause; however, as in v. 25, it is a masculine singular noun.

The phrase in question, לא תמשך עוד כל דברי אשר אדבר דבר ויעשה in v. 28 is not present in the A-group manuscript 410. Many critics evaluate for error in 410's text.[77] However, 410's 'error' may reflect the grammatical difficulty with the phrase. As a divergent minus from p967, 410's reading could stand as a textually independent witness to the difficulty with v. 28b. Thus three textual factors warrant further inquiry into the reliability of p967 as an early witness: Lust's late linguistic argument, the case of the verb תמשך, and the independent reading of 410.

Formally, the literary unit that begins in 12:17 is structured by the phrase και εγενετο λογος κυριου προς με λεγων υιε ανθροπου which is repeated four times (12:17, 21, 26, and 13:1). Each instance serves as the introduction to a new disputation on the subject of prophecy. p967's text omits the entire third section running from vv. 26–28. The argument from form *counters* Filson's argument for *homoioteleuton* given the form-critical role of the phrase in question.

Verses 27–28, the content of the third disputation, are largely a catena of phrases and words from the immediate context. According to Zeigler's Greek text, v. 27 includes four common theme-words from its surrounding context: ορασις (vv. 22, 23), ημερας (vv. 22, 23, 25), καιρους (v. 23 in L), and μακρους (v. 22). Verse 28, the disputation, offers even greater repetition; whole phrases repeat from the context:

v. 28aα	δια τουτο ειπον προς αυτους ταδε λεγει κυριος
v. 23aα	δια τουτο ειπον προς αυτους ταδε λεγει κυριος
v. 19aα	και ερεις προς τον λαον της γης ταδε λεγει κυριος
v. 28aβ	ου μη μηκυνωσιν ουκετι
v. 25bα	ου μη μηκυνω ετι
v. 28bβ	λαλησω λαλησω και ποιησω λεγει κυριος
v. 25bβ	λαλησω λογον και ποιησω λεγει κυριος
v. 25aβ	λαλησω και ποιησω

---

[76] Gesenius, *Hebrew Grammar*, §146c. In the cases of exception, the verb is masculine.

[77] Ziegler's apparatus attributes 410's omitted phrase to *homoioteleuton*; however, this would place the burden of paraplepsis on the largely dissimilar כה אמר אדני יהוה and נאם אדני יהוה, weakening the basis for his evaluation.

The Hebrew of v. 28 runs even more closely with the parallel phrases listed above: תִּמְשֵׁךְ lies beneath both μηκυνωσιν (v. 28aβ) and μηκυνω (v. 25bα), and אֲדַבֵּר דָּבָר lies beneath both λαλησω λαλησω (v. 28bβ) and λαλησω λογον (v. 25bβ). The Hebrew, like the Greek, also preserves the perfect repetition between vv. 28aα and 23aα. Thus three shared phrases suggest that v. 28 is constructed from material lifted from its surrounding context, either directly or mediated as glosses.

In short, v. 28 is quite probably a later addition, especially in light of its content, which is repeated from the context. The previous textual, form, and redactional considerations support the view that p967 represents a phase when vv. 26–28 did not yet appear in Ezekiel 12. As I will demonstrate below (§4.4.3) a possible rationale for the insertion of the verses might be found in the word-play with the verb משך "Meshech." The plus material in MT v. 28 affirms that God's word would not *meshech* (stretch out) any longer.

4.4.3. *Ezek 32:24–26*

32:24bβ—26

p967 ^{24bβ} οι δεδωκοτες τον φοβον αυτων επι της ζωης αυτων (39-<u>word minus</u>)
        ^{26bα} παντες απεριτμητοι τραυματιαι απο μαχαιρας οι δεδωκοτες τον φοβον
        αυτων επι γης ζωης

B ^{24bβ} οι δεδωκοτες τον φοβον αυτων επι της ζωης αυτων και ελαβοσαν την
        βασανον αυτων μετα των καταβαινοντων εις βοθρον ^{25} εν μεσω τραυματιων
        (<u>24-word minus</u>) ^{26} εκει εδοθησαν μοσοχ και θοβελ και πασα η ισχυς
        αυτων περικυκλω του μνηματος αυτου παντες τραυματιαι αυτου παντες
        απεριτμητοι τραυματιαι απο μαχαιρας

L" 62' ^{24bβ} οι δεδωκοτες τον φοβον αυτων επι της ζωης αυτων και ελαβοσαν την
        βασανον αυτων μετα των καταβαινοντων εις βοθρον ^{25} εν μεσω τραυματιων
        εδοθη κοιτη αυτης συν παντι τω πληθει εκαστου περικυκλω η ταφη αυτων
        (+ παντων) απεριτμητων τραυματιων μαχαιρα (<u>13-word minus</u>) ^{26} εκει
        εδοθησαν μοσοχ και θοβελ και πασα η ισχυς αυτων περικυκλω του μνημα-
        τος αυτου παντες τραυματιαι αυτου παντες απεριτμητοι τραυματιαι απο
        μαχαιρας

MT ^{24}אֲשֶׁר נָתְנוּ חִתִּיתָם בְּאֶרֶץ חַיִּים וַיִּשְׂאוּ כְלִמָּתָם אֶת יוֹרְדֵי בוֹר ^{25}בְּתוֹךְ
        חֲלָלִים נָתְנוּ מִשְׁכָּב לָהּ בְּכָל הֲמוֹנָהּ סְבִיבוֹתָיו קִבְרֹתֶהָ כֻּלָּם עֲרֵלִים
        חַלְלֵי חֶרֶב כִּי נִתַּן חִתִּיתָם בְּאֶרֶץ חַיִּים וַיִּשְׂאוּ כְלִמָּתָם אֶת יוֹרְדֵי בוֹר
        בְּתוֹךְ חֲלָלִים נִתָּן ^{26}שָׁם מֶשֶׁךְ תֻּבָל וְכָל הֲמוֹנָהּ סְבִיבוֹתָיו קִבְרוֹתֶיהָ
        כֻּלָּם עֲרֵלִים מְחֻלְלֵי חֶרֶב כִּי נָתְנוּ חִתִּיתָם בְּאֶרֶץ חַיִּים

p967 lacks 39 words of MT's text in 32:24bβ–26. While only p967 lacks this much text, it is partially supported by B's 24-word minus in overlapping material. p967's text is certainly connected with the evidence not only from B, but also from L's 13-word minus. Previous textual study has only focused on B's minus, but a rehearsal of that discussion will prove helpful towards understanding p967's text.

B lacks most of v. 25. Ziegler considered B the OG reading in his critical text. Previous textual explanations accepted Ziegler's estimation that B represented the OG and sought to explain only the extra MT material in v. 25 from נתנו משכב לה to the end. Because v. 25 is variously represented in the versions, Zimmerli proposes that it is a doublet of secondary status, derived from v. 26 and v. 24. Indeed, the material in v. 25 is highly repetitive; vv. 25 and 26 are especially similar as the following table shows:

	v. 25	v. 26
aα	בתוך חללים נתנו	שם
aβ	משכב לה בכל המונה	משך תבל וכל המונה
aγ	סביבותיו קברתה	סביבותיו קברותיה
bα	כלם ערלים חללי חרב	כלם ערלים מחללי חרב
bβ	כי נתן חתיתם בארץ חיים	כי נתנו חתיתם בארץ חיים
bγ	וישאו כלמתם את יורדי בור בתוך חללים נתן	
bδ	בתוך חללים נתן	

In direct contrast to Zimmerli, Allen, following Rost, considers v. 26 the secondary verse, added as an annotation on v. 25 and comprised of corrections.[78] Allen tabulates 6 variants in v. 26, showing how they could be viewed as a corrected edition of v. 25. Allen presents his argument for reconstruction thoroughly, and not without evidence. Here follows my rendering of his data:[79]

(i) בתוך חללים נתנו. v. 25aα בתוך חללים נתנו and v. 25bδ בתוך חללים נתן: נתן for נתנו.
(ii) משך תבל in v. 26aβ for the graphically similar משכב לה in v. 25aβ.
(iii) בכל המונה. v. 25aβ וכל המונה and v. 26aβ בכל: וכל for בכל.
(iv) סביבותיו קברותיה and v. 25aγ סביבותיו קברתה: קברתה for קברותיה קברתה.

---

[78] Allen, citing the 1904 work of Rost, argues that "v. 25a-bγ was heavily annotated and now stands as v. 25bδ–26." Allen, *Ezekiel*, 2:135 n25a.

[79] I follow Allen's enumeration, but the versification is my own, consistent with the preceding table.

(v)   What Allen calls a mistaken correction, מחללי for the preferred חללי:
      v. 26bα מחללי חרב and v. 25bα חללי חרב.

(vi) נתנו for נתן: v. 26bβ כי נתנו חתיתם and in 25bβ כי נתן חתיתם.

In fact, there is manuscript support for five of Allen's six variants, most
obviously for (iii), (v), and (vi). Three HUBP Hebrew variants in v. 25 show
the corrections offered by v. 26 which Allen postulated:

(iii) in v. 25aβ   בכל MT] וכל HUBP[III-96 150] (cf. v. 26aβ)
(v)   in v. 25bα[80] חללי MT] מחללי HUBP[III-30] (cf. v. 26bα)
(vi) in v. 25bβ   נִתַּן[1st] MT] נתנו HUBP[96 G-BEb 10(pm) Eb 16] (cf. v. 26bβ) | נָתַן HUB-
                      P[III-G-BEb(sm?) 10]

Textual information indirectly supports (i) and (ii) as well.

(i)   in v. 26aα

      שם משך MT] εκει εδοθησαν μοσοχ Z rel. | (minus in context 967)

In v. 26aα, εδοθησαν is a plus in all Greek witnesses (except p967 which
does not contain its material). The reconstructed phrase in Hebrew would
thus be שם נִתְּנוּ משך. The reconstructed נִתְּנוּ obviates Allen's suggestion
that v. 25bδ corrects v. 25aα. Instead, v. 26aα שם נִתְּנוּ משך corrects v. 25aα
בתוך חללים נתנו, harmonizing with the formally consistent (ה)שם found
also in vv. 22, 24, 29, and 30 for the national population register.[81]

(ii) in v. 26aβ

      משך תבל וכל MT] μοσοχ και θοβελ και πασα Z rel. (cf. MT +
                      copula) | *cubile eorum* Hi. σ'θ' (HUBP[V-recon.]
                      משכבם/משכב להם) cf. v. 25aβ

Jerome, represented in Symmachus and Theodotian reads *cubile eorum*,
which HUBP[V] reconstructs as משכבם/משכב להם. The similarity with v.
25aβ משכב לה is striking, and strongly supports my earlier proposal that
the MT reading משך תבל was either a correction or a word-play on v.
25aβ.

From the text-critical discussion and density of evidence, Allen's proposal is probably correct, that v. 26 is the later addition, based on v. 25. It
is quite possible that משכב לה in v. 25 provided the opportunity to add
Meshech and Tubal to the population of the pit, and thus occasioned the
Hebrew addition. This type of scribal innovation should not surprise. As

---

[80] Despite Allen's determination that מחללי was a mistake, ms. 30 shows it as a variant
for חללי, in keeping with the same in v. 26.

[81] The extraneous בתוך חללים נתן found in v. 25bδ may have been the introduction
to v. 26 before the speculated משכבם became משך תבל.

Block points out, Ezekiel has a "penchant for using words with more than one sense in a given context."[82] The idea that later scribes would capitalize on the double significations of language like משכב / משך is in keeping with the style of the book of Ezekiel.

As for Zimmerli's evaluation, it is less likely to be correct. However, the Greek witnesses in v. 25, p967, B, and L require an explanation. It is most probable that the three witnesses represent three stages of growth, from the 39-word minus of p967 to the 24-word minus of B to the 13-word minus of L. As v. 25 grew longer through in-line additions, the marginal corrections were absorbed, explaining the origins of v. 26. These stages likely reflect the stages of growth in the Hebrew of the proto-MT.

4.4.4. *Ezek 36:23c–38*

We have already mentioned the arguments for error in the case of p967's minus of 36:23c–38 in chapter 2 (§2.5). The Princeton editors, Filson, Wevers, and Spottorno argued for various mechanical explanations for the omission which were found unsatisfactory.[83] Filson makes the case that the scribe of p967's text is the culprit of the omission.[84] Hence, his argument requires parablepsis of *p967's* last line in v. 23b with the end of v. 38:

v. 23b in p967	και γνωσεται τα εθνη οτι εγω ειμι κυριος
v. 38b in A	και γνωσονται οτι εγω ειμι κυριος
v. 38b in BQ	και γνωσονται οτι εγω κυριος

Filson reveals his arguments' own weaknesses in his discussion. First, he states, "in some way which we cannot reconstruct with certainty, the scribe was led by *homoioteleuton* to omit 36:23c–38."[85] In this statement, he implied his previously discussed proposals for a scribe skipping a page or for a lost leaf in p967's parent codex. In fact, the correlation of *both* a lost leaf *and homoioteleuton* seems quite unlikely. This would require that the exact phrases perfectly aligned atop two separate columns of Greek text. Second, Filson overstates the case for the extent of the phrase for *homoioteleuton*. He claims:

---

[82] Block, *The Book of Ezekiel*, 2:469.

[83] J.W. Wevers, *Ezekiel* (NCB; London: Nelson, 1969), 273. M.V. Spottorno, "La omisión de Ez. 36, 23b–38 y la transposición de capítulos en el papiro 967," *Emerita* 50 (1981): 93–99.

[84] Filson, "Omission," 31.

[85] Ibid., 31.

the fact that the part of verse 23 which it [p967] does contain ends with words which are identical with the ending of v. 38 in A and almost identical (the last word *is* identical) with the ending of verse 38 in B and Q.[86]

A's reading is not identical with p967, though they do share the last four words (οτι εγω ειμι κυριος). p967 contains the term τα εθνη in v. 23b, which is lacking in v. 38 of BAQ. Not only are the phrases in p967 and BAQ dissimilar, B's reading in v. 38b diverges even further from A's. B is the closest text-type to p967's and would more likely correspond to p967's parent text. Hence, Filson's *homoioteleuton* argument is weakened for its basis in A. Additionally, Lust argues that an omission of 1451 letters is unprecedented for parablepsis in Ezekiel's text.[87] The appeal to *homoioteleuton* is, therefore, unsatisfactory.[88]

The second set of arguments for error in p967 which carry some merit concern the break at v. 23b. Block raised the question as to whether the oracle in 36:16–23b is sufficiently long to be an oracular unit unto itself. In p967, 36:16–23b serves as the final utterance before ch. 38 and the Gog-Magog oracles. Block argues that leaving these eight verses alone makes for a "very short, fragmentary oracle" that is "bland and truncated."[89] According to Block, vv. 23c–38 extend the chapter into an oracle of sufficient length, and therefore must have been original to ch. 36. However, as Lust points out, vv. 16–23b is by no means the shortest oracle in Ezekiel. Immediately preceding it, vv. 13–15 comprise a two-verse oracle unit.[90] Crane adds multiple other cases of short oracles in Ezekiel.[91] Further, in Lust's 1981 study, he adduces the evidence from the Coptic-Sahidic manuscript published by A. Erman.[92] Among its three complete Ezekiel oracles, the manuscript contains 36:16–23b as a stand-alone oracular unit. This evidence confirms, at the very least, that these short verses could be taken as

---

[86] Ibid., 31.

[87] Lust, "Ezekiel 36–40," 520.

[88] For an extended and thorough discussion of these arguments, see Crane, *Israel's Restoration*, 211–216. Crane finally agrees with Lust that p967's omission is not erroneous.

[89] Block, *The Book of Ezekiel*, 2:341.

[90] Lust also challenges Block's "truncated" critique, that 36:16–23b does not articulate how Yhwh will vindicate his holiness. The silence is equally true of vv. 13–15. This oracle also lacks word of how Yhwh will fulfill his promises. Lust, "Textual Criticism of the Old and New Testaments," 30.

[91] Crane, *Israel's Restoration*, 295.

[92] A. Erman, "Bruchstücke der oberägyptischen Übersetzung des Alten Testaments," in *Gesellschaft der Wissenschaften zu Göttingen, Nachrichten* (Göttingen: Vandenhoeck & Ruprecht, 1880).

an independent oracular unit, and provides further evidence that Ezekiel
originally lacked 36:23c–38.[93]

A related concern was raised with the separation of content between
v. 23b and c.

MT   v. 23a   וקדשתי את שמי הגדול המחלל בגוים אשר הללתם בתוכם
     v. 23b   וידעו הגוים כי אני יהוה נאם אדני יהוה
     v. 23c   בהקדשי בכם לעיניהם

All manuscripts contain the 'recognition formula' וידעו הגוים כי אני יהוה /
και γνωσεται τα εθνη οτι εγω ειμι κς . Immediately following, נאם אדני יהוה
appears in verse 23b in the MT, but λεγει αδωναι κυριος, well supported by
the versions, is missing in p967. The combined formulas mark the end of
the oracle in 36:16–23b, and, as Lust states, "the 'recognition formula' followed by *ne'um Yhwh* in v. 23b makes a good conclusion."[94] According to
Lust's argument, the Hebrew scribe responsible for the MT provided the
preceding material with a suitable formulaic ending (doubling the prophetic ending with the declarative formula) before adding the new oracular material in vv. 23c–38. The double formula was taken up in all Greek
manuscripts except p967. p967's text testifies to the earlier oracle, which,
according to Lust, ended only with the recognition formula.

Lust's reasoning about the double formula raised a critique from Block
who shows that the 'recognition formula' can often appear in the *middle*
of an oracle in Ezekiel.[95] Block tried to eradicate the significance of the
formal oracle unit in MT vv. 16–23b by showing that such formulae do not
always signify an ending. However, Block misses the point. The reading at
issue is not the *recognition* formula alone, but the addition of the *declarative* formula, which constitutes the variant between the MT and p967.
Lust's original point was that the *combination* of the 'recognition' and
'declarative' formulas makes for a fitting conclusion.[96] Crane carries Lust's
point further and shows that the combined 'recognition' and 'declarative'
formulas *never* appear in the middle of an oracle in Ezekiel.[97]

Additionally, several factors argue *for* p967's text. First, H. St. J. Thackeray's
linguistic analysis of 36:24–38 concluded that its text-type was foreign
to all but Theodotian's text. Two of his examples: (1) in 36:24, הארצות

[93] Lust, "Ezekiel 36–40," 525.
[94] Ibid.
[95] Block, *The Book of Ezekiel*, 2:340.
[96] Lust, "Textual Criticism of the Old and New," 29.
[97] Crane, *Israel's Restoration*, 290–291.

is translated τῶν γαιων/γεων in BAQ where χωραι would be expected. Indeed, Theodotian employs γαια again in Ezek 29:12 against LXX's χωρα. (2) In v. 25, גַּן עֵדֶן is translated κηπος τρυφης in θ' and BAQ. However in this construction, גַּן is always rendered with παραδεισος in BAQ; only in Theodotian is κηπος τρυφης repeatedly used (cf. Ezek 28:13; 31:8).[98]

Second, the linguistic argument applies to the Hebrew of 36:23c–38 as well. Thackeray pointed to several *hapax legomena* in this section of text,[99] and late linguistic features such as אָנֹכִי "I" in v. 28, מַעֲלָל "deed" in v. 31, תַּחַת אֲשֶׁר "instead" in v. 34, and הַלָּזוּ "this" in v. 35.[100] Lust telescopes the significance of this fact, pointing out that 36:23c–38

> has the character of an anthology. Most of its expressions are to be found elsewhere in Ezekiel. In such a pericope one does not expect to find so many *hapax legomena*.[101]

Lust adds to these examples a short study of the correspondences between 36:23c–38 and Deuteronomistic language in Jeremiah.[102]

Third, and especially interesting for the present project, are the three cases Lust identifies in which linguistic correspondence may be found between 36:23c–38 and other MT pluses. Lust's clearest example draws on the shorter text in LXX and especially on P.M. Bogaert's evidence in the Latin witnesses.[103] The MT plus in 34:31 אָדָם אַתֶּם, "you are men," occurs in the context of a promise oracle using a parable about Israel dispersed and gathered as sheep. This addition corresponds with the phrase in 36:37 כְּצֹאן אָדָם, "like a flock of men," where the pastoral metaphor also applies to restored Israel.

Fourth, the MT plus begins in v. 23b with נְאֻם אֲדֹנָי יהוה. As the *Tendenzen* of the present project reveal, the formulae for divine speech comprise a larger set of variants in prophetic formulae across the text of Ezekiel. Especially important are the four instances in which a prophetic formula marks the beginning of a more significant MT plus. The MT plus in 43:12, הִנֵּה זֹאת תּוֹרַת הַבָּיִת begins with the formula "behold!" The MT plus in

---

[98] See Thackeray, "The Greek Translators," 407.

[99] Thackeray, *The Septuagint and Jewish Worship*, 126.

[100] Taken from Zimmerli's review of the four most impressive cases. Zimmerli, *Ezekiel*, 2:245.

[101] Lust, "Ezekiel 36–40," 521–522.

[102] Ibid., 522–524. So also Nicholson, who demonstrates connections between Ezekiel 36 and Jeremianic passages where Dtr. influence is most probable: Jeremiah 31:31–34; 32:37–40. E.W. Nicholson, *Preaching to the Exiles: A Study of the Prose Tradition in the Book of Jeremiah* (Oxford: Blackwell, 1970), 81–84.

[103] Bogaert, "Le témoigne de la Vetus Latina," 390–391.

36:23b נאם אדני יהוה והשיבו וחיו begins with the formula for a divine say-ing, the same phrase which opens 36:23c–38. Finally, MT's 28–word plus in 33:25 opens with the divine messenger formula כה אמר אדני יהוה. Thus, a certain coherence in form exists among these MT pluses which begin with a prophetic form.

Fifth, the above introduction to the *Tendenzen* (chapter 3) shows that the alignment for the recognition formula was highly divergent among the witnesses. p967, MT and B all contain independent occurrences of the phrase against the other two. The MT plus in 36:23c–38 supplies the con-tent for the nation-recognition formula, clarifying the event which would produce recognition. The fluidity of the formula elsewhere supports view-ing it similarly here at the beginning of the textual variant.

Sixth, Lust rightly points out the requirement on textual critics to con-sider p967's edition, lacking of 36:23c–38, together with its unique chapter order.[104] The fifth century Latin manuscript Wirceburgensis shows p967's chapter order for Ezekiel 37–39.[105] La[W] is an independent witness giving stronger support to p967's text. On the basis of the length of the non-extant sections, P.M. Bogaert observes that the Latin manuscript probably also lacked 36:23c–38, which would provide otherwise unattested manu-script support for p967's minus.

Finally, it should be noted that the content of all three pluses discussed in the present section (12:26–28; 32:24–26; 36:23c–38) are phrases repeated from elsewhere in Ezekiel. In preceding discussions, I showed that 12:25 probably served as the basis for most of 12:28, and that 32:26 was copied almost word-for word from 32:25. Ezekiel 36:23–38 is also highly repetitive of material from elsewhere in Ezekiel. The full comparison is taken up in chapter 5's literary discussion (especially §5.4.1), but is well recognized by most critics.[106] In addition, all three variants show some connection to the term "Meshech." While the term does not occur in 36:23c–38, it is signifi-cant to the transposition of chs. 38–39, a textual feature that is arguably connected to 36:23c–38.

One may conclude that p967 is a viable edition of Ezekiel 36. The real debate now should be whether p967 is a reliabile witness to an early Hebrew *Vorlage*. Some data concerning this issue have been presented above.

---

[104] Lust, "Ezekiel 36–40," 520.
[105] Johnson Gehman, and Kase, *The John H. Scheide Biblical Papyri*, 11–13, 42–48; Bogaert, "Le témoignage de la Vetus Latina," 384–395; Lust, "The Sequence of Ez," 45–46.
[106] See Lust and Zimmerli, op. cit.

Thackeray's linguistic argument suggests that 36:23c–38 was not in OG. Rather, it was inserted into the Greek tradition based on an edition like Theodotian's. Although circumstantial, additional evidence suggests that the Hebrew *Vorlage* also lacked the passage. Thackeray and Lust's work with the late linguistic features and *hapax legomena* in the Hebrew of 36:23c–38 as well as the later Jeremianic language suggests redaction in the Hebrew textual tradition. Finally, the plus in 36:23c–38 participates in a trend within the MT to begin plus material with a prophetic formula (See chapter 5 §5.2.3.)

Only one piece of evidence could suggest activity in the Greek text-tradition; it is the use of the recognition formula. Because B, MT, and p967 show such divergent alignment in pluses or readings with this formula, a unique problem presents itself. A text-critical explanation for the variety may not be possible. However, the phenomena seem inter-related in ways that other literary variants are not, as if the Greek and Hebrew scribal traditions remained in active flux about the instances which occasioned knowledge of the divine.

4.5. Conclusions

Before drawing text-critical conclusions from the preceding analysis, I want to accurately reflect on the specific data set. The data set is comprised of variants that participate in literary *Tendenzen*, which I will examine from a literary perspective in chapter 5. Any text-critical conclusions offered here apply only to those variants which demonstrably differentiate p967 from MT's edition. The text-critical analysis above is contingent on the success of the literary arguments in chapter 5. Taken together, the two chapters offer a stratum or strata of variants which most likely result from scribal activity. Thus, the conclusions here reflect text-critical observations about the variant literary editions.

First, p967's meaningful variants do not support mechanical arguments for error. The three variants in 32:24–26 and 36:23c–38 (as well as the transposition of chapters in 37–39) offer no evidence to otherwise discount p967's witness as a text of Ezekiel. Further, none of the 45 minor variants analyzed in this chapter presented a case for mechanical error in p967's text. In the final analysis, an exclusively textual argument for error in 12:26–28 still holds some merit,[107] but far more often, p967

---

[107] In addition to the arguments mounted above in §4.4.2, a set of variants in the MT that display coherence with 12:26–28 (presented in chapter 5 §5.2.2.1) leads me to conclude

demonstrated itself to be a reliable witness to Ezekiel, what I have called a 'viable' text.

Second, text-critical analysis did not overwhelmingly clarify the relationship between p967 and B. Previous scholarship already held that the two witnesses best reflect the Old Greek and yet frequently diverge from one another. While no great advances have been made on these conclusions, some light was shed on a few specific issues. More often than not, a variant Hebrew text lay beneath the divergence between B and p967, (see 11 examples in §4.3.2). This trend is striking. It implies a close connection between the Greek textual tradition (both the OG and subsequent corrections), and the developing Hebrew text. Inner-Greek error only accounts for two of the divergent readings: both of B's mistakes in 24:9 and 39:11. In a few cases, it was possible to discern which text was likely corrected back to the more developed Hebrew text represented by MT: three times in p967 and twice in B. Perhaps most importantly, B represented the more strongly supported reading over isolated p967 pluses in 35:8; 38:20; 38:18; and 39:4. While B is certainly to be trusted in these four cases, the origin of p967's reading cannot be known from the available textual data, especially given other evidence supporting p967's reliability and relationship to the Hebrew. This leads directly to the next conclusion.

Third, p967's readings frequently reflect a variant Hebrew *Vorlage*. Of the 45 minor variants analyzed above, p967 could arguably reflect a variant Hebrew *Vorlage* 39 times, many with considerable certainty.

Fourth, at many points, MT appears to reflect a more developed textual stage of Ezekiel beyond that of the Old Greek. The weight of evidence from Origen's asterisks indicates that the MT readings are developed beyond OG: in 63 out of 64 cases. MT presents an isolated reading, unsupported by any of the Versions, 68 times; p967 just 31 times. Additionally, OG could be shown to reflect a variant Hebrew *Vorlage* from MT with great certainty; in all 18 cases, the MT was best explained as the more developed text (see §4.3.3).

An enduring question that remains is: how often does p967 represent an innovative text in the Greek tradition? A case can be made for this position, namely that p967 results from inner-Greek development. In 35:8,

---

that even in 12:26–28, p967 represents a viable text in which the verses did not appear. So while I recognize that text-critical arguments for error are warranted, the weight of evidence from multiple angles of analysis, including form and redaction-criticism, along with the wider scope of thematically related variants, present the better case in favor of p967's text.

p967 presents a one-word plus; in 38:20, a 10-word plus; and in 39:4, a 7-word plus. These unique, likely inner-Greek pluses along with p967's essentially unsupported minuses in 12:26–28; 32:26; and 36:23c–38 could indicate the maverick status of p967's Greek text. It *is* possible for a manuscript to have an Old Greek text-type, strongly reflect a Hebrew *Vorlage*, and yet still be a developed Greek literary edition.[108] In point of fact, p967 Daniel fits this description. Its text-type is Old Greek but its literary edition reflects Theodotian's LXX Daniel. Thus, p967's unique pluses and minuses in 35:8; 38:20; 39:4; 12:26–28; 32:26; and 36:23c–38 could reflect inner-Greek development on a very early text-type of Ezekiel. However, in Ezekiel, this is probably not the case for two major reasons.

First, the above analysis did not examine p967's text-type primarily but rather sets of meaningful variants characterized by literary *Tendenzen*. According to the coherence approach, described in chapter 3, the nature of the data set already presupposes compositional issues, not solely transmissional ones. In light of the inherent compositional possibilities in this data set, p967's imunity from arguments for error takes on increased significance; p967's readings are reliable in 41 of 45 minor variants. So while *four* isolated variants could reflect inner-Greek development, *eight* isolated variants showed that p967 could reflect a variant Hebrew text (see §4.3.1). This means that in 8 out of 13 instances (62%), an isolated p967 reading reflects not a developed Greek text, but a variant Hebrew *Vorlage*.

Second, the discussions in §4.4 showed that 36:23c–38 and 32:26 were not inner-Greek developments. Rather they were probably Hebrew developments with p967 reflecting its shorter Hebrew *Vorlage*. Analysis of 12:26–28 suggested the same.

One outstanding problem that is raised by this chapter is: how do critics adjudicate between types of arguments in the case of variant literary editions. In the analyses of §4.4, several types of arguments apply to p967's major textual variants. Linguistic, formal, redactional, and exegetical analysis revealed information obscured by text-critical analysis alone. For example, in 12:26–28, the *homoioteleuton* argument suggested a possible parablepsis, however on the basis of the exact phrases that provide the unit its formal structure. From an exclusively textual point of view, the data point to a mistaken omission. However, from a formal and redactional point of view, the data point to the insertion of a similar formal

---

[108] Refer to chapter 2's discussion of Gehmans' work for the correlation of p967's text type with a Hebrew *Vorlage* different from the MT.

unit, suggesting that p967's shorter text reflects the earlier edition of the disputations. In the case of 32:24–26, the issue was easier to decide in favor of p967's text. 32:24–26 provided no strong argument for textual error; on the contrary, the versions presented many different readings of the verses which probably signal a fluid textual tradition. In addition, the Hebrew data provided evidence for diachronic development. Finally, textual data showing correction of the letters משך hinted at a redactional rationale for editorial activity: the character of "Meshech".

Adjudication among options requires a strongly weighted matrix of evidence. The case of 36:23c–38 is exemplary: after several considerations, the weight of evidence developed towards a probable conclusion. Formal analysis of prophetic and recognition formulae explained the textual break at v. 23c. Redaction arguments, of the sort mounted by Lust and my own in §5.4.1.4 suggest late editing. Linguistic evidence shows translational anomalies and late Hebrew forms.

In addition to textual, linguistic, formal, and redactional arguments, the study of literary *Tendenzen* provides another layer to the matrix. Literary *Tendenzen* will show that additional MT pluses, beyond just the one in 36:23c–38, begin with prophetic formulae. Literary *Tendenzen* also show that divine speech and the temporality of prophecy carry 12:26–28's concerns into the smaller details of MT's scribal variants. The collation of variants into literary *Tendenzen* provides a different type of lens onto textual data. By demonstrating coherence, the variants become knit into a scribal phenomenon of meaningful change instead of surgically removed on the basis of transmission mechanics, where change is always only the result of error. Text-critical analysis of variant literary editions requires a dynamic model of author-transmitters.

In the final analysis, p967 has proven a formidable text. Its literary edition of Ezekiel is more often than not faithful to a Hebrew *Vorlage*, lacking in textual errors, and rarely reflects Greek innovation. Though the case-by-case evidence continues to require individual attention, the data set I've delineated in this project strongly suggests that p967's literary edition is a viable, early text of Ezekiel. Where once Tov declared it "a far reaching assumption" that p967's text reflects an accurate Hebrew *Vorlage*, the above analysis strongly suggests that p967 frequently reflects an early edition of a Hebrew text that differs from the MT.[109]

---

[109] Tov, *The Hebrew & Greek Bible: Collected Essays on the Septuagint* (VTSup 62; Leiden: Brill, 1999), 409.

CHAPTER FIVE

THE *TENDENZEN*: EXEGETICAL READINGS OF P967 AND MT AS VARIANT LITERARY EDITIONS

5.1. INTRODUCTION

As indicated in chapter 3, the present chapter will present readings of a specific set of variants between MT and p967. The data set derives from a comprehensive examination of variants that distinguish MT and p967's editions according to *Tendenzen*. This chapter will answer the question: what types of literary, thematic, or ideational features distinguish p967 from MT?

The four main *Tendenzen* which organize the exegetical readings in this chapter characterize the 'intertextual centers' as well. The intertextual centers, as indicated in chapter 3, each contain a major variant that Lust already deemed significant in his work with p967 as a variant literary edition. Hence, the presentation begins with an exegetical analysis of the intertextual center, proceeded by exegetical readings of the variants associated with its *Tendenzen*. The selected terminology, 'intertextual centers' and '*Tendenzen*' point to the principle of coherence that grounds the argument of the chapter. By intertextuality, I mean the interdependent ways in which texts (and textual variants) relate meaningfully to each other.[1] So for example, a density of terms, themes, and meaningful exegetical connections constitute strong evidence for the type of intertextuality examined here.

---

[1] On the development of intertextuality more generally, see Graham Allen, *Intertextuality* (New York: Routledge, 2000). My usage is quite mundane and distanced from highly theoretical notions that have been taken up in many diverse areas of literary and cultural studies. However, one theoretical concept that is relevant to the present analysis is the movement away from intertextuality as the determination of diachronic relations. Rather, as Julia Kristeva points out, intertextuality in this new sense involves a synchronic appreciation of texts as embedded within a field of discourse; the question of priority falls away. To a large extent, this is the type of intertextual analysis advanced in the present chapter, one that eschews models of linear textual production and reliance. See Julia Kristeva, "Word, Dialog, Novel" in *Desire in Language: A Semiotic Approach to Literature and Art* (ed., Leon S. Roudiez; New York: Columbia University Press, 1980), 64–91.

To take an example developed further below, Ezekiel 12–13 forms an intertextual center about the nature of prophecy. The *Tendenzen* associated with the center involve such themes as prophecy-fulfillment and the role of delay in Ezekiel's prophecies. Indeed, a wider scope of variants was identified that relate to the *Tendenz* of 'Prophetic Temporality.' Thus, the readings of the variants in this *Tendenz* explore how strong the variants' intertextual features are.

Ultimately, the readings that follow inquire whether a proposed *Tendenz* is strong enough to differentiate MT from p967's editions of Ezekiel. Thus the question becomes: from an exegetical/intertextual perspective, do the variants of any specific *Tendenz* form a layer of coherent features that distinguish MT and p967 as two literary editions of Ezekiel?

One final comment, by way of introduction: the larger project has dealt, at times, with the question of the diachronic development in Ezekiel's textual tradition. Indeed, it is difficult to focus squarely on variants and to refrain from commenting on impressions of editorial intent or even priority. Because p967 is most often the shorter text, it is conventionally simpler to speak about how MT differs from the shorter text. Hence, I have been careful about describing the MT variants as pluses (not additions) and the variant readings as differences or substitutions (and not changes).[2] On a few occasions, the impressions of editorial activity are strong enough that I suggest redactional dynamics; however, literary analysis alone is ill-equipped to determine textual questions such as priority. I intend to provide some comments on the issue of priority in the conclusion. Only there, upon appreciating the full significance of the previous textual studies, and the forthcoming codicological analysis, can questions of priority be duly addressed.

It is to a literary analysis of p967 and MT that I now turn.

5.2. 'Prophecy' *Tendenzen*

5.2.1. *Intertextual Center—Disputation on Prophecy in Ezekiel 12–13*

The textual situation found in chapters 12–13 justify calling it an intertextual center for variants about prophecy. In MT, Ezek 13:2, 3, and 7 contain pluses in the chapter's discussions about prophecy. The proceeding chapter also concerns prophecy and hosts one of the major variants, Ezek

---

[2] See Tov, *Textual Criticism of the Hebrew Bible* (2d ed.; Minneapolis: Augsburg Fortress, 2001), 236.

12:26–28, material missing in p967. In addition to this textual evidence, most redaction critics of MT find a strong case for editorial layers in chs. 12–13. They argue without reference to the textual variants just listed. Merely on the basis of redaction cues in the chapter, critics concur that chapter 12 in MT is updated from an earlier prophecy of Ezekiel to affirm a prophecy and fulfillment scheme.[3] Specifically, Ezekiel's sign act in 12:3–7 about an exile's baggage is interpreted in 12:10–16. In vv. 10–16, up-dating touches specify Ezekiel's originally vague or open sign actions such that they predict the events of Zedekiah during the Babylonian invasion of Jerusalem, *ex eventu*.[4]

The four textual variants about prophecy, as well as the independent conclusions about redaction in MT strongly suggest that Ezekiel 12–13 became a site for editorial activity about the nature of prophecy in general and Ezekiel's prophecies in particular.

Turning to a literary analysis, the MT plus in 12:26–28 is a self-contained unit within a series of prophetic disputations concerning prophecy and fulfillment. Lust argued that vv. 26–28 were an insertion on the basis of several factors one of which is the standpoint of literary analysis.[5] He demonstrated that the verses cohered with what he found to be the broader historicizing character of MT's variants.[6] The following analysis of *Tendenzen* defends a similar case for coherence, although on different bases.

Form-critical analysis highlights the significance of vv. 26–28 as a unit. The material in 12:17–28 is structured by the phrase "and the word of the LORD came to me saying, 'son of man,'" (ויהי דבד יהוה אלי לאמר בן אדם).

---

[3] The updating concerns modifications to the sign-act in ch.12 so that it describes Zedekiah's departure from Jerusalem. Zimmerli cites the then recent work of Hölscher, Cooke, van den Born, and Fohrer as a consensus position that material about Zedekiah's inconspicuous departure by night was added to account for the exile of both Israel and the "prince" (Ezek 12:10). See Zimmerli, *Ezekiel*, 1:267.

[4] There is a modest textual basis for redaction arguments here, however incoherently preserved. For example 12:4b–6a presents slight variants: [MT] "in their sight" versus [Greek] "before them" (three times), [MT] "in the dark" versus [Greek] "in secret", and [MT] "carry it (baggage)" on your shoulders versus [Greek] on shoulders "you will be lifted up." These variants in the description of Ezekiel's sign-act do provide some indication of scribal activity, but such activity largely lies in stages behind our present manuscript witnesses.

[5] Lust also argued that the MT plus was a later insertion. We have already discussed his late linguistic evidence in chapter 3.

[6] Ezekiel 12:26–28 advances the claim that God's prophecies are true and immediately fulfilled, which is in keeping with Lust's larger diagnosis of the MT's historicizing tendencies. In light of the literary context, linguistic factors, and the wider horizon of coherence with other variants, the above discussion demonstrates that the textual evaluation for error in p967 in this passage should not be maintained.

The phrase, which repeats four times in the larger unit (12:17, 21, 26, and 13:1), provides literary structure for the passage's form-critical breaks. Each instance of the phrase serves as the introduction to a new disputation on the subject of prophecy.[7] p967's text omits the entire third section running from vv. 26–28.

Structurally, the content of 12:21–13:7 can be broken up as follows:

> 12:21–25   A disputation of the proverb, "days are prolonged and visions come to nothing," raising issues of fulfillment and false prophecy.
>
> 12:26–28   A disputation of the saying, "the vision that he sees is for many years ahead; he prophecies for distant times."
>
> 13:1–7   A woe-oracle against false prophets.

Lust argued that 12:26–28 interrupts the thematic development of chs. 12–13.[8] Before examining the case for interruption, it should be pointed out that vv. 26–28 are not utterly foreign to their context. Ezekiel 12:21–25 is a disputation about a lack of true prophecy. Chapter 13's oracles against false prophets immediately follow the variant. Because 12:26–28 also concerns prophecy, the context retains its topical coherence. Thus, while topically coherent, Lust contends that a *thematic* interruption isolates vv. 26–28.

Thematically, Ezek 12:21–25 refutes a proverb about the futility of visions. The retort insists on fulfillment (v. 23, 25) and the eradication of false prophecy from the house of Israel (v. 24). The passage amounts to a vigorous defense of the potency and truth of prophecy, concerns which are carried into ch. 13's oracles against false prophets. These verses directly confront the threat of false prophets to true and potent prophecy. Lust argues that 12:26–28 interrupts this thematic coherence since the verses debate not *false* prophecy, but *Ezekiel's true* prophecy. The saying in 12:27 does not confront the unreliable prophecy that is bemoaned in the surrounding context. On the contrary, it deals with the temporal aspect of *reliable* prophecy, presenting two opposing positions about how correctly to interpret reliable prophecy. Further, the saying in v. 27 specifically concerns the prophecies of *Ezekiel*, "the vision that *he* sees is for many years ahead." The verse affirms prophetic potency as fulfillment in the

---

[7] The content of vv. 17–20 is not properly a disputation. However, its structure is continuous with the disputations that follow. For the form-critical term "disputation" see Zimmerli, *Ezekiel*, 1:36 and 283.

[8] For his original work with this variant, see Lust, "Major Divergences," 85–86; idem, "Textual Criticism of the Old and New Testaments," 24–26.

immediate present, not the distant future. Reference to Ezekiel and the disputations about true prophecy are lacking in the surrounding context.[9] In these two details, vv. 26–28 do establish different themes than those developed in the surrounding context.

However, Lust's claim for thematic interruption does not extend to all aspects of the MT plus. Especially problematic is the repeated notion about fulfillment in vv. 23, 25 and 28. In fact, vv. 25 and 28 contain virtually the same language: "words will no longer be delayed." Both the context and the MT plus affirm the immediate fulfillment of prophecy. Thus, it is problematic to argue for disruption on the basis of theme, when theme can also be adduced to show continuity among the verses.

Lust is no doubt correct that the verses stand out against the surrounding context. However, his focus on theme does not sharply distinguish the unit. Instead, attention to the rhetorical context highlights the fractures introduced by the MT plus. The first disputation (vv. 21–25) addresses a faltering confidence in the validity of prophecy. Specifically, the audience rejects visions as empty, having waited on them without result. Then the woe oracles in 13:1–7 address false prophets who deliver such empty visions as in 13:6, "and yet they [the false prophets] wait for the fulfillment of their word." In both rhetorical contexts, an impatiently waiting audience finds no basis to trust unfulfilled prophetic visions.

A different rhetorical situation is assumed in 12:26–28. The implied audience holds that visions *require* distended periods of time for fulfillment. Not only is the audience immune from the context's disappointment in waiting, it relishes the postponed, future-orientation of visions.[10] Additionally, the issue in 12:26–28 is specific to *Ezekiel's* visions. From a rhetorical perspective, 12:26–28 implies a new audience who is engaged in a different debate from that of the context.

Finally, a philological feature shows that the content of the disputation in vv. 26–28 belies a later concern, suggesting again that the MT plus is secondary. The verses contain a third-person reference to the prophet. As just mentioned, the debate in vv. 26–28 concerns Ezekiel's prophecies,

---

[9] So Zimmerli, who emphasizes the independence of the disputation as "thematically separate throughout." However, he concludes, with Filson, for scribal error in p967. Zimmerli, *Ezekiel*, 1:283.

[10] On the basis of this future-orientation, Lust argues that this second disputation deals with apocalyptic interpretation of visions. He points out that certain terms in vv. 26–28 occur in Daniel, Chronicles, Ezra-Nehemiah, in one case as characterizing Danielic interpretation of visions. (See chapter 3 above.) Lust, "Textual Criticism of the Old and New Testaments," 26.

specifically. Rather than merely a debate about the fulfillment of visions in general, the audience is engaged in a debate concerning the specific visions of Ezekiel. Such a debate implies some notoriety for Ezekiel's prophecies, a situation which is likely to have developed over time. Elsewhere in the book, Ezekiel speaks in the first person, breaking this style only a handful of times (e.g. 1:2–3 and 24:24). Thus the third person reference to the prophet in 12:26–28 is all the more indicative of later discussions about him. Further the debate in vv. 26–28 concerns the time-delay of Ezekiel's visions. Such a debate would not arise until such a point when fulfillment and its timing would become an issue. Both the specific focus on Ezekiel's visions and a concern for time-delayed fulfillment suggest a later audience concerned with the reception of Ezekiel's visions. Hence, the secondary nature of the MT plus is strengthened by the nature of its content and presumed rhetorical context.

5.2.2. 'Prophetic Temporality' Tendenz: *Time and Fulfillment in Ezekiel*

One issue that characterizes the MT plus in 12:26–28 is time. The disputations involve debates about the fulfillment of Ezekiel's visions and reflect a more general concern for the temporal dimension of prophecy. A number of textual variants across Ezekiel affect both the theme of time, but also the book's temporal structure. All of these variants participate in the *Tendenz* of 'Prophetic Temporality.'

5.2.2.1. *Programmatic Statements about Prophecy and Fulfillment*

Programmatic statements about prophecy rarely occur in the book of Ezekiel. Nevertheless, on the few occasions in which Ezekiel muses about the nature of prophecy, textual variants occur. An important programmatic statement about prophecy for Ezekiel is the phrase "my eye will not spare, I will not have pity." Often found in conjunction with details about divine judgment, the phrase underscores the fixity of the divine intention. The phrase occurs seven times in Ezekiel;[11] four of these instances present textual variants:

1) Ezekiel 7:4 and 9
Ezekiel 7:5–14 is not extant in p967. However, the textual issues between B and MT have led some critics to consider it the *main* basis for two edi-

---

[11] Ezek 5:11; 7:4, 9; 8:18; 9:5, 10; 24:14.

tions of Ezekiel.[12] Its importance to MT's edition of Ezekiel warrants its consideration here.

Ezekiel 7:5–14 contains two instances of the phrase "my eye will not spare, I will not have pity." This section of text is animated by several textual issues, over which much ink has been spilled.[13] A transposition (vv. 3–6aα occurs after v. 9 in B), and several pluses and variants indicate that 7:5–14 was heavily worked over. The main theme in this section of text is "the end" and its approach and arrival. The textual variants in this section deal with the issue of the fixity of the end. Thus, the temporal aspect of prophecy warranted scribal re-working, although the precise distinction between the LXX and MT is not clear.

2) Ezekiel 8:18

Immediately following the shared phrase in 8:18a "I will act in my wrath; my eye will not spare, nor will I have pity...," MT presents seven words of plus material over B.

| MT | וקראו באזני קול גדול ולא | *and though they call in my hearing with* |
| | אשמע אותם | *a great voice, I will not listen to them.* |

The MT plus further underscores deity's intention to act. The people cannot persuade God away from his fixed determination.

3) Ezekiel 24:14

Ezekiel 24:14 represents the most programmatic formulation of Ezekiel's philosophy of prophecy outside of 12:21–13:23. It does so by rendering God as the subject of a longer list of verbs, all expressing the fixity of the prophecy. For example, it includes, "I will act." The MT list is longer, with a plus over p967/B ולא אנחם, *"I will not relent."*[14]

Even beyond these four variants that occur in programmatic statements about prophecy, MT presents the stronger philosophy of prophecy-fulfillment in several other places. The idea that God will not relent is a common theme in other MT variants as well. In 7:13, the second half of the verse in MT is a unique plus.

[12] Tov, *Textual Criticism of the Hebrew Bible,* 333–4.

[13] J. A. Bewer, "On the Text of Ezekiel 7:5–14," *JBL* 45 (1926): 226–231; J. Goettsberger, "Ez 7,1–16 textkritisch und exegetisch untersucht," *BZ* 22 (1934): 195–223; Zimmerli, *Ezekiel,* 1:193–4.

[14] "LXX* omits the last clause, but in favor of its retention (contra Zimmerli, 496 et al.)," Allen, *Ezekiel,* 2:55.

כי חזון אל כל המונה לא ישוב

For the vision concerns all its horde, it will not be revoked

In the verse preceding, MT reads הגיע היום "the day draws near," while B merely states ιδου η ημερα "behold the day." The idea of the day drawing near is reminiscent of קרבו הימים "the days draw near" in 12:23, examined above.

Similarly, in 21:7, MT is the longer text once again,

ונהיתה   *and it will be fulfilled*

p967/B lack the phrase ונהיתה which would emphasize fulfillment. This same construction ונהיתה, occurs in 39:8 where the MT presents the more emphatic edition with regard to prophecy.

MT   ונהיתה
        and *it will be fulfilled*

967   και γνωση οτι εσται
        and *you will know that it will be*

All of the above variants share an emphasis on the fixity of prophecy. The extended section of textual variation in chapter 7 contained two instances of the phrase "my eye will not spare." Two additional MT pluses in the context of the statement "my eye will not spare," show the significance of fixity to MT's edition. Outside of these otherwise rare statements of fixity, MT offers increased assurance of fulfillment in six additional instances. In comparison with the shorter Greek text (always B, and p967 where extant,) the MT presented the more emphatic edition, one that articulates a stronger belief in the fulfillment of prophecy.[15]

5.2.2.2. *Date Reckoning*

The date references assigned to specific oracles fall into the 'Prophetic Temporality' *Tendenz*.[16] A full seven of the eleven date references extant

---

[15] Because p967 is not extant in chs.1–11, some of this evidence only distinguishes MT from B. As the discussion in chapter 2 showed, B and p967 do diverge from one another, and cannot thus be said to reflect the same Greek text. However, it is true that B and p967 agree against MT more often (see chapter 3); Hence, B's evidence is more likely to reflect p967's text. Regardless of the conjecture about p967's text, MT's consistent divergence from the Greek tradition within this *Tendenz* remains important information about *MT* as a unique literary edition.

[16] Many redaction studies of Ezekiel rely on the dates offered in Ezekiel. See Zimmerli, *Ezekiel*, 1: 1–3, 8, 73, and especially pp. 9–11. W. Eichrodt, *Ezekiel: A Commentary* (OTL;

in p967 diverge from those in MT: 26:1; 29:1; 30:20; 31:1; 32:1, 17; 33:21.[17] In MT, these dates all share the distinction of falling between the 10th–12th years after the deportation of Jehoiachim in 597/6. Thus they fall within the crucial years immediately before and after the 587 destruction of Jerusalem.[18]

In contrast, the tenth year is particularly central in p967; six of its seven divergent date references occur in the tenth year. In 29:1, p967 reads with MT, "tenth year". In the other five cases, p967 *alone* among the major codices and MT reads "the tenth year:" 26:1; 30:20; 31:1; 32:17; 33:21. The prominence of the tenth year in p967 suggests a temporal trend. The variant chronologies in p967 and MT are as follows:

p967's Chronology

Year	Month	Day	Citation and Episode
7	5	10	20:1—Historical review of Israel's rebellion (focus on Egypt)
9	10	10	24:1—Babylon begins its siege; metaphor of the burning pot
10	1	7	30:20—Egypt's arm is broken, never to be strong again
10	1	15	32:17—Pharaoh relegated to the pit of nations
10	3	1	31:1—Pharaoh and hordes: symbolic tree of Assyria scattered
(10	5	7)	—587 destruction of Jerusalem[19]
10	10	5	33:21—Announcement of Jerusalem's fall
10	12	1	29:1—Against Pharaoh—Israel will never again rely on Egypt
10	?	1	26:1—Tyre's permanent destruction (chs. 26–29)
12	12	1	32:1—Lament, Egypt strewn on field
25	1	10	40:1—Temple Vision
27	1	1	29:17—Tyre under siege of Nebuchadrezzar

Philadelphia: Westminster, 1970), 18–22. Irwin, *The Problem of Ezekiel: An Inductive Study* (Chicago: University of Chicago Press, 1943), 263–268. See especially Howie's critique of Torrey for two opposing positions. C.C. Torrey, *Pseudo-Ezekiel*, 58–70; C.G. Howie, *Date and Composition of Ezekiel* (JBLMS; Vol. IV; Philadelphia: SBL, 1950), 27–34. Few commented on the differences between the Greek and Hebrew. When Cooke offered his textual analysis of date reckoning in 1936, he suggested that some of the differences between the then extant Greek and Hebrew witnesses were intentional; however, he was not only unfamiliar with p967 but unfortunately refrained from further comment. Cooke, *A Critical and Exegetical Commentary*, xvii.

[17] There are fourteen altogether, but Ezek 1:1, 3:16, and 8:1 fall in the missing chapters of the p967 manuscript.
[18] For the logic of the date reckoning in Ezekiel, see Zimmerli, *Ezekiel*, 1:9–11.
[19] Zimmerli, *Ezekiel*, 1:9–16.

MT's Chronology

Year	Month	Day	Citation and Episode
7	5	10	20:1—Historical review of Israel's rebellion (focus on Egypt)
9	10	10	24:1—Babylon begins its siege; metaphor of the burning pot
(10	5	7)	— 587 destruction of Jerusalem
10	10	12	29:1—Against Pharaoh—Israel will never again rely on Egypt
11	1	7	30:20—Egypt's arm is broken, never to be strong again
11	3	1	31:1—Pharaoh and hordes: symbolic tree of Assyria scattered
11	?	1	26:1—Tyre's permanent destruction (chs. 26–29)
12	10	5	33:21—Announcement of Jerusalem's fall
12	12	1	32:1—Lament, Egypt strewn on field
12	(12?)	15	32:17—Pharaoh relegated to the pit of nations
25	1	10	40:1—Temple Vision
27	1	1	29:17—Tyre under siege of Nebuchadrezzar

Several observations pertain to these dates. First, 24:1 places the announcement of Babylon's siege of Jerusalem in the ninth year in both MT and p967. The next year, in the tenth year, Jerusalem and her temple falls to the Babylonians. Of the variant dates in p967, all but one (32:1) occurs in the same year as the 587 destruction of Jerusalem, most of them immediately preceding Ezekiel's receipt of the news.[20] This temporal simultaneity in p967 may indicate the strength of Ezekiel's prophetic timing for p967's edition. Though he is in Babylon and knew nothing of the events in Jerusalem, his visions and oracles are dated such that they coincided with the one-year window of events that led up to Jerusalem's fall. Such simultaneity bespeaks a view of Ezekiel's word as immediately potent. The dates also contribute to the portrait of Ezekiel as a visionary, able to see events though he is spatially removed from them. In addition to authorizing Ezekiel's prophetic office, the temporal simultaneity points to the dramatic focus in p967. p967's dates collect in the year of Jerusalem's greatest trauma. The largess of that violent destruction dominates the dramatic world constructed in p967, drawing increased focus on the judgments of God in that year.

Second, all but one of p967's variant dates occur in oracles against foreign nations. 26:1 is an oracle against Tyre and 29:1; 30:20; 31:1; 32:1; and 32:17 fall in oracles against Egypt. Variance between p967 and MT in this

---

[20] Ezek 29:1 is dated to the 12th month of the tenth year in p967, which is two months after Ezekiel receives the news in Ezek 33:21.

context suggests that the oracles against foreign nations were not 'set' in time;[21] editorial activity gave different interpretations of especially Egypt's role in the 587 destruction of Jerusalem.

Third, the sequence of Egypt's fate presents an important detail. In MT, the last two oracles against Egypt occur in the twelfth year at 32:1 and 32:17. Fifteen days likely separate the two oracles, for although the month is not specified in 32:17, the twelfth month in 32:1 likely extends through the chapter. In this sequence, the final oracle against Egypt reports the apocalyptic end of the nation in the pit of 32:17–32. This oracle acquires prominent significance in the discussion below where the fate of enemies will be discussed in greater detail (§5.3). Here it is enough to note that MT places the pit in a culminating position. p967, on the other hand, dates the pit to *before* Jerusalem's destruction. Further, p967 contains several oracles against Egypt that are subsequent to the apocalyptic pit, (31:1, 29:1, and 32:1). Hence, in p967, the pit cannot represent a truly apocalyptic end to Egypt, given Egypt's continued role in Ezekiel's oracles of judgment.

5.2.2.3. *Ezekiel's Temporal Structure*

The date references are not the only temporal differences between MT and p967.[22] In 4:4–6, MT and LXX manuscripts offer alternate accounts for the discrete number of years that Israel must endure her guilt. p967 is not preserved in these early chapters. However, the matter still merits consideration in order to further illumine MT's temporal features. Ezekiel 4:4–6 is concerned with fixing the number of years of Israel's guilt. In most LXX manuscripts, v. 4 reads "150 years" which is a minus in MT. Verse 5 then expands: the LXX providing 190 years vs. MT 390 years for the house of Israel.[23] I agree with Zimmerli's assessment that this section of ch. 4 is layered with additions and interpretation, all afforded by an originally unspecified מספר in v. 4.[24]

> It appears probable that we are not dealing with one single addition, made at one time, but that several phases of such activity are discernible. In the

---

[21] The variant date references in Ezekiel's oracles against foreign nations may represent a similar phenomenon as the rearrangement of chapters in Jeremiah's variant editions of the oracles against foreign nations.

[22] For the theory that the date reckoning of oracles was a later redactional fiction, see the famous arguments in Torrey, *Pseudo-Ezekiel*, 58–70.

[23] In v. 6, all witnesses agree that the house of Judah will endure forty years of guilt.

[24] Zimmerli, *Ezekiel*, 1:165.

different numbers given in MT and LXX, which are not simple scribal errors, we can follow still further the interpretive work which molded the text.[25]

While the full significance of these differences remains elusive, for the present discussion it is enough to note the inadequacy of mechanical explanations for error to explain them (see ch. 3). The MT's temporal scheme regarding the period of guilt is different from that of the LXX tradition.

In addition to variants in date reckoning, the textual tradition shows some manipulation with regard to the phrase "on that day." The phrase "on that day" (ההוא ביום) has long occupied a special place in redaction-critical arguments in prophetic books. As early as Duhm's work in Isaiah, scholars have seen in the phrase an attempt by later redactors to update prophecies for their times, often extending the prophecy to an eschatological horizon.[26] As Joseph Blenkinsopp has stated, "this formula provides us with a distinct possibility of tracing a line of development in the editorial history of prophetic books."[27]

The phrase appears in four MT pluses and in three alternate readings.[28] Since the phrase, ביום ההוא appears in MT only 13 times, a large percentage of cases are affected. Not surprisingly, the phrase is most prominent in chs. 38–39 which describe the day of Gog's invasion; There it occurs five times. However, these instances of the phrase are consistent in MT and p967, except for a small variant in 38:14 about what will happen with Gog on that day.

---

[25] Ibid., 1:164.

[26] The idea may have originated with Bernhard Duhm in his now famous redaction-critical studies of the prophets, especially Isaiah. Bernhard Duhm, *Jesaia* (4th ed.; Göttingen: Vandenhoeck & Ruprecht, 1922). See also idem, *Jeremia* (Tübingen: Mohr Siebeck, 1901). Most scholars now just assume this to be the case, so Hibbard who states "this rubric [ביום ההוא] marks off a particular kind of exegetical expansion of or comment on earlier material," James Todd Hibbard, *Intertextuality in Isaiah 24–27: the Reuse and Evocation of Earlier Texts* (FAT 16; Tübingen: Mohr Siebeck, 2006), 71.

[27] J. Blenkinsopp, *A History of Prophecy in Israel* (Rev. and enl.; Louisville: Westminster, 1996), 233. According to Blenkinsopp, the phrase served but is not limited to its function as an early prototype to *pesher* interpretation in which an early passage was interpreted in light of contemporary events or future/eschatological horizons. Following Blenkinsopp's suggestion, we could approach "on that day" as a shared literary convention between biblical authors and tradents or copyists who edited texts, what S. Talmon calls "biblical stylistics." Talmon, "Textual Study of the Bible: A New Outlook," in *Qumran and the History of the Biblical Text* (eds. F.M. Cross and S. Talmon; Cambridge: Harvard University Press, 1975), 321–400.

[28] p967's minuses occur in Ezek 20:6; 23:38, 39; and 24:27. p967's alternate readings occur in Ezek 24:2a, 2b; 38:14; and 40:1. (Ezek 24:2a-b offer alternate readings of היום הזה, and thus should not be counted among the MT's thirteen instances of ביום ההוא.)

The main variation between p967 and MT in the phrase "on that day" occurs in chs. 20–24. There, MT presents the phrase in four pluses. An interest in Egypt is prominent across these variants. The MT plus in 20:5–6 describes God helping the Israelites while they are in Egypt. The MT pluses in 23:38, 39 group the sins of Oholah and Oholibah into one day's events, sins that are intimately related to their fornications with Egypt. These pluses reinforce the focus on Egypt in two "on that day" phrases that are shared by MT and p967. In 29:21, when Egypt is plundered to supply military wages for Nebuchadrezzar's invasion of Tyre, the oracle proclaims that a horn will spring up in Israel "on that day." Then in 30:9, "on that day" marks the destruction of Egypt, a more clearly eschatological passage owing to the presence of the additional phrase, "behold it comes" (הנה באה). While the last two instances of the phrase also occur in p967, MT's pluses in 20:5–6, 23:38 and 39 contribute to an Egyptian-orientation for the eschatological phrase. "That day" appears to be one of divine aid to Israel while in Egypt (20:5–6) but of judgment and destruction for Egypt (23:38, 39; 29:21; 30:9). This Egyptian-orientation, while not absent in p967, is more pronounced in MT.

One additional factor may be involved in the MT's unique uses of the phrase in chs. 20–24. "On that day" uniquely marks the temple desecration in MT. Ezekiel 23:38 and 39 both use the phrase to temporally correlate acts that defiled the sanctuary. Additionally, in 24:27, "on that day" qualifies the temporal prediction about when Ezekiel's mouth will be opened: the day he learns that his judgment oracles against Jerusalem and its temple were fulfilled.[29] (These three MT pluses may be fruitfully read alongside the phrase "on that day" in 45:22 where the prince supplies a sin offering to make atonement for himself and the people. This sacrifice is legislated to occur during Passover, two weeks after the purification of the temple.)[30] Thus, MT presents three pluses of the phrase "on that day" in passages describing the temple's defilement, possibly as a complement to the phrase's significance in Ezekiel 45 regarding the purification of the temple and the people.

In addition to a general focus on Egypt and the destruction of the temple, MT seems to place notable emphasis on a quite specific event:

---

[29] Additionally, the reference to "on that day" in Ezek 29:21 correlates the the opening of Ezekiel's mouth with the "horn" that springs up, understood in Daniel 7–12 as the one responsible for the abomination that desecrates the temple.

[30] Ezek 45:18 and 21 prescribe the purification of the temple and the Passover atonement sacrifice for the first and the fourteenth days of the first month.

the moment when Ezekiel receives his speech. First, MT *uniquely* marks the moment with "on that day" (24:27). Second, MT dates that event to the 12th year as opposed to p967's date in the 10th (33:21–22). In this alternate dating, MT dislocates "that day" further from the actual destruction of the temple in the 10th year. Instead, MT forges a possible connection between the *speech* of Ezekiel and "that day." In contrast, p967 lacks the phrase "on that day" for Ezekiel's speech, but by its dating achieves temporal simultaneity between Ezekiel's speech and the destruction of the temple.

One possible conclusion from the variant dates and uses of "on that day" is that MT imagines the 'opening' of Ezekiel's mouth in a time after the first temple's destruction. As a metaphor, the opening of Ezekiel's mouth signifies the potency of Ezekiel's oracles. Certainly, Ezekiel produced oracles before his muteness is said to have ended (i.e., the ones dated to before the 12th year). Hence, his returned speech marks the moment at which these 'mute' oracles achieve their potency as prophetic utterances. That is to say, Ezekiel's muteness may represent the dormancy of his prophecy, whereupon a second 'speaking' is possible with the return of the prophetic voice.[31] Since his returned speech is dated to the 12th year in MT, two years after the destruction of the temple, Ezekiel's prophetic words must refer beyond that event.[32]

5.2.2.4. *Summary of 'Prophetic Temporality'* Tendenz

The topic of prophetic temporality was not just an isolated concern in MT 12:26–28. The *Tendenz* characterized a wider range of variants across Ezekiel. p967 and MT's date reckoning as well as the phrase "on that day" extend the editorial reach of the *Tendenz*. Programmatic statements in 14:7 and 7:13 further supported the presence of the *Tendenz* in MT pluses and variant material.

The MT edition of Ezekiel shows a considerable interest in the immediate fulfillment of prophecy. Some hint, however, did emerge in the above analysis regarding how MT dealt with delayed fulfillment. Through the

---

[31] A similar philosophy of the prophetic word can be found in 1QpHab 7, which holds that the true meaning of prophecies was not revealed to the original prophet, but required an intended time-frame before their meaning could be known.

[32] If "that day" is read synchronically as an eschatological day, then further speculation is possible. "That day" could refer to the events of a second invasion (chs. 38–39) by a ruler from the north which involves events in Egypt and the desecration of the temple. A speculative reading to be sure, MT does generate more of a basis for the later application of Ezekiel's oracles through its date reckoning and extra uses of "on that day."

MT's use of "on that day" with Ezekiel's speech, MT creates a period of delay. Almost like a time release capsule, Ezekiel's oracles linger until "that day" arrives in which they are activated. The activation "on that day" seems to involve events in Egypt and the desecration of the temple.[33]

However, some inconsistencies with date reckoning and the phrase "on that day" render the MT less than clear. Perhaps primary is the issue of the 12th year in MT.[34] As discussed above, several prophecies are dated to the 12th year, two years after Jerusalem's fall. However, these same prophecies contain the phrase "on that day" to refer to events in Jerusalem's temple, a temple which, given the date, cannot still be standing. This inconsistency suggests one of two interpretive options: Either we should not impose eschatological synchronicity onto all "on that day" passages (i.e., one "on that day" may refer to isolated events and not one cosmic day of the Lord) or we should not read the date reckonings as literally referring to the years after the first deportation in 597 BCE. Whatever the case, the MT pluses and variants examined under the heading 'Prophetic Temporality' *Tendenz* certainly throw light on the distinguishing temporal features of p967 and MT. The dislocation of some of Ezekiel's prophecies from the 10th year destruction of Jerusalem does not necessarily undercut the MT's philosophy of immediate fulfillment; I proposed that the return of Ezekiel's speech allows for delayed actualization of dormant oracles in a one-time fulfillment event. From this perspective, MT presents a prophetic book that has already exhausted its fulfillment applications. However, it does so by creatively maintaining its programmatic statement about the immediate fulfillment of Ezekiel's prophecies through concern for Ezekiel's muteness and speech. p967, in comparison, offers no such programmatic statement about immediate fulfillment.

5.2.3. *'Divine Speech' Tendenz: Prophetic and Oracle Formulae*

Programmatic statements about temporality are not the only variants represented in the intertextual center. Ezekiel 12–13 contains variants that deal with the nature of divine speech. Specifically, MT is host to three pluses in vv. 2, 3, and 7 which develop the topic. In all three verses, the

---

[33] Adding the conclusions drawn above from the MT's date references, the final demise of Egypt also occurs subsequently to the 587 BCE destruction (the twelfth year in Ezek 32:1 and 32:17).

[34] The dates could hold numerological significance, as suggested of numbers more generally in prophetic books by Fishbane, *Biblical Interpretation*, 450.

MT plus, loosely supported by various versions (often the hexaplaric notations) reads against p967, B, and various Latin texts.[35]

> v. 2   Son of man, prophesy against the prophets of Israel; Prophesy and say
> *to those who prophesy from their own heart*[36] "Hear the word of the
> LORD."
>
> v. 3   Thus has the LORD said, *Woe to the foolish prophets who follow their
> own spirit*[37] without having seen anything.
>
> v. 7   Have you not seen delusive visions and spoken lying oracles *and said
> "oracle of the LORD" when I have not spoken?*[38]

The three pluses evince a similar scribal tactic of incorporation through
subtle expansion of an idea. The addition in v. 2 specifies the problem
with false prophets who rely on their heart. Then in v. 3b, MT presents a
variant that avoids the redundancy with v. 2. Thus, where v. 3b read (following p967) "woe to those who prophesy out of their own hearts," MT
creates a pair with v. 2 by including the spirit. Similarly, v. 7b builds on
the indictment in v. 6 against false prophets. False prophecy in v. 7 refers
specifically to those who claim their specious speech to be an "oracle of
the Lord." The plus, then, extends the prophetic disputes to include the
specific problem of the way that traditional prophetic formulae can be
used to authorize the speech of false prophets.

The three variants in MT do not radically change the overall meaning
of 13:1–23, which inveighs against sources of alternate inspiration than the
LORD himself. The variants in MT do, however, strengthen and specify
the critique. Particularly relevant to the present study is the MT's anxiety
over the spurious attribution of נאם יהוה[39] to false oracles. A concern for
deceptive speech attributed to the divine voice differentiates the MT edition from p967.

In light of the editorial concern for spurious use of divine speech, particularly the use of oracle formulae to authenticate false prophecies, I turn
next to examine prophetic formulae. In several cases, the witnesses reveal
editorial activity surrounding the use of oracle formulae, including but not
limited to נאם יהוה.

---

[35] Note that p967 is damaged and therefore does not preserve Ezek 13:7.

[36] p967 substitutes: them.

[37] p967 substitutes: Woe to those who prophesy out of their own hearts.

[38] Ezek 13:7b is a minus in B; p967 is not preserved.

[39] This is captured more formally in Q and Theodotian, which uncharacteristically
translate נאם אדני as φησιν κυριος instead of the expected λεγει κυριος.

5.2.3.1. *Formulae for Prophetic Speech*

Any variant having to do with phrases as common as "oracle of the Lord" in prophetic literature must first be placed into larger perspective. What follows here is a list of variants dealing with phrases like כה אמר אדני, כה אמר יהוה, וידעו כי אני יהוה, and נאם אדני. In Ezekiel, כה אמר אדני appears upwards of 110 times. However, only three or four of these are affected by textual variation. The statistics are similar for the phrase, נאם אדני. Hence, before proceeding, we should pause to appreciate the overwhelming consistency between the editions of p967 and MT of Ezekiel's oracles. Nevertheless, variants in formulaic material are highly relevant for the *Tendenz* of divine speech. In fact, variants in formulaic material are all the more significant given the otherwise remarkable consistency of use.

Redaction critics often rely on prophetic formulae as aids in determining the fractures in the development of a text. As Zimmerli has pointed out for Ezekiel,

> An external help towards a more penetrating analysis of the sections, behind which such a process of growth lies hidden, is to be found in the formulaic material of the prophetic sayings. Its consideration can occasionally (but by no means always) point to seams and gaps in the text.[40]

In chapter 3, I listed 19 variants in prophetic formulae. From these we discover an important pattern. In ten cases, p967 lacks a formulaic phrase that is present in MT (16:59; 36:7; 18:32; 36:23c; 25:7; 37:2; 43:12; 34:9; 33:25; and 33:27). In eight of those cases, p967's minus is supported by B. Once, B reads alone (16:59), and once it agrees with MT (18:32). There are no cases where MT lacks a formulaic phrase that is present in p967.

MT is the more expansive text, more liberally using prophetic formulae throughout the divine speeches in Ezekiel. At the most basic level, this could point to a scribal trend to provide section breaks or to 'close' and 'open' oracles.[41] However, these statistics may not be very meaningful in distinguishing the two editions of Ezekiel unless the formulae correspond

---

[40] Zimmerli, *Ezekiel*, 1:26.

[41] Insufficient study renders these options speculative. However, see John Olley's contribution to the correlation between prophetic formula and paragraphing in 1QIsaᵃ: John W. Olley, "'Hear the Word of Yahweh': The Structure of the Book of Isaiah in 1QIsaᵃ," *VT* (1993): 34, 44–45. For different views, although not ones specific to prophecy, see Emanuel Tov, "The Background of the Sense Divisions in the Biblical Texts," in *Delimitation Criticism* (eds. Korpel and Oesch; Pericope I; Assen, The Netherlands: Van Gorcum, 2000), 336–341.

with other variant readings or pluses. Indeed, we are especially interested in those cases where a prophetic formula authorizes content that is not unanimously attested in our texts. Hence, the correlation between formula and variant content can shed light on potentially contestable uses of Ezekiel's speech. There are four cases where this correspondence obtains. In each one, MT is the longer text.

1) Ezekiel 18:32 (נאם אדני יהוה)
Ezekiel 18 is a didactic refutation of the proverb in v. 2. The overall point of the chapter deals with the individual responsibility to do righteousness and not sin. Adherence will lead to life rather than death. The chapter ends in MT with the following plus (in v. 32.)

> v. 31   Cast away from yourselves all your transgressions by which you transgressed, and make for yourselves a new heart and a new spirit. Why will you die, O house of Israel?

> v. 32   For I do not delight in the death of the one who is dying, *says the Lord. Turn then, and live.*

Following the divine saying, λεγει (αδωναι) κυριος / נאם אדני יהוה only MT and Theodotian/L expand. MT provides a summative statement of the point of the entire chapter with the words "turn then, and live" (והשיבו וחיו).[42] p967, on the other hand, finishes the chapter on a less emphatic note. Indeed, emphasis appears to characterize this variant, given MT's use of an imperative verb which is a unique verbal form in the chapter.

2) Ezekiel 36:23c–38 (נאם אדני יהוה)
The MT plus in 36:23c–38 contains promises to Israel concerning her return to the land and new life there. This material is treated more thoroughly elsewhere (see text-critical discussion in ch. 4 and below in §5.4). However, because the plus is introduced by a prophetic formula, it deserves mention here.

The declarative formula, נאם אדני יהוה appears in v. 23b in MT right before its multiple verse plus. The formula is missing in p967's shorter text. Interestingly, although B reads with p967 in the minus, λεγει αδωναι κυριος is well supported by several other Greek witnesses and versions. Immediately before the contested formula, all texts, including p967, contain the 'recognition formula' וידעו הגוים כי אני יהוה / και γνωσεται τα εθνη οτι εγω ειμι κυριος (in v. 23a).

---

[42] See discussion of this variant below in the "New Life" *Tendenz* in §5.3.2.5.

In MT, the combined formulas in v. 23 mark the end of the oracle in 36:16–23b. As Lust states, "the 'recognition formula' followed by *ne'um Yhwh* in v. 23b makes a good conclusion."[43] According to Lust's argument, the Hebrew scribe responsible for MT provided the preceding material with a suitable formulaic ending (doubling the prophetic ending with the declarative formula) before adding the new oracular material in vv. 23c–38. The *double* formula was taken up in all Greek texts except p967 and B.

Lust's reasoning that the MT's double formulae provided a prophetic *ending* was critiqued by Block who shows that the 'recognition formula' can often appear in the *middle* of an oracle in Ezekiel.[44] Block tried to eradicate the significance of the formal oracle unit in MT vv. 16–23b by showing that the recognition formula need not mark a break within the longer oracle unit of vv. 16–32. However, Block missed Lust's point. The reading at issue is not the 'recognition formula' alone, but the coordination of it and the 'declarative formula,' the latter of which constitutes the variant between MT and p967. Lust's original point was that the *combination* of the 'recognition' and 'declarative' formulas makes for a fitting conclusion.[45] Hence, Block's critique carries no weight. On the contrary, Crane carries Lust's point further and shows that the combined 'recognition' and 'declarative' formulae *never* appear in the middle of an oracle in Ezekiel.[46]

3) Ezekiel 33:25 (כה אמר אדני יהוה)

p967 and B preserve a minus of 28 words in 33:25–27 against MT. The MT plus opens and closes with the divine messenger formula; chapter 4 of the present work already showed the weakness of the *homoioteleuton* argument for explaining the minus even here where the full phrase is repeated at the opening and close of the MT plus.

The content of the MT plus provides the rationale for the surrounding pronouncements of judgment against those who inhabit the waste places of Israel. The list of abominations include shedding blood, idolatry, and relying on swords. Both vv. 25 and 26 end with a rhetorical question "will you possess the land?" Thus, the MT plus concerns competing claims to

---

[43] Lust, "Ezekiel 36–40," 525.
[44] Block lists Ezek 28:22; 35:12; 37:13; 38:23; and 39:28 and cites an independent study by Samuel A. Meier, *Speaking of Speaking: Marking Direct Discourse in the Hebrew Bible*, (VTSup 46; Leiden: Brill, 1992), 230–242. Block, *The Book of Ezekiel*, 2:340.
[45] Lust, "Textual Criticism of the Old and New," 29–30.
[46] Crane, *Israel's Restoration*, 290–291.

the land and provides a rationale to exclude those dwelling in the waste-places of the homeland.

4) Ezekiel 43:12b (הנה)

The case of Ezek 43:12b involves the MT plus *"behold this is the law of the house"* (הנה זאת תורת הבית). In MT, "this is the law of the house" is a repetition of the same phrase in v. 12a, but is here introduced by the prophetic formula הנה. The particle of attention, הנה appears frequently in chs. 40–48, usually as an object clause (a non-verbal clause) and 43:12 is no exception.

Verse 12b in p967 lacks the prophetic formula and MT plus. Additionally, in v. 12a, p967 refers to the diagram (διαγραφη) of the house as opposed to the MT's law. These seemingly minor variants have interpretive significance for the issue of genre. Specifically, is the genre of the unit that begins in Ezekiel 43:12 that of a *law-code for* the temple or a *diagram of* the temple. Indeed, Ezekiel 43:12b marks an important transition in the content of Ezekiel's temple vision. While chs. 40–43 are solely concerned with the temple architecture, the material that runs from 43:13–44:31 combines architectural design with legal/ritual material.[47] The MT reading in 43:12b serves to introduce 43:13–44:31, indeed to draw attention to it as the "law" and not the "diagram" of the temple.[48] In contrast, p967 does not bring emphasis to the legal elements in its introduction to 43:13–44:31. Instead, p967 characterizes it as the *diagram* of the temple. Hence, the two editions differ about which aspects of the temple are emphasized in Ezekiel 43–44.

5) Ezekiel 24:14 An Exception (δια τουτο)

I earlier examined cases in which an MT plus included *both* a prophetic formula and a textual plus. The four cases highlighted the editorial function of prophetic formulae, as a scribal convention for expansion, most likely. In every case, p967 was the shorter text. However, in working with the formulae, a notable pattern emerged that would serve as the only

---

[47] See Zimmerli's comments on the ritualistic character of these laws in Zimmerli, *Ezekiel*, 2:430.

[48] So Michael Fishbane and Shemaryahu Talmon who argue that the formula here, "this is the torah of…" operates like a title-line or colophon. See Michael Fishbane and Shemaryahu Talmon, "The Structuring of Biblical Books: Studies in the Book of Ezekiel," in Annual of the Swedish Theological Institute X (ed. B. Knutsson; Leiden: Brill, 1976), 129–153; esp. 138–153.

exception. In five of the cases where p967 reads διὰ τοῦτο, MT preserves a minus where we would otherwise expect to see לכן.[49] This situation is never reversed. While διὰ τοῦτο is not exactly a prophetic formula, it plays an important role in the syntax of prophetic speech. Additionally, it is often combined with prophetic formulae, i.e., *"therefore*, thus says the Lord." It bears considering here.

The striking presence of διὰ τοῦτο in the Greek textual pluses may signal a scribal convention unique to the Greek. As above, I will consider the one case where διὰ τοῦτο introduces a more extensive plus against MT. In 24:14, p967 reads,

> I, the Lord, have spoken; and it shall come, and I will do it. I will not delay, neither will I have any mercy. I will judge you, says the Lord, according to your ways, and according to your devices. *Therefore (διὰ τοῦτο) I will judge you according to your blood, and according to your devices you will be judged, says the Lord, you unclean, notorious, and abundantly provoking one.*

Verse 14 culminates the unit of vv. 24:3–14. The p967 plus highlights the metaphor of the cooking pot as symbolic of God's actions to clean Jerusalem of its uncleanness and abominations. (The literary context and content of this verse will be discussed in greater detail in §5.3.2.4.) The effect of the additional sentence in p967, however, heightens the significance of v. 14aβ. It also adds blood to the list of reasons Jerusalem will be judged.

In light of the earlier discussion of MT and p967's prophecy-fulfillment themes, the shared text of v. 14aα refers to prophecy and fulfillment. Due to the p967 plus, the two editions differ in *emphasis*. Both texts include a sequence of short statements emphasizing the certainty of God's intentions to fulfill his word (i.e., "I will do it. I will not delay.") Only the final statement "I will judge you" strays from the pattern of succinct statements to include two short prepositional phrases "according to your ways and according to your devices." Thus ends the oracle unit in MT. p967's plus does not extend this theme of fulfillment that characterizes each short statement. Rather, p967's plus extends the concept of judgment to include additional rationale, "blood" and "devices." The emphasis shifts from the promise of God's action to the behaviors and identity of the people who, in p967's concluding words, are called the "unclean, notorious, and abundantly provoking one."

---

[49] In the sixty cases where the Greek reads, διὰ τοῦτο, fifty-eight times לכן occurs in the MT, while the other two read על כן (in Ezek 22:4 and 42:6).

Since both editions share God's fulfillment statements, both p967 and MT relate the same ideas about the viability of prophecy. Both editions affirm the fulfillment examined above in the Prophecy Temporality *Tendenz*. However, in MT's edition the oracle culminates with this theme. As we will see below, variants in Ezekiel 24 throw light on this prophecy. For now, it is enough to note that p967's plus shifts the emphasis onto the judgment of Israel as opposed to the viability of God's word.

By way of conclusion, variants involving prophetic formulae, while not numerous, were illuminating. Above, I have examined four instances where MT plus material included a prophetic formula.[50] In one case, p967 exhibited the same phenomenon using terminology seemingly distinctive to the Greek tradition (δια τουτο). In the modest number of cases adduced here, there was certainly enough of a trend, in terms of distribution, to say that MT and p967 witness to possibly different conventions for expansion/editing using different formal conventions: δια τουτο for p967 and הנה for MT.[51] and נאם אדני ,כה אמר אדני יהוה

5.2.3.2. *Recognition Formula*: "They/you will know that I am the Lord" (וידעו כי אני יהוה / και γνωσονται οτι εγω ειμι κ̄ς ο θ̄ς)

The recognition formula merits separate treatment from the other prophetic formulae for two reasons. First, the Greek and Hebrew traditions *both* contain the phrase in plus material. In this uneven distribution, the recognition formula is distinct from other prophetic formulae just examined. The use of the recognition formula may still be a scribal convention, but it would be one shared across the versions. Second, the recognition formula interacts with its context differently than the previously considered formulae. The formulae of divine speech attribute oracles to the

---

[50] One important observation made in this section is that the presence of a prophetic formula at the beginning of variant/minus material is not a strong basis to evaluate for *homoioteleuton*. Consciousness of scribal conventions must accompany the textual evaluation of scribal mistakes. In this case, we have the basis to assume a scribal practice of inserting (excluding?) material under the heading of prophetic formula. As already pointed out, we detected the possibility of such scribal conventions in the Hebrew or the Greek. It is possible that all of the MT pluses derive from intentional Greek omission. However, the far more likely conclusion is for a Hebrew scribal convention that expanded content under the heading of a prophetic formula.

[51] While p967 and MT can be distinguished according to their use of prophetic formulae, a brief examination of the Greek textual tradition shows that Greek witnesses (especially L) contain pluses in prophetic formulae. For example, B and L present an asterisked plus "thus says the Lord" in Ezek 21:3(8).

mouth of God.[52] In contrast, the recognition formula is directed at audience perception. It throws light on particular knowledge as more accurately or effectively revealing God. In this sense, the recognition formula operates quite similarly to how Fishbane describes inner-biblical exegesis of prophecy:

> The initial oracle retains its authoritative status as a divine word—but requires redirection, respecification, revivification.[53]

The formula, if inserted, can shift the emphasis of an oracle onto a specific sentence or phrase. Indeed, material associated with the recognition formula enjoys a special kind of highlighting. Even if the dominant themes in a unit differ, the recognition formula directs the implied audience towards a specific prophetic message. Hence, the formula can redirect the message of an oracle.

The recognition formula, "you/they will know that I am the Lord" appears roughly 72 times in MT of Ezekiel.[54] Some redaction critics have suggested that it was a late editorial feature in Ezekiel. Although the textual evidence cannot substantiate the claim in most instances, it does provide some warrant for this view.[55] MT has the phrase in a unique plus twice, while p967 had a unique plus only once. The greatest number of unique variants occurred in B against MT and p967, with three occurrences. While the *variants* just listed are interesting, each of the editions (MT, p967, B) has one unique *plus* of the whole formula. It is these three cases which are discussed here.

---

[52] הנה is an exception. It does not introduce divine speech, but it is typical to the formal presentation of Ezekiel's visions, giving it some role, albeit more modest, in indicating divine content (i.e., significant elements of the vision.)

[53] Fishbane, "Revelation and Tradition: Aspects of Inner-Biblical Exegesis," *JBL* 99 (1980): 355.

[54] For accurate numbers of "pure" and adapted formulae, see Zimmerli, 1:38. Cf. idem, *I am Yahweh* (trans. Douglas W. Stott; Atlanta: John Knox, 1982).

[55] See, for example, Gustav Hölscher, *Hesekiel, der Dichter und das Buch* (BZAW 39; Giessen: Töpelmann, 1924). Hölscher is not the only one to suggest the view, and while his work was stimulating, it was reductive and largely rejected. See Zimmerli, *Ezekiel*, 1:4–6. In fact, on redaction-critical grounds alone, the arguments are based on debated points. For example, Blenkinsopp points out that the phrase "already occurs in these early prophetic legends [the Elijah and Elisha narratives]." Blenkinsopp, *A History of Prophecy in Israel*, 177. Similarly, Zimmerli argues that the formula "consists of two parts, which from a form-critical viewpoint each have a different origin and setting in life." He goes on to show similarities with H material, the Joseph story, and self-revelation proclamations associated with Sinai. Zimmerli, *Ezekiel*, 1:37. All of this evidence, even the Elijah and Elisha narratives, are subject to redaction-critical debates. Nevertheless, one cannot argue that the phrase is *always* late on redaction criteria alone.

1) Ezekiel 20:26 in MT

> I defiled them through their very gifts, in their offering up all their firstborn,
> in order that I might horrify them, *so that they will know that I am the Lord.*

In Ezek 20:26, MT claims that Israel has been defiled, despite obedience to God's ordinances, (i.e., child sacrifice). The recognition of God is linked to Israel's horror upon realizing what she has done and become.

2) Ezekiel 38:20 in p967

> The fish of the sea will quake at the presence of the Lord, and the birds
> of the sky and the wild beasts of the field, and all the reptiles that creep
> upon the earth, and all the men that are on the face of every land; and the
> mountains will be rent, and the valleys will fall, and every wall on the land
> will fall, *and the nations will know that I am the Lord.*

In 38:20, p967 claims knowledge of God for the nations. Verse 20 describes the nature-upheaval characteristic of day of the Lord imagery: quaking fauna, rent mountains, and destroyed walls.[56] The context connects the day of the Lord with the outworking of God's wrath upon Israel by means of the invasion of Gog-Magog. According to p967, this event causes the nations to know God.

It is probably significant that the next verse (v. 21) speaks about God summoning against Gog "every fear of the sword" (παν φοβον μαχαιρας.) μαχαιρα is a p967 plus in 38:21. Both the ideas of 'fear' and 'sword' are important in 32:17–32, another passage about international judgment. There, the portrayal of Assyria (v. 23), Elam (v. 24), and God through Pharaoh (v. 32) included the spread of their "fear [φοβον] in the land of the living." Further, 'sword' (μαχαιρα) plays an instrumental role as the means of death for most of the nations in the pit (vv. 20, 21, 22, 27, 28, 29, 30, 32).

By means of the recognition formula and the reference to sword in v. 21, p967 forges the stronger intertextual connection between 38:20–21 and ch. 32. Both units implement apocalyptic imagery, respectively the day of the Lord and the underworld, imagery that is embellished in p967.

---

[56] The imagery combines the Gen 1 taxomony of the natural world with a matrix of destruction images, found in such texts as Isa 2:12–17; 37:36; and Ezek 13:12–13, among many others.

3) Ezekiel 34:15 in B

> I will feed my sheep and give them rest *and they will know that I am the Lord.*

Ezekiel 34:15 develops the allegory of Israel as lost sheep. In v. 15, B claims that Israel will know God when Israel is fed and resting. A textual variant in v. 15a differentiates B further from MT.[57] Where B reads "I will feed my sheep," MT says "I am a shepherd of my flock." The difference is subtle: B's text draws greater attention to the way that God satisfies the people in their basic human needs.[58]

5.2.3.3. *The Nation-Recognition Formula*

As we just saw, p967's unique recognition formula referred not to Israel but to the nations. The 'nation-recognition' formula occurs five times in the Hebrew Bible, all in Ezekiel, clustered in chs. 36–39. Two of these instances in MT occur in 36:23c–38. Thus, while p967 uniquely contains the phrase in 38:20, MT also presents the phrase in material unique to its edition. Because the phrase occurs so infrequently, it strongly distinguishes MT and p967 as variant editions.

In 36:23c, the nation-recognition formula appears as the last line of the text shared by p967 and MT, immediately before the contested נאם אדני יהוה (see §5.4.1.1.3). The MT plus begins with a qualifying temporal clause, "*when through you [Israel] I display my holiness before their [the nations'] eyes.*" This qualification is further specified in vv. 24–28 which refers ahead to ch. 37. A second nation-recognition formula occurs within MT's plus (v. 36).

In p967 and MT, different events prompt the nations to recognize God. p967 points to God's summoning of Gog against Israel as the protracted outworking of God's wrath. p967's divine fulfillment uses the instrument of the invading army: εν σοι, "through you," referring to Gog.[59] Alternatively,

---

[57] p967 supports B in this variant.

[58] B might be connected to 34:23–24, already appreciated for displaying Septuagintal interest in messianic reflection. See Lust, "Le Messinaisme et al. Spetante D'Ézékiel," in *Messianism and the Septuagint: Collected Essays by J. Lust* (ed., K. Hauspie; BETL 178; Leuven: Leuven University Press, 2004), 32–33; reprinted from Lust, "Le Messinaisme et la Spetante D'Ézékiel," *Tsafon* 2/3 (1990).

[59] The nation-recognition formula here touches on the issue of prophecy and fulfillment as well. εν σοι is a textual plus in p967. MT's "through you [Israel]" is in a textual plus. We have already seen a similar distinction in (§5.2.2.1) where the MT asserted that God

MT stresses that nation-recognition will occur "through you [Israel]" in 36:23c. Ezekiel 38:18–25 portrays Gog's invasion with imagery of the day of the Lord.[60] Hence, p967 forges a strong connection between nations' knowledge of God and the apocalyptic day of the Lord depicted in Ezekiel 38. In contrast, the MT points to ch. 37 and the vision of dried bones as the event that will inspire the nations to knowledge of God. Specifically, God will be known to the nations through *Israel's* miracle (MT), and not *Gog's* invasion and destruction (p967).

In conclusion, the recognition formula occurred in contexts that exhibit traces of scribal editing. We saw evidence of the *Tendenz* in many of the witnesses, marking the formula as a wide-spread scribal technique. Both the Hebrew and Greek editions produced evidence for editorial activity. The straight recognition formula in MT and p967 did not produce coherently differentiated readings. However, a meaningful divergence is more likely in the case of the nation-recognition formula. MT and p967 can be sharply distinguished, offering different perspectives on the events of chs. 36–39.

5.2.4. *Summary of Section: 'Prophecy'* Tendenzen

The major variant in 12:26–28 does not represent an isolated MT plus about prophecy. The foregoing analysis showed the extent of textual variants which differentiate p967 from MT according the Prophecy *Tendenz*. Especially pronounced were variants related to the temporal features of prophecy and fulfillment. The MT plus in ch. 12 provided its edition with a programmatic statement about the immediate fulfillment of Ezekiel's prophecies. Likewise, in ch. 7, an MT plus offered a similar statement about visions, namely, that they are irrevocable. Such statements stand out even more in light of the variants in ch. 4 concerning the number of years of Israel's guilt. Variation in the number of years suggests that oracles were modified *ex eventu* to comply with a particular fulfillment interpretation.

The Prophecy *Tendenz* also highlighted differences in the temporal structure of the book. The date of Ezekiel's oracles in p967 clustered

---

would fulfill prophecies himself. In Ezek 14:7, p967's variant explains that he will answer "through him" (Ezek 14:7). p967's nation-recognition plus in Ezek 38:20 is consistent with the variant from Ezek 14:7, advancing a theology in which God uses mediating devices to fulfill his purposes.

[60] See especially Zimmerli who characterizes Ezek 38:18–25 as apocalyptic material that was not penned by Ezekiel. His discussion points out resonances with later apocalyptic-cosmic imagery. Zimmerli, *Ezekiel*, 2:312–314.

around the tenth year, the same year as the destruction of Jerusalem. MT spread the same oracles over the eleventh and twelfth years. Additionally, the temporal phrase "on that day" was deployed more frequently in the MT's edition. In some cases, the correlation of "on that day" with date references complicated the temporal structure of MT's edition. Nevertheless, some emphases were discernible in the MT's alternate temporal structure. For example, MT dated Egypt's apocalyptic demise in the pit last among the Egyptian oracles, underscoring the finality of Egypt's fate.

In addition to differences in prophetic time, the Prophecy *Tendenz* also encompassed variants dealing with prophetic speech. The issue was already present in the intertextual center, especially in MT's edition of 13:7. The MT plus in v. 7 warned about false prophets using prophetic formulae to authorize speech derived from their own hearts and spirits as opposed to that from divine origins. In the forgoing analysis, this MT statement introduced analysis of variants in prophetic formulae across the book. The patterns among the small percentage of variant material yielded a striking trend. MT uses divine speech formulae more frequently than p967.[61] Further, it did so in conjunction with content-pluses in four instances. This evidence raises the intriguing question about whether these content pluses in MT can be seen as candidates for the claim of false-speech prohibited in Ezek 13:7. That is to say, in these content-pluses, we may be looking at prophetic debate in action, staged by scribes on the site of the text itself. Arguing against this intriguing possibility is the significance of 36:23c–38 to the MT edition, for example. It is unlikely that the MT plus in ch. 36 was viewed as specious speech, authorized falsely by the divine oracle formula, particularly as it deals with the reanimation of the very heart and spirit denounced in 13:1–7. However, the example does throw light on how 36:23c–38 participates in a wider trend in the MT's more expansive edition of Ezekiel, a trend which correlated content-pluses with prophetic formulae.

In contrast to the differentiation between p967 and MT according to speech formula, the recognition formula formed a complex pattern among the witnesses. MT, p967, and B presented plus material, differently signaling content that would stimulate knowledge of God. Most notably, MT and p967 differ about what scenario would produce nation-recognition: p967 in the Gog invasion and MT in the valley of dried bones.

---

[61] The only exception was δια τουτο, discussed in §5.2.3.1.

5.3. 'Fate of the Slain' *Tendenzen*: Filling the Plains,
Valleys, and Pits

The prophecies of Ezekiel devote substantial attention to death. Specifically, the prophecies exhibit a concern for the *location* of slain bodies (חלל/τραυματιας), both native and enemy bodies, variously in Sheol, the pit, valleys, graves, plains, on the mountains, and other locations. Frequently, the material that exhibits a concern with the slain also serves as a site of textual divergence between MT and p967. In chapter 3, these variants were grouped as the 'Fate of the Slain' *Tendenzen*. The present discussion returns to those passages in which the *Tendenz* occurs to give an exegetical account of their meaning and literary function in Ezekiel.

The most prominent locus of the fate of the slain *Tendenz* appears in 32:17–32. One of p967's notable minuses (32:24bδ–26) occurs in this passage. However, additional textual issues in the immediate context and elsewhere participate in the *Tendenz* as well. I will deal with 32:17–32 as an intertextual center for the *Tendenz* and then turn to the more isolated occurrences elsewhere.

5.3.1. *Intertextual Center: The Pit in Ezekiel 32:17–32*

Ezekiel 32:17–32 hosts several variants that fall into the 'Fate of the Slain' *Tendenz*. Its very topic is the descent of Israel's enemy slain into the underworld. Verse 17 frames the description of the underworld within a 'lament' oracle over Egypt's fate.[62] Verses 17–32 are separated from what precedes by a new date formula in v. 17, but the first half of the ch. 32 is also a lament for Egypt. In the main, the lament consists of a register of the nations who already populate the pit (vv. 22–30). Then in vv. 31–32, Pharaoh responds to the events just described to him, and God's instrumental role is emphasized. The general point of the lament is to predict and perform Egypt's fated descent into the pit. Indeed, vv. 18–32 introduce a spatial cosmology characteristic of the apocalyptic genre.[63]

MT is the more expansive text. Most notably, Ezek 32:24bδ–26 is plus material in MT. Accordingly, MT's edition uniquely relegates Meshech

---

[62] In v. 18, the son of man is exhorted to lament (נהה/θρηνεω) over the hordes of Egypt.

[63] See Collins whose seminal classification of "apocalyptic literature" is still useful. In his definition, he recognized the significance of the spatial cosmos to the genre. J.J. Collins, *The Apocalyptic Imagination: An Introduction to Jewish Apocalyptic Literature* (2d ed.; BRS; Grand Rapids: Eerdmans, 1998), 1–42, especially 5.

and Tubal to the underworld. They join a register of Israel's otherwise historical enemies in the pit: Assyria, Elam, Edom, and the Sidonians.

Ezekiel 32:17–32 is structured by a poetic refrain, a refrain that bears on the extent of MT's plus in vv. 24bδ–26. In fact, Hölscher's analysis of MT led him to solve the textual difficulties in 32:17–32 using poetic analysis; He isolated the refrain,

> All of them slain, fallen by the sword
> Who caused terror in the land of the living
> And they bear their shame with those who have gone down to the pit.[64]

Hölscher conjectures that the text of 32:17–32 was once punctuated by the entire refrain, but as it currently stands, 32:17–32 only shows a repetition of quite similar phrases throughout 32:22–30. Even if Hölscher's reconstruction is unlikely, he is correct to note the way the repeated phrases provide a stylistic structure to the passage.[65] The repeated phrases in vv. 24bγ and 26bβ follow Hölscher's refrain closely; other verses repeat only segments of this refrain.[66]

Lust analyzed the MT plus in 32:24bδ–26 and connected it with a wider scope of editorial activity in MT.[67] For Lust, MT's plus cohered with its divergent presentation of the eschaton, owing mostly to the mention of Meshech and Tubal. Lust pointed out that the same protagonists of Ezekiel 38–39 also occurred in MT's edition of the pit, hence demonstrating coherence between 32:26–28 and the alternate sequence of chapters 37–39.[68] By including Meshech and Tubal among the company of Israel's

---

[64] Hölscher proposed such a poetic analysis for the textual difficulties in vv. 19–22 and 25. Hölscher, *Hesekiel*, 1924. I extend Hölscher's observation to the situation in vv. 26–28, which was not known by him in 1924. Cooke adopts Hölscher's "experiment" in his discussion of 32:17–32. Cooke, *A Critical and Exegetical Commentary*, 350. See also Boadt, who comments "the passage does not lack order, but the opposite," Lawrence Boadt, *Ezekiel's Oracles Against Egypt: A Literary and Philological Study of Ezekiel 29–32* (BEO 37; Rome: Biblical Institute Press, 1980), 151.

[65] The refrain is partially or wholly present in vv. 23, 24, 25, 26, 29, and 30.

[66] In light of the textual debates presented in chapter 4, it should be pointed out that vv. 24bγ and 26bβ, which frame the MT plus in Ezek 32:25–26, form the repeated phrases adduced in arguments for *homoioteleuton*. Such textual evaluations, which operate in isolation from literary analysis, fail to consider the literary role of stylistic features. Rather than conclude that our texts are erroneous, an evaluation already greatly problematized in chapter 4, we should appreciate the refrain as an opportunity for scribal elegance. That is to say, a scribe would have added (removed?) material in keeping with the poetic structure of the context.

[67] Lust, "Major Divergences," 87–89.

[68] See also Marco Nobile, "Beziehung zwischen Ez 32, 17–32 und der Gog-Perikope (Ez 38–39) im Lichte der Endredaktion," in *Ezekiel and His Book* (ed. J. Lust; BETL 74; Leuven: Leuven University Press, 1986), 255–59.

historical enemies in chapter 32, MT characteristically presents the more 'historicizing' interpretation of the eschatological invasion in Ezekiel 38–39.[69] Indeed, the issue of historical vs. mythic enemies constitutes perhaps the most intriguing aspect of the MT's list of nations.

Undoubtedly, any literary analysis must address the connection between Meshech and Tubal in both chapters 32 and 38–39. However, no one has examined the variants in the immediate context of chapter 32. The section is textually difficult, compounded by the fact that "individual verses swarm with difficult grammatical relationships."[70] Daniel Block notes the textual dilemmas astutely

> Seldom since Ezekiel's opening vision has a unit been plagued by such a concentration of truncated sentences, grammatical inconsistencies, and redundancy...The plethora of deviations from the MT in the LXX suggest that the Alexandrian translators...were as frustrated with the text as modern interpreters are. On the one hand, this early Greek version omits 15–18 percent of the material found in MT; on the other hand, it fills in several lacunae.[71]

The textual issues have been difficult to solve. However, p967's new evidence for an even shorter Greek edition of the passage sheds new light on the whole, suggesting that some of the textual issues derive from an editorial process upon which p967 may shed some new light.

MT's plus in 32:24–26 covers a longer list, over p967, of national bodies who are fated to the pit. However, this variant is by no means an isolated phenomenon in 32:17–32. Slain bodies play a significant role in differentiating MT from p967's editions of this lament, justifying the designation of 32:17–32 as an intertextual center for the 'Fate of the Slain' *Tendenz*. Issues such a nationality, circumcision, and notoriety are the salient categories for identifying bodies fated to the pit.

5.3.1.1. *Exegesis of Ezekiel 32:17–32 in p967*

In p967's edition of the lament, descriptions of the giants are more central than in MT; additionally, they form something of an inclusio for vv. 21–28. p967 opens its list of nations with the giants (v. 21). In between

---

[69] Lust, "Major Divergences," 87.

[70] Boadt, *Oracles Against Egypt*, 151.

[71] D.I. Block, *The Book of Ezekiel*, 2:212. So Blenkinsopp who says it is "more than usually corrupt." Joseph Blenkinsopp, *Ezekiel* (Interpretation; Louisville: John Knox, 1990), 141.

the scenes involving the giants (vv. 21 and 27,) the lament describes Assyria and Elam's existence in the pit.

The ancient giants preceded the rest of the company in p967's pit, having descended "long ago" (v. 27).[72] They speak a direct address "to you" in v. 21, commanding "be in the pit" and "go down and lay with the uncircumcised." In addition to these commands to Egypt, the giants ask a rhetorical question "than whom are you better?" This question signals to Egypt that they are in no better repute than the list of nations, and thus Egypt's fate is deserved.

The report at the beginning of v. 27 joins Assyria and Elam with the giants: "and *they* were laid with the giants who fell from long ago, the ones who went down to Hades." "They" probably refers to *both* Assyria and Elam. After this concise and neatly structured episode, v. 28 resumes its direct address to Pharaoh, alerting him, as anticipated by the rhetorical question, that Assyria, Elam, and the giants will be his nether-neighbors. Hence, the giants in vv. 21–28 provide an inclusio to this section of the enemy list with a summative statement about the pit's inhabitants.

Somewhat unexpectedly, vv. 29–30 resume after the giants in v. 28, adding the "rulers of Assyria" and the "rulers of the North, all the commanders of Assyria" to the list.[73] In these verses, p967's edition emphasizes two different categories of Assyrian leadership, rulers and commanders, perhaps specifying the statement already made in v. 22 of the first half of the list, "Assyria and *all his company*."[74] Certainly, the descriptions of these Assyrian cohorts follow the poetic refrain of the list in vv. 21–28. Thus, while vv. 29–30 share stylistic structure with vv. 21–27, they are set apart by virtue of coming after the inclusio about the giants in v. 28.

Aside from the largely tight literary structure of vv. 21–28, few other details emerge to organize p967's edition. The poetic refrain repeats its phrases throughout, "those slain by the sword," and "those who lay down with those descending to the pit." Elam (v. 24) and the rulers of Assyria

---

[72] απο αιωνος in p967 differs from the MT מֵעַרְלִים. The significance of the uncircumcised עֲרֵלִים will be discussed below. Zimmerli emends the MT on the basis of this Greek reading. Zimmerli, *Ezekiel*, 2:168 n27b.

[73] Many critics have noted that v. 28 (even in MT) seems a fitting conclusion. They are struck by the structural shift, which is even more pronounced in p967. See Wevers, *Ezekiel*, 244; Cooke, *A Critical and Exegetical Commentary*, 354; Zimmerli, *Ezekiel*, 2:779.

[74] It may also be significant that the lament in v. 17 is directed to Egypt and its hordes, while the end of the lament specifically mentions Pharaoh in v. 31. Perhaps at some point, a redaction of the lament saw fit to emphasize leadership, and thus returned to Assyria's rulers and commanders in order to underscore the address Pharaoh specifically.

(v. 29) are described as uncircumcised, undoubtedly bringing greater ignominy to the 'othered' status of the pit.

A final detail worth mention is the variety of Greek terminology used for the underworld. The passage locates Egypt and the first mention of Assyria in the "depth of the pit" (εν βαθει βοθρου), Elam in the "underworld" (εις γης βαθος), and the Assyrian rulers and commanders in the "pit" (εις βοθρον). In v. 27, Elam is laid to rest with the giants from long ago in "Hades" (αδης). Perhaps these terms refer to levels of ignominy, with the giants occupying the extreme, or perhaps they preserve different cultural ideas about death.[75]

5.3.1.2. *The Population in the Pit: MT and p967*

The MT's pit is a busier place. The nations depicted in its underworld are: Assyria (vv. 22–23), Elam (vv. 24–25), Meshech and Tubal (vv. 26–28), Edom (v. 29), and the Sidonians (the "princes of the North" in v. 30). Preceding all of these in v. 21 are the "mighty men," to be discussed in more detail below. While p967 lacks Meshech and Tubal and presents a truncated version of Elam's paragraph, still further differences exist. p967 does not list Edom or the Sidonians in the pit. Instead, the list of nations in p967 focuses on Assyria and more specific categories of the Assyrian cohort.[76]

In terms of geography, p967's edition of the nations is the more consistent of the two, though it is not without problems. Elam allied itself with its neighbor Babylon and fought against Assyria in the 7th century BCE. Thus, all of p967's nations come from remote locations in the wider ancient Near Eastern geography.

---

[75] For example, the Greek giants in Hesiod are laid to rest in Hades.

[76] The importance of Assyria may also be seen in the MT expansions in vv. 22–23. The MT plus of most of v. 23 is asterisked in Origen's Hexapla and Hi as well as Lucian mss., but is lacking in B p967 and Co. The reason these are minuses and not variants of the same verse is because of the Lucianic and Hexaplaric decision to include both verses—meaning these early witnesses understood the two verses as *meaning* differently enough to retain the two. Allen's explanation is appealing in that it explains all of the phrases in the MT plus, and it may explain the misreading of בירכתי in v. 23 by all the Greek readings, εν μηροις λαχχου (among the thighs/leg bones of the pit) as an interpretive interpolation. However, it is difficult to explain the Lucianic plus at the end of v. 23 with Allen's theory since its material does not repeat anything in the preceding verses. Allen does hit upon a section of text, however, in which corrective, clarifying glosses do accrue, although I see interpretive and compositional interpolations as well, like in the Lucianic reading just mentioned. Again, the variant material deals with the pit and its contents, having to do with Assyria.

Also, possibly relevant to the "Bones" *Tendenz* (§5.3.2.4), is the Greek reading εν μηροις λαχχου (among the thighs/leg bones of the pit).

Compared with p967, MT brings the national identity of the slain into closer geographical proximity. In place of the Assyrians in vv. 29–30, MT reads Edom and the Sidonians, respectively, which brings the geographical focus of these isolated verses (discussed above) closer to the regions of ancient Israel/Palestine. The difference in geography between the two editions likely bespeaks different historical horizons against which the lament for Egypt is articulated.[77]

Finally, even already in 32:18, at the start of the prophetic lament over Egypt, the editions exhibit a variant concerning the population of the pit.

v. 18[78]   και καταβιβασουσιν αυτης τα εθνη τας θυγατερας νεκρας
And *her nations* will bring down *the dead daughters*

v. 18   והורדהו אותה ובנות גוים אדרם
And bring *it* [the crowd of Egypt] down *with her and the daughters of the majestic nations*

In p967, Egypt's dead (νεκρας) daughters are brought to their fate in the pit at the hand of the nations. Conversely, in MT the prophet pronounces the descent of two parties, the crowd of Egypt and the daughters of majestic nations.

5.3.1.3. *Emphasis of MT: The Uncircumcised*

p967's edition of the pit mentions circumcision, but not consistently. Elam and the commanders of Assyria (v. 30) were marked as uncircumcised, increasing their condemned status in the pit. However, there is no mention of uncircumcision in the earlier reference to Assyria in v. 22 or the rulers of Assyria in v. 29. The term does not occur in these verses of p967.

---

[77] Elam and Assyria are easiest to locate historically since the height of Assyria and Elam's struggles occurred in the 7th century BCE. Edom and the Sidonians were active political forces during the Babylonian period. However, it is difficult to determine "what actual political polemic is involved" for the Sidonians (צדני). Zimmerli, *Ezekiel*, 2:177. According to Miller and Hayes' discussion of this period, a six-nation conclave met in Jerusalem (597 BCE) which included Edom and Sidon, to plot a rebellion against Babylon. However, in 587 when Zedekiah and Judah rebelled, records suggest that only Ammon and Tyre carried out rebellions. Edom and Sidon's adherence to the alliance is entirely unknown. However, given this and other periods of political inter-action, the referents were likely generated from historical events. In contrast, Meshech and Tubal remain anomalies as mythic figures.

[78] I translate "her nations" for p967 because αυτης is in the predicate position and probably modifies "nations," although the different syntax in B probably reads "*the* nations bring down *her* dead daughters."

In striking contrast, MT constructs a systematic narrative of the pit with respect to the status of circumcision. Uncircumcision is definitional for the shameful death attributed to those fated to the pit.[79] This is signaled by the beginning of the lament in v. 19: "Be laid to rest with the uncircumcised" (וְהִשְׁכְּבָה אֶת עֲרֵלִים). The point is seconded by the speech of the *Gibborim* (גבורים) in v. 21. In their opening line, they introduce the list of nations with the statement "they have come down, they lie still, the uncircumcised, those killed by the sword" (יָרְדוּ שָׁכְבוּ הָעֲרֵלִים חַלְלֵי חֶרֶב). Hence, the MT edition frames the list of nations by identifying the pit as a site of uncircumcision.

The term 'uncircumcision' (עֲרֵלִים) occurs five more times in MT than p967.[80] By increasing the density of the term, MT explicitly indicates each nation's relationship to circumcision.[81] Elam (vv. 24, 25), Meshech and Tubal (v. 26), and the princes of the North (v. 30) are described as uncircumcised. Egypt (vv. 19, 28, 32) and Edom (v. 29) will descend into the pit "*with* the uncircumcised."[82] Thus, either by nature or by association, the nations in the pit are brought to shame through uncircumcision.

One group in MT, the *Gibborim* (גבורים), has a unique relationship with the shame of uncircumcision. MT attributes to the גבורים their traditional status of valor in v. 27b, where their death is described in arguably honorable terms.[83] Additionally, several textual critics have seen allusions to Gen. 6 in v. 27a with the term נְפִלִים.[84] MT points נְפִלִים while

---

[79] Elsewhere in MT, uncircumcision holds significance that is not attributed to it in p967. In Ezek 44:7, the MT and all other Greek witnesses disallow people "uncircumcised in heart *and flesh*" into the temple. In the same phrase, p967 is only concerned to exclude those uncircumcised in heart. Fleshly circumcision is only an issue in MT. (For more on 44:7a, see §5.4.2 on the "Heart" *Tendenz*.)

[80] The MT addition in vv. 24b–26 contains the word twice. It also appears as a single-phrase plus in vv. 27 and 29. The fifth MT plus occurs in v. 21b, where the phrase in the Greek is a *translocation* of vv. 19–20.

[81] The only exception is Assyria in vv. 22–23.

[82] Grammatically, vv. 19 and 29 render "with (אֶת)" while vv. 28 and 32 have "in the midst (בְּתוֹך)." The MT inclusion of Sidon (the princes of the North) and Edom, apparently cultures that *practiced* circumcision, as did the Egyptians to whom the lament was directed, groups them with those punished and separated as unclean in death. See Zimmerli, *Ezekiel*, 2:173–4.

[83] Their swords are placed under their heads and their "shields" upon their bones. The translation "shields" is based on a reconstructed text taken up by Zimmerli and initially proposed by Cornill who read צִנּוֹתָם (their shields) for עֲוֹנֹתָם (their iniquities). Zimmerli, *Ezekiel*, 2:168 n27c. Cornill, *Das Buch*, 390. This conjecture will be challenged below in §5.3.2.4.4. Compare Isa 14:11 "your pride is brought down to Sheol, along with the sound of your harps, worms were spread out beneath you and weevils are your covering."

[84] We would expect to see a form of the verb יָרַד which is used consistently elsewhere in the pericope to describe the descent into the pit (vv. 18(2x), 19, 21, 24(2x), 25, 27, 29,

Cornill, Ehrlich, and Herrmann read נְפִלִים, the famed *Nephilim*, warriors of renown from Israel's primeval history.[85] In an unvocalized text, of course, both options would be possible. It seems that MT capitalized on the association with the *Nephilim*. For the MT, the association emphasizes the identity of the *Gibborim* as Israel's men of valor. Supporting this positive interpretation of the *Gibborim,* the heroes are nowhere shamed by uncircumcision in MT. On the contrary, the heroes of antiquity are granted a space in v. 27a which is *exempt* from uncircumcision's shame.

v. 27a ולא ישכבו את גבורים נפלים מערלים

And they will *not* lie with the heroes, those who fell *apart from* (מִן) the uncircumcised.[86]

The unique variants in MT's edition make a spatial distinction within the pit by means of the partitive מִן, quarantining apart the heroes.[87] The spatial distinction sets up, as Zimmerli argues, a space for an honorable death of the heroes (of old) and the dishonorable death of everyone else in the pit.[88] The descent of Edom in MT captures the significance of this division. Edom, a nation which was known to practice circumcision, could on that basis, join the heroes in being set apart from those uncircumcised nations in the pit. However, the MT plus in v. 29 את ערלים (with the uncircumcised) clarifies to which space in the pit this circumcised nation will go namely, to the space of shame. Thus, Edom is guilty by association, unlike the *Gibborim*.

MT offers a systematic account of the ritual status of the bodies in the pit. Just as it systematically identifies the 'uncircumcised,' MT is also more direct about the shame associated with these ritual/political identities.

30(2x)). The verb נפל occurs five times in Ezek 32:17–32: here, and four other times always describing death by the sword, with the phrase, "falling by the sword" (vv. 20, 22, 23, and 24). Thus, נפלים in v. 27a is a semantic anomaly for the chapter.

85 Zimmerli, *Ezekiel*, 2:168 n27b. Zimmerli states "the negation in missing in LXX, La^C, and Peshitta, and this considerably alters the meaning."

86 "They" refers to the uncircumcised, Meshech and Tubal from v. 26.

87 The partitive *mem* could also mean "some from." However, the context renders this option nonsensical, particularly given the negative particle, a unique plus in MT's edition. Zimmerli relies solely on the partitive construction here to develop his notion of an underworld with spatial distinctions. While I happen to agree with him, it should be noted that he ignores his own textual decision to read with the LXX here, substituting מעולם for מערלים. Zimmerli, *Ezekiel*, 2:168 n27b. He does so in order to strengthen his referential preference for "heroes of old" as opposed to "giants." He considers the MT variant about circumcision to "represent an accommodation to the context: the heroes of old lie apart from the uncircumcised." Ibid., 2:176.

88 Ibid., 2:176.

The phrase "they bear their shame" (כלמתם וישאו) occurs three times (vv. 24, 25, 30) and "ashamed" (בושים) occurs once (v. 30) in MT's edition. In contrast, p967 does not mention 'shame' at all in its edition. In three of these cases, MT is the longer edition. As for the fourth variant in v. 30, where MT reports that the Sidonians bear their **shame**, p967 reads "they bear their **torment**" (και απηνεγκαν την βασανον αυτων).[89] Thus, through its pluses and variants, MT characterizes the pit as a place of shame emphasized by the uncircumcised status of its inhabitants. Only the heroes of old enjoy a death in the underworld without shame. In this regard, it may be important to note that MT reserves the term *Sheol* for the "mighty men" (Greek "giants"). Otherwise, MT overwhelmingly uses "pit" (בור).[90]

5.3.1.4. *The Giants in p967*

According to p967, the 'giants,' along with everyone else in the pit, descend to their ignominy. p967's negative characterization, captured in part by the Greek translation οι γιγαντες (v. 21), is consistent with the traditio-development of these primeval beings.[91] Traditionally, the *Gibborim* גבורים were associated with Israel's ancient heroes.[92] However, the 'giants' came to be associated with the illicit sexual transgression of heaven and earth, described without judgment in Gen 6:4. Indeed, in Ezek 32:27a, p967 describes them as απο αιωνος, an allusion to the antiquity of the Genesis characters. In a large body of Second Temple Jewish literature, the giants became emblems of evil on the earth. No longer 'men of renown,' their destruction is described in extensive detail in works such as Jubilees and 1 Enoch.[93] Some of the textual variants in Ezekiel 32 reflect these negative characterizations.

---

[89] βασανος occurs seven times in the LXX of Ezekiel. Four of those cases translate כלמה (Ezek 16:52, 54; 32:24, 30). However, the *Vorlage* is not consistent: once דאגה (Ezek 12:18) and twice מכשול (Ezek 3:20 and 7:19).

[90] בור occurs in vv. 18, 23, 24, 25, 29, and 30; while שאול occurs in the two verses about the heroes in vv. 21 and 27. The only other term for the underworld is ארץ תחתיות in v. 24, but the verse also uses בור. As mentioned above, p967 displays various translational terms, but does not maintain the consistency of the giants in שאול the MT.

[91] This translation is consistent with the LXX of Gen 6:4, where the Greek witnesses read οι γιγαντες for both הגברים and הנפלים.

[92] The LXX translates the נפלים with οι γιγαντες. The גברים only secondarily acquired the valences ascribed to the נפלים in Genesis by association.

[93] See J. VanderKam, "Enoch Traditions in Jubilees and Other Second Century Sources," *JBL* 13 (1978): 229–251, and also George W. E. Nickelsburg, *1 Enoch: A Commentary on the Book of 1 Enoch Chapters 1–36; 81–108* (Hermeneia; Mineapolis: Winston, 1985), 165–169. Some support for understanding the גבורים as giants may be found in Ezek 27:19 where MT reads "Uzal" (אוזל), a maritime source of wrought iron. A reads "Asael" (ασαελ); (p967 reads ασηλ). The Shemihazah and Asael narratives are combined in 1 Enoch 6–11 as an

Indeed, rather than open up a space of honorable burial, the giants reinforce the negative valences of the pit. Verse 27a, which in MT served to differentiate two types of burial, offers no such distinction.

> v. 27a και εκοιμηθησαν μετα των γιγαντων των πεπτωκοτων απο αιωνος
> and they were (*minus*) laid with the giants, the ones who fell *from of old.*

The uncircumcised nation joins the giants in the pit.[94] p967 lacks the negative particle and the partitive construction that were present in MT. Thus, p967 maligns all the company in the pit; there is no place of honor in the underworld. The uncircumcised nations join the giants in one undifferentiated space of banishment.[95]

5.3.2. *'Fate of the Slain' Tendenzen: Variants across the Rest of Ezekiel*

Chapter 32 shows a concern for the fate of enemy nations, particularly those slain by the sword and condemned to a disgraceful death in the pit. This concern participates in a wider scribal *Tendenz* across the book of Ezekiel to locate the slain in valleys, on plains, in pits, on mountains, in the sea, and sometimes to distinguish whether they received proper burial or lay unburied.

5.3.2.1. *Tyre's Fate in the Midst of the Sea*

The oracles against Tyre occur in chs. 26–28. According to both editions, Ezek 28:8 describes how Tyre comes to its end in the midst of the sea. Zimmerli understands this as merely a reference to the geography of Tyre as an island city.[96] Of the two editions, p967 comes closer to Zimmerli's

---

etiology for the origins of evil on the earth. The giants, born of the transgressions of the former, are responsible for the havoc on the earth.

[94] For p967, which lacks vv. 25–26, this nation is Elam. This change in subject does not bear on the issue of circumcision, however, given that Elam is described as uncircumcised in v. 24.

[95] Indeed, Zimmerli has to go to great lengths in order to exegetically maintain the honorable death for the mighty men in the MT. He emends the text צִנֹּתָם or צִנּוֹתָם on the basis of conjecture in v. 27, "their **shields** lie on their bones" where all the versions attest עֲוֹנֹתָם "their iniquities". Zimmerli, *Ezekiel*, 2:168. Additionally, v. 27 ends with the phrase, כִּי חִתִּית גִּבּוֹרִים בְּאֶרֶץ חַיִּים (for the terror of the heroes was in the land of the living). Zimmerli, *Ezekiel*, recognizing this phrase challenges his exegesis, pointed out that all other villainous nations actively spread terror (נָתְנוּ חִתִּית) in vv. 23, 24, 26(25). Zimmerli demotes the causal כִּי to a neutral clause and rests his exegesis on the passive nature of the heroes' terror. Both decisions are dubious and seek to eradicate the clear presence of judgment against the heroes, even in the current form of the MT.

[96] Zimmerli, *Ezekiel*, 2:78–79.

claim, where Tyre's fate resembles that of a sinking island. In contrast, MT contains four variants that construe Tyre's fate in parallel terms to Pharaoh's in the pit of 32:17–33, the passage just examined. Three of these variants occur in 28:8–10.

First, p967's edition:

> v. 8   They will bring you down, and you will die the death of the slain in the heart of the sea.

> v. 9   Will you indeed say before your killers, "I am God." But you dress like a man[97] and not God.

> v. 10   You will die by the hands of uncircumcised strangers.

According to p967's edition, the island city of Tyre will fall because of an invasion of strangers. On account of Tyre's boasting and claims to divinity, the oracle pronounces Tyre's death with condemning language. They die the death of the slain and die among the uncircumcised.

The MT edition contains the following relevant two pluses and one variant:

> v. 8   *To the pit* they will bring you down, and you will die the death of the slain in the heart of the sea.

> v. 9   Will you really say "I am God" before your killers? You are a man and not God. *By the hand of the ones slaying you;*

> v. 10   you will die *the death of the uncircumcised* by the hands of strangers.[98]

MT contains similar phrases and ideas as the description of Israel's enemies in the pit of ch. 32. The verb ירד and the 'death of the slain (חלל)' were already extant in p967 (καταβιβάζω and τραυματίας). However, MT brings these and two other details into close alignment with the pit of

---

[97] p967's text presents a curious variant here. συ δε ει ανθρωπος in BAQ follows MT. However, p967 uniquely reads συ δε ησθα ανθρωπος. I take ησθα as a 2pf pass. 1cs of εννυμι. (A 2pf affixes -α as opposed to -κα, according to Smyth, *Greek Grammar*, §561).

[98] 28:8   και καταβιβασουσιν σε και αποθανη θανατω τραυματιων εν καρδια θαλασσης
    And they will bring you down; and you will die the death of the slain in the heart of the sea.

לשחת יורדוך ומתה ממותי חלל בלב ימים

To the pit they will bring you down; and you will die the death of the slain in the heart of the sea.

28:10   απεριτμητων απολη εν χερσιν αλλοτριων
    You will die by the hands of uncircumcised strangers.

מותי ערלים תמות ביד זרים

You will die the *death of the uncircumcised* by the hands of strangers.

ch. 32. The most striking MT plus occurs in v. 8, where it explicitly describes Tyre's descent (ירד) as "to the pit" (v. 8).[99]

The other variants more subtly shift the emphasis towards the pit of ch. 32. The MT plus in v. 9 uses the verb חלל (to slay) to re-emphasize the type of death Tyre will suffer. Additionally, MT rephrases p967's "by the hands of uncircumcised strangers" as "the death of the uncircumcised." p967's participial phrase shames by association, while MT shames through identity, expressed through the predicate construction. Given the importance of uncircumcision in ch. 32, particularly in MT, the following tabulation of parallels reveal the connections.

Tyre in ch. 28	Nations in ch. 32	Term/Phrase in MT
v. 8 (Hiph. impf.)	v. 18 (Hiph. impv.) v. 18, 24, 25, 29 (Qal ptc) v. 19, 27, 30 (Qal impv.) v. 21, 24 (Qal pft.)	thrust down (ירד)
v. 8	vv. 20, 21, 22, 23, 24, 25(3), 26, 28, 29, 30(2), 31, 32	death of the slain (חלל)
v. 8 (שחת)[100]	vv. 18, 24 (ארץ תחתיות) vv. 18, 23, 24, 25, 29, 30 (בור)	to the pit
v. 10	vv. 19, 21, 24, 25, 26, 27, 28, 29, 30, 32	death of the uncircumcised (ערלים)

The end of ch. 27 also describes Tyre's fate and echoes the death of Pharaoh from ch. 32. A rhetorical question posed to Tyre in 27:32 parallels the question posed to Egypt in 32:19. Both questions are pluses in MT, and both introduce the quoted speech opening an oracle of lament.[101] In 27:32,

---

[99] The specific term שחת is not used in ch. 32. However, as we saw earlier, both editions employ various terms for the pit; שחת is one of those terms in MT. The MT characterizes the sea as the pit in this verse for two reasons. First, the MT adds a stronger critique of Tyre's sins against God in this passage, where Tyre is accused of claiming to "be a god" (vv. 2, 6, and 9). Second, in 28:2, Tyre claims to be a god, reigning in the heart of the seas. The MT "pit" ensures that the sea is not taken as a place of power to reign, but rather as the shameful fate of enemy nations.

[100] The noun is rare in the MT: Ezek 19: 4, 8, and the present verse. Translation studies would be especially helpful with the many words for underworld; unfortunately McGreggor does not deal with the noun שחת, but only the verb. McGregor, *The Greek Text*, 25–26.

[101] p967 opens with a question as well, "How large is your reward which you have found in the sea?" All critical texts leave an LXX minus in v. 32b and a plus in v. 33a to signal the meaningful variant between MT and the Greek. In any case, p967's question is directly related to its immediate context and does *not* echo the fate of Egypt in ch. 32.

the mariners (v. 29) raise up laments (בניהם and קינה) and chant dirges
(וקוננו) over Tyre. They open with the question "who was destroyed like
Tyre in the midst of the sea?"[102] The answer comes in 28:8–10: *Egypt* was
destroyed like Tyre. Egypt suffered the death of the uncircumcised, was
slain, and fell into the pit. In these details, Tyre's fate closely parallels the
descent of nations into the pit of ch. 32.

In addition to these parallels with ch. 32, one additional variant in ch.
26 amplifies the significance of Tyre's fate, raising some as yet unseen
issues.

> 26:20–21
>
> οπος μη κατοικηθης μη δε αναστaθης επι ᵗⁿⁱ ζωης απωλειαν σε δωσω και ουχ
> υπαρξεις ετι
> so that you would not be inhabited nor *arise into life*;[103] I will make you a
> destruction and you will never exist again.
>
> למען לא תשבי ונתתי צבי בארץ חיים בלהות אתנך ואינך ותבקשי ולא
> תמצאי עוד
> in order that you will not remain and *I will give beauty in the land of the liv-
> ing*; I will make you a destruction until you no longer exist, *and though you
> will be sought after, you will never be found* again

Of the two editions, MT emphasizes the good conditions in the land of the
living after Tyre's ultimate end. The MT plus in v. 21 indicates that some
continue to search for the nation, despite the finality of Tyre's absence.
p967, the briefer of the two editions, pronounces the finality of Tyre's fate
against a different idea, namely that Tyre will not rise, presumably from
its permanent place in the underworld.[104]

5.3.2.2. *"Hordes" Tendenz: The End for Enemy Hordes*

The variants between MT and p967 frequently differ about the fate of
enemy hordes. The Hebrew term המון, usually meaning "horde" or "crowd"
(metonymically standing for the noise a crowd makes,) connotes a military entourage. The oracle of 32:17–32 is addressed to Egypt *and her hordes*

---

[102] In Ezek 27:32, p967 is a minus, while MT reads מי כצור כדמה בתוך הים.

[103] B reads, οπος μη κατοικηθης μη δε αναστῃς επι της γης ζωης "so that you would not be
inhabited nor **that you would rise up** on the **land** (BAQ) of the living." The definite article
in p967 is written in secondarily as a super-script, probably a correction.

[104] Perhaps a similar concern is expressed in the variant of 39:6 about "coastlands/
islands." The MT reads "I will send fire against Magog **and against** the inhabitants of the
islands (וישבי האיים) while LXX (cf. Latin) reads "I will send fire on Magog; and the
islands **will be** inhabited (και κατοικηθησονται)."

(32:18, 20, 31, 32). The MT plus in vv. 25–26 locates the hordes of Elam and Meshech and Tubal in the pit. Thus, the term המון is amply reflected in the MT edition of 32:17–32.

There are seven instances in which המון stands in an MT plus. All seven pluses amplify or extend the militaristic context onto an apocalyptic temporal or spatial plane. MT's pit of ch. 32: 17–32 uniquely acts as a repository for the המון of enemy nations. Further, המון shows up in the Day of Yahweh against Egypt (30:1–19) and in similar eschatological expressions in ch. 7. p967 is the shorter text in these instances. However, p967 does contain "horde" pluses against MT as well, mostly focusing on Tyre.

5.3.2.2.1. *Hordes in the Pit of Chapter 32*
In the twenty-four instances of the term המון in MT of Ezekiel, only one does not refer to the captivity or death of masses of people in a military context.[105] The term actually serves such an etiological function in Ezek 39:11 where Gog's burial place is named גיא המון גוג "the valley of Hamon-gog" or the "horde of Gog." In MT, the term dominates in the oracles against Egypt, referring to Egypt's military entourage in chs. 29–32. Ezekiel 30:10 offers a paradigmatic use, "I will destroy the *hordes* of Egypt by the hand of King Nebuchadrezzar of Babylon."

p967 translates המון with πλῆθος in Ezek 30:10, 15; 31:2, 18; 32:32. This is a common Septuagint translation for המון, especially in Ezekiel.[106] However, the Greek terminology for המון varies significantly in the other instances. Whereas MT denotes a fallen military entourage, p967 often translates with a more general term, such as "strength." While this may be the mere effect of a translator, nevertheless, the terminological choice has literary significance.[107]

---

[105] In Ezek 23:42, the harlot plays with a carnavalesque horde. In a small number of instances of the term "horde," the meaning is more vague. Even still, the association with military death is strong. So, in 26:13 where המון refers to the "sound" of Tyre's harps, Ezekiel's oracle is about silencing the harps in a final battle. Finally, it is possible to translate המון as "wealth" in a few cases (Ezek 29:19; 30:4, 15), but given the military context, captive slaves are arguably also in view.

[106] המון occurs in MT Ezekiel twenty-four times, the most of any biblical book. πλῆθος is by no means the only translation equivalent for המון, but πλῆθος is the most common translation in Ezekiel. Hatch and Redpath, "Appendix A," 250.

[107] In the "Hordes" *Tendenz*, some of the variants can be attributed to translation as opposed to "redactional" or "compositional" activity. However, because the variants effect the literary editions of MT and p967, they are treated among the data set of variants. This example serves as an important reminder that translation is difficult to distinguish from composition in some cases. The translation issue with המון will be discussed briefly below.

In the apocalyptic space of ch. 32's pit, MT frequently uses "horde" to describe the entourage of the descending enemies. MT addresses the oracle of 32:17–32 to the "hordes" of Egypt and offers Elam (twice) and Meshech and Tubal's hordes as examples of an apocalyptic fate in the pit.[108] By way of contrast, p967 does not use the term "horde ($\pi\lambda\eta\theta o\varsigma$)" frequently; it only occurs in v. 32 in the summative statement at the end of the passage. Otherwise, Egypt's "horde" is translated "strength ($\iota\sigma\chi\upsilon\nu$)." Thus, p967 lacks the opening rhetorical address that would interpolate Egypt's horde into the pit. Indeed, the "horde" does not appear *within* the pit either. p967 lacks the two occurrences of Elam and Meshech and Tubal's "horde" in the vv. 25–26 minus. Even in p967's extant description of Elam (v. 24), where MT used המון, p967 reads $\delta\upsilon\nu\alpha\mu\iota\varsigma$ (power). These Greek terms do not denote the concept of a multitude. Egypt's *strength* is addressed while Elam's *power* descends into the graves of the pit. Thus, p967 obscures the MT's semantic reliance on the term through an inconsistent translation of MT's המון. However, the lexical consistency in MT, as well as the MT המון-pluses in vv. 25–26 make the pit a site of the hordes' end.

The wordplay just described, and p967's use of "power" and "strength" convey a different interpretation of the population in the pit. Generally, p967 condemns national political traits, "strength" and "power." In contrast, MT seems to imply a more literal understanding of national strength, specifically condemning the military entourage to the pit. Overall, the "hordes" *Tendenz* in the pit owes to dynamics of translation.[109] However, the translation issue here coheres with textual variants elsewhere, as the following discussion will show.

5.3.2.2.2. *Hordes of Egypt*

p967 locates Egypt's fallen horde on the mountains. We already saw that in ch. 32, p967 lacks the term horde ($\pi\lambda\eta\theta o\varsigma$), despite MT's repeated use of המון in the pit. Instead, p967 mentions the $\pi\lambda\eta\theta o\varsigma$ of Egypt in its unique plus earlier in the chapter, in 32:6:

---

[108] Neither MT nor p967 describe Assyria (vv. 22–23), Edom (v. 29), or the princes of the North (v. 30) as surrounded by a horde. Assyria does descend with an entourage, but the term used is קהל / $\sigma\upsilon\nu\alpha\gamma\omega\gamma\eta$.

[109] It is unclear whether p967's terminology reflects an alternate distribution of Hebrew terms; in other words, there is no way to know if p967's terms reflect translation decisions or a variant Hebrew *Vorlage*, although the latter is less likely.

p967　απο του πληθους επι των ορεων

> (And the land will be drenched from your excrement) *as a result of the multitude on the mountains*; (I will fill the ravines because of you.)

MT　　מדמך אל ההרים

> (And I will drench the land with your flowing blood,) *your blood (will flow) to the mountains.* (And the ravines will fill because of you.)

In contrast, MT displays two המון-pluses concerning the fate of Egypt's hordes. The MT המון-pluses occur in 29:19 and 30:4.

1) Ezekiel 29:19

p967　(minus)

> (Behold I will give the land of Egypt to Nebuchadrezzar, king of Babylon and) *minus* (he will plunder her plunder and spoil her spoil; it will be the wages for his power.)

MT　　ונשא המנה

> (Behold I am giving the land of Egypt to Nubuchad king of Babylon.) *And he will carry off her horde,* (he will plunder her plunder and spoil her spoil; and she will be the wages for his army [power].)

2) Ezekiel 30:4

p967　(minus)

> (And the sword will fall on Egypt and disorder will emerge in Ethiopia and the slain will fall in Egypt) *minus* (and her foundations will collapse)

MT　　ולקחו המונה

> (And the sword will come upon Egypt and anguish will emerge in Cush when the slain fell in Egypt) *when they take her hordes* (and her foundations are thrown down.)

These two MT pluses occur in close proximity to each other. Chapter 30 takes the mundane military report of ch. 29 and infuses it with more cosmic imagery of destruction. Both contexts involve Egypt's hordes. In 29:19, King Nebuchadrezzar carries off Egypt's horde along with plunder and spoil, as God's payment on behalf of Babylon's labor.[110] Then in 30:4, Egypt

---

[110] Perhaps relevant to the larger significance of the enemy nations, v. 18 clarifies that Nebuchadrezzar's army "labored hard against Tyre" and required funds. God promptly solicits Egyptian plunder for Babylonian reserves. According to the MT plus, it seems that the Egyptians were probably indentured into Babylon's army as it pursued Tyre.

falls, slain by the sword, and her hordes are carried off. Both of these contexts seem to have a form of captivity in view where the fate of Egypt's hordes lies in exile. The latter MT plus occurs in a passage with similar "day of the Lord" phraseology as found in ch. 7.[111]

5.3.2.2.3. *Hordes on the Day of the Lord in Chapter 7*
Chapter 7, while not extant in p967, presents three MT המון pluses against the LXX and should be considered here for their relevance to the "hordes" *Tendenz* in MT's edition.

1) Ezekiel 7:12

> MT בא העת הגיע היום הקונה אל ישמח והמוכר אל יתאבל כי חרון
> אל כל המונה
>
> The time comes, the day draws near; let not the buyer rejoice and let not the seller mourn, *for wrath is upon all its horde.*

2) Ezekiel 7:13

> MT כי המוכר אל הממכר לא ישוב ועוד בחיים חיתם כי חזון אל כל
> המונה לא ישוב ואיש בעונו חיתו לא יתחזקו
>
> For the seller shall not return to the merchandise as long as they are among the living, *for the vision concerns all its horde, it will not be revoked*; and each man will not stand firm because of his iniquity.

3) Ezekiel 7:14

> MT תקעו בתקוע והכין הכל ואין הלך למלחמה כי חרוני אל כל המונה
> They blew the trumpet and fixed everything; *but no one goes to battle for my wrath is upon its whole horde.*

These pluses in MT expand on the notion of the fate of the "hordes". The hordes are the object of God's wrath according to Ezekiel's reliable and permanent visions. Given the apocalyptic context in which the pluses appear (i.e., בא העת הגיע היום in v. 12), the mythic trope strengthens the divine word (visions) and the divine intentions (wrath). In these three ways, the fate of the hordes is sealed in permanent eschatological destruction.[112]

---

[111] Note especially the phrase "the day is near" קרוב יום in Ezek 30:3 and 7:7. These are the only two instances of the phrase in Ezekiel; (and the only two instances of the word קרוב).

[112] This section of ch. 7 contains a dense set of references to the eschatological "day" discussed above in the "Prophetic Temporality" *Tendenzen*. See especially §5.2.2.3.

5.3.2.2.4. *Hordes and Tyre*

"Horde" (πληθος) occurs in four p967 pluses and signals a wider interpretive pattern that differentiates p967 from MT. The rare p967 pluses, in Ezek 27:25; 28:10, and 17, concern the oracles against Tyre. These instances amplify the already dense pattern of πληθος in chs. 26–28. In what seems to be a Greek play on words, the Tyrians are characterized as traders of economic *abundance* (πληθος—27:12, 16, 18, 25+, 33) and then indicted for the *abundance* (πληθος) of their iniquities (28:10+, 16, 17+, 18).[113] Finally, Tyre is said to be destroyed by *hordes* (πληθος—26:10; 28:9).

The same play on words does not exist in MT.[114] Tyre's aggressor in 26:10 is called שִׁפְעַת "an abundance." Further, in 28:9, p967 retains the wordplay when Tyre is killed and humiliated εν πληθει "by the horde," whereas MT reads בְּיַד מְחַלְלָיִךְ "by the hand of those who slay you." MT retains a more modest lexical consistency in the wordplays regarding economy (27:12, 16, 18, 33) and iniquity (28:16, 18), but switches terms from המון to רב. p967's pluses reinforce the strong pattern of wordplay with the term πληθος. Its edition makes a stronger connection between Tyre's fate at the hand of a horde, and Tyre's economic sins. This pattern of p967's use of πληθος could reflect ideas about economic conduct and divine retribution, in that Tyre falls to the same power that characterized its economic excesses.[115]

5.3.2.3. *'Death on the Field'* Tendenz

Among the issues that have emerged in the 'Fate of the Slain' *Tendenz* thus far, the theme of location most densely characterizes the variants. The underworld of chapter 32 summoned many issues related to the 'slain' including circumcision, the status of military hordes, and geography. However, all of the variants in the intertextual center reflect an interest in the "pit" as the final destination for Israel's enemies. In addition to the pit of ch. 32, other locations became relevant for the fate of the slain; for

---

[113] Where + signifies pluses in p967 using the term πληθος.

[114] המון, like the Greek πληθος, can mean "abundance" or "horde" and thus serve the same play on words.

[115] We already saw (in §5.3.2.2.3) that the MT edition of ch. 7 contained three "horde" pluses. In the immediate context, vv. 12–13 deal with mercantile life and the rest of the chapter goes on to indict additional economic practices. It is worth noting this connection in the MT between "hordes" and economics, in light of p967's edition of Tyre in chs. 26–28. We might have expected the word plays in MT chs. 26–28 to be as strong or even stronger than p967 as a result. However, in this failed expectation, the המון-pluses in ch. 7 probably do not intertextually refer to issues with Tyre.

instance, p967 reports that Egypt's hordes find their end on the mountains. Another location that is differently emphasized in MT and p967 is the field.

πεδιον (field) occurs 29 times in the LXX of Ezekiel.[116] The occasions on which it is used may be divided into three types: 1) the site of a vision;[117] 2) an agricultural reference (for example, beasts or trees of the field);[118] and 3) the site of death, usually by the sword or by animals. The last is the most common occurrence.

The third category, death on the field, first occurs in 7:15. Ezek 7:15 speaks about the mythic 'end' and reports that he who is on the field will die by the sword.[119] Though the chapter is replete with a rapid sequence of mythic references (i.e., phrases related to the day of the Lord), here the sword can *also* be understood in its mundane military sense. Indeed, v. 14 introduces the context of battle and invokes the 'four-fold judgment' scheme for both those who remain and those who escape the city during its siege.[120] In other sections of Ezekiel, most notably the sword-song in ch. 21, the sword takes on a mythic status as God's instrument of judgment.[121] Thus, the phrase in 7:15 about those who die on the field could likewise be understood as invested with mythic significance.

In the present reading, 'Death on the Field' acquires at least some of its significance because of the πεδιον in chapter 37. The significance of ch. 37 to 'death on the field' is certainly not exhaustive nor exclusive. However, the revivification of bones scattered on a field (בקעה / πεδιον) increased

---

[116] Edwin Hatch and Henry A. Redpath, "πεδιον," in *A Concordance to the Septuagint and Other Greek Versions of the Old Testament* (Oxford: Clarendon Press, 1906), 1114.

[117] Ezek 3:22, 23; 8:4; 37:1, 2.

[118] Ezek 17:5, 8, 24; 31:4, 5, 6, 15; 34:8, 27; 38:20; 39:4, 10, 17.

[119] p967 is not extant in Ezekiel 7. Incidentally, some variation exists with the word "sword." For example, the sword song in ch. 21:8–17 is very broken and the subject of numerous isolated textual studies. See Freedy, "The Glosses," 142; G.R. *Driver*, "Linguistic and Textual Problems: Ezekiel," *Bib* 19 (1938): 67–68; J. Noel Hubler, "Introduction to Iezekiel," in *A New English Translation of the Septuagint* (eds., Albert Pietersma and Benjamin G. Wright; Oxford: Oxford University Press, 2007), 946. Additionally, the term "sword" proved to be involved in several other textual variants as well. Among eight or so instances, p967 reflects a plus of the word "sword" in Ezek 26:15, a description of the fall of Tyre. MT, on the other hand, reflects a plus of the word "sword" in Ezek 32:20 and 32:31, both about the fate of Egypt and Pharaoh.

[120] The four-fold judgment here is modified into a binary one: those inside and outside the city die different deaths. See Zimmerli, *Ezekiel*, 2:208.

[121] See especially Ezek 21:14–15.

the importance of this locale for an intertextual reading of Ezekiel's oracles. It is to this issue that we now turn.

The announcement of death on the field occurs ten times, all of which use πεδιον for "field".[122] MT reads שדה in all but two cases where the term for a "channel" (אפיק) occurs instead. Several parties suffer death on the field: Israel (7:15; 16:5; and 33:27), the daughters of Tyre (26:6, 8), Egypt (29:5; 32:4; and implied in 31:12), Assyria (31:12), Edom (35:8), and Gog (39:5).[123] All of these parties, except for Israel, also end up in MT's edition of the pit in 32:17–32.[124]

A few of these instances of death on the field are variants and thus fall into the 'Fate of the Slain' *Tendenz*.

5.3.2.3.1. *Egypt and Pharaoh in Ezekiel 29:5*

p967   επι προσωπον του πεδιου σου πεση ου μη συναχθης ουδ ου μη περισταλης τοις θηριοις της γης και τοις πετεινοις του ουρανου δεδωκα σε εις καταβρωμα
   On the face of your field you will fall; you will not be assembled nor shall you be *buried*.[125] To the animals of the earth and to the birds of heaven, I gave you as food.

MT   על פני השדה תפול לא תאסף ולא תקבץ לחית הארץ ולעוף השמים נתתיך לאכלה
   On the face of the field you will fall; you will not be assembled *nor gathered*. To the animals of the earth and to the birds of the heaven, I gave you as food.

Verse 5a in MT and p967 read essentially the same, indicating that Egypt will fall on the field (πεδιου/שדה).[126] However, the reading in p967 disallows Egypt's burial using a negated passive of περιστελλω "you shall not

---

[122] p967 has nine; since the manuscript is not extant in Ezek 7:15. All LXX witnesses read πεδιον.

[123] In all these instances, the party dies by the sword except in Ezek 29:5; 32:4; and 39:5. In these three cases, the party's death is not reported, but the corpse is left for the birds and beasts to consume.

[124] Egypt, Assyria, Edom, and Gog were discussed in detail in §5.3.1.2. Assyria offers additional echoes, where in Ezek 31:12, a similar rhetorical moment obtains. Chapter 31 symbolizes Assyria as the great tree that is cut down on the field. Egypt is called to watch Assyria's fall (31:2–3) just like it is called to watch the nations descend into the pit in ch. 32. Compare MT's edition, where, as we saw in §5.3.2.1, Tyre's fate was schematized towards the pit of ch. 32.

[125] Also "wrapped as a corpse."

[126] The change of tense within the verse, though shared by both MT and p967, remains curious.

be wrapped." "Wrapped" or "taken care of" supply the simple sense of the
verb, although the connotation of dressing a corpse is probably in view;
thus, "buried."[127]

5.3.2.3.2. *Edom in Ezekiel 35:8*

και εμπλησω των τραυματιων σου τους βουνους και τας φαραγγας και εν πασι
τοις πεδιοις σου εσονται τετραυματισμενοι μαχαιρα πεσουνται εν σοι
And I will fill *(minus) the hills and your valleys* with the slain *and they will be
in all your fields*; those slain by the sword will fall *in you*

ומלאתי את הריו חלליו גבעותיך וגאותיך וכל אפיקיך חללי חרב יפלו בהם
And I will fill *its [Edom's] mountains* with its slain, *your hills and your valleys
and all your channels*; those slain by the sword will fall *in them*

MT provides the more expansive list of locations for the slain Edomites:
mountains, hills, valleys, and channels. p967 omits mountains and presents the variant "plains" (πεδιον) as opposed to "channels" (אפיק).[128] The
syntax of p967 creates a new clause with the phrase "they will be in all
your fields." p967's edition syntactically isolates the death on the field
where MT's undifferentiated list does not anywhere imply "field."

5.3.2.3.3. *Exegetical Significance of Death on the Field*

Earlier, I suggested that p967's "field" of ch. 37 may help to explain the
significance of death on the field in its edition. Through the lens of ch.
37's revivification, it is thus quite significant that p967 leaves Egypt, Edom
and Gog on the open field. Likewise, Edom, Gog, and the hordes of Egypt
do not appear in p967's underworld (in ch. 32). Thus, nothing in p967's
edition eliminates their candidacy for the miracle of ch. 37.[129] By way of
contrast, MT runs no risk of reviving enemy nations. All of them are
in the pit: Edom and Gog on account of the MT plus (see §5.3.1.2), and
Egypt's hordes, as discussed in §5.3.2.2.2 above.

---

[127] The Greek verb only occurs four times in the LXX according to Hatch and Redpath,
A Concordance to the Septuagint, 1126. Once it stands for אסף (Isa 58:8) and Hatch and
Redpath list Ezek 29:5 as קבץ. Sirach and Tobit do not have Hebrew counterparts, but the
context of Tobit 12:13 concerns death (νεκρος). In Attic and Herodotus' Greek, the term
simply means "to bury."

[128] p967's "field" (πεδιον) and MT's "channel" (אפיק) represent a translation which is
unique to Ezekiel and even there only occurs twice. Hatch and Redpath, "πεδιον," in *A
Concordance to the Septuagint*, 1113–4. φαραγξ is otherwise expected for אפיק in Ezekiel
(five times according to Hatch and Redpath, "φαραγξ," in *A Concordance to the Septuagint*,
1424).

[129] Note that *Pseudo-Ezekiel* specifies to whom Israel refers in its interpretation of
ch. 37.

The MT's term for "field" in ch. 37 further disallows ambiguity about the identity of those on the "field." MT's term in 37:1, 2 is בקעה, a "valley-plain" or a "broad valley." In MT, this term is always (and only) associated with the site of one of Ezekiel's visions (3:22, 23; 8:4; 37:1, 2). p967 does not distinguish between the type of field for visions and for death; it uses πεδιον in all instances. Thus, MT makes a strict spatial distinction between the visionary geography of Ezekiel's oracles for Jerusalem (and the judgments and promises therein) and the oracular pronouncements of death for nations on the fields of battle. p967 does not manifest the same terminological distinction.

It seems that the interpretive tradition, as captured by the Masoretic system of pointing, also eliminated any foreign candidates from the "field" of ch. 37's vision. A textually interesting verse in MT involves an alternate pointing of בקעה. MT of 26:10b reads "he enters your gates as men enter a breached city." "Breached" is a 3fs Pual ptc. of בקע (מְבֻקָּעָה). The Greek translated with εκ πεδιου, "from the plain," reading the Hebrew as if it was a noun with the prepositional מן (מִבַּקְעָה). The significance of this translation lies not in whether the Greek *misread* the Hebrew, but in the ambiguity of the Hebrew consonantal form. Rather than the Greek misreading, it is possible that the Masoretes pointed the phrase to ensure against the reading "from the plain" and hence to maintain the distinction regarding Ezekiel's visions that occur on the בִּקְעָה. In this scenario, p967 would preserve a possible original meaning; of course, this cannot be known for sure.

Nevertheless, a distinction in MT between שדה and בקעה is all the more possible given one of the observations made by Crane about the editions of Ezekiel 36–39. He showed that the implied Davidic ruler in MT was a militant leader and that ch. 37 depicts the revivification of an "exceedingly great army (37:10)" (חיל גדול מאד מאד).[130] If the field-vision revivifies a great army, it is crucial to MT that the vision *not* empower an enemy's national military. This could explain why MT reserves the term for visions concerning Jerusalem and its people. We already see this clarification in 37:12 where an MT plus adds עמי.[131] "My people," that is, those

---

[130] Crane, *Israel's Restoration*, 251–252, and especially 255.

[131] Already in Ezek 37:11, both MT and p967 identify the bones as the "whole house of Israel" whoever that may include. The added emphasis in MT moves beyond simply the social designation to ensure the *spiritual* identity, namely the relationship between God and *his* people. It is probably important that both of these identifiers occur in the interpretive frame for the vision (Ezek 37:12–14), material that follows the basic vision (Ezek 37:1–10). Who is included in the "house of Israel" (a political term for regional jurisdiction in most periods)? MT clarifies, only "my people."

identified by the deity, will be revivified, implying that enemy nations will not.[132] Thus, when read in this light, the Masoretic pointing for מבקעה "from the field" in 26:10b would allow for the renewal of an enemy nation, not associated with "my people." The specific context of ch. 26 refers to the king of Babylon coming against Tyre. MT, perhaps, did not want a resurgence of this particular kingdom from the North. p967's more broad use of "field" in both instances, at the very least, leaves its edition open to interpretation. While much of the preceding discussion is merely suggestive, one final interpretation brings increased significance to the militaristic meanings of the vision of ch. 37. In Ezek 37:10, MT revivifies a "great army," whereas p967 reads "συναγωγη πολλη σφοδρα, a great congregation." p967's congregation could imply a bold vision of the inclusion of foreigners.[133]

5.3.2.4. *"Bones"* Tendenz

As just discussed, the site of the vision in Ezekiel 37 may hold significance for the 'Fate of the Slain' *Tendenzen*. p967's deaths on the field would allow for the resurrection of foreign bodies, while MT's carefully distinguished spaces only permit "my people" Israel. Ezekiel 37 is, indeed, a chapter about the fate of the slain, albeit one that moves from death to life. The most prominent symbol for death in Ezekiel's vision is the dry bones. Thus, variants about bones take on increased significance in light of the intertextuality of death and the 'Fate of the Slain' *Tendenzen* already examined. Outside of Ezekiel 37, the term "bone" only occurs a few times, most densely in chapter 24. Several of these occurrences represent variants between p967 and MT.

5.3.2.4.1. *Bones in the Pot of Ezekiel 24*
Ezekiel 24 presents an allegory of a boiling pot.[134] The chapter uses the image to vividly depict the fate of Israelites in Jerusalem; hence, the chapter already lends itself to ideas about the fate of slain bodies.

---

[132] See Crane who makes the same point about Ezek 37:12. Crane, *Israel's Restoration*, 104–105.

[133] p967's congregation is characterized by what Crane calls p967's call to purity within the new "covenant of peace." Crane, *Israel's Restoration*, 251–252. Possible indications of p967's inclusive vision would be the variant in Ezek 44:7a, discussed below in §5.4.2.2. MT excludes all uncircumcised from the temple, while p967 only excludes those not circumcised of heart. p967's spiritual understanding of purity and identity is perhaps an indication that right-hearted foreigners were accepted in the "navel of the earth" (i.e., Jerusalem's temple).

[134] For a thorough discussion of the image and style of 24:1–14, see W.H. Brownlee, "Ezekiel's Copper Cauldron and Blood on the Rock," in *For Me to Live: Essays in Honor of*

In Ezekiel 24, the MT edition of the cook pot allegory exaggerates the bones. p967 and MT present variants in vv. 2, 4, 9, 10, and 11, all of which affect the specific allegory of the cooking pot. The end result is two different editions of the allegory, including alternate interpretations with different horizons of significance for the wider book of Ezekiel.[135] In p967, the pot retains general symbolic significance for the destruction of Jerusalem. MT, on the other hand, specifies the intertextual horizon towards Ezekiel 37 through the symbol of the stewing bones.

Ezekiel 24:1–14 is an allegory (*mashal*) about a burning cauldron. The interpretation of the *mashal*, offered by means of prophetic address and invective, concerns the destruction of Jerusalem and the fate of its inhabitants.[136] The controlling metaphor of a burning pot continues throughout. Within specific sections, however, the allegory is specified by two different images: a cooking pot for meat and a smelting pot for metals. For the most part, the images are artfully woven together. Nevertheless, inconsistencies are introduced by the two competing images, leading many commentators propose redaction solutions.[137] While some differences of opinion persist, most agree that the core *mashal* in vv. 3b–5 was inspired by a domestic

---

James Leon Kelso (ed. R.A. Coughenour; Cleveland: Dillon/Liederbach, 1972) , 24; and L.C. Allen, "Ezekiel 24:3–14: A Rhetorical Perspective," *CBQ* 49 (1987): 410.

[135] In considering the scribal phenomenon evinced by these variants, I was reminded of the apocalyptic mode of dream- or vision-interpretation. For example, the generic juxtaposition of dreams and interpretations, particularly characteristic of Daniel, takes the interpretation of symbols as divine revelation. See J.J. Collins, "The Court-Tales in Daniel and the Development of Apocalyptic," JBL 94 (1975): 218–234, esp. 234. The idea that later scribes redacted symbolic visions for the sake of apocalyptic interpretation finds precedent in 1QpHab. Timothy Lim, Brownlee, and Stendahl have pointed out the eccelctic textual nature of 1QpHab's biblical citations. Lim and Brownlee suggest that scribes altered the base text for the sake of their interpretive interests. The parade example occurs in the pesher on Hab 2:17, discussed in Timothy Lim, "Eschatological Orientation and the Alteration of Scripture in the Habakkuk Pesher," *JNES* 49 (1990): 185–194, esp. 190–191. K. Elliger develops a theory of interpretation that similarly correlates Hellenistic notions about revelation and dream interpretation. Elliger attaches his theory to the scribal eclecticism of 1QpHab. K. Elliger, *Studien zum Habbakkuk-Kommentar vom Toten Meer* (Tübingen: Mohr Siebeck, 1953), 155. In short, textual variants between the versions may reflect stages in the development of Jewish visions due to the effects of scribes adopting apocalyptic modes of interpretation.

[136] The interpretation of the metaphor of the cooking pot is also offered in Ezek 11:3, היא הסיר ואנחנו הבשר "[the city] is the pot, we are the meat."

[137] Freedy thinks that we have two originally separate images/allegories, brought together because of the shared metaphor of the cooking pot. Freedy, "The Glosses," 139–140 n2. Zimmerli speaks of an everyday work song about a cooking pot for vv. 3b–5 as the משל with vv. 6–14 serving as its interpretation. However, Zimmerli breaks the interpretation into vv. 6–8 and vv. 9–14. Zimmerli admits that the section in vv. 6–8, mostly adds metallurgy to the allegory and does not properly interpret what precedes. "Thus the original

culinary setting. For instance, Freedy calls it a "secular cook song figuratively applied to the fate of Jerusalem."[138] Whatever the redaction history may be, it is interesting to note that p967 stands closer to the mundane cook-pot imagery than MT, as the following discussion will show.

The *mashal* of the stewing pot begins in vv. 3b–5 and expands in vv. 9b–10. Verses 3b–5 describe setting the pot, pouring water in it (v. 3b), filling it with meat (v. 4) and bringing it to a boil (v. 5). Then vv. 6–8 recast the metaphor for the smelting cauldron working off the same term in v. 6 for pot (סיר / λεβης) as in v. 3. Ironically however, this section does not emphasize the requisite levels of heat required to smelt rust from a cauldron. It is not until vv. 9–10 and the return to the metaphor of the cooking pot that the images of raging heat begin to reach such levels. Both editions share this same basic content and structure.

The pertinent variant material occurs in vv. 2, 4, 9, 10, and 11.

v. 4b	εξεσαρκισμενα απο των οστεων	(the parts) being *stripped off* the bones
	מבחר עצמים מלא	*fill it with choice* bones
v. 9aβ	(minus)	(minus)
	אוי עיר הדמים	*woe to the bloody city*
v. 10a	και πληθυνω τα ξυλα	I will multiply the *wood*
	הרבה העצים	multiply the *bones*
v. 10bβ	οπος ταχη τα κρεα και	*in order that the meat would melt, the*
	ελαττωθη ζωμος	*sauce would be diminished*
	והרקח המרקחה	*spice the ointment pot; the bones will be*
	והעצמות יחרו	*scorched*
v. 11a	και στη επι τους ανθρακας	stand it upon the coals
	והעמידה על גחליה רקה	stand it *empty* upon the coals

p967's edition presents as the more mundane cooking allegory to make a general point. This is especially clear in v. 10 which reads, "I will multiply the wood and flame the fire, in order that the meat would melt, the sauce would be diminished." Here in v. 10, the increased heat enriches the stew. Complementing this image, v. 4 depicts the original placement of the meat in the stew pot, describing the shoulder and loins as "being stripped

---

interpretation of the משל of vv.3b–5 is to be found in vv.9b–10a, whilst vv.10b, 11ff contain the development of the interpretation in regard to vv. 6–8." Zimmerli, *Ezekiel*, 1:497.

[138] Freedy, "The Glosses," 139 n2. So Zimmerli who cites the study of van den Born attributing vv. 3b–5 to an originally oral work song. Zimmerli, *Ezekiel*, 1:496. Even Greenberg points out stages of composition to assist his literary reading, calling vv. 3–5 "a ditty," in poetic verse without reference to the subsequent stages of the allegory. Greenberg, *Ezekiel*, 2:503.

off the bones". Special bones from the choice of the flock are added in v. 5, which is text shared by both editions. These bones are seamlessly integrated into the mundane cook allegory to add "strength and flavor to the broth".[139] p967 only refers to the bones as incidental objects from which choice meat is stripped; its edition does not mention the bones again. In contrast, MT presents four instances where the word 'bones' appears in a plus. In an allegory, details take on increased importance as elements of signification. Thus, the dense use of עצם over p967's edition warrants attention.

MT's edition emphasizes the great volume of bones in the pot. Verse 4b supplies a unique imperatival clause, "fill it with choice bones." In meaning, this reads quite against p967 which replaces the imperative "fill" with adjectival participle to describe the meat "*being stripped off* the bones." As a result, MT *fills* the pot *with bones* while p967 takes the meat *off the bones*. The same difference occurs in v. 10. MT reads, "multiply the *bones* . . .; the *bones* will be scorched" where p967 reads, "multiply the wood . . . the sauce will be diminished."[140] Especially in this verse, MT bestows particular significance on the bones, as Zimmerli remarks, "there also appears a new emphasis here which breaks up the image: the destruction of human bones by burning them."[141]

The MT reading in v. 10 acquires added significance as being part of the woe oracle against the bloody city (vv. 9–13). The woe-form of the prophetic invective sets a tone of doom that was not present in the earlier, neutral presentation of the *mashal* (vv. 3b–5). The content of vv. 10–11 reinforces this tone of doom by bringing the image to a climax in description. Verse 10 describes flaming fire and the disappearance of flesh. This imagery goes well beyond the earlier description of melting the meat and boiling the sauce (v. 5). The verb חרר (to burn) in v. 10 especially raises the invective tone since burnt bones would hardly be consistent with the mundane culinary image. Indeed in v. 11, MT expresses the desired result of v. 10's burning, "stand it *empty* upon its coals". The word "empty" is an MT plus, as is the woe-form in v. 9.[142]

---

[139] Zimmerli, *Ezekiel*, 1:499. Most commentators take this detail for granted.

[140] Most commentators emend MT on the basis of the Greek to read "the logs", so the NRSV. However, the more difficult reading coheres with the "bones" *Tendenz* proposed here, and therefore represents a possible early reading.

[141] Zimmerli, *Ezekiel*, 1:495.

[142] Freedy argues that the word "empty" was added when the two images in vv. 3–11 came together. Freedy, "The Glosses," 139.

At the basic, most obvious level of the allegory, MT's edition of vv. 9–13 assigns unparalleled significance to the bones. The woe-oracle (v. 9) and the emphasis on burnt bones and the *empty* pot (v. 10) amplify the prophetic invective. Because the bones are featured in MT's edition, the judgment falls upon them and calls for their total incineration.

The present metaphor of the cooking pot draws on an earlier use of the same in chapter 11, where the pot is a metaphor of safety for the people. Ezekiel 11:7–11 describes how some Israelites will die *outside* of the pot/ Jerusalem where they will be killed by the sword. The MT variants in ch. 24 make the allegory include this category of Israelites, those who were killed outside of Jerusalem, among the bones. Just as MT harmonizes the fate of those outside the pot with ch. 11, it re-interprets the fate of those within. The empty pot annihilates that category of Israelites; their fate is destruction not protection. p967's edition of ch. 24's pot only re-interprets; it does not harmonize with ch. 11.

As an allegory, details take on increased exegetical significance. Hence, in allegorical detail, the *location* of the bones is as relevant to interpreting the passage as the bones themselves. The extra bones in the MT edition of the pot (ch. 24) are variously located with respect to the pot. This detail is likely significant given the prominent theme of the location of Israel's fate in Ezekiel. What may be called the 'four-fold judgment' theme may shed light on how to interpret the location of bones in ch. 24. Secondly, additional textual evidence in the interpretive frame of ch. 24 forms an intertextual horizon of interpretation with ch. 37. Both avenues will be addressed below.

5.3.2.4.2. *Location in the Pot Allegory*

The book of Ezekiel develops a four-fold understanding of Israel's fate. A paradigmatic statement of it occurs in 14:21 where the Lord names his 'four deadly acts of judgment' on Jerusalem: sword, famine, wild animals, and pestilence. Different iterations occur in 5:1–2; 5:12; 6:11–13; 7:15; and 33:27. These subtract or substitute 'judgments', adding fire and a scattering to the list of so-called 'four-fold' judgments.

Frequently, the act of judgment is associated with a location. This is especially the case where in 5:1–2, Ezekiel performs the sign-act of shaving his head, in order to demonstrate that 1/3 of the people will burn *within the city*, 1/3 will fall by the sword *all around the city* (סביבותיה), and 1/3 will be *scattered to the wind*. Of the last category, 5:12 qualifies that even those scattered abroad will be followed by the sword. Of course, the locations are far from systematic. In 6:12, those scattered abroad die of pestilence, not the sword. In 7:15, those in the *field* die by the sword. While no coherent pattern exists across Ezekiel, it is clear that Ezekiel's prophecies attach locative significance to the various judgments of God that overcome various groups of Israelites.

Returning to ch. 24 with these observations as a lens, some subtle issues of syntax between MT and p967 are relevant to allegorical interpretation. In v. 5aβ, MT reads, "and *also pile* the bones under *it*" וגם דור העצמים תחתיה while the Greek reads, "and *burn* the bones beneath *them*" και υποκαιε τα οστα υποκατω αυτων. The MT image of piling bones beneath the pot has troubled textual critics. Most read, העצים (sticks) instead of העצמים.[143] However, the emendation obscures the very allegorical element that begs interpretation in MT. The Greek likely envisions placing the bones beneath the choice (pl) cattle meat, all *within* the cauldron. On the other hand, the Hebrew certainly envisions some of the bones on the *outside* of the cauldron, being scorched by the fire below the pot. This is partially emphasized by the וגם that isolates the clause from the preceding one (only attested in late witnesses like V and Tht. with the translation καιγε); but also by the verbs (υποκαιε vs. דור) and the direct objects (sing. vs. plural). Thus, combining the images from vv. 4 and 5, MT depicts choice bones within, and bones under the pot, while p967 and B only have bones within the pot.

As noted earlier, ch. 24 develops the metaphor already presented in ch. 11. The ch. 11 metaphor of the cooking pot suggested that only those *outside* the pot would suffer destruction, implying that the meat within the pot would be safe. The MT edition of ch. 24 harmonizes the fate of those outside the pot with ch. 11, even as it re-interprets the fate of those within the pot as destruction, not protection.

The lens of the four-fold judgment heightens the allegorical importance of location in ch. 24. Since the pot stands for Jerusalem, MT depicts bones within and around the city. Presumably, all the bones are scorched, but certainly the ones in the pot are incinerated, due to the MT plus, "empty" discussed above. While the fate of the bones within the pot is sure in MT, the only thing we can say for certain about those outside is that they are numerous. In v. 9, MT declares that God will make great the pile, המדורה, (whose root is the same as the verb דור "to pile up" that uniquely appeared in MT v. 5aβ). p967 makes great the δαλον (firebrand), an image of a hot

---

[143] Driver, "Ezekiel," 175. This emendation is taken up in the NRSV.

and robust flame, certainly more in keeping with the original, mundane song.[144]

5.3.2.4.3. *An Interpretive Frame to the Pot Allegory*

As an allegory, ch. 24's bones are difficult to interpret without a prophetic explanation of their role in the *mashal*. While such an interpretation does not follow the allegory, the first few verses of ch. 24 do provide an interpretive frame for the allegory. While the introductory frame is not the same, form-critically, as a prophetic interpretation found so frequently after a *mashal* in Ezekiel,[145] it still indicates a form of interpretation. In MT 24:2–3a, Ezekiel is summoned to write down the day of Babylon's siege of Jerusalem and to utter the cooking-pot allegory to the rebellious house of Israel. These two exhortations frame the allegorical description and judgment that takes place in vv. 3b–13. By means of this frame, Ezekiel links Babylon's siege *of Jerusalem* with the destruction of the bones *within Jerusalem* (the pot). In the same way that MT's variants heightened the density of detail about the bones in the allegory (by means of pluses and variant readings,) the MT also presents the "bones" *Tendenz* in its interpretive frame. Verse 2, the announcement of destruction, includes two variants of the Hebrew word עצם.

v. 2αβ	της ημερας ταυτης	that day
	עצם היום הזה	that *very* (*'tsm*) day
v. 2bβ	απο της ημερας της σημερον	from that *same* day
	בעצם היום הזה	on that *very* (*'tsm*) day

Twice, v. 2 utilizes an idiom of Late Biblical Hebrew, "that very day," which deploys the term עצם. Neither instance in the Greek translates literally with οστεον. Indeed, if the Greek merely understood the idiomatic meaning of the phrase, we should not expect to find οστεον here.[146] However,

---

[144] In this variant, B, supported by a few versions, is exceedingly interesting—reading λαον. Perhaps this reading responds to MT's specific judgment on a certain group of Israelites by universalizing God's favor to the entire people.

[145] Chapters in Ezekiel that include *mashal* explanations or interpretations of visions are Ezek 15, 17, and 37.

[146] The adverb σημερον occurs in the Greek three times as a translation of the Hebrew idiom: Jos 10:27; Ezek 2:3, and here. However, in Ezek 24:2, the translation order της ημερας της σημερον suggests that the בעצם was not in the original translation, and that σημερον translates הזה. This is increasingly likely since a ב is not generally represented by απο. In cases where the Greek translates the Hebrew idiom literally, supplying translation equivalents for each term in עצם היום הזה the two examples are in Gen 17:26, τω καιρω της ημερας εκεινης and four places in Lev 23:14, 28, 29, 30 with only case variation from that in

if the Greek intended to extend the allegorical significance of the term "bones" to the interpretive-frame, it may have elected to include the term οστεον. MT once again, exaggerates the phrase with the term. In v. 2aβ, עצם is certainly an MT plus. I assert that the MT's two deployments of עצם here represent scribal pluses and not just non-literal translation issues, particularly for v. 2aβ.[147]

The significance of the MT's twice repeated phrase עצם היום הזה in 24:2, if I am correct about their status as scribal pluses, lies in its location. As part of the prophetic date-reckoning introduction to Ezekiel's prophetic words, the twice-repeated terms establish the thematic significance of the bones for what follows. They introduce the allegory as a 'day of bones'.

Additionally, the two phrases bookend the announcement of Babylon's siege of Jerusalem. Such repetition may be considered a highlighting device to emphasize the interpretation of the Babylonian destruction of Jerusalem for the bones in the pot-allegory.

The עצם -pluses in v. 2 gloss the allegory as a destruction of bones in Jerusalem. What happens when we read this allegory alongside ch. 37, where bones are an obvious feature of the vision?

5.3.2.4.4. *Bones in Ezekiel 37 and 24*
One of the most important visionary settings for the image of bones in all of Ezekiel is ch. 37. In this vision (37:1–10), dried bones strewn about a valley/plain (בקעה / πεδιον) are raised into a great living, breathing, fleshly company. The interpretation of the vision follows (vv. 11–14) whereby the revivified company signifies the whole house of Israel, having been raised up from their graves (קרב / μνημα).

---

v. 14, αυτην την ημεραν ταυτην. In these two instances, the Greek used καιρος and the intensive use of the Greek pronoun to translate עצם. It is not clear whether σημερον (today) ever represents עצם. The two other instances of σημερον in Jos 10:27 and Ezek 2:3 are unclear. Did εως της σημερον ημερας in Jos 10:27 have the idiom in its source text? Either the Greek translator followed word order, translating σημερον for עצם and just left off the Hebrew הזה at the end. In support of this is the correct translation of the preposition, εως for עד. However, the Greek idiom could just as easily have been chosen to translate היום הזה. The exact situation obtains (in Hebrew and Greek) in Ezek 2:3 as Jos 10:27.

[147] Translational versus textual variants remains an important contimuum for scholars of ancient texts. The lens of translational variants, when applied to this verse, highlights the opportunity for linguistic word play that cannot transcend the target language. What I am advancing here is the possibility that MT's Hebrew word-play with עצם was a scribal addition, in light of the Greek witness to the verse, and not just a Hebrew idiom that was not reproduced in the Greek.

Arguably, the MT edition of ch. 24 has ch. 37 in view.[148] Out of twenty-one occurrences in MT Ezekiel, the word "bone" occurs ten times in ch. 37:1–11 and six times in ch. 24:1–10 (MT). In the former, the vision revivifies the bones. In the latter, the vision incinerates the bones. Through allegorical elements, the incineration in ch. 24 excludes the Jerusalem-population from the restorative vision of ch. 37.

The same exemption of bodies can be seen elsewhere. Indeed, the pit of ch. 32 serves the same function, removing unwanted enemies from the face of the land to a permanent fate far beneath the earth. In most cases, the graves of each enemy are depicted within Sheol, erasing their chances of being among those who are raised up from their graves (37:12, 13). In one instance in the pit, iniquity is said to rest upon bones (ותהי עונתם על עצמותם).[149] This is the only place in all of Ezekiel in which bones hold iniquity. Otherwise, the body is susceptible or holds iniquity in the heart, the eyes, the face, the forehead, etc.[150] However, only within the pit are bones described as bearing iniquity.

5.3.2.4.5. Summary of "Bones" Tendenz

The MT edition of ch. 24 contains four extra instances of the word "bones" and several variants that affect the allegory of the cooking pot for Jerusalem's destruction. I have argued that MT forges an interpretive-horizon between the frame of ch. 24 and the vision of bones in ch. 37. Additionally, the allegory in MT takes special care to distribute bones within and outside the pot, likely connected to the importance of location that we see explicitly established in Ezekiel's four-fold judgments. These locations create categories of Israelites and either exempt or elect them for

---

[148] So Rendtorff, who notes the terminological connection, R. Rendtorff, "Ez 20 und 36, 16ff im Rahmen der Komposition des Buches Ezechiel," in *Ezekiel and His Book: Textual and Literary Criticism and their Interrelation* (Leuven: Leuven University Press, 1986), 261 n5. An English translation is available in R. Rendtorff, "Ezekiel 20 and 36:16ff. in the Framework of the Composition of the Book," in *Canon and Theology* (OBT; Minneapolis: Fortress, 1993), 190–195.

[149] Ezek 32:27 refers to the iniquity that rests on the bones of the heroes of old. Many commentators emend עונתם in order to read "their shields were upon their bones," but this proposal lacks a textual basis. So Zimmerli, *Ezekiel*, 2:168, though he finds Cornill's solution "fully satisfactory."

[150] The phrases that address body parts as the basis for judgment are numerous: idols in the heart (14:3), hard-hearted (3:7), lifting up eyes to idols (33:25), don't see with eyes (12:2), stumbling-block before the face (14:3), hard forehead (3:7), hands commit iniquity (18:17), evil hands (34:10), evil mouths (34:10), do not hear with ears (12:2).

participation in ch. 37's revivification. Lacking all of these editorial elements, p967's connection to ch. 37 is not as strong.[151]

The specific referents for MT's allegory are not clear. The incineration of "choice" bones in MT ch. 24 definitely annihilates one category of Israelites from the promised fate-reversal to take place in ch. 37. The bones *within* the pot are scorched and ultimately destroyed, leaving the smoldering pot *empty*. The bones without are piled up beneath the pot, presumably succumbed to the intense heat of the stewing pot. Both groups' bones are emphasized. The former, those who died *within* Jerusalem, leave no trace. Since even their skeletons burn up, they cannot benefit from the revivification of ch. 37. However, the fate of the many who died outside of is not particularly clear in ch. 24's allegory. On the one hand, their fate is embedded into a woe-oracle form, which suggests a negative fate. On the other, the variants in MT do not make any definitive claims on them, unlike those inside the *empty* pot. Would not the variant material emphasize such an important point if it were there to be made? Regardless, those bones which pile up outside the pot are given special attention, and thus the question is raised in MT: how does this category relate to the vision of bones in ch. 37?

5.3.2.5. *'New Life'* Tendenz

The fate of the slain in Ezekiel 37 does not end with dried bones, of course, but reverses the finality of death towards life. The concept of new life also characterizes a set of variants between p967 and MT. Indeed, there are ten cases where the theme of new life characterized variant material. However, these variants exhibited an unusual pattern across the witnesses: 1) p967 refers to the *Tendenz* against MT in four cases and 2) MT refers to the *Tendenz* in two cases.[152]

---

[151] Zimmerli's interpretation of Ezek 24:1–14 insightfully speaks about the way the pot-image is reversed from that in ch. 11, which could point to the function of p967's edition of the pericope. Zimmerli, *Ezekiel*, 1:496–501, esp. "Aim," 499–500.

[152] Two additional variants in the section in 37:6–8, present odd situations, yet are not significant enough to discuss here.

5.3.2.5.1. *'New Life' Tendenz in MT*
MT presents two cases where the 'New Life' *Tendenz* occurs:

1) Ezekiel 18:32

In 18:32, MT includes a plus phrase about new life (examined already in §5.2.3.1 above). Verse 32 is the final verse in chapter 18, a section of Ezekiel about retribution. The chapter moves between life and death, repeatedly answering questions with dictums about life-resulting or death-resulting actions. Verse 31 forms a theological conclusion for the chapter, equating Israel's casting off transgressions with its reception of a new heart and spirit. The verse goes onto ask "why will you die?" In p967, the rhetorical question of v. 31 is followed only by the terse statement (v. 32) that God does not desire death. MT, however, adds a final imperative, "so turn and live."[153] The imperatival form is unique and breaks the rhetorical-voice/audience developed throughout the chapter.

2) Ezekiel 33:5

In 33:5, p967 lacks another new-life phrase (v. 5b) which is present in MT. The first half of the verse assigns blood-guilt to Israel. p967 uses αν with subjunctive clauses to communicate contingency of guilt in vv. 2–4. But v. 5a contains a rare declarative statement (οτι-clause) about those Israelites who must bear their blood-guilt because of their actions. In MT, this statement is followed by v. 5b, "but if he had taken warning, he would have delivered his soul (נפשׁו)." MT makes amends for those among the guilty who took warning. Essentially, this holds out the possibility for life for people that would otherwise have been condemned by their blood-guilt.

5.3.2.5.2. *'New Life' Tendenz in p967*
The new life Tendenz occurs four times in p967 variants:

1) Ezekiel 17:23

In 17:23, p967 seeks to save some of the branches of the vine: "and his branches will be restored" (και τα κληματα αυτου αποκατασταθησεται). A restoration of the Davidic line can be read here. Other elements of the chapter gloss 'life' as an important theme of vv. 11–24: twice repeated is

---

[153] 62 *L"* Arm Tht. share MT's imperatival phrase, but contain additional content about casting off iniquities, elaborating even further on the MT's conclusion.

ζω εγω (חַי אָנִי) (vv. 16, 19). Verse 22 was already featured in the heart/spirit-*Tendenz* above.

2) Ezekiel 26:20

In 26:20, discussed in §5.3.2.1, we already noted that with this variant, p967 ensures that Tyre would not rise to life again; "nor will you rise to life." MT reads instead "and I will give beauty in the land of the living."

3) Ezekiel 31:17

In 31:17, p967 reads "in the midst of his life they were destroyed." MT reads "in the midst of the nations." The verse is about the tree of Assyria descending into the pit, while the specific phrase-variant refers to those who lived under her shade. MT is the mundane description while p967 spiritualizes the phrase.

4) Ezekiel 38:14

38:14 begins the second strophe of the Gog-Magog episode. Verses 14–16 are the proof for the nation-recognition statement in v. 16. However, v. 14 in MT already introduces a recognition fragment תֵדָע "you will know." p967 reads "you will be woken up" (εγερθησῃ). While many textual critics believe MT should have read תֵעֹר "you will arouse yourself," the lexeme εγειρω is frequently used to mean awaken.[154] There is not enough information to determine the intended sense in p967. However, it is possible that Gog's invasion was understood as a revivification of the enemy from the North.

5.3.2.5.3. *Summary of the 'New Life'* Tendenz

The *Tendenz* of 'new life' was certainly worth exploring, however, the variants yielded little coherence. The two verses in MT which exhibit the theme *did* both concern Israel, while three of p967's variants concerned the life of enemy nations: Tyre, nations protected by Assyria, and Gog. The conclusion to be made about the 'New Life' *Tendenz* is that it does not represent a strong intertextual tendency and therefore does not sharply distinguish MT from p967.

---

[154] Henry G. Liddell and Robert Scott, "εγειρω," in *Greek-English Lexicon* (Cambridge: Clarendon Press, 1959), 469. According to Hatch and Redpath, the most common Hebrew *Vorlage* is קוֹם "εγειρειν." Hatch and Redpath, *A Concordance to the Septuagint*, 364.

5.3.3. *Summary of Section: 'Fate of the Slain'* Tendenzen

The intertextual center for the 'Fate of the Slain' *Tendenzen,* Ezekiel's pit (32:17–32), proved its importance to the alternate literary editions in two respects. First, the well-known major variant at 32:26–28 was not an isolated feature; additional variants differente MT's edition of the pit from p967. MT's description of the pit itself differed in several significant respects from p967's shorter text. Second, variants across Ezekiel shared the theme of death and cosmic fate. For this reason, it was helpful to identify 32:17–32 as an intertextual center.

p967 and MT dealt differently with, not only the death of Israel, but also of Egypt, Tyre, Edom, Gog, hordes, and the like. The fate of these slain nations frequently emphasized specific locations: the pit served as the most important location for enemy nations. Indirectly, it also provided a mythic schema that could animate more mundane locations, such as MT's edition of Tyre's death "in the middle of the sea."

The MT edition of the pit was the more expansive text. This was most obviously the case with the major plus in vv. 26–28, where Meshech and Tubal joined the list of enemies. MT variants also included Edom and the Sidonians in the population. These nations were systematically identified by their relationship to circumcision. A space of shame opened for *both* those uncircumcised nations that did not practice circumcision *and* those who acquired the status through proximity and association. The only exception in MT was the differentiated space for the death of Israel's heroes, who were separated from the uncircumcised. MT stands out as the edition that ritualizes the cosmic space for death on the basis of this Jewish practice.

MT also emphasized the shameful condition under which the nations descended to their fate. The reproach (כלמה) borne by the nations, distinctive to the MT, conveyed this edition's stronger indictment against foreigners, generally. Significant to the intertextual whole of MT's edition, 39:26 announces that Israel will bear her reproach (כלמה/ἀτιμία) in the restored land, not in the pit, as is the case for the nations on the pit's list of nations. Thus, the divine reproach against the nations bears them to the underworld while Israel's divine reproach remains upon her as she returns to her life in the land.

The shorter edition in p967 simplifies the ignominy of the pit in two distinct ways. First, p967's focus on Assyria, her commanders, her leaders, and her neighboring war-state Elam, characterizes the pit as *geographically* remote. Second, p967's references to the giants "of old" bring a *temporal* remoteness to the pit as well. Already, the concept of the pit as underworld occupies a cosmically remote position. The cosmic, geographic, and temporal remoteness of the population in the pit heightens its otherness. Particularly p967's interpretation of the giants as the progenitors of the pit's negative valences generates a totalizing ignominy, without nuance or distinction.

The two editions bore traces of different ideas about the death of foreign nations. It was clear that the MT edition brought the fates of Egypt and Tyre into closer and stronger association with the pit. MT's ch. 28 rendered Tyre's death in the midst of the sea in terms of the שחת. Further, MT's pit was uniquely the site for the fate of Egypt's hordes. Egypt's fate was certainly a pre-occupation for the scribes who differentiated the two editions. While MT placed Egypt's hordes in the pit, p967 avoided interpolating Egypt's hordes into the pit. Instead of Egypt's hordes, spiritualized concepts such as Egypt's "strength" (ισχυν) as well as Elam and Assyria's "power" (δυναμις) are relegated to the pit. In p967, Egypt's "horde" does not lie in the pit, but rather on the mountains (32:6). Further, p967 leaves Egypt unburied on a field in 29:5. While both of these details are suggestive of ch. 37, the connections are not strong enough to make claims about scribal intention.[155] Nevertheless, p967's edition opens itself to a provocative intertextual connection between Egypt's unburied status on the field and the revivification of dried bones in chapter 37.

An examination of the site of chapter 37's vision reveals that MT, once again, introduced spatial distinctions that were not present in p967. The Hebrew term בקעה is reserved for the site of Ezekiel's visions of Jerusalem, while שדה was the location of the enemy slain. Several enemy nations died on the field (שדה): Egypt, Assyria, Edom, Gog, and their daughters. These same nations were placed in MT's edition of the pit, suggesting an intentional attempt to disallow their participation in Israel's restoration.[156] A similar dynamic was observable in MT's edition of the Pot

---

[155] The mountains play an important role in the restoration. See Jon Levenson, *Theology of the Program of Restoration of Ezekiel 40–48* (HSM 10; Missoula: Scholars Press, 1976; repr., Cambridge: Books on Demand, 2006), 37–42. Particularly relevant to this passage about Egypt, Ezek 37:22 describes the restored nation on God's holy mountain. This location is significant elsewhere to the restoration vision as well. Ezek 34:13–14 predicts that God will feed his sheep on the mountains; and 36:8 describes how the mountains will yield fruit for Israel who will come home. However, none of these references indicate any special significance for those who *die* on the mountains (except for ch. 37, indirectly,) merely for those Israelites who return to the mountains.

[156] See Nobile who discusses the significance of the seven peoples in MT's underworld of chapter 32 with the seven nations in Gog's entourage in 38:2–6. Nobile, "Beziehung zwischen Ez 32, 17–32 und der Gog-Perikope," 256.

allegory in chapter 24, where those who died in Jerusalem were incinerated and preemptively excluded from chapter 37's vision of restoration.
Hence, not only foreign nations, but categories of Israelites fall into the
'Fate of the Slain' *Tendenzen*. This problem with foreign nations characterized additional details in MT as well. In ch. 44, MT pronounced those
uncircumcised in heart *and flesh* from entrance into the restored temple.
Additionally, MT included the caveat in ch. 37 to specify that the vision
referred to "my people."

In contrast to this anti-foreigner vision of restoration, the openness
of p967's edition comes into greater focus. p967 does not locate Gog
or Edom in the pit; neither does it strongly depict Egypt's presence in
ch. 32. In fact, a p967 plus in 35:8 indicated that Edom died on a field. The
oracle against Mt. Seir (Edom) in ch. 35 strongly suggests that Edom is not
favored by Ezekiel's book. However, the same harsh tone found within
judgment oracles is levied against Israel as well. If a reversal of judgment
to mercy is possible for Israel, it is perhaps possible for Edom as well. MT,
by including Edom in the pit, annihilates that possibility. However, p967's
edition is ambiguous about Edom's role in the restoration vision.

Additionally, p967, unlike MT, did not restrict the vision in chapter 37
to "my people." p967's openness extends even to Gog-Magog. According
to p967's chapter order, the revivification of bones occurs after the Gog-
Magog battle. In 39:5, Gog is said to fall on the open field (שדה/πεδιον).
While the chapter does go on to depict Gog's burial, its bones placed in
a mass grave, p967 is characteristically ambiguous about whether the
drama of chapter 37 could include Gog and his entourage. Just as Gog's
death occurred on the field, so the revivification occurs on a πεδιον; and
Meshech and Tubal are not in p967's pit. Of course, both editions share
the scene in 39:15–16 where the Israelites carefully collect the enemy's
bones from the battle field. Especially in p967's edition, this scene cannot be understood apart from Ezekiel 37 which immediately follows. It
captures the Israelite desire, shared in p967 and MT, to exclude military
invaders from the population of revivified Israel. However, MT presents
the more emphatic edition on this point.

5.4. *Tendenzen* Related to Ezekiel 36:23c–38

Ezekiel 36:23c–38 constitutes the most substantial variant between p967
and MT. Missing in p967, MT is the longer text by fourteen and a half

verses. Up until now, no study has thoroughly examined the exegetical significance of the variant to the two editions.[157]

5.4.1. *Intertextual Center: The Promises in Ezekiel 36:23c–38*

Chapter 36 falls in the section of the book dealing with restoration from exile. In content, the chapter provides several details about the return of Israel as well as a divine motive for the event. Ezek 36:23a locates this motive in God's need to sanctify his name and display his holiness in the sight of the nations. These aspects of chapter 36 are shared by MT and p967.

While the oracles in chapter 36 concern the return of Israel to the land, the direct promise to the people occurs in the MT plus (vv. 23c–32). Previously in the chapter, promises were made to the mountains of Israel in 36:8–12 that the children of Israel would "soon come home" (v. 8). This is an indirect promise to the people of Israel, treating them as instruments of the restoration of the *land*.

The promise to the *people* of Israel in 36:23c–32 is embedded in a nation-recognition formula. Verse 23c provides a temporal clause to qualify the nation-recognition formula begun in v. 23a. It states, "when *through you* I display my holiness." By embedding the promise in the nation-recognition formula, Israel's restoration serves specific purposes in the dramatic plot of *God's* restoration. In this sense, the people are promised their return indirectly, as 36:22 indicates, "it is not for your sake that I am about to act."

In very general terms, the Lord's display (v. 23a) is the restoration of Israel after the exile. Verses 23c–38 are comprised of two oracular units which specify this concern. The first in vv. 23c–32 extends the preceding oracle that began in v. 22. Verse 22 and the end of the oracle in v. 32 are structured with an inclusio-like statement, "it is not for your sake that I am about to act." The act is performed in order to "display my holiness before their eyes" (v. 23). Thus, vv. 24–32 provide a motivation for the restoration, namely as God's display to foreign nations.

Verse 33 begins a second promise; hence, it does not participate in the nation-recognition formula from v. 23a. Nevertheless, the oracle in vv. 33–38 is in service of watching eyes. Verse 34 summons "the sight of all

---

[157] See my critique of Crane in chapter 1.

who pass by" and v. 36 emphasizes that the nations will know that it was God who rebuilt the land. The whole of v. 35 contains the quoted reaction of those for whom God's restoration is performed. Clearly here, as above, a specific promise to Israel is not prominently in view.

Thus, while the two oracles in vv. 22–32 and vv. 33–38 contain promises to the people of Israel, the promises are largely indirect. Rather, the focus of the oracles is on the divine plan for the restoration of the land and the sanctification of God's name. The role of the people is subsumed to these larger divine concerns. Indeed, vv. 22–38 contain two promises and present two solutions to two different problems. As the following discussion will develop, the MT plus develops a 'two-aspects' vision of restoration.

The two oracles present different promises. Verses 24–30 promise agricultural health, both through the productivity of vegetation and through the cessation of famines. In contrast, the second set of promises (vv. 33–35) focuses on architecture: Waste places will be rebuilt and towns refortified. The different types of promises suggest a two-aspect nature of the restoration. Indeed, the implicit problems and solutions in both oracles reinforce a two-aspect restoration.

The passage should also be considered in light of the various problems and solutions it envisions. In vv. 25–30, the solution is quite clear; the verses describe an act of cleansing the people from their uncleanness (טמאה). God provides a *new* heart and *his* spirit to replace the problem of the old, unclean body (vv. 26–27). The problem is undeniable: the people need to be cleansed from their uncleanness (v. 29). This cleansing will mark the beginning of a new era of vegetation in which the people will not suffer famine again (vv. 29–30). This aspect of the restoration 'solves' the problem of Israel's uncleanness (טמאה) for the sake of the land.

The second aspect is alluded to in v. 31 where a new problem surfaces. Despite her new 'clean' constitution, Israel must remember and loathe her evil ways (דרכי הרעים), bad practices (מעללים אשר לא טובים), iniquities (עונות), and abominations (תועבות). The verse is dense with heightened condemnatory language. These problems endured beyond, and thus are not solved by, the cleansing in vv. 26–27.[158] Thus we are left with two problems, uncleanness and evil iniquity, the latter of which seems to fol-

---

[158] The cleansing is described in v. 25 as a sprinkling of water. Num 19:19–20 describes an act of sprinkling water on an unclean person, where the terms טמא and טהר (unclean and clean) are also used. According to this ritual, the one who is not sprinkled with water is unclean טמא (v. 20). Relevant to the context in ch. 36, the passage in Numbers does not indicate whether cleansing a person also solves the problem of human iniquity and abomination.

low Israel into her restoration. She is called to remain ashamed and dismayed at these problems, as indicated in the final sentence of the promise oracle (v. 32). Thus, the oracle ends on a negative note, despite the fact that this is the first promise addressed directly to the people of Israel. This negative conclusion further indicates the incompleteness of Israel's return, a return which, as we saw earlier, God largely performs for the nations.

Indeed, elsewhere in Ezekiel, we are led to believe that restoration does not imply Israel's immediate or total perfection. In 34:17–22, the first stage of restoration is assumed since the flock of Israel is already grazing on the land (vv. 12–13). Then in v. 17, God addresses the sheep directly, accusing them of trampling and fouling their water. God announces his intent to judge between "sheep and sheep" (v. 17), "rams and goats" (v. 17), and "fat and lean sheep" (v. 20). The judgment also targets the strong who ravage or push out the weak. Thus we have the post-restoration announcement that the bad sheep will be weeded out (cf. 20:38).

Returning to 36:23c–38, vv. 37–38 invoke the sheep allegory just discussed. According to v. 37, post-restoration Israel seeks to increase like a flock. The image of increasing a flock, seen through the lens of chapter 34, summons two meanings: continued 'gathering' of the scattered sheep, and weeding out bad sheep. Both seem to be in view in chapter 36 as God grants their request, saying that he will increase Israel like a flock *for sacrifices*. Invoking "sacrifices" strongly implies that increasing Israel involves handing some sheep over to death, albeit a sacrificial one.[159] In short, while the intertextuality between the sheep in 36:37–38 and 34:17–22 is merely suggestive, it would only reinforce what was already clear in MT's vision of restoration: Israel will be cleansed for her return to the land, but the problem of iniquity will continue to vex the restoration of Israel. The problem of iniquity does not preclude the death of the unrighteous.[160]

5.4.1.1. *Literary Function of 36:23c–38 in MT*

Some have called 36:23c–38 a fitting introduction to chapter 37. Lust argued that 36:23c–38 was composed as a link between chapters 36 and 37.[161] He

---

[159] This idea is found already in Ezek 34:20–21, that God is on the side of the weak sheep and will feed the strong with judgment, ארענה במשפט.

[160] The purity concerns involved in MT's two-aspect vision of restoration will become significant again in the analysis below.

[161] Lust, "Ezekiel 36–40," 525–27. While I happen to agree with Lust on this issue, his position about the priority of the shorter text where 36:23c–38 is absent has been challenged, most significantly by Block. See Block, *The Book of Ezekiel*, 2:341–42. Lust responded

adduced several unique literary-linguistic parallels. Most significantly, the promise of "his" [i.e., the Lord's] spirit in 36:27 matches Ezek 37:14 "where God is said to give *his* spirit to the people."[162] The triple set of verbs for the return "לקח, קבץ, and בוא (Hif.)" only appear together in 37:21 and 36:24. Finally, the unique combination of purity and divine deliverance is shared by the two chapters.[163] Several other phrases increase the amount of shared material of the two passages.[164] All of this evidence does suggest a close compositional connection between the two chapters, particularly 36:23c–38 and the second half of chapter 37.

Ashley Crane, who likewise envisions a late editorial function for 36:23c–38 agrees with Lust. His study focuses only tangentially on the literary structure and function of the 'insertion;'[165] among his very few comments about 36:23c–38, he speculates,

> those changing the chapter order now insert 36:23c–38 as support for their chapter reorder.[166]

Unlike Lust, however, Crane bases his exegesis on speculative, though stimulating, historical-critical arguments.[167] He envisions the major editorial activity in MT occurring during Hasmonean times and calls the MT's alternate sequence of chs. 37–39 a "call to arms."[168] However, according to Crane, 36:23c–38 was inserted as a call to purity. Significant for Crane's argument is the fact that chapter 37 precedes the military invasion and victory described in chapters 38–39. Thus, ch. 36:23c–38 smooths the introduction to chapter 37 and secures the purity of messianic Israel's militant cause.[169] Crane glosses the passage as a call to purity, although

---

decisively in 2002 saying that once the editorial character of the section is proven, which he largely accomplished on the basis of a neutral philological argument, it is perfectly reasonable to recognize its bridge function, subsequently. See Lust, "Textual Criticism of the Old and New Testaments," 30.

[162] Italics original to emphasize that elsewhere in Ezekiel we read "new spirit," "one spirit," and "another spirit." See Lust, "Ezekiel 36–39," 526.

[163] See especially in Ezek 36:29 and 37:23.

[164] See Lust, "Ezekiel 36–40," 525–527.

[165] See my critique in chapter 1.

[166] Crane, *Israel's Restoration*, 255.

[167] In all other cases in chapters 36–39, Crane used his text-comparative method (see chapter 1). However, with the MT plus in chapter 36, Crane switches to a different mode of analysis.

[168] Crane, *Israel's Restoration*, 255. Many would challenge this historical proposal; these scholars have dated the redaction activity "not beyond the period of the exile." Allen, *Ezekiel*, 2:176–178. See also Zimmerli, *Ezekiel*, 1:9–16.

[169] Although, the content of 36:23c–38 lacks a basis for Crane's claim to see Davidic national unity in its vision of restoration.

he seems to hold that chapter 37 wholly accomplishes Israel's purification. It is difficult to engage Crane further; his discussion is too truncated to discern the full significance of his observation. Suffice it to say, he finds 36:23c–38 to be a fitting introduction to chapter 37 in MT.

While ch. 36:23c–38 does serve to introduce chapter 37, especially in light of Lust's observations, one glaring discontinuity involves the prediction of a new heart (36:26). Certainly, the new heart is important to the MT plus; 36:26 mentions the heart three times. Verse 26b reads:

והסרתי את לב האבן מבשרכם ונתתי לכם לב בשר

I will remove the heart of stone from your flesh, and I will give you a heart of flesh.

However, chapter 37 nowhere contains the word לב, much less the phrase לב חדש. Most commentators assume the flesh (בשר) that re-assembles on the bones of chapter 37 includes the "heart of flesh לב בשר" from 36:26b, and by extension, the "new heart" of 36:26a.[170] However, it is striking that 36:23c–38, presumably composed after chapter 37 was set, presents a linguistic emphasis on the heart that is lacking in chapter 37. Indeed, a comprehensive linguistic analysis of 36:26 and chapter 37 reveals no shared phrases regarding the heart.[171] Since the promise of the new heart is arguably one of the major themes in ch. 36:23c–38, talk about the heart is unlikely to be *only* or even *primarily* an introduction to chapter 37.[172] The explanation for the new heart in 36:23c–38 must lie elsewhere.

---

[170] So Greenberg who describes the heart's purification as a return to flesh, "the same element as the body." Greenberg, *Ezekiel*, 730. Ezek 37:23 does speak about purifying the people, which as Block argues, "had associated the experience with a heart-transplant [from 36:25–28]." Block, *Ezekiel*, 2:355. Jaqueline Lapsley, whose study is strong in the main, does not deal with the distinction between heart and sprit. Instead, she considers the new spirit in ch. 37 to be the fulfillment of 36:27's promise of a new heart and new spirit. In her defense, she was focused on intractable impurities requiring a new moral self which, in ch. 36 is an external gift. Hence, a new heart and spirit had to come from outside. Jacqueline E. Lapsley, *Can These Bones Live?: The Problem of the Moral Self in the Book of Ezekiel* (BZAW 301; New York: de Gruyter, 2000), 169–171.

[171] Additionally, the term "new spirit" in 36:26a does not occur in chapter 37's ten uses of רוח. As Lust pointed out, only the construction in 36:28 'my spirit' (רוחי) is parallel, in 37:14.

[172] Paul Joyce considers Deuteronomistic and Jeremianic influence in 36:23c–38 to explain the presence of language about the heart and the spirit. Joyce concludes that Ezekiel was very much influenced by the "deuteronomistic movement" and Jeremianic ideas here. However, overall Ezekiel's emphases focus more on the spirit language and a radical theocentricity. Paul Joyce, *Divine Initiative and Human Response in Ezekiel* (JSOTSup 51; Sheffield: Sheffield Academic Press, 1989), 122–124. Several have closely examined the connections with Jeremiah. Lust lists several phrases which secure this connection. Lust, "Ezekiel 36–40," 52–533. Likewise, Tov develops the argument. Tov, "Recensional Differences,"

In point of fact, Ezek 36:23c–38 has been called an "anthology of expressions found elsewhere in Ezekiel."[173] Rolf Rendtorff's redaction-critical study concludes that 36:16–38 takes up material found in ch. 20.[174] He argues that similar phrases and "die gleiche Einteilung der Geschichte in zwei Epochen findet sich nun auch Kap. 20 einerseits und 36,16ff anderseits."[175] The epochal shift occurs within the *Bundesformel*, or the changed relationship between God and the people. Divine anger marks the patterns in Israel's history until a new epoch of knowing God's holy name begins. For Rendtorff, 36:16–38 brings the periods of judgment to completion following the pattern laid out in chapter 20, and marks the beginning of a new epoch for Israel in the land.

Rendtorff's work on chs. 36 and 20 offers insight into a possible intertextual relationship between 36:23c–38 and ch. 20. In his analysis, he also mentions the significance of chapter 11 to Ezek 36:16–38. In fact, Rendtorff and Lust *both* pointed out the connections between the two passages, such as the word for word repetition between 11:17–19 and 36:24–26. Because of these purported connections, chapter 11 merits a more thorough analysis, especially since Ezekiel 11 mentions the "heart."

397–410. However, much less work has been done to view the insertion intertextually *within* the book of Ezekiel.

[173] Lust, "Ezekiel 36–40," 525. Leslie Allen concentrates on the way in which 36:16–38 carries the salvation message forward by repeating terms and ideas from Ezekiel 34–35. Allen, *Ezekiel*, 2:180. Some scholars think ch. 36:23c–38 is intertextual with Jeremiah primarily. Lust lists several phrases which secure this connection; Likewise, Tov contributes to this perception. Crane, *Israel's Restoration*, 222–223. While these connections stand and remain important, they do not serve the present project directly. More important here, few have bothered to see the intertextual nature of the insertion with material *within* the book of Ezekiel.

[174] R. Rendtorff, "Ez 20 und 36, 16ff," 260–265.

[175] "The same organization of history into two epochs may be found in both ch. 20 and 36:16ff." Rendtorff, "Ez 20 und 36, 16ff," 261. Rendtorff's overall argument maintains that 36:16–28 (possibly to v. 32) was never an independent unit. Rather, it consists of collected material (from chs. 20 and 11 primarily) in order to produce a composition of the genre 'Prophetenbuch'. His primary analysis shows how 36:16ff (by which he generally means vv. 16–23,) serves as a continuation of the pattern laid out in ch. 20. According to the pattern, God holds generations of Israelites under judgment in the wilderness (his anger in 20:8, 13, 21 and 36:18). God's announcement of anger is coupled with his announcement of the rationale: for the sake of his holy name (20:9, 14, 22 and 36:20). Ezek 36:19, a verse about scattering, finds its parallel in 20:23. Rendtorff then connects the 'Bundesformel' with the purification of the wicked cult (36:25); cf. 11:20; 14:11; 37:23–27. The 'Bundesformel,' is the changed relationship between God and Israel and includes their inheritance of the land of their fathers (36:28).

5.4.1.2. *Ezekiel 36:23c–38 and Chapter 11 in MT*

Commentators have long noted the connection between 36:26 and 11:19.[176] Closer inspection reveals that the surrounding verses in each passage are even more extensively related.[177] All of the verses in 11:16–21 show thematic and/or linguistic parallels with chapter 36. Further, the passages follow the same order of presentation. Both of these claims require some justification. Thus, the relevant phrases from each verse are listed and analyzed below.

	Chapter 11		Chapter 36
16	…though I removed them far away among the nations, and though I scattered them among the countries	19	I scattered them among the nations, and they were dispersed through the countries
	כי הרחקתים בגוים וכי הפיצותים בארצות		ואפיץ אתם בגוים ויזרו בארצות
17	I will gather you from the peoples and assemble you out of the countries where you have been scattered, and I will give you the land of Israel	24	I will take you from the nations and gather you from all the countries and bring you into your own land.
	וקבצתי אתכם מן העמים ואספתי אתכם מן הארצות אשר נפצותם בהם ונתתי לכם את אדמת ישראל		ולקחתי אתכם מן הגוים וקבצתי אתכם מכל הארצות והבאתי אתכם אל אדמתכם

---

[176] Lust, "Textual Criticism of the Old and New Testaments," 30. Most commentators point this out as well. So Block, *The Book of Ezekiel*, 355. Greenberg, *Ezekiel*, 730. Zimmerli, *Ezekiel*, 2:249.

[177] Rolf Rendtorff identifies a correspondence in the nation-covenant formula between 36:28 and the end of chs. 8–11 in his redaction-critical study of ch. 36, a verse that is not under discussion here. He includes a brief discussion of the correspondences to 11:17–20. See R. Rendtorff, "Ez 20 und 36, 16ff," 260–265, esp. 263.

Table (*cont.*)

	Chapter 11		Chapter 36
18	When they come there, they will remove from it all its detestable things and all its abominations	25	I will sprinkle clean water upon you, and you shall be clean from all your uncleannesses, and from all your idols I will cleanse you
	ובאו שמה והסירו את כל שקוציה ואת כל תועבותיה ממנה		וזרקתי עליכם מים טהורים קטהרתם מכל טמאותיכם ומכל גלוליכם אטהר אתכם
19	I will give them one heart and put a new spirit within them; I will remove the heart of stone from their flesh and given them a heart of flesh	26	A new heart I will give you and a new spirit I will put within you; and I will remove the heart of stone from your body and give you a heart of flesh.
	ונתתי להם לב אחד ורוח חדשה אתן בקרבכם והס־ רתי לב האבן מבשרם ונתתי להם לב בשר		ונתתי לכם לב חדש ורוח חדשה אתן בקרבכם והסרתי את לב האבן מבשרכם ונתתי לכם לב בשר
20	So that they may follow my statutes and keep my ordinances and do them. And they will be my people and I will be their God.	27b–28	…and make you follow my statutes and be careful to observe my ordinances and do them. (28) and you will dwell in the land that I gave your fathers; and you will be my people and I will be your God.
	למאן בחקתי ילכו ואת משפטי ישמרו ועשו אתם והיו לי לעם ואני אהיה להם לאלהים		ועשיתי את אשר בחקי תלכו ומשפטי תשמרו ועשיתם (28) וישבתם בארץ אשר נתתי לאבתיכם והייתם לי לעם ואנכי אהיה לכם לאלהים
21	But as for the heart that goes after their detestable things and their abominations, I will bring their deeds upon their own heads	31	Then you will remember your evil ways and your dealings that were no good, and you shall loathe yourselves for your iniquities and your abominable deeds
	ואל לב שקוציהם ותועבותיהם לבם הלך דרכם בראשם נתתי		וזכרתם את דרכיכם הרעים ומעלליכם אשר לא טובים ונקטתם בפניכם על עונתיכם ועל תועבותיכם

Several of the verses show *direct* parallels. There is a particularly close correspondence (nearly word for word) between 11:19 and 36:26.[178] Both 11:20 and 36:27–28 contain the *Bundesformel,* also called the renewed covenant.[179] 11:16, 17 are respectively parallel with 36:19, 24 in both theme and language, referring to the scattering and gathering of the people.[180] Finally, the triple set of verbs for obeying the divine ordinances, (הלך, שמר, and עשה) repeat in both chapters.[181]

Two sets of verses, 11:21/36:31 and 11:18/36:25, while connected in theme, are more indirectly related. Each deserves more extended discussion. First, the pair, 11:21/36:31 deals with how the people relate to moral wrongs *after* their return to the land (which happened in 11:18 and 36:28 respectively). In this sense, the two verses agree. However, they are also in tension. Ezekiel 11:21 speaks about the לב that returns to wicked dealings, focusing on the bad outcome of restoration. Ezek 36:31 calls for *remembrance* (זכר) of wicked dealings as a way to avoid them and hence focus on a good outcome.[182]

11:21a	(For) the heart that goes after	שקוציהם	and	תועבותיהם
11:21b	I will give them	דרכם בראשם		
36:31a	You will remember	דרכיכם הרעים	and	מעלליכם אשר לא טובים
36:31b	You will loathe yourselves for	עונתיכם	and	תועבותיכם

---

[178] Ezek 36:26 uses 2mpl possessive and independent pronouns while 11:19 uses 3mpl (except for one 2mpl that is, however, not attested by all Hebrew witnesses). Further, 36:26 contains את the direct object marker once over against 11:19. The only literary difference is one/new heart. 36:26 reads חדש; Witnesses for אחד in 11:19 vary, although MT has it. One witness does read חדש (see the reading in the fourth apparatus for v. 19(3) in HUBP on page לח).

[179] This is Rolf Rendtorff's term for the changed relationship that allows the people to inherit the land. R. Rendtorff, "Ez 20 und 36, 16ff," 262–263. Zimmerli simply designates "covenant formula," but always relies on Jeremianic understandings of the concept to explain Ezekiel. Zimmerli, *Ezekiel,* 1:262; 2:249.

[180] Both communicate the idea that the people were scattered among the nations and then gathered on the land. The verbs פוץ and קבץ repeat, as do the nouns גוים, ארצות (twice in both), and אדמה.

[181] Discussing Ezekiel 11:20 and 36:27, Joyce likewise concludes that the new heart and new spirit refer to "the gift of a renewed capacity to respond to Yahweh in obedience." Joyce does not emphasize the significance of the purity language here, as my analysis will argue. Joyce, *Divine Initiative and Human Response in Ezekiel,* 111.

[182] On the semantic level, the לב of 11:21a corresponds with the verb זכר in 36:31a. In the Hebrew lexicon, the heart is the site of intellectual capacities, including perception, insight, deliberation, and *memory*. See F. Stoltz, "לב Lēv heart," in *TLOT* (eds. Ernst Jenni and Claus Westermann; trans. Mark E. Biddle; vol. 2; Peabody, Ma: Hendrickson, 1997), 639.

Second, the pair, 11:18/36:25, raises an even larger issue. Both verses share the theme of purification.[183] Moreover, the two verses share the idea of abominable dangers to purity. However, the two chapters demonstrate a different understanding of purity and restoration. In ch. 11, the purity of the land is the concern, as 11:18 indicates, "they will remove from it [the land] all its detestable things." The people serve an instrumental function; an act is required of them, to remove the dangers posed to the land's purity.[184] The new heart and spirit of vv. 19–20 promote their *maintenance* of that purity. However, the post-restoration threat (presumably to the land) lies in those Israelites whose heart persists in abominable deeds in v. 21.

The sets of verses in chapter 36 cover much the same general plot, but re-interpret the 'mechanics' of purity. Ezekiel 36 is also concerned with the land.[185] Verse 25 announces how God intends to ensure the land's purity, by cleansing the people of their uncleanness (36:26–27). Hence, in ch. 36, the people are cleansed in order to *be able to* dwell on the land which happens subsequently (v. 28). The implication is that the land is not filled with detestable things (as in 11:18), but rather has already achieved a new clean status that requires preservation. The insurance against post-restoration abominable acts is memory (36:31) and shame (36:32) regarding past wrongs. Presumably, these emotional and intellectual states would not be possible without the clean heart and spirit granted them in vv. 26–27. The ability to obey divine ordinances here (36:27) is contingent on *memory* and not, as in chapter 11, on the *will* or *decision* to follow the good as opposed to the bad heart.

Thus, to summarize, the connections between 11:16–21 and 36:24–32 concern restoration and purity. The shared language and order of presentation between 11:16, 17, 19, 20 and 36:19, 24, 26, 27, 28, suggests that chapter 36 is a reinterpretation of ch. 11. In chapter 11, the people *actively cleanse the land* of impurities. For their post-restoration life, they receive

---

[183] The contamination of the land is a common concern of priestly theology. Lev 18:24–30 is especially important in this regard, a passage which correlates human conduct with defilement of the land, the subsequent solution to which is vomiting the people from the land.

[184] Lev 18:3b–4, 24–28 and 20:22–24 describe the land's reaction to the defilement caused by its inhabitants. Lev 25 describes the year of release (Jubilee), though Ezekiel does not seem to draw strongly on the concept. Similarly, Ezekiel does not seem to draw on the concept of the Sabbath years that, according to Lev 26:34–43, come after the people are expunged from the land.

[185] Note especially the promise oracle to the land in vv. 6–15 and the claim in v. 17 about the land.

a new moral self but face an old moral drama based on the *will* of the heart. In contrast, chapter 36 cleanses the people *in order to bring them* to the land, but initiates a new understanding of the moral self as lying in memory and shame. Remarkably, chapter 36 distinguishes yet correlates the relationship between the people's cleanness and their freedom from abominations.[186] Chapter 11 is not interested in the people's cleanness; it does not even employ the lexeme (טהר).[187] The MT plus in Ezekiel 36 then, follows and interprets 11:16–21 very closely. Linguistic parallels as well as views of restoration, purity, and the roles of the people and the land resonate between them.

Returning to the claim that 36:23c–38 is an "anthology of expressions," we may go even further. Ezek 36:23c–38 interweaves and reinterprets previous passages and serves as a lens through which to read the remainder of the book. Lust's work showed that it functioned as a bridge to chapter 37. Rendtorff's analysis of chapter 20's intertextual relationship with ch. 36 may also shed light on the break in p967 at 36:23b. As it stands, p967 completes the patterns Rendtorff identified in chapter 20, bringing Israel up to the potential brink of a new epoch in which God will, once again, act on behalf of his holy name. In MT, 36:23c–38 converts the *potential* of this new epoch into an actual one, filling in its details with ideas, theology, and predictions from typical divine utterances elsewhere in Ezekiel. It draws on chapter 37 and updates material from chapters 11 and 20 in order to redefine the temporal, religious, social, and cultic significance of the restoration period. It serves as an exegetical interpretation of Ezekiel's prophecies from earlier in the book and as a lens through which to understand Israel's restoration as stages of purification.

5.4.1.3. *Ezekiel 36 as a Transition to Chapters 38–39 in p967*

In p967, verse 23b concludes chapter 36 and hence immediately precedes Ezekiel 38–39. Hence, Ezekiel 36:1–23b introduces the Gog-Magog drama in p967. As noted above, some of the main themes among the promises

---

[186] According to Klawans, one who is morally impure is not also ritually impure; the concepts are distinct in the Hebrew Bible. Jonathan Klawans, *Impurity and Sin in Ancient Judaism* (New York: Oxford University Press, 2000), 21–32 and 36–38. However, Klawans argues that in the Qumran literature the two become "one conception of impurity that has both ritual and moral connotations." Ibid., 68, see also 67–68 and 75–88. The MT plus in Ezekiel 36 approaches this latter conceptualization.

[187] The concept of cleanness occurs surprisingly infrequently in Ezekiel. The verb טהר occurs only thirteen times, eight of which are in 36:23c—ch. 48. The lexeme does not occur anywhere in chs. 1–21.

in 36:1–23b are the profanation and sanctification of God's holy name and
the promise of Israel's return. These two themes function prominently in
Ezekiel 38–39 as well. God announces that his holy name will be sancti-
fied in 38:16 and 23 on the occasion of Gog's invasion and destruction.
An even stronger connection with Ezekiel 36 comes in 39:27 where God
announces:

> when I have brought them back from the nations, and gathered them out
> of the countries of the nations: and I will be sanctified among them in the
> presence of the nations.

This verse shows the same connection between the promise of Israel's
return to the land and God's sanctification as already found in 36:1–23b.

The connection between Israel's return and the sanctification of God's
name is echoed elsewhere in Ezekiel. For example, in Ezek 20:41 and
28:25, the promise to gather Israel to the land involves the sanctification
of God. These instances of the combined promise in chapters 20, 28, and
38–39 are amplified in the promises of Ezek 36:1–23b. The importance
of both themes is underscored through dense repetition in chapter 36:
God's 'name' occurs four times in vv. 20, 21, 22, and 23, and the promise
for Israel's return occurs three times in vv. 10, 11, and 12.[188]

In p967, 36:1–23b → 38–39 connects Israel's return with the holiness
of God. Specifically, chapters 38–39 provide the event which enacts the
combined promises of return and divine sanctification. Similarly, as discussed in §5.2.3.3, the transition also underscores the significance of the
Gog-Magog battle for the nation-recognition formula in 36:23a.

The transition from 36:1–23b to chapters 38–39 in p967 promotes dramatic anticipation. Nowhere in the book of Ezekiel does a reader ever find
anything specific about how God will accomplish his promise to sanctify himself. In p967, the repeated phrases in chapter 36 give way, not
to a statement of completion or assurance, but to an unfolding event in
chapters 38–39. Hence, Gog's invasion and defeat provide a heightened
dramatic effect with respect to the fulfillment of God's promises.

The most obvious difference between MT and p967 with regard to the
transition between chapter 36 and the rest of the book is the alternate
chapter order. For p967, as just discussed, the drama of the Gog-Magog
invasion becomes the occasion for God to sanctify his name in the sight

---

[188] Israel's return is twice more implied in vv. 8 and 9 which are promises about recul-
tivating and building the land.

of the nations. Ezekiel 36:23a provides the frame for this understanding of chapters 38–39. In contrast, MT's plus in 36:23c begins "when I display my holiness through you before their eyes" (בהקדשי בכם לעיניהם). The plus goes on to describe the two-aspect vision of restoration and then immediately proceed into the vision of the bones in chapter 37. Hence, MT indicates that Israel will be the instrument through which God makes his holiness known, suggesting that not the Gog-Magog battle, but the revivification of dried bones will induce this knowledge (see §5.2.3.3).

5.4.2. *"Heart/Spirit"* Tendenz

The new heart and spirit of 36:26–27 form the dominant lens through which the people of Israel are to understand their role in restoration. Indeed, there are eleven variants that contain reference to the heart/ spirit. Some are very strongly connected to the theme/theology developed in chs. 36:23c–38 and 37, others less-so. This makes sense since the distri- bution of the variants among the witnesses did not yield any significant pattern. 1) MT included the *Tendenz* over p967 six times; 2) p967 over MT four times; and 3) once MT and p967 agree against other Greek versions. Thus, the variants do not support viewing ch. 36:23c–38 as an intertextual center for the "Heart/Spirit" *Tendenz* in any coherent way. A brief exami- nation into the nature of the variants will support this thesis.

5.4.2.1. *Heart/Spirit*-Tendenz *in MT*

MT contains six variants in the *Tendenz:* 1) 13:2, 2) 13:3, 3) 16:30, 4) 31:10, 5) 36:5bβ, and 6) 36:5bγ.

1 & 2) Ezekiel 13:2 and 3
Chapter 13, already examined above in §§5.2.1 and 5.2.3, evinces special attention to the heart and spirit's role in prophecy on the part of MT. Two variants in vv. 2 and 3 serve to critique illicit prophecy that incorrectly stems from the heart and spirit.

3) Ezekiel 16:30
The variant in 16:30 concerns the heart of personified Israel. p967 asks about making a perpetual covenant with her daughters, in keeping with the allegorical genre of the chapter. However, MT renders the same phrase, "how sick is your heart?" Thus, in MT, the problem with Israel's heart is more squarely in view, while p967 makes no connection between

the practices of chapter 16's unfaithful wife and the drama of the heart developed later in the book.[189]

4) Ezekiel 31:10

The MT reference to heart in 31:10 also occurs in an extended allegory. Pharaoh is presented with the allegory of Assyria as the enormous cedar in order to describe its fall and perform Egypt's demise, ultimately into the pit, according to chapter 32. 31:10 serves as the transition from the dirge describing the tree's glory (vv. 3b–9) to God's specific actions of judgment against such trees. The variant in 31:10 is the content of the divine motivation clause which begins with "because" (ανθ ων/ יען אשר). p967 merely describes the tree's self-exaltation (και ειδον εν τω υψωθηναι αυτον) while MT specifies the problem "his heart was proud of its height" (ורם לבבו בגבהו).[190]

5) Ezekiel 36:5bβ

The MT variant in 36:5bβ talks about Edom and other historical enemies as whole-heartedly joyous about Israel's fall. p967, which is well-supported by a number of Greek witnesses, lacks the construction "whole-hearted."[191]

6) Ezekiel 36:5bγ

The variant in 36:5bγ about the heart was a rare example of inner-Hebrew disagreement among the witnesses. Hebrew manuscript 93 reads "in order that its heart would be expelled."[192] p967 reads with Z "to destroy it by plunder."

From these six cases, some words of synthesis may be offered. MT locates the problem with Israel in its sick heart (16:30) and rejects prophetic activity that speaks incorrectly from the heart/spirit (13:2, 3). The other three cases concern the heart of enemy nations, locating the basis for their judgment in their hearts, Assyria and Edom specifically.

---

[189] The other Greek witnesses show significant development. Manuscript 62 reads "in order that I should make a covenant with your heart," while the Lucianic and Theodotian witnesses ask "why should I purify your heart?" The latter's concern with purification of the heart makes it most obviously connected with the issues developed in 36:23c–37:28, more so than MT.

[190] Greek manuscript 46 combines the heart *and the spirit* in this instance.

[191] The MT, supported once again the Lucianic mss. and Tht. include the heart-reading.

[192] MT reads "in order that her open land would become plunder." HUBP[III-93] is quite odd, possibly indicating that Edom's heart will be removed in the same way as promised to Israel in the same chapter (36:26–27).

5.4.2.2. *Heart/Spirit*-Tendenz *in p967*

Four variants in the "Heart/Spirit" *Tendenz* occur in p967: 1) 17:22, 2) 20:24, 3) 22:15, and 4) 44:7.

1) Ezekiel 17:22
The variant in 17:22 occurs in the eagle and the vine allegory. Verses 22–24 focus on the branches of the vine and are commonly taken as a later messianic allegory.[193] p967 speaks about the sprig Yahweh will replant on Mount Zion (v.22b) as "the highest point of their heart." It is probably significant that the Greek tradition speaks about the sprig as "choice" through the lexical term επιλεκτος (vv. 3, 22). The MT's reading in v. 22 is more in keeping with the mundane level of the allegory, retaining a literal description of the tree's sprig as "from the topmost of its tender twigs." In neither v. 3 nor v. 22 does MT describe the branch as "chosen."

2) Ezekiel 20:24
The variant in 20:24 provides the divine rationale for the dispersal of Israel among the nations (v. 23). Verse 24 accuses Israel of disobeying divine commands on account of the "thoughts of their hearts." In contrast, MT locates the root cause of Israel's disobedience in the "idols of their fathers."[194]

3) Ezekiel 22:15
The variant in 22:15 occurs in another verse about the scattering of Israel. In this instance, God's intentions for those Israelites living among the nations drive the variant. p967 reads "and *your heart* will leave from you" while MT reads "and *your uncleanness* (טמאה) will leave from you." While the textual analysis presented in §4.3.1 showed that p967 could be an error/inner-Greek development, the context in MT presented notable textual fluidity in its use of the term טמאה. Hence, the MT's variant merits further literary analysis here.

---

[193] See Zimmerli, *Ezekiel*, 1:367–368. The shoot symbolically stood for the exaltation of the Davidic line. Slight variants in Ziegler's LXX favor a Christian messianic interpretation, though p967 probably preserves the pre-Christian Greek. See Lust, "Messianism in LXX-Ezekiel," 418; and his earlier idem, "'And I Shall Hang Him on a Lofty Mountain': Ezek 17:22–24 and Messianism in the Septuagint," in *IX Congress of the International Organization for Septuagint and Cognate Studies*, (ed. B.A. Taylor; SBLSCS 45; Atlanta: SBL, 1997), 231–250.

[194] Z synthesizes the two readings, "the thoughts of their fathers."

By speaking about uncleanness, MT diagnoses dispersed Israel with
the problems identified in chapters 24 and 36. Indeed, chapter 22 is an
oracle of judgment against the bloody city and uses metallurgic imagery
to communicate the modes of purification (vv. 17–22). In these details the
chapter is highly intertextual with chapter 24. Additionally, uncleanness
(טמאה) is a repeated concern in 36:23c–38 (vv. 25–29). Outside of these
three contexts, 22:15, and chapters 24 and 36, the noun only occurs one
other time.[195] Thus this variant achieves significance in *both* p967 and
MT by means of its intertextual connections with other chapters in which
Tendenzen have been identified. Specifically, while it is p967 that speaks
about the heart of Israel, MT reinforces its purity concerns for the restoration of Israel.

4) Ezekiel 44:7a

The heart-variant quoted in 44:7 is quite important and merits a presentation of the two versions:

p967   του μη εισαγαγειν υμας υιους αλογενεις απεριτμητους καρδια του
        γεινεσθαι εν τοις αγιοις μου.
        In order that you *not* admit[196] foreigners who are uncircumcised in
        heart to be in my sanctuary.

MT   בהביאכם בני בכר ערלי לב וערלי בשר להיות במקדשי
        When you admit foreigners, uncircumcised in heart *and flesh*, to be
        in my sanctuary.

Both MT and p967 exclude foreigners from the temple who are not circumcised in heart. The verse goes on to explain how these people from
v. 7a will profane (חלל) God's house. However, MT includes the qualification of fleshly circumcision, indicating that exclusion from the sanctuary
is not merely a matter of the heart. Indeed, MT reinforces its focus on
fleshly circumcision using the same flesh plus in 44:9 as well.

The four p967 variants about the heart in 17:22; 20:24; 22:15; and 44:7,
9 occur in contexts about foreignness. The first three are explicitly contexts of dispersal and return. The fourth is about foreigner's access to the
temple. The first three variants especially do not demonstrate a clear connection with the theology of chapters 36–37. They do, however, reflect an
interest in the state of the Diaspora's heart.

---

[195] The noun occurs in 39:24, which is sometimes taken to be the latest redactional
composition, written to connect the Gog-Magog oracles with the rest of Ezekiel's book.

[196] The genitive of the articular infinitive is used to express purpose, often a negative
purpose. Smythe, *Greek Grammar*, §2032e §1408.

5.4.2.3. *"Heart/Spirit" Tendenz: Two Cases Where p967 and MT Agree Against Other Greek Witnesses*

Two verses contain the variant in which p967 and MT agree: 1) 21:12(7) and 2) 29:16.

1) Ezekiel 21:12(7)

In 21:12(7), p967 and MT essentially read together "every spirit will expire." The connotation in p967 is certainly death (i.e., breath its last), while the MT verb (מסס) refers more to weakening. The full list of weakened body parts in v. 12 (7) is: "every heart, all hands, every spirit, all knees." The notable difference, however, occurs in B which adds "all flesh." This addition in the list forms a unique dual subject for the verb εκψυχω: "and all flesh and every spirit will breathe its last," (και εκψυξει πασα σαρξ και παν πνευμα).

Verse 12 occurs in the context of the sword song of Ezekiel 21. Israel is commanded to moan in grief for the destruction rendered against her by the sword. Theologically, the idea that the heart is weakened by this mourning, repeated in vv. 12(7) and 20(15), may serve an important role towards the change of heart expected in chs. 36–37, although nothing in the chapter indicates as much. However, in adding flesh to the list of expired body parts, B emphasizes the bodily failure of Israel. Such a corporal notion of the problem and solution is characteristic of Ezekiel 37.[197]

2) Ezekiel 29:16

The second variant in which MT and p967 agree is in 29:16. The verse runs, "the Egyptians will never again be the reliance of the house of Israel; they will recall their iniquity, when they follow after them." A, however, reads "when they follow after the hearts."

The two variants shared by MT and p967 do not generate any trends worth noting. While disappointing in terms of meaning, it is important information to see that though p967 and MT do not overwhelmingly share theology, they have shared readings in these two cases.

---

[197] p967 lacks "flesh" and abbreviates the term πνευμα here. If this abbreviation is supposed to refer to a divine name, then either p967 has not understood the context, or a curious theological assertion is being made; "the Spirit will expire". Perhaps B adds "flesh" in order to clarify that the term for spirit, (unabbreviated according to Z,) refers to human life.

5.4.2.4. *Summary of Section: "Heart/Spirit" Tendenz*

All of the instances of heart-variants in p967 concerned the Diaspora heart. Where 22:15 claimed that the Diaspora heart would leave, a Hebrew reading in 36:5bγ says the same of Israel's. Both editions contain variants stating that a bad heart is a problem: MT in 16:30 that a sick heart is connected to sin; and p967 in 20:24 that Israel was cast into dispersal because of the thoughts of her heart.

The two MT heart-variants depict life as an achievable goal of a penitent agent. Especially in 18:32 and 33:5, the agent may live by turning from iniquity. This theology, as Jacqueline Lapsley suggested, is not connected with that in chapters 36–37 regarding the source of human's moral capacity.[198] In chapters 36–37, the capacity for moral change lies in God and God's actions towards his guilty people.

5.4.3. *Summary of Section:* Tendenzen *Related to Ezekiel 36:23c–38*

Ezekiel 36:23c–38 provides MT with a two-aspect vision of restoring the purity of the land, of God's name, and of the people. As shown above, 36:23c–38 draws on the theology and structure of chapter 11 to develop a more complex notion of human agency and purity. While 36:23c–38 does provide an introduction to chapter 37, it also draws on elements in chapters 11 and 20 to form a larger lens through which to read MT's edition of restoration. The detail of the new heart, promised in 36:23c–38 especially demonstrated this. The new heart in MT chapter 36 represented a re-crafting of chapter 11, more than an introduction to chapter 37. Examination of "heart" variants demonstrated, at least, that MT's variant features do not exhibit a coherent theology of the heart. Further, p967 exhibited its own distinctive uses of heart. This complex and incoherent set of variants actually helps to show that human moral constitution is not largely at stake in differentiating p967's edition from MT. Instead, it supports viewing 36:23c–38 as a reinterpretation of the heart passage in chapter 11, a reinterpretation that included the heart, but did not invest greater significance to it as a coherent compositional interest throughout MT's edition.

---

[198] It more strongly resembles the notion in chapter 11, where the agent could choose one heart over another. By contrast, chs. 36–37 affirm the need for cleansing by granting a "new heart." See Lapsley, *Can These Bones Live?*.

5.5. 'GOG-MAGOG' *TENDENZEN*: VARIANTS RELATED TO EZEKIEL 38–39

Ezekiel 38–39 describes the invasion of Gog-Magog into the restored nation of Israel. Because p967 and MT present a different arrangement of chapters 36–39, the Gog-Magog events occur at different moments in the plot of restoration. Additionally, Gog's army captain, Meshech, appeared in an MT plus in another intertextual center, 32:17–32. Indeed, variants related to Gog-Magog occur across the book of Ezekiel, further distinguishing p967 from MT along the lines of what is here called the 'Gog-Magog' *Tendenzen*.

5.5.1. *Gog's Entourage of Nations*

In chapter 38, Gog descends on Israel accompanied by an entourage. Strikingly, Gog's living army is never called a horde (המון) in MT.[199] The term *is* used in association with Gog, but only as the name of his burial ground. 39:11 and 15 prescribe the name for the grave-site as "the valley of Hamon-gog" (גיא המון גוג). 39:15 sounds yet another affirmation, calling the name of the "city" Hamonah (המונה). Thus, Gog's "horde" denotes his *slain* entourage, those with whom he is buried. Gog's *living* entourage is described as "many peoples" (עמים רבים);[200] "peoples" (עמים);[201] an "assembly" (קהל);[202] "bands" (אגפים);[203] a "great army" (חיל רב);[204] and "brothers" (אחים).[205]

In addition to the nomenclature for Gog's armies, specific nations are named as part of his entourage: Meshech and Tubal (38:2); Persia, Ethiopia (Cush), and Put (Libya) (38:5); Gomer and Beth-togarmah (38:6). Additionally, Sheba, Dedan, and Tarshish (38:13) are on the scene during his invasion, questioning his militant motives. A handful of variants outside of chs. 38–39 include these geographic names.

The oracles against Tyre (chs. 26–28) associate the economic island state with several of Gog's associates. Both MT and p967 list the nationalities of some of Tyre's warriors in 27:10 as Persia, Lud, and Put (Libya).

---

[199] We have already examined the hordes in §5.3.2.2.
[200] Ezek 38:6, 9, 15, 22.
[201] Ezek 39:4.
[202] Both noun and verbal forms of this root are found in Ezek 38:4, 7, 13(2), 15.
[203] Ezek 38:9, 22, and 39:4.
[204] Ezek 38:15.
[205] Ezek 38:21.

Additionally, in 27:14, both editions report that Beth-togarmah's horses and horsemen join Tyre's army. Tyre's military entourage in ch. 27 and Gog's in ch. 38 comprise shared material in MT and p967.

MT furthers the intertextual resonances between Tyre and Gog's associates. Chapter 27 recounts a 21-verse list (vv. 5–25) of all the nations who traded with Tyre.[206] Among them, MT lists Dedan (v. 15), Sheba (v. 23), and Meshech and Tubal (v. 13). In lieu of these, p967 reads Rhodes (v. 15), a minus (v. 23), and "the whole world" (v. 26), respectively. There are no variants that work the other way: to bring p967's edition closer to the entourage of Gog. Thus, MT manifests a sharper connection between the Tyrian oracles and chapters 38–39.

The intertextuality between the two episodes is made all the more striking given the echoes between Tyre's fate in the sea and the nations' fate in the pit. We saw that Tyre's fate in the sea was shaped in MT to more strongly parallel the description of ch. 32's pit. (§5.3.2.1). Indeed, just as Meshech and Tubal appear in MT's pit (32:26), they show up here in the Tyrian traders' list of chapter 27. The Tyrian trade-list culminates in v. 27 with the fateful declaration that everyone involved in Tyre's economic engine will "sink into the heart of the seas on the day of your [Tyre's] ruin." The last colophon of v. 27 "and with all the company that is within you," implies the whole list of traders that preceded it.[207] Thus, MT allegorically sinks Gog's entourage and associates from chapters 38–39—Dedan, Sheba, and Meshech and Tubal—into chapter 27's heart of the sea.[208]

A much more modest variant involving Dedan occurs in 25:13. A brief oracle against Edom, 25:12–14 prophesies Edom's fall at the hands of *Israel*. The agency of Israel here is "remarkable" according to Zimmerli, and to Wevers "a notion otherwise completely foreign to the book of Ezekiel."[209]

---

[206] This trade-list is often taken to be secondary. See Zimmerli, *Ezekiel*, 2:63.

[207] So Zimmerli, Zimmerli, *Ezekiel*, 2:69. For a different interpretation, Block seems to see all of Tyre's trade partners as grouped with those who mourn in vv. 28b–32a. Block's interpretation, however, does not eliminate the intertextuality between the population in the pit and Tyre's fall into the sea. It does, however, shift the emphasis onto the generic as opposed to the allegorical parallels. In other words, the intertextual parallel becomes that of the lament genre and the rhetorical strategy of interpolating the narrative audience, (i.e., the trade-list observers in ch. 27 and Egypt in ch. 32). Block, *The Book of Ezekiel*, 2:84–85.

[208] Both editions of ch. 27 list Sidon, Edom, and Egypt among Tyre's traders. These nations also went down into MT's pit in ch. 32:17–32. For a thorough discussion of the trade-list, its historical setting, and its redactional features, see Greenberg, *Ezekiel*, 2:568–569.

[209] Zimmerli, *Ezekiel*, 2:16–18. Wevers, *Ezekiel*, 198. Greenberg and Block note the distinction, but in passing. Greenberg, *Ezekiel*, 2:523. Block, *The Book of Ezekiel*, 2:25.

MT signifies the range of Edom's collapse in v. 13 using the metonym "from Teman to Dedan."[210] In contrast, p967 narrates "those who are pursued from Teman." Not only does MT include Dedan, one of Gog's associates in chs. 38–39, but it does so in the context of an oracle in which Israel uniquely plays a role in the military victory. Here, too, we can see the parallel with chapters 38–39, which strongly imply that Israel participates in her defense against the Gog invasion.

5.5.2. *Wordplays with Meshech* (משׁך)

Earlier in §5.3.1, I suggested that the verb משׁך in 32:20 was used in a deliberate wordplay. There, the nations "drag" (משׁך) Egypt and its hordes into the pit. It is certainly striking that the verb occurs in an intertextual center in which Meshech and Tubal are important variants. The deliberateness of wordplays can only ever be made suggestively, but since the verb occurs in one other salient intertextual center, I consider the possibility here.[211]

In chapter 12, the verb משׁך is used in an MT plus within the intertextual center on prophecy. 12:28 reads "none of my words will be delayed (תמשׁך) any further." The Niphal of משׁך meaning "be delayed" refers to the temporal issue addressed in the disputation on prophecy. The same construction occurs in v. 25, the line immediately before the MT plus. Were the MT plus a later addition and the wordplay intentional, v. 25 provides an opportune location for a disputation on temporality in prophecy, particularly if the addition was made in conjunction with the alternate sequencing of chapters 38–39 and 37 as Lust originally suggested. If all of these possibilities were true, MT may have used the wordplay with משׁך to historicize one of Ezekiel's more apocalyptic prophecies.

The present study cannot do more to support the proposal for wordplay with Meshech. However, that these are the only three instances in Ezekiel where the verb appears (12:25, 28 and 32:20) and that they do so in intertextual centers is both striking and evocative.

---

[210] The expression is curious to all commentators, but that the two geographic names are associated with Edom is certain.

[211] Neither of these word-plays is possible in the Greek, since μοσοχ is not semantically related to the concept of dragging. It is *possible* that p967 harbors its own play on words in 39:18, where victorious Israel eats her victor. The word for young bull (μοσχος) is phonetically similar enough to Meshech so as to raise the possibility; μοσχος occurs twice in the verse.

5.5.3. *Plunder and Spoil*

Ezekiel's military judgments often include the threat that Israel would become spoil and plunder. A survey of the dynamics of plunder reveals that the progressive use of the term charts an important reversal for Israel's fate. In ch. 36:4–5, the mountains of Israel were devastated as the plunder (בז/προνομη) of the enemy nations. In a parallel fashion, the threatening plan of Gog's invasion in 38:12–13 includes his intentions to take Israel as both plunder and spoil (שלל/προνομη and בז/ σκυλα). In chs. 38–39, Israel was at risk of becoming plunder once again. However, the reversal of the plunder-dynamic occurs in chs. 38–39 as part of the more dramatic reversal of Israel's status, fate, and relationship with God. God destroys Gog and instructs Israel to burn the weapons and bury the remains of Gog. In 39:10, Israel directly participates in the reversal of her fate through the directive to plunder and spoil (שלל/προνομευω and בזז/σκυλευω) those who plundered Israel.

Because chs. 38–39 reverse this theme for Israel, the variants dealing with plunder merited consideration among the 'Gog/Magog' *Tendenzen.* One particularly important plus in MT establishes this reversal in an oracle of promise to Israel, a promise that is lacking in p967. In 34:8, a set of promises to Israel (allegory of the sheep), MT alone includes a provision that *Israel will not become spoil* (בז). Here in 34:8, p967 and MT promise the sheep that they would not suffer this form of post-mortem disgrace as food for wild animals. MT expands to include immunity from plunder as well. The MT plus adheres to its theory of prophecy. The promise of reversal in ch. 34 is fulfilled in ch. 39, immediately and without delay.

Two other "plunder" variants concern Egypt but split between p967 and MT.[212] In 30:24, the two editions report the king of Babylon's invasion into Egypt. In a p967 variant, the verse extends to say that he will "plunder its plunder and spoil its spoil." MT on the other hand, reads, "and he will groan before him with groans of the slain." The second variant, an MT plus, also occurs in a passage about Egypt. The shared text of 29:19 speaks about Egypt as plunder and spoil to Nebuchadrezzar's army. In MT, the phrase is preceded by "he will carry off his horde (ונשא המנה)." We saw in §5.3.2.2.2 that the horde of Egypt in 29:19 involved another prophecy and fulfillment pattern. In 29:19, King Nebuchadrezzar carries off Egypt's horde along with plunder and spoil, as God's payment on behalf of Baby-

---

[212] The third plunder-variant in 26:12 will not be discussed here since MT and p967 were in agreement against B. Ezek 26:12 concerns Tyre's horde.

lon's labor. Verse 18 clarifies that Nebuchadrezzar's army "labored hard against Tyre" and required funds. God then promptly solicits Egyptian plunder for Babylonian reserves. The MT plus implies that Egyptians were probably indentured to Babylon's army in their continued quest against Tyre. This oracle is fulfilled in 30:4 when Egypt's hordes are carried off by the Babylonian army. In 30:4, two features affirm the prophecy-fulfillment pattern. First, the hordes of Egypt are an MT plus, fulfilling the MT plus in 29:19. Second, the lexemes for plunder and spoil (שלל and בזז) do not occur in this verse. In fact, the lexemes do not occur again in Ezekiel's book with reference to Egypt. Thus, only the horde-prediction, and not the plunder-prediction, is fulfilled in MT.

The contrast with p967 becomes clearer at this point. p967 depicts a different fate for Egypt's horde. 32:6 reports that Egypt's horde (πλῆθος) would drench the land with blood from the mountains, a reading not found in MT. Additionally, we saw too that Egypt's horde does not appear in p967's edition of the pit in ch. 32. By way of contrast, MT addresses the pit oracle to Egypt's hordes explicitly.

5.5.4. *Summary of Section: 'Gog-Magog'* Tendenzen

With respect to the variants in the Gog-Magog *Tendenz*, MT is the more expansive text. Gog's entourage was more closely replicated in the Tyrian trade-list of chapter 27. Israel's agency against Edom in 25:12–14 mimicked her role in chapters 38–39 against Gog. The MT edition of the Edom oracle also echoed Gog's associates. We may see here the influence of the MT's theory of prophecy and fulfillment. The dynamics of plunder provided us a specific instance where MT's concern for fulfillment was clear. MT hosted a unique promise to Israel in chapter 34 that would be fulfilled in chapters 38–39. The same prediction-fulfillment was seen with regards to Egypt's hordes in chapters 29–30. Though the shared text predicted that Egypt would become plunder and spoil, MT's two pluses emended *both* the promise and the fulfillment to be about Egypt's horde.

The important role played by prophecy-fulfillment in the MT variants increases the significance of the proposed word plays with the verb משך. The verb is deployed only three times in MT: all in intertextual centers, twice in unique MT variants, and twice to directly refer to the immediate fulfillment of prophecy. These highly freighted resonances now appear to be stronger indications that MT may have applied its theory of prophecy, articulated in ch. 12:26–28, to both the fate of enemies in the pit and to the Gog-Magog episode in its edition of chapters 32 and 38–39, respectively.

5.6. SUMMARY OF CHAPTER: P967 AND MT AS VARIANT LITERARY EDITIONS

We began the present analysis with two guiding questions: 1) in what sense are p967 and MT variant literary editions? 2) What is the scope and nature of the variants that distinguish them? Examination of the *Tendenzen* sheds new light on both questions. For example, analysis of the *Tendenzen* revealed sets of variants that, though numerous, did not produce coherent exegetical readings and cannot therefore be used to sharply distinguish the editions. For example, *Tendenzen* like 'New Life' and "Heart," did not produce a coherent relationship to one another or to the intertextual centers. Compounding the matter, these two *Tendenzen* characterized *both* p967 and MT variants; this uneven distribution did not help to crystallize any strongly distinguishing features between p967 and MT's editions of Ezekiel.

Other *Tendenzen* did show coherent trends, but did not foster coherent exegetical readings. This was the case with MT's dating scheme and its more frequent use of "on that day." In the case of dating, it seemed likely that p967's tenth year increased the dramatic effect of the destruction of Jerusalem in correlating oracles with that same year. However, MT's dating scheme was more idiosyncratic, which probably means a different logic is at work in them.[213] Both MT's dating, and its use of "on that day" represent strongly distinguishing trends, but the preceding analysis did not uncover overwhelmingly striking exegetical meanings for these differences.

Several *Tendenzen* constituted a set of variants with strongly intertextual features which may therefore be used to distinguish p967 and MT as variant literary editions. One general theme which *did* distinguish MT's edition from p967 was its interest in spatial distinctions, particularly for the sake of purity. Drawing on the Ezekelian notion of the four-fold fate for Israel, which suggests that location is meaningful to Ezekiel's book, MT emphasized spatial locations for death and life. Several details underscored this emphasis: 1) MT's distinction between the שדה as the site of enemy slain and the בקעה as the field for Ezekiel's visions; 2) MT's creation of two locations in the Pot-allegory of chapter 24; 3) MT's more

---

[213] One obvious possibility is that they reflect actual dates, which would therefore, not necessarily possess a strong "literary" structure. Alternatively, the dates could hold numerological significance. See Fishbane, *Biblical Interpretation*, 450.

abundantly filled pit in chapter 32; 4) MT's spatial distinction within the pit of chapter 32 according to the status of uncircumcision; 5) MT's relegation of Egypt's "hordes" to exile in 29:19 and 30:4, and to the pit in ch. 32; and finally 6) MT's attention to cleansing the people for the sake of the purity of the *land* of Israel in 36:23c–38. In addition to these spatial distinctions, MT and p967 occasionally differed about the location of enemy slain: so 32:6 and 35:8.

A second theme that sharply distinguished the two editions was the treatment of foreign nations. As we saw, the nation-recognition formula in p967 was employed to show that the nations will come to know God as catalyzed by the Gog-Magog invasion and defeat. Indeed, that knowledge will be achieved when "through you [Gog-Magog]" (38:20) God reveals his holiness. In contrast, MT's edition privileges the vision of dried bones and the restoration of Israel as "my people" (37:12) through whom God's holiness is revealed. In comparing p967 and MT's understandings of the nation-recognition, a striking sense of debate emerges. Indeed, the instrument of God's self-revelation to the nations is cast in exactly the same terms, "through you." For p967, εν σοι occurs in 38:20 referring to Gog-Magog. For MT בכם occurs in 36:23c referring to Israel. Both occur in plus material. This detail sheds some light on the different chapter order: p967 and MT place different and varying emphasis on chs. 37 and 38–39 as fulfilling the divine requirement for self-sanctification.

Beyond the alternative uses of the nation-recognition formula, p967 and MT treat foreign nations differently. p967 presented the edition that was more amenable to the inclusion of foreigners in Israel's restoration vision. Compared with MT, p967's ambiguous presentation of foreign bodies strewn about the lands yields the impression that MT sought to tidy up the land. Most significantly, p967 did not explicitly disallow Edom or Egypt's hordes from the reversal of fate that takes place in the vision of dried bones. For p967's edition, the "field" represented an undifferentiated space of hope for revivification. The importance of the 'hope of the field' seems all the more likely given the emphasis placed on picking up Gog-Magog's bones from the "field" in both editions. MT looks like a swift refutation of national inclusion compared to p967's more open edition. MT ensured Gog-Magog's fate in the grave by relegating the enemy from the North to the pit. Egypt's "hordes" and Edom were similarly relegated to the pit. The exegetical significance for this understanding of MT is entirely comparative, since the meaning of MT derives from differentiation with p967. Nevertheless, the two editions can be distinguished on this point. MT presents an edition that fastidiously ensures the fate of bodies: foreign

enemy nations to the pit, Israel to the land of Israel. In fact, MT displays
further specificity. According to MT's edition of the Pot allegory in ch. 24,
MT restricted the surviving bones to those 'outside the Pot.' Thus, MT prepared a negative fate for the bodies that died in Jerusalem; their fate was
utter incineration. While the historical referents are difficult to determine,
it is clear that identity was at issue in MT's edition of restoration. MT's
plus in Ezekiel 37 of "my people" seemed to have as its corollary, variants
that determined who are *not my people*, as well.[214]

In addition to these general issues over foreign nations, the editions
showed some differentiation with respect to their treatment of Tyre and
Egypt, and to a lesser extent, Edom. The oracles about Tyre showed several
differentiating features between MT and p967's editions. The frequency of
Tyre's involvement in the variant editions deserves a summary presentation: 1) MT fused Tyre's fate (especially in 28:8) with the apocalyptic end
of enemy nations in the pit of ch. 32; 2) Tyre's fate *could* be in view again
when in 32:18 an MT variant places the "daughters of the majestic nations"
(בנות גוים אדרם) into the pit;[215] 3) MT's edition of the Tyrian trade-list in
ch. 27:5–26 includes three variants that bring Tyre's economic allies into
alignment with Gog-Magog's entourage, including Meshech and Tubal
(27:13). This further underscores the associations in the MT between Tyre
and Gog-Magog; 4) In p967, the "hordes" (πλῆθος) wordplay underscored
Tyre's sin and resultant fate with respect to economic overindulgence;[216]
5) In 26:20–21, MT and p967 both offer variants about life after Tyre. In
p967 we find a simple promise that Tyre would not rise again. However,
MT elaborates that beauty will return to the land and Tyre, as an object of
desire, will be defunct; and finally, 6) The Tyrian oracles (chs. 26–29) are
dated in p967 to the tenth year and in MT to the eleventh.

Similarly, the oracles about Egypt displayed variant material. Egypt
has been discussed more thoroughly above; thus the following summary
will be brief: 1) The alternate dating between p967 and MT especially
affected the oracles against Egypt. MT placed the pit of 32:17–32 last in

---

[214] Some hint about the issue of identity may lie in MT's manifest concern with circumcision. Both its edition of the pit, and its plus in 44:7 show a concern with this ritual
marker of identity. See §5.3.1.3.

[215] The suggestion is based on reading Ezek 32:18 in light of Ezek 26:6 and 8 where
the "daughters of Tyre" die on the field. (The readings in Ezek 26:6 and 8 are not variants
between MT and p967.)

[216] While more pronounced in p967, MT captured some elements of this wordplay, and
could therefore, be significant to MT's three pluses in chapter 7 concerning the economic
sins and apocalyptic destruction of "hordes."

the sequence of Egyptian oracles, perhaps to emphasize the apocalyptic finality of Egypt's fate; 2) Four MT pluses of the phrase "on that day" concerned Egypt;[217] 3) Egypt's "hordes" suffered captivity by the Babylonian army and went into exile in MT pluses (29:19 and 30:4); 4) MT frequently repeated that Egypt's "hordes" went down to the pit, while the translation Egypt's "strength" occurred in p967; 5) The significant differences in the pit of Ezekiel 32:17–32 all affect Egypt, over whom the lament is uttered; and 6) According to p967, Egypt's death in 29:5 does not involve "wrapping" the corpses, leaving the bodies exposed on the field.

Temporal matters distinguished the two editions as well. Certainly, the different chapter orders (MT 37→38–39 and p967: 38–39→37) affect the plot for Israel's restoration. The alternate date references and instances of "on that day" similarly affect the editions' temporal structures. Most importantly, MT offered a more explicit philosophy of prophecy in the plus at 12:26–28. This philosophy of immediate fulfillment extended to several other MT pluses and variants as well. These represented a strong set of coherent variants, and thus perhaps the strongest *Tendenz*. In other words, the *Tendenz* was numerously attested and widely distributed in MT's edition. The variants between MT and extant Greek witnesses in ch. 4:4–6 showed that prophecy and fulfillment produced variant assertions for the length of Israel's exile.[218] An additional example of MT's implementation of the prophecy-fulfillment pattern occurs in the variant in ch. 34:8 where MT promises that Israel will not become plunder; a promise which is fulfilled in chs. 38–39. Thus, MT presents the edition that more strongly and frequently articulates its ideas about prophecy and fulfillment.

The plus material in MT affects the issue of prophecy in two specific ways. Perhaps most obviously, the pluses in 13:2 and 3 specify the 'mechanics' of false visions. That is to say, false visions come from prophets who look to the musings of their own hearts (v. 2) and spirits (v. 3). Such false prophets not only get the mechanics of visionary experiences wrong, but they are further condemned for speaking in the name of Yahweh without having been sent for the task (v. 3). Second, the MT plus in 12:26–28 affirms new aspects of visionary prophecy. Further, variants in the context of chs. 12–13 share this reflection on the nature of Ezekiel's prophetic

---

[217] The MT plus in ch. 29:21 referred, not only to the plundering of Egypt, but indicated that a "horn would spring up."

[218] However, as was the case with several of the variants in the 'Prophecy-Fulfillment' *Tendenz*, MT can only be distinguished from the best witnesses to the Old Greek and not p967 in these chapters.

"vision" חזון. The proverb in 12:22 reveals that people are frustrated by the time-delay of visions. They are left to conclude that visions eventually just expire. 12:23–24 affirms three points in the face of this problem: 1) visions are robust, their fulfillment is trustworthy; 2) the time of fulfillment is "near;" 3) there is no such thing as false vision in Israel "anymore." In direct contrast to the last statement, false visions are are the very problem in 13:1–7 which warrant condemnation. Ezekiel 13:3 speaks about prophets who have not seen anything, and again in v. 6, those who envision emptiness. So while 12:21–28 affirm the robust nature of visions, 13:1–7 still sees fit to deal with the threat of false visions. The false visions of ch. 13, and the expired visions of ch. 12 both threaten prophetic expectation and crush people's confidence in visions.

As a final note of conclusion, the role of literary genre played an important role in the preceding discussion of variants. Especially noteworthy, textual variants in Ezekiel's 'allegories' warranted exegetical attention. For example, in the allegory of the cooking pot in ch. 24, the vision of dried bones in ch. 37, and the metaphor of the sheep in ch. 34, variant details took on increased significance.[219] An allegory, by definition, structures details for figurative meanings.[220] Ezekiel is arguably meant to be read through the lens of its allegories;[221] indeed, in one instance of first-person speech in Ezekiel, the prophet asks "Ah Lord God, they are saying of me

---

[219] For example, of ch. 24, critics widely agree that the details in the pot allegory almost overload the production of meaning. See Allen who states "the allegorical text seems to bombard a hearer with too much material to assimilate at once." Allen, *Ezekiel*, 2:57. So Zimmerli, *Ezekiel*, 1:497.

[220] For example, Northrop Frye comments on allegory in the Bible:

> In allegory this harmonic chord is the symbol...Note that allegory may be polyphonic, like Spencer's, or romantic and evocative, like Shelley's. The sense of infinite meaning we derive from symbols is partly the romantic sense of vague or indefinite meaning.

Northrop Frye, *Northrop Frye's Notebooks and Lectures on the Bible and Other Religious Texts* (eds. Northrop Frye and Robert D. Denham; Toronto: University of Toronto Press, 2003), 53 §133.

In speaking about symbol as polyphonic, Frye uses the notion of "harmony" (similar to how I have used "intertextuality") to evoke the way in which an allegory constructs figurative meanings from the sets of symbols it employs. That is to say, symbols are static details in the production of the "harmonies" of allegorical meaning. For a textual critic, variants in detail are thus, of increased significance.

[221] For comments about the role of allegory in Ezekiel specifically, see Joel Rosenberg, "Jeremiah and Ezekiel," in *The Literary Guide to the Bible* (eds., Robert Alter and Frank Kermode; 2d ed.; Cambridge: Belknap Press, 1990), 194–204.

'he is just a maker of allegories'" (20:49).[222] However one appreciates the role of allegory for understanding the entire book of Ezekiel, specific allegories within the book featured several important textual variants. This suggests that allegories became one specific site for interpretation and editorial activity. Perhaps most importantly, the genre of allegory plays a central role in the MT of chs. 12–13 about the nature of Ezekiel's "visions" (חזון).

---

[222] Such a comment resembles a strikingly rare instance, where the prophet is spoken of in the third person: 12:26–28 in MT states "the visions that *he* sees are for distant times." See the discussion of this variant in chapter 4 and §5.2.1 above. For a discussion of first-person speech in Ezekiel, see Zimmerli, *The Fiery Throne: The Prophets and Old Testament Theology* (ed., Kenneth C. Hanson; FCBS; Minneapolis: Fortress, 2003), 107–108.

CHAPTER SIX

CODICOLOGICAL ANALYSIS OF P967 EZEKIEL

Manuscripts have many stories to tell if you listen closely to the sounds of the details they preserve for today's world, such as the forms of letters, their layout, their being part of a collection, the other texts written down either on the same or reverse side of a leaf, or the background of their provenance if known.[1]

6.1. INTRODUCTION

Textual critics focus narrowly on the text of manuscripts and in an even greater act of abstraction, the *Ur*-Text. These texts, one reified and one ideal, continue to dominate the interests of those who work with ancient manuscript evidence. The situation is so entrenched that often the critical edition of a 'text' will not even include other manuscript information such as reading marks, as is the case with Jahn's publication of p967[Köln].[2] Codicology, the study of the text in its codex form, reminds us that what scholars isolate as textual histories should be understood in light of literary production and use.

The discipline of codicology can open up scholarship beyond text-myopia where manuscripts are viewed as merely conduits of an earlier text. Rather, codicology reminds us that the text is a *physical* object, and its various features can shed light on the communities who used the text and how the text was read and understood. As Gamble has noted,

> By observing precisely how the text was laid out, how it was written, and what it was written on, one has access not only to the technical means of its production but also, since these are the signs of intended and actual uses, to

---

[1] T.J. Kraus and T. Nicklas, "The World of NT Manuscripts: 'Every Manuscript Tells a Story'," in *New Testament Manuscripts: The Texts and the World* (eds. T.J. Kraus and T. Nicklas; TENT 2; Leiden: Brill, 2006), 4.

[2] Jahn, *Der griechische Text.* The same problem motivated J.W. Olley's "Texts Have Paragraphs Too: A Plea for Inclusion in Critical Editions," *Textus* 19 (1998): 111–125.

the social attitudes, motives, and contexts that sustained its [a codex's] life and shaped its meaning. [3]

In this chapter I will present, analyze, and assess p967's codicological features towards understanding how its text of Ezekiel was read and understood.[4] This approach to the manuscript of p967 coheres with the interest in literary and interpretive history at the heart of the larger project. For instance, chapters 3–5 explored how textual criticism may be a tool towards greater understanding of the literary interests affecting Ezekiel's later textual development. In the present chapter, I will use codicology in order to understand p967's reading community.[5]

All aspects of the codex will be presented, focusing on the Ezekiel portion. Once the descriptive work is complete, I will examine features which shed light on interpretive/exegetical interests and reading function. For instance, Ezekiel's text is more densely marked with marginal notations than Daniel and Esther providing a more significant lens into its readership. In light of these conclusions, I will then devote some discussion to the way in which Daniel and Esther participate in the readership of the codex.

6.2. DESCRIPTION OF P967 CODICOLOGICAL FEATURES

For the codicological features, I follow the checklist outlined by Robert Kraft.[6] The six major categories to be considered are, 1) Manuscript Identification, 2) Overall Form and Format, 3) Overall Style of Writing (Within Blocks of Text), 4) Use of Internal Spacing (Absence of Ink), 5) Explicit

---

[3] Harry Y. Gamble, *Books and Readers in the Early Church: A History of Early Christian Texts* (New Haven: Yale University Press, 1995), 43. See also Steve Delamarter, "Communities of Faith and Their Bibles: A Sociological Typology." The study of Medieval manuscripts supplies several examples of the type of sociological studies possible. See Malachi Beit-Arié, *Hebrew Manuscripts of East and West: Towards a Comparative Codicology* (The Panizzi Lectures, 1992; London: The Brittish Library, 1992), especially 1–24 and 79–103. See also Colette Sirat, *Hebrew Manuscripts of the Middle Ages* (ed. and trans., Nicolas de Lange; Cambridge: Cambridge University Press, 2002).

[4] This chapter is similar to the subject area of biblical studies usually referred to as the *Nachleben* of a book. However, I would distinguish the approach in this chapter as the *Leben* of the p967 text.

[5] Hereafter "reading community," "the readers," or "the community."

[6] Robert A. Kraft, "The 'Textual Mechanics' of Early Jewish LXX/OG Papyri and Fragments," in *The Bible as Book: The Transmission of the Greek Text* (eds. S. McKendrick and O.A. O'Sullivan; New Castle, De.: Oak Knoll, 2003), 70–71. Kraft's checklist is roughly based on the previous checklist of Aland.

In-Line Marks (Presence of Ink), and 6) Marginal Markings (Outside of Blocks of Text). These categories are detailed below for p967.

6.2.1. *Manuscript Identification*

The Ezekiel manuscript is known by several different names: p967, Chester Beatty IX–X,[7] and the Schiede manuscript.[8]

6.2.1.1. *Circumstances and Origins of Discovery*

Little is known about the discovery of the codex except that it came from Egypt and is connected to the larger manuscript collection represented by the Chester Beatty library.[9] In 1930, Mr. A. Chester Beatty acquired 12 manuscripts in Egypt which included portions of Ezekiel.[10] The discovery was announced for the first time on November 19th, 1931.[11] In the London Times, F.G. Kenyon noted that their provenance was not known with certainty, but then in his 1933 *General Introduction* to the collection, he says,

> From their character, however, it is plain that they must have been discovered among the ruins of some early Christian church or monastery; and there is reason to believe that they come from the neighbourhood of the Fayum.[12]

Van Haelst provides a good summary of the subsequent theories of origins for the Chester Beatty manuscripts.[13] For instance, in 1931, C. Schmidt reported having spoken with the venders and named Aphroditopolis as the region of the church ruins.[14] Later, H.A. Sanders made a case for a Coptic cemetery in

---

[7] The number assigned by Sir Frederick Kenyon.

[8] The manuscript of p967 Ezekiel is housed in four international locations, as indicated in chapter 2. Images of the Ezekiel pages are available in various locations. p967^Köln was made available on-line in 2001. [Cited 24, October, 2008]. Online: http://www.uni-koeln .de/phil-fak/ifa/NRWakademie/papyrologie/Ezechiel/bildereze.html. The plates of p967^CB are available in F.G. Kenyon, *Fasciculus VII: Ezekiel, Daniel, Esther* (Vol. 2, PLATES; London: Emery Walker, 1937). The plates of p967^Sch are available in Johnson, Gehman, and Kase, *The John Schiede Biblical Papyri.* I have not been able to acquire the plates for p967^Mad.

[9] For a detailed discussion of Egyptian codices and archeology, see E.G. Turner, *Greek Papyri: An Introduction* (Oxford: Clarendon, 1980), 76–88.

[10] The original Beatty collection included manuscripts of the Gospels/Acts, the Pauline Epistles, Revelation, Genesis, Numbers/Deuteronomy, Isaiah, Jeremiah, Ezekiel/Daniel/ Esther, Ecclesiasticus, as well as Enoch and a Christian homily.

[11] F. Kenyon, *General Introduction, Fasciculus I: The Chester Beatty Biblical Papyri Descriptions and Texts of Twelve Manuscripts on Papyrus of the Greek Bible* (London: Emery Walker, 1933), 5.

[12] Kenyon, *General Introduction*, 5.

[13] J. van Haelst, *Catalogue des papyrus litteraires juifs et chritiens* (Paris: Sorbonne, 1976), 30.

[14] Carl Schmidt, "Die neuesten Bibelfunde aus Ägypten," ZNW 30 (1931): 291–292.

Panopolis as the discovery site of the manuscripts.[15] G.D. Kilpatrick, upon noting the Coptic glosses on the Isaiah manuscript (Chester Beatty VII,) which he called "Vieux Fayoumique," located the collection in the region of the Fayum.[16] If Kilpatrick is correct, the epigraphic evidence could help narrow the provenance; however the precise location may forever elude us.

6.2.1.2. *Contents of the Codex*

p967 contains Ezekiel, Daniel, Bel and the Dragon, Susanna, and Esther. (For a discussion of the Greek texts of p967 Daniel and Esther, see §6.4). Page calculations indicate that approximately 9 pages (sides), now missing, once stood at the end of the codex.[17] Fernández-Galiano notes that Tobit, which appears after Esther in codex *Alexandrinus* (A,) could therefore conclude p967.[18] Obviously, unless the missing pages are found, the last section of the codex cannot be assigned with any certainty.

6.2.1.3. *Probable Date*

Most date the Ezekiel portion of the manuscript to the early 3rd century, although some disagreement still persists. Ezekiel comes first in the codex, and dates, on most assessments, significantly earlier than Daniel and Esther. "Two scribes were employed on this codex, one writing Ezekiel and the other Daniel and Esther."[19] According to Fernández-Galiano, the *terminus post quem* for Daniel and consequently Esther is 130 CE based on a textual reading of Aquila in Daniel 1:6.[20] However, one textual reading from the

---

[15] H.A. Sanders, *A Third Century Papyrus Codex of the Epistles of Paul* (UMSHS 38; Ann Arbor: University of Michigan Press, 1935), 13–14.

[16] G.D. Kilpatrick, "The Bodmer and Mississippi Collection of Biblical and Christian Texts" *GRBS* 4 (1963): 38.

[17] According to Fernández-Galiano, who tallies the contents according to the number of sides, Ezekiel runs from 1–122, Daniel 123–185, Susana and Bel 186–196, and Esther 197–227, leaving blank from 228–236. This estimate relies on a speculative length for the Esther portion since only 22 sides (197–218) are extant. Fernández-Galiano finds that p967 preserves 438 lines of Rahlf's Esther edition. He then estimated that the remaining 178 lines would fill 9 sides. Fernández-Galiano, "Nuevas Paginas," 14.

[18] "Cabe teóricamente que hubiera otro libro en ellas. Tobit, que sigue en A, tiene muchas más líneas de las aproximadamente 200 admitidas por unas diez páginas. ¿Podríamos pensar en Rut, que abarca 171 líneas? Todo ello es mera especulatión." "Theoretically, it's possible that there could be another book in them. Tobit, which follows in A, has many more lines, more than the approximately 200 permissible lines throughout ten pages. Maybe we could we think of the book of Ruth which covers 171 lines? All this is merely speculation." Fernández-Galiano, "Nuevas Paginas," 14.

[19] Kenyon, *Fasciculus VII, Ezekiel, Daniel, Esther*, viii.

[20] Fernández Galiano, "Nuevas Paginas," 16. While p967's Daniel is the Old Greek text type, its literary edition is essentially that of Theodotian. Aquila's recension is based on

recensionists is not strong evidence. Nevertheless, the paleography certainly points to a different hand for Ezekiel than that of Daniel and Esther.

The first dates for Ezekiel were proposed on the basis of the uncial script as well as the miniscule notations to be discussed below. JGK "see no reason to put the MS far into the 3rd century, if it is not even as early as the 2nd. 'Early 3rd' is perhaps safest."[21] Fernández-Galiano agrees, citing additional contemporaneous studies, all of which placed the manuscript in the late 2nd / early 3rd century.[22]

Subsequent dating arguments weighed factors related to the development of the codex-form: Roberts and Skeat maintained the proposed date of the early 3rd century.[23] Eric Turner, on the other hand, would push Ezekiel much later into the 3rd century. He reevaluates the relationship between the Ezekiel and Esther script and sees them as more temporally proximate than previously determined. However, he concedes that codicological factors would warrant an earlier date.[24] Given that Turner is alone in dating the Ezekiel script so late,[25] and the codex-format seems to indicate an earlier date, Ezekiel should remain dated to the late 2nd/ early 3rd century CE.

---

proto-Theodotian, and though dating is speculative, 130 CE is a cautious *terminus*. See Dominique Barthélemy, *Les Devanciers d'Aquila*.

[21] JGK consider the work of Kenyon, Wilcken, and H.I. Bell to arrive at their estimate. Johnson, Gehman, and Kase, *The John H. Schiede Biblical Papyri*, 5.

[22] Fernández Galiano cites the studies of A. Geissen and W. Hamm. Fernández Galiano, "Nuevas Paginas," 16 n27 and n28, respectively.

[23] Roberts and Skeat examine p967 among the 175 biblical manuscripts or fragments written before 400 CE. They propose a short list of 15 Christian codices to be dated from the 2nd century, but do not include p967 in that list. However, they offer that the list could be too restrictive, citing the debated dating of the Ezekiel codex from Chester Beatty. Colin H. Roberts and T.C. Skeat, *The Birth of the Codex* (London: Oxford University Press, 1983), 41 n3.

[24] Turner uses p967 as a parade example of the troubles involved in dating manuscripts. He argues that Kenyon's dates for Esther and Daniel's scripts (late 3rd and early 3rd respectively) presumed an unlikely 75 to 100 years between the time the two portions were copied. E.G. Turner, *Typology of the Early Codex* (Philadelphia: University of Pennsylvania Press, 1977), 3. In assigning the date to the Ezekiel portion, Turner adheres to his early judgment that the handwriting reflects a late 3rd century for both Ezekiel and Esther. He finds the closest handwriting parallels to 3rd and 4th century manuscripts. "But if this handwriting date is correct, it is fair to note that the format classification (aberrant Class 1 of Group 8) and the large number of lines per page would allow the manuscript to be placed earlier." Ibid., 99–100.

[25] Like Turner, Wilken independently dated Ezekiel and Esther as contemporary hands. However, against Turner, Wilken brought Esther's script *down* into the 2nd century and even considered its date more certain than Ezekiel's. By contrast, Turner brings Ezekiel *up* to the late 3rd century on the basis of Esther alone. Without more support, Turner's date cannot be followed.

6.2.2. *Overall Form and Format*

6.2.2.1. *Mega-Format*

p967 is a single quire (as opposed to a multiple gatherings) papyrus codex.[26] The codex is made of up 59 sheets to make 236 sides (pages hereafter).[27] Ezekiel runs from page 1 to 122, Daniel 123–185, Bel and Susanna 186–196, and Esther 187–227 leaving the non-extant 228–236 for speculation.[28] The 18 missing pages of Ezekiel in the beginning of the codex could contain a 64 line omission, which would amount to almost two pages of Rahlfs' edition.[29] Of course, a blank cover or title page could account for some/all of that space.

The codex may have been folded at one point due to the even break in the middle of each page.[30] Frayed edges on the outer margins, slightly below the center suggest that the codex was tied with a cord.[31] Such a cord may have been the means by which the codex was held together, as the gutters, where preserved, do not indicate any other forms of binding.

6.2.2.2. *Format Characteristics*

The measurements of p967's format features are as follows:[32]

---

[26] Turner, *Typology*, 59.

[27] According to Jahn, whose p967[Köln] contained the middle of the quire, p967 contained 59 sheets, 118 leaves, and 236 sides, folded at leaves 59[r] (ριη) and 60[r] (ριθ). Jahn, *Der griechische Text*, 8. Kenyon accurately proposed these numbers, (Kenyon, *Fasciculus VII, Ezekiel, Daniel, Esther*, vi–vii), but on the basis of incorrect speculations, as Fernández-Galiano points out in sufficient detail. Fernández Galiano, "Nuevas Paginas," 13–14. JGK's estimate of 62 sheets is certainly not correct. Johnson, Gehman, and Kase, *The John H. Scheide Biblical Papyri*, 1–3. Kenyon surmised that a blank side was left between the two books, which p967[Köln] repudiates. Ezekiel runs from the beginning of the codex to leaf 61[v] (ρκβ), although the leaves up to 9[r] (ιη) are not extant. Daniel begins on the top of 61[r] (ρκγ), leaving no blank page in between the two books. Jahn published a table summarizing the information of p967 which includes leaf number, codex's page number, where the leaf is housed, and the textual contents of each page. Jahn, *Der griechische Text*, 9–13.

[28] This estimate relies on a speculative length for the Esther portion since only 22 sides (197–218) are extant. Fernández-Galiano finds that p967 preserves 438 lines of Rahlf's Esther edition. He then estimated that the remaining 178 lines would fill 9 sides. Fernández dez Galiano, "Nuevas Paginas," 14.

[29] Fernández-Galiano calculates the average lines/page against Rahlf's text, showing that extant pages 18–122 total 2423 lines. If the first 18 pages are consistent with the rest of the manuscript, they would hold roughly 419 lines. However, this calculation is 64 lines shy of the requisite 483 to match the content in Rahlf's edition. Fernández Galiano, "Nuevas Paginas," 15–16.

[30] JGK correlate this proposal with Sander's suggestion that the codex was buried in a grave. Johnson, Gehman, and Kase, *The John H. Scheide Biblical Papyri*, 3.

[31] Ibid., 3.

[32] These dimensions are reproduced from JGK's calculations—although comparative data from the other critical editions are footnoted and discussed when *divergent*. Johnson, Gehman, and Kase, *The John H. Scheide Biblical Papyri*, 4.

Leaf height: 13 ½ in. (34.4 cm.)[33]
Page width: 5 in. (12.8 cm.)
Column height: 11 ½ in. (29.3 cm.) to ~ 11 ¾ in. (30 cm.)[34]
Column width: 3 ½ in. (9 cm.) to 3 ¼ in. (8.4 cm.)[35]
Upper Margin: about 1 in. (2.5 cm)[36]
Lower Margin: 1 ½ in. (3.8 cm)[37]
Inner Margin: variable but always less than ¾ in. (2 cm.)[38]
Outer Margin: ½–¾ in. (1.4–2 cm.)[39]

The number of lines per column is anywhere between 49 and 57.[40] JGK report an average of 51.1 lines on the verso and 53.8 lines on the recto.[41]

The number of letters per line is more varied. The scribe usually maintained a straight right margin, but was not always consistent.[42] JGK reported

---

[33] Kenyon calculated the height of p967[CB] at 14 in. Kenyon, *Fasciculus VII, Ezekiel, Daniel, Esther*, vii.

[34] JGK observe that the recto is generally longer, measuring closer to the upper limit. Kenyon reports that p967[CB]'s columns measure "about 11 ¾ in." high. It is possible that the columns at the outer-most leaves (represented by p967[CB]) were taller, diminishing as they come closer to the inner fold. Kenyon, *Fasciculus VII, Ezekiel, Daniel, Esther*, vii.

[35] As suggested above, the column width also decreases as the leaves come closer to the inner fold. Kenyon reports the column width at 3 ¾ in. JGK are careful to report that the 3 ½ in. (9 cm.) measurement applies to pages 39–40 while the 3 ¼ in. (8.4 cm.) measurement applies to pages 89–90. Johnson, Gehman, and Kase, *The John H. Scheide Biblical Papyri*, 4. Fernández-Galiano make the same observation, that the columns are wider on the outer leaves. He agrees with JGK that the upper limit is 9 cm., but reports that the inner leaves yield values between 8.21 and 8.8 cm. Fernández Galiano, "Nuevas Paginas," 17.

[36] Only Kenyon reports. Kenyon, *Fasciculus VII, Ezekiel, Daniel, Esther*, vii.

[37] Only Kenyon reports. Ibid., vii.

[38] Kenyon reports at ¾ in. Ibid., vii.

[39] Kenyon merely observes that the outer margin is "narrow." Ibid., vii. Fernández-Galiano claim that this measurement is rendered problematic because of the cuts from the dealers' blade. Fernández Galiano, "Nuevas Paginas," 18.

[40] Eric Turner categorizes p967 in Table 14: "Codices having fifty or more lines to a page," although he calculates the number of lines per page at 45–57, the lower number not reported by any of the critical editions of Ezekiel, and thus perhaps referring to Daniel or Esther. Turner, *Typology*, 96–97. The 25 complete sides from p967[Köln] hold from 50–57 lines per column, with 53.4 being the average.

[41] JGK report the range for the verso as 49–53 lines and the recto as 52–57 lines. Johnson, Gehman, and Kase, *The John H. Scheide Biblical Papyri*, 4. Kenyon reports "the number of lines in the Ezekiel varies between 49 and 57, but is generally about 53." Kenyon, *Fasciculus VII, Ezekiel, Daniel, Esther*, vii. He goes on to note that, "in the Daniel and Esther (where it can only be arrived at by calculation) it seems to have been less, about 44–46." Ibid., vii.

[42] JGK observe that letters were occasionally crowded or spaced out to preserve the alignment, with some attention to the rules of syllabification. For example, JGK notes that the final *nu* was often stretched to fit the space. "Normally, this letter is an eighth of an inch wide (.3 cm.), but as a space-filler it is sometimes widened to five-sixteenths of an inch (.8 cm.). This last device is characteristic of the Ezekiel scribe and does not appear to

16–27 letters per line in p967[Sch], rarely exceeding 22 letters.[43] Fernández-Galiano report 17 to 25 letters per line in p967[Mad], with an average of 21.[44]

6.2.3. Style of Writing (Within the Blocks of Text)

Kenyon described the Ezekiel script as,

> large, square in build, with well-rounded curves in such letters as ε and σ. It is very clear, but heavy and by no means elegant, unevenly written and spaced, and plainly not the work of a trained professional scribe.[45]

Kenyon does not indicate the criteria by which he judged the professionalism of the script. However, his assessment of Ezekiel's less formal scribal character seems to rely on the lack of decorative elements, such as serifs, final hooks or loops.[46] While Kenyon's comparative eye detected less professional characteristics to the Ezekiel script, each letter is singly formed, without ligatures. Letters such as α and δ are written with two strokes. Letters are not slanted; an upright orientation is maintained throughout. Finally, Kenyon did not have access to the Köln portion of the codex, which revealed a large decorative element below the inscription of the Ezekiel's final verse (see below §6.2.6.3.1). Thus the manuscript, though not exceedingly formal, was by no means slavishly inscribed.

From the above discussion, one wonders if the distinction between professional and non-professional is altogether useful for analyzing scripts. p967 contains far too many conventions of professional scribalism to be considered non-professional. Several of these conventions are described below in more detail, but they include: *ekthesis*, justification, plus/minus corrections by the original scribe, and awareness of minus conventions. Hence, a slightly less careful letter formation does not point to non-professionalism. Rather, the questions become: what various markets did professional scribes serve, and what does slightly less formal handwriting indicate about the audience who consumed the scribe's product? To answer the latter, it would seem that p967 was not inscribed for a highly formal setting.

---

be used in the other texts of the Chester Beatty papyri". Johnson, Gehman, and Kase, *The John H. Scheide Biblical Papyri*, 4–5. For more on the way the scribe dealt with the rules of syllabification at the end of lines, see Fernández Galiano, "Nuevas Paginas," 18–19.

[43] Johnson, Gehman, and Kase, *The John H. Scheide Biblical Papyri*, 4.

[44] Fernández Galiano, "Nuevas Paginas," 18. See below for discussion of format traits.

[45] Kenyon, *Fasciculus VII, Ezekiel, Daniel, Esther*, viii.

[46] For a detailed discussion of deciphering paleography for sociological information, including sloppier handwriting, see Turner, *Greek Papyri*, 88–96.

Letter formation does present some oddities. Smaller uncials appear, most often at the end of a line (towards the right margin) where the scribe sometimes crowded letters. In such a situation, letters could be even half the normal size. Scoring the right margin however, produced the opposite effect as well. The scribe would stretch letters, mostly affecting final *nu*.

> Normally this letter is an eighth of an inch wide (.3 cm.), but as a space-filler it is sometimes widened to five-sixteenths of an inch (.8 cm). This last device is characteristic of the Ezekiel scribe and does not appear to be used in the other texts of the Chester Beatty papyri.[47]

The only other cases of enlarged letters occur in the left-hand side of the block text and extend slightly into the margin. However, this phenomenon is called *ekthesis* and will be discussed below under paragraphing.

About individual letters, Kenyon provided detailed commentary,

> α is triangular, with straight strokes. β is rather large. ε is well rounded, with the cross-stroke in the centre. ζ is square, with the lower stroke slightly curved. ξ has the top stroke separate, while the middle stroke is a curve united with the bottom stroke. υ is Y-shaped (the two upper extensions being curved outward and down,) but deeply forked, so that the upright portion almost disappears; the whole is formed with one stroke of the pen. All the letters are firmly formed, with thick strokes.[48]

6.2.4. *Use of Internal Spacing (Absence of Ink Within the Blocks of Text)*

The letters in p967's block text are continuously wrapped as scriptio continua. Internal spacing is rare and therefore notable when present. Large multiple-line spaces occur in two places: at the end of Ezekiel and of Daniel; in both cases, the scribe left the remainder of the page blank.[49] The only other blank lines occur in Daniel where 3–4 line spaces provide breaks between each chapter.[50] These chapter divisions are unique to Daniel, they were applied neither to Ezekiel nor Esther.

---

[47] Johnson, Gehman, and Kase, *The John H. Scheide Biblical Papyri*, 5.

[48] Kenyon provides more information about how the script compares with Daniel and Esther, in Kenyon, *Fasciculus VII, Ezekiel, Daniel, Esther*, ix.

[49] Ezekiel ends on page 122 (61ᵛ, ρχβ). The block text extends through lines 22 leaving a space of approximately 27–32 lines. Similarly, Daniel, or rather Susanna ends at line 8 on page 198 (37ᵛ) leaving approximately 43 lines blank. In both spaces, the books end with a subscription, noted below.

[50] The block spaces contain Greek numerals, although not every LXX chapter receives a number, i.e. chs. 11–12 are blocked as one chapter. Bel and Susanna are not enumerated.

Two in-line spaces of considerable size stand out against the continuously wrapped text.[51] On page 90 (Q qoph,) a space of approximately 5 letters occurs in the middle of the line.[52]

Page 90
xxxix. 22–29; xxxvii. 1–4

Figure 1. 5-letter width space at Ezek 39:29[53]

A similar space of 4–5 letters occurs in Daniel on page 142 in the middle of line 39.[54] The space separates Dan 3:90 from v. 91 and following.

---

[51] Of the four major uncials, only Codex Alexandrinus exhibits similar wide spaces at the beginning of a new pericope. However, there it corresponds with an enlarged letter at the beginning of the next line, not attested in either instance in p967. See W.M. de Bruin, "Interpreting Delimiters: The Complexity of Text Delimitation in Four Major Septuagint Manuscripts," in *Studies in Scriptural Unit Division* (eds. M. Korpel and J. Oesch; Pericope 3; Assen: van Gorcum, 2000), 73 and §4.4 on page 86.

[52] The space appears on Plate XLII of the John H. Scheide papyri. The plate has 53 lines with an average of 20 letters of continuously wrapped text per line. The space occurs about 4/5ths of the way down, in the middle of line 41. There are 14 letters of text on line 41 and approximately 5 letters worth of space: ΚΣΟΘΣ" ΚΑΙΕΓΕΝΕ. (" indicates the end of a paragraph in p967, presented below.)

[53] p967[Sch] Plate XLII

[54] There are 12 letters of text on line 39 and approximately 4 letters worth of space: ΩΝΩΝ÷ΚΑΙΕΓΕΝΕ. (On the spaces and the ÷ mark, see analysis and discussion below.)

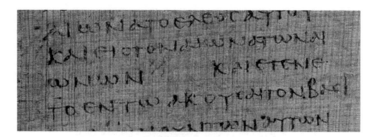

Figure 2. (÷) and 4-letter-width space at Dan 3:90[55]

Concerning such spaces within the manuscripts from the Judean desert, Tov states that they denote the "segmentation of a larger unit" on comparison with the closed sections of the Masoretic tradition.[56] While this may the case, here in p967 the discussion of Daniel 3:90–91 will problematize theories that interpret large unit delimitations on thematic bases alone. (See §6.4.3.4.1).

p967 does not utilize indentations or end of line gaps. Occasionally, a one letter space will occur at paragraph units, (see §6.2.5.3 below) or a ½ letter space at sense units (see §6.2.5.4 below).[57]

6.2.5. *Explicit In-Line Markings (Presence of Ink Within the Blocks of Text)*

6.2.5.1. *Plus Corrections*

Uncial corrections were made above the line. Most frequently, the error was otherwise unmarked in the text (i.e. no strikethrough or a marginal mark). According to JGK, the corrections were made in the original hand during inscription.[58] The plus corrections, within each portion of the manuscript, are as follows:

p967[Sch]

ε'πα (20:8; 40 line 2); οικον ᵗᵒᵘ ισραηλ (20:13; 40 line 25); ᵉᵝεβηλουν (23:38; 53 line 8); ᵗⁿˢ ζωης (26:20; 60 line 16); ˣᵃⁱ τα (27:13; 61 line 22); θᵖηνησει (32:16; 73 line 41); ᵗᵃᵟᵉ λεγει (35:13; 82 line 32);—σᵒηνται (23:48; 54 line 3); ˙χειχη (26:10; 59 line 6); εγοᵉνον (27:9; 61 line 3);—οντᵅⁱον (31:4; 72 line 43).

---

[55] p967[Köln] Theol. 17ᵛ.

[56] Tov, *Scribal Practices*, 145.

[57] See Marjo Korpel, "Introduction to the Series Pericope," in *Delimitation Criticism: A New Tool in Biblical Scholarship* (eds. M. Korpel and J. Oesch; Pericope 1; Assen: van Gorcum, 2000), 14.

[58] Johnson, Gehman, and Kase, *The John H. Scheide Biblical Papyri*, 5.

p967^{CB}

εκδικησ^{ε}ι^{ς}ν (16:41; 30 line 43).

p967^{Köln}

ισραηλ (20:40; 43 line 25), ^{εκ}τη (25:6; 57 line 7), ψυχης ^{σ}ου (25:6; 57 line 7);[59] ε^{αι}σειμουθ (25:9; 57 line 21), αμαρτι^{ας}ων (43:22; 106 line 35), μ'ηα (45:18; 112 line 42).[60]

p967^{Mad}—(?)

6.2.5.2. *Minus Corrections*

As stated above, most corrections did not mark the erroneous text with any special marker. However, some minus corrections do sporadically appear in the manuscript. Two systems seem to have been applied, dots above the letters and a strike-through. However, based on p967^{Sch}'s two instances of dotted letters, JGK point out that in 26:12, the word σου occurs in all other manuscripts witnesses. This instance raised the question about the function of the dots for the scribe, JGK concluding, "we cannot be sure of his use of this device."[61] However, an additional dotted word occurs in p967^{Köln} which does seem to function as an erasure. The minus corrections are as follows:

p967^{Sch}

σου with a dot above each letter (26:12; 59 line 21); και with a dot above each letter (27:18; 61 line 45)

p967^{CB}

p967^{Köln}

κ (18:16; 36 line 17); α/ε (21:6; 44 line 22);[62] με (25:17; 58 line 9).

6.2.5.3. *Punctuation: Paragraph Marks*[63]

The paragraphing exhibited in p967 is already well-understood. Kenyon, JGK, and Fernández-Galiano discuss the features in their respective

---

[59] Jahn reproduced the correction incorrectly in his transcription, writing ψυχη^{ς} σου instead of ψυχης ^{σ}ου. Jahn, *Der griechische Text*, 73.

[60] Only two are corrected with a strikeout through the erroneous letter(s).

[61] Johnson, Gehman, and Kase, *The John H. Scheide Biblical Papyri*, 5–6.

[62] Jahn leaves out this minus correction altogether from his transcription, underscoring the inaccuracies of that critical edition, especially regarding paratextual marks.

[63] For a general discussion of paragraphing trends in all the versions including Hebrew, Greek, Syriac, and the Samaritan Pentateuch, see Emanuel Tov, "The Background of Sense Divisions in the Biblical Texts," in *Delimitation Criticism* (Korpel and Oesch, eds.; Pericope 1; Assen: van Gorcum, 2000), 342–348.

critical editions of p967.[64] Kenyon and JGK even replicate paragraphing features in their transcriptions, Johnson's being the most attentive to
observable differences in styles of mark. E.J. Revell, writing in 1976, conducted a modest study showing p967's relationship with the MT system
of *petuhot* and *setumot*, open and closed paragraph divisions. However,
it is really the work of John Olley that sheds the most light on p967's
paragraphing.[65]

Paragraphs in p967 are clearly indicated by three coordinated features:
an in-line space of approximately one letter containing two dots/slashes on
an angle along with *ekthesis*.[66] *Ekthesis*, a Greek system of paragraphing,[67]
was already observed by Kenyon who describes

> The initial letter of a new section is enlarged, and projects a little into the
> margin; or, if the section begins in the middle of a line, the first letter of the
> first complete line is so treated.[68]

John Olley counted 85 such paragraphs across all extant portions of p967.[69]

Olley compares p967 to four major Hebrew MT manuscripts and the
three Greek uncials in order to study the diachronic development of
paragraphing.[70] With the results of his data, Olley posits development

---

[64] Jahn is inattentive to the paragraphing and cannot be trusted.

[65] John Olley, "Paragraphing in the Greek Text of Ezekiel in p967: With Particular Reference to the Cologne Portion," in *Studies in Scriptural Unit Division*, (Pericope 3; ed. M. Korpel and J. Oesch; Assen: van Gorcum, 2002), 202–225. Idem, "Trajectories in Paragraphing of
the Book of Ezekiel," in *Unit Delimitation in Biblical Hebrew and Northwest Semitic Literature*
(Pericope 4; ed. M. Korpel and J. Oesch; Assen: van Gorcum, 2003), 204–231.

[66] The horizontal lines or "paragraphos," found in p967 Daniel for example, do not
occur in Ezekiel.

[67] Tov says "the numbers of sources using *ekthesis* is small, and no patterns such as
frequent occurrence in a certain type of text or period, is detectable." Tov, "Scribal Features of Early Witnesses of Greek Scripture," in *The Old Greek Psalter* (eds. R.J.V. Hiebert,
C.E. Cox, and P.J. Gentry; JSOTSup 332; Sheffield: Sheffield Academic Press, 2001), 145. For
Tov's summary of p967's paragraph division, see Tov, "The Background" 343. C.H. Roberts
provides a description and parallels in *Manuscript, Society, and Belief in Early Christian
Egypt* (London: Oxford University Press, 1979), 16–18.

[68] Kenyon, *Fasciculus VII, Ezekiel, Daniel, Esther*, ix.

[69] Olley, "Trajectories," 206. Olley's carefull work and excellent presentations in two
essays (2002, 2003) can only invite the occasional disagreement, based merely on quite
subtle differences in perception. For example, I see reason for a paragraph mark at Ezek
18:10—despite the brokenness of the leaf at this point. The space and the double dash
are clearly visable before the καί. *Ekthesis* cannot be determined on the following line. I
would also strike the paragraphs at 12:1 and 15:1 as undeterminable from the evidence. At
12:1, the text is damaged where we would expect the double stroke and *ekthesis*. The same
is true for 15:1.

[70] Olley, "Trajectories," 205. He compared the Aleppo, Cairensis, Leningrad, and Reuchlin-
ianus Hebrew codices, along with Greek codices Alexandrinus, Vaticanus, and Marchalianus.

from early minimal paragraphing (best represented by p967) towards expansion.[71] The relative consistency among the *shared* Greek codices suggests a paragraphing 'tradition" independent from the Hebrew, although p967 shares 90% agreement with both traditions, indicating its proximity to the common core.

Olley also indicates the stastical implications of his paragraphing data across all manuscripts. The greatest diversity of paragraphing occurs in chs. 1–11 and 40–48. Olley suggests varying exegetical interests likely explains this phenomenon. Further, p967 exhibits a striking break from the Greek tradition towards the Hebrew in chs. 18–20.[72]

6.2.5.4. *Punctuation: Sense Marks*

In addition to the obvious paragraphing divisions, two types of sense divisions are present in p967: slight ½ letter spaces and a variety of in-line dots. The slight spaces were produced during inscription. However, the dots are different sizes, orientations, and density, leading me to believe they should be attributed to later hands.[73] W.M. De Bruin agrees, calling them

> two different, partially overlapping systems: a system of narrow spaces and a later one (or several ones) of dots.[74]

Dots occur above, at the top of, and within the middle of lines of text. Initial study scrutinized the dots according to ancient systems of punctuation. For instance, JGK compared p967[Sch] with the system of punctuation devised by Aristophanes of Byzantium, a comparison they ultimately found baseless.[75] More generally, scholars who work with ancient unit divisions conclude that

---

[71] The closest Greek manuscript to p967's 85 paragraphs is Codex Vaticanus at 180 paragraphs. Vaticanus is already greatly expanded beyond the Hebrew, which contain 135. (A and Q contain 273 and 340 respectively).

[72] Six of p967's 14 double dots (to be discussed below) also occur in this section.

[73] So Kenyon in Kenyon, "The Chester Beatty Biblical Papyri," ix; Revell, (1976, 133).

[74] W.M. de Bruin, "Interpreting Delimiters: The Complexity of Text Delimiters," in eds. M.C.A. Korpel and J.M. Oesch, *Studies in Scriptural Unit Division*, (Pericope 3; Assen: van Gorcum, 2002), 69.

[75] Johnson, Gehman, and Kase, *The John H. Schiede Biblical Papyri*, 16–17.

the function of high, intermediate, and low dots is not easy to define and seems to differ widely in several manuscripts and even in parts of one and the same manuscript.[76]

p967's uneven distribution of dots supports this and further critical consensus that high, medium, and low dots were an "idiosyncratic" system of reading marks.[77] According to Tov, the dots were "a Greek system which became more prevalent in the 3rd century."[78] Ulrich calls the dots scribal impressions, further clarifying that they were unique to individual manuscripts and not characteristic of the wider text-tradition.[79] JGK also understood the dots as indicators of reading interests, suggesting that the they facilitated oral reading.[80] This is quite likely given that reading wrapped uncial texts aloud required prior knowledge of the content, in most cases.[81] In any case, the dots derive from subsequent hands, providing a glimpse into the reading interests of the codex's owners. More precisely, these marks indicate that the readers of p967 were wrestling with the importance of sense systems. Our manuscript preserves a few approaches to this seemingly unresolved issue.

Among the 'overlapping systems' of dots, Olley detected one notable pattern in p967. Olley counted 11 instances were two dots are vertically aligned falling at possible paragraph sections. Indeed, he called them a secondary system of paragraphing.[82] This system lacks the paragraphing features that undeniably stem from inscription (i.e. *ekthesis,*) and thus provides a lens into the practices of p967's *owners.*

---

[76] W.M. de Bruin, "Interpreting Delimiters," 86. See also Kathleen McNamee, *Sigla and Select Marginalia in Greek Literary Papyri* (Fondation Égyptologique Reine Élisabeth, 1992), 7. This is the same conclusion of E. Ulrich, "Impressions and Intuition: Sense Divisions in Ancient Manuscripts of Isaiah," in *Unit Delimitation in Biblical Hebrew and North West Semitic Literature* (M. Korpel and J. Oesch , eds.; Pericope 4; Assen: van Gorcum, 2003), 301–304.

[77] JGK note the uneven distribution of dots in p967[Sch]. Johnson, Gehman, and Kase, *The John H. Schiede Biblical Papyri,* 17. More generally, see E. Ulrich, "Impressions and Intuition," 301–304. See also Tov, "The Background," 327–332.

[78] Tov, "Scribal Features of Early Witnesses of Greek Scripture," in *The Old Greek* Psalter (eds. R.J.V. Hiebert, C.E. Cox, P.J. Gentry; JSOTSup 332; Sheffield: Sheffield Press, 2001), 137–139.

[79] Ulrich, "Impressions," 301–304.

[80] Johnson, Gehman, and Kase, *The John H. Schiede Biblical Papyri,* 17.

[81] For a discussion of the development of Greek manuscripts from continuously wrapped text towards providing sense units, see E. Maunde Thompson, "Palaeography," in *The New Werner Twentieth Century Edition of the Encyclopaedia Brittanica* (9th edition; Vol. 18; Akron: Werner Company, 1907), 167.

[82] Olley, "Paragraphing," 204, 207.

Olley points out that only 35% of the eleven double dots correspond with paragraphs in Vaticanus and Alexandrinus, meaning that 65% of these paragraphs would represent p967 innovations.[83] However, we should be careful not to over-interpret the double dots in p967. The 'innovative paragraphing' argument quickly becomes circular. The divergence between p967's double dots and the Greek paragraphing tradition could equally undermine the conclusion that they functioned as paragraph marks at all; instead the double dots may point to a different kind of separate function. Additionally, the double dots are also subject to greater observational error. The double dot is an isolated mark, while the paragraph marks discussed above involved three coordinated features, making them easier to identify with certainty. In fact, two of Olley's vertical double dots are reproduced as *diagonal* dots in JGK's transliteration (20:2, 39 line 18; and 23:32, 52 line 32,) revealing disagreement among even critical observers. The manuscript editors pointed out the difficulty differentiating dots on account of material deterioration or the original quality of the papyrus.[84] In many cases, I agree with Olley that vertical double dots *are* clearly present, and do stand out compared with the singular dots that dominate the in-line text. However, the only conclusion to be reached supports what was already said above, that the double dots represent another overlapping system and probably functioned as a type of sense division. In the end, we are assured of the vibrancy of the ongoing tradition of sense division evinced by the in-line marks in p967.

6.2.5.5. *Breathings*

Breathing marks in p967 are marked with curved hooks over initial vowels. For example, p967[Köln] contains nine breathing marks: εις three times (19:3; 38 line 10), (20:38; 43 line 14), (43:16; 105 line 45); εν once (45:15; 112 line 20); εξ three times (46:1, 4; 113 lines 32, 54), (46:6; 114 line 6); ου once (46:20; 115 line 34); and ας once (18:24; 37 line 13).

6.2.5.6. *Accents*

In p967, like most Greek manuscripts, proper names usually have hooks or acute dashes, (or occasionally raised dots) at the end of the word.

---

[83] Olley, "Paragraphing," 210.
[84] See Johnson, Gehman, and Kase, *The John H. Schiede Biblical Papyri*, 16–17.

However, the practice is not always consistent.[85] For example, in 25:10, αμμων has the final accent (57; line 26), but on the same page, the two instances of αμμων (57; lines 2 and 24) are not accented. Another example, again on the same page (57,) μωαβ gets the accent in line 19, but not in lines 15 and 27. JGK observe,

> These marks are in the same ink as the text, but it is difficult to say whether
> they were inserted at the time of the writing or later.[86]

6.2.5.7. *Contractions: Numbers*

In p967, contracted or abbreviated numbers are marked with a super-stroke ⁻, which extends horizontally into a slight space preserved by the scribe to the right of the symbol. They distribute across the manuscript as follows:

p967^Sch—none
p967^CB—none

p967^Köln—4 = δ̄ once (43:15; ρε line 43); 5 = ε̄ once (45:6; ρια line 17 for 5,000); 7 = ζ̄ four times (44:26; ρι line 12), (45:23x2; ριγ lines 13 and 14), (45:25; ριγ line 24); 10 = ῑ four times (48:10x2; ριθ lines 30 and 32), (48:18x2; ρκ lines 32 and 34); 12 = ιβ̄ once (ριζ line 28); 18 = ιη̄ once (48:35; ρκβ line 17); 20 = κ̄ four times (45:5; ρια line 11), (48:9; ριθ line 25), (48:13; ριθ line 56), (48:21; ρκα line 1); 25 = ε̄ και κ̄ ten times (45:5; ρια line 10), (45:6; ρια line 18), (48:8; ριθ line 17), (48:9; ριθ line 24), (48:10x2; ριθ lines 28–29 and 33), (48:13; ριθ line 53), (48:15; ρκ line 8), (48:20; ρκ line 43–44), (48:21; ρκα line 4); 30 = λ̄ twice (46:22x2; ριε lines 49 and 50); 45 = φ̄ και δ̄ three times (48:16; ρκ lines 14, 16, and 18); 50 = ν̄ once (45:2; ρι line 51).

p967^Mad—(?)

There are some strange anomalies. For example, 25,000 is rendered ε̄ και κ̄ ten times, but once as πεντε και κ̄ (48:21; ρκα line 1). This example could be explained as the result of the scribe turning to the top of a new page, however, we should not rule out the possibility that some significance lies behind such anomalies. Indeed, according to Smyth, classical Greek

---

[85] For more information on the Greek writing practice, see Leslie Threatte, *The Grammar of Attic Inscriptions: Phonology I* (Berlin: de Gruyter, 1980), 85–88.
[86] Johnson, Gehman, and Kase, *The John H. Schiede Biblical Papyri*, 15–16.

contracted numbers are usually marked with a ΄.[87] Whether there is more than a functional connection between numbers and the *nomina sacra*, (described below,) is beyond the scope of this study, but remains an interesting question.[88]

6.2.5.8. *Contractions:* Nomina sacra

In p967, the divine names κυριος, θεος, and πνευμα (rare) are contracted, like numbers, with a superstroke ‾ which extends horizontally into a slight space preserved by the scribe to the right of the name. We have already reviewed the issues associated with the *nomina sacra* above. (See chapter 2 in §2.4).

6.2.5.9. *Contractions and Suspensions:* Nu *at End of Line*

Nu's at the end of the line receive special treatment. The scribe would either stretch the letter to fill a short line or would contract the word, replacing the *nu* with a superstroke ‾. The phenomenon of contraction occurs in p967[Sch] 42 times, p967[CB] 7 times, and p967[Köln] 34 times. In general, it appears the *nu* was contracted in order to prevent the line from extending too far into the margin, (e.g. 48:6–7; 119 lines 5–9). However, occasionally the *nu* is included on a line that extends into the right margin (e.g. την 46:8; 114 line 16), indicating that the margins, which are not perfectly aligned anyway, were not always the scribe's primary concern. In one case, both the dash and the nu are present, ημεραν̄ (45:23; 113 line 17); the scribe wrote the dash, and either he or a secondary scribe thought better of the remaining space, and wrote in the final *nu*.

6.2.5.10. *Diple*

The diple " > " frequently occurs at the end of a line. Its function is difficult to determine and merits further study. In p967, it can stand in the middle of a word that wraps to the following line, (akin to the English hyphen,) as in μνησθω > σιν (18:24; 37 line 16). However, with similar frequency, the diple can stand at the end of a line dividing separate words, for example ποιηση > κατα (18:14; 36 line 9). In Greek scribal practices, the diple was used in a variety of ways. Turner shows that Greek commentators used

---

[87] Smyth, *Greek Grammar*, §348c.
[88] For such an exploration, see Bruce Grigsby, "Gematria and John 21:11—another look at Ezekiel 47:10," in *ET* 95 (1984): 177–178.

the diple as a reference mark for notes, presumably written on another manuscript.[89] Fernández-Galiano discuss the mark as a space-filler at the end of the line, but this is just not possible. ">" generally appears outside of the right hand margin, obviating Fernández-Galiano's explanation.[90] The diple occurs 45 times in p967^{Sch}, 10 times in p967^{CB}, and 29 times in p967^{Köln}.

6.2.5.11. *Dieresis*

Dieresis marks occur over the beginning vowels of several words. Especially common are ὕμος, ὕιος, and ϊσραηλ. Words are marked consistently, with rare exceptions, (as with ισραηλ in 20:30; 42 line 27). From my observations, it is possible that they were added by a second hand because the ink is notably more faded (see 18:5; 36 line 13). They most certainly facilitated reading, helping to distinguish the wrapped text.

6.2.6. *Marginal Markings (Outside the Blocks of Text)*

6.2.6.1. *Page Numbers*

Page numbers appear in the upper margin, centered over the column of text. All pages which are not broken bear page numbers, which suggests that the entire manuscript was numbered. Comparing the script of the numbers with the block text, some differences in style are probably to be attributed to a different scribe.[91] Especially distinctive are the α and the ξ.

The page numbers from 43–122 are completely preserved. All of the leaves from p967^{CB} (pages 19–34) are broken at the top, leaving no trace of the page numbers. Pages 35–42 in p967^{Köln} are in various states of legibility, mostly broken or faded. Finally, page 85 in p967^{Sch} is partially broken, perhaps by a worm. The following is a list of the state of the page numbers for Ezekiel:

> 1 [α] (missing), 2 [β] (missing), 3 [γ] (missing), 4 [δ] (missing), 5 [ε] (missing), 6 [ς] (missing), 7 [ζ] (missing), 8 [η] (missing), 9 [θ] (missing), 10 [ι] (broken), 11 [ια] (missing), 12 [ιβ] (missing), 13 [ιγ] (missing), 14 [ιδ] (missing), 15 [ιε] (missing), 16 [ις] (missing), 17 [ιζ] (missing), 18 [ιη] (missing), 19 [ιθ] (broken), 20 [κ] (broken), 21 [κα] (broken), 22 [κβ] (broken), 23 [κγ] (broken), 24 [κδ] (broken), 25 [κε] (broken), 26 [κς] (broken), 27 [κζ] (bro-

---

[89] Turner, *Greek Papyri*, 117–118.

[90] Fernández Galiano, "Nuevas Paginas," 19.

[91] JGK suggested that the numbers are later, though their suggestion is probably now disproved. Johnson, Gehman, and Kase, *The John H. Schiede Biblical Papyri*, 5.

ken), 28 [κη] (broken), 29 [κθ] (broken), 30 [λ] (broken), 31 [λα] (broken), 32 [λβ] (broken), 33 [λγ] (broken), 34 [λδ] (broken), 35 [λε] (broken), 36 [λς] (broken), 37 [λζ] (broken/faded), 38 [λη] (broken), 39 [λ]θ, 40 [μ] (broken), 41 [μ]α, 42 [μβ] (broken/faded), 43 μγ, 44 μδ, 45 με, 46 μς, 47 μζ, 48 μη, 49 μθ, 50 ν, 51 να, 52 νβ, 53 νγ, 54 νδ, 55 νε, 56 νς, 57 νζ, 58 νη, 59 νθ, 60 ξ, 61 ξα, 62 ξβ, 63 ξγ, 64 ξδ, 65 ξε, 66 ξς, 67 ξζ, 68 ξη, 69 ξθ, 70 ο, 71 οα, 72 οβ, 73 ογ, 74 οδ, 75 οε, 76 ος, 77 οζ, 78 οη, 79 οθ, 80 π, 81 πα, 82 πβ, 83 πγ, 84 πδ, 85 π[ε], 86 πς, 87 πζ, 88 πη, 89 πθ, 90 Q,[92] 91 Qα, 92 Qβ, 93 Qγ, 94 Qδ, 95 Qε, 96 Qς, 97 Qζ, 98 Qη, 99 Qθ, 100 ρ, 101 ρα, 102 ρβ, 103 ργ, 104 ρδ, 105 ρε, 106 ρς, 107 ρζ, 108 ρη, 109 ρθ, 110 ρι, 111 ρια, 112 ριβ, 113 ριγ, 114 ριδ, 115 ριε, 116 ρις, 117 ριζ, 118 ριη, 119 ρι, 120 ρκ, 121 ρκα, 122 ρκβ.

6.2.6.2. *Marginal Words / Marginal Notations*

In the upper margins of Ezekiel, seven brief notations appear in cursive script.[93] My transliterations rely on the work of the critical editors of the various p967 sections, but some discussion is necessary to defend my decisions.

Moving through Ezekiel in order, the notation on page 64 probably reads, εμ]πορω[ν. In this I am in agreement with JGK. However, JGK's transcription on page 68 needs correction. JGK only reproduce συντελει in their transcription of p967[Sch], but upon closer examination, and in comparison with the marginal word on the top of page 107 of p967[Köln], a θ (short for θεος) can clearly be seen.

The notation on page 75 is the most elusive. Fernández-Galiano offers a good possibility in συ]νεστωτ(ων) but indicates, "el posible … está poco claro."[94] One of the primary problems is that the lexical meaning, "to unite," is difficult to interpret (see §6.3.3.1.3). αναστασεως is clearly discernible on page 90.[95] Likewise, Fernández-Galiano testifies that μετανοιας on page 104 is clear. Page 107 has two notations on the top and the bottom margins. Jahn transliterates, π θ ιερου [π(ερι) θ(εου) ιερου] on top and π μετανοιας [π(ερι) μετανοιας] on the bottom.[96] While I agree with the readings, I find

---

[92] I use the "Q" for the letter κοππα of the Greek alphabet, not present in the Koine or Septuagint Greek alphabets. See discussion of the development of Greek numerals, including the use of κοππα for 90 in A.N. Jannaris, "The Digamma, Koppa, and Sampi as Numerals in Greek," in *The Classical Quarterly Vol. 1* (ed. J.P. Postgate; London, 1907), 37–40. See also Bruce M. Metzger, "The Greek Alphabet," *Manuscripts of the Greek Bible: an Introduction to Greek Palaeography* (Oxford: Oxford University Press, 1981), 6–10.

[93] The one exception is that one notation on page 107 occurs in the lower margin.

[94] "The possibility … it is scarcely clear." Fernández Galiano, "Nuevas Paginas," 20.

[95] With Johnson, Gehman, and Kase, *The John H. Schiede Biblical Papyri.*

[96] "Auf Seite ρζ finden sich zwei Randglossen, jeweils eine am Kopf und am Ende der Kolumne. Die obere kann man als π(ερι) θ(εου) ιερου lesen. Der entsprechende Hinweis zum Text steht als Schrägstrich am Ende von Zeile 4 zu dem Satz: και ποιησουσιν οι ιερεις

some letters indiscernible and offer two corrections. For π θ ιερου, I read, π- θυ ιε(ρ)ου. The *pi* is followed by a stroke, perhaps a ligature or to indicate the missing letters of περι. Also, I read θῡ, against Jahn's θεος, for the case is determined with a clear stroke over the *upsilon*.[97] A similar stroke should be supplied over the *pi* in the lower notation, although I find the script is difficult to read with fewer certain letters, : π- μ(ε)ταν(οι)α(ς).

As for translation, six of the seven notations are in the genitive. In the two notations on page 107, the genitive case follows περι, which should be translated "concerning..." In light of these two translations, it is reasonable to supply περι for the remainder of the genitive notations. Only θεος συντελει on page 68 diverges from the grammatical form, as a present indicative conjugation to be translated, "God fulfills."

Table 1: Marginal Words in Cursive Script

Greek cursive	English translation	Page and Edition	Reference
εμ]πορω[ν	(concerning) merchants	ξδ (64) p967[Sch]	Ezek 28:9–19
θ συντελει[98]	God fulfills	ξη (68) p967[Sch]	Ezek 30:1–13
συ]νεστωτ(ων)	uniting	οε (75) p967[Mad]	Ezek 32:30—33:8
αναστασεως	(concerning) resurrection	Q (90) p967[Sch]	Ezek 39:23–37:4
μετανοιας	(concerning) repentence	ρδ (104) p967[Mad]	Ezek 43:1–9
π-- θυ ιε(ρ)ου	concerning God's temple	ρζ (107) p967[Köln] [top margin]	Ezek 43:26–44:7
π- μ(ε)ταν(οι)α(ς)	concerning repentence	ρζ (107) p967[Köln] [bottom margin]	Ezek 43:26–44:7

επι του θυσιαστηριου τα ολοκαυτωματα. Das zweite Zeichen, zwei Schrägstriche am linken Rand, findet sich bei Zeile 20 zu dem Satz: και εσται (η πυλη) κεκλεισμενη κτλ. Die Glosse dazu am Fuß der Kolumne: π(ερι) μετανοιας. [My translation]: "On page ρζ are two marginal notes, one above and one below the column. One can read the upper as π(ερι) θ(εου) ιερου. The corresponding textual reference is marked by a diagonal stroke at the end of line 4 to the phrase: και ποιησουσιν οι ιερεις επι του θυσιαστηριου τα ολοκαυτωματα. The second mark, two diagonal strokes on the left-hand side of the column, occurs at line 20, to the phrase: και εσται (η πυλη) κεκλεισμενη κτλ. The additional gloss at the foot of the column reads: π(ερι) μετανοιας." Jahn, *Der griechische Text*, 15.

[97] The dash over the *upsilon* elsewhere denotes an abbreviation, especially common for the *nomina sacra*.

[98] Johnson, Gehman, and Kase, *The John H. Schiede Biblical Papyri*.

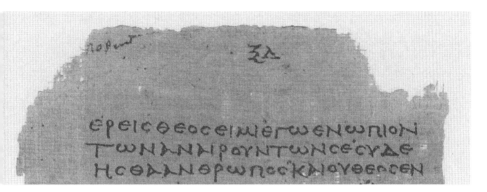

Figure 3. εμ]πορων "(concerning) merchants"[99]
Page 64
Ezek 28:9–19

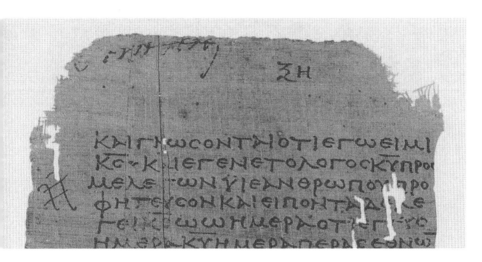

Figure 4. θ συντελει "God fulfills"[100]
Page 68
Ezek 30:1–13

---

[99] p967ˢᶜʰ Plate XXII.
[100] p967ˢᶜʰ Plate XXIV (note the cat. 2 double hatch mark at 30:1–2).

Figure 5. αναστασεως "(concerning) resurrection"[101]
Page 90
Ezek 39:23–37:4

Figure 6. π—θυ ιε(ρ)ου "concerning God's temple"
Page 107 (upper margin)
Ezek 43:1–9

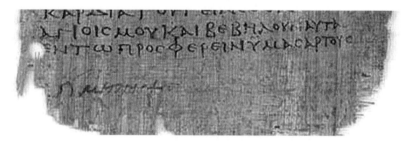

Figure 7. π- μ(ε)ταν(οι)α(ς) "concerning repentance"
Page 107 (lower margin)
Ezek 43:1–9

---

[101] p967[Sch] Plate XLII.

The cursive script of the notations would certainly be contemporary with or later than the block text. Since Ezekiel alone contains marginal notations, an earlier date in the early 3rd century becomes quite possible.[102] Two hands penned the notations in p967[Sch], θ συντελει on page 68 exhibits unique features from those on 64 and 90. Fernández-Galiano believes the notations on pages 75 and 104 were done by the same hand.[103] Jahn does not comment on the cursive script, although in my estimation, they seem like still another different hand. If I am correct, there were three separate hands who penned the marginal notations.

6.2.6.3. *Marginal Marks and Symbols* [*Tables of Ezekiel Marks*]

In addition to marginal notations, the codex contains a number of scribal/ reader marks. The formation, density of use, and no doubt importance varies. I have divided the marginal marks into seven categories. In this section, I focus exclusively on the marks in the Ezekiel portion of the manuscript.[104]

1) Greek cursive notations appear on six pages of p967. (See §6.2.6.2 above).

2) Ecclectic marks appear in the margins of several pages. This category consists of marks that seem to be uniquely formed and distinctive.

3) 20 diagonal slashes with the same orientation (NE to SW) appear in the left and right margins.

4) 21 horizontal slashes of similar length, tending to occur on the left margin.

5) 20 idiosyncratic slashes in the left and right margins.

6) 26 larger ink blots with little discernible regularity in the left and right margins.

7) 15 clusters of 2 to 10 small dots in the left and right margins.

---

[102] H.I. Bell of the British museum examined pages 64, 68, and 90 of p967[Sch] and said, "these cursive notes seem to me pretty certainly not later than the 3rd century (συντελει is in a hand not easy to fix exactly, but the others look to me typically 3rd century)," as quoted in Johnson, Gehman, and Kase, *The John H. Schiede Biblical Papyri*, 5.

[103] Fernández—Galiano, "Nuevas Paginas," 20.

[104] For my analysis, I have analyzed the portion of p967 housed by Princeton, and used the facsimilies of the Köln and Chester Beatty portions. For the Madrid portion, which only comprises 7% of Ezekiel, I have only benefitted from Fernandez-Galiano's graphic descriptions, but did not obtain a facsimile. Thus, while Fernández-Galiano provided significant discussion useful for interpretation, the following data is incomplete.

The tables in the following sections provide information as indicated (unless otherwise noted):

Critical edition of p967[105]	Edition reference •	Page Num.	Line of text	Left/right Inner/outer margin	Reference in Ezekiel (ch.:verse)

6.2.6.3.1. *Category 2: Ecclectic Marks*

= arrow mark

p967[Sch]	XVI.r.	56 νϛ	Upper Margin	Centered	Ezek 24:22–25:5

= ink blot

p967[Köln]	16(7)v.	120 ρχ	Upper Margin	Left, outer	Ezek 48:14–21

= ink blot

---

[105] For clarity, I will refer to each portion of the manuscript by their critical editions, annotated as follows: Chester Beatty = p967[CB], Schiede/Princeton = p967[Sch], Universität Köln = p967[Köln], Madrid = p967[Mad].

p967^{Köln}	16(8)r.	121 ρκα	Upper Margin	Right, outer	Ezek 48:21–31

The two upper marginal marks on pages ρκ and ρκα are on facing pages, in the outer margin. The mark on page 121 (ρκα) is certainly original. It is posible that the mark on page 120 (ρκ) resulted from closing the codex before the ink had dried since the page 121 (ρκα) mark is larger and somewhat resembles its neighbor. However, careful attention to the lines and ink blots on the ρκ mark shows discernible lines that do not have a counterpart. Both marks appear to be an attempt to cross out previous, now indiscernible marks. The other possibility is that the two blots were made during the production of the codex, to clean the stylus. However, this seems unlikely for two reasons, 1) judging by the thickness and density of strokes, the stylus that penned the marginal mark was considerably larger than that for the block text; and 2) there are no other such marks across the codex. If the scribe needed to clean his stylus, it is unlikely that these two pages alone would show traces. I prefer the possibility that they blot out earlier marks/writing/symbols.

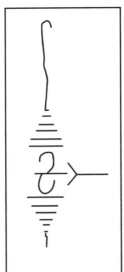 = Ezekiel's decorative book-end

p967^{Köln}	16(8)v.	122 ρκβ	Lines 18–21+	Left, inner	Ezek 48:35

This is the decorative end mark for the book of Ezekiel before half a page of space. The page is broken across the bottom half of the symbol. It is entirely probable that the symbol extended into the broken section of the papyrus and retained its point-symmetry. Perhaps a similar style of decoration introduced the book of Ezekiel, although this cannot be known since the first several pages are lost. No such mark introduces Dan 1:1 on the next page.[106]

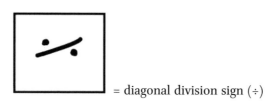 = diagonal division sign (÷)

| p967^{CB} | 16.r. | 32 λβ | Line 30 | Right, in text | Ezek 17:1 |

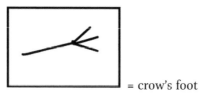 = crow's foot

| p967^{Köln} | 11v. | 107 ρζ | Line 4 | Right, outer | Ezek 43:27 |

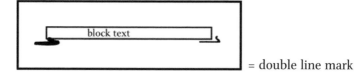 = double line mark

---

[106] The symbol which appears at the end of Ezekiel also appears at the conclusion of Enoch's Epistle (ch. cvii:3) of the Chester Beatty collection. It can be found on plate f.13.r of that edition. The symbol appears there twice, flanking both margins of the block text. There is an added feature, a herringbone horizontal line 2/3 down the symbol. See Frederic G. Kenyon, *The Chester Beatty Biblical Papyri, Descriptions and Texts of Twelve Manuscripts on Papyrus of the Greek Bible: Fasciculus VIII Enoch and Melito* (PLATES; London: Emery Walker Limited, 1941).

| p967^{Sch} | XXXV.v. | 83 πγ | Line 40 | Left, inner and right, outer | Ezek 36:9 |

 = double hatch mark

p967$^{Sch\,*}$	XXII.r.	64 ξδ	Lines 48–49	Left, outer	Ezek 28:18
p967^{Sch}	XXIV.r.	68 ξη	Lines 3–4	Left, outer	Ezek 30:2
p967$^{Sch\,*}$	XLII.r.	90 Q	Lines 40–41	Left, outer	Ezek 37:1
p967^{Köln}	16(3)v.	111 ρια	Upper margin	Left, inner	Ezek 45:3–11

* indicates a symbol that lacks one of the vertical slashes.

 = double crossed line

p967^{CB}	16.v.	31 λα	Line 10	Left, inner	Ezek 16:49
p967^{Köln}	16(1)v.	105 ρε	Line 6	Left, inner	Ezek 43:10
p967^{Köln}	16(3)v.	111 ρια	Line 38	Left, inner	Ezek 45:8

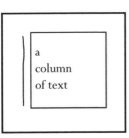 = elongated   vertical   line   (imperfection   as appears)

p967^{Sch} *	XLI.v.	89 πθ	Lines 4–6	Left, inner	Ezek 39:14
p967^{Köln}	11v.	107 ρζ	Lines 6–9	Right, outer	Ezek 43:27
p967^{Köln}	11r.	108 ρη	Lines 6–10	Left, outer	Ezek 44:9

* Indicates that the vertical line is supplemented with a short horizontal dash pointed inwards towards the block of text.

6.2.6.3.2. *Category 3: Diagonal Slashes*
20 diagonal slashes with the same orientation (NE to SW) appear in the left and right margins.

p967^{CB}	14.r.	28 κη	Line 10	Left, outer	Ezek 16:19
p967^{CB}	17.r.	34 λδ	Line 18	Left, outer	Ezek 17:18
p967^{Köln}	12+42abcr.	36 λς	Line 51	Left, outer	Ezek 18:21
p967^{Köln}	13v.	37 λζ	Line 6	Right, outer	Ezek 18:22
p967^{Sch}	I.v.	39 λθ	Line 15	Right, outer	Ezek 20:1
p967^{Köln}	0.I.v.	41 μα	Line 16	Right, outer	Ezek 20:20
p967^{Sch}	VII.v.	47 μζ	Line 13	Right, outer	Ezek 22:3
p967^{Sch}	X.r.	50 ν	Line 45	Left, outer	Ezek 23:12
p967^{Sch}	XV.v.	55 νε	Line 37	Right, outer	Ezek 24:18
p967^{Sch}	XVII.v.	59 νθ	Line 16	Right, outer	Ezek 26:12
p967^{Sch}	XVIII.r.	60 ξ	Line 35	Left, outer	Ezek 27:6
p967^{Sch}	XXI.v.	63 ξγ	Line 10	Left, inner	Ezek 27:34
p967^{Sch}	XXII.r.	64 ξδ	Line 17	Left, outer	Ezek 28:13
p967^{Sch}	XXIV.r.	68 ξη	Line 10	Left, outer	Ezek 30:4

p967[Sch]	XXVIII.r.	72 οβ	Line 48	Left, outer	Ezek 32:5
p967[Sch]	XXXI.v.	79 οθ	Line 13	Right, outer	Ezek 34:8
p967[Sch]	XXXII.r.	80 π	Line 19	Left, outer	Ezek 34:18
p967[Köln]	16(2)v.	109 ρθ	Line 14	Right, outer	Ezek 44:18
p967[Köln]	16(3)r.	112 ριβ	Line 25	Right, inner	Ezek 45:15
p967[Köln]	16(7)r.	119 ριθ	Line 11	Right, outer	Ezek 48:7

6.2.6.3.3. *Category 4: Horizontal Slashes*
21 horizontal slashes of similar length, tending to occur on the left margin.

p967[Köln]	12+42abcv.	35 λε	Line 30	Yes*	Left, inner	Ezek 18:8
p967[Köln]	12+42abcr.	36 λς	Line 32	Yes	Right, inner	Ezek 18:18
p967[Köln]	o.I.v.	41 μα	Line 17	No	Left, inner	Ezek 20:20
p967[Köln]	o.I.v.	41 μα	Line 23	No	Left, inner	Ezek 20:21
p967[Sch]	XI.v.	51 να	Line 38	No	Left, inner	Ezek 23:23
p967[Sch]	XVI.r.	56 νς	Line 21	No	Left, outer	Ezek 24:25
p967[Sch]	XX.r.	62 ξβ	Line 1	No	Left, outer	Ezek 27:19
p967[Sch]	XXVI.r.	70 ο	Line 52	No	Left, outer	Ezek 31:8
p967[Sch]	XXVIII.r.	72 οβ	Line 43	No	Left, outer	Ezek 32:4
p967[Sch]	XXXIV.r.	82 πβ	Line 24	No	Left, outer	Ezek 35:11
p967[Köln]	16(1)v.	105 ρε	Line 31	No	Left, inner	Ezek 43:13
p967[Köln]	16(1)r.	106 ρς	Line 27	No	Left, outer	Ezek 43:21
p967[Köln]	16(2)v.	109 ρθ	Line 26	No	Left, inner	Ezek 44:19

p967^{Köln}	16(3)r.	112 ριβ	Line 16	Yes	Left, outer	Ezek 45:14
p967^{Köln}	16(4)v.	113 ριγ	Line 26	No	Left, inner	Ezek 45:25
p967^{Köln}	16(5)v.	115 ριε	Line 37	No	Right, outer	Ezek 46:20
p967^{Köln}	16(5)r.	116 ριϛ	Line 9	No	Right, inner	Ezek 47:1
p967^{Köln}	16(5)r.	116 ριϛ	Line 37	No	Left, outer	Ezek 47:6
p967^{Köln}	16(6)r.	118 ριη	Line 31	Yes	Right, inner	Ezek 47:23
p967^{Köln}	16(7)r.	119 ριθ	Line 3	No	Left, inner	Ezek 48:5
p967^{Köln}	16(7)r.	119 ριθ	Line 5	No	Left, inner	Ezek 48:5

* A 'Yes' indicates that the horizontal line extends into the block of text, while 'No' indicates a horizontal line that is restricted to the margin.

6.2.6.3.4. *Category 5: Idiosyncratic Slashes*

20 idiosyncratic slashes in the left and right margins.

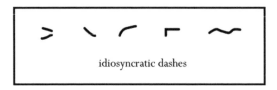

idiosyncratic dashes

p967^{CB}	12.r.	24 κδ	Line 15	Left, outer	Ezek 14:7
p967^{Köln}	43v.	43 μγ	Line 26	Left, inner	Ezek 20:40
p967^{Sch}	VIII.r.	48 μη	Line 3	Left, outer	Ezek 22:11
p967^{Sch}	XII.r.	52 νβ	Line 45	Left, outer	Ezek 23:35
p967^{Sch}	XIV.r.	54 νδ	Line 17	Left, outer	Ezek 24:22
p967^{Sch}	XIX.v.	61 ξα	Line 11	Right, outer	Ezek 27:11
p967^{Sch}	XX.r.	62 ξβ	Line 26	Left, outer	Ezek 27:26
p967^{Sch}	XXXVII.v.	85 πε	Line 52	Right, outer	Ezek 38:10
p967^{Sch}	XXXVIII.r.	86 πϛ	Line 16	Left, outer	Ezek 38:12
p967^{Sch}	XLII.r.	90 Q	Line 24	Left, outer	Ezek 39:26
p967^{Köln}	16(1)r.	106 ρϛ	Line 18	Left, outer	Ezek 43:19

p967^Köln	16(1)r.	106 ρς	Line 32	Right, inner	Ezek 43:22
p967^Köln	11v.	107 ρζ	Line 19	Left, inner	Ezek 44:3
p967^Köln	11v.	107 ρζ	Line 33	Left, outer	Ezek 44:5
p967^Köln	16(2)r.	110 ρι	Line 2	Left, outer	Ezek 44:24
p967^Köln	16(3)v.	111 ρια	Line 12	Right, outer	Ezek 45:5
p967^Köln	16(3)r.	112 ριβ	Line 6	Left, outer	Ezek 45:11
p967^Köln	16(6)v.	117 ριζ	Line 27	Left, inner	Ezek 47:13
p967^Köln	16(7)v.	120 ρκ	Line 9	Right, inner	Ezek 48:15
p967^Köln	16(7)v.	120 ρκ	Line 19	Left, outer	Ezek 48:16

6.2.6.3.5. *Category 6: Larger Ink Blots*

26 larger ink blots with little discernible regularity in the left and right margins.

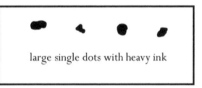

large single dots with heavy ink

p967^CB	12.v.	23 κγ	Line 4	Left, inner	Ezek 13:20
p967^CB	12.v.	23 κγ	Line 10	Left, inner	Ezek 13:21
p967^CB	14.r.	28 κη	Line 9	Left, outer	Ezek 16:18/19
p967^CB	15.v.	29 κθ	Line 30	Left, inner	Ezek 16:34
p967^CB	17.v.	33 λγ	Line 20	Right, outer	Ezek 17:7
p967^Köln	12+42abcr.	36 λς	Line 18	Right, inner	Ezek 18:16
p967^Köln	13v.	36 λζ	Line 17	Left, inner	Ezek 18:24
p967^Sch	XIX.v.	61 ξα	Line 24	Left, inner	Ezek 27:13
p967^Sch	XIX.v.	61 ξα	Line 29	Left, inner	Ezek 27:15
p967^Sch	XIX.v.	61 ξα	Line 36	Left, inner	Ezek 27:16
p967^Sch	XXX.r.	74 οδ	Line 17	Right, inner	Ezek 32:22

p967^Sch	XXXV.v.	83 πγ	Line 3	Right, outer	Ezek 36:4
p967^Sch	XXXVI.r.	84 πδ	Line 23	Left, outer	Ezek 36:16
p967^Sch	XXXVII.v.	85 πε	Line 8	Right, outer	Ezek 38:1
p967^Sch	XXXIX.v.	87 πζ	Line 38	Right, outer	Ezek 39:1
p967^Sch	XLI.v.	89 πθ	Line 28	Left, inner	Ezek 39:17
p967^Köln	16(1)r.	106 ρϛ	Line 10	Left, outer	Ezek 43:18
p967^Köln	16(1)v.	107 ρζ	Line 47–48	Left, inner	Ezek 44:6
p967^Köln	16(2)v.	109 ρθ	Line 46	Left, inside	Ezek 44:24
p967^Köln	16(2)r.	110 ρι	Line 11	Left, outer	Ezek 44:26
p967^Köln	16(4)v.	113 ριγ	Line 9–10	Left, inner	Ezek 45:22
p967^Köln	16(4)v.	113 ριγ	Line 24	Left, inner	Ezek 45:25
p967^Köln	16(7)v.	120 ρκ	Line 22	Left, outer	Ezek 48:17
p967^Köln	16(7)v.	120 ρκ	Line 38	Left, outer	Ezek 48:18
p967^Köln	16(8)r.	121 ρκα	Line 40	Right, outer	Ezek 48:28
p967^Köln	16(8)r.	121 ρκα	Line 47	Right, outer	Ezek 48:30

6.2.6.3.6. *Category 7: Clusters of Small Dots*

15 clusters of 2 to 10 small dots in the left and right margins.

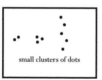

small clusters of dots

p967^Köln	o.I.r.	40 μ	Line 41	Left, outer	Ezek 20:15
p967^Köln	o.I.r.	40 μ	Line 45	Left, outer	Ezek 20:15
p967^Köln	o.I.v.	41 μα	Line 4–9	Left, inner	Ezek 20:17
p967^Sch	XIX.v.	61 ξα	Line 21–42	Left, inner	Ezek 27:13–17
p967^Sch	XXIII.v.	68 ξη	Line 34–36	Left, inner	Ezek 29:18–19
p967^Sch	XXIV.r.	68 ξη	Line 35–48	Right, inner	Ezek 30:10–12

p967^Sch	XXIX.v.	73 ογ	Line 9	Left, inner	Ezek 32:9
p967^Sch	XXXVI.r.	84 πδ	Line 5	Left, outer	Ezek 36:12
p967^Köln	16(1)r.	106 ρς	Line 16–27	Left, outer	Ezek 43:19–20
p967^Köln	16(1)r.	106 ρς	Line 37	Right, inner	Ezek 43:22
p967^Köln	11r.	108 ρη	Line 31–33	Left, outer	Ezek 44:13
p967^Köln	16(3)r.	112 ριβ	Line 21	Left, outer	Ezek 45:15
p967^Köln	16(6)r.	118 ριη	Line 17–23	Left, outer	Ezek 47:20–22
p967^Köln	16(7)v.	120 ρκ	Line 17	Left, inner	Ezek 48:16
p967^Köln	16(7)v.	120 ρκ	Line 42	Left, inner	Ezek 48:19

6.3. Relation of Features to Reading Tradition

6.3.1. *Christian Features*

p967 was likely a Christian manuscript. We saw above that all the theories of provenance (§6.2.1.1) connect its discovery with Christian locales, whether a church, archive, or grave.

The thrust of scholarship tends to conclude that the codex form, for the most part, functioned in Christian communities. It is indisputable that Christians favored the codex form for the first three centuries CE.[107] C.H. Roberts advanced the first serious proposal for the Christian preference for the codex in 1954.[108] The argument took account that some Christian texts were manufactured on rolls. However, subsequent manuscript finds confirm that Christians most often preferred the codex form.[109]

---

[107] With the discovery of numerous manuscripts from Egypt over the 20th century, scholars began to recognize the distribution of literary form: in the first three centuries CE, Jewish and Greek/Latin literature appeared in roll form, while Christian texts appeared in the form of a codex. By the 6th century, the roll went largely out of favor. See Roberts and Skeat, *The Birth of the Codex*, 75.

[108] C.H. Roberts, "The Codex," *PBA* 40 (1954): 169–204. However, the suggestion was already in circulation fifty years earlier, so Caspar R. Gregory, *Canon and Text of the New Testament* (ITL; New York: Charles Scribner's Sons, 1907), 322–323.

[109] Turner refined and developed the work of C.H. Roberts and developed his now famous typology of codices. His typology presents clear data reflecting Christian preference for the codex form. Turner, *Typology*, 1 *et passim*. Roberts and Skeat show that of the 172 Christian biblical manuscripts before 400CE, 158 adopt the codex, while only 14 are on rolls. Roberts and Skeat, *Birth of the Codex*, 40. Their conclusion: "the Christian adoption

In addition to the codex form, scholars have also charted the close relationship between Christian manuscripts and scribal practices regarding the *nomina sacra*. T.S. Skeat's 1969 discussion established the contraction of the *nomina sacra*'s observed connection with the codex form. He argued that both were characteristic of Christian texts.[110] While some disagreement persists about the genealogy of the *nomina sacra*, it is certainly true that Christians abbreviated κυριος and θεος and extended the practice to Trinitarian names.[111] So, in p967, we find πνευμα contracted at Ezek 18:31; 21:12, although the Daniel section furnishes at least three more cases.[112]

p967's codex form and its *nomina sacra* largely warrant the conclusion that the reading community was Christian.[113] However, some isolated

---

of the codex seems to have been instant and universal." Ibid., 53. Most recently, Larry W. Hurtado provided renewed discussion on the basis of subsequent manuscript publications. Hurtado, *Earliest Christian Artifacts: Manuscripts and Christian Origins* (Grand Rapids: Eerdmans, 2006), 47 n15.

Various theories of origins give more or less weight to possible Christian influence. C.H. Roberts proposed that the earliest Christians developed the codex in order to distinguish their Scriptures from the Jewish rolls, (see the longer discussion of the 'hypothesis' in C.H. Roberts and T.C. Skeat, *Birth of the Codex*, 54–61). Harry Gamble proposes that Paul's writings were the catalyst for the popularity of the codex-form and influenced the later Christian near-exclusive use of the form. Gamble, *Books and Readers in the Early Church: A History of Early Christian Texts* (New Haven: Yale University Press, 1995), 42–81. Others place much less weight on the influence of Christians for the development of the form. For instance, Turner emphasizes materialist-social factors, believing the papyrus codex was a "second-class" book. Turner, *Typology*, 37. Similarly, G. Cavallo argued in 1975 that the codex was typical of lower class works, such as the popular romance. Guglielmo Cavallo, *Libri, editori e pubblico nel mondo antico: Guida storica e critica* (BUL 315; Rome: Laterza, 1975), 83–86. However, Roberts and Skeat convincingly refute the quality of Cavallo's evidence. Roberts and Skeat, *Birth of the Codex*, 69. Finally, Roberts and Skeat claim the codex was originally a Roman invention, popularized by Christians. Ibid., 24. All scholars advance the similar suggestion, first proposed by Roberts and Skeat, that the parchment notebook is the prototype from which the codex form developed. Ibid., 15–23, 54.

[110] T.C. Skeat, "Early Christian Book-Production: Papyri and Manuscripts," *The Cambridge of the Bible: Volume 2, The West from the Fathers to the Reformation* (ed. G.W.H. Lampe; Cambridge: Cambridge University Press, 1969), 72–73. Ludwig Traube offered the pioneer study on *nomina sacra*, coining the term. See the discussion of L.W. Hurtado, *Earliest Christian artifacts*, 95 especially n2.

[111] For a good discussion, see Hurtado, *Earliest Christsian Artifacts*, 96–98. Hurtado's full theory on the development of the Christian *nomina sacra* deserves mention. He proposes that the contraction of Trinitarian names and Jesus in particular were related to gematria (symbolism which assigns numerical value to alphabetical characters). He relates the contraction of the divine name to the Greek convention of placing horizontal strokes over numbers. Ibid., 116–117.

[112] The contractions of πνευμα occur at Dan 3:86; 5:23; 6:3 in p967[CB].

[113] This conclusion is most recently challenged by theories about the emergent relationships between Jewish and Christian textual practices. So in 1973, Kurt Treu argued that *nomina sacra* and the codex form were originally taken up by Christians from Jewish prototypes. Robert Kraft accepted and developed Treu's position. However, their position is convincingly refuted by Hurtado with respect to the specific features of the codex-form

evidence could point away from a Christian identity. Contracted numbers are only arguably a sign of Christian copyists. p967 presents several cases of contracted numbers (see §6.2.5.7).[114] Turner demonstrates that number contraction was a Greek "documentary" influence that *became* characteristic of Christian practices.[115] In other words, the phenomenon of number contraction is a somewhat ambiguous marker of identity.

More significantly, p967 contains a curious case of a contracted divine name. As seen above, contraction for the term πνευμα "spirit" did occur in a few places. However, p967 presents a contracted form of πνευματα "spirits" at Dan 3:65 with the form πνᾱ. The last three words of line 23 read, παντα τα πνᾱ. The contraction appears on a leaf in p967[Köln] which is partially broken on the left margin; the beginning of line 24 is broken at the first letter, but I read [τ]ον κ(ν) υμνειται. Even with the broken first letter on the next line, it is clear that πνα is not part of a word that wraps to the next line; Indeed, all other witnesses read πνευματα for πνα. The anomaly here is the contraction of the *plural* form of πνευμα, so "spirits." Even more curious, the context of the verse warrants the translation "winds." It is possible that πνευματα was contracted because it occurs at the end of a line, but elsewhere this practice only affects the final *nu*, not a longer ending such as—ευματα. It is also possible that the scribe rendered the term as a contraction out of habit. However, the word πνευμα is usually written out instead of contracted, such that the "habit" would argue in the other direction. The only explanation left is that πνευματα, like πνευμα elsewhere in the manuscript, was recognized as a divine name. This raises the question about the religious identity/beliefs of the scribe that would treat plural "spirits" as divine; they cannot certainly refer to the third person of the Trinity. Further, since the context suggests a natural connotation "winds," is this even distinctly Christian nomenclature? To answer this question is outside the scope of this study; but the question itself raises the kind of nuance necessary in characterizing a 'manuscript' as distinctly Christian.

---

and *nomina sacra*. Hurtado, *Earliest Christian Artifacts*, 107–108. Nevertheless, Robert Kraft's more broadly conceived argument invites scholars to reconsider the extent to which early Christianity relies on its Jewish heritage in its practices of textual mechanics. The merit of Kraft's position is an important cognizance of the social fluidity of the identity designations we use to characterize texts and their readers. R. Kraft, "Textual Mechanics," 68.

[114] Hurtado suggests (footnote above) that number symbolism may have been a factor in the development of the contracted *nomina sacra*. Perhaps too, the contraction of numbers betray an interest in gematria, although I have not inquired into the issue here. It would certainly be an interesting line of inquiry, as already suggested by Kraft, "The 'Textual Mechanics'," 53.

[115] E.G. Turner, *Greek Manuscripts of the Ancient World* (Oxford: Oxford University Press, 1971), 18. See also C.H. Roberts, *Manuscripts*, 18.

Finally, p967's format does not resemble typical biblical codices. Eric Turner, whose typology of the codex is still a reliable catalogue, places p967 in Group 8. This group consists of considerably tall codices, a feature which Turner singles out as significant to its manufacture.[116] p967 is still further singled out as even taller than the others, in its membership in "Aberrant Class 1 of Group 8."[117] The only other similarly sized biblical codex is Luke's gospel from Oxyrhynchus. Meanwhile, the other manuscripts in p967's class are two copies of Homer, Zenophon, Sophocles, Aristophanes, and two magic texts.

In a second, more general comparison of format, Turner lists early codices with 50 or more lines per page.[118] On this list, p967 is once again in the clear minority as one of only 3 biblical texts.[119] Among the 33 Greek texts listed are two copies of Hesiod's *Theogony*, Plato's *Republic*, and several copies of Homer.

It is important to point out that, in general, extant Greek literary texts are more numerous than biblical ones.[120] However, biblical texts occur far more frequently in Turner's other categories. For instance, 80% of the codices in group 11 (miniature-sized format) are biblical or identifiably Christian.[121] Thus, the relative paucity of biblical/Christian texts with formats similar to p967 remains noteworthy. p967 is, in format, an unusual codex.

It is clear from the above discussion that a variety of factors bear on the identity of p967. It is more probably still the case that p967 derives from Christian circles.[122] The contractions of θεος, κυριος, πνευμα, the Christian

---

[116] Turner, *Typology*, 23.

[117] Ibid., 20–21.

[118] Turner, "Table 14," *Typology*, 96–97.

[119] Turner actually calls p967 the only identifiably Christian codex; he disqualifies Numbers-Deuteronomy, as an OT book, and Codex Alexandrinus as a very large *parchment* codex. Turner, *Typology*, 97.

[120] Even still, Roberts and Skeat demonstrated that Greek literature more often appeared in roll form. See footnote above.

[121] Groups 5, 6, 7, and 9 all contain roughly half biblical or Christian texts.

[122] The study of specific manuscripts needs diligently to attend to the complexities inherent in identity. As a comparison, see David W. Johnson, "Anti-Chalcedonian Polemics in Coptic Texts, 451–641," in *The Roots of Egyptian Christianity* (ed. B.A. Pearson and J.E. Goehring; Studies in Antiquity and Christianity; Philadelphia: Fortress, 1986), 216–234. See also the provocative but apt claims of Bart D. Ehrman, *The Orthodox Corruption of Scripture: The Effect of Early Christological Controversies on the Text of the New Testament* (New York: Oxford University Press, 1993); and the related and well received work of Ehrman's student, Wayne C. Kannady, *Apologetic Discourse and the Scribal Tradition: Evidence of the Influence of Apologetic Interests on the Text of the Canonical Gospels* (SBLTCS 5; Atlanta: SBL, 2004). This issue is similar to the one that plays out regarding Jewish precursors to Christian codicological mechanics and manufacture. As Robert Kraft argues there, we must proceed with a nuanced sensitivity to the hybridity of social identities and

preference for the codex format, along with the theories of provenance largely favor Christian identity. Further, the manuscripts of the Chester Beatty collection, which include the gospels and other New Testament books, probably represent an ancient Christian archive.[123] However, p967 shows closer affiliation with non-Christian, Greek literature in some format characteristics and documentary practices.

6.3.2. *A Liturgical Function?*

6.3.2.1. What the Codex Format Says about Function

Despite the Greek documentary features of p967's codex, a very likely function for a Christian manuscript is liturgy. The strength of this sociological niche invites a discussion on p967's liturgical and religious study functions.

More generally, the codex format is conducive to repeated and/or oral reading. In addition to easily accessed free pages of the book-format, pagination supports the codex's reading functions. It is well established that the primary function of pagination aided in the manufacture of codices, preventing leaves from getting out of order. However, they surely functioned secondarily as references for repeated reading.[124] Additionally, several scribal mechanics would aid a reader such as dieresis, breathing marks, sense marks, and paragraphing. For a continuously wrapped text, these features would bring needed guidance to facilitate reading or oral performance.[125]

Eric Turner postulates a difference between codices for study and those meant to be read aloud.[126] He distinguishes on the basis of handwriting

---

commitments reflected by codicological information. Robert Kraft, "Textual Mechanics," 51–72. Scholars are showing growing support for the idea that Christianity and Judaism in Egypt participated in a closer nexus. See A.F.J. Klijn, "Jewish Christianity in Egypt," in *The Roots of Egyptian Christianity* (ed. B.A. Pearson and J.E. Goehring; Philadelphia: Wipf and Stock, 1986), 161–175. See also in the same volume, B.A. Pearson, "The Earliest Christianity in Egypt: Some Observations," in *The Roots*, 150.

[123] See Roger S. Bagnall, *Reading Papyri: Writing Ancient History* (New York: Routledge, 1995), 40–47 who offers a measured discussion on the relationship between archives and manuscripts of individual texts. G.D. Kilpatrick, who speculates that the Chester Beatty collection consists of those cloistered library manuscripts which survived the Christian persecutions under Diocletian, has no evidence. G.D. Kilpatrick, "The Bodmer and Mississippi Collection of Biblical and Christian Texts," *GRBS* 4 (1963): 38.

[124] Roberts and Skeat, *Birth of the Codex*, 49–51, especially n5.

[125] See discussion in Hurtado, *Earliest Christian Artifacts*, 177–185.

[126] Bernard Knox believes that all codices are for reading aloud. Bernard M.W. Knox, "Silent Reading in Antiquity," *GRBS* 9 (1968): 421. See also G.L. Hendrickson, "Ancient Reading," *CJ* 25 (1929): 182–96.

and its readability. In his discussion, Turner lifts up p967 (CB IX–X) as an
example of a congregational codex, pointing out its unique paleography:

> Scholars have not been able to point to any precise palaeographic parallel
> for Chester Beatty Codex IX–X (OT 183). The handwriting has at one and
> the same time elements that are familiar and unfamiliar. As explanation I
> suggest that in it handwritings that are practiced and clear but of no special
> merit have been produced to a greater size than normal to ease the task of
> reading aloud.[127]

p967 presents several unique features beyond its paleography which many
attribute to a liturgical function. As discussed above, p967's height is an aberrant feature as well. Kenyon originally reported that the p967 codex was
"exceptionally tall and narrow,"[128] which Fernández-Galiano considered a format especially suited for handling in liturgy.[129] In fact, Stanley Porter asserts
that the burden of proof lies on the claim that codices were *not* used in liturgy.[130]
Turner, Fernández-Galiano, and Porter offer reasonable judgments, but by no
means provided sufficient argumentation for their speculations.

With significantly more basis, Hurtado brought Turner's data to bear
on function, arguing that codex p967 was meant to be read aloud. We
already saw above Turner's point about the larger height and more easily
legible script. Turner already surmised that this aberrant feature was to
"ease the task of public reading aloud."[131] Hurtado adduces p967's narrow
columns of text as aids for oral reading. He further draws on p967's height
as an important indicator of function.[132] Many codices were quite small or
"compact" (10–15 x 15–20 cm) which Hurtado suggests were for personal
use, their size increasing the likelihood that they functioned as personal
traveling texts. In contrast, p967's height militates against the designation
"compact." So while some would characterize all codices as compact, p967
likely functioned differently than these smaller, travel-size codices.[133]

---

[127] Turner, *Typology*, 85.

[128] Kenyon, *Fasciculus VII, Ezekiel, Daniel, Esther*, vii.

[129] Fernández Galiano, "Nuevas Paginas," 18.

[130] Stanley E. Porter, "Why So Many Holes in the Papyrological Evidence for the
Greek New Testament?," in *The Bible as a Book: The Transmission of the Greek Text* (ed.
S. McKendrick and O.A. O'Sullivan; New Castle, De.: Oak Knoll, 2003), 175.

[131] Turner, *Typology*, 85 and Hurtado, *Earliest Christian Artifacts*, 173 n64.

[132] Hurtado, *Earliest Christian Artifacts*, 163 n27.

[133] Hurtado challenges scholarly assumptions like those advanced by Eldon Epp that *all*
codices were small and thus convenient for travel, (p. 157). Hurtado's ten page discussion
concludes that difference in size, however insignificant to scholars like Epp, "*does* permit
some inferences about their intended uses," (p. 165, emphasis mine). Hurtado, *Earliest
Christian Artifacts*, 155–165.

It is worth noting that liturgical function is often adduced to explain the origin of the Greek translations.[134] While this explanation comes under considerable scrutiny, few would disagree that *later* Greek manuscripts functioned in liturgical settings.

The weight of the above discussion supports the theory that p967 served a public reading function, likely liturgical.[135] However, some further clarification may be possible and is certainly desirable. Second and third century Christian worship included reading, preaching, singing, and catechetical instruction.[136] Reading could either be *lectio continua*, the continuous reading of the whole book, or follow a set of select chapters or verses. Preaching would follow these readings, although it might occasionally be offered extemporaneously.[137] A biblical manuscript could also serve as a basis for music.[138] Finally, catechetical instruction was an

---

[134] Thackeray mounted the original and long-withstanding argument for the liturgical rationale for the Old Greek. However, his theory was strongly refuted by Perrot, especially for the Prophets. C. Perrot, "La lecture de la Bible dans la diaspora hellénistique," in *Études sur le judaïsme hellénistique* (ed. R. Kuntzmann and J. Schlosser; LD 119; Paris: Éditions du Cerf, 1984), 109–132. See also the very good summary discussion in J.M. Dines, *The Septuagint* (New York: T&T Clark, 2004), 47–50.

[135] For a discussions of scribalism in Egyptian Christianity, see Peter van Minnen, "Greek Papyri and Coptic Studies, 1996–2000," in *Coptic Studies on the Threshold of a New Millennium: Proceedings of the Seventh International Congress of Coptic Studies, Leiden 2000* (ed., Mat Immerzeel and Jacques van der Vliet; 2 Vols.; OLA 133; Leiden: Peeters, 2004), 423–446. Van Minnen offers some general observations on the contributions of papyrology to the study of early Egyptian Christianity. His essay builds on the earlier essay of Bagnall which devotes a short section to the same question. Roger S. Bagnall, "Greek and Coptic Studies, 1990–1995," in *Hellenstic and Roman Egypt: Sources and Approaches* (Burlington: Ashgate Publishing, 2008), 219–230, esp. 224ff; originally published in *Ägypten und Nubien in spätantiker und christlicher Zeit 2* (ed., Schrifttum, Sprache und Gedankenwelt; Wiesbaden: Ludwig Reichert Verlag, 1999), 219–230. On an earlier assessment of the paucity of papyrological evidence for the history of Gnostic manuscripts, see C.H. Roberts, *Manuscript*, 52–54.

[136] Justin Martyr, Tertullian, and others indicate the important role of the Septuagint and especially the prophets in worship. See the helpful discussion of Hughes Oliphant Old, *The Reading and Preaching of the Scriptures in the Worship of the Christian Church: Volume 1 The Biblical Period* (Grand Rapids: Eerdmans, 1998), 245–352, especially 251–277. See also J.A. Lamb, "The Place of the Bible in the Liturgy," in *The Cambridge History of the Bible: Vol 1, From the Beginnings to Jerome* (ed., P.R. Ackroyd, C.F. Evans, G.W. Lampe, and S.L. Greenslade; Cambridge: Cambridge University Press, 1970), 563–583.

[137] Eusebius tells us that Origen preached *extempore* towards the end of his career. Eusebius, *Ecclesiastical History*, VI, 36, I.

[138] For example, some marks indicate directions for choral lyric. Turner, *Greek Papyri*, 116–117. See also Robert F. Taft, "Christian Liturgical Psalmody: Origins, Development, Decomposition and Collapse," in *Psalms in Community: Jewish and Christian Textual, Liturgical, and Artistic Tradition* (eds., Harry Attridge and Margot Fassler; SBLSS 25; Atlanta: SBL, 2003), 7–32; and Edward Foley, *Foundations of Christian Music: The Music of Pre-Constantinian Christianity* (AEL; Collegeville: The Liturgical Press, 1996), 96–97.

important function of both traveling and institutional teachers.[139] Thus, various liturgical elements could form the functional context for p967's use, and indeed, we need not isolate just one.

6.3.2.2. *What the Marginal Marks in p967 Say about Function*

As we just saw, many scholars suggest that several codicological features of p967 point to a liturgical function. Indeed, one of the formatting capacities distinctive of a codex is the space provided by the margins. As Eric Turner noted,

> There can, indeed, be little doubt that the codex form gave an active encouragement to the practice of marginal annotation. The columns of writing are much more distinctly separated from each other than in the roll, and the outside margins of the pages invite annotation.[140]

While the marginal marks in p967 may have helped facilitate liturgical readings, their variety and density deserve more careful attention. A body of critical scholarship on the matter is only in early stages; a comprehensive study of the types of marginal marks that appear in Greek codices should certainly be taken up in further work. For the present, in light of this scholarly lacuna, my analysis will be a measured exploration of the marks' liturgical and reading functions. Emanuel Tov's comprehensive study of scribal practices in the Hebrew manuscripts from the Judean desert can serve as a useful comparison. In some cases, he provides some observations about Greek manuscripts, but the focus is clearly on the Hebrew manuscripts.[141] However, his discussions of section and highlighting marks are comparable to the analysis of similar features below.[142]

6.3.2.3. *Marginal Marks and Reading Use*

Some of the questions of function may be answered by the numerous marginal marks that appear around the columnar text.[143] I divided these

---

[139] The Didache 11.1; 11.10; and 15.1 indicates as much. Chapters 11–13 of the Didache are devoted to the topic of traveling teachers. 15.1–2 speaks about appointing institutional teachers. See discussion of H.O. Old, *Reading and Preaching*, 251–265.

[140] Turner, *Greek Papyri*, 122.

[141] See especially, Tov, *Scribal Practices*, 303–316.

[142] Tov, *Scribal Practices*, 178–236.

[143] For a similar proposal and study, see Porter who analyzes markers in lectionary texts and compares them with those found in biblical manuscripts. Stanley E. Porter and Wendy J. Porter, *New Testament Greek Papyri and Parchments: New Editions* (MPER NS 29 & 30; Berlin: de Gruyter, 2008).

marks into seven categories (see §6.2.6.3). These marks are distributed across the portion of Ezekiel according to the following chart. The chart calculates the percentage of marks per extant verse.

Table 2: Reading Marks per Chapter: (% of verses)

Chapter	% of marks per verse	Verses missing because of broken (b) text or in p967^{Mad} (Mad), which has not been examined by me. [% is calculated without the missing verses.]
12	0	10 vv. b
15	0	
19	0	
21	0	
25	0	
46	4.2	
14	4.8	2 vv. b
26	4.8	
31	5.6	
23	6.1	
22	6.5	
35	6.7	
34	8	6 vv. Mad
13	9.5	2 vv. b
16	10.3	5 vv. b
28	10.5	7 vv. Mad
29	11.1	12 vv. Mad
30	11.5	
38	13	
39	13.8	
32	14.3	2 vv. Mad
24	14.8	
20	16.3	
17	16.7	
36	17.4	
18	18.8	
47	21.7	
27	25	
37	25	24 vv. Mad
44	32	
48	37.1	
45	40	
43	55.6	9 vv. Mad
33		All vv. Mad
40		All vv. Mad
41		All vv. Mad
42		All vv. Mad

As the following discussion will demonstrate, marks that fall into categories 1–2 are best classified as 'reading marks,' either as aids for public reading or for personal study. The marginal words (category 1,) can hardly be explained otherwise.[144] The same is true of category 2, the eclectic marks in §6.2.6.3.1.[145] The latter are distinctive enough, often prominently displayed, and in most cases carefully formed. These two categories offer

---

[144] See C.D. Osburn, "The Greek Lectionaries of the New Testament," in *The Text of the New Testament in Contemporary Research: Essays on the Status Quaestionis* (eds., B.D. Ehrman, M.W. Holmes; Grand Rapids: Eerdmans, 1995), 61–74. The presence of marginal notations does not immediately signal a liturgical function. In fact, in other cases where they appear, scholars have concluded otherwise. For example, the manuscript of Chester Beatty Isaiah (p965), dated by Kenyon to the 3rd century, contains 47 Coptic glosses in the margins. W.E. Crum provided the analysis for publication, stating, "no other Greek bible [sic] ms. thus annotated with Coptic glosses has hitherto come to light," (p. ix). He sees private edification, not liturgy as the probable function. Although several factors of manuscript corruption rendered Crum's conclusions admittedly "anything but reliable," in the cases he could work out, the function seemed to be grammatical correction (p. x). In this sense, the Isaiah manuscript does not serve as a real comparison for p967 Ezekiel whose notations cannot be explained by grammatical concerns. W.E. Crum, "The Coptic Glosses," in *The Chester Beatty Biblical Papyri Descriptions and Texts of Twelve Manuscripts on Papyrus of the Greek Bible: Fasciculus VI: Isaiah, Jeremiah, Ecclesiasticus* (ed., Frederic G. Kenyon; Oxford: Oxford University Press, 1937), ix–xii. Codex Sinaiticus is another example of a Greek uncial with marginal notations serving corrective and commentary not liturgical functions. (See John J. Brogan, "Another Look at Codex Sinaiticus," in *The Bible as Book: The Transmission of the Greek Text* (eds. S. McKendrick and O.A. O'Sullivan; New Castle, De.: Oak Knoll, 2003), 17–32. Brogan updates the standard work by H.J.M. Milne and T.C. Skeat, *Scribes and Correctors of the Codex Sinaiticus* (London: The British Museum, 1938). It is even possible that marginal notations have a magical function. See Roberts, *Manuscripts*, 82–83. With respect to the marginal notations in p967 Ezekiel, Fernández-Galiano thought that the five words of which he was aware (from p967^{Sch} and p967^{Mad}) indicated a liturgical function. "Tambien en el margen superior encontramos pequenas indicaciones cursivas que, sin duda, servian para facilitar al lector la busqueda de determinados pasajes para el rito." Fernández Galiano, "Nuevas Paginas," 20.

[145] De Bruin's study of Scriptural unit division suggests that a cross/plus mark, which I would label category 2, "may be liturgical." W.M. de Bruin, "Interpreting Delimiters," 87. For more on the cross sign, see Turner, *Greek Papyri*, 116–117. Turner provides another interesting more general suggestion regarding critical signs. He showed that *hypomnemata*, or Greek commentary texts (which somewhat resemble *pesharim*) reproduce running lemmata for commentary on a text furnished with critical signs. Turner asks the logical question, is it possible "that a text furnished with critical signs implies the existence of a commentary to explain the signs? The presence of critical signs in literary papyri has been recognized for a long time especially in papyri of Homer, but in practice they have been neglected by textual critics and treated as without significance." Turner, *Greek Papyri*, 115. For instance, Turner adduces the evidence of Aristophanes' commentary texts which were penned in a separate book in the third century CE (contemporary with p967), but by the fifth century, the comments appeared directly in the margins of the codex. It is certainly an interesting possibility that certain marks in p967 correspond with a commentary text, now lost. Whatever the case, these marks may still be recognized as 'reading marks' signaling, at minimum, important sections of text.

the strongest indication of what passages held special significance for the reading community who interpreted p967 Ezekiel.

The function of the remainder of the marks, categories 3–7, is less clear at a casual glance.[146] Johnson hypothesized that they were the marks of the scribe cleaning his stylus. However, the highly uneven distribution, as noted in Table 2 above, makes this explanation unlikely.

Categories 3 and 4, the horizontal (–) and diagonal (/) dashes are the most systematic in form and hence point to a more routinized function. In Tov's analysis of Hebrew manuscripts, he determined that similar types of marks indicated paragraphs and readings sections.[147] However, in p967 the dashes do not offer a system of sense divisions. The horizontal dash (–) corresponds with the beginning or ending of a sense unit only 7 times (18:18; 20:20, 21; 24:25; 43:13; 45:25; 47:1, 6, 23), while even fewer diagonal dashes (/) do (18:21; 20:1; 22:3; and 24:18). The remaining 10 occurrences of the horizontal dash (–) occur in the middle of a sense unit (18:8; 23:23; 27:19; 31:8; 32:4; 35:11; 43:21; 44:19; 45:14; 46:20; 48:5 x2),[148] while the diagonal dashes (/) do so 16 times (16:19; 17:18; 18:22; 20:20; 23:12; 26:12; 27:6; 27:34; 28:13; 30:4; 32:5; 34:8, 18; 44:18; 45:15; 48:7).

Likewise, the dashes are not a system of text-critical marks as a result of textual comparison. From the manuscripts known to Septuagint scholars today, the horizontal dash (–) corresponds to a meaningful textual variant only 8 times (18:8, 18; 27:19; 35:11; 43:13; 46:20; 47:1, 6) and the diagonal dash (/) only 8 times (17:18; 26:12; 27:6; 28:13; 30:4; 32:5; 34:8; 45:15). Thirteen horizontal dashes (–) (20:20, 21; 23:23; 24:25; 31:8; 32:4; 43:21; 44:19; 45:14; 45:25; 47:23; 48:5 x2) and 12 diagonal dashes (/) (16:19; 18:21, 22; 20:1, 20; 22:3; 23:12; 24:18; 27:34; 34:18; 44:18; 48:7) do not correspond with meaningful text-critical issues.[149]

---

[146] Turner discusses marks in the context of Greek literary manuscripts that I have labeled categories 3–7. The practices extend across literary genres and authors, including Homer and prose authors. In this wider context, Turner agrees, "the most frequently occurring signs have no precise intrinsic signification, and need an explanation to make them intelligible." Turner, *Greek Papyri*, 116.

[147] Tov, *Scribal Practices*, 179–187. p967 goes against Greek cases as well. See Aristotle's *Rhetoric* 3.8 1409a.20.

[148] With respect to sense units, the dashes that extend into the block of text do not hold any special significance. The dashes (–) that extend into the text at 18:18 and 47:23 mark sense units, but the ones at 18:8 and 45:14 do not.

[149] As above, the horizontal dashes (–) which extend into the textual block divide evenly between marking textual issues (18:8, 18) and having no relationship to textual issues (45:14; 47:23).

Finally, as discussed above, the marks are not left by the scribe cleaning his stylus. Having ruled out three viable hypotheses for the function
of the marks, it is increasingly likely that the system of dashes represent
some sort of interpretive reading marks, probably highlighting sections
of text with more dense or repeated use.[150] Of course, this hardly solves
the problem of their significance, since the marks could highlight the text
in several different ways. For example, the dashes could highlight a set
of passages, verses, or phrases that are meant to be read sequentially,
that are thematically related, or they may have little system to them at
all, representing rather, idiosyncratic marks according to scribal/reading
interests.

6.3.3. Analysis of the Interpretive Interests of the Reading Community

The preceding discussion has shed some light on p967's function and
reading community. Some of the features arguably point to reading interests. Marginal marks categories 1–4 provide the best window into sections
of text that held particular interest for the reading community. In particular, all of the marginal words relate thematically with the contents of the
pages on which they appear. Some marginal marks may reflect a liturgical
function.

By way of a general introduction to the discussion below, one clear
interest of p967's readers was the temple. Table 2 above shows sections
of relative readings use in p967. Chapters 40–48 stand out as the chapters
with the greatest number of marginal marks. Chapter 43 was the most
heavily annotated; 55.6% of its verses were marked in some way. Six chapters are notated at a density of over 20%: chs. 43, 45, 48, 44, 27, and 47
in descending order. The strikingly high percentage of reading marks in
chs. 43, 44, 45, 47, and 48 appear to reflect a concerted interest in the
content of Ezekiel's temple vision.

The importance of the temple is underscored by the work of John
Olley on the paragraph marks in p967. Olley's valuable studies on the
paragraphing in Ezekiel manuscripts showed that the sense divisions in
chs. 40–48 developed in notably distinctive trajectories. In chs. 40–48,

---

[150] Compare the remarks of Epiphanius that types of marks refer to different subject
matters (e.g., an X marks passages concerning the messiah). Epiphanius, *Weights and Measures* cf. *Patrologia graeca* (ed., J.P. Migne; 163 Vols.; 1857–1886), 43:237. See also J.E. Dean,
Epiphanius' Treatise on Weights and Measures: The Syriac Version (SAOC 11; Chicago: Chicago University Press, 1935), 15.

Olley finds that p967's sparse paragraphing is significantly developed in the Greek manuscript tradition. The Hebrew tradition also develops, but less so and in different ways than the Greek.[151] These disparities in the alternate paragraphing of chs. 40–48 led Olley to ask whether liturgical/exegetical explanations produced the divergent trajectories.[152] It may be the case that different reading sections prompted divergences in paragraphing. It is certainly true that the marked density of interest and the history of paragraphing in chs. 40–48 suggest that the reading community was especially interested in Ezekiel's temple vision.

6.3.3.1. *Marginal Words / Marginal Notations*

The marginal words provide clear insight into the interpretive interests of the reading community. In this section, I will explore the relationship between the marginal words and the exegetical content of the leaves on which they appear. I am interested in how the words thematize or highlight aspects of the Ezekiel text.

6.3.3.1.1. *Ezek 28:9–19*

εμ]πορω[ν   "(concerning) merchants"[153]
Page 64 (ξδ)

  The entire unit of vv. 11–19 fits on the page, suggesting the marginal word relates to this lament. Ezek 28:9–19 is part of a longer oracle against the king of Tyre. However, the marginal notation appears to re-contextualize it for a mercantile audience. Exegetically, the verses support a universalizing application. Verses 11–19 offer a critique of human economic proclivities, wherein Edenic abundance gives way to the violence of trade (v. 16). In fact, the intertextual allusions to Adam and the garden of Eden from Genesis 2–3 summon primeval and paradigmatic human behaviors. In this case, the king of Tyre's beauty and access to splendor leads him to his destruction, being cast from the dwelling of the gods. As Zimmerli points out, vv. 11–19 concern themselves to "an unusual degree with material of a mythic nature."[154] Mythic material lends itself to universalized behaviors and easily refers beyond any one specific horizon of significance. Indeed, it would seem that p967's readers found in the lament over Tyre, a major

---

[151] Olley, "Paragraphing," 214; and idem, "Trajectories," 209.
[152] Olley, "Trajectories," 221; and idem, "Paragraphing," 215.
[153] See discussion and analysis of marginal words in §6.2.6.2 above.
[154] Zimmerli, *Ezekiel*, 2:73.

center of trade in the Mediterranean world, a critique of human economic proclivities relevant to their own day.

The manuscript reveals an even more specific concern with trade. A category 2 mark (a double hatch mark), amplifies verse 28:18, "in the unrighteousness of your trade you profaned your sanctuaries". In this sense, it seems the reading community intended to refer, not only to mercantile life in general, but specifically to the ways in which trade defiles sanctuaries.

6.3.3.1.2. *Ezek 30:1–13*

θ συντελει   "God fulfills"
Page 68 (ξη)

Chapter 30:1–13 falls within the larger sequence of seven oracles against Egypt in chs. 29–32 (29:1–16; 29:17–20; 30:1–19; 30:20–26; 31:1–18; 32:1–16; and 32:17–32). Of the seven oracles, 30:1–19 is the only one not introduced by a date formula.[155] The reading community of p967 may have seen fulfillment of the timeless oracle in more recent events of their past for a prophecy-fulfillment re-contextualization. Whether they interpreted a literal 'end' to Egypt, or whether Egypt held symbolic meaning, the codex does not indicate. In either case, it does seem significant that a codex hailing from Egypt would hold the fulfillment of an ancient Jewish prophecy against Egypt important to its own time. It may be significant that the marginal notation renders the verb "to fulfill" in the present tense, perhaps indicating that the prophecy is continuously fulfilled in a non-literal/spiritual sense.

6.3.3.1.3. *Ezek 32:30–33:8*

συ]νεστωτ(ων)   "uniting" (?)
Page 75 (οε)

Some difficulty reconstructing the notation on page 75 affects the uncertainty of its relationship with the contents of the page.[156] I will

---

[155] Perhaps it is significant that a double hatch mark occurs at 30:1–2, where one would expect to see the date formula.

[156] Recall, the page is slightly broken at the top, and a lexical definition was difficult to determine without using context. Even with context, as the current discussion reveals, the lexical meaning is unclear.

explore a few lexical possibilities on the basis of their exegetical strength.[157]
1) συνιστημι, "set together": συνεστωτων, "(concerning) matters read
together". It is possible that the content of this folio, Ezek 32:30–33:8 is
meant to be 'read together' with another passage. One possible partner
passage is ch. 30 with its marginal notation on page 68 regarding the fulfillment of an oracle against Egypt. Chapter 32 concludes the oracles against
Egypt; thus the shared material could warrant viewing the two as 'united'
texts. However, in §6.2.6.2, we saw that the script of the notation on page
68 is unique and probably penned by a different hand than the one on
page 75. The suggestion loses some of its merit on this account. A second
possibility is that the two pericopes on page 75 should be read together,
the end of chapter 32 with the words of 33:1–8, an exegetical possibility to
be discussed as number three. 2) συνιστημι, "to form a union (in a hostile
sense)". In this sense, συνεστωτων could read, "(concerning) the conspira-
tors" and refer to the nations of ch. 32 who are fated to the pit. Indeed, the
nations are "set together" as the previous definition indicates. 3) συνιστημι,
"arise, become, take place". As a perfect participle, συνεστωτων could mean,
"(concerning) matters that took place". This notation could refer to either
ch. 32:30–32 or to ch. 33:1–8. In 33:1–8, the son of man serves as the watch-
man and warns his people of the coming of judgment. If the notation refers
to 33:1–8, the significance could be messianic, indicating that a son of man
arose to enact the matters described in this passage. If the notation refers
to 32:30–32, it may indicate that the reading community understood world
powers to be eliminated and interned in permanent captivity. Phrases
such as, "gone down in shame" and "for all the terror which they caused"
(v. 30) affirm the depravity of political aspirations to power, and the ultimate
powerlessness the enemy nations have as a result of divine judgment.

However, none of these possibilities is fully satisfactory, and after further inquiry, the marginal notation may yield a different interpretation
altogether.

6.3.3.1.4. *Ezek 39:23–29 and 37:1–4*

αναστασεως   "(concerning) resurrection"
Page 90 (Q)
The page contains the last seven verses of ch. 39 (vv. 23–29), but the
notation probably refers to the beginning of ch. 37 which begins about

---

[157] Lexical entries based on Henry G. Liddell and Robert Scott, *Greek-English Lexicon*
(Cambridge: Clarendon, 1959).

two thirds of the way down the page. Chapter 37 is marked with the double hatch mark, likely directing the reader's attention to the beginning of the 'resurrection' reading. The mark may indicate the beginning of a liturgical reading.

Ezekiel 37 was not always read in light of eschatological ideas about resurrection. Its life in post-exilic Israel bore the historical hopes for restoration of its audiences.[158] As Zimmerli states, the chapter "expresses the event of the restoration and regathering of the politically defeated all-Israel."[159] The interpretation of Ezekiel's vision as resurrection may be found in 4 Macc. 18:17; Sib. Or. 2.221–226 and 4.179–182; Barnabas 12:1; and the Apocalypse of Peter 4:7–9. Christian patristic authors overwhelmingly took Ezekiel 37 to be about resurrection as well.[160] Even Jewish tradition understood the vision of the bones as resurrection, as evinced by the frieze at Dura Europas.[161] The frieze depicts a real resurrection of the dead, not a repatriation of an historical Israel. However, other Jewish commentaries continue the traditions that understood the 'resurrection' in historical terms. Most interesting is the tradition that understood the dried bones as the Northern Kingdom. According to a fragment of the Palestinian Targum, the dead who die in exile refers to the Ephraimites.[162]

---

[158] Zimmerli, *Ezekiel*, 2:258; Greenberg, *Ezekiel*, 2:741; for a slightly different view, see Eichrodt, *Ezekiel*, 507. More generally, see Jon Levenson, *Resurrection and the Restoration of Israel: The Ultimate Victory of the God of Life* (New Haven: Yale University Press, 2006), 161–162, 199. R. Judah b. Ilai *b. Sanh* 92b says "in truth it is an allegory" recognizing its symbolic meaning for national restoration. Even *Pseudo-Ezekiel*'s use of Ezek 37 refers to an historical restoration. See Johannes Tromp, "'Can These Bones Live?' Ezekiel 37:1–14 and Eschatological Resurrection," in *The Book of Ezekiel and Its Influence* (eds., J.J. de Jonge and Johannes Tromp; Aldershot: Ashgate, 2007), 61–78. For the opposite position on the "resurrection" in *Pseudo-Ezekiel*, see Dimant, "Pseudo-Ezekiel," *Encyclopedia of the Dead Sea Scrolls* (eds., Lawrence H. Schiffman and James C. VanderKam, New York: Oxford Press, 2000), 283. For the critical edition of *Pseudo-Ezekiel*, see Devorah Dimant, *Discoveries in the Judaean Desert XXX*, 7–88.

[159] Zimmerli, *Ezekiel*, 2:264.

[160] For a list see Zimmerli, *Ezekiel*, 2:264 n. 35.

[161] Carl H. Kraeling, *The Synagogue, The Yale University Excavations at Dura-Europos final report 8, part 1* (New Haven: Yale University Press, 1956). See Rachel Wischnitzer-Bernstein, "The Conception of the Resurrection in the Ezekiel Panel of the Dura Synagogue," *JBL* 60 (1941): 43–55.

[162] Alejandro Díez-Macho, *Neophyti 1, Targum Palestinense ms. de la Biblioteca Vaticana: Edición príncipe, introducción y version castellana [por] Alejandro Díez-Macho* (Madrid: Consejo Superior de Investigaciones Científicas, 1968–1979), 201. For another good digest of early Christian and Jewish interpretation of 37:1–14, see Moshe Greenberg, *Ezekiel*, 2:749–751.

As the marginal notation indicates, the reading community of p967 clearly read chapter 37 as referring to resurrection (αναστασις—"raising up").[163] However, it is unclear whether p967's distinctive chapter order held any special significance.[164] The marginalia do not shed much light on the issue (see chapters 3 and 4). In p967, chapters 38–39 are marked with three category five, three category six, and one category two marks. These marks represent only 13% density per verse, and can hardly be used to argue that the contents of chs. 38–39 held any special place among the readers of p967. Even less do they point to a definite interpretive connection between the Gog-Magog battle with the resurrection. Lacking marginal words or a clear pattern of idiosyncratic marks, it cannot be known to what extent the reading community was interested in p967's alternate eschatological sequence. It may be that they were more concerned with the connections between the resurrection and the military fulfillments in the Egyptian oracles, if the notation at chapter 30 is any indication.

6.3.3.1.5. Ezek 43:1–9 and Ezek 43:26–44:7

μετανοιας   "(concerning) repentance"
π- θυ ιε(ρ)ου   "concerning God's temple"
π μ(ε)ταν(οι)α(ς)   "concerning repentance"
Pages 104 and 107 (ρδ and ρζ)

Chapter 43 was the most heavily used chapter in the entire codex, according to the number of reading marks. We already saw that 55% of the text was marked in some way. (See Table 2 above.) Chapter 43 describes Ezekiel's visit to the holy of holies, his sanctification of the altar, and the return of God to dwell in the temple forever. The notation, π- θυ ιε(ρ)ου

---

[163] αναστασις is the term used in the New Testament to refer to "the resurrection." Some headway on various interpretations of Ezekiel 37 may be found in textual pluses that were inserted at the beginning of verse 1 as glosses: νεκρων αναβιωσις in Q[mg] and περι αναστασεως των νεκρων in Syh[mg].

[164] See Lust's now retracted ideas about Pharisaic eschatological theology. Lust, "Ezekiel 36–40 in the Oldest Greek Manuscript," 532. Lust goes onto comment in a footnote that, "this does not contradict the Pharisaic belief in an individual resurrection." Ibid., 532 n70; Lust's modified position remains helpful, that the sectarian climate of the Second Temple Period would have read this section of Ezekiel according to different eschatological views. Lust, "Major Divergences," 92. Such eschatological readings were taken up in John's Apocalypse. See Lust, "The Order of the Final Events in Revelation and in Ezekiel," L'Apocalypse johannique et l'apocalyptique dans le Nouveau Testament (BETL 53; ed. J. Lambrecht; Gembloux: Duculot; Leuven: University Press, 1979), 179–183.

(concerning God's temple), no doubt refers to what, in the Hebrew, is the glory of Yahweh returning to his dwelling among his people.

The two notations which both include the term μετανοια (repentance) provide an interpretive frame to the material running from 43:1–44:7. According to p967, the divine commission of the unit is to arrange one's heart according to the way (ο οδον) of the house (in 44:5). Indeed, a category 2 mark appears beside 43:10, "describe to the house of Israel the temple and its appearance and plan (διαγραφη,) that they may be ashamed of their iniquities." Theologically, shame is likely linked with the interest in repentance as that act which prepares the altar/heart for the indwelling of God's holiness. In this context, the ειλαστηριον το μεγα (the great mercy seat) of verse 14 could function symbolically as the central architecture of the repentant heart: an altar, anointed by Ezekiel (the son of man) which acts as a place for expiation.[165]

6.3.4. Description of the Interpretive Interests of the Reading Community

The marginal notations are largely theological. They highlight God's holy temple and his act of fulfillment and might say something about the reading community's understanding of God. Resurrection and repentance provide insight into theological anthropology. As the previous analysis demonstrated, the marginal notations, often theological, proved to provide interpretive lenses that resulted in coherent exegesis of the passages. In other words, they were thematically related to the content of the pages on which they occur. Each of the interpretive interests identified by the marginal notations may be further supported by isolated verses marked with categories 2–7. From the exegetical observations above, three pronounced interests emerged.

First and primary, the reading community was interested in the temple, God's presence there and its sanctity. Closer inspection reveals the centrality of the altar in the reader's interpretive world. Nine marks, two of them category 2, appear beside verses in ch. 43 about the altar. The verses describe the altar's measurements, ordinances, atonement, and priestly sacrifices.[166]

---

[165] Paul, in Romans 3:25, refers to Jesus Christ as he "whom God set forth as an expiation (ιλαστηριον)," cf. Hebrews 9:5.

[166] Cat.2 at 43:27 (2x); cat. 4 at 43:13; cat. 5 at 43:19, 22, and 44:3; cat. 6 at 43:18; cat. 7 at 43:19–20, 22.

Second, the readers were concerned with economy and issues raised by mercantile life. Second only to the temple, passages about trade wares and economic practices dominate. Two pages of the codex seem to highlight economic issues with their category 2 marks in the upper margin: the first, page 111 (ρια) shows marked concern for economic oppression (category 2 at 45:8) and ensuring the maintenance of just weights and measures (category 5 at 45:11).[167] The second, page 120 (ρχ) bears four additional marginal marks calling for land, food, and dwellings for the workers in the temple-vision.[168] Additionally, at 16:49 and 45:8, isolated category 2 marks highlight economic injustice. Taken together, these prominent category 2 marks are supported by a large number of category 3–7 marks at passages about economy.[169] The specificity of these interests suggest that p967 was reappropriated as instructive about contemporary issues in business, trade, economic power, and economic sin. More specifically, it could reflect grievances within a religious community that found the temple a useful metaphor for social relations (i.e., the workers in the temple are religious subjects and the temple personnel are those who occupy positions of power).

Third, the readers were interested in Egypt and the prophecies predicting Pharaoh's fall. A double hatch mark (category 2) appears at 30:2 emphasizing the day Egypt falls. Four other marks echo this interest in Egypt's end.[170] A Diaspora theme is evident as well. At 34:8 the shepherd is upbraided for not seeking after scattered sheep.[171] Further, the readers highlighted 48:28 in which the borders for the tribe of Gad are made to extend into Egypt.[172] These two marks reveal a concern for the status of Diaspora Egypt with respect to the temple vision and the shepherd of Israel.[173]

---

[167] Page 111 bears a double hatch mark in the upper margin.

[168] Category 2 on the upper margin of page 120; category 7 at 48:19; category 6 at 48:17, 18; and category 5 at 48:15.

[169] Ezek 28:13; 18:8, 16, 18; 26:12; 27:6, 13, 15, 16, 13–17, 19, 26, 34; 31:8; 45:15, 22, 25 (x2), 48:6–7, 13.

[170] Category 3 at 30:4; category 4 at 32:4; category 7 at 30:10–12 and 29:18–19.

[171] Category 3.

[172] Page 121 (ρκα) bears a category 2 mark at the top of the page, and a category 6 at 48:28.

[173] See the related conclusion about the LXX translator's view of the Profane leader in Arie van der Kooij, "The Septuagint of Ezekiel and the Profane Leader," in *The Book of Ezekiel and its Influence* (eds., H.J. de Jonge and Johannes Tromp; Burlington: Ashgate, 2007), 43–52.

The exegetical interest in Egypt does not necessarily relate to the previous two. Indeed, two material factors suggest that the interest in Egypt was an isolated concern, perhaps even a 'layer' of the reading tradition. First, the paleography and grammatical form of θ συντελει on page 68 (ξη) was distinctive from the other marginal notations. Thus, the fulfillment concerns regarding Egypt were probably penned by a unique hand. Second, I proposed that the marks in the upper margins of pages 120–121 (ρκ-ρκα) are ink blots which crossed out earlier notations. These blots occur on pages that show a marked interest in several materialist details in equal land allotments. For example, 48:28 is marked as the land allotment for Gad (Egypt).[174] The marked verse at 45:8 adds to the importance of tribal justice with the negative command against the prince whose oppression involves tribal land inheritance.[175] On the literal level, these concerns are historical/materialist. It is possible that symbols in the upper margin on these pages once emphasized the importance of these materialist concerns, but were later blotted out. Certainly, the marginal notations about resurrection and economic sin are better understood as theological/spiritual interpretation. It is possible the Egypt-specific, literalist interpretations of Ezekiel's temple (ch. 48) were rejected in favor of more allegorical ones (visions as symbolic of spiritual realities). While this is a speculative explanation for the ink blots on pages 120–121, the discussion has highlighted the modes of interpretation evinced by p967's marginal words. Indeed, literal and allegorical constituted two important modes of interpretation in the early church. In this observation, perhaps we have arrived at the time when we can revive the question put aside in 1977 by C.H. Roberts who said

> the origin and development of the Church in Egypt to which not only the form but the content of some of the early papyri will contribute is a matter for later consideration.[176]

---

[174] Recall that a category 6 appears at this verse. It may also be significant that Ezekiel's allocation of land to Gad is innovative. Gad is displaced from its traditional location east of the Jordan (Num 32:34–36). Moving and extending Gad's boundary to the Nile would have been all the more striking.

[175] Category 2 at 45:8.

[176] C.H. Roberts, *Manuscript*, 25. For a general introduction on modes of biblical interpretation in the early church, see Karlfried Froehlich, *Biblical Interpretation in the Early Church* (ed., William G. Rusch; SECT; Philadelphia: Fortress, 1984), 1–29.

6.4. THE WHOLE CODEX: EZEKIEL IN LIGHT OF P967
DANIEL AND ESTHER[177]

6.4.1. *Introduction*

The three books contained in the p967 codex are an interesting combination, although not inexplicable.[178] The order, Ezekiel, Daniel, and Esther does occur in codex Alexandrinus.[179] However, this order was by no means standard. Codex Vaticanus separates Esther who comes after the wisdom books, and sets Ezekiel and Daniel at the end of the prophets.[180] Further, the Greek version of Daniel includes Susanna and Bel and the Dragon, which our codex contains, but they appear in reverse order, unique to p967. Thus, p967 has no known exact counterpart for its edition and collection. This situation coheres with a more general scholarly impression regarding codices and canon. Specific to p967, Esther's canonical status was contested within Judaism and Christianity up to the 3rd century, which is when p967 was inscribed.[181] More generally, Roberts and Skeat argue that the codex format played little to no role in canonical groups, although they may overstate the case.[182] Instead, a codex facilitates a kind

---

[177] For the critical publications of p967 Daniel and Esther, see Frederic G. Kenyon, *The Chester BeattyBiblical Papyri: Descriptions and Texts of the Twelve Manuscripts on Papyrus of the Greek Bible. Fasc. 7: Ezekiel, Daniel, Esther* (London: Walker, 1937 [Text], 1938 [Plates]); Angelo Geissen, *Der Septuaginta-Text des Buches Daniel, Kap. 5–12, zusammen mit Susanna, Bel et Draco, sowie Esther Kap. 1, 1a-2,15, nach dem Kölner Teil des Papyrus 967* (PTA 5; Bonn: Rudolf Habelt, 1968); W. Hamm, *Der Septuaginta-Text des Buches Daniel, Kap. 1–2, nach dem Kölner Teil des Papyrus 967* (PTA 10; Bonn: Rudolf Habelt, 1969); R. Roca-Puig, *Daniel. Dos semifolis del còdex 967, Papir de Barcelona, Inv. no. 42 i 43,* (Barcelona, 1974); W. Hamm., *Der Septuaginta-Text des Buches Daniel, Kap. 3–4, nach dem Kölner Teil des Papyrus 967* (PTA 21; Bonn: Rudolf Habelt, 1977).

[178] See Henry B. Swete, *An Introduction to the Old Testament in Greek: The History of the Greek Old Testament* (Cambridge: Harvard University Press, 1900), 197–230.

[179] Ezekiel is the 32nd book, Daniel the 33rd, and Esther the 34th. Codex Alexandrinus is a 5th century uncial and is housed in the British Royal museum as B.M. Royal MS 1D V–VIII.

[180] Vaticanus is dated to the 4th century CE. *Codex vaticanus graecus 1209* (Bibliorum sacrorum graecorum; Vatican City: Bibliotheca Apostolicae Vaticanae & Instituto Poligrafica e Zecca della Stato, 1999). The Hebrew canons likewise differed, with Daniel coming after Esther (not before), and Ezekiel grouped separately with the prophets.

[181] For a discussion on the debates about Esther's canonical status see Moore, *Additions,* 156.

[182] Roberts and Skeat state emphatically, "as regards the Christian Bible as a whole, any possible influence of the codex on its contents can be immediately dismissed." Roberts and Skeat, *Birth of the Codex,* 62. Even smaller 'canonical' collections had only a *loose* relationship to the codex format. By way of example, Roberts and Skeat show how the four gospels, while considered a spiritual unity in early Christianity, circulated in codices

of "comprehensiveness," or an ability to bring disparate texts into one manuscript. They write:

> A comprehensive codex might consist either of a single literary work extending over a number of rolls; a 'collected edition' or a representative selection of works by a single author or on a single theme; or quite simply a miscellany.[183]

Thus, p967's books are not likely to have been assembled on the basis of an emerging notion of canon. Given the fluid status of canon, the later 2nd/early 3rd century inclusion of Esther, and the unique literary editions of both Ezekiel and Daniel, p967 is probably best understood as a "collected edition."

In the analysis that follows, I use exegetical and codicological analysis to identify the interests of p967's reading community which used the codex. In many cases, it is possible to establish thematic or exegetical connections that the reading community may have appreciated among the books or sections of books.

In considering the connections between Ezekiel and the rest of the codex, attention to the paleography is necessary. Daniel and Esther are written in a different and probably later hand than Ezekiel (see discussion above). Although most of the arguments for dating assigned several decades between the hands of Ezekiel and that of Daniel and Esther, the p967 codex is a single quire. It seems unlikely that the Ezekiel portion would have stood alone for multiple decades before the remainder of the codex was filled. More likely, a second scribe who was trainded in a newer style, prepared the second portion of the codex. Whatever the case, the inscription by two different hands, ones removed in time or else style, already points to a manufacturing break between the two sections of the codex. More importantly, the paratextual marks in Daniel and Esther do not overwhelmingly resemble those in Ezekiel, as if a different reader was responsible for them. With these facts in mind, the designation 'reading community' that has facilitated the above analysis is further problematized. From the potentially divergent dates, we might conclude that the 'reading community' stretches over some length of time and may not represent an historically coherent community. Nevertheless, the Daniel and

---

separately, in smaller groups, or with additional books, i.e. not as a standard codicological canon. Ibid., 62–66.

[183] Ibid., 48–49.

Esther portions of p967 further illumine the practices of reading which sustained the codex. In what follows, we will examine the features distinct to Daniel and Esther's reading audiences, and expand the analysis to include a total reading portrait of p967 in antiquity.

6.4.2. *Discussion of the Editions of Daniel and Esther in p967*

6.4.2.1. *The Texts*

The version of Daniel in p967 is that of the Old Greek not Theodotian.[184] However, it represents a developed Greek text with an editorial transposition[185] and the Greek additions. The rearrangement of chapters 5–8 in p967 Daniel, clearly secondary, brings the fictional settings of the

---

[184] p967 of Daniel serves as the sole witness to the OG (except for later hexaplarically expanded ms 88 and Syh). All the major codices contain the revision of Theodotian. Thus noted Kenyon upon the initial publication of the Daniel portion. Kenyon, *Chester Beatty*, x. The Old Greek and p967's Greek edition disappeared, supplanted by the Theodotionic LXX, which became universal. Eugene Ulrich provides a detailed discussion of the way in which Theodotian supplanted p967's text in light of Origen's Hexapla. Since p967 is pre-hexaplaric, it should not surprise us that it resembles the text Origen used for his o' column. However, p967 lacks several of the "Origenian hexaplaric changes and additions taken from the Theodotianic text that are now found in the single extant Greek witness to Origen's revised o' text, MS 88." Ulrich, *The Dead Sea Scrolls*, 208. Fernández-Marcos offers a good recent discussion of the relationship between the OG and the LXX of Daniel in Fernández-Marcos, *The Septuagint in Context: Introduction to the Greek Versions of the Bible* (trans. Wilfred G.E. Watson; Boston: Brill, 2000), 88–92.

[185] Because of the section numbers on the top of the papyrus pages in the codex, Kenyon was able to confirm early on, "it will be observed that chapters vii and viii are placed before v and vi." Kenyon, *Chester Beatty*, vi. The sequence variance may be seen in Geissen, *Der Septuaginta-Text des Buches Daniel, Kap 5–12*, 96–191.

So while p967 Daniel does not preserve the original OG translation of the Hebrew, having been edited in the Greek stages of transmission, its text type does stand closer to the OG than the Theodotian mss. See also, Alexander A. Di Lella, "The Textual History of Septuagint-Daniel and Theodotian-Daniel," in *The Book of Daniel: Composition and Reception* (vol. 2 of *The Book of Daniel*; eds., John J. Collins and Peter W. Flint; Boston: Brill, 2002), 589–590. Although on the same page in Di Lella, Lust thinks that the redaction occurred in a Semitic text:

> ... The different order of the chapters in the LXX [of 967] and in MT may be due to an alternative arrangement of originally independent episodes. The major differences between the MT and LXX in chs. 4 and 5 are connected with the heavily redacted composition of the Semitic text. Lust, "The Septuagint Version of Daniel 4–5," in *The Book of Daniel in the Light of New Findings* (ed., A.S. van der Woude; BELT 106; Louvain: Peeters, 1993), 52–53.

visions and tales into chronological order.[186] Less clear is the rationale for the (re)arrangement of Bel and the Dragon before Susanna. It may be thematic, as I will discuss below.[187]

Kenyon identified the text of Esther as the Septuagint version, the additions appearing in their expected order.[188] The additions significantly transform the story, a fact which could bear on Esther's inclusion in p967.

6.4.2.2. General Thematic Connections Among the Books

Before looking at the codex's paratextual marks, some thematic connections may be pointed out among the three editions. In general, apocalyptic eschatology, fulfillment of God's word, and Diaspora identity link the three Greek books.

First, p967 Ezekiel, LXX Daniel, and LXX Esther share an interest in apocalyptic eschatology. As we have already noted, the edition of Ezekiel in p967 represents a particular eschatological perspective. As Lust has famously stated, p967 Ezekiel is the more apocalyptic edition of the book. Daniel, a paradigmatic member of the apocalyptic genre, is famous for its eschatological themes. The visions in Dan 7–12 communicate a promise for deliverance from present persecution and include a promise for a new

---

[186] Of this sequence variance, J.J. Collins states,
the sequence of chapters in papyrus 967, the oldest witness to the OG, has chs. 7 and 8 before chs. 5 and 6. Yet chs. 7 and 8 clearly belong with chs. 9 and 10, in terms of both literary genre and historical setting. The placement in Papyrus 967 resolves a problem in the Hebrew-Aramaic text by keeping the kings in chronological order (chs. 7 and 8, like ch. 5, are set in the reign of Belshazzar, whereas ch. 6 is set under Darius the Mede). Here again, the Greek is clearly secondary. John J. Collins, *Daniel* (Hermeneia; Philadelphia: Fortress, 1993), 6.

[187] In p967, Susannah comes *after* Bel and the Dragon. This is a unique feature not found in other manuscripts. Collins does not provide an explanation for the alternate sequence. Collins, *Daniel*, 4–5.

[188] Kenyon, *Chester Beatty*, viii. The Septuagint version (of the B text) is a paraphrastic translation of the MT; see Carey A. Moore, *Daniel, Esther, and Jeremiah: The Additions* (AB 44; New York: Doubleday, 1977), 162–163. The Lucianic text (or Alpha text, AT) is much shorter; it is debated whether it is another translation, or a midrashic recension. See Moore, *The Additions*, 163–165; or Tov, *Septuagint*, 255. For the state of the question, see Kristen de Troyer, *Rewriting the Sacred Text* (TCS 4; Atlanta: SBL, 2003), 62–66. In chapter 3 of *Rewriting*, De Troyer treats the question as a case study. Ibid., 59–89. For an earlier sustained argument, see idem, "Translation of Interpretation? A Sample from the Books of Esther," in *X Congress of the International Organization for Septuagint and Cognate Studies, Oslo 1998* (SBLSCS 51; Atlanta: SBL, 2001), 343–353.

kingdom of God.[189] Finally, the additions in the B-Text of Esther recast God as the main actor and include eschatological elements.[190] Additions A and F, respectively, present an apocalyptic vision and its fulfillment/interpretation.[191] These additions frame the book and in so doing, transform the genre of Esther's story into the fulfillment-drama of an apocalyptic vision.[192]

Second, the interest in the efficacy of divine predictions found in LXX Esther can also be found in p967 Daniel and Ezekiel in their concerns for historical fulfillment. As we saw in the case of the marginal words, Ezekiel invited continued reuse of prophecy for new fulfillment-situations.[193] Daniel's interest in the fulfillment of prophecy and apocalyptic visions is more inherent to the content of the book. Daniel 9 begins and ends with a prediction and an angelic discourse revealing an *ex eventu* prophecy that betrays an interest in fulfillment.[194] Daniel 10–12, to an even greater

---

[189] The alternate sequence of chs. 5–8 does not affect the eschatological content of each of the chapters; (the order is chs. 7, 8, 5, 6). However, it may be significant for how p967 Daniel was thought to interact with history.

[190] Additions labeled A–F, so Robert Hanhart, *Esther* (2d ed.; Septuaginta, Vetus Testamentum Graecum, vol. 8/3; Göttingen: Vandenhoeck & Ruprecht, 1983).

[191] As Emmerson states about these two additions,

> The whole perspective of the Greek tale is changed. Through the first and last additions (particularly 11.5–11; 10.4–12) the court intrigue of the Hebrew version takes on an eschatological perspective as a cosmic struggle between Jews and Gentile nations, Haman appropriately becoming the apocalyptic 'Gogite'. (cf. Ezek 38–9).

G.I. Emmerson, "Esther," in *The Dictionary of Biblical Interpretation* (ed. R.J. Coggins and J.L. Houlden; London: SCM Press, 1990), 205. These elements affirm God's providential care for his people through the event of a miraculous intervention in history (Addition D, affirmed in Addition F).

[192] The Greek additions to Esther and Daniel are part of the Old Testament Apocrypha. See the wonderful English translation of Bruce M. Metzger, *Oxford Annotated Apocrypha, Revised Standard Version* (New York: Oxford University Press, 1977). Good introductions to the Apocrypha include D.A. de Silva, *Introducing the Apocrypha: message, context, and significance* (Grand Rapids: Baker Academic, 2002); and D.J. Harrington, *An Invitation to the Old Testament Apocrypha: Approaches to the Mystery of Suffering* (Grand Rapids: Eerdmans, 1999). For a good comprehensive bibliography, see Craig Evans, *Ancient Texts for New Testament Studies: a Guide to the Background Literature* (Peabody: Hendrickson, 2005), 13–14 (Esther,) 18 (Prayer of Azariah,) and 19–20 (Bel and the Dragon).

[193] Indeed, as we saw above in §6.3.3.1.2, the fulfillment concerns of the reading community regarding Egypt capitalized on the only oracle against Egypt that did not have a date formula. This was supported even further by the double hatch mark at 30:1 where the date is conspicuously missing. How the reading community read ch. 30 serves as evidence for the type of re-contextualization permitted by p967's edition.

[194] Daniel 9:2 introduces the 70 year prophecy of Jeremiah that Dan 9:22–27 re-interprets. The schema of 70 weeks breaks the history of Israel into periods, leaving the remaining week for the present/future. Such a feature is consistent with the genre of "historical

extent, communicates its fulfillment interests in relation to contemporary history, although its eschatological hope is not realized; the hope extends notably beyond the horizon of history.[195] Finally, Greek Esther is crafted to show that the events of Esther's struggle on behalf of the Jews are the fulfillment of God's word. Addition B, which appears at the opening of the version, is also an *ex eventu* prophecy. So while each book retains its distinctive eschatological features, the three share an interest in the validity of God's word, expressed through visions, historical surveys, and prophetic oracles.

Third, the three Greek editions address Diaspora dynamics and identities. Ezekiel writes from Babylon. His book depicts a displaced community envisioning its homeland as a past failure and a future hope. Daniel and Esther's narratives take place in foreign courts where Jewish Diaspora identity is asserted over the threat of cultural integration and indeed subjugation. Daniel and Esther are certainly more similar with respect to Diaspora themes. However, as the discussion below will indicate, some Diaspora themes do seem to characterize the reading community of Ezekiel in p967. While purely speculateive, the scribes who combined Daniel and Esther with Ezekiel in the original codex could have been participating in wider Diaspora discourses.

6.4.3. *The Reading Community's Marks in Daniel and Esther*

In p967, the books of Daniel and Esther are not nearly as heavily marked as was the case in Ezekiel. The following table presents the reading marks according to the seven categories for each extant page of Daniel, Bel, Susanna, and Esther.

---

apocalypses." J.J. Collins, *The Apocalyptic Imagination*, 63–64 and 155–157. See also Michael Stone, who places more significance on the connection between prophecy and apocalypticism particularly the fulfillment concerns. Michael Stone, Apocalyptic Literature," in *Jewish Writings of the Second Temple Period* (ed. M.E. Stone: CRINT 2.2; Philadelphia: Fortress, 1984), 390.

[195] See especially Daniel 11, where a detailed description of the Hellenistic period is framed as *ex eventu* prophecy.

Plate numbers	Lines extant	Page #	Content	Significant Markings
p967^{Köln} Theol. 16,9^{r}	1–44	123	Daniel 1:1–8	
p967^{Köln} Theol. 16,9^{v}	1–46	124	Daniel 1:8–17	
p967^{Köln} Theol. 16,10^{r}	1–48	125	Daniel 1:17—2:4	Cat. 7 marks at lines 38–41 [Dan ~2:3]
p967^{Köln} Theol. 16,10^{v}	1–48	126	Daniel 2:4–11	
p967^{Köln} Theol. 16,11^{r}	1–46	127	Daniel 2:11–19	
p967^{Köln} Theol. 16,11^{v}	1–46	128	Daniel 2:19–26	
p967^{Köln} Theol. 16,12^{r}	1–46	129	Daniel 2:27–34	
p967^{Köln} Theol. 16,12^{v}	1–45	130	Daniel 2:34–42	
p967^{Köln} Theol. 16,13^{r}	1–45	131	Daniel 2:42–48	
p967^{Köln} Theol. 16,13^{v}	1–43	[132]	Daniel 2:48–49–3:1–3	B̄ (new chapter)[196] Cat. 3 mark at beginning of ch. 3
p967^{Köln} Theol. 16,14^{r}	1–43	133	Daniel 3:3–11	
p967^{Köln} Theol. 16,14^{v}	1–45	134	Daniel 3:12–17	
p967^{Köln} Theol. 16,15^{r}	1–45	135	Daniel 3:17–23	
p967^{Köln} Theol. 16,15^{v}	1–44	136	Daniel 3:23–30	
p967^{Köln} Theol. 16,16^{r}	1–43	<1>37[197]	Daniel 3:30–39	Cat. 2 mark at line 13[198] [Dan 3:33]
p967^{Köln} Theol. 16,16^{v}	1–43	138	Daniel 3:39–47	
p967^{Köln} Theol. 16,17^{r}	1–42	139	Daniel 3:47–56	Cat. 7 marks at lines 1–4 [Dan. 3:48] Cat. 3* (8)[199]
p967^{Köln} Theol. 16,17^{v}	1–46	140	Daniel 3:57–71	Cat. 2 (÷) in upper margin Cat. 4 marks at regular intervals (3–5 lines) along left margin Cat. 3* (9)

[196] A new chapter is marked with a transition mark consisting of roughly 3 lines of blank page with the chapter numeral centered in the space.

[197] <> = erroneous omission in the original text.

[198] The mark is unusually heavy and uneven; it is possible that the mark is a mistaken ink drop that was slightly smeared.

[199] Throughout sections of Daniel and all of Esther, Category 3 marks (/) appear within the blocks of text, sometimes appearing at the end of line. They are inserted above the first word of a new phrase, and in many cases, correspond with MT versification. They function to mark sense units.

Table (*cont.*)

Plate numbers	Lines extant	Page #	Content	Significant Markings
p967^{CB} f.71.r.	1–24	141	Daniel 3:72–78	Cat. 4 marks at regular intervals (3–5 lines) along left margin Cat. 3* (6)
p967^{Köln} Theol. 17^r	23–43	141	Daniel 3:78–81	Cat. 4 marks at regular intervals (3–5 lines) along left margin Cat. 3* (4)
p967^{CB} f.71.v.	1–27	142	Daniel 3:81–88	Cat. 2 (÷) in line 5[200] [Dan. 3:83] Cat. 2 (÷) in line 23[201] [Dan 3:88] Cat. 4 marks at regular intervals (3–5 lines) along left margin Cat. 3 (6)
p967^{Köln} Theol. 17^v	26–47	142	Daniel 3:88–92 (25)	Cat. 2 (÷) in line 39[202] [Dan 3:90] Cat. 3* (2)
p967^{CB} f.72.r.	1–26	143	Daniel 3:92 (25)–95 (28)	Cat. 3* (8)
p967^{Köln} Theol. 18^r	24–46	143	Daniel 3:95 (28)– 3:96 (29)	Cat. 3* (2)
p967^{CB} f.72.v.	1–25	144	Daniel 3:96 (29)–4:9	Cat. 2 (÷) in line 7 [Dan 3:97; end of ch.] Γ̄ (new chapter)
p967^{Köln} Theol. 18^v	24–45	144	Daniel 4:9 (12)–4:11 (14)	
p967^{CB} f.73.r.	1–25	145	Daniel 4:11 (14)–11a (14)	
p967^{Köln} Theol. 19^r	23–45	145	Daniel 4:14a (17)– 4:16 (19)	
p967^{CB} f.73.v.	1–26	146	Daniel 4:16 (19)–19 (22)	
p967^{Köln} Theol. 19^v	24–45	146	Daniel 4:19 (22)–4:22 (25)	

---

[200] τουσαιων÷ευλογειτεισ
[201] ωνας ÷οτιεξειλατοη
[202] ωνων÷　　　καιεγενε. See image on page 234.

able (*cont.*)

Plate numbers	Lines extant	Page #	Content	Significant Markings
p967^{CB} f.74.r.	1–26	147	Daniel 4:22 (25)–25 (28)	
p967^{Köln} Theol. 20^r	25–45	147	Daniel 4:25 (28)–4:28 (31)	
p967^{CB} f.74.v.	1–26	148	Daniel 4:28 (31)–29 (32)	
p967^{Köln} Theol. 20^v	26–44	148	Daniel 4:29 (32)–4:30a (33)	
p967^{CB} f.75.r.	1–25	149	Daniel 4:30a (33)–30c (33)	
p967^{Köln} Theol. 21^r	25–43	149	Daniel 4:30c (33)–4:34 (37)	
p967^{CB} f.75.v.	1–24	150	Daniel 4:34 (37)–34a (37)	
p967^{Köln} Theol. 21^v	24–42	150	Daniel 4:34a (37)–4:34b (37)	
p967^{CB} f.76.r.	1–24	151	Daniel 4:34b (37)–34c (37)	
p967^{Köln} Theol. 22^r	22–42	151	Daniel 4:34c (37) and 7:1	Δ̄ (new chapter)
p967^{CB} f.76.v.	1–26	152	Daniel 7:1–6	
p967^{Köln} Theol. 22^v	23–44	152	Daniel 7:6–8	
p967^{CB} f.77.r.	1–24	153	Daniel 7:8–11	
p967^{Köln} Theol. 23^r	22–42	153	Daniel 7:11–14	Cat. 2 (=) in left margin at line 30 [Dan. 7:12]
p967^{CB} f.77.v.	1–25	154	Daniel 7:14–19	
p967^{Köln} Theol. 23^v	22–43	154	Daniel 7:19–22	
p967^{CB} f.78.r.	1–24	155	Daniel 7:22–25	
P. Barc.42^r	24–41	155	Daniel 7:25–28	
p967^{CB} f.78.v.	1–26	156	Daniel 7:28–8:4	Ē (new chapter)
P. Barc.42^v	27–46	156	Daniel 8:4–7	Cat. 7 marks at lines 44–45
p967^{CB} f.79.r.	1–28	157	Daniel 8:7–12	
p967^{Köln} Theol. 24^r	27–46	157	Daniel 8:11–15	
p967^{CB} f.79.v.	1–28	158	Daniel 8:15–20	
p967^{Köln} Theol. 24^v	27–45	158	Daniel 8:20–24	
p967^{CB} f.80.r.	1–26	159	Daniel 8:24–5 pref.	F̄ (new chapter)
p967^{Köln} Theol. 25^r	26–45	159	Daniel 5 pref.	
p967^{CB} f.80.v.	1–27	160	Daniel 5: pref.-5	
p967^{Köln} Theol. 25^v	26–44	160	Daniel 5:5–7	
p967^{CB} f.81.r.	1–26	161	Daniel 5:7–12	
p967^{Köln} Theol. 26^r	25–44	161	Daniel 5:11–17	
p967^{CB} f.81.v.	1–26	162	Daniel 5:17–29	

Table (*cont.*)

Plate numbers	Lines extant	Page #	Content	Significant Markings
p967^{Köln} Theol. 26^v	25–42	162	Daniel 5:29–6:1	Z̄ (new chapter)
p967^{CB} f.82.r	1–24	163	Daniel 6:1–4	
p967^{Köln} Theol. 27^r	24–42	163	Daniel 6:4–5	
p967^{CB} f.82.v.	1–25	164	Daniel 6:5–8	
p967^{Köln} Theol. 27^v	24–43	164	Daniel 6:8–12	
p967^{CB} f.83.r.	1–25	165	Daniel 6:12–13	
p967^{Köln} Theol. 28^r	25–43	165	Daniel 6:13–16	
p967^{CB} f.83.v.	1–24	166	Daniel 6:16–18	
p967^{Köln} Theol. 28^v	24–41	166	Daniel 6:19–22	
p967^{Köln} Theol. 29,1^r	1–41	167	Daniel 6:22–28	
p967^{Köln} Theol. 29,1^v	1–40	168	Daniel 6:28; 9:1–6	H̄ (new chapter) Cat. 2 mark in margin beside lines 8–9
p967^{Köln} Theol. 29,2^r	1–42	169	Daniel 9:6–12	
p967^{Köln} Theol. 29,2^v	1–40	170	Daniel 9:12–17	
p967^{Köln} Theol. 29,3^r	1–41	171	Daniel 9:17–23	
p967^{Köln} Theol. 29,3^v	1–42	172	Daniel 9:23–27	
p967^{Köln} Theol. 29,4a+b^r	1–44	173	Daniel 9:27–10:6	Θ̄ (new chapter) Cat. 2 (–) at line 6 [Dan. 10:1] Cat. 2 mark in margin beside lines 8–9 [Dan. 10:1]
p967^{Köln} Theol. 29,4a+b^v	1–41	174	Daniel 10:6–13	
p967^{Köln} Theol. 29,5^r	1–41	175	Daniel 10:13–20	
p967^{Köln} Theol. 29,5^v	1–42	176	Daniel 10:20–11:4	Ī (new chapter)
p967^{Köln} Theol. 29,6^r	1–33	177	Daniel 11:5–8	
p967^{Köln} Theol. 29,6^v	1–33	178	Daniel 11:10–15	
p967^{Köln} Theol. 30^r	1–22	179	Daniel 11:16–20	
p967^{Köln} Theol. 30^v	1–22	180	Daniel 11:23–26	
P. Barc.43^r	1–22	181	Daniel 11:29–32	
P. Barc.43^v	1–24	182	Daniel 11:34–38	
p967^{Köln} Theol. 31^r	1–22	183	Daniel 11:40–45	
p967^{Köln} Theol. 31^v	1–23	184	Daniel 12:2–6	
p967^{Köln} Theol. 32^r	1–23	185	Daniel 12:8–13	
p967^{Köln} Theol. 32^v	1–23	186	Bel and the Dragon 4–8	
p967^{Köln} Theol. 33^r	1–22	187	Bel 10–14	
p967^{Köln} Theol. 33^v	1–23	188	Bel 1–22	
p967^{Köln} Theol. 34^r	1–22	189	Bel 26–30	
p967^{Köln} Theol. 34^v	1–23	190	Bel 33–39	
p967^{Köln} Theol. 35^r	1–23	191	Susanna 5–10	

able (*cont.*)

Plate numbers	Lines extant	Page #	Content	Significant Markings
p967^{Köln} Theol. 35^v	1–23	192	Susanna 19–29	
p967^{Köln} Theol. 36^r	1–21	193	Susanna 34–37	
p967^{Köln} Theol. 36^v	1–22	194	Susanna 44/45–52	
p967^{Köln} Theol. 37^r	1–21	195	Susanna 55–59	
p967^{Köln} Theol. 37^v	1–15	196	Susanna 62a–62b + Subscriptio	Subscription to Daniel[203]
p967^{Köln} Theol. 38^r	1–23	197	Esther 1:1a–1:1f	Cat. 3* (7)
p967^{Köln} Theol. 38^v	1–25	198	Esther 1:1m–1:1s	Cat. 3* (9)
p967^{Köln} Theol. 39^r	1–24	199	Esther 1:6–1:10	Cat. 3* (7)
p967^{Köln} Theol. 39^v	1–24	200	Esther 1:15–1:19	Cat. 3* (11)
p967^{Köln} Theol. 40^r	1–23	[201]	Esther 2:2–2:7	Cat. 3* (7)
p967^{Köln} Theol. 40^v	1–25	202	Esther 2:11–2:15	Cat. 3* (5)
p967^{CB} f.102.r	1–21	[203]	Esther 2:20–23	Cat. 3* (1)
p967^{CB} f.102.v.	1–24	204	Esther 3:4–9	Cat. 3* (9)
p967^{CB} f.103.r.	1–23	[205]	Esther 3:13–13:3	Cat. 3* (5) Cat. 2 mark in right column at line 9
p967^{CB} f.103.v.	1–22	[206]	Esther 13:5–3:14	Cat. 2 mark in right margin at line 20–21
p967^{CB} f.104.r.	1–21	[207]	Esther 4:3–7	Cat. 3* (7)
p967^{CB} f.104.v.	1–22	[208]	Esther 4:11–16	Cat. 3* (7)
p967^{CB} f.105.r.	1–20	[209]	Esther 13:12–17	Cat. 3* (8)
p967^{CB} f.105.v.	1–22	[210]	Esther 14:3–8	Cat. 3* (9)
p967^{CB} f.106.r.	1–20	[211]	Esther 14:13–16	Cat. 3* (9)
p967^{CB} f.106.v.	1–22	[212]	Esther 15:5–10	Cat. 3* (8)
p967^{CB} f.107.r.	1–19	[213]	Esther 15:16–5:4	Cat. 3* (8)
p967^{CB} f.107.v.	1–20	[214]	Esther 5:9–14	Cat. 3* (5)
p967^{CB} f.108.r.	1–18	[215]	Esther 6:3–6	Cat. 3* (7)
p967^{CB} f.108.v.	1–19	[216]	Esther 6:11–14	Cat. 3* (5)
p967^{CB} f.109.r.	1–17	[217]	Esther 7:6–9	Cat. 3* (30)
p967^{CB} f.109.v.	1–18	[218]	Esther 8:2–6	Cat. 3* (4)

[203] δανιηλ' / ... ει]ρηνη τω γραψαν / ...]και τοις αναγινωσκου / ...]ην. See directly below on the Subscription in Daniel.

The Subscription to Daniel in p967[204]

Line 1	δανιηλ'	Daniel
Line 2	... ει]ρηνη τω γραψαν	peace to the one who wrote
Line 3	...]και τοις αναγινωσκου	and to those reading
Line 4	...]ην	[grace / peace?]

The two forms at the end of lines 2 and 3 (γραψαν and αναγινωσκου) present some problems: their articles both suggest the dative case. Two explanations are possible. 1) The endings were left off in a form of shorthand; or 2) The endings appear in the broken text on the subsequent lines. By this explanation, the—τι ending to γραψαν wraps to line 3, yielding an Aorist, active, dative, singular, masculine participle of γραφω. This form agrees with its article, τω. Likewise, the expected—ντι ending to αναγινωσκου would appear at the beginning of line 4. The expected form, αναγινωσκοντι, a Present, active, dative, plural, masculine participle of αναγινωσκω, agrees with its article, τοις. Such orthographic variation from ο to ου in the -ουντι ending is certainly possible in Greek papyri.[205]

In favor of the former, the phenomenon of wrapping a subscription does not seem warranted. The line-format of the subscription is centered; it does not align with the margins of the columnar text. The freedom of this format seems to betray the necessity that explains a wrapped text. The format could obey an aesthetic with respect to a type of centered text. Whatever the case, the dative singular and dative plural form are intended, as reflected in my translation.

6.4.3.1. Sense Divisions (Sense Marks)

Sense divisions are the exception not the rule in p967 Daniel and Esther. Paragraphing is non-extant.[206] This is quite in contrast with Ezekiel where both scribal *ekthesis* combined with a double slash and the later verti-

---

[204] Thanks to Juan Hernandez for helpful conversation about wrapped text in Greek manusripts.

[205] See Francis Thomas Gignac, *A grammar of Greek papyri of the Roman and Byzantine periods: Phonology, Volume 1* (TDSA 55; Milan: Istituto editorial Cisalpino. La Goliardica, 1976), 215.

[206] Kenyon concurred, using the term *paragraphi* for what I more generally called "line breaks," given their multiple function across the entire p967 mauscript: "There is no punctuation, the reading marks have been inserted by a second hand in the Song of the Three Children and in Esther. The verses of the Song are also marked by *paragraphi*, but

cal double dots brought organization to Ezekiel's paragraphing. Instead, in the non-Ezekiel portion of the codex, one section is marked with line breaks (-) where horizontal lines extend from the left margin into the block text at 3–5 line intervals. These line breaks are, however, isolated to Daniel 3:57–88 and were inserted by a secondary scribe. Also secondary is a system of phrase breaks (/) that appears within the continuous block text or, when appropriate, at the end of lines. All of Esther is so marked, while only Dan 3:49–96 has the phrase marks. Both of these types of sense marks likely facilitated reading, raising the same issues as discussed above (§6.3). Finally, the original scribe is responsible for the chapter breaks in Daniel, indicated by three blank lines and a system of enumeration. Neither Ezekiel nor Esther are presented similarly.

6.4.3.2. *Marked Sections of Reading Activity*

Despite the phrase breaks throughout Esther, Daniel presents the more worked-over text. Daniel is more heavily marked than Esther with idiosyncratic marginal features. Daniel 3 has five (÷) marks.[207] These five marks appear at formal/structural breaks within The Hymn of the Three Young Men (vv. 57, 83, 88b, 90, and 97).[208] Four other category 2 marks appear in Daniel at 7:12; 9:2; and two at 10:1 (marking the beginning and the ending of the verse.) Neither Bel nor Susanna have any reading marks.

---

these are sometimes placed above the line in which a verse ends and sometimes below it." Kenyon, *Fasciculus VII, Ezekiel, Daniel, Esther*, ix.

[207] Orientation of the (÷) is diagonal. The fifth category 2 mark in Dan 3 comes at 3:33 and is likely an erroneous ink blot. If this is correct, the mistaken mark provides no information about the reading community. The contents of the verse, "we cannot open our mouth," and "shame is upon us," do not immediately connect to the content interests highlighted by the other four marks in ch. 3. Additionally, the fifth mark at 3:33 is unlike the other four, which are all highly standardized ÷ marks. The latter observation could indicate that the ÷ in Daniel 3 functioned as the obelos or metobolos of the Aristarchian symbols also used by Origen. Indeed, the mark occurs in LXX material that is not present in the MT. However, against this, see the similar mark at Ezek 17:1 and the observations in the note 208 below.

[208] No consistent connection exists between the (÷) marks and text-critical issues in the Greek text tradition. On the poisitive side, the mark at 3:90 corresponds with the end of the hymnic additions in the versions and the one at 3:97 corresponds with a short θ′ variant from both MT and OG. On the latter, see Collins, *Daniel*, 178, n70. However, on the negative side, the marks at 3:57 and 3:88 hold no text-critical significance for variant readings or text-critical corrections. Additionally, several more obvious variants that could have been marked were not. The (÷) mark was not a formal sign to indicate textual issues in p967 Daniel.

Esther bears only two category 2 marks both in ch. 13. The marks act as a frame for the chapter at vv. 2 and 7.

6.4.3.3. *A Liturgical Section: The Hymns in Daniel 3*

In the book of Daniel, the Prayer of Azariah (3:49–56) and The Hymn of the Three Young Men (3:57–97) are highly structured by a variety of reading marks, setting them distinctly apart from the remainder of the text. The only 'phrase marks' and 'line breaks' in Daniel occur in this section.[209] The 'line breaks,' or in this case *paragraphi*, correspond to most of the verses of the hymn, providing the reading community with reading stanzas. Moreover, the system of five (÷) marks break 3:57–97 into four readings: (3:57–82, 83–88a, 88b–90, and 90–97).[210] In addition to these secondary reading marks, the original scribe left in-line spaces throughout the Hymn of the Three Young Men. The spaces coincide with (÷) marks: at v. 83 (approximately two letters), at v. 88b (of approximately one letter), and at v. 91 (of approximately five letters).

The reading sections within the Hymn of the Three Young Men were created by scribal text-breaks. These spaces, which originate from the inscription of the codex, seem likely to mark a liturgical passage, and warrant such a literary reading. The first section (vv. 57–82) directly addresses "all the works of the Lord." The three 2nd person plural imperative verbs implemented in the text, ευλογειτε (bless), υμνειτε (sing praises), and υπερυψουτε (exalt,) repeat in each verse and provide hymnic structure to both this and the second reading section (vv. 83–88a).[211] While the addressees are not always human, the verses urge collective praise of the Lord and lend

---

[209] See Stanley Porter who similarly uses unit delimitation to discuss exegetical and liturgical significance. Stanley E. Porter, "The Influence of Unit Delimitation on Reading and Use of Greek Manuscripts," in *Method in Unit Delimitation* (eds. M. Korpel, J. Oesch, and S. Porter; Pericope 6; Boston: Brill, 2007), 44–60.

[210] The first mark rests just above ευλογειτε, the first verse beginning with an imperative (v. 57) in The Hymn of the Three Young Men. The second occurs at the end of 3:88a after the words, "highly exalt him forever and ever," which closes the section of imperatives. The third mark occurs at the end of The Hymn in v. 90 after the phrase, "his mercy endures forever and ever." This mark appears within a space equal to roughly four letters which was clearly left by the original scribe. The final mark designates the end of ch. 3 at v. 97. While I suggest that these marks indicate liturgical sections, it should be noted that other functions *may* be asserted. For instance, the (÷) marks in Codex Sinaiticus, refer to insertions that were written in the margin. However, p967 does not contain any such marginal material.

[211] In p967, the imperative form,—ειτε is not consistent. The form occasionally reads,—ειται or—ειτω.

themselves to a liturgical setting.[212] The progression of addressees in vv. 57–82 (1st reading section) includes the heavens, earth, and creatures and culminates in v. 82 with human beings (υιοι των ανθρωπων). The second section (vv. 83–88a) is entirely directed at humans, beginning with Israel and continuing to priests, servants, the righteous, holy, and humble ending with the three young men from the Daniel 3 narratives.[213] This section of the hymn contains two features that warrant a theory of liturgical use: 1) the (÷) mark within the two letter space at v. 83 as well as 2) the 2nd person plural address to humans.

The third reading section, beginning at v. 88b, is marked by a (÷) and a space of approximately one letter. However, some discussion is neccesary to explain this section break given the connections between v. 88b–c and v. 88a.

88a   Bless the Lord, Hananiah, Azariah, and Mishael; sing his praise and highly exalt him forever (÷).

88b   For (οτι) he delivered us (ημας) from Hades; and saved us from the hand of death

88c   and he rescued us (ημας) from the midst of the burning flaming furnace; and from the midst of fire, he rescued us (ημας).

On the grounds of content, the break is awkward. Verse 88b opens with a οτι-clause that completes v. 88a. The clause supplies a motivation for the three young men urged to praise the Lord in v. 88a. Verse 88b–c calls to mind the narrative context of the entire Hymn by reminding readers of the divine act that delivered Hananniah, Azariah, and Mishael. Thus, in terms of content, the section division divides closely connected material and is thus somewhat problematic.

However, conducive to a liturgical context, the mark occurs at a formal break. Verse 88a ends the first two reading sections with the triple-set of imperative verbs that consistently repeats throughout all of vv. 57–88a. As in each verse of this section, the addressee is specified; in v. 88a, it is the three young men.[214] At the opening of the third reading section, v. 88b–c

---

[212] The changes in subjects addressed may be divided as follows: "vv. 58–63: the heavenly realm; vv. 64–73: the natural elements (rain, wind, etc.); vv. 74–81: the earthly bodies; vv. 82–90: human beings. See Collins, *Daniel*, 204–205.

[213] These three, claimed in 1 Macc. 2:59 to have survived the flame, correspond to Shadrach, Meshach, and Abednego from the narrative section of Dan. 3. See B.T. Dahlberg, "Shadrach, Meshach, and Abednego," *Interpreter's Dictionary of the Bible* (Nashville: Abingdon, 1962), 4:302–303.

[214] The first and second sections (vv. 57–82 and 83–88a) meet the formal criteria laid out by Westermann for Imperative Psalms. Claus Westermann, *The Praise of God in the*

can be grammatically differentiated by its use of "us" (ημας). If v. 88b–c
were meant to be read with the shared content that preceded in v. 88a, we
would expect to read "for he rescued *them*" (αυτους) referring to the three
men.[215] Instead, the third reading section (vv. 88b–90) directs its attention to a collective audience in a short poetic reading honoring the God
who delivers people from Hades and the fiery furnace.[216] If this is right,
v. 88b–c opens a liturgical section which affirms the power of the Lord
over death. The section culminates in calls for thankfulness and praise
(vv. 89–90) rendered in 2nd person plural imperatives. The secondary (÷)
mark and the scribal space of 5 letters after v. 90 commend a definite
break to the third reading section.[217] In short, a liturgical context nicely
explains the movement from imperatives to an audience response starting in v. 88b.

6.4.3.4. *Analysis of Interpretive Interests*

6.4.3.4.1. *Dan. 3:57–82, 83–88a, 88b–90, 91–97*
Four ÷ marks and an in-line space
Pages 140–144 (ρμ-ρμα)

As indicated by the preceding discussion, Daniel 3 was more densely
worked over by the reading community. The second and third reading
sections (vv. 83–88a and 88b–90) shared the theme of deliverance from

---

Psalms (trans. Keith R. Crim; Richmond: John Knox, 1965), 130–132. Westermann concludes
that the form, a later development among the Psalm-forms, "was determined liturgically
and designed for liturgical use. Ibid., 130.

[215] Many scholars take vv. 88–89 to be secondary to the original hymn. So Moore, *Daniel,
Esther, and Jeremiah: The Additions*, 74. However, the formal discontinuities, noted above,
between v.88a and 88b–c suggest that v. 88a may have been written to link the originally
independent hymn of v. 88b–c to the conventions of the longer poem. Thus, while v. 88a
may have been the craft of the redactor, it could also have been the device of the original
author. Either way, v. 88a serves as the bridge to the interpretive content of v. 88b–c.

[216] The third reading (vv. 88b–90) affirms a later Christian interpretation of Daniel 3 and
the deliverance of the three men from the fiery furnace. See Aage Bentzen, *Daniel* (HAT
19; 2d ed.; Tübingen: Mohr Siebeck, 1952), 39. See the similar conclusions of McGowan
and Mowry. McGowan argues that NT texts and their narratives were read liturgically as
"interpretive etiologies of a catechetical nature." Andrew McGowan, "Is There a Liturgical
Text in this Gospel? The Institution Narratives and Their Early Interpretive Communities,"
JBL 118 (1999):86. Mowry argues that the literary form of the songs in Rev 4–5 suggest the
liturgical setting for the lyric poems. Lucetta Mowry, "Revelation 4–5 and Early Christian
Liturgical Usage," *JBL* 71 (1952): 75–84. These two studies connect narrative setting and
liturgical hymns and offer interesting parallel cases to the situation in Daniel 3.

[217] Of the four reading sections, the fourth is the least likely to have been read liturgically, and thus does not receive attention here.

death.[218] The theme is carried into the fourth reading section as well. In p967, v. 91 reports that Nebuchadnezzar heard the three men's singing and saw that they were alive.[219] Then Nebuchadnezzar offers praise to the Jewish deity for, "there is no other God who is able to save (εξελεσθαι)". In this fourth section, as in the preceeding two, the exegetical insterests focus on praise and divine deliverance.

The Hymn of the Three Young Men in Daniel 3 may have been read in connection with Ezekiel 37 as a resurrection text. Even beyond their thematic connection, Ezekiel 37 and the hymn in Daniel 3 share an important scribal feature. The scribe who prepared Daniel left a five-letter width space after Dan 3:88b-90. A space of nearly the same size occurs before Ezekiel 37. These two gaps in the continuously wrapped text constitute the *only spaces of such notable length* in the entire extant manuscript. Such a scribal technique suggests an appreciation for the connection between the two passages on the part of the scribe of Daniel.

It is important to point out, however, that the in-line spaces were produced by the scribe who inscribed the manuscripts and were a part of the manufacturing process. The reading community who placed the secondary (÷) marks in Daniel did not similarly mark Ezekiel 37. In fact, the (÷) mark only occurs once in the Ezekiel portion of the text, at 17:1 (see §6.2.6.3.1 and images on pp. 233–234).

6.4.3.4.2. *Daniel 7:12*

Category 2

Page 153 (ρνγ)

Resurrection is not the only apocalyptic element that interested the reading community; the remainder of the reading marks draws attention to passages critiquing imperial power using apocalyptic tactics common to the genre. Already in Dan 3, Nebuchadnezzar's role as tyrant was dramatically reversed as he praised the Jewish God for his power for deliverance (v. 29).

---

[218] Verses 57–88a only hint at the theme in v. 88a through mention of the three young men. This mention, however, summons the fiery furnace narrative. Certainly, vev. 88b–90 are quite directly about deliverance from death.

[219] The text of p967 follows G at this point, but diverges somewhat from all versions as well. For instance, in v. 91 "and their *singing was in the hearing of the King*, and he saw that they were alive." The highlighted phrase is rendered according to Hebraic word order, an Hebraism which is not found in G or in Theodotian, and is clearly closer to the semitic version.

The marked verse in Dan 7:12 sheds light on apocalyptic political ideas about the fate of empires.[220] Following on the vision of the four beasts which represent a succession of evil empires, vv. 11–12 describe their destruction. However, only the fourth beast is completely destroyed (v. 11). The initial three beasts are not annhiliated, but rather "the duration of their life was given to them until the appointed time" (v.12).[221] Verse 12 is sober to the persistent existence of imperial powers and holds out a future hope for an appointed time of their demise. The symbolic nature of the beasts lends itself to re-contextualization. It is quite possible that the reading community applied the concept to their contemporary political realities.

6.4.3.4.3. *Daniel 9:2*
Category 2
Page 168 (ρξη)

The apocalyptic conception of the future according to appointed times recurs in the marked verse at Dan. 9:2. It cites Jeremiah's 70-year fulfillment period for the desolation of Jerusalem.[222] In the Danielic interpretation, 70 *weeks* of years (vv. 25–27) are re-contextualized and recalculated

---

[220] It is possible that the mark refers to Dan 7:13 in which "one like the son of man appeared on the clouds." However, the phrase ιδου επι των νεφελων του ουρανου, which opens the scene, is a full five lines below the mark. Despite how popular this verse was in early Christianity, the reading community of p967 did not directly mark the messianic imagery. For references on the role of this verse in early Christianity, see Arthur J. Ferch, *The Son of Man in Daniel 7* (AUDDS 6; Berrien Springs, Mi.: Andrews University Press, 1979), 4–9.

[221] Collins holds that v. 12 refers to the remaining three beasts. However, variant explanations do exist. As he notes, H.L. Ginsberg argues that the "remaining beasts" refer to residual Persian and Median powers that persisted beyond the period of Antiochus IV. Harold L. Ginsberg, *Studies in Daniel* (TS 14; New York: Jewish Theological Seminary of America, 1948), 7. Ginsberg's interpretation may be less appealing for the original sense, but his comes closer to how the reading community may have read the verse, as referring to contemporary powers, not least because the fourth beast was often taken to stand for Rome. Both Jewish and Christian interpretation attest such continued recontextualization of Daniel's visions. See especially Collins' thorough discussion in Collins, *Daniel*, 88.

[222] Jeremiah's prophecies in 25:11–12 and 29:10 address an exilic audience. See William L. Holladay, *Jeremiah* (Hermeneia; 2 vols.; Minneapolis: Fortress, 1989), 2:139–140. Holladay argues for redactional activity regarding the 70 years. However, the different ideas about the 70-years, according to Holladay, were catalyzed by the destruction in 587 BCE and thus involve a pre-exilic and an exilic audience. 2 Chronicles 36:21, Ezra 1:1, and Zechariah 1:12 all reference the 70 years with respect to the Persian period restoration of Yehud. See, Reinhard Kratz, "The Visions of Daniel," in *The Book of Daniel: Composition and Reception* (eds. J.J. Collins, and Peter Flint; 2 vols.; Boston: Brill, 2002), 1:109–111.

to predict the temple desecration under Antiochus IV.[223] Why the reading community of p967, centuries after the Maccabean events, would be
interested in this number is unclear. It may be because the weeks of years
in Dan 9 did not work out perfectly, that the community attempted to
recalculate the number for a third application in their own time. However, without more evidence, this is merely speculation.

6.4.3.4.4. *Daniel 10:1*
Two category 2
Page 173 (ρογ)
   The two marginal marks beside Dan. 10:1 strongly indicate an interest
in the efficacy of Daniel's visions. The verse asserts that Daniel's "vision
is true" (αληθες το ορα) and filled with great power (το πληθος το ισχυρον.)
The vision referred to in 10:1 runs through chs. 10–12, describing a military
conflict (ch. 11 especially) and culminating in the deliverance of the elect
(in ch. 12).[224] Daniel 11 originally offered an *ex eventu* prophecy about the
Syrian wars of the Hellenistic period, while ch. 12 extended hope for resurrection across the literary horizon into the future. As in Ezekiel, we see
the theme of divine deliverance promised within the context of imperial
wars and threat. The marks, however, occur at points that emphasize the
strength and truth of Daniel's vision.

6.4.3.4.5. *Esther 13:1–7*
Two category 2
Pages 205–206 (σε-σς)
   The two marks in Esther occur at the beginning and end of Addition
B (ch. 13).[225] The content in Esther 13:1–7 consists of a letter from the

---

[223] Daniel's interpretation of the 70 years was written long after the advent of the Persian Yehud to which it originally referred. However, Collins perhaps overstates the case
that Daniel "rejects" the Persian period fulfillment schemes. Collins, *Daniel*, 359. Indeed,
the literary setting places ch. 9 during the reign of Cyrus, inviting at least a two-fold fulfillment interpretation, the original Persian one and the updated fulfillment contemporary
with the book of Daniel.

[224] Daniel 12 constitutes the only clear example of resurrection from death in the
Hebrew Bible. As commentators have noted, the vision does not hold out hope for a
miraculous political deliverance for the Jews, as is usually the case. Instead, the future
for the Jews takes the form of resurrection from the dead in 12:2–3. Collins calls these two
verses, "the only clear attestation of a belief in resurrection in the Hebrew Bible." Collins,
"Excursus: On Resurrection," in *Daniel*, 394.

[225] Addition B, of the five in Esther, is the most likely to have been originally written
in Greek, which helps to understand its literary tradition. So C.A. Moore, *Daniel, Esther,
and Jeremiah*, 193–199; See his original argument in C.A. Moore, "On the Origins of the
LXX Additions to the Book of Esther," *JBL* 92 (1973): 382–93; and the supporting study of

Persian king Artaxerxes to his governors. In that letter, he articulates various rationales for instituting his anti-Semitic pogrom against the Jews. That this passage is isolated raises questions. If the section is taken out of its running context, it would merely read as a diatribe against the Jews. Indeed, the exegetical connections with the language of Ezekiel may support this view that p967 demonstrates its readers' anti-Semitic interests. Chapter 13's pogrom includes a direction that the Jews would be "completely wiped out by the swords of their enemies" and "go violently down into Hades (αδης)" (vv. 6–7). In Ezekiel, the same phrases describe the fate of foreign empires,[226] who as we saw, found their end in Ezekiel's pit (chapter 32.) Consistent with this exegetical connection, p967's readers may seek to relegate their Jewish contemporaries to the pit.

The opposite reading is also possible. *Within* its literary context, Addition B describes the wicked plot of the antagonist, Haman. p967's readers may have understood themselves in the role of Esther's Jews, facing great persecution. Historically, the charges in Esther levied against the Jews, particularly that they "pervert society with strange laws" (v. 5) were also mounted against Christians, for instance, in the first century CE by Tacitus.[227]

The case of Esther 13:1–7 in p967 is instructive. The reading marks highlight a text whose antagonism (interior binaries) can generate opposite meanings depending on the context in which they are read and understood. The codex supplies no further assistance with this much-needed supplemental information. In this case, conclusions about the "reading community" are ambiguous and underscore the limitations of the modern pursuit for ancient meanings. Nevertheless, the cosmic revenge and polarizing language of Addition B in Esther tells us something about the reading community's religious climate, in which rhetorical foment was more intensified.

R.A. Martin, "Syntax Criticism of the LXX Additions to the Book of Esther," *JBL* 94 (1975): 65–72.

[226] Death by the sword is a recurrent refrain throughout Ezekiel. So threatened are the Ammonites in ch. 21, Edom in ch. 25, Pharaoh and Egypt in chs. 17, 29, 30 and 32, and Israel in chs. 6, 7, 11, 12, 14, 21, 24, and 33. As for the pit, "Hades" appears three times in Ezek 31:15–17 referring to Assyria and once of Egypt in ch. 32:27. However, Ezekiel's words for the pit include שאול (Sheol), שחת (pit), בור (cistern/pit), and ארץ תחתית (underworld). These may be translated into Greek somewhat loosely as αδης (Hades), βοθρος (pit), λαχχος (cistern/pit), and γη βαθος (underworld).

[227] Tacitus, *Annals* xv 44.

6.4.3.5. *Discussion of Interpretive Interests*

The preceding discussion identified several thematic concerns that cut across the books. The theme of deliverance from death is found in Daniel 3 (marked five times with ÷), and Ezekiel 37 (marked by a category 2). Both texts highlight praise and deliverance and even claim God's power to save from death. Secondly, marks in both Esther and Daniel point to passages about foreign nations and the negative context of imperial power dynamics. This interest resonates with the passage in Ezek 30 annotated as a divine fulfillment of Egypt's destruction. The themes of death and deliverance occupy many of the Jewish and Christian apocalypses which often focus on resurrection and mythologize the tension of life under imperial power.

As mentioned in §6.2.1.2, it is possible that Tobit followed Ezekiel, Daniel, and Esther in p967. A connection certainly exists between Tob 8:5 and Dan 3:52–53 since both begin with the phrase, "you are blessed, Lord, God of our fathers" and emphasize the natural world's words of blessing.[228] Further connections exist but are not strong. For example, Tobit, Esther, and Susannah describe female exemplars of the faith, serving as counterpoints to Ezekiel's wicked women in chs. 16 and 23.[229]

More generally, Tobit, Daniel, and Esther are Diaspora texts. They depict Jews living under foreign rule: Daniel between the Babylonian and Persian reigns, Esther under Persian rule, and Tobit under Assyrian captivity. These Diaspora contexts in p967's books highlight Ezekiel's literary setting in Babylon, by the river Chebar. Consistent with these prominent literary settings, codex p967's historical setting in Egypt may prove important to further inquiry into re-contextualized readings of the codex (i.e. "God fulfills," or how the Exodus chapters were read.) Of course, Tobit's presence in p967 is merely speculative.

6.5. CONCLUSION

The codex of p967 bears witness to its reading community in numerous ways. As the preceding discussion revealed, the codex's production,

---

[228] For the connections, see Collins, *Daniel*, 205.
[229] Tobit 3:14–15 and 6:12 describe Sarah as "beautiful and God-fearing," a phrase used also of Susannah (Sus 2) and Esther (Esth 2:7, 20 in the LXX).

contents, notations, and reading marks reveal the character and interests of a Christian community of readers.

With a few caveats, I characterized the codex as Christian. The codex format and its use of contraction for the *nomina sacra* serve as the most widely regarded markers of Christian origin. Scattered textual variants and the larger Chester Beatty collection add support to the characterization. However, these features merely scratch the surface of the religious identity of the reading community. For instance, the contraction of πνευματα, the plural of πνευμα (spirit/wind), whatever it may be, cannot refer to the Trinity. Likewise, the demonstrated interest in the pogrom described in Esther 13 or life in Diaspora nations could indicate p967's function within emerging Jewish-Christian identities and relations.

Throughout the above discussion, I have used 'reading community' very loosely to refer to any number of p967's consumers. It is clear that some individual readers of p967 worked with a stylus in hand, not as scribes, but as active readers in the textuality of p967. These hands that held the styluses could reflect individual idiosyncrative reading/study practices, or could more closely represent authority readings within a worship context. Hence, the 'reading community' could refer to the congregations within which p967 circulated, or, at the other extreme, a diachronic Egyptian Christian tradition of reading. These types of distinctions cannot be determined from the individual marks on p967's pages, but would rather benefit from considerable comparative study.

Whomever it may represent, the marginal symbols and notations comprise one of the most definitive lenses into the religious ideas of the 'reading community.' The seven categories of marks saturate the pages, however unevenly, and indicate an active readership. Ezekiel's marginal words offer rare linguistic evidence for ancient practices of reading and interpretation. Six of the seven marginal notations in the Ezekiel portion coherently refer to themes in, or exegetical interpretations of, the content of their pages.[230] Of particular interest as regards the more general life of the codex, the theme of resurrection worked across the books. Both the marginal notation, αναστασεως at Ezek 37 and the hymnic section-marks of Dan 3 brought the theme to the fore. If it can be shown that indeed, the category 2 double hatch mark of Ezek 37 and the five (÷) marks in Dan 3

---

[230] The one exception, as indicated in §6.3.3.1.3 is the marginal notation in Ezek 32:30–33:8 on page 75.

mark liturgical sections, one can imagine the two texts being fruitfully read together.

Judging by the density of marks, both linguistic (category 1) and non-linguistic (categories 2–7), Ezekiel's temple generated the greatest interest. The interpretation of the temple bore both materialist and spiritual concerns, which I suggested, may relate to modes of patristic exegesis. The theme of economy, more strongly emphasized through the marginal annotation "(concerning) merchants," emerged in chs. 40–48 as well. Scattered marks beside verses about land allotments, just measures, and non-oppressive leadership suggest that p967's readers read their contemporary political life through the lens of temple-symbolism. Such materialist-historical concerns were also reflected in the fulfillment-interest pointed at Ezekiel 30's oracle against Egypt. In short, the historical nature and conditions of the Egyptian community that read and used p967 may be dimly reflected by this codicological analysis.[231] We see that Jewish prophecy concerning Egypt and the temple vision maintained some measure of symbolic significance for a 3rd century reading community.

Beyond the temple's symbolic meaning, its spiritual significance is apparent by the three marginal words at Ezek 43. The chapter describes the ritual of sanctifying the altar in preparation for the deity's return. This event was understood as symbolic of repentance. The return of the Lord was affirmed as central to this symbolic ritual. This text likely offered an important teaching about early Christian piety and the moral constitution of a religious person.

Few obvious material/scribal connections exist among the biblical books contained in the codex. The marginal marks across the codex appear consistent only within a particular book (so Esther's phrase breaks) and even within a singular passage (so the ÷ marks in Dan 3). Thus both according to paleography and reading marks, the books stand separately. The only exception is the theme of resurrection in Ezekiel and Daniel; however, the reading marks do not overwhelmingly point to their functional connection. Only the 5 letter in-line spaces, created during the inscription of Daniel, suggest that any intentional connection should be made between

---

[231] It should be pointed out that the interest in Egypt, characteristic of some of p967's marks, extends to the other LXX witnesses as well. Textual plusses at the start of Ezek 29:1 are consistent with Egyptian readers' interests and probably represent glosses that were incorporated into the front matter of the chapter. So φαραω βασιλει αιγυπτου in A^mg-410 534–306^mg, επι φαραω βασιλεα αιγθπτου βαβυλωνος in 130, επι φαραω ετει ι′ μηνι ι′ ημερα in α′ Q, and επι αιγθπτον και φαραω in Syh.

the two passages. This is all the more striking given the above discussion (§6.3.4) about the strong literary connections among the three books. The logic of p967's collected edition does not seem to lie in a functional explanation. There does not appear to have been a consistent readership or an official type of reading across the codex. Indeed, the paratextual elements, especially those in the margins, offer little indication, if there even was a note-worthy rationale, for why the three books came together in one codex.

The liturgical function proposal, explored above, does not seem to obtain for p967 as a whole. Indeed, it seems clear that p967 was used in more than one way. However, liturgical function may best explain the features of certain passages. A number of scholars have suggested a liturgical function for various features adduced throughout the discussion above: Fernandez-Galiano for marginal words, Hurtado for format, McGowan for hymns within etiological narrative sections, Westermann for imperative psalms, Stanley Porter for unit delimitation, and De Bruin for specific category 2 marks. However, the idiosyncratic presentation of the marks suggests personalized use; if liturgical, p967 was by no means an official guide to readings. The evidence mounted here for reading use may better support private study, devotion, or teaching functions. It could equally suggest a blurred line between liturgy and study in p967's reading community.

As Turner indicated, the marks in codices are often-times quite idiosyncratic and elusive.[232] The historian's reliance on analogical reasoning has not yet uncovered a system to the marks of our ancient readers. Certainly, evidence from parallel cases in other manuscripts may shed light on a reading practice that has gone unexplained here. However, I suspect that many of p967's marks are so idiosyncratic as to be lost to our modern capacities for observation and analysis, beyond the general reading function I assumed here. Additionally, a number of more specific functions could not be adequately explored. Choral marks, magical uses, and symbols for a separate commentary text or 'oral script' provide at least three additional lines of investigation into p967's otherwise un(der)explained marks.

---

[232] Turner, *Greek Papyri*, 116.

CHAPTER SEVEN

CONCLUSION

7.1. SUMMARY

The present study focused on p967 and MT as a variant literary editions of Ezekiel. The project, rooted in textual criticism, considered the way in which literary and text-critical methods work in tandem to answer questions about variant literary editions. Behind variant literary editions (in this case, MT and p967) lies a fluid textual tradition. Such fluidity raised questions about textual transmission and textual relationships as well as the nature of the sources that host our textual evidence. The project opened up these relevant areas of study in order to shed new light on the text, literary edition, and manuscript of p967.

7.1.1. *The Text of p967*

The text of p967 is extremely important for understanding the textual transmission and growth of Ezekiel. The earliest scholarship on p967's text concluded that p967 was perhaps the most important Septuagintal text for determining OG and its Hebrew *Vorlage*. This phase of research had a stronger basis in textual evidence than subsequent work (especially that of Ziegler). The textual analysis in chapter 4 largely supported this positive evaluation for p967's text, providing new evidence in four areas of textual study. First, p967 represents a strong witness to an alternate literary edition, affirming textual fluidity for Ezekiel's transmission history. In all the variants analyzed in this study, text-critical arguments for error did not withstand increased scrutiny. Hence, in the major variants originally identified by Lust, as well as many of its more minor details, p967's text cannot be dismissed as an accident of transmission history. Second, p967 and B, as the two earliest Greek witnesses to Ezekiel, continue to present a textual puzzle. Frequently, in the variants analyzed, the divergence between B and p967 likely arose from variant Hebrew texts or alternate interpretations of a Hebrew reading. While more focused attention to their relationship is still necessary, p967 and B's texts seem to be the result of the Greek tradition following closely beside a developing Hebrew text tradition.[1] Third, p967's textual status is more certain: p967's text lies impressively close to its Hebrew parent text. In fact, the evidence strongly suggests that p967 frequently reflects an early edition of a variant Hebrew text from MT. Fourth, MT often reflects a more developed textual stage of Ezekiel beyond that of the Old Greek.

From the textual conclusions reached in chapter 4, it is now essential that textual critics consider p967 as a witness to an early Hebrew text and to the Old Greek. As shown in chapter 2, several modern critical studies distanced p967's textual evidence from both Aleppo (MT) and B as less significant for the early stages of Ezekiel. This distancing may be the effect of one sole textual study: Floyd Filson's 1943 essay on 12:26–28 and 36:23c–38.[2] The timing of Filson's study, which established the basis for error in p967 especially in 12:24–26, perhaps led many scholars to over-generalize that p967 was full of errors and only significant to the later development in the Greek textual tradition.[3] As the present study showed, the case for error in 36:23c-38 is untenable, and Filson's evaluation in 12:26–28 is not as strong as was once assumed. Indeed, the weight of evidence supports p967's testimony to a text in which 12:26–28 did not occur. Moreover, several other evaluations for error in p967 minuses could not withstand greater scrutiny from multiple lenses of analysis. Hence, the scholarly *hesitation* to view p967's variants as important textual information for early stages of Ezekiel cannot persist. Perhaps this over-reaction against p967s text can also explain Lust and Crane's overstated embrace of p967's text. As shown in chapter 1, Lust and Crane swung the pendulum too far in the other direction, declaring p967's text to be earlier than the MT. Such a sweeping statement is not entirely accurate either: p967 and MT do not share text-types, and the diversion between p967 and B's text types point to the kind of continued study required. p967's text did, on occasion, show some development beyond that of the OG.

With appropriate words of text-critical caution, a modest claim is possible. p967's base text is, in many cases, closer to a shorter Hebrew parent text. This shorter text likely resembles the basis for many of MT's

---

[1] The study of p967's paragraphing, presented in chapter 6, afforded an additional piece of information that may shed light on the relationship between p967 and B. p967's 85 paragraphs showed 90% agreement with both the Hebrew (MT) and Greek traditions, indicating that p967 is most proximate to a common core. According to this angle of analysis, B represents a more developed text, with 180 paragraphs, over twice that of p967.

[2] Filson, "The Omission," 27–32.

[3] Filson's study was widely cited, for example, by Zimmerli, Tov, and Block, who all remained skeptical of p967's textual information. See chapter 1.

developments. This assertion is sufficiently general to allow, for example, the possibility that MT and p967's Hebrew *Vorlage* represent different attempts by scribes to affix ch. 37, chs. 38–39, and chs. 40–48 to the previous 36 chapters of the book. The assertion is also sufficiently cautious to retain the awareness that p967's text is, in a few cases, the more developed text beyond B, for instance in 35:8; 38:20; 38:18; and 39:4. Chapter 6 of the present study, which focused on p967's codex, underscores this point. p967 functioned as a copy of Ezekiel for a 3rd century audience, reminding us that every witness to a text is also a piece of functioning literature with potential actualizing touches within its text. As in the case of any manuscript, the p967 codex is not a neutral repository of textual information, any more than is the Masada copy of Ezekiel or the supposed excerpted texts of Ezekiel. For example, resurrection was important to the p967 scribal community, as indicated by the marginal notation "concerning resurrection" and the two unique in-line gaps at Ezekiel 37 and Daniel 3. While I do not attribute any text-critical significance to this fact, as discussed below (§7.1.3), the awareness of such material features remains essential to any abstract discussions of textual priority.

Beyond the conclusions just reached, this project highlighted two important areas of textual study that require further attention. First, a more thorough study of p967's relationship to B especially, as well as the other versions could bring additional clarity to the question of the Old Greek translation, inner-Greek transmissional issues, and the stages of development in the Hebrew text. Second, this study did not attempt to answer the specific arguments, set forth in chapter 2, about the linguistic non-homogeneity evidenced in the Greek witnesses. Thackeray and McGregor explained breaks in linguistic style as the work of different translators, whereas other scholars, such as Tov and Fernández-Marcos, proposed theories of revision.[4] Especially important to these theories is the section in chs. 26–39, demarcated by McGregor as S2. These chapters encompass the oracles against Tyre and Egypt and, especially in the case of Ezek 32:17–32, proved significant to the literary study of chapter 5. Indeed, McGregor's

---

[4] Tov, "The Relationship Between the LXX of Jer, Ez, and the MT," in *The Septuagint Translation of Jeremiah and Baruch: A Discussion of an Early Revision of the LXX of Jeremiah 29–52 and Baruch 1:1–3:8* (Missoula: Scholars Press, 1976), 135–155. Fernández-Marcos, "On Symmachus and Lucian in Ezekiel," in *Interpreting Translation: Studies on the LXX and Ezekiel in Honour of Johan Lust* (ed. F. García Martínez and M. Vervenne; Leuven: Leuven University Press, 2005), 153. Barthélemy provided a modest basis to attribute S2 to a kaige revision. Barthélemy, *Les Devanciers D'Aquila* (Leiden: Brill, 1963), 42–43 n4.

translation data includes some linguistic terms that were significant to
the present literary study, for example: (5.6) "prophesy and say to them"
(הנבא...ואמרת);[5] (5.17) "plunder" (בזז/בז); and (5.18) "plunder" (שלל). (see
Table V in the Appendix). A deeper study of linguistic non-homogeneity,
along the lines proposed here, will shed important additional light on p967's
text as well as on the textual history of Ezekiel.

7.1.2. *p967 and MT as Variant Literary Editions*

In addition to textual conclusions, the present study clarified the scope
and nature of the variants that distinguish p967 from MT as variant literary editions. Variants were grouped according to *Tendenzen* in order to
appropriate the principle of coherence from redaction criticism. The *Tendenzen* connected details across Ezekiel to four intertextual centers:

Intertextual Center	*Tendenzen*	Number of Variants
Ezekiel 12–13	'Prophecy' *Tendenzen*	87 variants
Ezek 32:17–32	'Fate of the Slain' *Tendenzen*	99 variants
Ezek 36:23c–38	*Tendenzen* Related to Ezek 36:23c–38	21 variants
Ezekiel 38–39	'Gog-Magog' *Tendenzen*: Variants Related to Ezekiel 38–39	49 variants

The four general *Tendenzen*, to varying degrees, furnished substantial sets
of coherent variants that can be used to distinguish the editions. First,
MT's plus at 12:26–28 was not an isolated variant. The content of the
verses enjoyed thematic intertextuality with several variants about prophetic temporality and the reliability/authority of Ezekiel's speech. MT
displayed variants in programmatic statements about prophecy and material that affected the temporal structure of the book. The tendency of MT's
edition towards increased precision about prophetic prediction provides
important evidential support for the intentionality of the plus at 12:26–28.
Within the intertextual center, Ezekiel 13 furnished additional variants
about the nature of prophetic speech. Consistent with the variants about
prophetic temporality, MT exhibited the edition with increased attention
to speech and prophetic speech formulae.

---

[5] McGregor, *The Greek Text of* Ezekiel, 110–111.

Second, the variants that fell into the 'Fate of the Slain' *Tendenzen* constitute considerable evidence for a thematic distinction between MT from p967. Frequently, MT's edition provided increased precision and detail about the nature and location of slain bodies. In these details, the variants clustered within the oracles about foreign nations, particularly in Ezekiel 32's pit. MT presented a more populous pit, with greater attention to shame and the circumcised status of slain bodies. Additionally, MT described Tyre's fate in the pit of the sea and the hordes of Egypt's fate in the pit (ch. 32:17–32) and in exile (29:19 and 30:4). It is possible, given the density the "hordes" *Tendenz* in chapter 7, that MT's edition forges a connection between the day of the Lord and the fate of the slain. However, since p967 is not extant in chapter 7, my conclusions about MT were more cautious. MT certainly displayed a concern for the day of the Lord (according to the variants in the 'Prophetic Temporality' *Tendenz*) and linked such details with the fates of various peoples. Finally, Israel's fate seems to have been in view in the details of MT's pot allegory (chapter 24,) particularly those variants about bones. These, as well as variants about 'death on the field,' present a reasonably strong connection to Israel's fate in Ezekiel 37 and the vision of the dried bones. Once again, MT's edition presents the increased details that would fix the interpretation of these visions of Ezekiel.[6] In contrast to all of these trends in MT, p967's edition furnishes fewer details about the precise nature and location of slain bodies, leaving its edition more open to multiple interpretations.

Third, Ezek 36:23c–38 did not generate coherence with as many variants as the above two *Tendenzen*. The variants about a new heart/spirit were exegetically ambiguous and occurred in p967 as well as MT. Perhaps the most striking feature of 36:23c–38 in MT (and its minus in p967) is the way in which it differently frames the event that would produce nation-recognition of Israel's deity. Certainly, the recognition formula, and the nation-recognition formula specifically, occurred in several variants (analyzed in the *Tendenz* about Prophetic speech.)

Fourth, the variants that fell into the 'Gog-Magog' *Tendenzen* extend the significance of chs. 38–39 in the two editions to other passages. The nations listed in Gog's entourage (Ezekiel 38) occur in MT variants elsewhere, for example, in Tyre's trade list of chapter 27. While few in number, the variants about plunder show MT's edition is more concerned with

---

[6] However, as noted in chapter 5, the variants in the "new life" *Tendenz* did not offer a striking scenario of differentiation between p967 and MT.

the fulfillment of the promise that Israel would not become plunder in the Gog-Magog invasion (see MT plus in 34:8). Most significantly to the 'Gog-Magog' *Tendenzen* are the word plays with the term "meshech" (משך). Of the three occurrences of the verb, two are in MT pluses (12:28 and 32:20). The lexical connection between Meshech's name (chapters 38–39) and the verb "to stretch out" form a suggestive link between MT's edition of chapters 38–39, its edition of the pit (Ezek 32:17–32), and its statements about prophecy and fulfillment (Ezek 12:26–28).

From the evidence, p967 and MT can be classified as variant literary editions of Ezekiel. To claim that p967 and MT are variant literary editions requires immediate specification and nuance since the two texts share tremendous amounts of material. The textual basis for their variance involves the gross differences present in Ezekiel 12–13, 32, and 36–39.[7] While one could limit the designation 'variant literary edition' to only these few passages, two points militate against this overly cautious option: 1) the content of Ezekiel 12–13, 32, and 36–39 impacts such larger issues as the book's vision of restoration, its structuring principle of prophecy, and its notion of enemy fate; and 2) variants in smaller details, coherent with these gross differences, cut across the book. With respect to the latter point, limiting the designation to only a few chapters would obscure the literary significance of the smaller variants in, for example, the oracles against Tyre. It is probably overstating the case to say that p967 and MT are variant literary editions of the oracles against Tyre. Nevertheless, textual variants in those passages *do* support differentiating features that are more pronounced elsewhere. Hence, designating p967 and MT variant literary editions captures the significance that such smaller details carry within the context of the two editions. To push the idea further, in the case of Ezekiel 24, it is *more* appropriate to talk about variant literary editions of the pot allegory. As argued in the conclusion to chapter 5, the allegorical genre would invest variants in descriptive detail in Ezekiel 24 with meaningful significance for interpretation. Lacking awareness of p967 and MT's status as variant literary editions, however, would obscure the significance of variants in Ezekiel 24. Adopting the designation 'variant literary edition' for the whole of p967 and MT alerts the exegete that textual variants may yield rich literary analysis within the context of the respective edition. Hence, we have in the Tyrian oracles and the pot

---

[7] Unfortunately, since p967 is not extant in chs. 1–11, ch. 7, which is variant between MT and LXX, cannot be included in this list.

allegory two different examples of how the designation 'variant literary edition' brings variants to light that would otherwise be obscured. On this last point, the designation 'variant literary edition' achieves an important methodological feat as well. Variants such as those in the Tyrian oracles and the pot-allegory have long been assessed according to textual criticism alone. Working against this methodological parochialism, the status 'variant literary edition' creates a methodological imperative to consider, not only textual information, but literary intertextuality, as this project has done throughout. For this methodological reason, as well as the other reasons listed above, we should appreciate p967 and MT as 'variant literary editions' of Ezekiel.

The variant literary editions of p967 and MT differ primarily in their views of restoration.[8] The different plot sequences for chs. 36–39 are only one aspect of the story. MT's variants about prophecy probably occupy a more prominent place in its edition of restoration than was previously given them.[9] Given its firm statements about prophecy's interpretation and fulfillment, MT presents a fixed vision of restoration. In this fixity, MT actualizes its visions of restoration; the visions cannot fulfill new potential applications. MT's treatment of משך especially captures this dynamic. In Ezekiel 12, MT declares that Ezekiel's visions would not "be delayed" any longer (משך). Then 'Meshech' is relegated to MT's pit in Ezekiel 32 and appears in the oracle against Tyre's trade list in 27:13. Finally, Gog-Magog is the chief prince of Meshech in chs. 38–39. In every instance where משך occurs, MT presents a variant or is the longer text. Hence, for MT, the invasion in chs. 38–39 is a fulfilled vision, new applications are arrested, and "Meshech" or 'prophetic delay' is forever relegated to the pit. In these details, this study simply deepens Lust's original conclusion that MT was the more historicizing edition of Ezekiel. However, this study places new significance on the role of prophecy-interpretation in distinguishing p967 from MT.

Lust's original theory also argued that p967 was the more apocalyptic of the editions. However, this second point cannot stand. MT displayed certain apocalyptic features not present in p967. In some cases, MT presented the *more* apocalyptic edition over p967, showing extensive variation in the apocalyptic pit, as well as the increased use of the eschatological phrase

---

[8] Ashley Crane's study is to be credited for identifying the importance of restoration, despite the study's limited scope.

[9] Lust suggested as much, though his work on MT's views about prophecy was limited to Ezek 12:26–28.

"on that day." Clearly, the temporal concerns revealed by comparing the two editions are more complex than Lust originally suggested. Lust's observations about p967's eschatological significance remain true, in the main. The chapter order in p967 *does* place the visions of chs. 37 and 40–48 at the end of the book, divorcing them from the 'plot' of restoration that culminates in chs. 38–39. Thus, as Lust suggests, p967's visions refer not to past events, but are projected forward into a post-exilic eschaton in which an ideal state is envisioned (chs. 40–48). Even though MT still exhibits the historicizing tendencies noted by Lust, it does so in conjunction with distinctive apocalyptic features.

The conclusions I am offering regarding apocalypticism and the interpretation of prophecy raise the question, originally posed by Lust, about sectarianism. Here at the end of the study, we are finally in a position to reconsider the possible effects of the Jewish sectarian debates of the Greco-Roman period on the transmission of Ezekiel. I have already expressed extreme caution in using these debates exclusively to *determine* textual evaluations about priority. However, the difference between the two editions do reflect known sectarian debates. In addition to Lust's original speculation about sectarian notions of Israel's national eschatology, the findings of this study show that opinions about prophecy differentiate the two editions, as well. Josephus tells us that the Pharisees, Sadducees, and Essenes held different opinions about divine determination, whether God's word determines the future or is contingent upon a freely unfolding future.[10] p967 and MT show signs of these known sectarian ideas. We could add that MT displayed a more dense interest in the death of specific national identities and may have had sectarian distinctions about outsiders and insiders in mind. Of course, these are by no means the only features that differentiated the two editions, as this study has shown, so one cannot conclude that an exclusive sectarian debate, as Josephus presents the sects, occasioned editorial activity in Ezekiel's textual transmission. Nevertheless, one feature of these two pieces of literature is their more general participation in sectarian types of discourses, some of which we know characterized the Second Temple Period.

Finally, Crane's assertion that MT's edition distinctively functioned to rally the troops does not seem correct. The question of Israel's military role in history rarely emerged as significant to the set of variants analyzed in this study. Military dynamics played a stronger role in MT's edition

---

[10] Josephus, *Antiquities* 13.171–73[13.5.9].

of the apocalyptic and *mythic* fate of Israel's enemies in the pit. While MT was certainly the more militaristic edition on this point, the military demise of enemy nations was theological; Israel played no role in their defeat. Hence, it is difficult to conclude from the evidence examined in this study, that MT calls Israel to arms.[11] Crane's case is already weak within the results of his own study. Crane places a great deal of emphasis on the variant in Ezekiel 37 where MT reads "army" (חיל) as opposed to p967's "congregation" (συναγωγη); These two terms, in both the Hebrew and the Greek, are not restricted to the denotations Crane supplies them. Indeed, even if these common translations are warranted, it is difficult to extend the significance of this detail to the much larger question of p967 and MT as variant literary editions! While the observation is interesting and important for Ezekiel 37, the variant appears to be an isolated feature and thus, generalization from it, without additional supporting evidence, is misleading.[12]

I suspect that chapters 40–48 are key to the final stages of Ezekiel's composition. While the present study did not endeavor to conduct redaction criticism *qua* redaction criticism, the nature of the textual evidence, as indicated in the introduction, resembles redaction-critical data. Hence, some speculation is warranted. It would seem that the redactional history of ch. 36, ch. 37, and chs. 38–39 is connected to the redactional history of chs. 40–48. For example, most scholars note the connection between 37:24–28 and chs. 40–48. Further, 36:17–23 and 38:14–16 invite similar conclusions. Finally, 37:1–12, ch. 43, and 36:23c-38's interest in a new heart may have been connected at one time. This is all very speculative. However, in the main, p967 represents something of the culmination of this compositional, redactional process. Its order, 36→38–39→37, was probably set when chs. 40–48 were affixed to the end of the book.[13] I see MT's alternate sequence as occasioned by a subsequent historical or even ideological moment in Second Temple Judaism. The flexible application of Ezekiel's visions, that was permitted by p967's edition and drove its compositional development, eventually reached a limit. MT represents

---

[11] Indeed, a variant in 43:2, outside the scope of Crane's study, involves military imagery that is unique to p967. p967 specifies that sounds of an "army (παρεμβολη)" accompany God's return to the temple; MT does not include the militaristic detail.

[12] Further, Crane is incorrect that p967 is the peaceful edition vis à vis MT's militaristic edition. I would suggest a potential military application of p967's edition related to the narrative in Second Maccabees.

[13] The somewhat similar Temple Scroll, dated to the 3rd, possibly the 4th century B.C.E. may reflect a contemporary interest to Ezekiel 40–48.

the text that sought to close Ezekiel's oracles and fix the historical plot to which they refer, simultaneously lacing the book with the insider/outsider distinctions we noted in chapter 5, particularly in the 'Fate of the Slain' *Tendenz*. It does seem possible to imagine sectarian debates about the interpretation of prophecy and divine determination contributing to the editorial activity.

7.1.3. p967's Literary Edition and its Codex

Having studied p967's unique literary edition as well as its reception in a 3rd century codex, this study is in a unique position to comment on diachronic interpretive issues. To what extent do p967's paratextual data generate interpretations consistent with p967's unique textual edition?

The paratextual marks in p967's codex maintain two large areas of continuity with p967's edition: the fulfillment or reuse of oracles and the new life offered in Ezekiel 37. First, several of p967's paratextual marks pointed to an interest in prophecy and fulfillment and further indicated a readership who reapplied Ezekiel's prophecies to its contemporary context. The notation at Ezekiel 30 that "God fulfills" (θ συντελει) is a clear indication that readers remained interested in the concept of fulfillment. Additionally, the paratextual marks indicated that p967's reading community reapplied several of Ezekiel's oracles about economics to its contemporary time. Such reapplication of Ezekiel's oracles could be found in the chapter on Tyrian trade and in the temple vision's economic details. p967's paratextual interest in fulfillment and the reapplication of prophecy echoes in p967's text vis-à-vis MT. Because MT's edition so frequently emphasizes the immediate fulfillment of Ezekiel's prophecies, by comparison, p967's edition lends itself to reapplication.[14] Thus, p967's reception is consistent with its literary edition on the matter of prophetic interpretation and fulfillment.

A second continuous feature in p967 is its view of the new life offered in Ezekiel 37. As argued in chapter 5, p967's variant literary edition lacked the details present in MT that would determine the identity of the bones in Ezekiel 37. In other words, p967's edition shows less fixity than MT in its interpretation of Ezekiel 37. Additionally, p967's edition positions the chapter right before the vision of chapters 40–48, thereby unifying the genre of the conclusion of the book: p967 concludes on a visionary and

---

[14] In light of this observation, it is probably significant that the marginal notation "God fulfills" (θ συντελει) occurs at the only undated oracle against Egypt.

not an historical plane. The effect of p967's edition of Ezekiel 37 not only lifts the event onto the same visionary plane as the temple vision, but also dislocates the event from the otherwise historically-oriented oracles of chs. 36 → 38–39 in the plot of restoration. Hence, the placement of Ezekiel 37 in p967 permits understanding its vision as applied to the realm beyond history, such as the eschaton. These features of p967's text invite or at least more easily allow for the later reading community to take Ezekiel 37 as a chapter about resurrection. The reading community's interest in resurrection not only focused on Ezekiel 37, but also highlighted the significance of resurrection in Daniel 3.

Discontinuities between p967's text and its paratextual information, however, also obtain on topics such as the temple, economic matters, and the recognition of God. First, the marks on the p967 codex showed substantial attention to Ezekiel's temple. By way of contrast, this study did not furnish unique variants related to the temple. p967's text did offer a different dating scheme than MT, dates which correlate with the destruction of the temple. However, p967 did not show marked textual variance in chs. 40–48 along any discrete *Tendenzen*. Hence, the codicological evidence for interest in the temple does not correlate with the same interest in p967's unique edition. Second, the paratextual density in passages about economic matters does not extend to p967's unique edition. p967's reading community showed a concern for merchants, for economic sin, excess, and injustice. These same themes did not characterize any of p967's textual variants. Third, p967's literary edition included a unique textual variant in Ezek 38:20 concerning the recognition of God. As argued in chapter 5, both the recognition formula and the nation-recognition formula proved exegetically meaningful for MT and p967's editions of Ezekiel. However, the paratextual marks in the p967 codex did not echo this concern.

In addition to the continuities and discontinuities between p967's text and the paratextual marks in its codex, a third type of diachronic observation presents a more puzzling picture. In the case of the topic of enemy fate, the paratextual marks in p967 exhibited interpretive themes consistent, not with p967, but with *MT's* edition. MT's unique literary edition showed considerable consistency in variants about the fate of slain enemies. This same concern occupied the readers of p967's codex. The paratextual notation at Ezekiel 30 highlighted the fate of Egypt. For the users of p967's codex, Egypt's fate seemed a matter of fulfilled prophecy.[15]

---

[15] As Eugene Ulrich pointed out to me, the readers' marks in 1QpHab and 1QIsaᵃ appear to have functioned similarly.

Specifically, Ezekiel 30 contains 'Day of the Lord' imagery, such as the phrase "day drawing near" and the coming of thick clouds. The biblical text on this leaf speaks about the sword, and culminates in 30:10–12 where a more specific oracle attributes Egypt's fate to Babylon. These themes did not characterize p967's unique edition, but could be found in MT variants. For example, MT pluses in 29:19 and 30:4 predict Nebuchadnezzar's destruction of Egypt's horde. In this and several other details, MT variants gave increased attention to the end of Egypt.

Similarly the fate of Tyre is a consistent theme between MT's edition and the paratextual marks in p967's codex. The paratextual notation at Ezek 28:9–19 likens the end of Tyre to the fate of merchants. In comparing the variant literary edition, it was MT, not p967, that showed an increased interest in Tyre's fate. For example, MT contained variants that would bring Tyre into closer association with Gog-Magog, adding Meshech to its trade list, and condemning it to the pit along the same lines as MT's edition of Ezekiel 32. Hence, MT's treatment of the end of Tyre corresponds to p967's paratextual interpretive interests.

The coherent topical interest in the fate of the slain exhibited between p967's paratextual marks and MT's unique edition is certainly curious. The phenomenon could bespeak a wider interpretive trend in the reception of Ezekiel, regardless of literary edition. The strength of an interpretive interest may transcend any specific text or edition. Indeed, this seems likely. However, the limited data set examined here requires these impression to remain suggestive. So while the shared interpretive trends in MT's edition and p967's paratextual marks cannot necessarily support larger claims about the interpretive reception of Ezekiel, the curious phenomenon does raise an important caution for how scholars use materialist philological information in study of variant literary editions. On the latter point, more needs to be said.

The continuities between p967's text and its paratext could represent important information for the textual analysis of p967. While I do not defend the following arguments, I consider them for argument's sake. So, for example, because p967's codex clearly exhibits an interest in Ezekiel 37 as a chapter about resurrection, one could argue that p967's chapter order was a late development, attributable to inner-Greek scribes with demonstrable interest in resurrection. Certainly, p967's paratextual notation at Ezekiel 37 cannot be ignored; it constitutes materialist information about the non-neutrality of the source that furnished us p967's unique text. Additionally, the five-letter in-line gap at Ezekiel 37, formed during scribal inscription, could support the theory for inner-Greek development.

However, several factors work against this conclusion. First, Ezekiel 37 was not the exclusive interest of p967's scribes; the chapter featured already in *Pseudo-Ezekiel*, pointing toward a vibrant interpretive tradition that grew up around the chapter, even among Hebrew scribes. Thus, p967's paratextual marks cannot be viewed as entirely unique or discontinuous with a wider, somewhat timeless interest in the chapter. Second, if the inner-Greek scribes responsible for p967 saw fit to alter the chapter order, we should expect to see additional coherent textual features across its unique text, which however, we did not find. Third, if we rely on p967's paratextual marks to explain *this* textual puzzle, we should expect to find a strong connection between p967's *other* paratextual features and p967's text, which again, we did not find. Thus, p967's non-neutral interest in resurrection does not seem, in this case, to explain p967's textual variance.

Indeed, while I affirm the non-neutrality of p967's manuscript, the total paratextual information does not present a clear picture. For example, the interest in the fulfillment of oracles presents complicated evidence for diachronic consistency between p967's edition and paratext. p967's edition is only open to the delayed fulfillment of oracles *in comparison* to MT's edition which is more emphatically against such delay. In other words, to say that p967's variant edition inherently promotes delayed fulfillment of Ezekiel's oracles is overstating the case. Of course, it is possible to argue that p967's edition is the result of scribes who wanted to *excise* passages about prophecy that presented ideas different from their interests. However, a brief survey of the high density and wide distribution of textual variants in MT (see chapter 5 §5.2.2) makes this proposal unlikely. Hence, in the case of prophecy and fulfillment, p967's paratextual information is only at best, an example of p967's openness to continued reapplication, and at worst, simply a coincidence.

The cautious approach, taken here, to using p967's paratextual information for text-critical conclusions is supported by the preceding discussion. Both the discontinuous trends between p967's text and paratextual marks, as well as the continuity demonstrated between MT's edition and p967's paratextual marks further underscore the complex relationship between p967's text and its life as a codex. Conclusions from codicology have a complex relationship to text-critical arguments. Instead, codicology more directly yields information about the interpretation of Ezekiel from a diachronic perspective.

7.2. SCRIBALISM AND VARIANT LITERARY EDITIONS OF
PROPHETIC BOOKS

Study of variant literary editions raises questions about the nature and
role of scribes in the production of biblical texts. As a final note, I want to
place this study on Ezekiel into a wider discussion of scribalism, particularly as it pertains to prophetic books.[16]

The issue of scribes' roles in the formation of prophetic books specifically, is by no means new to biblical studies.[17] However, recent scholarship
shifts the focus from the formation of a prophetic book *qua* book and onto
the role of scribes as interpreters and esoteric authors.[18] This shift can be
seen in the work of scholars like Wolfgang Lau and Burkhard Zapff who
talk about the composition of new prophetic texts as "scribal prophecy
(*schriftgelehrte Prophetie*)."[19] Similarly, Blenkinsopp talks about the "scribalization of prophecy."[20] Alongside this shift runs a parallel development in
Second Temple studies about prophecy, wherein the model of prophets as

---

[16] Ulrich notes that, for biblical books, and prophetic books particularly, "the pattern is
dynamic growth." This 'growth' requires a model of scribalism which would take interpretive
practices seriously. See the heretofor unpublished essay, shared with the author's permis-
sion. Ulrich, "Qumran Witness to the Developmental Growth of the Prophetic Books," 1.

[17] See Zimmerli, "From Prophetic Word to Prophetic Book," in *"The Place is too Small for
Us": The Israelite Prophets in Recent Scholarship* (ed., R.P. Gordon; trans., Andreas Köstenberger; SBTS 5; Winona Lake, Ind.: Eisenbrauns, 1995), 419–42; repr. from "Vom Prophetenwort zum Prophetenbuch," *TL* 104 (1979): cols. 481–96. For a literary/redactional approach
to the same question see David Petersen, *The Prophetic Literature: An Introduction* (Louisville: John Knox, 2002), 33–36. Petersen identifies four types of literary growth according to
prominent redactional theories in exemplary passages: "collecting," "commenting," "updating," and "linking." For a new take on this old question, see the recent essay by Michael H.
Floyd, "The Production of Prophetic Books in the Early Second Temple Period," in *Prophets, Prophecy, and Prophetic Texts in Second Temple Judaism* (eds., Michael H. Floyd, Robert
D. Haak; New York: T & T Clark, 2006), 276–297. In the specific case of Ezekiel, many
scholars find writing to be central to the production of the book. So Blenkinsopp, *Prophecy
and Canon: a Contribution to the Study of Jewish Origins* (South Bend: University of Notre
Dame Press, 1986), 71. See also Joachim Shaper, "The Death of the Prophet: The Transition
from the Spoken to the Written Word of God in the Book of Ezekiel," in *Prophets, Prophecy,
and Prophetic Texts in Second Temple Judaism* (eds., Michael H. Floyd, Robert D. Haak; New
York: T & T Clark, 2006), 63–79.

[18] See C.R. Matthews, "Appointing Desolation: Contexts for Interpreting Edom's Fate
and Function in Isaiah," in (ed., E.H. Lovering Jr.; SBLSP; Atlanta: SBL, 1995), 265. See also
Benjamin D. Sommer, *A Prophet Reads Scripture: Allusion in Isaiah 40–66* (Stanford: Stanford University Press, 1998), 23–25.

[19] Wolfgang Lau, *Schriftgelehrte Prophetie in Jes 56–66* (BZAW 225; Berlin: de Gruyter,
1994), 1–21. Burkhard Zapff, *Schriftgelehrte Prophetie—Jes 13 und die composition des Jesajabuches* (FB 74; Würzburg: Echter, 1995). See also O.H. Steck, *Studien zu Tritojesaja* (BZAW
203; Berlin: de Gruyter, 1991).

[20] Blenkinsopp, *Prophecy and Canon,* especially 71.

inspired messengers yields to the model of inspired *interpreters* of texts.[21] Increased interest in the *Pesharim* and citations of Israelite prophecy in texts like 1QS, CD, and the New Testament have put Israel's prophecy and Second Temple scribalism in a new and central light.

Michael Fishbane's voluminous work on inner-biblical exegesis is widely hailed as relevant to both developments in that he examines the phenomenon of interpretation within the context of scribal textual production. Fishbane included "mantological" interpretation among his three types of scribal modes of exegesis.[22] According to Fishbane's introductory remarks

> scribal practice provides the most concrete context for the transmission of a *traditum*... whatever the origins and history of our biblical materials, then, they became manuscripts in hands of scribes, and it is as such that we have received them.[23]

Study of variant literary editions of prophetic books should be included in the data set for such approaches to inner-biblical exegesis. However, it remains for text-critical scholars to refine our understanding of the roles and modes of scribalism in the production of variant literary editions.

Indeed, study of variant literary editions has occasioned further reflection on textual models of scribalism. While textual criticism traditionally conceives of scribes as 'transmitters' of the biblical text, variant literary editions cannot have been produced without some author-fuction within the textual tradition. The phenomenon of variant literary editions invites

---

[21] See William M. Schniedewind, *The Word of God in Transition: From Prophet to Exegete in the Second Temple* (JSOTSup 197; Sheffield: Sheffield Academic Press, 1995). See also Alex P. Jassen, *Mediating the Divine: Prophecy and Revelation in the Dead Sea Scrolls and Second Temple Judaism* (STDJ 68; Leiden: Brill, 2007). See also David Aune's "Charismatic Exegesis in Early Judaism and Early Christianity," in *Apocalypticism, Prophecy, and Magic in Early Christianity: Collected Essays* (WUNT 199; Tübingen: Mohr Siebeck, 2006), 126–150.

[22] Michael A. Fishbane, *Biblical Interpretation in Ancient Israel* (New York: Oxford University Press, 1984), 443–99. While Fishbane's category has been readily cited, scholars who have engaged the category find it to be inadequate to cover the range and types of interpretation found in prophetic books. See Matthias Henze, "Daniel and Jubilees," in *Enoch and the Mosaic Torah: the Evidence of Jubilees* (eds., Gabriele Boccaccini and Giovanni Ibba; Grand Rapids: Eerdmans, 2009), 53–66, esp. 61. Indeed, as Brevard Childs, in his review of the book, judiciously comments

> Perhaps because of the complexity of the material, this section [Mantological Exegesis] did not seem to me to carry the same compelling force as the earlier portions of the book.

Brevard S. Childs, "Review of Fishbane's *Biblical Interpretation*," *JBL* 106 (1987): 512.

[23] Fishbane, *Biblical Interpretation*, 23. For his entire discussion on scribalism and inner-biblical exegesis, see Ibid., 23–43.

a model of textual transmission whereby the text becomes an active site of scribal activity. As Tov advances

> It is assumed that large scale differences displaying a certain coherence were created at the level of the literary growth of the books by persons who considered themselves actively involved in the literary process of composition.[24]

Tov cites the principle of coherence, the same principle operating in chapters 3, 4, and 5. Such coherent large scale differences, according to Tov, are part of the literary growth of a text, albeit the latter stages of that growth. He calls those responsible for such coherence, "author-scribes," and identifies their role as the "last editors and the first scribes of transmission."

Unfortunately, however, textual criticism has not adequately developed a way to accommodate this model of scribal production. Traditional textual criticism frequently eschews issues of literary growth. For example, Tov comments that textual criticism's proper object of study is *transmission* and cannot be any stage of literary growth.[25] Tov certainly recognizes the issues of literary growth implied by the phenomenon of variant literary editions. For example, he speaks about a transitional phase between composition and transmission of a biblical book in which scribes inserted elements and became "small-scale partners in the creation of biblical books."[26] However, Tov's focus on the "creation of biblical books" enforces the concept of canon on period(s) in which the category did not yet exist or in a way in which it was not meaningful. Hence, textual criticism's task of eliminating the corruptive forces of transmission dominates the traditional model of textual criticism. Instead, with Ulrich, we must insist on a model of scribalism which affirms the "composition-by-stages" of ancient texts

> "composition-by-stages" is the method by which the Scriptures were produced from the beginning, and...for some of the latter stages we now have manuscript evidence documenting two or more *literary editions* of some of the biblical books.[27]

In this model, as Watts states about redactional studies in Jeremiah,

> redactional development and textual transmission overlap. One cannot distinguish them diachronically as if redactors first produced the finished

---

[24] Tov, *Textual Criticism of the Hebrew Bible*, 314.
[25] Tov repeatedly insists that content alterations are by definition secondary and therefor not the proper object of text-critical study. See Ibid., 258.
[26] Ibid., 314.
[27] Ulrich, *Dead Sea Scrolls*, 24–25.

text, which copyists then corrupted . . . textual history began long before its redactional history ended.[28]

In other words, scribes who affected changes and developments on their parent texts did so in tandem with their copying task. As Watts goes on to state,

> there is no evidence . . . to indicate that the editorial and duplicative tasks were sharply distinguished in the early period of textual transmission, much less assigned to different people.[29]

According to this model of scribalism, variant literary editions are the result of *both* a mechanical process of copying *and* an authorial function.

The 'composition-by-stages' model of scribalism prepares textual criticism to engage the larger question, raised initially, about the role of scribes in the transmission of prophetic books. It does so by affirming each stage of the text, as potentially revealing of distinctive scribal practices.

In the case of p967 and MT as variant literary editions, significant textual evidence points to the role that prophecy-interpretation played in distinguishing the editions. In most cases, MT's longer text reflected the type of 'scribalization of prophecy' of which Blenkinsopp speaks. MT's interest in fulfillment and prophetic speech even extends to its demonstrable interest in details about enemy fate and Israel's restoration. Only the text-critical model of composition-by-stages allows the scholar to appreciate the phenomenon of scribalization evinced in Ezekiel's textual evidence. The conclusions drawn in this study produce a new sphere of evidence for the activity of scribes, ripe for comparison with Second Temple interpretation and reception of prophecy.

---

[28] James Watts, "Text and Redaction in Jeremiah's Oracles," 437. Making a similar point about redaction and transmission, Kristen de Troyer notes that the Bible itself is the product of redactional activity and is thus, rewritten in a very important sense. De Troyer, *Rewriting the Sacred Text,* 1.

[29] Watts, "Text and Redaction in Jeremiah's Oracles," 438. Watts is indebted to Michael Fishbane who wrote before Tov's *Text Criticism of the Hebrew Bible*, and who works out of a premise quite different from Tov. Fishbane focuses on editorial features of inner-biblical and post-biblical exegesis. He attends to, among other things, scribal techniques and transmission process. Fishbane maintains a broad definition of the transmission process to include everything from the updating of traditions to the copying of texts. Fishbane, *Biblical Interpretation*, 23, 31–32, 37. Kristen de Troyer mounts a similar plea in *Rewriting the Sacred Text.*

APPENDIX

---

[1] Chapsters 38–39 come before chap. 37 in p967^Sch.

[2] p967^Mad does not include chaps. 38–39 since they are transposed and appear in p967^Sch.

p967^Köln   *Der Griechische Text des Buches Ezechiel: Nach dem Kölner Teil Papyrus
967*
P. Leopold Günther Jahn
(1972)
- Transcription of chaps. 11:25–21:14; 25:5–26:9; 43:9–48:35 with criti-
cal apparatus
- Description of Papyrus
- Rendition of Text and Critical Apparatus
- List of homoioteleuta readings
- List of readings according to Hexaplaric marks
- Notes to more important readings

TABLE II: ALIGNMENT OF P967 AMONG THE GREEK VERSIONS

p967^CB

Kenyon's enumeration of agreement/disagreement with p967^CB :[3]
   Variants from A: 121   Agreements with A: 56
   Variants from B: 34   Agreements with B: 142
   Variants from Q: 76   Agreements with Q: 100
   Variants from Γ: 4   Agreements with Γ: 13

Payne's enumeration of agreement/disagreement between p967^CB and B:[4]
   with A: 42
   with B: 32
   with Q: 30

Payne's enumeration of agreement between the miniscules and p967^CB
   against B:[5]

I (Egyptian)	1
II (Palestinian)	4
III(Antiochian)	4
I, II	7
I, III	5
II, III	4
I, II, III	16
Misc. Mss.	17

---

[3] Kenyon, Chester Beatty, x.
[4] Payne does not collate Γ since it is minimally extant. Payne "The Relationship," 256.
[5] The miniscule groups are according to Procksch. See Payne for more detailed assessment of the conclusions of Procksch and Gehman about the miniscule categories. Payne,
"The Relationship," 257–258.

p967^Sch

JGK's enumeration of agreement and disagreement:[6]
    Variants from A: 441   Agreements with A: 95
    Variants from Q: 197   Agreements with Q: 39
    Variants from B: 129   Agreements with B: 168

p967^Köln   No such figures available

p967^Mad   No such figures available

TABLE III: DIAGRAMS OF GREEK TEXTUAL HISTORY

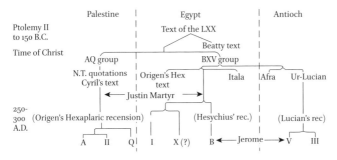

Payne's Diagram of LXX Ezekiel with p967 (Beatty text)[7]

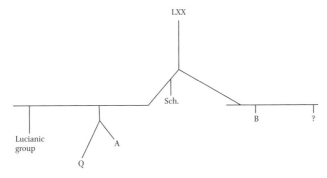

Gehman's Diagram of LXX Ezekiel with p967 (Sch.)[8]

---

[6] Johnson, Gehman, and Kase, *The John H. Schiede Biblical Papyri*, 33.
[7] Payne, "The Relationship," 265.
[8] Gehman, "The Relations Between the Text of the John H. Schiede Papyri and that of the Other Greek MSS. of Ezekiel," *JBL* 57 (1938), 286.

Table IV: Ziegler's 1977 Text Groups

B-Texts[9]
B—Codex Vaticanus (4th century)
967—(3rd century)
988—Antinoopolis Papyri (4th century)[10]

A-Texts
A—Codex Alexandrinus (4th–5th centuries)
26—(10th century)
106—(14th century)
410—(13th century)
544—(11th century)

Hexaplaric Texts
Q—Codex Marchalianus (6th century)
88—(10th century)
Syh—Codex Syrohexaplaris (8th century)
62—(11th century)
147—(12th century)
407—(9th century)
922—(3rd–4th centuries)

L-Group
22—(11th–12th centuries)
36—(11th centuries)
48—(10th–11th centuries)
51—(11th century)
96—(11th century)
231—(10th—11th centuries)
763—(11th century)
311—(12th century)
538—(12th century)
V—Codex Venetus (8th century)
46—(13th–14th centuries)
449—(10th–11th centuries)
Z^V—Codex Zuqninensis (6th–8th centuries)
456—(11th century)

---

[9] Ziegler also includes the Latin, Coptic and Old Latin quotations in the B-Group. ("La Co altlat. Zitate") Ziegler, *Ezechiel* (1952) 23.

[10] C.H. Roberts, (ed) *The Antinoopolis Papyri. Part I* (London: London Egypt Exploration Society, 1950), S. 19–23 Nr. 10. Ziegler did not have access to these fragments until after he had completed his work on Ezekiel. Thus, he published the collation of variants in 1954 in *Susanna, Daniel, Bel et Draco* (ed. Ziegler; *Septuaginta Gottingensis* XVI, 2, Göttingen 1954), S. 77–78.

Catena group
  87—(10th century)
  91—(11th century)
  490—(11th century)
  49—(11th century)
  90—(11th century)
  764—(13th–14th centuries)
  130—(12th–13th centuries)
  233—(10th century)
  534—(11th century)

Mixed Codices
  86—(9th–10th centuries)
  198—(9th century)
  239—(written in 1046)
  306—(11th century)
  380—(12th century)
  393—(8th century)
  403—(written in 1542)
  611—(16th century)
  613—(13th century)
  710—(10th century)
  927—Codex Melphictensis rescriptus (6th century, rewritten in 11th–12th centuries)

TABLE V: MULTIPLE TRANSLATOR THEORY
SELECT DATA FROM MCGREGOR'S 1985 STUDY

	English / Hebrew	S1 (chs. 1–25)	S2 (chs. 26–39)
5.1–3	you will know that	(επι) γινωσκειν διοτι	γινωσκειν οτι
5.1	I am Yahweh[11]	/ οτι	εγω ειμι xxxx
5.2	....	εγω xxxx	....
5.3	יָדַע	....	γινωσκειν
	כִּי	(επι) γινωσκειν	οτι
	אֲנִי (יהוה)	διοτι / οτι	εγω ειμι xxxx
		εγω xxxx	

---

[11] McGregor, *The Greek Text of Ezekiel*, 97–100. This evidence was adduced by Thackeray but his primary witness, B evinced the break at 26:6 / 28:23. However, p967 reads εγω ειμι at 26:6, and thus supports the break at the end of ch. 25. The Zeigler text reads with B in this instance, not having p967 at his disposal.

Table (*cont.*)

	English / Hebrew	S1 (chs. 1–25)	S2 (chs. 26–39)
5.4	sword (חרב)[12]	ρομφαια	μαχαιρα
	(to fall) by the sword[13]	εν ρομφαια	μαχαιρα (in the dative case)
5.5	(he) said to (me)[14] (אמר אל/ל)	(speaking verb) + προς	(speaking verb) + dative case
5.6	prophesy and say to them[15] (הנבא...ואמרת)	impv. + future	impv. + impv.
5.7	iniquity/sin (עון)[16]	αδικια	Inconsistent (αδικια, ανομια, ασεβεια, αμαρτια)
5.8	people (עם)[17]	λαος	εθνος
5.9	assembly (קהל)[18]	οχλος	συναγωγη
5.10	scatter (זרה)[19]	διασπερω / διασκορπιζω / σκορπιζω	λικμαω
5.11	be scattered (פוץ in the Hiphil)[20]	διασκορπιζω	διασπερω
5.12	devestation, waste (שממה)	αφανισμος	απωλεια / ερημος / ηφανισμη[21]
5.13	sin (רשע)	ανομος (λοιμος in one case)	αμαρτωλος / ασεβεια / ανομος
5.17	plunder (בז/בזז)	διαρπαζειν / διαρπαγη (spelling?)	προνομη / σκυλευσει

[12] Ibid., 101–105. Sword is used as synedochy to express the violent retribution which will befall Israel. McGregor does not see any contextual cause for the lexical variation in the Greek term. χιφος appears in 16:40 and 23:47 but the context is shared—the slaughter of an adulterous woman. According to O'Connell (1972:288) the Kaige used ρομφαια and Aquila and Symmachus used μαχαιρα. Ibid., 105.

[13] Ibid., 104–105.

[14] Ibid., 105–110. The sections are not totally consistent. προς was used with the first person pronoun in all three sections (*i.e.* S2 has προς με where we would expect μοι in 37:3, 4, 9, 11, 18). Thus, this constitutes weak evidence. Ibid., 109–110.

[15] Ibid., 110–111.

[16] Ibid., 111–113.

[17] Ibid., 113–116. S2 only but not always uses ethnos "in contexts where there is a strong sense of foreignness." Otherwise, λαος does stand in when Israel as "my people" is rendered. Ibid., 116. "Cf. Turner (156:16)".

[18] Ibid., 116–117.

[19] Ibid., 118–119.

[20] Ibid., 119–120. The Hifil is the only stem which exhibits consistency. The Qal and Nifal are mixed with no distinction between the sections.

[21] This unique form in 36:34 is in 36:23c–38.

Table (*cont.*)

	English / Hebrew	S1 (chs. 1–25)	S2 (chs. 26–39)
5.18	plunder (שלל)	σκυλα	προνομευω / σκυλευω
5.23	possession (מורשה)	κληρονομια	κατασχεσις
5.24	ruins (חרבה)	ερημος	ερημος / ερημοω (verb—spelling?)

TABLE VI: TEXTUAL LEMMATA IN CANONICAL ORDER

4:4 πεντηκοντα και εκατον Z rel. (obel. *O*) (967 not preserved)] ενενηκοντα και εκατον
O Q^mg-147 538 534–239'-710 | ενενηκοντα και τριακοσιας 410 |
(minus) *C'* = MT

4:5 ενενηκοντα και εκατον Z rel. (967 not preserved)] ενενηκοντα και τριακοσιας *C'*-403'
410 Hi. = שלש מאות ותשעים MT

4:6 το δεξιον Z rel. (967 not preserved)] το δεξιον (obel. *O*) δευτερον *O*-62 Arm = הימיני
שנית MT ≈ *L''*-311 Tht. 147'

7:12 (minus) ZB La^S Co Aeth (967 not preserved)] (ast. *O*) οτι οργη εις παν το πληθος
αυτης rel. = כי חרון אל כל המונה MT

7:13 (minus) ZB 233 La^S Co Hi.(967 not preserved)] (ast. *O* 86') και ετι εν ζωη το ζην
αυτων οτι ορασις εις παν το πληθος αυτης ουκ ανακαμψει rel. ≈
α'σ'θ' = ועוד בחיים חיתם כי חזון אל כל המונה לא ישוב =
MT

7:14 (minus) ZB La^S Co Hi. (967 not preserved)] (ast. *O* 86 449) και ουκ εστι(ν) πορευομενος
εις τον πολεμον οτι η οργη μου εις παν το πληθος αυτης rel. =
ואין הלך למלחמה כי חרוני אל כל המונה MT

8:18 (minus) ZB La^S Hi.(967 not preserved)] και κεκραξονται εις τα ωτα καλεσουσιν εν
τοις ωσιν μου φωνη μεγαλη και ου μη εισακουσω αυτων *L*-311-
V-46-Z^V Tht. | (ast. *O*) και καλεσουσιν εν τοις ωσιν μου φωνη
μεγαλη και ου μη εισακουσω αυτων ≈ rel. = וקראו באזני קול
גדול ולא אשמע אותם MT

12:26 (minus) 967] και εγενετο λογος κυριου προς με λεγων Z rel. = ויהי דבד יהוה
אלי לאמר MT

12:27 (minus) 967] υιε ανθρωπου ιδου οικος ισραηλ ο παραπικραινων λεγοντες
λεγουσιν η ορασις ην ουτος ορα εις ημερας πολλας και εις καιρους
μακρους ουτος προφητευει Z ≈ rel. ≈ בן אדם הנה בית ישראל
אמרים החזון אשר הוא חזה לימים רבים ולעתים רחוקות
הוא נבא MT

12:28 (minus) 967] δια τουτο ειπον προς αυτους ταδε λεγει κυριος ου μη μηκυνωσιν
ουκετι παντες οι λογοι μου ους αν λαλησω λαλησω και ποιησω
λεγει κυριος Z ≈ rel. ≈ לכן אמר אליהם כה אמר אדני יהוה
לא תמשך עוד כל דברי אשר אדבר דבר ויעשה נאם אדני
יהוה MT | δια τουτο ειπον προς αυτους ταδε λεγει κυριος (om.
ου μη μηκυνωσιν—*fin.*) 410
(minus) 967 410] ου μη μηκθνωσιν Z rel. = לא תמשך

13:2   προφητευσεις 967 (obel. *O*) Z B Sa Hi.] (ast. *O*) τους προφητευοντας rel. =
       הנבאים MT

       προς αυτους 967 (obel. O) ZB Sa Hi.] (ast. O) τοις προφηταις τοις
       προφητευουσιν απο καρδιας αυτων rel. θ'α' ≈ לנביאי מלבם MT
       | אליהם לנביאי מלבם HUBP[III-96]

13:3   προφητευουσιν 967 Z rel. (recon. הַנְּבִיאִים)] הַנְּבִיאִים MT
       απο καρδιας αυτων 967 Z rel.] (ast. *O*) τοις πορευομενοις οπισω του πνευματος
       αυτων *O'L"* 403 410 Arm Or. Tht. ≈ הנבלים אשר הלכים אחר
       רוחם MT

13:7   (minus) ZB Sa Hi.[(967 not preserved)]] (ast. *O*) και ελεγετε φησι(ν) κυριος και εγω
       ουκ ελαλησα Q θ' ≈ A Arab rel. = ואמרים נאם יהוה ואני לא
       דברתי MT

16:30 την θυγατερα 967 Z ≈ rel. (recon. לְבִתֵּךְ)] την καρδιαν *O* (Syh[txt])-62' *L"* Tht.
       Or.[lat]VIII400.401 Hi. = לְבָתֵּךְ MT | *testamento* Bo (διαθηκη)
       Arab

16:44 ταυτα εστιν 967 Z rel.] הנה MT

16:59 (minus) 967 Z rel.] (ast. *O*-Q) οτι *O*-Q-62 Arm = כי MT | *propter quod*
       Or.[lat]
       (minus) La[C]] ταδε λεγει κυριος Z rel. = כה אמר אדני יהוה MT

17:9   δια τουτο 967 Z rel.] (minus) MT

17:12 οταν 967 Z Syh[mg] rel.] ιδου Q[mg]-Syh *L"* Chr.II 193 Tht. 86 α'σ'θ' = הנה MT

17:22 κορυφης 967 B La[C] Bo Arab Cyr.II372 Or.[lat]VIII438 Spec.Hi.[test]] κορυφης +
       (ast. *O* 86 Hi.) και δωσω απο κεφαλης παραφυαδων αυτης ≈ rel.
       = ונתתי מראש ינקותיו MT
       καρδιας αυτων 967 Z rel.] εκ καρδιας κορυφης αυτης *L"* Tht. | ינקותיו רך
       MT

17:23 και τα κληματα αυ]του αποκ[ατασταθησεται] 967 ≈ (obel. *O* Hi.) Z rel.]
       (minus) 764 = MT

18:32 (minus) 967] λεγει κυριος ZB La[S] Co rel. = נאם אדני יהוה MT
       (minus) 967 ZB La[S] Co Arab Hi.] (ast.O) και επιστρεψατε και ζησατε ≈ rel.
       = השיבו וחיו MT | והשיבו וחיו MT | επιστρεψατε και ζησατε 534 =
       HUBP[III-96-150] | ως το επιστρεψαι αυτον απο της οδου αυτου της
       πονηρας και ζην αυτον λεγει αδωναι κυριος και επιστρεψασται
       και ζησεται επιστρεψατε ουν και ζησατε ≈ *L"* Arm Tht. 62

20:5   (minus) 967 534 106] λεγων εγω κυριος ο θεος υμων Z rel. = לאמר אני
       יהוה אלהיכם MT

20:6   τη χειρι μου αυτω̣ν̣ τ̣ου εξαγαγειν 967 534 106] [(v 5)] τη χειρι μου αυτων λεγων
       εγω κυριος ο θεος υμων [(v 6)] εν εκεινη τη ημερα αντελαβομην τη
       χειρι μου αυτων του εξαγαγειν Z rel. = MT

20:24 καρδιων αυτω(ν) 967 147' 407 106 (*cordis* Ir.[lat])] πατερων αυτων Z rel. =
       אבותם MT

20:26 (minus) 967 ZB La[CS] Sa Iust.Hi.[test]] (ast. O) ινα γνωσιν οτι εγω κυριος rel. =
       למען אשר ידעו אשר אני יהוה MT

20:33 δια τουτο 967 Z rel. (obel. *O*)] (minus) 62 Tyc. = MT

21:2(7) δια τουτο προφητευσον υιε ανθρωπου 967 Z rel.] υιε ανθρωπου δια τουτο
       προφητευσον A"0239'-403' Bo Arab | δια τουτο υιε ανθρωπου
       προφητευσον La[S] Tyc. | υιε ανθρωπου *O*-Q-147 *C"*-86' 106 = בן
       אדם MT

και προφητευσον επι 967 26' 147' Hi. = וְהִנָּבֵא אֶל MT] και προφητευσον
περι L'⁻⁴⁴⁹ Tht. | και προφητευσεις επι Z rel.

21:3(8) (minus) 967 48 C'-233 544 Sa Tyc.] και ερεις προς την γην του ισραηλ Z rel.
= וְאָמַרְתָּ לְאַדְמַת יִשְׂרָאֵל MT

τάδε λεγει κς 967 Bᵐᵍ rel. (ast. Q) = כֹּה אָמַר יְהוָה MT] (minus) Z Bᵗˣᵗ 106
| כֹּה אָמַר אֲדֹנָי יְהוָה HUBPᴵᴵᴵ⁻³⁰, ⁹³, כֹּה אָמַר אֲדֹנָי יְהוָה HUBPᴵᴵᴵ⁻¹⁵⁰ |
⁹⁶, G-BEb 22

ιδου εγω 967 Z rel. = הִנְנִי MT] (minus) Bᵗˣᵗ

21:12 παν π̅ν̅α̅ (πνευμα) 967 = כָּל רוּחַ MT] (obel. O) πασα σαρξ και παν πνευμα
Z rel. | παν πνευμα πασα σαρξ 62

22:13 εαν δε 967 Z rel.] ιδου ουν L'³⁶ Tht. ≈ הִנֵּה HUBPᴵᴵᴵ⁻¹⁵⁰ | και ιδου θ' 86 = וְהִנֵּה
MT | ecce Arm | et ego Arab

επαξω 967 ZB V] παταξω rel. ≈ εκροτησα θ' 86 = הִכֵּיתִי MT

χειρα μου προς χειρα μου 967 Z rel.] χειρα μου B V 490 Co = כַּפִּי MT

22:15 η καρδια σου 967] η ακαθαρσια σου Z rel. = טֻמְאָתֵךְ MT | (minus)
HUBPᴵ⁻Peshitta

22:27 (minus) 967 rel.] (ast. O) του απολεσαι ψυχας O' III Arm. Tht. = לְאַבֵּד
נְפָשׁוֹת MT (pr. copula HUBPᴵᴵᴵ⁻¹⁵⁰) | נֹקִי לְאַבֵּד נְפָשׁוֹת
HUBPᴵᴵᴵ⁻⁹⁶

22:28 αλειφοντες αυτους 967 Z rel.] ηλειφον αυτους Q ≈ טָחוּ לָהֶם MT | חֹזוּ לָהֶם
HUBPᴵᴵᴵ⁻⁹⁶

πεσουνται 967 Z rel. (recon. יִפֹּלוּ)] αναρτυτω πεσουνται Qᵐᵍ III (recon.
תִּפֹּל יִפֹּלוּ) | (ast.ˢᵘᵇ Q) πηλω Q = תָּפֵל MT

23:38 (minus) 967 Z rel. ≈ cII-239' ll 26' 544 Cyr.] (ast. O) εν τη ημερα εκεινη O'
III Arm Tht. Qᵗˣᵗ 86 = בַּיּוֹם הַהוּא MT

23:39 (minus) 967 Z rel.] (ast. O) εν τη ημερα εκεινη O' V-449 Aeth Tht. α'σ'θ'
Qᵗˣᵗ 86 = בַּיּוֹם הַהוּא MT | αφυλακτως 26' 239' 403' 410 544 |
αφυλακτως εν τη ημερα εκεινη A

24:2 γραψον εκει σεαυτω εις ημεραν 967] γραψον σεαυτω εις ημεραν Z rel. |
γραψον σεαυτω το ονομα της ημερας III Tht. = כְּתָב לְךָ אֶת
שֵׁם הַיּוֹם MT cf. omnia (nomen?) in diem Laˢ

απο της ημερας ταυτης 967 Z rel.] ταυτης 449 Tht. | אֶת עֶצֶם הַיּוֹם הַזֶּה
MT

απο της ημερας της σημερον 967 Z rel.] απο της ημερας ταυτης σημερον L'³⁶
≈ בְּעֶצֶם הַיּוֹם הַזֶּה MT | (minus) 46

24:4 και εμβαλε 967 Z rel.] אֱסֹף MT

εξεσαρκισμενα απο των οστεων 967 ≈ Z rel.] מִבְחַר עֲצָמִים MT
(minus) 967 Z rel.] πληρη 62 θ' (recon. הַמַּלֵּא) | (ast) πληρης α' | πληρωσον
σ' = מַלֵּא MT | מַלְּאוּ HUBPᴵᴵᴵ⁻⁸⁹

24:5 υποκαιε 967 Z rel.] דּוּר MT

τα οστα 967 Z rel. = הָעֲצָמִים MT] הָעֲצוּמִים HUBPᴵᴵᴵ⁻⁹⁶

24:9 (minus) 967 ZB ll Laˢᵂ Sa] (ast. O) ουαι πολις των αιματων rel. = אוֹי עִיר
הַדָּמִים MT

δαλον 967 Z rel.] λαον B 130 Laˢ | מְדוּרָה MT | תַּבְרָה HUBPᴵ⁻Tar | מַעֲמָרָא
HUBPᴵ⁻Peshitta

24:10 τα ξυλα 967 Z rel. = הָעֵצִים MT] הָעֶצֶם HUBPᴵᴵᴵ⁻⁹³ ≈ ossa Vul.
(minus) 967 ZB ll 106 Laˢᵂ Co Ambr.] (ast.O) και τα οστα συνφρυγησονται
rel. = וְהָעֲצָמוֹת יֵחָרוּ MT

24:11 ανθρακας 967 ZB *ll* La^SW Co] ανθρακας (ast. *O*) αυτης rel. = גחליה MT
(minus) 967 ZB *ll* La^SW Co] (ast. *O*) αυτης εξηψηθη Q V-46 *C'*-86'-239'-403'
106' 544 Aeth ≈ A' *O'*^Q 48–449 130–233 Arm. Tht.Hi.| κενη
εξηφθη *L*^-36 48 cf.^MT | רקה MT (= κενη)

24:14 διαστελω 967 Z rel.] אפרע MT | אמנע TarJ | Peshitta | אגרע HUBP^III-96
ουδε μη ελεησω 967 Z rel.] ου φεισομαι ουδε μη ελεησω *L* 86 | ουδε μη
ελεησω (ast. *O*) ουδ ου μη παρακληθω *O'*-62 Arm Hi. ≈ ουδε
φεισομαι και ου μη παρακληθω 62 *III* Tht. ≈ אחוס ולא אנחם
ולא MT | ולא אחוס ולא ארחים HUBP^I-TarJ (cf. ולא ארחם
HUBP^I-Peshitta)
δια τουτο 967 Z (obel. *O* Hi.)] (minus) MT
(minus) 967 Z rel.] ιδου Q 26 Tht. | (minus in context) MT
εγω κρινω σε κατα τα αιματα σου και κατα τα ενθυμημ*α*τα σου κριθησει λεγει
κς η ακαθαρτος η ονομαστη και πολλη του παραπικραινειν 967
≈ Z rel. (obel. *O* Hi.)] η ακαθαρτος η ονομαστη και πολλη του
παραπικραινειν *ll* 764 La^S | (minus) MT
κριθησει λεγει κς 967] κρινω σε Z rel. | (minus) La^W | (minus in context)
ll 764 La^S = MT

24:27 (minus) 967] εν εκεινη τη ημερα ZB *L''* La^CS Tht. | εν τη ημερα εκεινη rel. =
ביום ההוא MT

25:7 (minus) 967 ZB 87 *L'*^-36 La^C Bo] (ast. *O*) ιδου εγω rel. = הנני MT

25:15 οτι 967] δια τουτο Z rel. | (minus) 106 147 239 *III* Bo Aeth Tht. = MT

26:1 δεκατω 967 538 *cII*-86 26 544 Bo] ενδεκατω Z rel. = עשתי עשרה MT |
δωδεκατω A

26:10 εκ πεδιου 967 Z rel. (recon. (מִבְקָעָה)] מִבְקְעָה MT
απο πληθους 967 ≈ Z rel.] משפעת MT | מרפסת Tar ≈ HUBP^I-Peshitta (HUBP^V-
שפע-II, 'stamp (hoofs)')

26:12 και σκυλευσει 967 Z rel. ≈ ובזזו MT
τον πλουτον σου 967 A''-106' Arab] τα υπαρχοντα Z rel. | רכלתך MT

26:20 μη δε αναστα*θ*ης 967 Z ≈ μη δε αναστης B *III* Tht.] ונתתי צבי MT | תשב צבי
HUBP^III-30(pm) 89(pm)
επι ^της ζωης 967 *ll* 91-764] επι γης ζωης Z ≈ rel. = בארץ חיים MT

26:21 ετι 967 ZBL La^CW Co Arab] ετι (ast) και ζητηθηση και ουχ ευρηθηση (+ ετι
62) rel. = ותבקשי ולא תמצאי עוד MT

27:12 απο πληθους πασης ισχυος σου 967 Z rel.] απο πληθους πασης δυναμεως σου
III Tht. | מרב כל הון MT

27:13 και συμπασα ^και τα παρατεινοντα 967 Z rel. (recon. συμπασα ≈ (הכל or תֵּבֵל]
και μοσοχ και θοβελ 87–91 86 α'σ' ≈ (tr.) תֵּבֵל ומשך MT (תובל
HUBP^III-30 96 150)

27:15 ροδιων 967 Z rel.] αραδιων A''-106 | drn HUBP^I-Peshitta | δαδαν 86 α'σ'θ' Hi. =
דדן MT

27:16 ανθρωπους 967 Z rel. (recon. (אָדָם)] ארם MT | (εδωμ) HUBP^I-Peshitta (recon.
(אָדָם
απο πληθους του συμμεικτου σου 967 Z rel.] מרב מעשיך MT | מרב כל הון
HUBP^III-30

27:18 εκ πληθους δυναμεως σου 967 Q 233 Arab] εκ πληθους πασης δυναμεως
σου Z rel.| (ast. *O'*^Syh) εν πληθει εργων σου εκ πληθους πασης

δυναμεως σου O' L' Tht. Hi. = ברב מעשיך מרב כל הון MT | מרב ברב ≈ HUBP^{III-30 ≈ 93}

27:23 (minus) 967 ZB L' Co Arab] (ast. O) και δαιδαν rel. (recon. ודדן) | ועדן MT (= edne Hi.)

ουτοι εμποροι σου 967 ZB L' Co Arab = (obel. Syh)] ουτοι εμποροι σου (ast. O^{-Q}) σαβα O^{-Q}62—› α'σ'θ' 86 (sabba Hi.) cf.^{MT} | רכלי שבא MT (שבה HUBP^{III-96})

27:25 εν τω πληθει 967 Z rel.] εν αυτοις καρχηδονιοι Q^{mg} | εν τω πληθει εμποροι σου O' 106 Aeth Arab Arm | (minus) MT

27:32 (minus) 967 ZB Co Arab Tyc.Hi.^{test}] (ast. O) τις ωσπερ τυρος κατασιγηθεισα εμμεσω θαλασσης ≈ rel. = מי כצור כדמה בתוך הים MT

27:33 απω του πληθους σου 967 Z rel.] απω του πληθους σου του πλουτου 62' ≈ ברב הוניך MT

28:8 (minus) 967 rel. Z] לשחת MT

28:9 εν πληθει 967 ZB La^C Co Arab Hippol. Tyc.] εν χειρι (ast. O^{-Syh}) τραυματιζοντων σε ≈ rel. = ביד מחלליך MT

28:10(9) εν πληθει 967 Z rel.] εν χειρι L'' Tht. = ביד MT

απεριτμητων 967 ZB La^C Co Arab Hippol. Tyc.] (ast. O^{-Syh}) τραυματιζοντων σε θανατοις απεριτμητων ≈ rel. = מחלליך מותי ערלים MT

28:16 απο πληθους 967 Z rel.] ברב MT

28:18 δια το πληθος των αμαρτιων σου 967 Z rel.] δια το πληθος των ανομιων σου Syh^{mg} L'' Tht. = מרב עוניך MT

28:26 (minus) 967 62 = MT] (obel. O^{-Syh}) και ο θεος των πατερων αυτων Z rel.

29:1 δεκατω 967 Z rel. = העשרית MT] δωδεκατω B Syh^{mg}-62' L⁻³⁶–311 233–613 927 Co Arab Hi.

29:5 περισταλης 967 Z rel.] συσταλης 26 | תקבץ MT

29:16 αυτων 967 Z rel. = MT] των καρδιων A''-410 Syh 36 C'-86-239'-403' Arm

29:17 δια πληθος αμαρτιων σου 967 Z rel. (obel. O)] (minus) MT

29:19 (minus) 967 BZ La^S (vid.) Co] (ast.Q) και λη(μ)ψεται το πληθος αυτης rel. = ונשא המנה MT

30:4 (minus) 967 Z B La^S Co Tyc.] (ast. O) και λη(μ)ψονται το πληθος αυτης rel. = ולקחו המונה MT

30:5 περσαι 967 Z rel.] αιθιοπια 86 α'σ'θ' = כוש MT

και κρητες 967 Z rel.] και φουδ 86 α'σ'θ' = ופוט MT

και λυδοι 967 Z = ולוד MT] wlwby 'HUBP^{I-Peshitta}; tr. L'' Tht. (cf.^{below})

και λιβυες 967 Z rel.] και λιβυες και αιθιοπες και λυδοι και πασα η αραβια L'' Tht. | (minus) MT

οι επιμεικτοι 967 Z rel. (recon. ~ הערב) ≈ reliquum] αραβια 86 Hi.^{lat.} α' ≈ σ' = הערב MT | + (ast. 86) και χουβα α'σ'θ' = וכוב MT

30:20 δεκατω 967 62' 763*-lI] ενδεκατω BAQΓ Syh rel. = עשרה אחת MT

30:24 και προνομευσει την προνομην αυτης και σκυλευσει τα σκυλα αυτης 967 Z rel.] ונאק נאקות חלל לפני MT (לפני cf. ενωπιον αυτου 62')

31:1 δεκατω 967 Q-62' 490–534 106 Tht.] ενδεκατω ΒΑ Γ Syh rel. = אחת עשרה MT

31:10 και ειδον 967 Z rel.] και επηρθη η καρδια αυτου Syh^{mg} L'' Tht. = ורם לבבו MT | και επηρθη το πνευμα η καρδια αυτου 46

31:17 ζωης αυτου απωλοντο 967 ≈ Z rel.] גוים MT

32:1   δωδεκατω 967 B Syh *duodecimo* La[H] rel. = שְׁתֵּי עֶשְׂרֵה MT] ενδεκατω Z
       A''-106 534–239' | δεκατω 88 L'-449* 130* 410 Tht. *decimo* Hi.

32:6   απο του πληθους 967] απο του πληθους σου Z rel. | מִדָּמְךָ MT

32:17 δεκατω 967 88 763–449 Tht. 86 α'θ'] δωδεκατω ZBAQ Syh *duodecimo* La[H]
       rel. = שְׁתֵּי עֶשְׂרֵה MT

32:18 τα εθνη 967 ≈ tr. Z rel.] גּוֹיִם אַדִּרִם MT | גּוֹיִם אַדִּירִים HUBP[III-96]
       τας θυγατερας νεκρας 967 ≈ tr. Z rel.] בְּנוֹת MT
       ισχυν 967 Z rel.] πληθος 86 σ'* θ' Syh.* = *multitudinem* Hi. = הֲמוֹן MT | γην A

32:19 (minus) 967 ZB Co Arab Hi.[test]] (ast. O 449 Hi.) εξ υδατων ευπρεπους
       καταβηθι και κοιμηθητι μετα απεριτμητων rel. ≈ מִמִּי נָעַמְתָּ
       רְדָה וְהָשְׁכְּבָה אֶת עֲרֵלִים MT

32:20 και κοιμηθησεται 967 Z rel. (recon. וְהֻשְׁכַּב cf.[v 32]] και ηλκυσαν αυτην 62'
       = מָשְׁכוּ אוֹתָהּ MT (om. copula) | και εξειλκυσαν αυτην 86
       α'σ'θ'
       πασα η ισχυς αυτης 967 Z rel.] (ast. α'σ'θ') το παν πληθος αυτης 86 α'σ'θ' ≈
       וְכָל הֲמוֹנֶיהָ MT

32:21 και ερουσιν 967 87 Bo ≈ יְדַבְּרוּ (om. copula) HUBP[III-96]] και ερουσιν σοι Z rel.
       ≈ 407 | יְדַבְּרוּ לוֹ MT
       οι γιγαντες 967 Z rel.] אֵלֵי גִבּוֹרִים MT | גְבוֹרִים HUBP[III-93 150] | אֵילֵי HUBP[III-96]
       καταβηθι 967 Z rel. (recon. רֵד)] יָרְדוּ MT
       κοιμηθητι 967 Z rel. (recon. שְׁכָב)] שָׁכְבוּ MT
       μετα απεριτμητων 967 Z rel. (recon. בַּעֲרֵלִים)] הָעֲרֵלִים MT | עֲרֵלִים
       HUBP[III-30] | כַּעֲרֵלִים HUBP[III-93]

32:24 δυναμις αυτου 967 Z rel.] הֲמוֹנָהּ MT | δυναμις αυτου και παν το πληθος αυτου
       L Tht. (Heb = fs. suffix vs. 967 ms. indep. pron.)
       (minus) 967] ελαβοσαν βασανον αυτων Z ≈ rel. | וַיִּשְׂאוּ כְלִמָּתָם MT
       (= ατιμιαν θ' 86 cf.[16:52; 36:7; 39:26] ≈ αισχυνην α'σ') | וַיִּשְׂאוּ אֶת
       כְּלִמָּתָם HUBP[III-96]
       (minus) 967 Ⅱ] μετα των καταβαινοντων Z rel. = אֶת יוֹרְדֵי MT

32:25 (minus in context) 967 Z rel.] (obel. pro ast. L) κοιτη αυτης συν παντι 62' L''
       Tht. = וְכֹל | מִשְׁכָּב לָהּ בְּכָל MT | מִשְׁכָּב לָהּ וְכֹל HUBP[III-96 150]
       (minus) 967 Z rel.] (ast. 86) και αρουσιν εντροπην αυτων 86 | וַיִּשְׂאוּ כְלִמָּתָם
       MT
       (minus in context) 967 Z rel.] (obel. pro ast. L) συν παντι τω πληθει εκαστου
       L 62 ≈ בְּכָל הֲמוֹנָהּ MT

32:26 (minus in context) 967] μοσοχ και θοβελ και πασα (recon. θοβελ וְתֻבָל) Z
       rel. ≈ מֶשֶׁךְ תֻּבַל וְכָל MT | μοσοχ και θοβελλι και πασα (recon.
       θοβελλι תֻּבְלִי) 233 | μοσοχ και βοβελ και πασα (recon. βοβελ
       בֹּבֵל) 538 | cf.[v25] *cubile eorum* Hi. σ'θ' (HUBP[V-recon.] /מִשְׁכָּבָם
       מִשְׁכָּב לָהֶם cf.[v 25])
       (minus in context) 967] παντες απεριτμητοι C 26 = כֻּלָּם עֲרֵלִים MT | כֻּלָּם
       חֲלָלִים HUBP[III-30] | παντες (obel. Q) τραυματιαι αυτου παντες
       απεριτμητοι ≈ Z rel.
       (minus in context) 967] η ισχυς αυτων Z rel. | η ισχυς εκαστου L | הֲמוֹנָהּ
       MT

32:27 και 967 Z rel.] και (ast.) ουκ O(Q*) Arm[p] Hi. = וְלֹא MT
       γιγαντων 967 Z rel. = גִבּוֹרִים MT] גִבּוֹרִים בָּאָרֶץ HUBP[III-96]
       απ αιωνος 967 Z rel.] מֵעֲרֵלִים MT

32:29 εδοθησαν 967 ZB Q^mg-Syh^mg Co] εδωμ rel. = אדום MT

(minus) 967 ZB La^C Co] (ast.O) και οι βασιλεις αυτης και παντες ≈ rel.
≈ וכל מלכיה MT | και μοσοχ οι βασιλεις αυτης και παντες
minisc.

οι αρχοντες ασσουρ 967 Z rel. ≈ A] οι αρχοντες 130' | οι αρχοντες αυτης O (Q^txt)
L'' C'- 233–86 106' La^C Arab Arm (= נשיאיה MT) | נשיאה
אשר MT

τραυματιων 967 Z rel.] ערלים MT | הערלים HUBP^III-30

32:30 στρατηγοι ασσουρ 967 Z rel.] צדני אֲשֶׁר MT | צדני אֲשֶׁר HUBP^III-G-BEb 10 |
σιδωνιοι α'σ' | σεδεκ θ' | venatores qui Vul

και απηνεγκαν την βασανον αυτων 967 Z rel.] και ελαβον την βασανον αυτων
A''-106' L''-456 Tht. | וישאו את כלמתם MT | וישאו כלמתם
HUBP^III-96

(minus) 967 Z rel.] (ast. Q^txt 86) αισχυνομενοι O Arm Hi. ≈ L''-456 Tht. =
בושים MT

32:31 ισχυν αυτων 967 ZB La^C Co Arab] ισχυν αυτων (ast. O) τραυματιαι μαχαιρας
φαραω και πασα δυναμις αυτου rel. = חללי חרב פרעה המונה
וכל חילו MT

32:32 πληθος αυτου 967 Z rel. = המונו HUBP^III-G-BEb 10 (sm) | המונה MT (q המונו /k
המונה HUBP^III-G-BEb 10 (pm))

33:21 δεκατω 967 88–Syh^txt 449* 86] δωδεκατω Z BA rel. = שתי עשרה MT |
ενδεκατω L

33:25 (minus) 967 Z rel.] כה אמר אדני יהוה MT

(minus) 967 Z B La^CS Co Hi.] (ast. O 449 534) επι τω αιματι φαγεσθε και
οφθαλους υμων λημψεσθε προς ειδωλα υμων και αιμα εκχειτε
και την γην κληρονομησετε (26) εστητε επι τη ρομφαια υμων
εποιησατε βδελυγμα και εκαστος τον πλησιον αυτου εμιανατε
και την γην κληρονομησετε ≈ rel. = על הדם תאכלו ועינכם
תשאו אל גלוליכם ודם תשפכו והארץ תירשו (26) עמדתם
על חרבכם עשיתן תועבה ואיש את אשת רעהו טמאתם
והארץ תירשו MT cf.39:17–19

33:27 (minus) 967 ZB La^CS Co Hi.^test] ερεις προς αυτους Syh + δια τουτο ειπον αυτοις
O^-Syh L'' 62 | δια τουτο ειπον αυτοις rel.^-Syh | ταδε ειπον αυτοις 106
(recon. ειπον) ≈ (אָמַר) כה תאמר אלהם MT

(minus) 967 Z rel. = MT] נאם אדני יהוה HUBP^III-30

34:8 (minus) 967 26 306* 410 La^CS Aug.] (ast. 88) εις προνομην και γενεσθαι τα
προβατα (subst. ποιμνια L'') μου Z rel. ≈ לבז ותהיינה צאני MT
| לבז ותהיינה (om. צאני) HUBP^III-96

34:9 (minus) 967 ZB Bo] ακουσατε λογον κυριου rel. = שמעו דבר יהוה MT

34:15 (minus) 967 Aug. = MT] (obel. O 86) και γνωσονται οτι εγω ειμι κυριος Z ≈
rel. = et scient quod ego sum dues La^Sg

34:30 (minus) 967 Z rel.] (ast.O) μετ αυτων O (Q^mg)-62' L'' Arm Tht. = אתם MT

35:8 (minus) 967 Z rel.] τα ορη σου L'' | (ast.O) τα ορη αυτου O-62 = הריו MT |
montes Arm

πεδιοις σου 967 Z rel.] אפיקיך MT

εσονται 967] (minus) Z rel. = MT

πεσουνται εν σοι 967 Z rel.] יפלו בהם MT | (minus) HUBP^III-150

36:5 (minus) 967 Z rel.] εξ ολης καρδιας 62 *L''*⁴⁶ Tht. = כל לבב MT
 εν προνομη 967 Z rel.] εις προνομην 147' 46 *cII* = לבז MT | לבב HUBP^III-93

36:7 (minus) 967 Z rel.] (ast.*O*) ταδε λεγει αδωναι κυριος *O*-62' *L''* Arm Tht. Hi. =
 כה אמר אדני יהוה MT

36:23 οτι εγω κς 967 62' 534 PsCypr. = כי אני יהוה MT] οτι εγω ειμι κς Z rel.
 (minus) 967 Z B 46 Bo La^Ver Tyc. PsCypr.] (ast. *O*) λεγει αδωναι κυριος rel.
 = נאם אדני יהוה MT
 (minus) 967] εν τω αγιασθηναι με εν υμιν κατ οφθαλμους αυτων Z rel. =
 בהקדשי בכם לעיניהם MT
 (minus) 967] Ezek 36:24–38 Z ≈ rel. ≈ MT

36:36 (minus in context) 967] και γνωσονται τα εθνη οσα αν καταλειφθωσι
 κυκλω υμων οτι εγω κυριος ωκοδομησα τας καθηρημενας και
 κατεφυτευσα τας ηφανισμενας Z ≈ rel. ≈ וידעו הגוים אשר
 ישארו סביבותיכם כי אני יהוה בניתי הנהרסות נטעתי
 הנשמה MT

36:38 (minus in context) 967] και γνωσονται οτι εγω ειμι κυριος A''-410 *L'*-46 233–403'
 | και γνωσονται οτι εγω κυριος Z rel. = וידעו כי אני יהוה MT

37:1 *init.* (minus) 967 Z rel. = MT] νεκρων αναβιωσις Q^mg | περι αναστασεως των
 νεκρων Syh^mg
 πνι κυ (πνευματι κυριου) 967 rel.] πνευματι κυριος ZB A' 62' Tert.Ambr.Ir.^lat |
 πνευματι τω αγιω κυριου Q^mg | πνευματι Or. Lo. | רוח יהוה MT
 οστω(ν) 967 Tert.Ir.^latConsult = עצמות MT] οστων ανθρωπινων Z rel.| οστων
 ανθρωπων *L''* 130*-534–403' Bo Arm Or.Tht.Hi.

37:2 (minus) 967 ZB Bo GregEl.Ambr.Ir.^lat Aeth Arm Hi.] και ιδου AQ = והנה
 MT

37:4 προφητευσον 967 ZB A V-449 Bo Aeth Or.IV 210 Tht.Tert.GregEl.Ambr.
 Ir.^latConsult = הנבא MT] προφητευσον υιε ανθρωπου *L'*-403
 Or.XI 387 Lo. | προφητευσον υιε ανθρωπου προφητευσον 26 544
 613 | (obel. Q) υιε ανθρωπου προφητευσον rel.
 επι τα οστα ταυτα 967 Z rel. = על העצמות האלה MT] επι τα οστα ταυτα
 προφητευσον υιε ανθρωπου V-449 Tht. | (minus) *L'*-46 Or.XI
 387 Lo.

37:5 πνα (πνευμα) ζωης 967 Z rel.] *spiritum et vivetis* Bo Tert. = רוח וחייתם
 MT

37:7 τα οστα 967 Z rel. = העצמות HUBP^II-PirkeRE32(201) = MasEzek] (minus) HUBP^III-96 |
 עצמות MT
 εκαστον προς τη αρμονιαν αυτου 967 Z rel.] οστεον προς τη αρμονιαν αυτου
 O (Q^mg) *C'*- 130'-239'-403' 410 Arab Arm | οστεον προς οστεον
 εκαστον *L''*-48–46 Tht. = עצם אל עצמו MT
 εν τω με προφητευσαι 967 ZB Ambr.Ir.^lat] εν τω με προφητευσαι φωνη 233 |
 (ast. *O*) φωνη εν τω με προφητευσαι rel. = קול כהנבאי MT

37:9 προφητευσον επι το πνα προφητευσον υιε ανθρωπου 967 Z rel. = MT] υιε
 ανθρωπου προφητευσον επι το πνευμα προφητευσον A''-106 υιε
 ανθρωπου προφητευσον επι το πνευμα *C''*- 239'-403' Arab Arm
 Hi. | προφητευσον υιε ανθρωπου 407 Ambr.
 σου πνευματω(ν) 967] πνευματων Z rel. = רוחות MT] ανεμων 407 36^txt-V |
 ανεμων του ουρανου A'' Arab Ambr.Spec.Aug.

(minus) 967 Z rel.] (ast. *O*) το πνευμα A''-403' *O' L'* Bo Arab Arm Tht.Tert. Ambr.Ir.[lat] Spec.Consult.Hi.PsVig. = הרוח MT

37:10 συναγωγη 967 Z rel.] δυναμις 87–91 Syh = *valentia* Tert. = חיל MT

πολλη 967 Z rel.] μεγαλη A''-106'-403' Bo Tert. = גדול MT

σφοδρα 967 Z rel.] σφοδρα (ast. *O*) σφοδρα O-62' 534 Arab Arm[p] Hi. = מאד מאד MT

37:12 προφητευσον και ειπον 967 Z rel. = MT] προφητευσονται υιε ανθρωπου και ειπε *L''* Tht.

(minus) 967 ZB Cypr.Ambr.Tyv.Spec.] (ast. *O*) προς αυτους rel. = אליהם MT

(minus) 967 Z rel.] (ast. *O*) λαος μου *O'* Bo Arab Arm Tert.Hi. = עמי MT

37:19 εν τη χειρι ιουδα 967 Z rel.] בידי MT

37:25 (minus) 967 ZB La[W] Eus.ecl.Tyc.] (ast. *O*[-Syh]) και οι υιοι αυτων και οι υιοι των υιων αυτων εως αιωνος ≈ rel. = ובניהם ובני בניהם עד עולם MT

37:26 (minus) 967 Z rel.] (ast. *O*) και δωσω αυτους και πληθυνω αυτους ≈ O-62' *L''* 87[mg]-91[mg] Bo Arm Tht.Hi. = ונתתים והרביתי אותם MT

37:28 και γ[ν]ωσονται τα εθνη οτι εγω ειμι κς 967 Z rel. = וידעו הגוים כי אני יהוה MT] *et scient omnes gentes quia ego Dominus* La[W] | και γνωσονται οτι εγω ειμι κυριος A Aeth Arab

(minus) 967 Z rel. = MT] λεγει κυριος A'-410 Arab Tyc.

38:2 ρως μεσοχ 967 B ≈ Z rel. = *ros mosoch* Hi. (translit. ראש)] ρωμεσοχ 410 ≈ 106 239' Arm | κεφαλης ρως μεσοχ 62 | κεφαλης μοσοχ α' Tht. = *capitis* μασεχ Bo = ראש משך MT

38:3 ρως μοσοχ 967 Z ≈ rel. (translit. ראש)] ρωμεσοχ 410 ≈ 106 239' Arm | *capitis* μασεχ Bo = ראש משך MT

(minus) 967 B Arm] γωγ Z rel. = גוג MT | μαγωγ 87 | γωγ και μαγωγ Tht.

38:4 (minus) 967 Z rel.] (ast. *O*) και περιστρεψω σε κυκλοθεν και δωσω χαλινον εις τας σιαγονας σου *O' L''* 87[mg]-91[mg]-239' 26 Bo Aeth Arm Tht. ≈ ושובבתיך ונתתי חחים בלחייך MT

συναξω σε 967 Z rel.] πλανησω σε 147 26 239' Aeth | והוצאתי אותך MT

ενδεδυμενους θωρακας παντας 967 Z rel.] לבשי מכלול MT

και μαχαιραι 967 Z rel.] επιλαμβανομενους και μαχαιραι 62 cf. תפשי MT | και μαχαιραι (ast. *O*) παντες αυτοι O 26 239' Arm θ' ≈ (תפשי) חרבות כלם MT

38:6 και παντες οι περι αυτον 967 Z rel.] και παντα τα υποστηριγματα αυτου Syh θ' | וכל אגפיה MT

38:8 επ εσχατων ετων 967 ≈ Z rel.] (minus) 106| באחרית השנים MT | באחרית השנה HUBP[III-96]

επι την γην ισραηλ 967 62' V-449 26 403' 410 544 ≈ Z rel.] επι την ιερυσαλημ 233 | על הרי ישראל MT

38:9 και παντες οι περι σε 967 Z rel.] וכל אגפיך MT

38:11 γην απεριμμενων 967 ≈ γην απεριμμενην Z rel.] ארץ פרזות MT

38:14 και εν τη ημερα εκεινη 967] ουκ εν τη ημερα εκεινη Z B *O'* 106 198 239' = *in die non* La[W] | ουχι εν τη ημερα εκεινη = הלוא ביום ההוא MT rel. = *nonne in die illa* La[Amb]

εγερθηση 967 Z rel. (recon: תֵעֹר)] εξεγερθηση A''; απαντησις 46; γνωση και εγερθηση *L''* Tht. | תדע MT

38:16   γωγ 967 O-62 La^SW (ast. O) = גוג MT] (ast. V) ω γωγ L"-46 Tht. o Gog Vul. |
(minus) Z rel. (Z rel.^-Bo tr.^v 17 (obel.O) γωγ)

γνωσιν παντα τα εθνη 967 L"-449 La^W Tht.] γνωσι παντα τα εθνη εμε Z rel. =
דעת כל הגוים אתי HUBP^III-30 | sciant me omnes gentes quod
ego sum dominus dues La^S | דעת הגוים אתי MT | דעת הגוים אתי
HUBP^III-93

38:17   συ ει περι ου 967 Z rel.] האתה הוא זה אשר MT | האתה הוא אשר
HUBP^III-30

των προφητων ισραηλ 967 ≈ Z rel.] των προφητων ισραηλ (ast. O) των
προφητευσαντων O-62 L" Bo Tht. σ'θ' = נביאי ישראל הַנִּבְּאִים
MT | נשיאי ישראל הַנִּבָּאִים HUBP^III-30 (om. נביאי ישראל)
הַנִּבָּאִים HUBP^III-96

του αγαγειν σε επ αυτους 967 Z ≈ rel. ≈ להביא אתך עליהם MT] להביא
אתך עולם HUBP^III-93

38:18   και εσται 967Z rel. = וְהָיָה MT] (minus) Peshitta
η ημερα εκεινη εν 967] εν τη ημερα 534 La^W Peshitta| εν τη ημερα εκεινη εν
ημερα Z rel. = ביום ההוא ביום MT

38:20   ινα γνωσιν παντα τα εθνη εμε εν σοι ενωπιον αυτων 967] (minus) Z rel. = MT

38:21   και καλεσω επ αυτον παν φοβον μαχαιρας 967 ≈ (om. μαχ.) Z rel.] και καλεσω
επι αυτον και παν φοβον B | + (ast. L) εις παντα τα ορη μου Syh
≈ L" Tht. cf.^MT | וקראתי עליו לכל הרי חרב MT | וקראתי
עליו למפל הרי חרב Tar

38:22   και επι παντας τους μετ [αυ]του 967 Z rel.] ועל אגפיו MT

39:1   ρως μοσοχ 967 Z ≈ rcl. (translit. ראש)] ρωμεσοχ 410 ≈ 106 Arm | capitis
μασεχ Bo | ראש משך MT | γης ρως μοσοχ L

39:4   και ου βεβηλωθησεται το ονομα το αγιον 967 cf.^39:7] (minus) Z rel. = MT

39:6   επι γωγ 967 Z rel.] μαγωγ O^Q C'-198–393–403' 106' Arm = במגוג MT

39:8   ιδου ηκει και εσται 967] הנה באה וְנִהְיָתָה MT | ιδου ηκει και γνωση οτι εσται
Z rel. (cf. scies quia erit La^Sg scies quoniam erit La^H

39:11   τοπον ονομαστον μνημειον 967 Z rel. = locum nominatum . . . La^S Vul ≈ מקום
שָׁם קבר HUBP^III-96 G-BEb24 | τοπον εχει ονομαστον μνημειον 62
cf.^MT | מקום שָׁם קבר (לבית MT | אתין לגוג אתר כשר
קבורא) Tar (אתר כשר cf. שָׁם MT)

εν ισραηλ 967 Z rel. = בישראל MT] εν ιερουσαλημ 26' | (minus) A*

το πολυανδρειον 967 Z rel.] גי MT

(minus) 967 Z rel.] ανατολης L" Tht. = קדמת MT

εκει τον γωγ και παν το πληθος αυτου 967 rel. = שם את גוג ואת כל הֲמוֹנה
MT

το γαι το πολυανδριον του γωγ 967 Z rel.] גיא המון גוג MT | המון גוג
HUBP^III-96 | גיא המון גיא HUBP^III-150

γαι 967 Z rel. = גיא MT ≈ γε O (γη Syh) C^-233 410 La^S (ge) Arm Ambr.Hi.] τε
B 26 Cyr. | (minus) 106 Arab

39:15   πολυανδριον 967 Z rel.] πληθος σ' | εβρ' αμωνα θ' Syh = המונה MT

39:28   εν τω επιφανηναι με αυτοις 967 Z rel. (recon. בהגלותי)] בהגלותי אתם MT
εν τοις εθνεσιν 967 Z rel.] + (ast. O) και συναξω αυτους επι την γην αυτων και
ου καταλειψω απ αυτων ουκετι εκει L"-403' 87^mg Bo Arm Tht. ≈
O-62' = וכנסתים על אדמתם ולא אותיר עוד מהם שם MT

39:29   εξεχεα τον θυμον μου 967 Z rel.] שפכתי את רוחי MT

40:1   εν τη ημερα εκεινη 967 Z rel.] εν οστεω τη ημερα εκεινη 62' = בעצם היום הזה
        MT | בעצם הזה היום הזה HUBP[III-93]

43:12   (minus) 967 ZB 106] (ast. O) εισιν rel. ≈ הנה MT
        (minus) 967 ZB] (ast. O) ουτος ο νομος του οικου rel. = זאת תורת הבית
        MT

44:9   δια τουτο 967 Z rel.] (minus) MT

BIBLIOGRAPHY

Aejmelaeus, A. *On the Trail of the Septuagint Translators: Collected Essays.* Kampen: Kok Pharos, 1993.

Allen, Graham. *Intertextuality.* New York: Routledge, 2000.

Allen, Leslie C. "Ezekiel 24:3–14: A Rhetorical Perspective," *CBQ* 49 (1987): 404–414.

——. *Ezekiel 20–48.* WBC 29. Dallas: Word Books, 1990.

Bagnall, Roger S. *Reading Papyri: Writing Ancient History.* New York: Routledge, 1995.

——. "Greek and Coptic Studies, 1990–1995." Pages 219–230 in *Hellenistic and Roman Egypt: Sources and Approaches.* Burlington: Ashgate Publishing, 2008.

Baillet, Maurice. "Ézéchiel (Pl. XVIII)." Page 94 in *Les 'petites grottes' de Qumrân: exploration de la falaise, les grottes 2Q, 3Q, 5Q, 6Q, 7Q, à 10Q, le rouleau de cuivre.* Edited by Maurice Baillet, Józef Tadeusz Milik, and Roland de Vaux. DJD 3. Oxford: Clarendon, 1962.

Barr, James. *The Typologies of Literalism in Ancient Biblical Translations.* MSU 15. Göttingen: Vandenhoeck & Ruprecht, 1979.

Barthélemy, Dominique. "Ézéchiel (Pl. XII)." Pages 68–69 in *Qumran Cave I.* Edited by Dominique Barthélemy and Józef Tadeusz Milik. DJD 1. Oxford: Clarendon, 1955.

——. *Les Devanciers d'Aquila.* Leiden: Brill, 1963.

——. "Trois niveaux d'analyse." Pages 47–54 in *The Story of David and Goliath: Textual and Literary Criticism: Papers of a Joint Research Venture.* Edited by D. Barthélemy, D. Gooding, J. Lust, and E. Tov. Göttingen: Vandenhoeck & Ruprecht, 1986.

Barthélemy, Dominique *et al.*, eds. *Preliminary and Interim Report on the Hebrew Old Testament Text Project.* 5 vols. New York: United Bible Societies, 1973–1980.

Barthélemy, Dominique. *et al.*, eds. *Critique textuelle de l'Ancien Testament: Tome 3. Ézéchiel, Daniel et les 12 Prophètes.* OBO 50/3. Göttingen: Vandenhoeck & Ruprecht, 1992.

Barthélemy, Dominique, D.W. Gooding, J. Lust, and E. Tov, eds. *The Story of David and Goliath: Textual and Literary Criticism: Papers of a Joint Research Venture.* OBO 73. Göttingen: Vandenhoeck & Ruprecht, 1986.

Barton, John. *Reading the Old Testament: Method in Biblical Study.* 2d ed. Louisville: Westminster, 1996.

Baudissin, W.W. Graf von. *Kyrios als Gottesname im Judentum und seine Stelle in der Religionsgeschichte.* 4 vols. Giessen: Töpelmann, 1929.

Baumgarten, A.I. "Bi-Lingual Jews and the Greek Bible." Pages 13–30 in *Shem in the Tents of Japhet: Essays on the Encounter of Judaism and Hellenism.* Edited by J.L. Kugel. JSJSup 74. Leiden: Brill, 2002.

Beck, J.A. *Translators as Storytellers: A Study in Septuagint Translation Technique.* STBL 25. New York: Peter Lang, 2000.

Beckwith, R. *The Old Testament Canon of the New Testament Church and its Background in Early Judaism.* Grand Rapids: Eerdmans, 1985.

Beit-Arié, Malachi. *Hebrew Manuscripts of East and West: Towards a Comparative Codicology.* The Panizzi Lectures, 1992. London: The British Library, 1992.

Bell, Maureen. "Introduction: The Material Text." Pages 1–4 in *Re-constructing the Book: Literary Texts in Transmission.* Edited by Maureen Bell, Shirley Chew, Simon Eliot, et al. Burlington: Ashgate, 2001.

Bentzen, Aage. *Daniel.* HAT 19. 2d ed. Tübingen: Mohr (Siebeck), 1952.

Bertholet, Alfred. *Hesekiel.* HAT 13. Tübingen: Mohr (Siebeck), 1936.

Bewer, Julius A. "On the Text of Ezekiel 7:5–14." *JBL* 45 (1926): 226–231.

——. "Review of Johnson, Gehman, and Kase (eds), *The John H. Schiede Biblical Papyri: Ezekiel.*" *JBL* 57 (1938): 421–425.

——. *English Bible 1949 Authorized.* HABS. New York: Harper & Bros., 1950.

——. "Textual and Exegetical Notes on the Book of Ezekiel." *JBL* 72 (1953): 158–169.

Blenkinsopp, Joseph. *Prophecy and Canon: A Contribution to the Study of Jewish Origins.* South Bend: University of Notre Dame Press, 1986.

——. *Ezekiel.* IBC. Louisville: Westminster, 1990.

——. *A History of Prophecy in Israel.* Rev. and enl. ed. Louisville: Westminster, 1996.

Bloch, R. Howard. "New Philology and Old French." *Spec* 65 (1990): 38–58.

Block, D.I. *The Book of Ezekiel: Chapters 1–24.* NIBCOT. Grand Rapids: Eerdmans, 1997.

——. *The Book of Ezekiel: Chapters 25–48.* NIBCOT. Grand Rapids: Eerdmans, 1998.

Boadt, Lawrence. *Ezekiel's Oracles Against Egypt: A Literary and Philological Study of Ezekiel 29–32.* BEO 37. Rome: Biblical Institute, 1980.

Bogaert, P.M. "Le témoignage de la Vetus Latina dans l'étude de la tradition des Septante: Ézéchiel et Daniel dans le Papyrus 967." *Bib* 59 (1978): 384–395.

Botte, B., and Bogaert, P.M. "Septante et versions grecques." Cols. 536–692 in *DBSup* 12. Paris: Letouzey et Ané, 1993.

Brock, S.P. "The Phenomenon of Biblical Translation in Antiquity." Pages 541–571 in *Studies in the Septuagint: Origins, Recensions, and Interpretations.* Edited by H. M. Orlinsky. LBS. New York: Ktav, 1974.

Brogan, John J. "Another Look at Codex Sinaiticus." Pages 17–32 in *The Bible as Book: The Transmission of the Greek Text.* Edited by S. McKendrick and O.A. O'Sullivan. New Castle, De.: Oak Knoll Press, 2003.

Brooke, George J. "The Biblical Texts in the Qumran Commentaries: Scribal Errors or Exegetical Variants?" Pages 85–100 in *Early Jewish and Christian Exegesis: Studies in Memory of William Hugh Brownlee.* Edited by C.A. Evans and W.F. Stinespring. Atlanta: SBL, 1987.

——. "Ezekiel in Some Qumran and New Testament Texts." Pages 317–337 in *The Madrid Qumran Congress: Proceedings of the International Congress on the Dead Sea Scrolls Madrid 18–21 March 1991.* Edited by Julio Trebolle Barrera and Luis Vegas Montaner. Vol. 1. STDJ 11. Leiden: Brill, 1992.

——. "Rewritten Bible." Pages 777–81 in *Encyclopedia of the Dead Sea Scrolls.* Edited by Lawrence H. Schiffman and James C. VanderKam. Vol. 2. New York: Oxford University Press, 2000.

Brownlee, William H. "The Scroll of Ezekiel from the Eleventh Qumran Cave." *RevQ* 4 (1963): 11–28.

——. "Ezekiel's Copper Cauldron and Blood on the Rock." Pages 21–43 in *For Me to Live: Essays in Honor of James Leon Kelso.* Edited by R.A. Coughenour. Cleveland: Dillon/Liederbach, 1972.

——. *Ezekiel 1–19.* Vol. 1. WBC 28. Waco: Word, 1990.

Cassuto, Umberto. "The Arrangement of the Book of Ezekiel." Pages 227–240 in *Biblical and Oriental Studies.* Edited by U. Cassuto. Translated by Israel Abrahams. Vol. 1. Jerusalem: Magnes, 1973.

Cavallo, Guglielmo. *Libri, editori e pubblico nel mondo antico: Guida storica e critica.* BUL 315. Rome: Laterza, 1975.

Collins, John J. "The Court-Tales in Daniel and the Development of Apocalyptic." *JBL* 94 (1975): 218–234.

——. *Daniel.* Hermeneia. Philadelphia: Fortress, 1993.

——. *The Apocalyptic Imagination: An Introduction to Jewish Apocalyptic Literature.* 2d ed. BRS. Grand Rapids: Eerdmans, 1998.

——. *The Library in Alexandria and the Bible in Greek.* VTSup 83. Leiden: Brill, 2000.

Cooke, G.A. "Some Considerations on the Text…" *Zeitschrift für die alttestamentliche Wissenschaft* 42 (1924): 105–115.

——. *A Critical and Exegetical Commentary on the Book of Ezekiel.* ICC. Edinburgh: Clark, 1936.

Cornill, Carl Heinrich. *Das Buch des Propheten Ezechiel.* Leipzig: J.C. Hinrichs, 1886.

Crane, Ashley. *Israel's Restoration: A Textual-Comparative Exploration of Ezekiel 36–39.* VTSup 122. Boston: Brill, 2008.

Cross, Frank M. *The Ancient Library of Qumrân and Modern Biblical Studies*. Rev. ed. Garden City, NY: Doubleday, 1961.

——. "The History of the Biblical Text in Light of the Discoveries in the Judaean Desert." *HTR* 57 (1964): 281–99. Repr., Pages 177–95 in *Qumran and the History of the Biblical Text*. Edited by Frank Moore Cross and Shemaryahu Talmon. Cambridge: Harvard University Press, 1975.

——. "The Contribution of the Qumrân Discoveries to the Study of the Biblical Text." *IEJ* 16 (1966): 81–95.

——. "Prolegomenon." Pages XLVI–LI in *Studies in the Septuagint*. Edited by S. Jellicoe. LBS. New York: Ktav, 1974.

Crum, W.E. "The Coptic Glosses." Pages ix–xii in *The Chester Beatty Biblical Papyri Descriptions and Texts of Twelve Manuscripts on Papyrus of the Greek Bible: Fasciculus VI: Isaiah, Jeremiah, Ecclesiasticus*. Edited by Frederic G. Kenyon. Oxford: Oxford University Press, 1937.

Dahlberg, B.T. "Shadrach, Meshach, and Abednego." Pages 302–303 in *Interpreter's Dictionary of the Bible*, IV. Nashville: Abingdon, 1962.

De Bruin, W.M. "Interpreting Delimiters: The Complexity of Text Delimitation in Four Major Septuagint Manuscripts." Pages 66–89 in *Studies in Scriptural Unit Division*. Edited by M. Korpel and J. Oesch. Pericope 3. Assen: Van Gorcum, 2000.

De Lagarde, Paul. *Mittheilungen I*. Göttingen: Dieterich, 1884.

——. *Anmerkungen zur griechischen Übersetzung der Proverbien*. Leipzig: Brockhaus, 1963.

De Silva, D.A. *Introducing the Apocrypha: Message, Context, and Significance*. Grand Rapids: Baker Academic, 2002.

De Troyer, Kristen. "Translation of Interpretation? A Sample from the Books of Esther." Pages 343–53 in *X Congress of the International Organization for Septuagint and Cognate Studies, Oslo 1998*. SBLSCS 51. Atlanta: SBL, 2001.

——. *Rewriting the Sacred Text: What the Old Greek Texts Tell us about the Literary Growth of the Bible*. TCS 4; Atlanta: SBL, 2003

Dean, J.E. *Epiphanius' Treatise on Weights and Measures: The Syriac Version*. SAOC 11. Chicago: Chicago University Press, 1935.

Delamarter, Steve. "Communities of Faith and Their Bibles: A Sociological Typology."

Di Lella, Alexander A. "The Textual History of Septuagint-Daniel and Theodotian-Daniel." Pages 586–607 in *The Book of Daniel: Composition and Reception*. Edited by John J. Collins and Peter W. Flint. Vol. 2 of *The Book of Daniel*. Boston: Brill, 2002.

Díez-Macho, Alejandro. *Neophyti 1, Targum Palestinense ms de la Biblioteca Vaticana*. 6 vols. Madrid: Consejo Superior de Investigaciones Científicas, 1968–1979.

Dimant, Devorah. "Literary Typologies and Biblical Interpretation in the Hellenistic-Roman Period." Pages 73–80 in *Jewish Civilization in the Hellenistic-Roman Period*. Edited by Shemaryahu Talmon. JSPSup 10. Sheffield: Sheffield Academic Press, 1991.

——. *Qumran Cave 4 XXI: Parabiblical Texts, Part 4: Pseudo-Prophetic Texts*. DJD 30. Oxford: Clarendon Press, 2001.

Dimant, Devorah and J. Strugnell. "4Q Second Ezekiel." *RevQ* 13 (1988): 45–58.

Dines, Jennifer. *The Septuagint*. New York: T&T Clark, 2004.

Dirksen, P.B., and M.J. Mulder, eds. *The Peshitta: Its Early Texts and History: Papers read at the Peshitta Symposium held at Leiden 30–31 August 1985*. MPI 4. Leiden: Brill, 1998.

Dorival, G., M. Harl, and O. Munnich, eds. *La Bible grecque des Septante—Du judaïsme hellénistique au christianisme ancien*. ICA. Paris: Cerf, 1988.

Driver, G.R. "Ezekiel: Linguistic and Textual Problems." *Bib* 19 (1938): 60–69, 175–187.

Duhm, Bernhard. *Jeremia*. Tübingen: Mohr (Siebeck), 1901.

——. *Jesaia*. 4th ed. Göttingen: Vandenhoeck & Ruprecht, 1922.

Duncan, Julie A. "Excerpted Texts of Deuteronomy at Qumran." *RevQ* 18 (1997): 43–62.

Dupont-Sommer, A. *The Essene Writings from Qumran*. Translated by Géza Vermès. Oxford: Blackwell, 1961.

Ehrlich, A.B. *Randglossen zur Hebräischen Bibel*. Vol. 5. Leipzig: J.C. Hinrichs, 1912.

Ehrman, Bart D. *The Orthodox Corruption of Scripture: The Effect of Early Christological Controversies on the Text of the New Testament.* New York: Oxford University Press, 1993.

Eichrodt, W. *Ezekiel: A Commentary.* OTL. Philadelphia: Westminster, 1970.

Eissfeldt, Otto. *Einleitung in das Alte Testament: unter Einschluss der Apokryphen und Pseudepigraphen sowie der apokryphen—und pseudepigraphenartigen Qumran-Schriften.* 3d ed. *NTG.* Tübingen: Mohr (Siebeck), 1964.

Elliger, K. *Studien zum Habbakkuk-Kommentar vom Toten Meer.* Tübingen: Mohr (Siebeck), 1953.

Emmerson, G.I. "Esther." *The Dictionary of Biblical Interpretation.* Edited by R.J. Coggins and J.L. Houlden. London: SCM Press, 1990.

Erman, A. "Bruchstücke der oberägyptischen Übersetzung des Alten Testamentes." Pages 401–440 in *Gesellschaft der Wissenschaften zu Göttingen, Nachrichten.* Göttingen: Vandenhoeck & Ruprecht, 1880.

Evans, Craig A. *The Interpretation of Scripture in Early Judaism and Christianity: Studies in Language and Tradition.* Sheffield: Sheffield Academic Press, 2000.

———. *Ancient Texts for New Testament Studies: A Guide to the Background Literature.* Peabody: Hendrickson, 2005.

Ferch, Arthur J. *The Son of Man in Daniel 7.* AUDDS 6. Berrien Springs, Mi.: Andrews University Press, 1979.

Fernández Galiano, M. "Notes on the Madrid Ezekiel Papyrus." Pages 133–138 in *Proceedings of the Twelfth International Congress of Papyrology.* Edited by Samuel, D.H. *ASP* 7. Toronto: Hakkert, 1970.

———. "Nuevas Paginas del codice 967 del AT griego." *SP* 10 (1971): 7–76.

Fernández Marcos, Natalio. *The Septuagint in Context: An Introduction to the Greek Versions of the Bible.* Leiden: Brill, 2000.

———. "On Symmachus and Lucian in Ezekiel." Pages 151–161 in *Interpreting Translation: Studies on the LXX and Ezekiel in Honour of Johan Lust.* Leuven: Leuven University Press, 2005.

Field, Frederick. *Origenis hexaplorum quae supersunt, sive veterum interpretum Graecorum in totum Vetus Testamentum fragmenta.* 2 vols. Oxford: Oxford University Press, 1875. Repr. Hildesheim: Olms, 1964.

Filson, F. V. "The Omission of Ezek. 12:26–28 and 36:23b–38 in Codex 967." *JBL* 62 (1943): 27–32.

Fischer, J. *In welcher Schrift lag das Buch Isaias den LXX vor? Eine textkritische Studie.* BZAW 56. Giessen: Töpelmann, 1930.

Fishbane, Michael. *Biblical Interpretation in Ancient Israel.* Oxford: Clarendon, 1985.

Fishbane, Michael and Shemaryahu Talmon. "The Structuring of Biblical Books: Studies in the Book of Ezekiel." Pages 129–153 in *Annual of the Swedish Theological Institute X.* Edited by B. Knutsson. Leiden: Brill, 1976.

Fleischer, Ezra. "Annual and Triennial Reading of the Bible in the Old Synagogue." *Tarbiz* 61 (1991): 25–43.

Floyd, Michael H. "The Production of Prophetic Books in the Early Second Temple Period." Pages 276–297 in *Prophets, Prophecy, and Prophetic Texts in Second Temple Judaism.* Edited by Michael H. Floyd and Robert D. Haak. New York: T & T Clark, 2006.

Fohrer, Georg. *Die Hauptprobleme des Buches Ezechiel.* BZAW 72. Berlin: Töpelmann, 1952.

Fohrer, Georg and K. Galling. *Ezechiel.* HAT 13. Tübingen: Mohr (Siebeck), 1955.

Foley, Edward. *Foundations of Christian Music: The Music of Pre-Constantinian Christianity.* AEL. Collegeville: The Liturgical Press, 1996.

Fraenkel, Detlef. "Nachtrag zur 1. Auflage von 1952." Pages 331–352 in *Ezechiel.* Septuaginta: Vetus Testamentum Graecum auctoritate Academiae Scientiarum Gottingensis 16:1, by Joseph Ziegler. 2d ed. Göttingen: Vandenhoeck & Ruprecht, 1977.

Freedy, Kenneth S. "The Glosses in Ezekiel I–XXIV." *VT* 20 (1970): 129–52.

Froehlich, Karlfried. *Biblical Interpretation in the Early Church.* Edited by William G. Rusch. SECT. Philadelphia: Fortress, 1984.

Frye, Northrop. *Northrop Frye's Notebooks and Lectures on the Bible and Other Religious Texts*. Edited by Northrop Frye and Robert D. Denham. Toronto: University of Toronto Press, 2003.

Gamble, Harry Y. *Books and Readers in the Early Church: A History of Early Christian Texts*. New Haven: Yale University Press, 1995.

Gehman, Henry Snyder. "The Relations between the Hebrew Text of Ezekiel and that of the John H. Schiede Papyri." *JAOS* 58 (1938): 92–102.

——. "The Relations between the Text of the John H. Schiede Papyri and that of the other Greek Mss. of Ezekiel." *JBL* 57 (1938): 281–287.

Geissen, Angelo. *Der Septuaginta-Text des Buches Daniel Kap. 5–12, zusammen mit Susanna, Bel et Draco sowie Ester Kap. 1, 1a–2,15, nach dem Kölner Teil des Papyrus 967*. PTA 5. Bonn: Rudolf Habelt, 1968.

Gesenius, Wilhelm. *Hebrew Grammar*. Rev. and enl. by E. Kautzsch. 2d English ed. Oxford: Clarendon, 2003.

Gignac, Francis Thomas. *A grammar of the Greek papyri of the Roman and Byzantine periods: Phonology, Volume 1*. TDSA 55. Milan: Istituto editoriale Cisalpino. La Goliardica, 1976.

Ginsberg, Harold L. *Studies in Daniel*. TS 14. New York: Jewish Theological Seminary of America, 1948.

Goettsberger, J. "Ez 7,1–16 textkritisch und exegetisch untersucht." *BZ* 22 (1934): 195–223.

Gooding, D.W. "An Approach to the Literary and Textual Problems in the David-Goliath Story." Pages 55–86 in *The Story of David and Goliath: Textual and Literary Criticism: Papers of a Joint Research Venture*. Edited by D. Barthélemy, D. Gooding, J. Lust, and E. Tov. Göttingen: Vandenhoeck & Ruprecht, 1986.

——. "Third Stage." Pages 114–121 in *The Story of David and Goliath: Textual and Literary Criticism: Papers of a Joint Research Venture*. Edited by D. Barthélemy, D. Gooding, J. Lust, and E. Tov. Göttingen: Vandenhoeck & Ruprecht, 1986.

Goshen-Gottstein, M.H. "Hebrew Biblical MSS: Their History and the Place in the HUBP Edition." *Bib* 48 (1966): 243–290.

Grabbe, Lester. "The Translation Technique of the Greek Minor Versions: Translations or Revisions?" Pages 505–56 in *Septuagint, Scrolls, and Cognate Writings*. Edited by George J. Brooke and Barnabas Lindars. SBLSCS 33. Atlanta: SBL, 1992.

Gregory, Caspar R. *Canon and Text of the New Testament*. ITL. New York: Charles Scribner's Sons, 1907.

Greenberg, Moshe. *Ezekiel*. 2 vols. AB. Garden City, NY: Doubleday, 1983.

Grenfell, Bernard P. *An Alexandrian Erotic Fragment and other Greek Papyri*. Oxford: Clarendon, 1896.

Grigsby, Bruce. "Gematria and John 21:11: Another Look at Ezekiel 47:10." *ET* 95 (1984): 177–78.

Haelst, J. van. *Catalogue des papyrus litteraires juifs et chretiens*. Paris: Sorbonne, 1976.

Hamm, W. *Der Septuaginta-Text des Buches Daniel, Kap. 1–2, nach dem Kölner Teil des Papyrus 967*. PTA 10. Bonn: Rudolf Habelt, 1969.

——. *Der Septuaginta-Text des Buches Daniel, Kap. 3–4, nach dem Kölner Teil des Papyrus 967*. PTA 21. Bonn: Rudolf Habelt, 1977.

Harford, John Battersby. *Studies in the Book of Ezekiel*. Cambridge: Cambridge University Press, 1935.

Harl, M. "Le renouvellement du lexique des Septante d'après le témoignage des recensions, révisions et commentaires grecs anciens." Pages 239–259 in *LXX: VII Congress of the International Organization for Septuagint and Cognate Studies Leuven 1989*. Edited by C.E. Cox. SBLSCS 31. Altanta: SBL, 1991.

Harrington, D.J. *An Invitation to the Old Testament Apocrypha: Approaches to the Mystery of Suffering*. Grand Rapids: Eerdmans, 1999.

Hatch, Edwin and Henry A. Redpath. *A Concordance to the Septuagint and Other Greek Versions of the Old Testament*. Oxford: Clarendon, 1906.

Hauspie, K., "πιπτω επι προσωπον μου: A Set Phrase in Ezekiel?" Pages 513–530 in *LXX: X Congress of the International Organization for Septuagint and Cognate Studies; Oslo, 1998*. Edited by B.A. Taylor. SBLSCS 51. Atlanta: SBL, 1998.

Hendrickson, G.L. "Ancient Reading." *CJ* 25 (1929): 182–96.

Hengel, Martin. *The Septuagint as Christian Scripture: Its Prehistory and the Problem of its Canon*. OTS. Edinburgh: T&T Clark, 2002.

Herbert, Edward D. "11QEzekiel (pls. II, LIV)." Pages 15–28 in *Qumran Cave 11 2: 11Q2–18, 11Q20–31*. Edited by Florentino García Martínez, Eibert J.C. Tigchelaar, and Adam S. van der Woude. DJD 23. Oxford: Clarendon, 1998.

Herrmann, Johannes. *Ezechielstudien*. BWANT 2. Leipzig: J.C. Hinrichs, 1908.

———. *Die Gottesnamen im Ezechieltexte*. Pages 70–87 in *Alttestamentliche Studien: Rudolf Kittel zum 60. Geburtstag*. Edited by R. Kittel. BWANT 13. Leipzig: J.C. Hinrichs, 1913.

———. "Die Septuaginta zu Ezechiel das Werk dreier Übersetzer." Pages 1–19 in *Beiträge zur Entstehungsgeschichte der Septuaginta*. Edited by J. Herrmann and F. Baumgärtel. BWANT 5. Berlin: Verlag von W. Kohlhammer, 1923.

———. *Ezechiel*. KAT 11. Leipzig: Deichart, 1924.

Hibbard, James Todd. *Intertextuality in Isaiah 24–27: The Reuse and Evocation of Earlier Texts*. FAT 16. Tübingen: Mohr Siebeck, 2006.

Holladay, William L. *Jeremiah*. 2 vols. Hermeneia. Minneapolis: Fortress Press, 1989.

Holmes, R. and J. Parsons. *Vetus Testamentum Graecum cum Variis Lectionibus*. 5 vols. Oxford: Clarendon, 1798–1827.

Hölscher, Gustav. *Hesekiel, der Dichter und das Buch*. BZAW 39. Giessen: Töpelmann, 1924.

Howie, C.G. *Date and Composition of Ezekiel*. JBLMS 4. Philadelphia: SBL, 1950.

Hubler, J. Noel. "Introduction to Iezekiel." Page 946 in *A New English Translation of the Septuagint*. Edited by Albert Pietersma and Benjamin G. Wright. Oxford: Oxford University Press, 2007.

Hulst, A.R., *Old Testament Translation Problems*. Leiden: Brill, 1960.

Hultsch, F. *Metrologicorum scriptorium reliquiae*. Vol. 1. Leipzig: Teubius, 1864.

Hurtado, Larry W. *The Earliest Christian Artifacts: Manuscripts and Christian Origins*. Grand Rapids: Eerdmans, 2006.

Hurvitz, Avi. *A Linguistic Study of the Relationship between the Priestly Source and the Book of Ezekiel: A New Approach to an Old Problem*. CahRB 20. Paris: Gabalda, 1982.

Irwin, W.A. *The Prophets and Their Times*. Rev. ed. Edited by J.M. Powis Smith. Chicago: University of Chigaco Press, 1941.

———. *The Problem of Ezekiel: An Inductive Study*. Chicago: University of Chicago Press, 1943.

Jahn, L.G., *Der Griechische Text des Buche Ezechiel nach dem Kölner Teil des Papyrus 967*. PTA 15. Bonn: Rudolf Habelt, 1972.

Jannaris, A.N. "The Digamma, Koppa, and Sampi as Numerals in Greek." Pages 37–40 in *The Classical Quarterly Vol. 1*. Edited by J.P. Postgate. London, 1907.

Jellicoe, S. *The Septuagint and Modern Study*. Oxford: Clarendon, 1968.

———. "Prolegomenon." Pages XLVI–LI in *Studies in the Septuagint: Origins, Recensions, and Interpretations: Selected Essays*. Edited by S. Jellicoe and H.M. Orlinsky. New York: Ktav, 1974.

Jobes, K.H. and M. Silva. *Invitation to the Septuagint*. Grand Rapids: Baker, 2000.

Johnson, A.C., H.S. Gehman, and J.E.H. Kase. *The John H. Scheide Biblical Papyri: Ezekiel*. PUSP 3. Princeton: Princeton University Press, 1938.

Johnson, David W. "Anti-Chalcedonian Polemics in Coptic Texts, 451–641." Pages 216–234 in *The Roots of Egyptian Christianity*. Edited by B.A. Pearson and J.E. Goehring. SAC. Philadelphia: Fortress, 1986.

Joosten, J., "On the LXX Translator's Knowledge of Hebrew." Pages 165–180 in *LXX: X Congress of the International Organization for Septuagint and Cognate Studies; Oslo, 1998*. Edited by B.A. Taylor. SBLSCS 51. Atlanta: SBL, 1998.

Joüon, Paul and T. Muraoka. *A Grammar of Biblical Hebrew*. Parts 1 and 2. SB 14/1. Rome: Editrice Pontificio Istituto Biblico, 2003.

Joyce, Paul. *Divine Initiative and Human Response in Ezekiel*. JSOTSup 51. Sheffield: Sheffield Academic Press, 1989.

Kahle, Paul. *The Cairo Genizah*. London: Oxford University Press for the British Academy, 1947.

Kannady, Wayne C. *Apologetic Discourse and the Scribal Tradition: Evidence of the Influence of Apologetic Interests on the Text of the Canonical Gospels*. SBLTCS 5. Atlanta: SBL, 2004.

Katz, Peter. "Rez. A. Rahlfs, Septuaginta." *TLZ* 61 (1936): 265–287.

———. "The Recovery of the Original Septuagint. A Study in the History of Transmission and Textual Criticism." Pages 165–182 in *Actes du Premier Congrès de la Fédération internationale des Associations d'études classiques 1950*. Paris: Klincksieck, 1951.

———. "Zur Textgestaltung der Ezechiel-Septuaginta." *Bib* 35 (1954): 29–39.

Kelley, P.H., D.S. Mynatt, and T.G. Crawford. *The Masorah of Biblia Hebraica Stuttgartensia: Introduction and Annotated Glossary*. Grand Rapids: Eerdmans, 1998.

Kenyon, F.J. *General Introduction: The Chester Beatty Biblical Papyri Descriptions and Texts of Twelve Manuscripts on Papyrus of the Greek Bible*. Fasc. 1. London: Emery Walker, 1933.

———. *The Chester Beatty Biblical Papyri: Ezekiel, Daniel, Esther*. Fasc. 7. 2 vols. London: Emery Walker, 1937.

———. "Reviews." *JTS* 39 (1938): 409–413.

———. *The Text of the Greek Bible*. 3d rev. and aug. ed. A.W. Adams. London: Duckworth, 1975.

Kilpatrick, G.D. "The Bodmer and Mississippi Collection of Biblical and Christian Texts." *GRBS* 4 (1963): 33–47.

Klawans, Jonathan. *Impurity and Sin in Ancient Judaism*. New York: Oxford University Press, 2000.

Klijn, A.F.J. "Jewish Christianity in Egypt." Pages 161–175 in *The Roots of Egyptian Christianity*. Edited by B.A. Pearson and J.E. Goehring. Philadelphia: Wipf and Stock, 1986.

Knox, Bernard M.W. "Silent Reading in Antiquity." *GRBS* 9 (1968): 431–35.

Kooij, A. van der. "The Septuagint of Ezekiel and Hasmonean Leadership." Pages 437–446 in *Interpreting Translation: Studies on the LXX and Ezekiel in Honour of Johan Lust*. Edited by F. García Martínez and M. Vervenne. BETL 192. Leuven: Leuven University Press, 2005.

———. "The Septuagint of Ezekiel and the Profane Leader." Pages 43–55 in *The Book of Ezekiel and its Influence*. Edited by H.J. de Jonge and Johannes Tromp. Burlington: Ashgate, 2007.

Korpel, Marjo. "Introduction to the Series Pericope." Pages 1–50 in *Delimitation Criticism: A New Tool in Biblical Scholarship*. Edited by M. Korpel and J. Oesch. Pericope 1. Assen: Van Gorcum, 2000.

Kraeling, Carl H. *The Synagogue*. The Yale University Excavations at Dura-Europos final report 8, part 1. New Haven: Yale University Press, 1956.

Kraft, Robert A. "The 'Textual Mechanics' of Early Jewish LXX/OG Papyri and Fragments." Pages 51–72 in *The Bible as Book: The Transmission of the Greek Text*. Edited by S. McKendrick and O.A. O'Sullivan. New Castle, De.: Oak Knoll, 2003.

Kratz, Reinhard. "The Visions of Daniel." Pages 91–113 in *The Book of Daniel: Composition and Reception*. Edited by J.J. Collins and Peter Flint. Vol. 1. VTSup 83. Leiden: Brill, 2002.

Kraus, T.J. and T. Nicklas. "The World of NT Manuscripts: 'Every Manuscript Tells a Story'." Pages 1–9 in *New Testament Manuscripts: The Texts and the World*. Edited by T.J. Kraus and T. Nicklas. TENT 2. Leiden: Brill, 2006.

Kristeva, Julia. "Word, Dialog, Novel." Pages 64–91 in *Desire in Language: A Semiotic Approach to Literature and Art*. Edited by Leon S. Roudiez. New York: Columbia University Press, 1980.

Lamb, J.A. "The Place of the Bible in the Liturgy." Pages 563–83 in *The Cambridge History of the Bible: Vol 1, From the Beginnings to Jerome*. Edited by P.R. Ackroyd, C.F. Evans, G.W. Lampe, and S.L. Greenslade. Cambridge: Cambridge University Press, 1970.

Lapsley, Jacqueline E. *Can These Bones Live?: The Problem of the Moral Self in the Book of Ezekiel*. BZAW 301. Berlin: de Gruyter, 2000.

Lau, Wolfgang. *Schriftgelehrte Prophetie in Jes 56–66*. BZAW 225. Berlin: de Gruyter, 1994.

Levenson, Jon. *Resurrection and the Restoration of Israel: The Ultimate Victory of the God of Life*. New Haven: Yale University Press, 2006.

———. *Theology of the Program of Restoration of Ezekiel 40–48*. HSM 10. Missoula: Scholars Press, 1976. Repr., Cambridge: Books on Demand, 2006.

Levey, S.H. *The Targum of Ezekiel*. The Aramaic Bible 13. Wilmington, Del.: Michael Glazier, 1987.

Liddell, Henry G. and Robert Scott. *Greek-English Lexicon*. Cambridge: Clarendon, 1959.

Lim, Timothy. "Eschatological Orientation and the Alteration of Scripture in the Habakkuk Pesher." *JNES* 49 (1990): 185–194.

Lust, Johan. "The Order of Final Events in Revelation and Ezekiel." Pages 179–183 in *L'Apocalypse johannique et l'Apocalyptique dans le Nouveau Testament*. Edited by J. Lambrecht. BETL 53. Leuven: Leuven University Press, 1980.

———. "De samenhang van Ez. 36–40." *TvT* 20 (1980): 26–39.

———. "Ezekiel 36–40 in the Oldest Greek Manuscript." *CBQ* 43 (1981): 517–33.

———. "'Gathering and Return' in Jeremiah and Ezekiel." Pages 119–142 in *Le Livre de Jérémie*. Edited by P.M. Bogaert. BETL 54. Leuven: Leuven University Press, 1981.

———. "The Sequence of Ez 36–39 and the Omission of Ez 36,23c-38 in Pap. 967 and in Codex Wirceburgensis." *BIOSCS* 14 (1981): 45–46.

———. "Messianism and the Septuagint: Ezek 21,30–32." Pages 174–191 in *Congress Volume Salamanca 1983*. Edited by J.A. Emerton. VTSup 36. Leiden: Brill 1985.

———. "Exegesis and Theology in the Septuagint of Ezekiel: The Longer 'Pluses' and Ezek 43:1–9." Pages 201–232 in *LXX: VI Congress of the International Organization For Septuagint and Cognate Studies; Jerusalem 1986*. Edited by C.E. Cox. SBLSCS 23. Atlanta: SBL, 1986.

———. "Ezekiel Manuscripts in Qumran: Preliminary Edition of 4Q Ez a and b." Pages 90–100 in *Ezekiel and his Book: Textual and Literary Criticism and their Interrelation*. Edited by Johan Lust. BETL 74. Leuven: Leuven University Press, 1986.

———. "The Final Text and Textual Criticism: Ez 39,28." Pages 48–54 in *Ezekiel and his Book: Textual and Literary Criticism and their Interrelation*. Edited by Johan Lust. BETL 74. Leuven: Leuven University Press, 1986.

———. "Introduction: Ezekiel and his Book." Pages 1–6 in *Ezekiel and his Book: Textual and Literary Criticism and their Interrelation*. Edited by Johan Lust. BETL 74. Leuven: Leuven University Press, 1986.

———. "Methodological Remarks." Pages 121–128 in *The Story of David and Goliath: Textual and Literary Criticism: Papers of a Joint Research Venture*. Edited by D. Barthélemy, D. Gooding, J. Lust, and E. Tov. Göttingen: Vandenhoeck & Ruprecht, 1986.

———. "The Story of David and Goliath in Hebrew and Greek." Pages 5–18 in *The Story of David and Goliath: Textual and Literary Criticism: Papers of a Joint Research Venture*. Edited by D. Barthélemy, D. Gooding, J. Lust, and E. Tov. Göttingen: Vandenhoeck & Ruprecht, 1986.

———. "The Use of Textual Witnesses for the Establishment of the Text: The Shorter and Longer Texts of Ezekiel." Pages 7–20 in *Ezekiel and his Book: Textual and Literary Criticism and their Interrelation*. Edited by Johan Lust. BETL 74. Leuven: Leuven University Press, 1986.

———. "The Septuagint Version of Daniel 4–5." Pages 39–53 in *The Book of Daniel in the Light of New Findings*. Edited by A. S. van der Woude. BETL 106. Leuven: Leuven University Press, 1993.

———. "אדני יהוה in Ezekiel and its Counterpart in the Old Greek, *ETL* 72 (1996): 138–145.

——. " 'And I Shall Hang Him on a Lofty Mountain': Ezek 17:22–24 and Messianism in the Septuagint." Pages 231–250 in *IX Congress of the International Organization for Septuagint and Cognate Studies*. Edited by B.A. Taylor. SBLSCS 45. Atlanta: SBL, 1997.

——. "The Delight of Ezekiel's Eyes: Ez 24:15–16 in Hebrew and Greek." Pages 1–25 in *LXX: X Congress of the International Organization for Septuagint and Cognate Studies; Oslo, 1998*. Edited by B.A. Taylor. SBLSCS 51. Atlanta: SBL, 1998.

——. "Exile and Diaspora. Gathering from Dispersion in Ezekiel." Pages 99–122 in *Lectures et Relectures de la Bible: Festschrift P.M. Bogaert*. Edited by J.M. Auwers and A. Wénin. BETL 144. Leuven: Leuven University Press, 1999.

——. "Syntax and Translation Greek." *ETL* 77 (2001): 395–401.

——. "The Spirit of the Lord, or the Wrath of the Lord? Ez 39,29." *ETL* 78 (2002): 148–155.

——. "Textual Criticism of the Old and New Testaments: Stepbrothers?" Pages 15–31 in *New Testament Textual Criticism and Exegesis*. Edited by A. Denaux. Leuven: Leuven University Press, 2002.

——"Major Divergences between LXX and MT in Ezekiel." Pages 83–92 in *The Earliest Text of the Hebrew Bible: The Relationship between the Masoretic Text and the Hebrew Base of the Septuagint Reconsidered*. Edited by A. Schenker. SBLSCS 52. Atlanta: SBL, 2003.

——. 'Messianism in LXX-Ezekiel: Towards a Synthesis." Pages 83–92 in *The Septuagint and Messianism*. Edited by M.A. Knibb. BETL 195. Leuven: Leuven University Press, 2006.

—— (ed.) *Ezekiel and His Book: Textual and Literary Criticism and Their Interrelation*. BETL 74. Leuven: Leuven University Press, 1986.

Lust, J., E. Eynikel, and K. Hauspie. *Greek-English Lexicon of the Septuagint. Revised Edition*. Stuttgart: Deutsche Bibelgesellschaft, 2003.

Marquis, Galen. "Word Order as a Criterion for the Evaluation of Translation Technique in the LXX and the Evaluation of Word-Order Variants as Exemplified in LXX-Ezekiel." *Textus* 13 (1986): 59–84.

——. "Consistency of Lexical Equivalents as a Criterion for the Evaluation of Translation Technique as Exemplified in the LXX Book of Ezekiel." Pages 405–424 in *VI Congress of the International Organization for Septuagint and Cognate Studies*. Edited by Claude E. Cox. SBLSCS 23. Atlanta: SBL, 1987.

Martin, R.A. "Syntax Criticism of the LXX Additions to the Book of Esther." *JBL* 94 (1975): 65–72.

McGann, Jerome J. "Theory of Texts." *LRB* 18 (1988): 20–21.

——. *A Critique of Modern Textual Criticism*. Chicago: Univesity of Chicago Press, 1983. Repr., Charlottesville, Va: University Press of Virginia, 1992.

McGowan, Andrew. "Is There a Liturgical Text in this Gospel? The Institution Narratives and Their Early Interpretive Communities." *JBL* 118 (1999): 73–87.

McGregor, Leslie. J. *The Greek Text of Ezekiel: An Examination of its Homogeneity*. SBLSCS 18. Atlanta: SBL, 1985.

McLay, Tim. *The OG and Th versions of Daniel*. SBLSCS 43. Atlanta: SBL, 1996.

McNamee, Kathleen. *Sigla and Select Marginalia in Greek Literary Papyri*. Bruselles: Fondation Égyptologique Reine Élisabeth, 1992.

Metzger, Bruce M. *Manuscripts of the Greek Bible: an Introduction to Greek Palaeography*. Oxford: Oxford University Press, 1981.

——. *Oxford Annotated Apocrypha*. Revised Standard Version. New York: Oxford University Press, 1977.

Milne, H.J.M. and T.C. Skeat. *Scribes and Correctors of the Codex Sinaiticus*. London: British Museum, 1938.

Minnen, Peter van. "Greek Papyri and Coptic Studies, 1996–2000." Pages 423–446 in *Coptic Studies on the Threshold of a New Millennium: Proceedings of the Seventh International Congress of Coptic Studies, Leiden 2000*. Edited by Mat Immerzeel and Jacques van der Vliet. 2 vols. OLA 133. Leiden: Peeters, 2004.

Moore, Carey A. "On the Origins of the LXX Additions to the Book of Esther." *JBL* 92 (1973): 382–93.

——. *Daniel, Esther, and Jeremiah: The Additions.* AB 44. New York: Doubleday, 1977.
Mowry, Lucetta. "Revelation 4–5 and Early Christian Liturgical Usage." *JBL* 71 (1952): 75–84.
Mulder, Martin J., ed. *The Old Testament in Syriac According to the Peshitta Version* 3/3: *Ezekiel.* Leiden: Brill, 1985.
——. "Some Remarks on the Peshitta translation of the book of Ezekiel." Pages 169–182 in *The Peshitta: Its Early Text and History, Papers read at the Peshitta Symposium held at Leiden 30–31 August 1985.* Edited by P.B. Dirksen and M.J. Mulder. Leiden: Brill, 1988.
Muraoka, Takamitsu. "Literary Device in the Septuagint." *Textus* 8 (1973): 20–30.
——. "The Greek Texts of Samuel-Kings: Incomplete Translations or Recensional Activity?" *Abr-Nahrain* 21 (1982–1983): 28–49.
——. "In Defense of the Unity of the Septuagint Minor Prophets." *AJBI* 15 (1989): 25–36.
——. *Hebrew/Aramaic index to the Septuagint: keyed to the Hatch-Redpath concordance.* Grand Rapids: Baker, 1998.
Nicholson, E.W. *Preaching to the Exiles: A Study of the Prose Tradition in the Book of Jeremiah.* Oxford: Blackwell, 1970.
Nickelsburg, George W.E. "The Bible Rewritten and Expanded." Pages 97–104 in *Jewish Writings of the Second Temple Period.* Edited by Michael Stone. CRINT 2. Philadelphia: Fortress, 1984.
Nobile, Marco. "Beziehung zwischen Ez 32, 17–32 und der Gog-Perikope (Ez 38–39) im Lichte der Endredaktion." Pages 255–259 in *Ezekiel and his Book: Textual and Literary Criticism and their Interrelation.* Edited by Johan Lust. BETL 74. Leuven: Leuven University Press, 1986.
Old, Hughes Oliphant. *The Reading and Preaching of the Scriptures in the Worship of the Christian Church: Volume 1 The Biblical Period.* Grand Rapids: Eerdmans, 1998.
Olley, John W. "'Hear the Word of Yahweh': The Structure of the Book of Isaiah in 1QIsaᵃ." *VT* (1993): 19–49.
——. "Texts Have Paragraphs Too: A Plea for Inclusion in Critical Editions." *Textus* 19 (1998): 111–125.
——. "Paragraphing in the Greek text of Ezekiel in p967 with Particular Reference to the Cologne Portion." Pages 202–225 in *Studies in Scriptural Unit Division.* Edited by Marjo Christina Annette Korpel, Josef M. Oesch. Pericope 3. Assen: Van Gorcum, 2002.
——. "Trajectories in Paragraphing of the Book of Ezekiel." Pages 204–231 in *Unit Delimitation in Biblical Hebrew and Northwest Semitic Literature.* Edited by M. Korpel and J. Oesch. Pericope 4. Assen: Van Gorcum, 2003.
Oloffson, Staffan. *The LXX Version: A Guide to the Translation Technique of the Septuagint.* ConBOT 30. Stokholm: Almqvist & Wiksell, 1990.
Orlinksy, Harry M. "On the Present State of Proto-Septuagint Studies." *JAOS* 61 (1941): 81–91. Repr. pages 78–109 in *Studies in the Septuagint: Origins, Recensions, and Interpretation: Selected Essays.* Edited by S. Jellicoe and H.M. Orlinsky. New York: Ktav, 1974.
Osburn, C.D. "The Greek Lectionaries of the New Testament." Pages 61–74 in *The Text of the New Testament in Contemporary Research: Essays on the Status Quaestionis.* Edited by B.D. Ehrman, M.W. Holmes. Grand Rapids: Eerdmans, 1995.
Patmore, Hector M. "The Shorter and Longer Texts of Ezekiel: The Implications of the Manuscript Finds from Masada and Qumran." *JSOT* 32 (2007): 231–42.
Patrologia graeca. Edited by J.-P. Migne. 162 vols. 1857–1886.
Payne, J. Barton. "The Relationship of the Chester Beatty Papyri of Ezekiel to Codex Vaticanus." *JBL* 68 (1949): 251–265.
Pearson, B.A. "The Earliest Christianity in Egypt: Some Observations." Pages 132–156 in *The Roots of Egyptian Christianity.* Edited by B.A. Pearson and J.E. Goehring. Philadelphia: Wipf & Stock, 1986.
Perrot, C. "La lecture de la Bible dans la diaspora hellénistique." Pages 109–132 in *Études sur le judaïsme hellénistique.* LD 119. Edited by R. Kuntzmann and J. Schlosser. Paris: Éditions du Cerf, 1984.

——. "The Reading of the Bible in the Ancient Synagogue." Pages 137–159 in *Mikra: Text, Translation, Reading and Interpretation of the Hebrew Bible in Ancient Judaism and Early Christianity*. Edited by M.J. Mulder. Philadelphia: Fortress, 1988.

Petersen, David. *The Prophetic Literature: An Introduction*. Louisville: Westminster, 2002.

Pfann, S. J. "4Q298: The Maskil's Address to All Sons of Dawn." *JQR* 85 (1994): 203–235.

Pietersma, Albert and Benjamin G. Wright, eds. *A New English Translation of the Septuagint*. Oxford: Oxford University Press, 2007.

Popović, M. "Prophet, Books and Texts: Ezekiel, Pseudo-Ezekiel and the Authoritativeness of Ezekiel Traditions in Early Judaism." Pages 227–251 in *Authoritative Scriptures in Ancient Judaism*. Edited by M. Popović. JSJSup 141. Leiden: Brill, 2010.

Porter, Stanley E. "Why So Many Holes in the Papyrological Evidence for the Greek New Testament?" Pages 167–186 in *The Bible as a Book: The Transmission of the Greek Text*. Edited by S. McKendrick and O.A. O'Sullivan. New Castle, De.: Oak Knoll, 2003.

——. "The Influence of Unit Delimitation on Reading and Use of Greek Manuscripts." Pages 44–60 in *Method in Unit Delimitation*. Edited by M. Korpel, J. Oesch, and S. Porter. Pericope 6. Boston: Brill, 2007.

Porter, Stanley E. and Wendy J. Porter. *New Testament Greek Papyri and Parchments: New Editions*. MPER NS 29 &30. Berlin: de Gruyter, 2008.

Procksch, Otto. *Studien zur Geschichte der Septuaginta-Die Propheten*. Leipzig: J.C. Hinrichs, 1910.

Rabin, C. "The Ancient Versions and the Indefinite Subject." *Textus* 2 (1962): 60–76.

Ranke, E. *Par palimpsestorum Wirceburgensium antiquissimae Veteris Testamenti latinae fragmenta e codd. Rescriptus*. Vienna: G. Braumüller, 1871.

Rendtorff, Rolf. "Ez 20 und 36, 16ff im Rahmen der Komposition des Buches Ezechiel." Pages 261–265 in *Ezekiel and His Book: Textual and Literary Criticism and their Interrelation*. Leuven: Leuven University Press, 1986.

——. "Ezekiel 20 and 36:16ff. in the Framework of the Composition of the Book." Pages 190–195 in *Canon and Theology*. OBT. Minneapolis: Fortress, 1993.

Roberts, Colin H. "The Codex." *PBA* 40 (1954): 169–204.

——. *Manuscript, Society, and Belief in Early Christian Egypt*. London: Oxford University Press, 1979.

Roberts, Colin H. and T.C. Skeat. *The Birth of the Codex*. London: Oxford University Press, 1983.

Roca-Puig, R. *Daniel. Dos semifolis del còdex 967, Papir de Barcelona, Inv. no. 42 i 43*. Barcelona, 1974. Repr., *Aegyptus* 56 (1976): 3–18.

Rooker, M.F. *Biblical Hebrew in Transition: The Language of the Book of Ezekiel*. JSOTSup 90. Sheffield: JSOT Press, 1990.

Rosenberg, Joel. "Jeremiah and Ezekiel." Pages 194–204 in *The Literary Guide to the Bible*. Edited by Robert Alter and Frank Kermode. 2d ed. Cambridge: Belknap Press, 1990.

Rylaarsdam, J. Coert. "Editor's Foreward." Pages iii–ix in Norman Habel, *Literary Criticism of the Old Testament*. GBSOTS. Philadelphia: Fortress, 1971.

Sanders, H.A. *A Third Century Papyrus Codex of the Epistles of Paul* (UMSHS 38; Ann Arbor: University of Michigan Press, 1935).

Sanderson, Judith E. "Ezekiel." Pages 209–220 in *Qumran Cave 4. X. The Prophets*. Edited by Eugene Ulrich et al. DJD 15. Oxford: Clarendon, 1997.

Schäfers, J. "Ist das Buch Ezekiel in der Septuaginta von einem oder mehreren Dolmetschern übersetzt?" *TGI* 1 (1909): 289–291.

Schenker, A. *Septante et texte massorétique dans l'histoire la plus ancienne du texte de Rois 2–14*. CahRB 48. Paris: Gabalda, 2000.

Schmidt, Carl. "Die neuesten Bibelfunde aus Ägypten." ZNW 30 (1931): 285–93.

Schwagmeier, Peter. *Untersuchungen zu Testgeschichte und Entstehung des Ezechielbuches masoretischer und griechischer Überlieferung*. Dr. Theol. Dissertation, University of Zurich, 2004.

Shaper, Joachim. "The Death of the Prophet: The Transition from the Spoken to the Written Word of God in the Book of Ezekiel." Pages 63–79 in *Prophets, Prophecy, and Prophetic Texts in Second Temple Judaism.* Edited by Michael H. Floyd and Robert D. Haak. New York: T & T Clark, 2006.

Sinclair, Lawrence A. "A Qumran Biblical Fragment 4QEzek^a (Ezek 10, 17–11, 11)." *RevQ* 14 (1989): 99–105.

Sirat, Colette. *Hebrew Manuscripts of the Middle Ages.* Edited and translated by Nicolas de Lange. Cambridge: Cambridge University Press, 2002.

Skeat, T.C. "Early Christian Book-Production: Papyri and Manuscripts." Pages 54–79 in *The Cambridge of the Bible: Volume 2, The West from the Fathers to the Reformation.* Edited by G.W.H. Lampe. Cambridge: Cambridge University Press, 1969.

Skehan, Patrick. "The Divine Name at Qumran, in the Masada Scroll, and in the Septuagint." *BIOSCS* 13 (1980): 14–44

Smyth, Herbert W. *Greek Grammar.* Rev. by Gordon M. Messing. Cambridge: Harvard University Press, 1984.

Sommer, Benjamin D. *A Prophet Reads Scripture: Allusion in Isaiah 40–66.* Stanford: Stanford University Press, 1998.

Sperber, A. *The Bible in Aramaic. Vol. 3 The Latter Prophets according to Targum Jonathan.* Leiden: Brill, 1962.

Spottorno, M.V. "Some Lexical Aspects in the Greek Text of Ezekiel." Pages 78–84 in *Ezekiel and his Book: Textual and Literary Criticism and their Interrelation.* Edited by Johan Lust. BETL 74. Leuven: Leuven University Press, 1986.

———. "La omisión de Ez. 36, 23b–38 y la transposición de capítulos en el papiro 967." *Emerita* 50 (1981): 93–99.

Steck, O.H. *Studien zu Tritojesaja.* BZAW 203. Berlin: de Gruyter, 1991.

Steuernagel, Carl. *Lehrbuch der Einleitung in da AT mit einem Anhang über die Apokryphen und Pseudepigraphen.* Tübingen: J.C.B. Mohr (P. Siebeck), 1912.

Stoltz, F. "לֵב Lēv heart." Page 639 in *The Theological Lexicon of the Old Testament.* Edited by Ernst Jenni and Claus Westermann. Translated by Mark E. Biddle. Peabody: Hendrickson, 1997.

Stone, Michael. "Apocalyptic Literature." Pages 383–441 in *Jewish Writings of the Second Temple Period.* Edited by M.E. Stone. CRINT 2.2. Philadelphia: Fortress, 1984.

Strawn, Brent A. "Excerpted Manuscripts at Qumran: Their Significance for the Textual History of the Hebrew Bible and the Socio-Religious History of the Qumran Community and its Literature." Pages 107–167 in *The Bible and the Dead Sea Scrolls,* Vol. 2: *The Dead Sea Scrolls and the Qumran Community.* Edited by J.H. Charlesworth. Waco: Baylor University Press, 2006.

———. "Excerpted 'Non-Biblical' Scrolls at Qumran? Background, Analogies, Function." Pages 65–116 in *Qumran Studies: New Approaches, New Questions.* Edited by Michael T. Davis and Brent A. Strawn. Grand Rapids: Eerdmans, 2007.

Swete, Henry Barclay. *Introduction to Old Testament in Greek.* Cambridge: Harvard University Press, 1900.

Taft, Robert F. "Christian Liturgical Psalmody: Origins, Development, Decomposition and Collapse." Pages 7–32 in *Psalms in Community: Jewish and Christian Textual, Liturgical, and Artistic Tradition.* Edited by Harry Attridge and Margot Fassler. SBLSynS 25. Atlanta: SBL, 2003.

Talmon, Shemaryahu. "The Textual Study of the Bible—A New Outlook." Pages 321–400 in *Qumran and the History of the Biblical Text.* Edited by F.M. Cross and S. Talmon. Cambridge: Harvard University Press, 1975.

———. "'Yād Wāšēm': An Idiomatic Phrase in Biblical Literature and its Variations." *HS* 25 (1984): 8–17.

———. "Fragments of an Ezekiel scroll from Masada (Ezek 35:11–38:14)." *OLP* 27 (1996): 29–49.

———. *Final Reports: Hebrew Fragments from Masada.* Pages 1–149 in *Masada 6, The Yigael Yadin Excavations 1963–1965.* Edited by S. Talmon and Y. Yadin. Jerusalem: Israel Exploration Society and the Hebrew University of Jerusalem, 1999.

———. "Textual Criticism: The Ancient Versions." Pages 141–169 in *Text in Context: Essays by Members of the Society for Old Testament Study.* Edited by A.D.H. Mayes. Oxford: Oxford University Press, 2000.

Thackeray, H. St. J. "Notes and Studies: The Greek Translators of Ezekiel." *JTS* IV (1902–1903): 407–408.

———. "The Greek Translators of Ezekiel." *JTS* 4 (1903): 398–411.

———. "The Bisection of Books in Primitive Septuagint Mss." *JTS* 9 (1907): 88–98.

———. *Grammar of the Old Testament in Greek.* Vol 1. Cambridge: Cambridge University Press, 1909. Repr., Hildesheim, Germany: Georg Olms, 1987.

———. *The Septuagint and Jewish Worship: A Study in Origins.* 2d ed. The 1920 Schweich Lectures. London: Oxford University Press, 1923.

Thompson, E. Maunde. "Palaeography." Pages 147–170 in *The New Werner Twentieth Century Edition of the Encyclopaedia Brittanica.* 9th ed. Vol. 18. Akron: Werner Company, 1907.

Thompson, J. David. *A Critical Concordance to the Septuagint: Ezekiel.* Lewiston, N.Y.: Edwin Mellen Press, 2000.

Threatte, Leslie. *The Grammar of Attic Inscriptions: Phonology I.* Berlin: de Gruyter, 1980.

Tisserant, E. "Notes sur la recension lucianique d'Ézéchiel." *RB* 8 (1911): 384–390.

Traube, Ludwig. *Nomina Sacra: Versuch einer Geschichte der christlichen Kürzung.* Munich: Beck, 1907. Repr., Darmstadt: Wissenschaftliche Buchgesssellschaft, 1967.

Torrey, C.C. *Pseudo-Ezekiel and the Original Prophecy.* 2d ed. New York: Ktav, 1970.

Tov, Emanuel. *The Septuagint Translation of Jeremiah and Baruch: A Discussion of an Early Revision of the LXX of Jeremiah 29–52 and Baruch 1:1–3:8.* HSM 8. Missoula: Scholars Press, 1976.

———. "Loan-Words, Homophony and Transliterations in the Septuagint." *Bib* 60 (1979): 216–236.

———. "Criteria for Evaluating Textual Readings: The Limitations of Textual Rules." *HTR* 75 (1982): 429–498.

———. "The Nature of the Differences between the MT and the LXX." Pages 19–46 in *The Story of David and Goliath: Textual and Literary Criticism: Papers of a Joint Research Venture.* Edited by D. Barthélemy, D. Gooding, J. Lust, and E. Tov. Göttingen: Vandenhoeck & Ruprecht, 1986.

———. "Recensional Differences between the MT and LXX of Ezekiel." *ETL* 62 (1986): 89–101.

———. "Some Sequential Differences Between the MT and LXX and their Ramifications." *JNSL* 13 (1987): 151–160.

———. "The Septuagint." Pages 161–188 in *Mikra: Text, Translation, Reading, and Interpretions of the Hebrew Bible in Ancient Judaism and Early Christianity.* Edited by M. Mulder. Assen: Van Gorcum/Philadelphia: Fortress, 1988.

———. "Excerpted and Abbreviated Biblical Texts from Qumran." Pages 27–41 in *Hebrew Bible, Greek Bible and Qumran: Collected Essays.* TSAJ 121. Tübingen: Mohr Siebeck, 2008. Repr. from *RevQ* 16 (1995): 581–600.

———. *The Text-Critical Use of the Septuagint in Biblical Research.* 2d ed. JBS 8. Jerusalem: SIMOR, 1997.

———. "The Dimensions of the Qumran Scrolls." *DSD* 5 (1998): 69–91.

———. *The Greek and Hebrew Bible: Collected Essays on the Septuagint.* VTSup 62. Leiden: Brill, 1999.

———. "The Background of the Sense Divisions in the Biblical Texts." Pages 312–348 in *Delimitation Criticism.* Edited by Korpel and Oesch. Pericope I. Assen: Van Gorcum, 2000.

——. *Textual Criticism of the Hebrew Bible*. 2d ed. Minneapolis: Augsburg Fortress, 2001.

——. *The Texts from the Judean Desert: Indices and an Introduction to the Discoveries in the Judaean Desert Series*. Edited by E. Tov et al. DJD 39. Oxford: Clarendon, 2002.

——. *Scribal Practices and Approaches Reflected in the Texts Found in the Judean Desert*. STDJ 54. Leiden: Brill, 2004.

Tromp, Johannes. "'Can These Bones Live?' Ezekiel 37:1–14 and Eschatological Resurrection." Pages 61–78 in *The Book of Ezekiel and Its Influence*. Edited by J.J. de Jonge and Johannes Tromp. Aldershot: Ashgate, 2007.

Tucker, Gene M. "Editor's Foreward." Pages iii–iv in Ralph W. Klein, *Textual Criticism of the Old Testament: From the Septuagint to Qumran*. GBSOTS. Philadelphia: Fortress, 1974.

Turner, E.G. *Greek Manuscripts of the Ancient World*. Oxford: Oxford University Press, 1971.

——. *Typology of the Early Codex*. Philadelphia: University of Pennsylvania Press, 1977.

——. *Greek Papyri: An Introduction*. Oxford: Clarendon, 1980.

Turner, Nigel. "Greek Translators of Ezekiel." *JTS* 7 (April 1956): 12–24.

Turner, P.D.M. "The Septuagint Version of Chapters I–XXXIX of the Book of Ezekiel." PhD diss., Oxford University, 1996.

Ulrich, Eugene. "The Old Latin Translation of the LXX and the Hebrew Scrolls from Qumran." Pages 121–165 in *The Hebrew and Greek Texts of Samuel: 1980 Proceedings IOSCS—Vienna*. Edited by E. Tov. Jerusalem: Academon, 1980. Repr. pages 233–274 in *The Dead Sea Scrolls and the Origins of the Bible*. Grand Rapids: Eerdmans, 1999.

——. "Double Literary Editions of Biblical Narratives and Reflections on Determining the Form to be Translated." Pages 101–116 in *Perspectives on the Hebrew Bible: Essays in Honor of Walter J. Harrelson*. Edited by James J. Crenshaw. Macon, Ga.: Mercer University Press, 1988.

——. "Pluriformity in the Biblical Text, Text Groups, and Questions of Canon." Pages 37–40 in Vol. 1 of *Proceedings of the International Congress on the Dead Sea Scrolls, Madrid, 18–21, March 1991*. Edited by J. Trebolle Barrera and L. Vegas Montaner. STDJ 11. Leiden: Brill, 1992.

——. "Multiple Literary Editions: Reflections Toward a Theory of the History of the Biblical Text." Pages 78–105 in *Current Research and Technological Developments on the Dead Sea Scrolls: Conference on the Texts from the Judean Desert, Jerusalem, 30 April 1995*. Edited by Donald W. Perry and Stephen D. Ricks. STDJ 20. Leiden: Brill, 1996. Repr. pages 99–120 in *The Dead Sea Scrolls and the Origins of the Bible*. Grand Rapids: Eerdmans, 1999.

——. *Dead Sea Scrolls and the Origins of the Hebrew Bible*. Grand Rapids: Eerdmans, 1999.

——. "Impressions and Intuition: Sense Divisions in Ancient Manuscripts of Isaiah." Pages 279–307 in *Unit Delimitation in Biblical Hebrew and North West Semitic Literature*. Edited by M. Korpel and J. Oesch. Pericope 4. Assen: Van Gorcum, 2003.

VanderKam, James. "Enoch Traditions in Jubilees and Other Second Century Sources." *JBL* 13 (1978): 229–251.

Walters, P. *The Text of the Septuagint: Its Corruptions and Their Emendation*. Cambridge: Cambridge University Press, 1973.

Watts, James. "Text and Redaction in Jeremiah's Oracles against the Nations." CBQ 54 (1991): 432–447.

Weber, R. et al., eds. *Biblia Sacra Iusta Vulgata Versionem*. 3d ed. Stuttgart: Deutsche Bibelgesellschaft, 1983.

Wenzel, Siegfried and S.G. Nichols, eds. *The Whole Book: Cultural Perspectives on the Medieval Miscellany*. Ann Arbor: University of Michigan Press, 1996.

Westermann, Claus. *The Praise of God in the Psalms*. Translated by Keith R. Crim. Richmond: John Knox, 1965.

Wevers, John William. "Evidence of the Text of the John H. Schiede Papyri for the Translation of the *Status Constructus* in Ezekiel." *JBL* 70 (1951): 211–216.

——. *Ezekiel*. NCB. London: Nelson, 1969.

——. *Studies in the Text Histories of Deuteronomy and Ezekiel*. Göttingen: Vandenhoeck & Ruprecht, 2003.

Wong, K.L. "The Prince of Tyre in the Masoretic and Septuagint Texts of Ezekiel 28:1–10." Pages 447–464 in *Interpreting Translation: Studies on the LXX and Ezekiel in Honour of Johan Lust*. Leuven: Leuven University Press, 2005.

Würthwein, Ernst. *The Text of the Old Testament: an Introduction to the Biblia Hebraica*. Translated by Erroll F. Rhodes. Grand Rapids: Eerdmans, 1979.

Yadin, Yigael. *Masada: Herod's Fortress and the Zealots' Last Stand*. London: Weidenfeld & Nicolson, 1966.

Zapff, Burkhard. *Schriftgelehrte Prophetie—Jes 13 und die Komposition des Jesajabuches*. FB 74. Würzburg: Echter, 1995.

Ziegler, Joseph. *Untersuchungen zur Septuaginta des Buches Isaias*. ATA 12/3. Münster: Aschendorffsche Verlagsbuchhandlung, 1934.

——. "Die Bedeutung des Chester Beatty-Schiede Papyrus 967 für die Textüberlieferung der Ezechiel-Septuaginta." *ZAW* 61 (1945/1948): 76–94.

——. *Ezechiel*. Vetus Testamentum Graecum XVI. Göttingen: Vandenhoeck & Ruprecht, 1952.

——. "Zur Textgestaltung der Ezechiel-Septuaginta." *Bib* 34 (1953): 435–455.

——. *Ezechiel, Septuaginta*. Vetus Testamentum Graecum XVI. 2d ed. Göttingen: Vandenhoeck & Ruprecht, 1977.

Zimmerli, Walther. *Ezekiel*. Translated by Ronald E. Clements. 2 vols. Hermeneia. Philadelphia: Fortress, 1979.

——. *I am Yahweh*. Translated by Douglas W. Stott. Atlanta: John Knox, 1982.

——. "From Prophetic Word to Prophetic Book." Pages 419–442 in *"The Place is too Small for Us": The Israelite Prophets in Recent Scholarship*. Edited by R.P. Gordon. Translated by Andreas Köstenberger. Winona Lake: Eisenbrauns, 1995. Repr. from "Vom Prophetenwort zum Prophetenbuch." *ThLT* 104 (1979): cols. 481–96.

——. *The Fiery Throne: The Prophets and Old Testament Theology*. Edited by Kenneth C. Hanson. FCBS. Minneapolis: Fortress, 2003.

INDEX OF MODERN AUTHORS

INDEX OF SUBJECTS

INDEX OF ANCIENT SOURCES

New Testament